THE SOPWITH PUP

N6183 or "Mildred H" of No.3 (Naval) Squadron being manhandled at either Marieux or Furnes in mid-1917.

THE SOPWITH PUP

J.M.BRUCE, I.S.O., M.A., F.R.Ae.S., F.R.Hist.S.,
GORDON PAGE and
RAY STURTIVANT, I.S.O.

'The little brown aeroplane that flew like a leaf on the wind.'
Sir Gordon Taylor, *Sopwith Scout 7309*

An AIR-BRITAIN Publication

Copyright © 2002
J.M.Bruce, Gordon Page, Ray Sturtivant
and Air-Britain (Historians) Ltd.

Published in the United Kingdom by:

Air-Britain (Historians) Ltd
12 Lonsdale Gardens,
Tunbridge Wells, Kent TN1 1PA

Sales Department:
41 Penshurst Road, Leigh,
Tonbridge, Kent TN11 8HL

Correspondence to:
R.C.Sturtivant, 26 Monks Horton Way,
St.Albans, Herts, AL1 4HA
and not to the Tunbridge Wells address

ISBN 0 85130 310 2

Printed in the United Kingdom by:
The Cromwell Press Ltd,
Aintree Avenue,
White Horse Business Park,
Trowbridge, Wiltshire BA14 0XB

Origination by Steve Partington, Glos.

Cover paintings by Professor Dugald Cameron OBE:

Front cover:
Captain S.W.Pratt of No.46 Squadron in Pup A7327,
just after sending down an Albatross D.V out of
control on 17th June 1917.

Rear cover:
Ships Pup N6431 taking off from the turret
platform of HMS Yarmouth.

Contents

Glossary of Terms and Abbreviations

A/c	Aircraft
AA	Anti-aircraft (fire)
AAF	Australian Air Force
AAP	Aircraft Acceptance Park
Actg	Acting
AD	(i) Air Department (of the Admiralty); (ii) Aircraft Depot (RFC)
ADAE	Assistant Director of Aeronautical Equipment
ADMA	Assistant Director of Military Aeronautics
AES	Armament Experimental Station
AFC	(i) Air Force Cross; (ii) Australian Flying Corps
AID	Aircraft Inspection Department (later Directorate)
Alb	Albatros
Alld	Allocated
AM	Albert Medal
AOS	Aerial Observers School
AP	Aeroplane Park
Arr	Arrived
ARS	Aeroplane Repair Section
ASD	Aeroplane Supply Depot
AT	Aerial Target
Att	Attached
B.A.	British Association standard screw threads for bolts of $^{1}/_{16}$ in. to $^{15}/_{16}$ in.
BASD	British Aviation Supplies Depot (Paris)
Bde	Brigade
B.E.	Bleriot Experimental
BEF	British Expeditionary Force
Brig	Brigadier
B.S.	Blériot Scout
B.S.F.	British Association standard screw threads for bolts of $^{1}/_{4}$ in. to $^{1}/_{2}$ in.
CAF	Canadian Air Force
Canc	Cancelled
Capt	(i) Captain; (ii) Captured
CBE	Commander of the Order of the British Empire
Cdr	Commander
CFS	Central Flying School
CID	Committee of Imperial Defence
CRAeS	Companion of the Royal Aeronautical Society
CSD	Central Supply Depot
CTD	Controller of Technical Department
DAD	Director of the Air Department (of the Admiralty)
DAE	Director of Aeronautical Equipment
DDGMA	Deputy Director-General of Military Aeronautics
Deld	Delivered (to)
Dept	Department
Dest	Destroyed; destruction of
Detd	Detached
DFC	Distinguished Flying Cross
DFW	Deutsche Flugzeug Werke
DGMA	Director-General of Military Aeronautics
D.H.	de Havilland
DoI	Died of Injuries
DoW	Died of Wounds
DSC	Distinguished Service Cross
DSO	(Officer of the) Distinguished Service Order
EA/ea	Enemy aircraft
ECD	Experimental Constructive Department (RNAS Isle of Grain)
EF	(British) Expeditionary Force
Exp	Experimental
ERA	Engine Room Artificer
F.E.	Farman Experimental, late Fighting Experimental
Fl Abt	Flieger-Abteilung
FL	Forced landing
Flt	Flight
Flt Cdr	Flight Commnder
Flt Cdt	Flight Codet
FPS	Fleet Practice Station
FS	Fighting School
FSL	Flight Sub-Lieutenant
Ft	foot/feet
FTL	Forced to land
FTR	Failed to return
FTS	Flying Training School
GBE	Knight Grand Cross of the Order of the British Empire
GCB	Knight Grand Cross of the Order of the Bath
GFSoAFG	Grand Fleet School of Air Fighting and Gunnery
HA	Hostile Aircraft
Halb	Halberstadt
HD	Home Defence
HMS	His Majesty's Ship
hp	horse power
Hptm	Hauptmann
hr	hour
J	Jagdstaffel
Jasta	*Jagdstaffel*
KB	Kite balloon
KBE	Knight of the Order of the British Empire
KCB	Knight Commander of the Order of the Bath
km	kilometre(s)
Lt	Lieutenant
Ltn	Leutnant
Ltn d R	Leutnant der Reserve
LVG	Luft-Verkehrs Gesellschaft
Maj-Gen	Major-General
MC	Military Cross
Mia	Missing in action

Mjr	Major		RS	Reserve Squadron
MM	Military Medal		SAD	Southern Aircraft Depot
Mod	Modified		SARD	Southern Aircraft Repair Depot
mph	miles per hour		Sct	Scout
(N)	Naval (in squadron numbers: eg, 8 (N) = No.8 Naval)		SD	Stores Depot
NFS	Naval Flying School		S.E.	Santos [Dumont] Experimental, later Scouting Experimental
NLC	Night Landing Ground		SEAFIS	South-eastern Area Flying Instructors School
OBE	Officer of the Order of the British Empire		SoAF	School of Air Fighting
Obltn	Oberleutnant		SoAG	School of Air Gunnery
OC	Officer Commanding		SoAF&G	School of Air Fighting & Gunnery
Offstv	Offizierstellvertreter		Soc	Struck off charge
OOC	Out of control		SoMA	School of Military Aeronautics
(O)SAG	Observers' School of Aerial Gunnery		SoN&BD	School of Navigation & Bomb Dropping
PFO	Probationary Flying Officer		SoSF	School of Special Flying
PoW	Prisoner of War		Sqn	Squadron
PRO	Public Record Office		SS	Steamship
RAAF	Royal Australian Air Force		SSW	Siemens-Schuckert Werke
RAE	Royal Aircraft Establishment, Farnborough		2-str	Two-seater
RAF	Royal Aircraft Factory to 31.3.18; Royal Air Force from 1.4.18		TDS	Training Depot Station
			Temp	Temporary
RE	Royal Engineers		TS	Training Squadron
R.E.	Reconnaissance Experimental		U/c	Undercarriage
RFC	Royal Flying Corps		U/s	Unserviceable
RFC (MW)	Royal Flying Corps (Military Wing)		Uffz	Unteroffizier
Rittm	Rittmeister		VC	Victoria Cross
RMS	Royal Mail Steamer		Vfw	Vizefeldwebel
RN	Royal Navy		W/e	Week ending
RNAS	(i) Royal Naval Air Service; (ii) Royal Naval Air Station		W/o	written off
			Wg	Wing
RNASTE	Royal Naval Air Service Training Establishment		Wg Cdr	Wing Commander

The fuselage of a Pup under construction in the Whitehead factory at Feltham.

Specifically conceived as a single-seat military scouting aircraft of high performance the B.S.1 was designed in 1912 at the Royal Aircraft Factory, Farnborough, by Geoffrey de Havilland. Here it is seen in its original form early in 1913.   *(Science Museum)*

Acknowledgements

Among the many people who have given help with information and photographs for this book are Tony Arbon, Trevor Boughton, Chaz Bowyer, Dugald Cameron, Frank Cheesman, Mark Collington, Dick Cronin, Mick Davis, Major John M Elliott USMC (Ret), Malcolm Fillmore, Brendan Goddard, Jim Halley, Trevor Henshaw, John Hopton, Lee Howard, Dave Howley, Paul Leaman, Alan Leishman, Stuart Leslie, Jan Mangelschots, Andy Marden, Geoffrey Negus, Mike O'Connor, Frank Olynyk, Colin Waugh, the staff of the RAF Museum especially Peter Elliott and Simon Moody and the staff of the Liddle Collection (Brotherton Library).

Also Dugald Cameron for the cover paintings,
Dave Howley for his coloured side-view drawings and Mick Davis for the three-view drawings

Foreword

As when a bird hath flown through the air, there is no token of her way to be found,
but the light air being beaten with the stroke of her wings and parted
with the violent noise and motion of them, is passed through, and
therein afterwards no sign where she went is to be found.
(From The Wisdom of Solomon)

The war of 1914-18 is now remote in time, since survivors of those who endured its satanic battles are now an aged and dwindling few. So urgent and indiscriminate are the demands of war that many inventions that should benefit mankind and enrich our world are all too soon adapted to be, or to contribute to, killing machines or processes. Perhaps to an extent greater than any earlier conflict, the First World War brought about many such perversions.

One of the foremost and most portentous of these was and is the aeroplane. In 1914 it was still at a primitive stage, virtually unproven as any kind of significant adjunct to a battle or campaign; yet during four frenetic years it was rapidly developed in several forms, to bomb, to reconnoitre, and to fight its own kind in the air over and beyond the battlefield, by day and by night.

The flying and fighting qualities of these martial aeroplanes differed widely; some were more pleasant to fly than others; the affection or dislike, respect or disquiet that aircraft inspired in their pilots varied accordingly. In terms of affection and warmth of recollection, none was more highly regarded than the Sopwith Pup, at least when considered as a flying machine. Pilots of those fighter squadrons that had to go on flying the Pup in combat after it had been outrun and outgunned (though never outmanoeuvred) might have taken a less euphoric view of the little aircraft; yet more than one of them could testify that they owed their lives to the Pup's agility, despite its other shortcomings.

The Pup's controllability made it ideally suitable for much experimental flying, most notably in the outstandingly inventive pioneering of deck-flying from and on to naval ships, pursued resourcefully by the Royal Naval Air Service and Royal Air Force. Indeed, that work alone entitles the Pup to a special place in aviation history, and a substantial part of it is recounted and illustrated in these pages.

Chronology is of fundamental importance in the interpretation of facts and events; yet, regrettably, it is necessary to warn readers that dates recorded in official documents and log-books are not always as correct and consistent as the historian would wish. Understandably, the heat and stress of operational circumstances must have affected the immediacy, clarity and correctness of at least some such records. All one can do, therefore, is to report such details as they stand recorded, but subject to this caveat. This applies especially to the entries in Appendix 13.

In relatively recent years it has become fashionable among certain historians, playwrights, media practitioners and others to denigrate and decry virtually everything and everyone involved in the 1914-18 war. So persistent and strident have these misrepresentations been that it can be difficult for later generations to identify and understand the general ethos of that stricken period. This book incorporates some quite substantial quotations from official documents both pre-war and wartime, and from books written by some of those who, as very young men, knew and flew the Sopwith Pup in its time; and it is hoped that these may provide a clearer, more authentic and better balanced insight into the contemporary circumstances, with their attendant difficulties, uncertainties, aspirations and disappointments, than do sophisticated representations fabricated by those who were not there, selectively and disparagingly derived from hindsight. In particular, these quotations demonstrate that the men concerned, at varying levels of responsibility, performed their duties conscientiously and bravely in circumstances of daunting difficulty. They were ordinary mortals who did their best, not the inept blunderers as which they have been too often maliciously caricatured.

Thus it is meet, indeed necessary, even at this remove from the Kaiser's war, to record the story of aircraft such as the Sopwith Pup and the actions and feelings of its gallant young pilots. Such men, such deeds, deserve a measure of immortality in the annals of their war, as do the aircraft that they flew. This monograph on a much-loved little aeroplane is therefore offered as a modest token of its way and an enduring sign where it went.

J.M.Bruce
January 2002

Jack Bruce

When this book was in its final stages we were saddened to learn that Jack Bruce had died on 26th May 2002. This present work is therefore the last of the many to appear from one of the greatest British air historians and the doyen of World War One aviation history.

John McIntosh Bruce, ISO, MA, FRHistS, MRAeS, was born at Scone, Perthshire, on 24th February 1923. He attended the Robert Douglas Memorial School in Scone and then the Perth Academy. In 1941 he was a founder member of the Edinburgh University Air Squadron, joining the RAF Volunteer Reserve the following year. Graduating as a pilot in June 1943, the following month he graduated in absentia from Edinburgh University as an MA. In 1944 he became a Staff Navigator, having gained first place in a course at No.1 General Reconnaissance School, Summerside, Prince Edward Island, Canada.

On leaving the RAF in 1946 he joined the civil service, working his way up through various executive and administrative posts with the Ministry of Employment in the Birmingham area. During this period he began private research into First World War aviation, and in particular British military aircraft of that period. In October 1952, *Flight* magazine published his critical study of the D.H.4, this being followed similar articles on other WW1 British types. Seventeen such articles appeared before his magnum opus, *'British Aeroplanes 1914 - 1918'*, was published by Putnam in 1957, at the then tremendous price of twelve guineas, to become the benchmark for all future works of this nature. It opened people's eyes to what could be achieved, and became a book which one had to have, whatever the price, setting a new standard for in-depth research and inspiring many others to research their particular subjects in great depth.

He became a member of the Historical Group of the Royal Aeronautical Society on its formation in 1959, serving on its committee for many years, and was also a Fellow of the Royal Historical Society. In 1966 he joined the staff of the embryo RAF Museum, a post he must have welcomed after his mundane years administering Employment offices, and when it opened at Hendon in 1972 he became Deputy Director and Keeper of Aircraft until eventually retiring in 1983, being then made a Companion of the Imperial Service Order. He next spent fifteen months as Charles A. Lindbergh Professor of Aerospace History at the Smithsonian Institution in Washington, D.C. before returning to England to spend his retirement continuing writing books and articles on his favourite topic.

He was a founder member of Air-Britain when it was formed in 1949, with contributions in the early days to *Air-Britain Digest*. He was also a member of the Cross & Cockade Society (later Cross & Cockade International) from its inception in 1960, becoming its vice-president in 1971, which post he still held at the time of his death.

He continued to write until the end, despite failing health in later years. In addition to articles in *Air Pictorial, Aeroplane* and *Air Enthusiast* magazines, he wrote 26 of the popular series of Profile Publications monographs, then later a series of Wind-Sock Datafile monographs for Ray Rimell's Albatros Productions.

In 1982 Putnam produced another epic book from his pen, *The Aeroplanes of the Royal Flying Corps Military Wing* (sadly he never managed a similar work on the Naval Wing), and in 1987 came *Britain's First Warplane: a Pictorial Survey of the First 400 Naval and Military Aircraft* from Arms & Armour Press.

We owe him a great debt.

Chapter 1

The Line
Of Pedigree

Long before man had created any kind of heavier-than-air flying machine, visionaries had foreseen, albeit in terms far from specific, fighting in the air in some distant future. In 1737, Thomas Grey (1716-71) had predicted:

'The time will come, when thou shalt lift thine eyes
To watch a long-drawn battle in the skies.'

Horace Walpole (1717-97) opined that

'There will be fights in the air with wind-guns
and bows and arrows.';

and Tennyson (1809-92), in his poem of 1842, 'Locksley Hall', had an expansive vision of an aeronautical future, but tempered his rapturous prediction of airborne commerce by an awareness of the darker side of humanity's propensity for self-destruction:

'For I dipt into the future, far as human eye could see,
Saw the Vision of the World, and all the wonder that would be;
Saw the heavens fill with commerce, argosies of magic sails,
Pilots of the purple twilight, dropping down with costly bales;
Heard the heavens fill with shouting, and there rain'd a ghastly dew,
From the nations' airy navies grappling in the central blue.'

Before and during the Battle of Fleurus, 26th June 1794, French military balloons served as observation posts; thereafter similar balloons participated in like manner in various campaigns. Perhaps this made it inevitable that later military thinking would regard the aeroplane merely as a mobile observation post and reconnaissance vehicle. Certainly at the time of the French military aeroplane trials of late 1911 the official specifications were for reconnaissance and spotting aircraft. In December 1911, Britain's War Office followed the same limited line of thought when setting out the requirements for aircraft participating in the Military Aeroplane Competition that was held at Larkhill in August 1912, specifically requiring them to carry two men, one the pilot, the other an observer. No provision for armament or communications equipment of any kind was specified.

One can only conjecture as to whether these official requirements might have been modified in any way if those responsible for drawing them up had seen the memorandum submitted by Capt Bertram Dickson, RFA, late in 1911, to the standing sub-committee of the Committee of Imperial Defence. In November 1911, the sub-committee, in a sudden reversal of official attitudes to aeronautics, began to consider 'the measures which might be taken to secure to this country an efficient aerial service'. By then the Air Battalion of the Royal Engineers had been in existence for some seven months: commanding No.2 Company was that remarkable officer Mjr Robert HM Brooke-Popham (whose name will appear frequently in this book) who, in delivering a lecture in 1910, said that he saw no reason why aviators should not shoot at one another in flight.

Capt Bertram Dickson was an early aviator of distinction and prophetic vision; and in his submission to the sub-committee of the CID he wrote:

'In the case of a European war between two countries, both sides would be equipped with large corps of aeroplanes, each trying to obtain information of the other, and to hide its own movements. The efforts which each would exert in order to hinder or prevent the enemy from obtaining information would lead to the inevitable result of a war in the air, for the supremacy of the air, by armed aeroplanes against each other. This fight for the supremacy of the air in future wars will be of the first and greatest importance, and when it has been won the land and sea forces of the loser will be at such a disadvantage that the war will certainly have to terminate at a much smaller loss in men and money to both sides.'

Dickson's predictions were to become grim reality in less than four years, but went unheeded in the Military Aeroplane Competition, which succeeded only in producing a grotesquely unsuitable winner in the Cody biplane, while all but ignoring those entrant aircraft that had real potential.

The official narrow outlook was not shared by the men of the Air Battalion, RE, and the succeeding Military Wing of the Royal Flying Corps, who clearly saw that aeroplanes could have other military uses. Even before the Military Aeroplane Competition started, they, and the staff of the Royal Aircraft Factory, Farnborough, had mounted machine-guns on aeroplanes, dropped missiles and experimented with wireless and other forms of signalling.

More significantly, in the field of aeroplane design, work had begun in the Royal Aircraft Factory on the design of the B.S.1 (Blériot Scout No.1) in the summer of 1912. This was a small single-seat tractor biplane with a span of 8.388m (27ft 6in) and a 100hp Gnome Omega-Omega 14-cylinder rotary engine. In terms of performance the B.S.1 was intended to realize the conviction of its designer, Geoffrey de Havilland, that it was possible at that time to build an aeroplane capable of exceeding 90mph, and thus provide a means of delivering reconnaissance reports to field commanders with minimum delay.

The B.S.1 had a further and significant potential that was not recognised at the time: as a small, high-speed single-seat scouting aircraft it was the progenitor of a whole class of military aeroplanes that, in their armed form, were the single-seat fighters that, from early 1915 onwards, were to form a vital component of every air service of any size. In British parlance the term 'scout' continued, during the 1914-18 war, to be applied to such aircraft for some time after they had ceased to perform any semblance of scouting.

Farnborough's portentous B.S.1 was, partly geometrically, though not structurally, a scaled-down B.E.3. It crashed on 27th March 1913 while being flown by Geoffrey de Havilland, and it appears that by that time Mervyn O'Gorman, the Superintendent of the Royal Aircraft Factory, had decided that this new category of aeroplane merited a more distinctly separate designation and had renamed it S.E.2. In respect only of the bizarre, unrelated and unsuccessful S.E.1, the initials had signified Santos [Dumont] Experimental: now, however, in the

A leading part in the design of the Sopwith company's fast single-engine biplane of 1913 was played by Harry Hawker. In this photograph, taken at Hendon, Hawker stands in front of the second Sopwith D.1, better known in its time as the Sopwith three-seater.

(Via Chaz Bowyer)

case of the S.E.2 and its successors they stood for Scouting Experimental.

As part of its repair process the S.E.2 was modified; in its revised form it did not fly again until October 1913. By that time another British aircraft of similar type was under construction in the works of the Sopwith Aviation Co Ltd at Kingston-upon-Thames. It was delivered to Brooklands on Thursday 27th November 1913, was assembled in about 1½ hours, and was immediately taken into the air by Harry Hawker, 'flying round the track at about 90mph', according to the weekly *Flight* of 6th December 1913. *Flight*'s report of these events continued: 'This machine Mr Hawker is taking to Australia with him shortly'.

This new Sopwith was a tiny tractor biplane with a wingspan of only 25ft 6in. and a 80hp Gnome Lambda engine;

The new Sopwith biplane, soon to be nicknamed Tabloid, as the cynosure of a group of admirers at Hendon after its dramatic arrival there on 29th November 1913. The universality of the cloth cap is evident: second from left, wearing his reversed in contemporary-aviator fashion, is the well-known Hendon pilot Marcus D. Manton. Adjusting his own cap, Harry Hawker is just behind and to left of the aircraft's interplane struts.

remarkably, in its prototype form it was a two-seater, accommodating pilot and passenger side by side in considerable discomfort.

It proved to be every bit as fast as *Flight*'s reporter had estimated, for its performance had been measured at Farnborough on the morning of Saturday 29th November 1913. There, with pilot, passenger and fuel for 2½ hours, it recorded a maximum speed of 92mph and a minimum of 36.9mph; it climbed to a height of 1,200ft in one minute. These figures must have impressed the staff of the Royal Aircraft Factory, for they were rather better than those of the B.S.1/S.E.2: not only did the Sopwith achieve these results with an engine of lower power than that of the B.S.1, and with a passenger aboard, but its fuselage was structurally simpler and aerodynamically less refined than that of Geoffrey de Havilland's design. Significantly, this made it a better production prospect than the S.E.2.

How much, if anything, was known outside Farnborough about the S.E.2 in the summer of 1913 is uncertain, though its existence can hardly have gone completely unnoticed. The official Reports & Memoranda No.86 (Report on Full Scale Work, by Mervyn O'Gorman, Superintendent of the Royal Aircraft Factory), dated March 1913, included seven paragraphs and four pages of graphs devoted to the B.S.1/S.E.2 and was incorporated in the Technical Report of the Advisory Committee for Aeronautics, 1912-13. The entire Technical Report bore the printing date 1914, and its contents, therefore, may not have been generally available for earlier scrutiny; but Geoffrey de Havilland's accident was immediately reported, and, despite efforts to maintain a measure of secrecy concerning the nature of the aircraft he was flying, there can be little doubt that it soon became clear that the S.E.2 was an unusually fast aeroplane.

It cannot now be known to what extent, if at all, it inspired Harry Hawker, to whom has been attributed a leading share in the design of the diminutive new Sopwith. Others believed to have participated therein were Fred Sigrist and, of course, Tom Sopwith himself; also closely involved were R.J.Ashfield, Harry Kauper and Frank Cowlin.

Such were the engaging simplicity of performance trials and the innocent trust in a new and, for the period, advanced aircraft that the Sopwith flew on to Hendon on 29th November 1913, as soon as its business at Farnborough had been completed. Its arrival was reported in *Flight*'s issue of 6th December 1913:

'A machine was then seen approaching at a great rate over West Hendon. This turned out to be the new 80hp Gnome Sopwith biplane, piloted by Mr Hawker. On entering the aerodrome he made two complete circuits at an astounding speed, which Mr Reynolds estimated at nearly 90 miles an hour.'

Clearly, a considerable impression had been made.

This was also apparent from the report that was published in *The Aeroplane* of 4th December 1913:

'On Saturday afternoon Mr Hawker arrived from Brooklands in a hurry on what is probably the fastest practical biplane in the world, and, before landing, flew a few times round the pylons just to show what a biplane can do if you will only let it. The machine in question was the "tabloid" Sopwith biplane, 80hp Gnome, which, despite its compactness, has all the qualities of an aeroplane with nothing of the horizontal helicopter about it, for although with tail up and engine all out, a speed of well over 90mph can be attained, yet it has flown officially at 35½ mph with full tanks and a passenger.'

Apart from that report's somewhat fulsome enthusiasm, it provided what was probably the first association in print of the

Also taken at Hendon on 29th November 1913, this photograph clearly illustrates the clean compactness of the Tabloid Prototype. The forward edge of the cockpit was raised to form a wind deflector in lieu of a separate windscreen.

term 'tabloid' with the little Sopwith, coming only five days after its appearance at Hendon.

In *Flight*'s report published on 6th December 1913, the new Sopwith was referred to as Hawker's 'Baby' tractor biplane. On page ix of the same issue of that weekly there appeared a modest advertisement by the well-known firm of manufacturing chemists, Burroughs, Wellcome & Co of London, for their

> '*Tabloid* Adjustable Head Dressing, Compressed (Regd Design): Cap-like, instantly applied without skill; stays in position; washable. EVERY AVIATOR SHOULD CARRY IT IN READINESS. 10d each, complete. All chemists.'

The Aeroplane of 11th December carried (on page 633) another Burroughs, Wellcome advertisement, promoting

> '*Tabloid* first-aid pocket outfits: No.706, 7/6; No.710, 2/0. Sold by all chemists.'

On the next-but-one page of that issue, a possibly apprehensive C.G.Grey sought to ward off the potential displeasure of one of his regular advertisers by printing this item:

> '*The Tabloid*
> In response to earnest enquirers the small speedy Sopwith biplane has been nicknamed the "Tabloid" because it contains so many good qualities in such small compass, and also because it is such a concentrated dose of medicine for certain gentlemen at the Royal Aircraft Factory. One hopes that Messrs Burroughs, Wellcome & Co, ever good friends to aviators, will not consider the nickname an infringement of their trade mark.'

In this rear view can be seen the relative width of the fuselage and the size of the cockpit opening for the two side-by-side occupants.

Typically, Grey had managed to work in a venomous side-swipe at the Royal Aircraft Factory while trying to wriggle off the hook of his own facetiousness.

Burroughs, Wellcome & Co had advertised in *The Aeroplane* from November 1911; they had been advertising in *Flight* from January 1912 and possibly earlier. They were not amused by what they regarded as an infringement of their brand name, and (so it was said) even considered taking legal action on that account. Fortunately, good sense prevailed: it was evident that the offending nickname was a popular appellation not a Sopwith company designation, and the threatened litigation was abandoned. Perhaps it was also recognised that such widespread publicising of the name *Tabloid* was an excellent form of free advertising. All of this, of course, merely served to ensure the immovable establishment and usage of the name for the aircraft.

In the Sopwith Works Order record against the date 25th October 1913 that first Tabloid was listed as *'one 80hp Tractor Two-seater Type St. B.'* The better-known designation *Type S.S.* apparently did not come into use until December 1913, and was more appropriate to the single-seat production version of the design than to the two-seat prototype.

Harry Hawker had flown the little Sopwith back to Brooklands from Hendon on 30th November 1913. After only a brief time he left for his visit to his native Australia. As foreshadowed, he took the prototype Tabloid with him, arriving at Fremantle in RMS *Maloja* on 13th January 1914. Assembly of the aircraft had been completed by 26th January, when it was exhibited at the CLC Motor & Engineering Works, Melbourne; and on the following day Harry Hawker flew it for the first time in Australia. His later public flights drew great crowds and aroused much public enthusiasm: a graphic account of his

These two photographs were taken during Hawker's visit to Australia with the Tabloid prototype. The aircraft was at Randwick racecourse, New South Wales; the date was 28th February 1914.
(Colin Owers)

Australian flying in the Tabloid was given by his widow Muriel Hawker in her book *HG Hawker, Airman: his life and work* (Hutchinson, London; 1922).

Harry Hawker returned to England on Saturday 6th June 1914, and was flying at Brooklands next day: his Tabloid did not arrive at Brooklands until 11th July, five weeks later. Events had moved portentously in his absence, for the Tabloid was then in production, and five single-seat examples had already been delivered to the Royal Flying Corps Military Wing. Notwithstanding the relentless barrage of contumelious criticism hurled *ad nauseam* at the War Office and Royal Aircraft Factory by journalists of the C.G.Grey persuasion – in particular, despite the allegation that the Military Wing was incapable of looking beyond the Factory for its aeroplanes – the War Office had placed an initial contract, No.A.2368, for nine Tabloids as early as 18th December 1913, a mere three weeks after the appearance of the prototype at Brooklands (though it appears that the effective date of the contract was regarded as 9th January 1914).

A further three were ordered under the same contract on 13th March 1914. The total cost of this order was £12,900; each Tabloid therefore cost £1,075.

It must be recorded that no production of the S.E.2 was ordered; hence the Sopwith Tabloid was the first military single-seat scout in history to be ordered and built in quantity.

The due delivery date for the first production Tabloid was 27th February 1914, but nearly two months were to elapse before the RFC received its first aircraft. The delay was probably accounted for by the diversion of Sopwith production resources to the non-military matter of participating in the 1914 contest for the Schneider Trophy.

Jacques Schneider had presented his trophy for a speed and seaworthiness competition between seaplanes. The first contest, held at Monaco in 1913, was won by Maurice Prévost, flying a Deperdussin monoplane; his average speed was a stately 73.63km/h (45.75mph). Britain was not represented in any way.

The adaptation of the Sopwith Tabloid to seaplane form included the sensible and necessary installation of a 100hp Gnome Monosoupape engine. Initially listed on 2nd April 1914 as Hydro Tractor (type HS), the aircraft was given a single central float of relatively broad beam and two small outboard floats, and arrangement that proved to be unsatisfactory. The Tabloid seaplane's construction was initiated under Sopwith Works Order No.56, dated, dated 2nd February 1914; when completed, it was taken to Southampton Water for its first tests, but did not become airborne on that occasion, probably on 1st April 1914. *The Aeroplane* of 9th April 1914 reported:

'In taxying one of the wing tip floats became immersed [sic], and the machine turned a somersault. Mr Pixton was thrown out as the machine turned over and merely received a wetting, though he says it is by no means easy to swim in an aviation costume.'

One of the shore-handling party was R.E.Nicoll, who described the mishap in a letter published 36 years later, in *Flight* of 28th December 1950:

'As a member of the small party of four who originally assembled the aircraft at Hamble, it is interesting to recall what actually happened. The aircraft, as at first built, had a single main float, and after Pixton had gone on board we launched the machine from the end of the slipway, holding the tail whilst the engine was started. After the let-go signal, and immediately the engine was opened out, the machine went straight over on its back, throwing Pixton (who had only just got out of bed after a very bad cold) into the icy waters of the Hamble River. The machine drifted out to mid-stream and after some time was made fast with a rope around its tail; finally it was pulled ashore on the change of the tide at about 2 o'clock the next morning.

'The considerably damaged wood and fabric structure was packed up and sent back to the Sopwith Works, where it was completely rebuilt in record time

Probably taken on 8th April 1914, this photograph shows the Tabloid floatplane Schneider Trophy entrant by the Thames. At that pre-contest date the aircraft's tail float was relatively small, had no water rudder and was attached by three struts. The man standing just behind the port wingtip wearing a muffler, is Victor Mahl.

(British Aerospace, Kingston-on-Thames)

Probably taken around the same time, the Tabloid floatplane Schneider Trophy entrant afloat on the River Thames.

and…fitted with twin floats. It was then quickly despatched to Monaco where, in due course, it secured the coveted trophy for Great Britain.'

Sir Tom Sopwith himself, in the first lecture to be delivered before the newly-formed Historical Group of the Royal Aeronautical Society on 21st November 1960, added some further details of the first attempt to fly the Tabloid floatplane:

'We dismantled the little biplane; took it back to Kingston; cut the main float longitudinally in halves and made them into two floats; built a new twin-float chassis and flew the revised machine off the Thames at Kingston, without permission, then shipped it to Monaco, all in 3$^{1}/_{2}$ days.'

After repair and modification, the Tabloid seaplane was taken to the Thames just below Kingston Bridge at about 5 am on 7th April 1914, in the hope of testing its new twin-float undercarriage and of flying it along the river above Teddington

The Tabloid seaplane at Monaco, now with a larger-volume tail float faired up to the underside of the rear fuselage, and fitted with a water rudder. The aircraft's contest number 3 has been painted on the rudder.
(Jean Nogl)

Lock. Despite the early hour Thames Conservancy officials objected and the Sopwith team had to content themselves with flotation tests.

Equally early on the following morning the little seaplane was transported to Richmond, which was within the bailiwick of the Port of London Authority, and was launched at Glover's Island. Water handling and taxying proved satisfactory, and Howard Pixton took off and flew towards Eel Pie Island. The Tabloid's Monosoupape was not running too well, and there was too little room for a proper flight to be made.

Photographs taken at the time show that the Tabloid seaplane had a triangular fixed fin and a new, plain rudder of considerable area. No doubt these new surfaces were provided primarily to balance the effect of the side area of the floats, but the fin and a generally similar rudder were to be standard features of the production Tabloids delivered to the RFC.

Considered against the circumstances of the time, the Sopwith decision thus to divert time, resources and effort to participation in the Schneider contest was breathtakingly bold, viewed against the company's rare contract to deliver Tabloids to the Military Wing. According to *The Aeroplane* of 16th April 1914, 'Mr Sopwith does not expect to win, he merely hopes that his machine will put up a respectable performance' - diplomatic modesty, no doubt, for hopes were obviously high enough to justify risking the displeasure of the War Office at delay in deliveries of its first Tabloids. It is, of course, possible - perhaps even probable - that the War Office was consulted and apprised of Sopwith's hopes, for a good Schneider-contest result could only redound to Britain's (and, of course, Sopwith's) honour. However that may be, this was the same War Office that had been the target of unrelenting journalistic vitriol for its alleged lack of vision and indifference to British-designed aircraft - a potential purchaser who (so it was implied) had to be propitiated to an exceptional extent to order any British aircraft in quantity; and to which, moreover, Sopwith was already a contractor - for the supply, in quantity, of the Sopwith D.2 tractor biplane, a version of the three-seater of February 1913. At the material time, the Tabloid was a quite revolutionary aircraft, and the War Office should be given at least some credit for ordering it so quickly, and in preference to

The Schneider entrant under tow at Monaco.   *(Jean Devaux)*

the S.E.2 of the Royal Aircraft Factory, which institution the War Office was alleged to favour to the exclusion of all others.

The well-merited victory of the Tabloid seaplane at Monaco on 20th April 1914 is a matter of history and is amply documented elsewhere. Piloted by Howard Pixton, it completed the required twenty-eight 10km laps in 2hrs 13.4secs; its average speed was 85.8mph. That mark passed, Pixton flew on for two more laps to cover a total of 300km (186.42 miles) in 2hrs 9mins 10secs: his overall average speed was 86.6mph, and he had succeeded in covering one 10km lap at 92.1mph. His final speed would have been greater had not his Monosoupape lost power from the 15th lap, when one of its nine cylinders cut out.

This handsome victory created something of a sensation, and continental opinions of the capabilities of British aircraft and pilots had to be considerably revised.

The success of the Tabloid floatplane led eventually to orders for a similar seaplane version from the Admiralty; and the production aircraft, known initially as the Sopwith Schneider, later as the Sopwith Baby, served the RNAS and Royal Air Force until the end of the 1914-18 war. In so doing they long outlived the production Tabloids, which were used in very small numbers by the RFC and RNAS.

Although the first standard production Tabloid landplane had flown on 11th April 1914 it was not delivered until 22nd April: perhaps its delivery was delayed until any possible need for spares for the Schneider aircraft was safely past (but that is speculation). It was flown to Farnborough by Harold Barnwell; in the course of its acceptance flights there it recorded maximum and minimum speeds of 94.9mph and 39.6mph, respectively. One official record suggests that this first Tabloid was damaged on arrival at Farnborough; however that may be, the aircraft was allotted the official number 378 and was subjected to structural testing in the Royal Aircraft Factory in June 1914.

Deliveries of the other Tabloids to the RFC proceeded throughout the spring and summer of 1914. The second (the due delivery date of which had been 9th March 1914) arrived at Brooklands on Friday, 24th April, was flown by Howard Pixton on 25th April and by Fred Raynham on the following day. It was flown several times during the ensuing week and on Sunday 3rd May Pixton demonstrated it to a visiting French commission. Not until Wednesday 6th May did he fly it to Farnborough, where he had the bad luck to overturn on landing. Damage was not irreparable however, and the Tabloid was quickly restored to be photographed wearing its official number 326. Its delivery date was officially recorded as 13th May 1914, perhaps a consequence of its landing mishap. Also delivered on that date was No.381.

Heavily oil-stained after the sustained effort that brought it victory, the little Sopwith had, as a charming Monegasque tribute, flowers bound to its forward centre-section struts.

The Sopwith assembly shop in early 1914. At least four Tabloids at different stages of advancement can be seen; at right is a hull for one of the larger, unequal-span Bat-Boats of which at least three were built.

Because the first production Tabloid was diverted to the Schneider Trophy contest, the first of the type to be delivered to the Military Wing of the RFC was this one, photographed at Brooklands in April 1914. It was flown to Farnborough by Harold Barnwell on 22nd April, was allotted the official number 378, but was subsequently tested to destruction and saw no squadron service. All production Tabloids delivered to the Military Wing were single-seaters: comparison with the lower photograph on page 13 shows how the size of the cockpit opening was reduced.

Pixton made the delivery flight of the second aircraft on 6th May,1914, but suffered a landing mishap on arrival at Farnborough, with the undignified result seen in this photograph.

One Tabloid that apparently never was delivered to the RFC was the winner of the Schneider contest. After its return from Monaco it retained its 100hp Monosoupape engine, and was fitted with a neat V-strut wheel undercarriage that was a marked improvement on the twin-skid structure that was retained, with lengthened skids, on those Tabloids that found their way to the RFC. It thus introduced the characteristic Sopwith undercarriage: two simple Vs of elliptical-section steel tubing transversely connected by two spreader bars on which were pivoted, centrally, the half-axles that carried the wheels. The upward displacement of these half-axles was restrained by rubber bungee cord which, wound round the axles and the apices of the V-struts, served as a shock absorber, giving a measure of independent suspension to each wheel. The entire undercarriage structure offered appreciably less resistance than

After repair, the RFC's second Tabloid was numbered 326 and was allocated to No.5 Squadron. Main component numbers were stencilled on in very small characters. Those visible in this photograph can be seen on the rudder (SAC 41), fin (SAC 45) and fuselage (SAC 42). The apparent bulge along the underside was formed by sagging fabric that had not been properly laced up.   (R.A.E. Crown copyright)

Another Tabloid at Farnborough, after delivery for the Military Wing, but before application of its official number.   (R.A.E. Crown copyright)

the twin-skid arrangement, an important consideration because it was intended to enter the 100hp Tabloid in the sporting contests that lay ahead in that last peaceful summer of 1914*.

The first of these was the third Aerial Derby, which was to be held on Saturday 23rd May 1914. With its new wheel undercarriage the Schneider Tabloid arrived at Brooklands on 20th May, the day on which the fifth standard production Tabloid was also delivered there. Next day Howard Pixton flew the 100hp aircraft, made several further flights on it on 22nd May, and on the 23rd set off for Hendon at 10.30am. The Sopwith company had also entered a standard Tabloid in the Aerial Derby: This could only have been one of the production aircraft built for the RFC, but it is virtually impossible now to determine which. It might have been intended that the fifth Tabloid should be the second-string Sopwith entry in the contest, but the weather on 23rd May was so unfavourable (and probably contributed to the loss of Gustav Hamel that day) that the Derby was postponed for two weeks.

On 26th May the sixth standard production Tabloid arrived at Brooklands to join the fifth; it seems likely that the third was also still there at that time. Pixton flew two of them to Farnborough, one on 2nd June to become 386, the other next day to become 387: presumably the third of this trio was the Tabloid flown, with the race number 18, by Pixton in the Aerial Derby on 6th June. The 100hp Schneider Tabloid, No.21 in the race, was piloted by Harold Barnwell.

Both Sopwiths performed well, but dangerously deteriorating visibility compelled both Barnwell and Pixton to abandon the race, which was won by Walter Brock on a Morane-Saulnier monoplane built by the Grahame-White company.

As noted on an earlier page, Harry Hawker returned to England from Australia on Aerial Derby day, 6th June 1914. Next day he was back at Brooklands, and lost no time before flying the 100hp Schneider Tabloid. Thereafter he flew it regularly and gave frequent exhibitions of looping. One of his flights took him to Farnborough on 15th June; while there the aircraft's speed was measured to be 111mph and other aspects of its performance and handling might have been evaluated, for Hawker did not fly it back to Brooklands until the following day.

---

* **Note:** *This form of undercarriage was the subject of the Sopwith company's British Patent No.109,146, dated 1st November 1916.*

The Schneider Tabloid with its neat and simple wheel undercarriage photographed at Hendon on the occasion of the 1914 Aerial Derby with its pilot in the race, Harold Barnwell. The fabric wheel covers were held in place by cord carried over the tyres.

A general view of some of the aircraft competing in the 1914 Aerial Derby, lined up at Hendon on 6 June 1914. At right are the two Sopwith entries, the 100hp Schneider Trophy winner (racing number 21) and the standard 80hp Tabloid, flown by Pixton, to which the racing number 18 was allotted.

Howard Pixton being photographed beside his Tabloid at Hendon, Aerial Derby Day, 1914.

Another production Tabloid that the Sopwith company apparently flew competitively in the summer of 1914 was this one; for a time at least it bore the identifying number 3 on the fuselage sides. This photograph is dated 11th June, 1914, but the aircraft was seen and photographed at Brooklands at an earlier date.   *(Fleet Air Arm Museum)*

By Wednesday 17th June Hawker was looping the aircraft with engine stopped. It was intended that he should give looping exhibitions every Sunday afternoon during that summer. On 20th June Hawker and the Schneider aircraft were entrants in the Hendon-Manchester-Hendon race, but he became ill while flying and was obliged to withdraw from the contest.

A week later, on the evening of 27th June, Hawker's career almost came to a premature end. Flying the 100hp Schneider Tabloid, he looped with engine off at a height of 1,200ft. It was reported by C.G.Grey that Hawker completed the loop,

> '... perfectly, but...as he came out of it, he started a vertical dive with a spin in it.' Aviation terminology at that time was neither securely established nor standardised, and Grey's meaning is not clear beyond doubt. He went on to describe how, in the initial stages of descent, the Tabloid was 'standing vertically on its nose' and its wings were rotating about the axis of the aircraft's centre line; subsequently '... the tail seemed to swing out and the vertical path became an irregular spiral to the right with the body nearly horizontal and the left wing up'

A more succinct and phlegmatic account printed in *Flight* of 3rd July 1914 suggested that in fact the Tabloid, so far from completing its loop perfectly, had stalled while inverted and 'fell out of the inverted position sideways'. Whatever the precise truth of the matter, Hawker had too little height to recover from the spin. By good fortune his aircraft fell into trees that broke his fall but folded the wings upwards; miraculously Hawker managed to extricate himself from the ruins unscathed, and was flying a standard Tabloid next day.

That next day was Sunday 28th June 1914. In distant, obscure Sarajevo, a young Serbian nationalist, Gavrilo Princip, fired the shots that murdered the heir to the Austro-Hungarian throne, the Archduke Franz Ferdinand, and his wife. A month later to the day Austria-Hungary, with the ready support of Germany, declared war on Serbia, and the world was dragged towards the abyss.

During that fateful month Harry Hawker delivered four Tabloids to Farnborough; on the day when Britain declared war on Germany, 4th August 1914, he delivered another standard Tabloid and the two-seat prototype to the RFC. By that time the prototype had been modified: its wings were re-rigged with no dihedral on the upper wing and apparently increased dihedral on the lower, providing what hindsight could regard as a foretaste of the Camel; a plain V-strut undercarriage replaced the twin-skid structure; and the rear fuselage was stripped of fabric, allegedly in the belief that this would enhance the aircraft's looping capability.

The modified prototype was still a two-seater, and on acceptance by the RFC it was allotted the official serial number 604. Its purchase price was £900, its engine an 80hp Gnome, No.3103. Only two more production Tabloids were flown to Farnborough for the RFC after the outbreak of war: these became 611, which was delivered on 6th August, and 654, flown from Brooklands to Farnborough by Howard Pixton on 29th August and handed to the RFC on 1st September.

Pilots of the Military Wing were becoming acquainted with the Tabloid during that summer of 1914. Because they understood that they would have to fly the type on military duties that would prove to be significantly different from light-hearted entertainment flights over and around a compatible aerodrome, their assessments were, not surprisingly, more penetrating and forward-looking than those of a display pilot.

The Tabloid's introduction to squadron service was delayed because modifications had to be made. On arrival at Farnborough the aircraft were inspected by the Aircraft Inspection Department, who, in addition to examining the airframe, apparently added minor fittings and installed instruments. The addition of safety clips to the valve rockers of the engine increased the Gnome's diameter just enough to necessitate slight enlargement of the engine cowling: the need for this was conveyed to the Sopwith company in a letter dated 12th June 1914 from the Director-General of Military Aeronautics (DGMA).

A later view of the 100hp Schneider Tabloid, again at Hendon, but this time wearing the racing number 14 for its participation in the Hendon-Manchester-Hendon race, flown on 20th June 1914. By that time it had new wheel covers that were more tidily fitted. The aircraft in the background of this photograph is the Grahame-White Lizzie.

The modified prototype Tabloid in the form in which it was taken over by the RFC on the outbreak of war, initially as 604; later transferred to the RNAS, it was renumbered 169.

RFC pilots might have wanted other modifications; indeed they might even have had some reservations about using their Tabloids. On 30th June 1914, Major J.F.A.Higgins, then commanding No.5 Squadron, RFC, flew a Tabloid from Farnborough to Netheravon, presumably for his squadron. Next day he submitted a detailed report that was communicated to the DGMA on 9th July by Lt Col. F.H.Sykes, OC Royal Flying Corps (Military Wing). This refers to the aircraft as the first of its type to be delivered to the Military Wing and indicates that it was 381, which had been the third to be flown to Farnborough but probably was the first to be formally delivered to the Military Wing proper.

The full text of Sykes's report, which largely embodied Higgins's manuscript text, is as follows:

Report on SA (Sopwith Scout Aeroplane No. 381)

The first Sopwith Scout Aeroplane delivered to the Military Wing was flown from Farnborough to Netheravon by Major Higgins on 30th June 1914, and as a result of his experience I wish to bring to notice the following points:-

1. The machine has a strong desire to climb when the engine is full on, and considerable force is necessary to keep it down, by means of the lever, to the level flying position. It would probably be advantageous if a spring were fitted to assist the pilot to keep the lever forward.
2. The allowance for engine torque in the design does not appear to be sufficient, as the machine flies with its left wing down the whole time, and considerable effort is necessary to keep it level. A spring might be fitted to assist the pilot as regards this, also. Both the springs mentioned in (1) and (2) should be fitted with a wire strainer to adjust the tension as necessary.
3. It is probably inadvisable that these machines should be flown at full speed (i.e. at full engine power) always, especially on a very gusty day, partly because they have to be held down to prevent them from climbing, and partly because they have a hard, unyielding action when struck by gusts. For this reason a throttle that can be worked by the pilot is very

necessary; the present one is in a most inconvenient position and practically has to be tied open as it jars to the shut position. A double Bowden control on the control lever would probably best answer the purpose.
4. The petrol tap lever (i.e., the one operating the needle valve) is not a convenient arrangement; a ratchet arrangement such as used on S.E.2 or the later Henry Farman is more convenient than the small twisting lever. This is not essential but would add greatly to the ease of adjusting the petrol to suit the amount of throttle opening.
5. The present form of 'cut-out' fitted to the control lever is an inconvenient one, and in the case of No. 381 not strong enough. It is of the push in and out type. A spring cut-out fixed at the top of the handle, as in S.E.2, is more convenient and not so liable to get out of order.
6. Most of the instruments are placed where the pilot can hardly see them. I suggest that I might perhaps be asked to send one of my pilots to Contractors to discuss this point when new types of machines are ordered in which the standard instrument board cannot be fixed.
7. The present undercarriage and wheels are too weak and could not stand landing on anything in the nature of rough ground. It is believed that several undercarriages have been broken by Sopwith pilots, landing even on perfectly smooth ground. I understand that a new undercarriage has been designed, and recommend that it be tried immediately and, if satisfactory, substituted for the existing type on all machines before delivery, as I consider it unwise to use the existing type.
8. I believe it has been suggested that the single lever should be done away with and a two-handled lever substituted. Most pilots dislike the two-handled type. The present lever is satisfactory, but springs should be fitted as suggested in (1) and (2).
9. General flying of the machine
   The machine flies well, does not seem to be affected by 'bumps' and corrects itself laterally. It is rather unstable fore and aft but controllable. With a stronger undercarriage it would be fairly easy to land.

Major Higgins reports that on the whole S.E.2 is a more pleasant machine to fly:

[From PRO File AIR 1/789/204/4/650]

The designation SA quoted in the heading to that report was part of the short-lived official scheme of aircraft nomenclature that was introduced on 10th June 1914 and abandoned from 26th August 1914. 'SA' was the type designation for the Sopwith Scout, 80hp Gnome.

Major Higgins's report indicates that 381 possessed what was a characteristic of many later Sopwith types in being tail heavy, and that it required from the pilot an amount of physical effort that was out of proportion to its size. The reference to the superiority of the S.E.2 has a certain piquancy.

The weakness of the Tabloid's undercarriage had been revealed by the mishaps suffered by the earliest deliveries. It was evidently, and understandably, enough to deter pilots from flying the Tabloid, and on 8th July 1914, seven days after submitting his report on 381, Mjr Higgins wrote to the Military Wing's Officer i/c Stores:

'Can you let me know the position as far as Sopwith Scouts are concerned? Are they to wait until a new undercarriage and wheels are fitted or may they be flown? I have one, 326, at Farnborough. I should be very much obliged if you would let me know early.'

The reply of 10th July informed Higgins that 'the Commanding Officer' (presumably Lt Col F.H.Sykes) had written to the War Office recommending that the strengthened undercarriage should be fitted to the Tabloids before they were taken into service, and that he had given a verbal instruction that they were not to be flown until that was done.

On 22nd July 1914, DGMA wrote to Sopwiths:

'Gentlemen,
With reference to your Contract A.2368 dated 9th January and 13th March last, for twelve Sopwith Scout biplanes, it is reported that the first machine delivered was found to be too weak in the undercarriage and wheels, and was unable to land on rough ground without damage.

'It is understood that in the later machines delivered, an extra strut has been provided which obviates this weakness, and that you are prepared to fit a similar strut and stronger wheels, free of charge, to the remaining machines, whether delivered or not, under the above Contract.

'Please confirm this.

'The matter is specially urgent as regards the Biplanes delivered and I shall be glad if you will arrange to carry out the above modification in these machines as early as possible.'

War Office confirmation of Sykes's verbal ban on flying Tabloids with the original undercarriage came in an instruction dated 23rd July 1914 and addressed to C.1A of the War Office and the OC Military Wing.
Signed by Major W.Sefton Brancker, this read:

'The firm have now been requested to fit the extra strut and stronger wheels into the undercarriages of all the machines on this order. Will you please keep these machines until this alteration has been carried out.

'Those delivered with the strengthened undercarriage should of course be handed over as soon as they have passed their tests.'

By that date, with war less than two weeks away, at least nine, possibly ten, of the RFC's Tabloids had been delivered to Farnborough, but it is not known how many had the strengthened undercarriage. Proof that 394 had it exists in a photograph; presumably 611 and 654 were delivered with it; 362, which had to be sent back to the makers on 8th July to have its longerons replaced, was returned to the RFC on 23rd July with 'new type chassis fitted'; 386, which had been delivered to Farnborough on 2nd June, was given its new undercarriage on 6th August, and apparently only then was officially handed over to the Military Wing next day, 7th August.

Misgivings about the strength of the Tabloid's undercarriage led to the introduction of an additional strut on each side, as seen here on 394 at Farnborough. This aircraft was also transferred to the RNAS; it was renumbered, first as 904, soon afterwards as 167. On 9th October 1914 it was flown by Flt Cdr Spenser Grey in his abortive attempt to bomb the airship sheds at Cologne, and was then abandoned at Antwerp.

(R.A.E. Crown copyright)

Chapter 2

Into War

On 31st July 1914, with war imminent, the Military Wing of the RFC drew up a list of aircraft and engines that were serviceable on that date, in or destined for the four squadrons (Nos. 2, 3, 4 and 5) that were to go to France to operate with the British Expeditionary Force. Possibly because several of the Tabloids still had to be modified at that time no aircraft of the type appeared in the list, but four (362, 386, 387 and 611) went to France in transit cases with the Aircraft Park, which unit arrived at Boulogne on 18th August. This set itself up at Amiens on 21st August, but was ordered to move to Le Havre four days later; only after a sequence of moves did it finally settle at St.Omer late in October.

Two of that quartet of Tabloids, 387 and 611, were allotted to No.3 Squadron on 24th August, but their careers were brief: both were reported wrecked and were struck off charge, 387 on 2nd September, 611 on the following day. Although one official record asserts that 386 went to No.4 Squadron on 26th December 1914, the aircraft's log book unequivocally states that it was handed to No.5 Squadron on 3rd December.

Pilots of that unit who flew it were Lt B.C.Hucks, Capt F.V.Holt, Capt G.I.Carmichael and Mjr A.C.H.MacLean, OC No. 5 Squadron. In 1957 Group Captain Carmichael recalled that the Tabloid was 'a joy to fly'; he flew it on several

reconnaissance missions before handing it over to No.4 Squadron on 9th January 1915.

In its new unit 386 underwent minor modifications, including the fitting of 'two boxes for shot dropping' on 18th January. Whatever these were they were never used, for on 20th January the Tabloid crashed in a dive at Dunkerque; Major G.H.Raleigh, OC No.4 Squadron, who alone flew 386 while it was with his unit, was killed.

It seems that none of the Tabloids that went to France was provided with any kind of armament before leaving England, but one that was flown with offensive intent and some success was 387.

Its aggressive pilot was 2/Lt Norman C.Spratt, who had acquired a reputation as a pre-war pilot at Hendon, and in August 1914 was one of four flying officers attached to the Aircraft Park. His log book records that on six flights on 387 between 29th August and 2nd September 1914 he was 'chasing Germans'; his armament was sketchy. In his book *Recollections of an Airman* Louis Strange credits Spratt with a combat victory:

'He flew a Sopwith Tabloid and forced the enemy [allegedly an Albatros two-seater] to land by circling

Norman Spratt was the first man to fly any type of Sopwith as a fighter in combat with enemy aircraft. In this photograph he is with the British-built Breguet biplane that he flew at Hendon in 1913. He later flew as a test pilot at the Royal Aircraft Factory, Farnborough, subsequently joining the RFC. As a pilot of No.7 Squadron he was brought down and made PoW on 28th September 1915 while flying an R.E.5.

Gordon Bell, another early RFC pilot of Tabloids in France, was a well-known pilot of the pre-1914 period, and was one of British aviation's most colourful personalities. He met his death on 29th July 1918 at Villacoublay, when the Vickers F.B.16E broke up in the air. In this photograph he is seen at Eastchurch, probably early in 1914, with a Bleriot XI of the Naval Wing.

round him and making pretence to attack him. As a matter of fact, he had run out of ammunition, but the bluff succeeded and the occupants of the German machine were taken prisoners.'

Precisely when this event occurred was not recorded by Strange, but his account suggests that Spratt must have had at least a revolver as weapon at the time.

Another witness of Spratt's success was James McCudden, then a mechanic in No.3 Squadron but later Major J.T.B. McCudden, VC, DSO, MC, MM, who in a long and distinguished career as a fighter pilot flew the Tabloid's descendant, the Pup, in combat with No.66 Squadron and on Home Defence sorties. In his own remarkable book *Five Years in the Royal Flying Corps*, McCudden recorded that two Tabloids joined No.3 Squadron at St Quentin on 26th August 1914:

'Soon after landing, we saw two very fast machines come in, and on inspection they proved to be Sopwith "Tabloids" (small single-seater scouts with 80hp Gnome engines), flown by Lieuts Norman Spratt and Gordon Bell. These machines were very speedy for those days, doing nearly 90mph as well as having a good climb.

'They did not avail us much as fighting machines, in that they were not fitted in any way with firearms, but they could and did perform excellently from the scouting point of view.'

These two Tabloids were, of course, 387 and 611, both moving with No.3 Squadron to La Fère on 26th August and to Compiègne two days later. It was at the latter place that McCudden witnessed Norman Spratt's duel with the putative Albatros (but indicated, perhaps in error, the date thereof as 28th August):

'About 5.30pm a large German biplane flew over us and dropped three bombs. One fell near the camp lavatory, and it was a most diverting sight to see a certain Sergeant doing a record sprint partially disrobed. However, the bombs did no damage at all.

'The German (an Albatros perhaps) was pursued by Mr Spratt on his Sopwith Tabloid armed with a handful of fléchettes, the Sopwith gaining on the German quickly and visibly. It was said afterwards that Mr Spratt forced the German down by circling round him, but I do not know whether that is correct.'

The flight was Spratt's second that day during which he was 'chasing German aeroplanes', but he did not record his victory in his log book.

No.3 Squadron moved to Senlis on 30th August, to Juilly on 31st August and to Serris on 2nd September. Spratt flew 387 to Serris at 4 am that day; two hours later he took off to chase German aeroplanes, as described by Louis Strange:

'As usual, the German airmen spotted our new aerodrome at Serris and paid us a visit. They had an uncanny knack of finding out where we were located almost as soon as we arrived, so that we were not at all surprised to see them there. Norman Spratt went up to have a go at one of these disturbers of our peace and managed to fire thirty rounds at him from his revolver at close range, but the enemy remained apparently undamaged. Spratt landed in desperation and tied a hand grenade on to the end of a long piece of control cable; he had the bright idea of flying over the Hun and hitting his propeller with the grenade, but I felt very sceptical about his chances of bagging a victim that way, and I do not think he ever did.'

Spratt's log book records only one last flight on 387 on 2nd September, but does not mention his desperate improvisation, noting only that the flight was of no more than ten minutes' duration. McCudden's account helps to explain the brevity of the flight:

'The following evening, just before dusk, a Zeppelin was reported near us, and in the north-eastern sky a large smoke blur could be seen. Two machines left in pursuit, a Sopwith Tabloid flown by Mr Spratt and an Avro flown by Captain Wilson, of No.5 Squadron. They were away some time and arrived back in the dark, the Sopwith unfortunately capsizing on the ground. Happily the pilot was unhurt.'

As an RFC Tabloid pilot, Bentfield C.Hucks was contemporary with Gordon Bell. Hucks was a celebrated British display and aerobatic pilot in the pre-war era; behind him is the Bleriot XI-2 that he flew in 1914.

These engagements so gallantly initiated and fought by Norman Spratt were the first true combats in which a Sopwith Scout was flown as a fighter aircraft: they were, in their primitive way, exemplary, for they provided a practical demonstration of how superior speed and manoeuvrability gave the essential combat advantage to a fighting aeroplane: all that was lacking was effective armament. Those were epoch-making days, their events perhaps enough to warrant naming Spratt as the first single-seat fighter pilot in history. In more down-to-earth matters, his historic Tabloid was not returned to the Aircraft Park and was struck off squadron charge on the day of its crash.

As a similar fate befell 611 next day, 3rd September, that left only 362 and 386 still with the RFC in France; but as noted on an earlier page, 386 was wrecked on 20th January 1915. Evidently 654 went to France, but official records are conflicting and appear to confuse 654 and 362.

Other Tabloids might have gone to France in the autumn of 1914, for on 4th November the Aircraft Park reported that there were three engine-less Sopwith Scouts in transit cases at Rouen awaiting shipment back to England. Unfortunately these Tabloids were not identified, nor was there any indication of whether they were complete, damaged, or partly robbed of components needed as spares.

No.362 had gone to France with the Aircraft Park in August, but was not issued to a squadron. Its engine (No.3533/WD.23) was removed and returned to store, probably on or shortly after 13th October 1914, whereafter it might have been robbed of its instruments: a further entry dated 9th December 1914 records the fitting of a new clinometer, altimeter, watch, air-speed indicator, tachometer and compass. A new engine must also have been found, for on 12th December the Tabloid was tested at St.Omer by Lt B.C.Hucks. Minor adjustments were made and a broken rib in the lower starboard wing was replaced before Capt. F.V.Holt made two flights in the aircraft on 20th December.

Later that month a rifle was fixed to a port centre-section strut: this was probably the only attempt to mount fixed-gun armament on an RFC Tabloid. The installation could hardly have proved practical, but it was never put to the test of combat, for 362 crashed at St.Omer while being flown by Capt Holt on 17th January 1915. It was handed over to the Aircraft Park Stores on 3rd February, and was struck off to England next day.

Tabloid No.654 had been delivered to Farnborough by Howard Pixton on 29th August 1914, and on its acceptance tests had climbed to 3,500ft in 4½ minutes and had returned a speed of 95.4mph. On the following day it was inspected and fitted with instruments, and on 1st September was handed over to the Military Wing. It had probably gone to France before 16th October, on which date its engine (No.3566/WD.28) was taken out and returned to store. On 18th November it was logged, for unexplained reasons, as 'Rebuilt machine', was again fitted with instruments, and was completely re-doped. On 1st December 1914 it made three brief local flights, two by 2/Lt B.C.Hucks and one by Capt G.I. Carmichael of No.5 Squadron (who, curiously, logged his only Tabloid flight of that day as on 362, which might not have been airworthy at that time).

Next day, 2nd December, Hucks flew 654 from St.Omer to Bailleul and back, and from St.Omer to Merville and back; but on the latter flight he had the misfortune to turn over on landing. With skids, rudder and upper wing damaged, the Tabloid was handed to the Aircraft Park for repair. Apparently it was not reconstructed, however, for on 4th February, in company with 362, it was struck off for return to England.

That marked the end of the RFC's use of Tabloids in France, and it is doubtful whether any of the other surviving three, or at most four, saw any significant use elsewhere.

After its early association with No.5 Squadron No.326 was apparently allotted to No.1 Squadron during that unit's formative period as an aeroplane squadron, but was transferred to Central Flying School on 8th December 1914. What, if anything, it did there remains unknown. No.381's flight to No.5 Squadron on 30th June 1914 has already been recounted on pages 21-22, but it probably did little flying thereafter. It was not included in the squadron's strength on 31st July and was struck off charge on 28th September. In the case of 392, a reported allocation to No.7 Squadron must have been fleeting and probably unproductive, for the aircraft joined the Military Wing only on 28th July 1914 and was re-allocated to a Reserve Aeroplane Squadron (i.e., a training unit), presumably the one at Farnborough, early in August.

Although the two-seat prototype had been purchased by the War Office for use by the Military Wing of the RFC, neither it nor 394 and 395 saw any service with the Military Wing, for all three were bought by the Admiralty from the War Office. On 8th September 1914, Squadron Commander Spenser Grey, RN, went to see the DGMA, evidently to sound out the prospects for such a deal, and the whole matter was concluded with astonishing celerity, probably a reflection of the RNAS's urgent requirement for the aircraft. That same day the Director of the Air Department, RN (Capt Murray Sueter, RN), wrote to the DGMA:

'Squadron Commander Gray [sic] was sent to see you this morning on the subject of whether you could allow the Admiralty to take over three or four of the small-span Sopwith tractor biplanes that the War Office have purchased. These biplanes would be useful to the Admiralty for the work the Naval Pilots are carrying out abroad.

'If this can be arranged will you kindly let me know where the aeroplanes are, and when delivery could be taken of them. Also what was the price paid for them.'

A pre-war photograph of R.L.G. Marix, pilot of Tabloid No.168 on the bombing raid that caused the destruction of the Zeppelin Z.IX on 9th October 1914.

This was acted upon, instantly it seems, by Lt Col W. Sefton Brancker, ADMA, who replied to DAD, still on 8th September:

'Three Sopwith Scouts can be spared. They are at Farnborough in the charge of the OC Military Wing (Col Trenchard, RFC). I believe that at present they are undergoing slight alteration under arrangements made with Mr Sopwith. The price was £1,075 with engine. Two of the three are quite new. They can be taken at once.'

On 10th September, 394 and 395 were handed over to the Naval Wing; the prototype, 604, was sent to the Sopwith works, ostensibly to be converted into a single-seater, for on 7th October Trenchard wrote to Brancker:

'...I think £800 would be a fair price for the third machine, providing the Naval Air Department pay cost of alteration by the Sopwith company.'

Thus the final statement of the amount due from the Admiralty for the three little Sopwiths was set out;

Aeroplanes	No.	Rate	£	s	d
Sopwith Scouts Nos. 904 and 905	2	£1,075	2,150	0	0
Add 9½% Departmental Expenses			204	5	0
Sopwith Scout No. 604	1	£800	800	0	0
			3,154	5	0

It was soon realised that the serial numbers 904 and 905 had already been allotted to the Short biplanes S.58 and S.80 (the latter being Frank McClean's aircraft used on his remarkable flight along the Nile, 2nd January - 22nd March 1914); consequently the two Tabloids were again renumbered, this time as 167 and 168; the prototype was also given the new identity of 169.

Whatever the Sopwith works did to 604 it took little time; the aircraft remained a two-seater and was reported to be ex-Works on 11th September. It was at Hendon on 13th September 1914, and at 3.30pm that afternoon it left for Eastchurch, piloted by Harry Hawker with FSL Lord Carbery (who had been a pre-war sporting pilot of note) as passenger.

By that time the RNAS had an aeroplane squadron in the field, equipped with an assortment of aircraft. It had gone first to Ostend, but soon moved back to Dunkerque. This unit was commanded by the redoubtable Wg Cdr C.R.Samson, RN, who firmly believed that war should be waged aggressively and to the maximum discomfiture of the enemy. To that end he set up an advanced base at Antwerp, and it was there that the two single-seat ex-RFC Tabloids 167 and 168 arrived on 18th September.

On 23rd September Samson's squadron set out to bomb the German airship sheds at Düsseldorf and Cologne. One of their number was the Tabloid No.168, flown by Lt R.L.G.Marix. Thick mist in the target areas largely frustrated the attack; in particular Marix was unable to locate his objective.

By that time Tabloid No.169 had joined the others, and all three were on the strength of No.2 Aeroplane Squadron, RNAS, at Antwerp. Unfortunately, 169 crashed on 25th September while being flown by FSL Lord Carbery, who had a passenger aboard, the Prince de Ligne. Sqn Cdr E.L.Gerrard, then commanding No.1 Squadron RNAS, decided to take advantage of the repair process to have the aircraft modified to standard single-seat form with fixed fin and plain rudder. It was sent to the works of the Belgian Bollekens firm in Antwerp, but it is not known how far the modification process was taken before Antwerp fell to the advancing Germans on 9th October 1914.

On 26th September Marix, in 168, gave chase to a German monoplane that was reconnoitring Antwerp, probably in preparation for the German bombardment that began on the 28th. On that day Marix flew 168 in what could have been little more than a token bombing attack on railway centres, for the only bombs that 168 could have carried would have done little more damage than hand grenades to such targets.

Curiously, Marix' feat was mildly commercialised in Germany. This postcard was sold by Photochemie *of Berlin: its legend reads 'Original photograph from the war zone. English armoured car with Lieutenant Marick (sic) of the English Royal Flying Corps, who dropped the bombs on the Düsseldorf airship shed.'*

(The late A.E.Ferko)

Nevertheless, on 9th October, after Samson's unit had withdrawn from Antwerp, the Tabloids 167 and 168 set off from the more-or-less deserted airfield to attack the airship bases at Cologne and Düsseldorf. Lt Cdr Spenser Grey flew 167 towards Cologne, but in poor visibility failed to locate his target; he therefore dropped his two bombs on the central railway station and returned to Antwerp.

Flt Lt Marix, on 168, found the sheds at Düsseldorf without difficulty, dropped his bombs from 600ft, and was rewarded by seeing the roof fall in and 500ft flames erupt: he had destroyed the Army Zeppelin *Z.IX*, a signal achievement. His Tabloid came under heavy ground fire and sustained several hits; one bullet severed his rudder control cables; another evidently punctured his petrol tank, for his fuel ran out when he was still 20 miles from Antwerp and he had to come down near the Dutch frontier. Obliged to abandon 168, he made his way back to Antwerp, partly by bicycle, partly on a railway locomotive.

The enemy began to shell the aerodrome at Antwerp that evening, badly damaging Spenser Grey's Tabloid and the B.E.2a No.49. He and Marix left Antwerp by car for Ostend, and their gallant little Tabloids were both lost. The fate of 169 can only be guessed at, but it is likely that it would be destroyed in the Bollekens works to prevent its use by the enemy. Whatever its fate, the end of such an exceptionally historic prototype was sad and obscure. Curiously, all three Tabloids (167-169) were still included in the December 1914 *List of HM Naval Aircraft*.

Official appreciation of this early bombing exploit was expressed on 28th December 1914, by Cdr Murray Sueter in a letter to the Sopwith company:

'Gentlemen,

With reference to the recent attack on the German Airsheds at Cologne and Düsseldorf, carried out by Squadron Commander Spenser D.A.Grey and Flight Lieutenant R.L.G.Marix, you may be interested to learn that the machines used were your "Sopwith Tabloid aeroplanes". I take the opportunity of expressing my appreciation of the excellent performance of these machines.

'It is reported from Berlin that a new Zeppelin fitted with the latest silent motors, which had just been moved into the shed at Düsseldorf, and a Machinery Hall alongside the Airship Shed, were destroyed by Flight Lieutenant Marix. The roof of the Airship Shed has fallen in.

I am, Gentlemen,

Yours faithfully,

(Signed) Murray F. Sueter

Director, Air Department'

Spenser Grey was less successful than Reggie Marix in his endeavour to attack a German airship shed. This photograph shows him in a moment of relaxation at Coudekerque in 1916.

Spenser Grey's abandoned Tabloid (at right) and the RNAS. B.E.2a No.49 stand engineless and forlorn on the airfield at Antwerp after the German advance and occupation of the area.

(The late A.E.Ferko)

Chapter 3

Design Development

A revised design had been drawn up in June 1914, distinguished by the Sopwith Drawing Office as the S.S.2. The main fuselage girder was generally similar to that of the S.S., but was 1⅟₁₆in shorter overall; the positions of spacers in the forward portion were altered, and the lower wings were to be located perceptibly higher above the lower longerons. Whereas on the S.S. the oil tank was immediately ahead of the cockpit, on the S.S.2 it was in the top decking, behind the pilot's shoulders. This change may have been made because the S.S.2 was to have a wheel on the control column to actuate the lateral control, and that needed greater clearance than a forward-mounted oil tank would have permitted. The shape of the top decking of the S.S.2 was subtly different, as was that of the engine cowling.

On the S.S.2 as drawn in June 1914 there was to be stagger of 13 degrees on the mainplanes, but the centre-section struts (and presumably the interplane struts) were to be of streamline-section steel tubing. A V-strut undercarriage, separately detailed on drawing No. 439, was to be fitted, carrying 26in x 2½in wheels on the centrally-pivoted half axles.

Although the profile of the fin and rudder was very similar to that of the production Tabloid, the areas of the two surfaces were greater, and the structure (steel tubing throughout) was simplified. New and enlarged horizontal tail surfaces were also designed; the tailplane had a straight leading edge and slightly raked tips; overall span was 9ft 2in, eleven inches greater than on the original design.

It is uncertain whether an S.S.2 was built in the form indicated by the few surviving drawings, but the design might have been modified to become the more orthodox of the two Gordon Bennett aircraft, which became 1214 on acquisition by the RNAS. Both are discussed below.

A further possibility is that the S.S.2 design could have been revised to become the distinctively different single-seater of which the RNAS ordered twelve under Contract No. C.P.58295/14. These had the Sopwith designation S.S.3; for them the serial numbers 1201 - 1212 were allotted, and the first completed aircraft appeared in the latter half of December 1914. The contract was apparently extended to embrace the

purchase of a thirteenth aircraft, numbered 1213, but it was elsewhere recorded with a separate identity as 'Sopwith R Scout', and it differed from the contractual dozen in having an 80hp Le Rhône engine, not the standard 80hp Gnome, and probably in other respects. Chronologically, it also preceded the twelve RNAS production Tabloids by about six weeks, for it arrived at Hendon from Brooklands, piloted by Harry Hawker, on 10th November 1914. No.1213 was probably very similar to the original S.S. design, for it was basically the Tabloid airframe that had been ordered by the Società Transaerea Italiana. It was originally intended to have a 50hp Gnome, but at least one official list attributes an 80hp Gnome.

At that time two other Sopwith single-seaters were in RNAS hands. These had been built as entrants for an international racing contest for the Gordon Bennett prize of £1,000, but the outbreak of war had precluded British participation, and the two Sopwiths were purchased by the RNAS under a separate contract, No. C.P.60619/14.

They were numbered 1214 and 1215, were officially listed together as 'Sopwith G.B.', but were not identical: the former looked generally much like a Tabloid of the original design, but had a simple V-strut undercarriage, and its interplane and centre-section struts were of streamline-section steel tubing. No.1215 was markedly different, having a slim fuselage faired out to a roughly circular cross-section, and an absurdly small fin and rudder. Unlike 1214, it had no stagger on its mainplanes, but its struts were of streamline-section steel tubing, and it had a V-strut undercarriage. Both 1214 and 1215 were reported to have (at least when in RNAS ownership) the 80hp Gnome engine; on 1214 the cowling was similar to that of the production Tabloid, whereas on 1215 it was of better aerodynamic form and circular section, but had an alarmingly small frontal opening that portended cooling problems.

Although Sqn Cdr E.L.Gerrard was reported to have recommended in September 1914 that the Gordon Bennett Sopwiths should be sent out to augment the equipment of the RNAS force in Belgium, it is questionable whether the aircraft had been completed at that time. Not until 19th October did Hawker deliver 1214 to Hendon from

The second Gordon Bennett showed greater aerodynamic refinement in the design of its fuselage, and appeared to have zero stagger. These photographs were taken at Hendon; in the front view of the aircraft the RNAS officer at left is Spenser Grey.

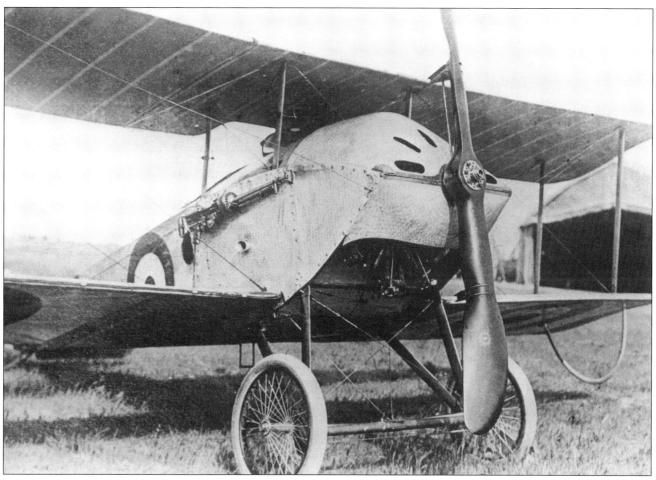

The Sopwith Gordon Bennett No.1214, photographed at Dunkerque after being fitted with a fixed Lewis gun and a Morane-Saulnier-type propeller with deflector wedges of the kind developed by Jules Hue, mechanic to Roland Garros, who had flown his Morane-Saulnier Type L, armed in this way, from Dunkerque in the early spring of 1915. This, the more conventional of the two Sopwith Gordon Bennett racers, probably owed at least part of its structure to the Sopwith S.S.2 design.

Brooklands, and 1215 was first reported at Hendon on 25th November, when it was flown by Spenser Grey. Its arrival enabled Hendon to report on 1st December 1914 that the station's six 'Machines available for defensive purposes' included the Sopwiths Nos.1213, 1214 and 1215. All three were still listed at Hendon on 11th March 1915.

A note in *The Aeroplane* of 21st October 1914 stated that:

'The latest "scout", built for the Gordon Bennett Race, does 105 miles an hour with an 80hp Gnome, and she is "slow" compared with the 100hp machine...'

Flight of 6 November 1914 printed a relevant item in its *Eddies* column:

'One of the latest Sopwith Scouts which are doing so well out at the front was seen at Hendon recently. It was fitted with a simple type Vee chassis of steel tubes, carrying a tubular non-sprung axle, springing being effected by the large diameter Palmer tyres. I understand that this 'bus is shortly going to the front.'

The former quotation probably referred to 1215, but the latter could hardly have done so, for when photographed at Hendon the special Gordon Bennett aircraft had the usual sprung half-axles in its undercarriage. Perhaps, then, the *Flight* paragraph referred to 1214 in its early existence: certainly by the time in 1915 when it was at Dunkerque it had the usual Sopwith sprung undercarriage.

And indeed *Flight* later published, in its issue of 27th November 1914, a remarkably explicit description of 1215:

'A new Sopwith biplane was seen at Hendon lately, which is expected to far out-class, as regards speed,

anything hitherto turned out by this enterprising firm. It would obviously not be wise to give a very detailed description of this new machine at the moment, but the following particulars should convey some idea of its general "lay-out". In shape, if not in construction, the new scout is of the "monocoque" type, having a circular section fuselage, which offers a minimum of head resistance. The engine is totally covered in by a hemispherical cowl, sufficient air for cooling being allowed to enter the cowl round the propeller shaft, and to escape underneath the fuselage, where the cowl does not quite touch the under surface. The planes are not staggered as in the usual type of scout, and are almost flat on the under surface. The tail is perfectly symmetrical, and the fixed stabilising plane placed on the centre line of the fuselage. The chassis is of the very simplest type, consisting of two Vs without any skids.'

On 4th May 1915, No.1214 was sent by road to Dover, and in the official *Disposition of Aircraft* as at 20th June 1915, both 1213 and 1214 were recorded as being on the strength of 'C' Squadron, RNAS Dunkerque. On 3rd July 1915 Sqn Cdr Spenser Grey, DSO, flew 1214 on a hostile-aircraft patrol from Dunkerque to Nieuport. Presumably by that time the aircraft had been fitted with the fixed Lewis gun and Morane-Saulnier-type deflector propeller seen in the illustration on this page, but Grey saw no enemy aircraft on that occasion.

On the evening of 13th July, three German seaplanes bombed the RNAS aerodrome at Dunkerque; two bombs struck a hangar and damaged three Henry Farmans. Accompanied by three Nieuport 10s, Spenser Grey took off on 1214 to attack the

Typical of the twelve developed Tabloids built for the RNAS, as 1201-1212, this aircraft, photographed at Eastchurch, may have been 1209. These had ailerons, steel-tubing wing struts, zero stagger, V-strut undercarriage, pylon-mounted tailskid, and enlarged tailplane.   (Fleet Air Arm Museum)

enemy seaplanes, but in bad visibility none of the RNAS defenders was able to do battle.

It is doubtful whether 1215 ever left Hendon, for on 25th May 1915 that station reported that this Sopwith had no engine and was out of true. That was still the position on 10th June, but by 20th June 1915 No.1215 was no longer listed anywhere and had presumably been deleted.

****

The S.S.3 aircraft delivered to the RNAS as 1201-1212 were of extensively revised design. In general appearance there were several points of similarity between them and the Gordon Bennett 1215, for the Tabloid had no stagger on the mainplanes, steel-tubing struts and a V-strut undercarriage; the gap between the mainplanes appeared to be greater than on the original production S.S.

In these RNAS Scouts the basic profiles of the fuselage were of Tabloid origin; whether they derived from the S.S. or the S.S.2 is uncertain, but the latter seems more probable. Changes in the disposition of spacers had been made to align them with the new positions and angles of the centre-section struts and lower-wing spars. The pilot was given an opaque wind deflector like that standardised on the production Sopwith Schneider seaplanes, of which the earliest must have been contemporary with the RNAS Tabloids in the Sopwith works; on most aircraft this wind shield was semi-conical in form. A small circular glazed aperture was provided on each side of the

fuselage just above the lower wing. In the tail unit the tailplane and elevator assembly appeared to be identical with that designed for the S.S.2; the fin and rudder were further enlarged, and appeared to be virtually identical with those of the early production Schneider seaplanes. A larger and presumably stronger tail-skid assembly was mounted on a pylon under the rear fuselage. Most significant of all, ailerons replaced wing-warping; these were fitted to upper and lower wings, their actuating cables running along the rear spars within the lower wings to emerge near the lower end of each rear interplane strut and then taken up to the underside of the upper aileron. Upper and lower ailerons were linked by strut-like connecting members, and there was a spanwise balance cable between the upper ailerons. This aileron-operating system was similar to that of the contemporary Sopwith Two-seat Scout, the so-called 'Spinning Jenny', which was one of several 'stretched' derivatives of the Tabloid. The mainplanes and ailerons of 1201-1212 were remarkably similar to those of the later production form of the Sopwith Schneider seaplane.

Deliveries of these S.S.3 Tabloids began shortly before Christmas 1914: the first (numerically), No.1201, was tested at Brooklands on 21st December. Together with 1202, and possibly others, it had been allotted to the seaplane carrier HMS *Ark Royal* as early as 28th November 1914. It was one of four, 1201-1204, that went to the Aegean in that ship, which sailed from Sheerness on 1st February 1915 and arrived in her war area on the 17th; by 11th March two more Tabloids, 1205 and 1206, were being prepared for shipment to the Aegean as

No.1211 apparently remained at Eastchurch throughout its existence. It was with No.2 Squadron (later renamed No.2 Wing), RNAS, late in May 1915, and by 3rd August was on the strength of No.4 Wing. Wrecked in October 1915, it was deleted on the last day of that month.
(Fleet Air Arm Museum)

The seaplane carrier HMS Ark Royal, in which the Naval Tabloids were taken to the Aegean. This photograph was taken at Malta, but its date is not known.

Tabloid No.1202 at Aliki Bay on Mudros. Its national markings consisted of Union Flags painted on the undersurfaces of the lower wings.

(RAF Museum)

part of the equipment of No.3 Squadron, RNAS, under the command of Wg Cdr C.R.Samson, RN.

Although it was apparently considered that take-offs could be made from *Ark Royal*'s forward deck by trolley-borne seaplanes or landplanes with wheel undercarriages, no known record states that any attempt to do so was ever made. That *Ark Royal*'s Tabloids were expected to operate from a shore base was made clear in an Admiralty paper of early 1915; yet it also indicated that deck take-offs were not impossible:

'The four aeroplanes carried, have a speed of 85 to 90 miles an hour and a fuel capacity of 3½ hours. They carry a pilot only and no passenger. They will carry four 20lb bombs or 1,000 steel spikes (fléchettes). In order to utilise these aeroplanes, a suitable base on land with level ground for 400 yards in every direction is required, but as before mentioned, they can be flown from the deck of the ship.'

The Tabloids of *Ark Royal* proved to be operationally useless: what the British force needed most of all was aircraft that could make productive reconnaissance flights and control the fire of the British warships that were supposed to bombard the Turkish positions in the Dardanelles. The little single-seat Sopwiths could do neither, a fact later lamented by Sqn Cdr R.H.Clark-Hall, *Ark Royal*'s captain.

While it seems unlikely that any of the carrier's pilots flew any of the ship's four Tabloids, it is known that 1202 at least was ashore at Aliki Bay seaplane station on Imbros for a time, possibly after 8th April 1915, on which date *Ark Royal* divested herself of her Tabloids. In a report dated 9th July 1915, on aircraft in the Dardanelles, Col. F.H.Sykes, RFC (who had been lent to the Admiralty for the purpose of inspecting and reporting on the entire air service in the Eastern Mediterranean), included this paragraph:

'HMS *Ark Royal* brought out four Sopwith single-seater land machines from England, but has sent three of them back to Malta. The fourth is still with the ship but is not flown. These could all be utilised if a good land aerodrome were made available.'

The Tabloid that did not go to Malta can only have been 1202: although all four, 1201-1204, were still attributed to *Ark Royal* in the official RNAS *Disposition of Aircraft* list dated 2nd October 1915, only 1202 was recorded as serviceable at that date. By December 1915, Nos 1203 and 1204 were at the White City Depot, somewhat the worse for wear. A survey report on both was submitted on 7th December: apart from torn fabric, both had badly damaged lower wings; 1203's bomb gear, undercarriage and cowling were also damaged; and 1204

had lost its fin. Deletion must have followed shortly afterwards.

To provide more aircraft for service in the Dardanelles campaign, No.3 Squadron, RNAS, was withdrawn from Dunkerque to Dover, where it prepared its equipment for its move to the Aegean. Its advance party arrived at Tenedos on 24th March 1915, but a gale delayed the disembarkation of the aircraft until the 26th and 27th. These were a motley assortment: in addition to the two Tabloids, 1205 and 1206, there were eight Henry Farmans (1518 - 1525), one Breguet (1390), three Maurice Farmans (1241, 1369, 1370), Samson's favourite B.E.2a (No.50), and two B.E.2cs (964 and 965).

In the climatic and operational conditions of the Dardanelles campaign the usefulness of this odd collection of aeroplanes was depressingly limited, as the official historian made clear in *The War in the Air, Vol. II, p24*. Specifically, he recorded:

'The Tabloids, owing to limited vision, were useful chiefly for single-seater fighting, and there was to be little opportunity for them to do the only thing they could do.'

A closer look at No.1202 reveals carriers for bombs under the fuselage.

No.3 Squadron's Tabloids were indeed armed. Surviving photographs of 1205 show a Lewis machine-gun mounted centrally above the centre section of the upper mainplane. This gun was in its basic infantry form, retaining the radiator casing and shoulder stock, and at that period could have carried only the 47-round magazine. As the Lewis was inaccessible to the pilot in flight, his gunnery potential was thus limited. At least one of the Tabloids in the Aegean had a rack under the fuselage, doubtless for the four 20lb bombs attributed by the Air Department. Perhaps it was realised that such a bomb load was over-optimistic, for RNAS Gunnery Memorandum No.4 of 28th January 1916 specified that the bomb armament of the Sopwith Scout was to be only 'One set grenade gear'.

That doughty warrior, Samson, had no real use for his Tabloids (or, indeed, for any of his unit's aircraft that were incapable of waging active war against the enemy). In describing his squadron's aeroplanes in his book *Fights and Flights* he included this reference:

'Two Sopwith Tabloids, which were single-seaters and not of very much use, as although they were fast and had a gun, they were not efficient as fighters in those days before inventors discovered how to fire through the propeller area. Also they had a habit of shaking out their engines.'

One further RNAS Tabloid went to the Aegean area. This was 1209, which was on the strength of No.2 Squadron at Eastchurch by May 1915; on 23rd May, in company with 1212, it flew a patrol seeking an Albatros seaplane that had dropped several bombs near ships in the area of the Goodwin Sands. The Tabloids were unrewarded, for they made no contact. Presumably they carried some form of armament, but details thereof have yet to be found. No.1209 went to Dunkerque with No.2 Wing, RNAS, on 1st August 1915, but merely as a stage in its journey to the Aegean. It was recorded on the combined strength of Nos.2 and 3 Wings on 1st October, on which date its predecessors, 1205 and 1206 were on their way back to Britain aboard the SS *Liverpool*.

There must have been nothing for 1209 to do, and it was sent back to Britain: by 16th December it had reached Dover, that station's daily report of that date stating that 1209 had been deleted and despatched to the White City Depot.

Of the five S.S.3 Tabloids that did not go overseas, 1207 and 1208 went to Great Yarmouth; they were delivered there by rail on 16th March 1915. They were assembled by Sopwith riggers, apparently at a leisurely pace, but their flight testing was delayed because their ailerons were returned to the Sopwith works on 24th March: for unrecorded reasons, the company had telegraphed a request for these components to be sent back. New ailerons were fitted on 7th April, and Harry Hawker tested 1207 next day, but overturned on landing and the aircraft was extensively damaged. Evidently Hawker was not, for on 9th April he successfully put 1208 through its acceptance trials

On 12th April, 1207 was sent to the Sopwith factory for repair; it was back at Yarmouth by 2nd May and Hawker flew its acceptance trials without mishap on 5th May. Both Tabloids were fitted with bomb racks on 19th May, and it was reported on 26th and 27th August that 1208 had flown on bomb-dropping practice. By 1st October it was at Bacton, one of Yarmouth's night landing grounds, where it had probably been sent as a potential anti-Zeppelin defender, but it was soon declared out of true. By 1st November both 1207 and 1208 were reported serviceable, but a month later 1207 was, in its turn, recorded as out of truc. It was restored to airworthiness and was flying at least until 24th March 1916, when FSL E.B.Thompson had to make a forced landing that may have marked the end of 1207's flying days, for, by 15th April 1916, it was awaiting deletion. Its stablemate, 1208, had already gone, deleted on 17th March 1916.

The remaining three Tabloids, 1210-1212, were initially (in May 1915) all with No.2 Squadron (No.2 Wing from June 1915) at Eastchurch, with 1212 detached to RNAS Westgate. In home-defence sorties on the nights of 26th/27th May and 31st May/1st June 1915, 1210 and 1212 made night flights, fruitlessly seeking Zeppelins. On the latter night 1210 was flown by Flt Lt Sydney Pickles, a well-known pre-war pilot (see also page 37); and 1212's pilot was FSL R.H.Mulock (later Col Mulock, CBE, DSO, and much involved in the early efforts to create a Canadian Air Force), who had, on the night of 16th/17th May, managed a single shot at the Zeppelin *LZ.58* before the Lewis gun of his Avro 504 jammed. He did not have even that opportunity on his Tabloid two weeks later. No.1210 was apparently still flying at Eastchurch as late as 24th May 1916, but 1212 had come to a tragic end at Westgate on 9th August 1915, when it crashed and overturned after a night flight in deteriorating weather, killing FSL R. Lord. It was deleted on 21st August 1915.

Although one or two of the RNAS Tabloids survived into 1916, the type was no longer regarded as effective in March of that year. The list of Naval aircraft for that month listed the six survivors (at the date of compilation), under the heading *Types of Aeroplanes of small fighting value which it is not intended to reproduce*: These were 1202, 1205-1208 and 1210. Also included was the Gordon Bennett 1214.

No.1207, photographed in front of one of RNAS Great Yarmouth's hangars (which were landscaped rather than camouflaged), had an underslung bomb rack and large RNAS roundels under the upper wings. *(RAF Museum)*

Tabloid No.1205 of No.3 Squadron RNAS at Tenedos aerodrome. Its overwing Lewis gun is obvious, and it had additional slots in its engine cowling to improve cooling. RNAS-style roundels (a red circle with large white centre) were applied to the undersides of upper and lower mainplanes and to the upper surface of the upper wings.

Chapter 4

Sincerest Foreign Flattery

The impression made by the Tabloid on the aviation world was great enough to lead to the design being copied in Germany and Russia. As early as 21st January 1914, the German periodical *Flugsport* published general arrangement drawings of the prototype Tabloid: although these were not wholly accurate they gave a fair representation of the disposition of principal structure members, and the printed dimensions (metric and rounded) were not too wide of the mark. The brief accompanying article described structural features, stated that the aircraft's maximum speed was 150 km/h (93.21mph) and referred to its speed range as 'extraordinary'.

Both the prototype and the Schneider Tabloid floatplane were illustrated in the 1915 edition of the *'Taschenbuch der Luftflotten'*, a modest little publication that included references to virtually every aeroplane and seaplane that might have had military potential, and a fair number that had none whatever. In view of the Tabloid's remarkable performance, however, it obviously merited serious consideration, and it was no secret that the type had been produced for military purposes.

These considerations might have sufficed to persuade the Schütte-Lanz company to build a single-seat scout that obviously owed its inspiration to the Sopwith Tabloid. It will probably never be known whether any detailed German examination of the remains of Spenser Grey's and Marix's Tabloids was undertaken after their capture, but the possibility cannot be excluded. Any report of such an examination might have been made available to German aircraft manufacturers, and its circulation might have included the Schütte-Lanz firm. There was, however, a connection between the Sopwith and Schütte-Lanz companies in the person of Wilhelm Hillmann.

In May 1914 Hillmann was in England, and he piloted the German Navy's Sopwith Bat-Boat on its delivery flight. It has been said that Hillmann was at that time an employee of the Schütte-Lanz company, and that licence production of the Bat-Boat by Schütte-Lanz was under consideration. If that were so, Hillmann might well have visited the Sopwith factory and might have seen Tabloids under construction.

The Schütte-Lanz design, which has been attributed to both Hillmann and Walther Stein, was a neat little single-bay biplane with a 100hp Gnome engine within a cowling that closely resembled that of the original Sopwith; it is possible that the 80hp Oberursel UO engine was considered as an alternative power unit. The undercarriage was a neat structure with two forward-raked V-struts. It is not entirely certain that the Tabloid *Doppelgänger* was officially designated SchüL D.I but as such it has become known.

It did not appear until the summer of 1915, yet it still had warping wings and a balanced rudder without fin. In overall dimensions the D.I was slightly smaller than the Tabloid, with its wing span of 7.5m (24ft 7.27in) and length of 5.4m (17ft 8.6in): the corresponding dimensions of the Tabloid were 25ft 6in and 20ft 4in. In flying trim the D.I weighed 680kg (1,499 lb), some 34 percent more than the Tabloid's modest 1,120lb.

The Schütte-Lanz company claimed that their D.I was the first German single-seat fighter biplane, and that it had been designed to have two fixed and synchronised machine-guns. Much careful thought had gone into the design of metal fittings, and special attachments made it possible for the wings to be fitted or detached by two men in 10-15 minutes. Yet, although the Schütte-Lanz accommodated its pilot farther aft than on the Tabloid and must have given him a

The Schutte-Lanz D.I was the German company's imitation Tabloid.
(A.E.Ferko)

At Mannheim-Sandhofen aerodrome, Walther Stein stands beside the Schutte-Lanz D.I: its design has been attributed to him.   (A.E.Ferko)

The Lebed VII was a near-perfect reproduction of the SS Tabloid.
(W.M.Lamberton)

This photograph of an upended Lebed VII emphasises its Russian roundels on wings and rudder, and confirms its retention of the warping wings of the SS Tabloid. There is a numeral 1 on the fin.
(Wim Schoenmaker via Harry Woodman)

better all-round field of view, it was nevertheless rejected because of poor outlook and defective structural details. The SchüL D.I was therefore abandoned. It was not the last design for a single-seat scout or fighter in which Hillmann was involved, however, for he later designed the Märkische D.I, of which only a single prototype was built by the Märkische Flugzeugwerke in 1918.

Another, though slightly later, German single-seater of somewhat similar type was the Rex scout of 1916, but it appeared to owe more to the Bristol Scout than to the Tabloid. Like the Schütte-Lanz D.I, the Rex did not progress beyond the prototype stage.

What appeared, in photographs, to be a well-nigh perfect copy of the S.S. Tabloid was built in Russia by the Aktsionyernoye Obshchestvo Vozdukhoplavania V.A. Lebedeva of Petrograd. Shortly before the war began, the Lebedev firm was one of the four leading aircraft companies in Russia; its output at that time was six aircraft per month. On 8th June 1914, V.A.Lebedev ordered an S.S. type Tabloid from Sopwith, and the Sopwith Works Order Book records that this aircraft was delivered, without engine, on 30th July. Obviously using this Tabloid as a model, Lebedev's factory built a number of copies under the designation Lebed VII. Like their British prototype, these had an 80hp Gnome engine. V.B.Shavrov indicates in his book *The History of Aircraft Construction in the USSR* (Moscow, 1969) that the Lebed VII was produced in small numbers and was used for training purposes.

The Lebedev company also built two examples of a kind of 'stretched' Tabloid as the Lebed VIII. This appeared to be a single-seater, but had two-bay wings with ailerons on the upper surfaces, a lengthened fuselage, and a V-strut undercarriage.

A Lebed VII in Russian service. This particular aircraft has no under-cowling at the nose, and there are louvres on each side in the forward nose panels, which suggest that the engine tended to overheat. There is also an access point with what appears to be a sliding door in the starboard flank panel.   (Wim Schoenmaker via Harry Woodman)

The Lebed VIII was an enlarged Lebed VII and had extended wings that needed two-bay bracing.   (Alexandrov via Harry Woodman)

Chapter 5

The Sparrow

The Sopwith company's test pilot, Harry Hawker, had to do a good deal of travelling, largely to put RNAS Sopwiths through their acceptance tests at various RNAS stations, and to test Sopwith types built by other contractors. This growing commitment may have been a reason for building Hawker a personal aircraft in the autumn of 1915.

Hawker himself is said to have laid out the outlines of this aircraft in chalk on the shop floor at Kingston. It was a single-seat, single-bay biplane of great simplicity, powered by a 50hp Gnome engine that, according to company lore, had powered the Burgess-Wright biplane bought by Tom Sopwith in 1911. Despite the use of ailerons on the S.S.3 Tabloids built for the RNAS, Hawker's little single-seater had wing-warping lateral control. The mainplanes, of 5ft 1½-in chord, had unusually shaped tips: these had a distinctive, slightly curving reverse rake; the large tailplane had corresponding reverse rake on its outboard extremities. In their general form the vertical tail surfaces established the basis of a characteristic design feature that was to reappear, with slight modifications, on many of the succeeding Sopwith types, but on the aircraft built for Hawker the fin had a short, straight and vertical leading edge.

The upper wings were attached to a narrow centre section that was supported on four vertical struts, of which the rear pair marked the back of the pilot's cockpit. He therefore sat directly under the centre section, where he had virtually no upward view. The undercarriage, of simple steel-tubing V-struts, was of typical Sopwith design; the Gnome engine was on an overhung mounting, and had a simple horseshoe-form cowling with open front.

It is not known precisely when Hawker's personal single-seater made its first flight, but some 27 years later, on 13th November 1942, the correspondence page of *The Aeroplane* carried a letter from Mr J.H.Williams, who had been in the Sopwith works when the aircraft was built. In this reminiscence he stated that he believed that it was '...first flown from the football ground in the Kingston Road leading to the Ham Boundary'.

Hawker flew his new single-seater over to Hendon on Sunday, 14th November 1915. In the recollection of the late Eric J.Arnsby, recorded in an earlier letter published in *The Aeroplane* of 30th October 1942, 'Hawker brought it over from Brooklands to show it to two Sopwith people (Watson and Ridley), then pupils at the Hall Flying School', where Eric Arnsby was himself learning to fly at that time.

'Watson' can only have been Basil George Watson, a compatriot of Harry Hawker's, who in 1914 had seen some of Hawker's demonstrations of the Tabloid prototype in Australia, and had been so fired with enthusiasm for aviation that he accompanied Hawker back to England. There he obtained employment, perhaps with Hawker's help, in the Sopwith works, and apparently did some flying in Sopwith aircraft, though whether as pilot or flight observer is not altogether clear. He was involved in the crash of a Sopwith aircraft on 22nd June 1915 and was reported to have suffered concussion and multiple cuts. He must have made a good and relatively speedy recovery from these injuries however, for he embarked on his course of flying training at the Hendon school of the Hall Aviation Co. later that summer and passed the tests for his aviator's certificate (No. 1910) on 18th October 1915. It was reported in *The Aeroplane* of 27th October that

'Mr B.Watson, who qualified at the Hall School a week ago, has now been engaged by the Sopwith Aviation Co. Ltd, to put new machines through their tests.'

In the circumstances and chronology, it seems likely that Watson must have been fully aware of Hawker's aircraft by 14th November 1915: that it had profoundly impressed him became clear some months later. Ridley, on the other hand, was first reported as actively under instruction at the Hall School during the week ending 28th November 1915, and did not gain his aviator's certificate (No.2474) until 20th February 1916.

Hawker's demonstration of his new mount at Hendon on 14th November 1915 left no doubt that the aircraft was aerobatic: the representative of *The Aeroplane* who was at

Design transition from the Tabloid to the Pup was made via this minimal single-seater that was built as a personal transport for Harry Hawker late in 1915. Its fin had a blunt, upright leading edge, and its 50hp Gnome engine had a cutaway cowling. *(Mrs Helena Lloyds via Chas Schaedel)*

Hendon that chilly afternoon recorded, in an unwontedly terse report:

'Also Mr H. Hawker, on 50 Gnome Sopwith (speed 22mph to 84.6; 6 loops, tea, 6 more, with tail-slides, nose-dives, etc., and home)'

One who saw this new Sopwith single-seater was Cecil Lewis, later to write that most satisfying and evocative of all personal accounts of wartime flying in his classic book *Sagittarius Rising*. In a later work, *Farewell to Wings*, he recalled this memory of Hawker's little aeroplane:

'I first saw what turned out to be the forerunner of the Pup at Brooklands in 1915. As trainee pilots, lumbering round the circuit in Longhorns, it seemed to our young eyes the most wonderful, beautiful aeroplane in the world. And when Hawker, the test pilot of Sopwiths, took it up and flew it stylishly round Brooklands, we were all enraptured. When, to cap it all, he flew the little thing under the Byfleet footbridge that spanned the banked track, we were Hawker fans for life.

'This feat, which certainly needed accurate judgement and nerves; was not quite so amazing as it sounds. Our Longhorns had a 55ft span while the Hawker mount was under 25ft across. It was a tiny aircraft, too small for a tall man to get into. It had a seven-cylinder Gnome engine that developed 50hp and I can still see its little white biplane wings and neat little tail. It was all so beautifully proportioned, a worthy forerunner of the whole stable of Sopwith aircraft, which, right through the war - and since - were of such outstanding design. They filled the eye, they "looked right", we used to say. A pilot knew beforehand when he took over a new type of Sopwith that it would handle like a thoroughbred.'

Curiously little more seems to have been recorded about this particular little Sopwith single-seater. In its time it was known, to some at least, as Hawker's Runabout. How much running about it did is unknown, but apparently it did not register significantly with anyone in the wartime aviation industry who wrote any memoirs or recollections of the period. Nor is it clear how long the original Runabout survived, though it has been said that Hawker used it until it was replaced by the tiny Bee, which is believed to have appeared in 1917.

Although the original layout drawings of Hawker's Runabout of 1915 were made in chalk, full size, on the floor of

the Sopwith experimental shop, true working drawings must have been made at a later stage, for several further examples of the type were built. These may not have been identical in every detail with the 1915 prototype, but in geometry and in all essential respects they were remarkably similar.

An example of these later warping-wing single-seaters was built and flown in Australia by Basil George Watson, who returned to his native land in 1916, arriving there early in June. Although he had been declared medically unfit for military service, he was determined to go on flying, and announced that he was going to build his own aeroplane. Evidently he started the construction of his aircraft before June was out, working at and in his family home at Brighton, Victoria.

Watson must have been an exceptionally talented and capable craftsman, and (if he did indeed fabricate every part of his aircraft) he must have had a well-equipped workshop at his home. It has been recorded that he was born on 12th October 1895, consequently he was only 18 when he landed in England in June 1914, soon to start work in the Sopwith factory at Kingston-upon-Thames, and was only a few weeks past his 20th birthday when he passed the tests for his aviator's certificate. By the time of his return to Australia he had had appreciably less than two years' factory experience: in his two years in England he had had to spend time recuperating from his injuries of 22nd June 1915, had spent several weeks at Hendon learning to fly, and a few more on his voyage back to Australia.

And yet, starting in late June 1916, he apparently built his Sopwith single-seater in little more than four months, for the aircraft was reported to be complete by November 1916, only a week or two after his 21st birthday. It was further reported that Tasmanian ash was used for the airframe, and that the propeller was made of Queensland walnut.

It is not known whether Watson had any assistance in his task or, indeed, whether he brought any parts of the aircraft with him from England. Surviving photographs suggest that the airframe was assembled in one of the rooms of the Watson home, and they clearly show that the completed aeroplane was beautifully finished. It differed externally from Hawker's original and the other Sopwith-built examples in having metal panels on the fuselage sides as far aft as the rear of the cockpit. They and the full-circular engine cowling were immaculately finished with the "spot-burnished" effect seen on many Sopwith-built types.

The engine, as on Hawker's personal aircraft, was a 50hp Gnome, acquired in Australia from H.C. ('Horrie') Miller, who had earlier fitted it to an aircraft of his own creation that he had flown briefly at Point Cook. Miller was yet another of the

Brooklands early in the spring of 1916, and Hawker's little Runabout stands in company with the third production 1½ Strutter No.1378, as if in anticipation of the scene that later greeted Brigadier-General W.Sefton Brancker and inspired his exclamation that gave the Pup it nickname (see page 42). *(Philip Jarrett)*

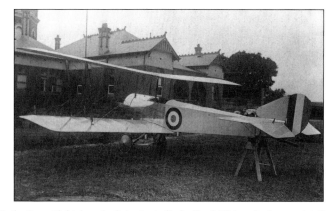

In all essential respects identical with the four Sopwith Sparrows of 1916, the Sopwith biplane built in Australia by Basil Watson had some detail refinements mentioned in the text
(The late A.E.Tagg)

Australians who had gone to England to further their interest in aviation and, like Hawker, Kauper and Watson, had worked for the Sopwith company. His own little single-seater bore a strong resemblance to the initial Sopwith Tabloid design.

It was at Point Cook that Watson, with official permission, made the first test flights of his Sopwith single-seater. Photographs of the aircraft taken shortly after its completion show that it bore British roundels on the fuselage sides, and the normal tricolour stripes on the rudder. Perhaps Watson's patriotism was sufficiently fervent to persuade him to apply these markings to the aircraft, thousands of miles removed from theatres of active warfare (and at the time few of the aircraft at the Australian Central Flying School at Point Cook bore any kind of national markings), but there is a possible, albeit tenuous, explanation not only for the use of the national markings but also for the presence of the aircraft in Australia.

In his excellent book *Military Aircraft of Australia, 1909-1918*, Group Captain Keith Isaacs, AFC, CRAeS, RAAF (retd) records:

'In 1915 Sydney Pickles recommended the purchase of a Sopwith, or Bristol, Scout for the Central Flying School at Point Cook. In January 1916 the Government [of Australia] ordered one fast scout of whichever type was available, together with two Grahame-White Boxkites and two Curtiss JN-3 Jennies. Initially only the Boxkites could be supplied and, on 16th June 1916, Lt-Col Reynolds recommended the purchase of two Maurice Farman Longhorns instead of the Jennies, and one Bristol Scout with an 80hp Gnome engine.'

The Bristol Scout arrived at Point Cook on 28th September 1916, while Basil Watson was still assembling his Sopwith single-seater. Although no evidence has been found of any Australian order for a Sopwith scout of any kind, it is not impossible that the Sopwith company - or at least its Australian employees, Harry Hawker, Harry Kauper, Harry Cato and Basil Watson - might have learned of Sydney Pickles' 1915 advice to the Australian authorities (for Pickles, too, was an Australian). Memories of Harry Hawker's successful Australian tour of 1914 with the Tabloid might have inspired the idea of demonstrating a suitable single-seater in Australia, with Basil Watson as project co-ordinator, aircraft builder and pilot. But all of that, one must emphasise, is speculation; and certainly no official Australian order was placed for a specimen of the Sopwith single-seater.

Watson flew his little Sopwith with skill and publicity sense, visiting many places to give flying displays that included aerobatics. On 9th February 1917 he left Hamilton carrying a quantity of air mail as an experiment; he picked up mail at several intermediate towns and finally delivered it to Melbourne on 27th February. Although this inspired proposals for further air-mail flights, these came to naught, for on 28th March, while Watson was flying from Albert Park to Point Cook, his aircraft's wings collapsed following a series of loops. The broken Sopwith fell into the sea near Laverton, Victoria, and Watson died of his injuries.

It is not known whether any enquiry into his death was held. If one was, its report has yet to be discovered, but it is possible that Watson's repeated enthusiastic aerobatic displays might have overtaxed the warping-wing structure, in which only single flying wires were fitted. Inevitably, there was no incidence bracing, and the fabric appeared to have been merely tacked to the ribs, not sewn round each rib.

In the case of Watson's ill-fated aircraft, dates are known with certainty. Much more obscure is the history of the origins of four further aircraft of the same basic type that were built, almost certainly in 1916, by the Sopwith company, apparently to some kind of official order.

A Sopwith works General Arrangement drawing, No.1719, survives. Drawn on 12th September 1916 and traced on 18th November, it names the aircraft simply as 'Type: 50hp Gnome'. In view of the drawing date it is possible that component drawings had been completed earlier; indeed, construction of the four Sopwith-built specimens might have been well in hand by May/June 1916, when Watson left England for Australia, for a year later, by 12th June 1917, the batch of four were apparently considered to be 'very old machines'. It seems unlikely that they would have been so described if they had been, say, merely six months old - and had they been that age they would have been precisely contemporary with Watson's aircraft; if, as seems probable, they were older then they must have preceded it.

Why, and for which Service, these four were built remains an enigma. They were belatedly allotted the serial numbers A8970-A8973, possibly about 16th/17th May 1917; the entry in the official record reads:

'A8970-A8973 Four Sopwith (small) scouts. No R.N.A.S. [numbers?] have been allotted.
A.E.2A, 2.5.17. Warping wings fitted for 50 Gnomes.
At Sopwiths, Brooklands, ready but without engines.'

These aircraft were evidently discussed at the 76th meeting of the Progress & Allocation Committee on 22nd May 1917, but it seems that no copy of the Report of that meeting has survived. The subject came up again at the Committee's 92nd Meeting on 11th June 1917. Under the heading *Sopwith Sparrows with 50hp Gnome* it was minuted:

'Lt-Col Whittington referred to the statement made on the 22nd May that an officer of the Technical Department would inspect these machines and say whether they were worth buying, and asked if any decision had been come to, as he had heard nothing since.
'Col Beatty arranged to report on this.'

At the next meeting, on 12th June, it was reported under the same heading that:

The late Sparrow of December 1918 that had an ABC Gnat engine; it is noteworthy that the interplane bracing was by wire cables, not streamline-section wires. The ¼-rear view provides an interesting comparison with that on page 35.

'Gen. Pitcher stated that he sent a report on this to D/DGMA about three weeks ago, advising strongly that they should not be bought, as they were very old machines and to make a thorough examination would entail taking them down.'

There can be virtually no doubt that these Sopwith Sparrows were the aircraft to which the numbers A8970-A8973 had been allotted in mid-May 1917; and it is of considerable interest to note that as early as May/June 1917 the name Sparrow was in use (and, indeed, serves to confirm the type identity of the four). Until relatively recent years it had been generally believed that that designation applied only, and at a later date, to a variant of the 50hp single-seater that was intended to be a radio-controlled pilotless aircraft capable of being used as a flying bomb. This particular variant had a 35hp ABC Gnat two-cylinder flat-twin engine, and its company photographs bear the date December 1918.

With the ultimate object of creating a pilotless flying bomb, experimental work on radio-control equipment and appropriate aircraft had begun in 1916 in great secrecy. In an early exercise in disinformation, such aircraft were designated ATs, signifying Aerial Targets. Various aircraft designs were drawn up, notably by the Royal Aircraft Factory, the Sopwith company, and Ruston, Proctor & Co. A Sopwith contender of unknown date was a very rudimentary biplane, apparently intended to have a four-wheel undercarriage; receiving aerials were wound round the rear fuselage and the extensions of the mainplanes. No record of the intended engine has yet been found, but the aircraft was apparently damaged before it could be flown, and it was abandoned.

Leading the early experiments with radio control was 2/Lt A.M.Low, later known (not altogether authentically) as Professor Low, and the first aircraft to be employed was a hastily concocted pilotless monoplane cobbled together from various airframe components and fitted with a 50hp Gnome engine. Early tests showed that the Gnome created such interference with the radio signals that an alternative power unit had to be sought.

One cannot but wonder, therefore, whether the four Sparrows intended for the Gnome engine might have been built as an alternative (perhaps even a first) Sopwith attempt at an AT, but shelved when the Gnome's radio interference rendered it unacceptable. Despite the uncertainty of the building date of A8970-A8973, it seems likely that they were built after the emergence of the prototype Sopwith Pup, or at least while it was being constructed; hence they could not, even at that time, have been seriously regarded as fighting scouts, and the fact that they were intended to have only the 50hp Gnome engine must have ruled out any thought of operational employment.

In view of the extreme secrecy that shrouded the flying bomb/AT project it is possible that any continuation of development after June 1917 might not have been made known even to the Progress & Allocation Committee.

Whether the later, Gnat-powered Sparrow of December 1918 was one of the 'very old' foursome refurbished and re-engined is not known. It is possible that the Gnat installation for the Sparrow was first tried out on Hawker's little Bee, for the similarity of installation and cowling on the two aircraft was strong. If this was what had to be done for want of readily available Sparrow airframes, it suggests that the Gnat-powered Sparrow might have been a new aircraft.

And yet, at least one of the original Sparrows survived the war. In 1919 it was bought at Northolt by Lt John Whitworth Jones (later Air Chief Marshal Sir John Whitworth Jones, GBE, KCB) and an ex-RAF friend named Nicholson. Reports of this aircraft indicate that it was dismantled and in a neglected condition, but that, in addition to its Service roundels and rudder stripes, it was painted overall with black and white stripes. Jones and Nicholson repaired and assembled their Sparrow, and both flew it.

Apparently the aircraft was never allotted a civil registration. Less than a year after acquiring the Sparrow both Jones and Nicholson re-joined the RAF. Nicholson was killed soon after arriving in the Middle East, and Jones did not return to England until 1925. The Sparrow had been stored in a barn in 1920, but Jones was unable to trace it. It had in fact passed into the hands of one Mr Mouser, a garage owner, who sold it in 1925 to Mr R.C.Shelley of Billericay. On a plate on the instrument panel, Ron Shelley found the inscription 'Machine type: SLTBP. Engine 50hp Gnome No.476' (the

The striped Sparrow that briefly belonged to Lt John Whitworth-Jones in 1919-20. It is virtually certain that this is the aircraft that was acquired by R.C.Shelley in 1925.   *(The late Air Chief Marshal Sir John Whitworth-Jones, GBE, KCB, via E.A.Harlin)*

The Sparrow after being repainted grey overall by Mr Shelley: the name Flycatcher can be distinguished on the flank panel behind the engine cowling. As on the late-1918 Sparrow, this aircraft had the trailing portion of the centre section removed, and the fin and rudder were of true Sparrow profile. *(The late E.J.Arnsby)*

engine in the aircraft was in fact No.683 3831, and had been rebuilt by F.W.Berwick & Co Ltd: its separate plate bore the date 6th August 1916). No authentic interpretation of the designation SLTBP has yet been found.

Ron Shelley took the aircraft to Billericay, where he overhauled the engine, painted the Sparrow grey, applied the name *Flycatcher* to the side of the forward fuselage, and taxied the aircraft until an unseen hole in the field caused it to stand on its nose.

In early 1927 it was sold to Lionel Anderson, who overhauled it, installed an 80hp Le Rhône engine, and fitted ailerons. It may have been the Sparrow-derived two-seater illustrated here, in which ailerons had been fitted to the lower mainplane only, a second cockpit had been formed, and an

overwing gravity tank (perhaps from an Avro 504K) had been installed. In the tail unit, what appeared to be a new fin and new rudder had replaced the original surfaces; although the rudder bore the national letter G, the aircraft had no formal civil registration. Whether this modified Sparrow was repaired after the incident recorded in the photograph is not known, but the aircraft was probably the last survivor of all the Sparrows. More curiously, it outlived all of the few Sopwith Pups that came on to the British civil register after the Armistice.

That it did so is an irony of history, for the essential significance of the Runabout/Sparrow/SLTBP design lies in the fact that in its general layout it established the lines and proportions of the Sopwith Pup.

Probably the same aircraft after conversion to a two-seater with ailerons on the lower wings and an overwing gravity tank. (The late E.J.Arnsby)

Chapter 6

The Pup: First Beginnings

On 3rd April 1915 a Conference was held in the Admiralty under the chairmanship of the first Lord, Mr Winston Churchill. It was to consider aircraft delivered to and on order for the RNAS, and the further orders that should be placed, in the light of operational experience and future requirements. This was a wide-ranging conference, and one of the papers laid before it had been prepared by Wg Cdr A.M.Longmore (the late Air Chief Marshal Sir Arthur Longmore, GCB, DSO). One of his several recommendations concerning aircraft for the RNAS was that a fast scout type should be ordered for attacks on enemy aircraft. At that time Longmore was in command of No.1 Wing, RNAS, at Dunkerque, and doubtless he subsequently took particular interest in the Sopwith Tabloid variant No.1214 with its fixed forward-firing Lewis gun (see page 29) when it was on the strength of his unit.

Although the first production Bristol Scouts were coming into service about the time of the Admiralty conference of April 1915, it seems that curiously few of them went to Dunkerque, though they were sent to other RNAS stations, ostensibly for use as envisaged by Wg Cdr Longmore. Also coming forward were Nieuport 10s, a two-seater type that had a good performance and could be modified to become a single-seat fighting scout. These were followed early in 1916 by a batch of Nieuport 11 single-seaters.

RNAS strength in single-seat fighters might have been enhanced in the spring of 1916 by the Nieuport 16, virtually a Nieuport 11 airframe in which the 110hp Le Rhône 9J replaced the 80hp Le Rhône 9C. The first few deliveries were made to RNAS Dunkerque from March 1916, but in an act that must have represented a substantial sacrifice by the Naval Service, all of the seventeen RNAS Nieuport 16s were transferred to the RFC from 18th March 1916 onwards.

It is possible that by that time the RNAS knew something of the new single-seat fighting scout that had been evolved by the Sopwith company from the Sparrow. The prototype of this new Sopwith scout had received the approval of the Sopwith experimental department on 9th February 1916. Precisely when the Air Department of the Admiralty was told about the aircraft is uncertain. It would have been understandable if the Sopwith company had wanted to wait until its own trials of the prototype had been successfully concluded; and at that time of year such trials would have been subject to the vagaries of the weather and might have taken time to complete. Whatever the circumstances might have been, it was not until the week ending 24th March 1916 that 'Y' Section of the Admiralty Air Department

> 'Put forward to purchase by wire one Sopwith Single-Seater 80hp Aeroplane. This will form part of the New War Programme, March 1916.
> 'Put forward to invite firm to tender for 2 Sopwith Fighters 80hp Aeroplanes. These will also form part of March 1916 Programme.'

In its turn, that submission might well have followed the Admiralty's tests of the prototype, flown earlier than 27th March (see page 42).

Whether the alacrity of response from higher levels matched the urgency implicit in the telegraphed submission is uncertain, for it was not until its report for the week ending 14th April 1916 that 'Y' Section recorded, in its reference to the Sopwith company

> 'Firm's tender received for one 80hp Le Rhône Single-seater Fighter Biplane and spares. Put forward to accept.
> 'Firm's tender for two 80hp Fighting Scouts received. Price under consideration.'

Agreement to purchase the prototype was readily forthcoming in the form of Contract No. C.P.109458/16, and the aircraft was allotted the serial number 3691, probably in April 1916. The 'two 80hp Fighting Scouts' for which Sopwith also tendered must almost certainly have been those that apparently had been regarded as on order as early as 3rd April 1916, with the serial numbers 9496 and 9497 already allotted (although the power unit then associated with them was the 100hp Gnome Monosoupape: see page 45).

The new fighter's derivation from the Sparrow was reflected in almost every line and proportion. In basic profile the fuselage was virtually identical, but it had an additional spacer in each bracing plane and the cockpit was moved aft to improve the pilot's view. Because the engine was of 80hp, and a Vickers machine-gun with its ammunition stowage and

An early, wintry appearance of the prototype Pup at Brooklands.
(Mrs Helena Lloyd, via Charles Schaedel)

empty-belt drum had to be carried, there can be no doubt that, in the forward fuselage at least, timber sections were slightly larger than those of their counterparts in the Sparrow.

Flight surfaces were similar to those of the Sparrow, most obviously in the reverse rake of the wing tips and tailplane/elevator extremities. On the fighter prototype, however, a centre section of greater span (4ft 8½in) was supported by four wooden centre-section struts that in end elevation diverged upwards; it had a central cut-out in the trailing edge to enlarge the pilot's field of view. A major difference between the new fighter and the Sparrow was the provision of ailerons in place of wing-warping; these were fitted to upper and lower mainplanes. This led to structural and bracing changes in the wing cellule. Interplane bracing, on the prototype, was by wire cables.

In the form in which it left the factory the fighter prototype had a fin and rudder that appeared to be virtually identical with those of the Sparrow. The undercarriage was a simple structure with the Sopwith articulated axle; the V-struts were of streamline-section steel tubing, and the entire assembly was relatively low, giving minimal ground clearance for the propeller.

An early RNAS performance report on the new Sopwith provided clear evidence of the aircraft's capabilities which, on the modest power of the 80hp Le Rhône 9C engine, bordered on the phenomenal. Its terse assessments were as follows:

Type   Sopwith Single-Seater Scout – 80hp Le Rhône

Crew   One

Fuel   Petrol   21 galls.
        Oil   8 galls.

Load   Pilot   170 lb
        Petrol   151 lb
        Oil   71 lb
        Gun   45 lb
        500 rounds 33 lb
                    470 lb

Climb   5,000ft in 4 mins 59⅘ secs   Revs 1070
        10,000ft in 12 mins 29⅘ secs Revs 1050

Speed   Ground   108mph Revs 1300
        6,500ft   110mph Revs 1260
        10,000ft   106mph Revs 1200

Note:
The above readings are corrected for pressure and temperature

Stability Longitudinal Very good
           Lateral   No [sic]
           Directional   Very good

Run to get off (in calm) 20 yards
Run after landing   50 yards

Remarks:
'This machine is remarkable for its performance, ease of handling, and for the quickness with which it can be manoeuvred. It is easy to land, landing at from 25 to 30mph.
The view is equal to that of the Nieuport with the exception of straight downwards. The propeller clearance is very slight, but it is understood that later machines will have a higher chassis. Later machines will be fitted with double streamlined wires instead of single cable, and also an adjustable tailplane to compensate for weight of different pilots.
The Vickers gun 500-round belt is fitted outside fuselage along top of cowl and trued through propeller.'

A copy of this report was sent to the War Office, and its circulation naturally included RFC Headquarters in France, where it was read by Maj Gen H.M.Trenchard, General Officer Commanding the RFC. Part of his pencilled marginal note is unfortunately indecipherable and undated, but it was addressed to Brig Gen H.R.M.Brooke-Popham, his Deputy Assistant Quartermaster General, and included the unqualified sentence, 'Let us get a squadron of these'.

Very early in its existence the new Sopwith fighter was nicknamed the Pup. Harald Penrose, in his book *British Aviation: the Great War and Armistice* (Putnam, 1969), credibly attributes the origination of the name to Brig Gen W.Sefton Brancker, presumably at about the time when Brancker took up post as Director of Air Organization:

'At Brooklands Harry Hawker had taken the new Sopwith single-seat fighter for its first flight, and found it delightful. It was the prettiest little aeroplane so far built. Hearing from his Admiralty colleagues of the successful test, Colonel Brancker drove down from the War Office to inspect the machine - for here at last was the vital answer: a single-seat tractor really capable of competing on decisive terms with the Fokker. Fitted with the first of the Sopwith-Kauper mechanical synchronising gears, its single Vickers gun mounted centrally on the turtle deck just ahead of the pilot would spray hell to the Germans.
'Arrived at the famous race-track Brancker found this latest Sopwith alongside the bigger 1½ Strutter. That they had come from the same stable was obvious. "Good God!" said Brancker. "Your 1½ Strutter has had a pup." And Pup it was ever after, capturing the affection of all who flew it...'

Perhaps there were in official places those who could not bring themselves to accept such a flippant name for a fighting aircraft, for the little Sopwith was only rarely referred to in official reports and records as the Pup (and then, so it might seem, almost by inadvertence). Indeed, the late Major Oliver Stewart, MC, AFC, (himself a Pup pilot of distinction), told in his evocative book *The Clouds Remember* (Gale & Polden, Aldershot) how:

'A minor comedy of officialism was enacted with the Pup. Those in high places were grieved to observe this name "Pup"; they regarded it as undignified, frivolous, slangy, unofficial and Heaven knows what else. So they found time, during the fury and trouble of war, to sit down and pen an order which called upon all officers and men to note that the Sopwith Pup was not the Sopwith Pup, but the Sopwith Scout Mark Something-or-Other, and it demanded that on all future occasions the aeroplane should be referred to under that title and none other. Everybody read the order and marvelled, and then referred to the machine as the Sopwith Pup. So another, more peremptory, order came out drawing the attention of all units to this prevalence of incorrect nomenclature. The aeroplane was in future always to be described as the Sopwith Scout Mark Something-or-Other. So I suppose that and the perverse state of mind of the fighting forces when it came to language, both good and bad, accounts for the fact that the aeroplane has ever after been known exclusively as the Sopwith Pup.'

That particular comedy was, of course, confined to the RFC, yet when the RFC's official Rigging Notes on the type were produced the pages were uniformly headed 'Sopwith Pup'.

The Pup prototype, 3691, itself had a considerable history. After its Admiralty tests it was sent to Central Flying School for performance trials. The speed trial flown on 27th March 1916, produced an average speed of 101.9mph at unspecified altitude (but probably at ground level); in the climbing trial two days later the Pup prototype reached 5,000ft in 5mins 10secs, 10,000ft in 13mins 10secs, and 15,000ft in 25mins. On these tests the aircraft had on board fuel for 4 hours but probably no ammunition; its loaded weight was just under 1,100lb.

Shortly afterwards, 3691 was officially allocated to 'Chingford for K Section'. It arrived there at 11.40am on 10th May 1916, flown by Flt Lt R.C.Hardstaff, who had brought the aircraft from Brooklands. Although Chingford was primarily a RNAS flying school, it also received several prototypes of aircraft intended for Naval service, including the AD Scout, Pemberton Billing PB.23 and 29, and the Sopwith Pup and Triplane. Presumably these were subjected to thorough examination and evaluation, but no detailed record of such testing has yet been found.

In the case of the Pup prototype, one particular aspect that was the subject of examination and, doubtless, modification was the armament installation. In respect of the week 27th May to 2nd June 1916, 'Y' Section of the Air Department reported 'Sopwith Scout, 80 Clerget: After gun trials to obtain satisfactory belt feed to Vickers gun machine flown and delivered to Dunkerque for trial under service conditions and report.'

At that date the only aircraft to which that could refer was 3691, yet no other known record suggests that it had a Clerget engine, nor that such an installation in that particular Pup was proposed. Perhaps this was a temporary and mistaken confusion with the intention (expressed about 19th June) to fit the Clerget to 9496, 9497 and the first Beardmore batch 9901 - 9950 (see page 45).

To revert to 3691's early history, it is known that it visited the RNAS Station, Isle of Grain, on 16th and 25th May, the latter visit apparently having been made to provide another aircraft type to be seen by the Lords Commissioners of the Admiralty, who were visiting Grain that day to see for themselves examples of aeroplanes and seaplanes then in, or intended for, use by the RNAS.

On these occasions the Pup prototype was flown by Hardstaff, and he was again its pilot on 28th May 1916, when the aircraft left Chingford at 12.15pm, bound for the RNAS base at Dunkerque in France. It was initially allocated to 'A' Squadron of No.5 Wing, then located at Furnes. Describing the equipment of RNAS Dunkerque at that time the official historian wrote:

'There had been reinforcements, also, of fighting aeroplanes. They were only two in number, but each had a performance which was remarkable for the period. They were the Sopwith Pup (80hp Le Rhône engine) and the Sopwith Triplane (110hp Clerget). The first Pup arrived at the end of May and the Triplane in the middle of June, and both were sent to the fighting squadron at Furnes where they caused something of a sensation. They could climb faster and higher than any aeroplane hitherto seen, were faster on the level, gave a splendid view and could be thrown about in the air with great ease and rapidity.'
(The War in the Air, Vol.II, p 438)

No.3691 had in fact been recorded as being on the strength of No.5 Flight of 'A' Squadron several weeks before Hardstaff delivered it to Dunkerque, which fact probably signifies only that administrative punctilio did not necessarily imply physical presence. Once there, the Pup apparently moved occasionally from unit to unit: after a brief period undergoing repair within the Dunkerque Depot its known locations followed this tabulated sequence (in which the dates are those of official returns, not of movements; regrettably, they cannot be regarded as wholly reliable, nor should this listing be regarded as complete):

22.6.16	'Ready' with Sopwith Fighter Flight, 'A' Squadron
29.6.16	Reported as in Composite Flight, 'A' Squadron
13.7.16	Reported as in Scouts Flight, 'A' Squadron, No.1 Wing (together with N500, the first prototype Sopwith Triplane)
27.7.16	Under repair
17.8.16	At Depot
31.8.16	With 'C' Squadron, No. 1 Wing
07.9.16	Under repair
21.9.16	In Sopwith single-seater Flight, 'C' Squadron, No.1 Wing
5.10.16	Still under repair, at Depot

Apparently 3691 was at that time still substantially in its original form, with low undercarriage, Sparrow-form fin and rudder, and minor details. By 21st September 1916 its companions in 'C' Squadron's Sopwith fighter Flight were four production Pups, N5182-5185, and it may be that the

The Pup prototype photographed at Dunkerque some time in 1916. It is seen in what is believed to be its original overall finish, namely natural fabric, bare metal and varnished plywood and interplane struts. Unfortunately the date of the photograph is not known, nor is it clear why the elevators bore the spanwise tricolour stripes that, at that time, normally denoted a Beardmore-built aircraft. (Frank Cheesman)

This side view of the prototype Pup clearly shows the retention of the Sparrow-form fin and rudder, and the original relatively low undercarriage.
(K.M.Molson)

The prototype, 3691, at a time and place unknown, but without stripes on its elevators. *(RAF Museum)*

prototype was compared unfavourably with them. On 19th October 1916, RNAS Dunkerque sent the following request to the Vice-Admiral, Dover Patrol:

'Submitted.
That the attached list of Machine Spares for Sopwith Scout No.3691 may be forwarded to Air Department, Admiralty, with a request that they may be ordered from Messrs Sopwith and forwarded to Dunkerque.
'This machine was the first of the type, and has now done 3 months' flying on Active Service.
'The later numbers of the type have various improvements embodied, and as the machine is now being overhauled in the Depot it is desired to embody these.
'Messrs Sopwith's representative was consulted during his visit here, and concurs in this proposal '

Presumably this request was approved and the appropriate modifications made, whereafter 3691 must have been virtually to production standard.

By 2nd November 1916 the aircraft was listed as being in Reserve at the Dunkerque Depot; a week later, apparently after being on the strength of 'B' Squadron, it was listed as an aircraft of 'D' Flight in the newly-formed Detached Squadron that was to serve with the 22nd Wing of the RFC. This new unit was later designated No.8 Squadron, RNAS, and fought with great distinction thereafter, flying Nieuports, Pups, Triplanes and Camels: it became better known as Naval Eight. Pilots known to have flown 3691 in the squadron included FSLs S.J.Goble and H.Jenner-Parson; and it has been reported that FSL N.E.Woods claimed to have shot down a Halberstadt on

26th December 1916, while flying 3691, but it is uncertain whether this was confirmed.

It was still with No.8 Squadron in January 1917 and was taken over by No.3 (Naval) in February when Naval Eight was withdrawn to re-equip with Triplanes and handed its Pups over to No.3 Squadron. No.3691 was reported to be in 'B' Flight of No.9 (Naval) Squadron on 22nd February, and by early March it was under repair. On 26th April it was listed as one of 20 Pups at Dunkerque Depot, and shortly after 10th May it went to Dover. From that station it flew at least two sorties as a Home Defence fighter against raiding formations of German bombers. On 25th May 1917, flown by FSL R.F.S.Leslie, it attacked one of the Gothas that had bombed Folkestone. Leslie's shots evidently struck home, but without conclusive result. Early in the morning of 4th July, No.3691 again took off to intercept another Gotha formation, but failed to make contact.

Although 3691 was subsequently withdrawn from active use and had been officially deleted before January 1918 it was not broken up. By 18th December 1917 the Pup prototype was in the USA as an exhibition piece, one of several British operational aircraft that were sent there to let the American public see something of Britain's armaments. Also on 18th December 1917 the President of the Air Board, Lord Rothermere, gave instructions that examples of every type of operational and training aircraft used in the war were to be preserved, and during 1918 surviving specimens of some 60 aircraft were progressively gathered together at the Agricultural Hall, Islington. A Pup was allocated on 26th March 1918, a Type 9901a Ship's Pup next day. The Pup that was eventually delivered, apparently from Manstone, on 13th September was, miraculously, 3691 itself (and, for the record, the earmarked 9901a was the Beardmore-built Pup 9945, delivery of which to Islington was predicted for mid-November 1918).

All of the aircraft gathered together at Islington were intended for the proposed National War Museum; and, had they survived, would have given Britain an unsurpassed collection of historic aircraft that would have been the envy of the world in later years. Yet of all those then brought together, only the Short 184 seaplane flown at Jutland was to survive beyond the early 1920s, and it was virtually torn to pieces by salvage teams following bomb damage to the Imperial War Museum in World War II. Perhaps the greatest losses of all were the Pup prototype and the Morane-Saulnier Type L monoplane flown by FSL R.A.J.Warneford, VC.

Chapter 7

Early Production and Introduction to Service

A precisely dated chronology of the initial contracts for Pups has yet to be established. An official record in respect of the week ending 3rd April 1916 states that there were on order two Sopwith single-seaters numbered 9496 and 9497; their designated power unit was, at that time, the 100hp Gnome Monosoupape. The contract for their supply, C.P.109545/16, was an Admiralty one.

By 19th June 1916 a change of intention was recorded, the engine for the two being quoted as the 80hp Clerget 7Z. To the two aircraft was added a batch of 50, numbered 9901-9950 and ostensibly intended to have the 80hp Clerget. Four weeks later (week ending 17th July), however, responsibility for building 9901-9950 was transferred to William Beardmore & Co, Ltd, of Dalmuir, Dunbartonshire, while a further batch of 20 (N5180-N5199) with the 80hp Le Rhône 9C engine had been ordered from the parent Sopwith company. Both contracts were for the RNAS, that for 9901-9950 being CP.117318/16, and for N5180-N5199 CP.119901/16.

In August 1916 the Admiralty adopted the designation Sopwith 9901 for the type, following their not always consistent system of nomenclature under which aircraft types were designated from the serial number of the first, or first production, example.

The record in respect of 14th August 1916 stated that there was on order one Sopwith 9901 that was to have a 110hp Clerget engine and the serial number N503. This high-powered singleton was included in the list every week up to and including 4th December 1916, whereafter it disappeared without explanation. It might reasonably be thought that the creation of such an aircraft would involve little more than the adaptation of a Sopwith Triplane fuselage, complete with Clerget installation already in place, to accept the Pup's biplane wing cellule. Yet it appears that an entirely new type was designed, for only three weeks later there appeared at Brooklands the first prototype of the Sopwith F.1 Camel, which had the 110hp Clerget. A possible inference from this development might be that the Sopwith design office had

perhaps learned something of RNAS operational use and opinion of the Pup (such as was to be expressed in the report of 29th November 1916, set out on page 50), and had decided that a biplane for the 110hp Clerget would have to have heavier armament in a heavier airframe. Such thinking could lead only to a complete re-design with twin guns and a closer concentration of major masses: hence the Camel.

That same entry dated 14th August included the addition of three more Pups to the batch ordered from Beardmore with the 80hp Clerget engine; the 53 aircraft were to be numbered 9898-9950. At that time it was estimated that the first Beardmore delivery would be made on 26th August, and that Sopwith would deliver 9496-9497 on 19th August. Whether the five aircraft numbered 9496-9497 and 9898-9900 should be regarded as prototypes of any kind or samples for any production purpose is questionable, but it is possible that 9496 and 9497 were regarded as evaluation aircraft.

Some official records of the period are, unfortunately, inconsistent and unreliable. One indicates that 9496 and 9497 were delivered during the week ending 11th September 1916, whereas another unequivocally states that 9496 had been officially accepted at Brooklands two months earlier on 10th July 1916. Its first official allocation was to No.3 Wing, the RNAS strategic bombing unit that was then settling in at its base at Luxeuil: perhaps it was hoped to assess the Pup as an escort fighter to protect the Breguets and Sopwith 1½ Strutters that were to form the Wing's primary equipment, but there must have been substantial differences in speed and range between the Pup and its potential charges that would have created operational difficulties. No.9496 went to No.3 Wing via 'C' Squadron of No.1 Wing, Dunkerque (see page 83).

No.3 Wing's weekly returns of aircraft might have been prepared by someone with a longish memory, for 9496 was initially recorded therein as a Sopwith Tabloid - even, on at least one occasion, as a Sopwith Pup Tabloid.

By 23rd February 1917, 9496 had been joined at Luxeuil by the Beardmore-built Pup 9906, which had been delivered to

This Clerget-powered Pup apparently bore no serial number when photographed but is believed to be 9496. Its centre section was entirely covered with transparent material, it had an adjustable tailplane, and on the leading edge of the starboard upper wing there was a rudimentary arrangement of static and pressure tubes for the air-speed indicator. As recounted in the texts 9496 was officially accepted on 10th July 1916, and was earmarked for No.3 Wing, RNAS. It went to that unit via 'C' Squadron of No.1 Wing at Dunkerque, where it was recorded on 20th July 1916.

The Beardmore-built 9906 was accepted at Dalmuir on 7th December 1916 and was delivered to Manstone on 12th December. By 23rd February 1917 it was with No. 3 Wing at Luxeuil, but suffered an in-flight split of the transparent covering of its centre section two days later while being flown by Flight Commander C. Draper, who is here seen in its cockpit. Late in March it was reported to need extensive repairs, and following a survey on 2nd April it was deleted.

Manstone (see page 198) for No.3 Wing on 12th December 1916, and was still at Manstone on 17th January 1917. By 30th March 9906 was reported to be in need of 'extensive repairs', but three days later was surveyed, presumably for deletion. On 6th April 1917, 9496 was similarly surveyed.

No.9497 had a very different and more productive career. It might have been used as a production guide-model by Beardmore, for it was at Inchinnan, Beardmore's airfield, by 5th October 1916. On that date, and again on 13th October, it was flown by A. Dukinfield Jones, Beardmore's test pilot. It is, of course, possible that he might have flown it at an earlier but unrecorded date, for he had flown the first Beardmore-built Pup, 9901, on 26th September. As early as 4th September, 9497 had been officially allocated to RNAS Isle of Grain, for use in deck-landing experiments, and official records aver that it arrived there on 27th October 1916. Jones, however, recorded that he delivered it to Port Victoria on 1st November.

When photographed at Grain on 7th December 1916, No.9497 was finished in typical Beardmore style, with tricolour spanwise stripes on the elevators, and its underwing roundels inboard of the lower ailerons; moreover, the fin was painted P.C.10 and did not bear the Sopwith company's name as did contemporary Sopwith-built Pups. Perhaps 9497 had been sent to Beardmore as an uncovered airframe, but was covered and painted by the Scottish contractors for delivery after it had served its purpose as a production reference model (but this is conjecture). This Pup's involvement in the Grain experiments will be related in Chapter 19 (see pages 125-126); it was still at Grain in the spring of 1918.

The three RNAS Pups numbered 9898-9900 might have been attributed to Beardmore in error. An entry in an official record of less than impeccable accuracy indicates that by 18th September 1916 their construction was being attributed to the parent Sopwith company (which did in fact build them). Statistics of predicted output suggest that the firm did not expect to deliver 9898-9900 until mid-November 1916 and only after it had delivered all 20 of the batch N5180-N5199. And indeed there are indications that that was how things turned out: one record indicates that 9898 was delivered on 18th November, 9899 about a week later, and that 9900 was expected on 9th December. All three saw much use with several operational squadrons, side-by-side with contemporary Pups from the bigger production batches, and can only be regarded as similar in all essential respects to mainstream production aircraft.

No.3 Squadron of No.1 Wing had 9898 by 30th November and 9900 by 28th December 1916; on the latter date 9899 was under repair at Dunkerque. While 9899 was with No.11 (Naval) Squadron its pilots included FSL A.R.Brown, later well-known for his involvement in the fighting of 21st April 1918 in which Rittmeister Manfred, *Freiherr* von Richthofen, met his death.

RNAS deliveries of production Pups were being made from Sopwith early in September 1916: these were of the batch N5180-5199. The first, N5180, was recorded on the strength of 'C' Squadron of No.1 Wing at Dunkerque by 7th September, but had evidently been with the squadron in August, for it had crashed on 21st August 1916; after this brief and undistinguished career it was deleted on 12th October. Of the Beardmore batch 9901-9950, A. Dukinfield Jones flew 9901 on 26th September 1916; the aircraft was officially accepted on 16th October, and was delivered to RNAS Eastchurch on 6th November. On arrival there it was immediately flown by Sqn Cdr Harry Busteed, who noted that the little Sopwith was 'tail heavy all speeds'. Unfortunately, he did not mention whether or not he had used the adjustable tailplane that was fitted to 9901. As recorded on page 42, this important modification was foreshadowed in the early official report on the prototype: Busteed's experience apparently confirmed the need for it, and might even have suggested that a greater range of incidence adjustment was necessary.

Dated 7th December 1916, these photographs are of 9497, which at that time had an 80hp Clerget engine, and the transparent covering on its centre section was over the area between the spars only. A possible explanation of the tricolour elevator stripes on this Sopwith-built Pup is suggested in the text.

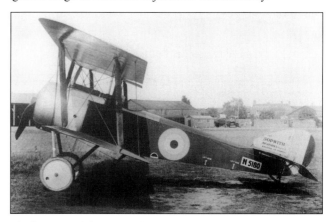

The first Sopwith-built Pup of the batch N5180 - N5199 photographed at Brooklands. As related in the narrative, N5180 had one of the briefest careers of any of the early production Pups. It had the adjustable tailplane.

The first Beardmore-built Pup, 9901, photographed at Eastchurch shortly after its arrival there in November 1916. Powered by an 80hp Clerget, it had an adjustable tailplane. Although by no means the first Pup to enter RNAS service, its serial number provided the original Admiralty designation for the Pup.

The production Pups were generally very similar to 3691, but had a revised design of fin and rudder, together with a higher undercarriage; in the interplane bracing, streamline-section wires replaced the cables of the prototype. Those first delivered to the RNAS had transparent covering on the centre section in an endeavour to improve the pilot's view upwards and forwards.

Apart from the change in shape and area of the fin and rudder, the early production Pups had an adjustable tailplane, the incidence of which could be varied in flight by the pilot. The variable-incidence tailplane of the Sopwith 1½ Strutter had proved to be successful, and it must have seemed sensible and desirable to fit a similar refinement to the Pup. In the smaller aircraft a simpler actuating system was employed, as described by Harald Penrose (*British Aviation: the Great War and Armistice*, Putnam 1969):

'To use the nut and worm gear patented for the 1½ Strutter would be unnecessarily expensive, so Hawker devised a simple crank hinged from the stern-post, connecting it at mid-length to a vertical push-tube attached to the rear spar, and operated it with wires running from a diagonal sliding knob on the right side of the cockpit.'

The RFC was quite as eager as the RNAS to obtain the Pup in quantity. At the time of the prototype's appearance the Sopwith company was primarily an Admiralty contractor: the RFC had earlier been obliged to turn to other manufacturers for the Sopwith 1½ Strutters that it wanted, and had to repeat the exercise with the Pup. Probably the RFC's demands for the 1½ Strutter were enough to stretch its contractors to the limit of their capacity; indeed Trenchard had recently sent an urgent request to the War Office for additional aircraft needed for the critical preparatory months preceding the 1916 Somme offensive, and this was met by the transfer, from April 1916 onwards, of many RNAS 1½ Strutters to the RFC.

Little time was lost in getting out a tender for an RFC production contract, or, indeed, in finding a constructor. Before the end of April 1916, under the reference MA/Aeros/714, a tender for 50 Pups was with the Standard Motor Co Ltd of Coventry who were to build the aircraft as sub-contractors to the Sopwith company. At the time Standard were building 50 B.E.12s (6136-6185), and the first had been delivered to the AID at Farnborough. The contract for the Pups (No.87/A/461) was dated 22nd May 1916, and the serial numbers A626-A675 were allotted for them. Standard's production followed that of the B.E.12s commendably quickly, for the first few Pups had been completed before the last of the B.E.12s had been delivered: the first official allocation of a Standard-built Pup was of A627 on 13th September 1916 when the aircraft, although still at Coventry, was allotted to the RFC with the Expeditionary Force.

RFC Headquarters in France were understandably anxious to get the new Sopwiths into squadron service at the earliest possible opportunity. Their anxiety was probably rendered more acute by the failure of the Somme offensive, and as early as 24th July 1916 Brig Gen Brooke-Popham wrote to the Director of Aeronautical Equipment (DAE):

'It has been found impossible to keep up the supply of Morane Scouts and it will therefore be necessary to replace one Flight in No.60 Squadron in the immediate future. It is proposed to do this by single-seater Sopwith Scouts with 80hp Le Rhône engines.

'Will you please say how soon the necessary number of these machines can be sent out?

'We would be willing to take all except the first two without engines. We should require eight to start with and replacements at the rate of one a week together with a supply of spare parts.'

DAE replied on 27th July, stating that the first two production Pups would be completed in August, and that a regular supply of 12 per month would follow from 1st September. This seemed to be confirmed by telegrams on 14th and 17th August, the latter reporting that the first Standard-built aircraft would be ready for its test flight on 31st August and would be sent to CFS and Orfordness for trials and evaluation. The second production Pup was promised for 8th September, the third five days later, and the fourth on 15th September.

As none had materialised by mid-September Brooke-Popham again wrote to DAE on the 18th, asking how the Sopwiths were progressing and how soon he could expect to have enough Pups to equip a Flight. No doubt he was by that time accustomed to failures of production promises, and therefore may not have been surprised to learn from ADAE's reply of 19th September 1916

'...that there have been further considerable delays in the construction of the Sopwith Scout fitted with the 80hp Le Rhône engine. The first machine is expected to have its trial flight on the 22nd inst., and should leave on the following day for its trials at Orfordness. Provided the first machine passes its tests satisfactorily, the next machines should follow at the rate of two for the next week, and three for the week after that.

'It is therefore improbable that we shall be able to send out sufficient machines to form and keep up a Flight before the end of the second week in October.'

Fortunately for No.60 Squadron, enough Nieuport 16s were delivered to the RFC for the unit to be progressively re-equipped with that type, and by mid-October 1916 the process was nearly complete. Thus No.60 Squadron never had the Pup, and the first RFC squadron to be equipped with the Sopwith was No.54, which arrived in France on 24th December 1916.

Meanwhile, the RNAS had been acquiring operational experience with the Pup. By 21st September 1916,

Second Pup of the first Sopwith-built batch, N5181 had a long and varied career. By 14th September 1916 it was with 'B' Squadron, No.1 Wing, RNAS Dunkerque, and was briefly reported with No.2 (Naval) Squadron on 28th September, but by 2nd November it was in 'D' Flight of the RNAS Detached Squadron that was soon designated No.9 (Naval) Squadron. N5181 transferred to No.3 (Naval) Squadron in February 1917 when Naval Eight was withdrawn to re-equip with Triplanes, but by 8th March was under repair at Dunkerque Depot. In June it was at Dover, and by October was with the RNAS War School at Manstone, fitted with an 80hp Gnome engine, and is also believed to have seen service at the RNAS Gunnery School, Freiston, at some time. *(RAF Museum)*

'C' Squadron of No.1 Wing, RNAS, could list its active strength of Pups as 3691, N5182, N5183 and N5184. In the squadron's reserve was N5185, while N5180 had been wrecked a month earlier and was theoretically under repair in the Depot: in fact it was deleted on 12th October. By 14th September N5181 had reached 'B' Squadron of No.1 Wing, and in the following week was joined by N5187.

On 30th October 1916, Section B of the Air Department of the Admiralty sent a signal to RNAS Headquarters, Dunkerque, intimating that a further 50 'Sopwith Le Rhône Aeroplanes Type 9901' were to be ordered, and requesting a list of such minor modifications as were felt to be necessary. Next day Sqn Cdr Alec Ogilvie replied to the Vice-Admiral, Dover Patrol, suggesting five modifications:

'(1) That the streamlining on the fuselage in the neighbourhood of the pilot's seat should be cut further down so as to allow the pilot to lean over the side with greater facility.

'(2) That the control stick should have a plain straight wooden handle instead of the Y-shaped handle, the disadvantages of which are that the stick is prevented from coming over so far as it would if it were straight,

A Pup with most of its centre section covered with transparent material presented a faintly bizarre appearance in flight.

and, being metal, under circumstances of low temperature at a great altitude, the metal chills the hands even through gloves and if the metal should touch the bare flesh, it is liable to take the skin off.

'(3) That flexible copper tubing be fitted in place of solid pipes. This tubing, when fitted with long nipples, has been found to entirely eliminate petrol pipe troubles. The rubber joints are found to be highly unsatisfactory as the rubber perishes and swells, sometimes blocking the jet and sometimes choking the pipes. No.1 Wing have been fitting flexible copper piping to their machines and maintain that they have eliminated breakdowns from this cause.

'(4) That the windscreen fitted to the handle of the gun be done away with and a small pad about 5" x 4" substituted. It is found that it is impossible to keep the oil from clouding the windscreen as at present fitted and that when this has happened it is impossible to sight the gun.

'(5) That the shields for the ammunition belt be fitted so as not to interfere with the manipulation of the gun mechanism. On some of the later machines this has been so fitted.

'There are one or two defects with regard to the synchronising mechanism on the Vickers light gun and in the ammunition belt wheel, but these points are being made the subject of a separate report by Headquarters G.'

Perhaps Ogilvie had no views on the adjustable tailplane or the transparent covering of the centre section; alternatively, he might have regarded any suggested modifications of these features to be major rather than minor. In respect of the centre section, however, the Air Department itself notified RNAS Dunkerque on 13th November that 'During trials with an 80hp Clerget Sopwith [this must have been 9901] at Eastchurch on 6th November, the celluloid window in the top plane burst while the machine was in the air', and enquired whether any similar failure had occurred on any Dunkerque Sopwith.

As a Flight Sub-Lieutenant in No.8 (Naval) Squadron, D.M.B. Galbraith won his squadron's first combat victory on 10th November 1916, flying Pup N5193. Here he is seen later in his career, with Camel B3926 at Manstone.

On 21st November, No.1 Wing replied through the Senior Officer, RNAS Headquarters, Dover Command:

'...the first Sopwith Scout sent to No.1 Wing was fitted with 80hp Clerget engine. This machine had the entire centre section covered with celluloid, and in this case the celluloid did actually burst in the air. The burst was not bad, but this type of centre section was unsatisfactory.

'Since the above, 80hp Le Rhône Sopwith Scouts have been sent, some with centre section entirely covered with fabric, and some with a celluloid window extending over the centre section between the main spars.

'In this case, the celluloid is more strongly secured, and of the three types this is the most satisfactory, e.g., N5187 with 80hp Le Rhône.

'The window is of considerable assistance in fighting and accompanying and the celluloid has showed no signs of giving away [sic], although these machines have been operating at great heights during very cold weather.'

RNAS Pups had combat successes before the end of 1916. One of the earliest was achieved by FSL S.J.Goble (later Air-Vice Marshal S.J.Goble, CBE, DSO, DFC, RAF), an Australian officer of No.1 Wing, on 24th September 1916, when he pursued and shot down in flames an LVG two-seater that had been one of a number of German aircraft that had bombed Dunkerque. Goble was later one of the original members of the RNAS Detached Squadron, soon to be named No.8 (Naval) Squadron, that was formed in October 1916 for service with the RFC. Initially it had one Flight of Nieuports (5 Nieuport 21s and one Nieuport 11), one of Sopwith 1½ Strutters, and one of Pups. By 2nd November it had, at least on paper, two Flights of Pups: 'C' Flight had N5182, N5183, N5190, N5192, N5193 and N5194; 'D' Flight 3691, N5181, N5184, N5186, N5196 and N5197. This was achieved by depriving No.1 Wing of virtually all of its Pups; and of the first Sopwith-built production batch, N5180-N5199, all but N5180 saw some service with Naval Eight at some time. Officially, the replacement of the squadron's 1½ Strutters by Pups had been completed by 16th November 1916, and it was an all-Pup unit by the end of 1916.

FSL S.J.Goble, who scored one of the earliest combat successes on a Pup on 24th September 1916. Behind him in this photograph is the B.E.2e No.1110, a Beardmore-built aircraft that was briefly at Dover late in July 1915. (K.M.Molson)

N5183 was one of Naval Eight's earliest Pups. Here it is seen after a landing mishap, probably in mid-February 1917: it was sent to the Depot at Dunkerque, 'crashed', on 18th February. It had been with 'C' Squadron, No.1 Wing, by 14th September, 1916, and was one of the earliest transferees to the RNAS Detached Squadron (later Naval Eight), on or shortly before 2nd November. It was taken over by No.3 (Naval) Squadron in February 1917. By June 1917, N5183 was with No.9 (Naval) Squadron, which returned it to the Depot on 12th July. There it was considered to be 'very old; not worth repair', and was reported to have been deleted on 16th July 1917.

A footnote to page 448 of Vol. II of *The War in the Air* casts a revealing light on the difficulties of engine supply at the time:

'To get the "Pups" Wing Captain Lambe had to undertake to supply the 80hp Le Rhône engines. This he did by taking them out of crashed Nieuports. A few he begged from the French naval air service. The engines, after being thoroughly overhauled in the Dunkirk depot, were taken across to Dover where they were fitted in the "Pups".'

The new RNAS squadron's first combat victory was won by FSL D.M.B.Galbraith, DSC, flying N5193, on 10th November 1916: his victim was an LFG (Roland) two-seater, which spun down out of control after his attack over Bapaume. On 16th November, closing to a range of 15-20 yards, he again drove down his opponent out of control; and a week later he attacked the rear aircraft of a formation of six, fired 60 rounds, and saw its port wings fold up. Goble, too, had victories on 16th, 17th and 27th November, and by the end of 1916 No.8 (Naval) Squadron had shot down a total of 20 enemy aircraft.

Several other victories had been won by Pups of No.1 Wing before the formation of Naval Eight, and RNAS pilots had acquired a fair amount of combat experience on the type by the end of November 1916. Doubtless that experience underlay the following RNAS report of 29th November: while rightly recognising the Pup's fine qualities, its forward-looking observations were realistic and to the point.

'Under the present conditions this machine is considered second to none as a fighting machine.

'At 16,000ft she has the speed and climb of every HA [Hostile Aircraft] encountered up to date and, although the Nieuport 110hp Le Rhône, for instance, manoeuvres much quicker, the height lost in doing so is very noticeable. In the Sopwith "Pup" it has been noticed that, in fast dives, the machine surges up and down considerably, making it very difficult to keep sights on target. Otherwise she dives splendidly at well over 120 knots [138mph] with no apparent harm to the machine.

'The following points in design, etc., require consideration, and it is pointed out that pilots are unanimous in their opinion that, although this machine is probably superior to anything in this area at present, it will not remain so for long and that, if we are to cope with the German scouts of the near future, a stronger, bigger-engined machine of much the same type with greater speed and climb will be required before the spring.

'Points of design. etc, for consideration
in present and future types:

1. Visibility is very bad and is a serious handicap to a pilot of a fighting machine.
2. No advantage appears to be derived from the adjustable tailplane.
3. Centre section struts are too weak.
4. Muzzle of Vickers gun is too far away from propeller, which (we think) accounts a good deal for holes being put in propeller.
5. It is recommended to have two synchronised guns in all new types of scout.
6. An interrupter gear should prove more satisfactory than a synchronised one and is shortly going to be tried. A design has been got out by Flight Commander Huskisson and Lieutenant d'Albiac.
7. Some method of preventing guns from freezing should be designed. At present the guns and belt cannot be worked at greater heights than 14,000ft owing to their frozen condition.
8. The above remarks also apply to the compasses.

'In conclusion it is considered that the life of these machines is not great and that, when they once start to lose their performance, they should not be patched up but relieved right away by new machines.'

The principal shortcomings identified in that significant assessment were the basic inadequacy of the single Vickers gun (and, by implication, the slowness of its rate of fire, which in turn was related to engine speed) and the lightness of the Pup's structure, with the consequentially short effective airframe life.

While the 'stronger, bigger-engined machine of much the same type with greater speed and climb' was under construction in the Sopwith experimental shop, it was still only an unflown prototype, would not emerge as the first F.1 Camel for another four weeks, and was a distant and uncertain production prospect. It seems curious that, at the date of that report, no mention was made of the Sopwith Triplane, the qualities of which had been greatly praised and were known to RNAS pilots; yet despite its more powerful Clerget engine the Triplane in its basic and most numerous form had, like the Pup, only a single gun.

****

Despite the production difficulties mentioned on page 47, the autumn of 1916 had eventually seen the delivery of the RFC's first production Pups, built in Coventry by the Standard Motor Co, Ltd. As decreed by the DAE's department in August 1916 the first aircraft, A626, was allocated to Central Flying School on 11th October 1916; it had been completed by 27th September. It was tested there over the period 12th to 21st October, and the results were recorded in the official trials report M.31, together with remarks and recommendations. The main contents of the report were:

Sopwith Scout A626

Engine:	80hp Le Rhône, No.35018
Airscrew:	L.P 1020, drawing No. 5740
	Diameter 2600mm, pitch 2200mm

Rev. counter, Aneroid, Air-speed Indicator
Vickers interrupter gear

Weight empty	787 lb
Petrol	18½ gals, Oil 5 gals

1. Petrol system consists of one gravity-feed tank.
2. A gun mounting and Vickers interrupting gear is fitted, but no gun at present.
3. Tailplane is adjustable from pilot's seat.

Tested at Upavon.
Consumption trials, 18th October 1916

Petrol about 6 gals per hr
Oil 10 pts

Speed trial at height, 21st October 1916

At	5,000ft	105mph
	7,000ft	103mph
	9,000ft	103mph
	11,000ft	101mph
	13,000ft	98mph
	15,000ft	85mph

Average speed over measured course 113.3mph (height about 10ft), tested 16th October 1916

Climbing trial, 12th October 1916

To	1,000ft in 1 min 5 sec	to	8,000ft in 12 min 0 sec
	2,000ft in 2 min 10 sec		9,000ft in 14 min 5 sec
	3,000ft in 3 min 30 sec		10,000ft in 16 min 25 sec
	4,000ft in 5 min		11,000ft in 19 min 20 sec
	5,000ft in 6 min 25 sec		12,000ft in 22 min
	6,000ft in 8 min 15 sec		13,000ft in 25 min 15 sec
	7,000ft in 9 min 55 sec		14,000ft in 28 min 40 sec
			15,000ft in 32 min 40 sec

The machine is very similar to a Bristol Scout but of lighter construction, giving better performance and lower stalling speed.

1. Stability
   Lateral   Good
   Longitudinal   Good
   Directional   Good

2. Amount of vibration in air   Slight

3. Whether the controls are conveniently placed and easily worked.

   (a) for engine   Yes, but throttle lever
   (b) for flying   should be placed ½ inch further from side.

4. Whether machine is tiring to fly   No

5. Length of run
   To unstick   About 40 yards
   To pull up (engine stopped)   About 60 yards
   Direction and strength of wind   Calm

6. Ease of landing   Moderate

7. Length of time to prepare engine for starting   3 minutes

Note: This machine is very uncomfortable to fly in rough weather, probably due to its light loading and small size. It is difficult to handle on the ground in a wind.

Suggestions for improvement in design

1. The longerons, where clips are fitted, should be covered with aluminium to prevent damage to the longerons.

2. The brackets carrying the rudder post fitted on rear of longerons are cut away to fit same, which weakens the rear of the fuselage. It is suggested that the brackets be made longer to fit the longerons.

3. Steel axles should be fitted in place of duralumin.

4. The fairlead through which the elevator cable passes out of the fuselage to be shaped so that the cable does not chafe on its ends; they should be belled out.

5. The wing-flap [i.e., aileron] interconnecting cable to be made to clear the rib on the top plane to prevent chafing of the cable.

6. The elevator hinge to be fitted so that the collar of the hinge bolt does not enter the tube.

7. Packing to be fitted around the cowl to prevent oil leaking over the windscreen on the gun.

8. The welding on the top sockets of the Vee undercarriage is weak; this must be made stronger.

9. The pitot tube should be fitted on the outside of the top plane.

10. The bracket carrying the skid wires on the rudder post are [sic] too near the ground. It is suggested that these be fitted higher up, and that springs be fitted in the control cables to the skid, similar to the B.E.2c.

11. The lacing to the fuselage to be overlapped.

12. The petrol tank is a single tank, gravity fed to the carburettor. The specification (No.2A.13(1)) requires duplicate tanks. EF require that where only one tank is fitted, it should be divided longitudinally. It is recommended that the tank be divided longitudinally and a two-way cock fitted, or another tank may be fitted under, or above, the top plane.

13. The centre section of the top plane should be covered with Cellon (i.e., transparent material).

14. The pilot's seat should be made more comfortable by fitting a rest for the pilot's back. This could be done in three-ply extending from his seat to the rail behind his shoulders.

15. It is recommended that the calculations of this machine be gone into at once and that it be sand tested. It is doubtful whether it is sufficiently strong to stand up to a dive and sharp flatten out. The ability to do so is necessary in this type of machine.

(Signed) M.K.Cooper-King
Secretary to CFS Test Committee

A copy of that report was sent to RFC Headquarters on 9th November 1916, by which date the first RFC squadron to be equipped with the Pup, No.54, was forming at Castle Bromwich under the command of Major K.K Horn. Its first Pup, A627, had been allocated on 22nd October 1916, A629-A632 on 8th November, and A633-A652 and A654 had all been allotted

A648 was first allocated to No 54 Squadron, RFC on 15th December 1916 and was listed on the squadron's strength on 6th January 1917. Later used by No.46 Squadron, it was one of the Pups that the unit flew to England on Home Defence detachment on 10th July 1917.

to the squadron up to 20th December. A628 had been allocated to Orfordness for trials on 6th November and probably did not go to France, and several others of the 26 early allocations to No.54 did not go with the squadron when it crossed the Channel on Christmas Eve 1916.

One of those that did not join No.54 Squadron, although allocated to it on 8th November 1916, was A631. Possibly in response to the concluding recommendation of the CFS Report on A626, this, the sixth Standard-built Pup, was sent to the Southern Aircraft Depot at Farnborough for delivery to the Royal Aircraft Factory, wherein it was subjected to structural testing by the primitive static-loading methods then practised. The Royal Aircraft Factory's report, *B.A.25: Test to Destruction of Sopwith Biplane Scout A651*, was dated January 1917, but unfortunately no copy is known to have survived in official records. The results and recommendations, if any, arising from these tests are unknown, and recorded Factors of Safety for the Pup appear to be inconsistent (but it should be remembered that modifications made during the type's service might have produced changes in such figures; indeed might have been specifically intended to do so). A table in a data manual produced in August 1917 by T6C of the Air Board gave, in respect of the Pup, a Factor of Safety of 4.46 on the front spars with Centre of Pressure at 0.3 of the chord, and 5.0 on the rear spars with CP at 0.5 of the chord. Substantially different figures were given on an undated drawing in the AID Aeroplane Pocket Book, wherein Factors of Safety on the front spars were 6.1 (upper) and 7.7 (lower), and on the rear spars 6 (upper) and 7 (lower). These were calculated on an assumed aircraft weight of only 1,030lb, whereas A626 weighed 1,225lb when tested at CFS. It appears, however, that an overall Factor of Safety of 7.95 was officially accepted as the standard for the Pup.

Other points made in the CFS report were picked up and acted upon: for instance, by 21st December 1916 alteration Sheet No.151 had appeared, showing a method of reinforcing Pup undercarriage struts. On one of the CFS suggestions, RFC Headquarters held different views, however. On 13th January 1917 Brig Gen Brooke-Popham wrote tersely to DAE:

'Cellon is not required on the centre section of Sopwith Single-Seater Scouts. Can this please be done away with on future machines and plain fabric substituted?'

Apparently Brooke-Popham expected this to be agreed, for on the same date he instructed both Aircraft Depots to replace Cellon with plain fabric on the centre sections of Pups overhauled by them.

If considered primarily as an RFC matter this presents a minor puzzle, for the only Pups delivered to the RFC at that time were all built by Standard: next day, 14th January, No.54 Squadron's strength consisted of 16 Standard-built Pups (A630, A633-A637, A639, A640, A642, A644-A649 and A652). Whether any of these had transparent covering on the centre section is uncertain, but seems unlikely: A626 left the factory with fabric covering thereon, and no known photograph of any of its batch successors shows anything but this opaque and conventional form of centre section. Nevertheless, on 9th March 1917, both Aircraft Depots reported to Headquarters that Sopwith Scouts were coming out with ordinary fabric on the centre section; and it seems unlikely that such reports would have been considered necessary if all earlier deliveries had had fabric-covered centre sections. A fair number of early production Pups for the RNAS, both Sopwith-built and Beardmore-built, had been delivered with Cellon covering, however, and Brooke-Popham's ruling may have been based at least as much on Naval Eight's combat experience with such Pups as on RFC opinions. One feels that it would have been out of character for Brooke-Popham, unilaterally and without advice or consultation, to have decided against a feature of the other Service's aircraft, and indeed the RNAS abandoned the transparent covering of the centre section relatively early in the Pup's service with its fighting squadrons.

B1721 might almost have been A6174's replacement in No.54 Squadron, for it was allocated to the unit on 10th May 1917, the day after A6174 was lost. It was reported as 'new' in the squadron on 19th May, but in its turn was brought down on 30th May; after combat near Hesbécourt Lt F.W.Kantel was obliged to land in enemy territory. The aluminium flank panel had apparently been replaced, and it incorporated en enlarged rectangular access panels probably a squadron modification.

A one-time No.54 Squadron aircraft that came safely home was B5926. While still at the Standard works this Pup was allocated to the E.F. on 25th August 1917. It was reported at No.1 ASD, St Omer, on 9th November 1917, and two days later it was with No.54 Squadron. By 22nd December it was again with No.1 ASD, St Omer, and on 13th January 1918 it was flown back to England. Here it is seen at a training unit, with an Avro 504A or 504J for company.

Another of No.54 Squadron's aircraft, A6174, is seen here in German hands after its capture on 9th May 1917. Although 2/Lt G.C.T.Hadrill, its pilot, was reported to have died of wounds, his name appeared in the post-Armistice Royal Air Force List. He had been shot down near Lesdain by Leutnant Werner Voss of Jasta 2, and was No.28 in Voss's extensive victory log.

Chapter 8

Production Progress

After the initial production contracts that had made possible the equipping of the first Pup squadrons, further orders were placed. From the Sopwith company the RNAS ordered a second batch, this time of 50 aircraft numbered N6160-N6209, under Contract No. C.P.100785/16. Thirty were also ordered, as N6100-N6129, from Beardmore under Contract No. A.S.14757, which was dated 12th February 1917, but these were delivered as Beardmore S.B.3s under Contract No. A.S.775/17 and are discussed under that heading (see pages 130-132). A further order under A.S.775 from Beardmore was for 30 Pups numbered N6430-N6459: not surprisingly, deliveries of the Pups preceded those of the S.B.3s. The last RNAS order for Pups was for 70 from Sopwith, to be numbered N6460-N6529, but 50 of these (N6480-N6529) were cancelled shortly before 13th March 1917 in order that the Sopwith company might concentrate its endeavours on the production of Camels.

Estimates of output of these RNAS Pups were made weekly, but were both over-optimistic and confused, and are best disregarded. The first of the initial Sopwith batch of twenty, N5180, had evidently been delivered not later than August 1916, for, as recorded on page 46, it crashed on 21st August. The last of the batch, N5199, was expected during the week ending 11th November 1916 and is known to have been on the strength of No.3 (Naval) Squadron by 30th November. In January 1917, 14 of the batch N6160-N6209 were delivered to Dunkerque (N6160, N6161, N6163-N6173 and N6209); those delivered in February were N6174-N6197. The balance of that batch had all been delivered before 12th April 1917, at which time deliveries from the last Sopwith-built batch (N6460-N6479) were coming through: of these, N6462, N6464, N6474, N6475, N6477 and N6478 were all at

Dunkerque Depot on 26th April 1917.

The Pups N6460-N6479 were delivered under Contract No.C.P.102622/17, which had originally been for 70 aircraft to be numbered N6460-N6529, but, as noted above, N6480-N6529 were cancelled. Nevertheless, the Sopwith company built, under the same Contract No.C.P.102622/17, a further 70 airframes that were delivered as spares. Official records indicate that deliveries began late in 1916 and ended early in May 1917; some weeks later the seemingly incongruous serial numbers C3707-C3776 were allotted to this batch, doubtless for administrative convenience and possibly in response to a War Office letter dated 27th July1917.

In February 1917 the RNAS was pressing hard for deliveries of Pups and Triplanes for service in France, and the Service perceived a bottleneck in the Sopwith organisation at Brooklands. On 14th February Capt A.V.Vyvyan RN, the Assistant-Director of Air Services, sent the following directive to the Captain Superintendent, Central Supply Depot, White City:

'Owing to the necessity of getting machines to Dunkirk as rapidly as possible, and the delays which have occurred in testing machines at Brooklands and then flying them to Dunkirk, the Fifth Sea Lord has approved of all Triplanes and Pups being sent direct by Naval Motor Lorries to Dover for erection and trial from Sopwith's works.

'They will be erected by Naval ratings at Dover and are to be put through their tests at Dover by Lt [F.G.] Andreae.

'Any Naval ratings now employed at Brooklands in testing, and erecting machines should be sent to Dover.

'It is requested that the necessary arrangements be made for the new procedure to come into force forthwith.'

This new procedure soon became a source of friction between the RNAS and Sopwith employees: evidently three of the latter had been sent to Dover as erectors. Word of

Among the 14 Sopwith-built Pups delivered to Dunkerque in January 1917 was N6160, first of the batch N6160-N6209. On 8th February it was in the Repair section of the Dunkerque Depot, probably being erected, and three days later went to No.3 (Naval) Squadron. In that unit it was flown by FSL R.Collishaw on 15th February and 4th March, on each of which dates he sent down an enemy aircraft out of control. Other victories won on this Pup occurred on 22nd and 23rd April (FSL H.S.Kerby). On the last-mentioned date two Albatros D.IIIs collided as a result of Kerby's attack; one of them was flown by Hptm Paul von Osterroht, Staffelführer of Jasta 12 (see also caption for N6172 on the next page). N6160 was at Dunkerque Depot on 16th August 1917, and was transferred to Dover on 11th October. On 30th March 1918, by which time it had acquired an 80hp Gnome engine, it was being erected at Cranwell. In this photograph it is seen at Freiston, a satellite landing ground for Cranwell and, in RNAS times, the home of that Service's Gunnery School. (L.A.Rogers)

Last of the 20 Pups of the initial Sopwith-built batch, N5199 had reached No.3 (Naval) Squadron on 30th November 1916 but was subsequently transferred to Naval Eight on 5th January 1917. It returned to No.3 (Naval) early in February 1917, but was reported wrecked in that squadron on 11th April; its deletion was recommended on 27th April and executed on 4th May, 1917.

difficulties at Dover had reached the Fifth Sea Lord, the redoubtable Commodore Godfrey Paine, to whom Wg Capt C.L.Lambe wrote, on 27th May, in terms of as much exasperation and bitterness as he could judiciously address to such a formidable senior officer:

'I am sorry that you think Osmond [Wg Cdr E. Osmond] is at fault over any friction which has occurred at Dover Aerodrome as regards the erection of Sopwith machines. I have gone into this question several times and in my opinion the firm is to blame. They have only got three men for erecting, which is far less than the number they would employ themselves if they had to erect the machines at Brooklands. We give them every assistance in the way of moving machines, working parties for erecting, etc., in fact the greater part of the erecting is done by Naval ratings.

'The truth is that the firm have always been dead against having to erect machines at Dover at all and have constantly placed difficulties in the way. It is very seldom that a machine arrives complete for erection, and some essential part such as compass, petrol gauge and other parts have to be supplied from the Dover Store, in order to get the machines out rapidly. Machines are also constantly arriving without flying wires.

'I only proposed the erection of the machines at Dover at the time when there were no Ferry Pilots, and I had to send pilots from Dunkirk to London and thence to Brooklands to get any machines out here at all. Now that there are a good many Ferry Pilots, and there is not such great urgency for machines owing to lack of pilots, I am prepared to have all machines accepted at Brooklands if you think this would be better. but I cannot possibly spare pilots to go to Brooklands, since once in London they are beyond my control and I never know what happens.'

That concluding, despairing admission is not without its humour.

Unfortunately, official papers do not include any account of the situation in the Sopwith works, but doubtless the firm did not lack problems of its own. At the time in question it was building 1½ Strutters, Pups and Triplanes side by side in the same assembly shop while initiating quantity production of the Camel, and the likelihood of confusion must have been great.

Because most of the Beardmore-built Pups were initially intended for use from ships, few of them went to Naval squadrons on the Western Front. They were never numerous at best, and just how thin on the ground, and in the Fleet, they were may be gauged from this tabular presentation of their initial distribution from the Beardmore works. As indicated on page 74, 9909-9949 and N6430-N6459 were of Type 9901a.

When Their Majesties King George V and Queen Mary visited the Sopwith factory at Kingston-upon-Thames on 19th April 1917, they saw Pups and Triplanes being built side-by-side. The identifiable members of this group are, from left, Mr R.O.Cary (General Manager), Colonel the Maharajah of Bikanir, Queen Mary, Mr G.H.Mitchell (Works Manager), Capt B. Godfrey-Faussett RN, King George V and Mr T.O.M.Sopwith.

A less fortunate Pup of the January 1917 consignment was N6161, another unwilling guest of the Germans. It was in 'B' Flight of No.3 (Naval) Squadron by 25th January, but was shot down on 1st February while being flown by FSL G.L.Elliott.   (A.E.Ferko)

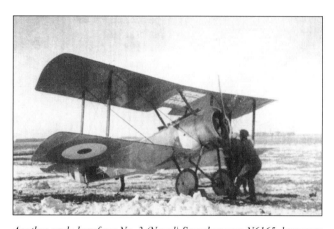

Another early loss from No. 3 (Naval) Squadron was N6165, here seen at Dover early in 1917. It was reported to be on the strength of the squadron on 15th February but apparently did not physically join the unit until 21st February. Although officially recorded as missing in a report dated 1st March 1917, the loss of the aircraft and its pilot, FSL J.P.White, was apparently not recorded as a casualty until 4th March. N6165 was deleted on 11th May 1917.   (P.S.Leaman)

Another of No.3 (Naval) Squadron's losses in that grim spring of 1917, N6172 fell into enemy hands intact on 12th April, having been driven down by Hptm Paul von Osterroht, Staffelführer of Jasta 12. Recorded as being in Reserve at Dunkerque on 8th February, 1917, this Pup went to No.3 (Naval) two days later. Although officially deleted by the RNAS on 11th May, N6172 was evidently flown by German pilots. Its own pilot, Flt Cdr R.G.Mack, was wounded and made PoW; his conqueror, von Osterroht was killed on 23rd April in a collision during combat with N6160 (see photograph on page 54).   (A.E.Ferko)

The second Beardmore-built production Pup, 9902, photographed shortly after it was completed. It had an 80hp Clerget engine, an adjustable tailplane, and transparent covering in its centre section. Test-flown by A Dukinfield Jones on 23rd October 1916, it was officially accepted on 8th November and was dispatched to Cranwell six days later. It was still there on 5th January 1918, but crashed on 6th February.

Initial delivery destinations of Beardmore-built Pups		
	Batch	
Destination	9901-9949	N6430-N6459
Cranwell	9902,9903,9908, 9909,9923,9924, 9925,9946	-
Dover	-	N6442
Dover for Walmer	9947	N6438-N6441
Dover for Dunkerque	9915,9916, 9928,9929	N6459
Eastchurch	9901	-
East Fortune	9917-9920	N6448, N6449
Grain	9922	N6445-N6447
Hendon	9948,9949	-
Killingholme	9930-9940	N6434-N6437
Manston(e)	9906,9907	-
Port Victoria	9912	-
Great Yarmouth	9904,9905	-
Carriers:		
HMS Manxman		
(a) through East Fortune	9913, 9914, 9943, 9944, 9945	N6430, N6431
(b) through Turnhouse	-	N6443-N6446
HMS Vindex		
(a) direct	9910, 9911	-
(b) through Felixstowe	9921, 9926, 9927	N6457, N6458
HMS Furious	-	N6450-N6454
Aegean	9941, 9942	N6432, N6433

Last of the four Beardmore-built Pups that were sent to the Aegean area, N6433 was test-flown and officially accepted on 7th May 1917. As related on page 88 it was one of four Pups that were handed over to the Greek government at the end of the war.

Most of these Beardmore-built Pups later moved on to other places and units: for example, the five delivered to Dover for Dunkerque all saw operational service, between them, with Naval Squadrons Nos.4, 9, 11, 12 and the Seaplane Defence Flight. Those delivered to Killingholme had obviously gone there for temporary storage, whence they progressed variously to Houton Bay, Cranwell, Grain, East Fortune and the Seaplane Defence Flight at Dunkerque.

It is one of the minor statistical curiosities of the 1914-18 war that Pups delivered against Naval contracts totalled no more than 176, including the prototype 3691 and the Beardmore-built 9950, which became the prototype S.B.3. Thus Naval Pups were outnumbered almost tenfold by those constructed for the RFC.

The RFC wanted more Pups than the Standard company could produce on the exigent time scale of war, and were obliged to turn to other constructors.. First approaches were made to the Darracq Motor Engineering Co Ltd of Townmead Road, Fulham, London S.W.6, with Contract No.87/A/1071, and to Whitehead Aircraft Ltd, Townshend Road, Richmond, with Contract No.87/A/1072: from each an initial order for 50 aircraft was proposed.

A further early contender was the Wells Aviation Co Ltd, of Elystan Street, Chelsea, from which 100 Pups were ordered under Contract No.87/A/885; the serial numbers A5138-A5237 were allocated on 28th September. 1916. On 2nd October a contract for 200 Sopwith 1½ Strutters numbered A5238-A5437 was given to the Wells company, whereupon the order for Pups was cancelled and the numbers A5138-A5237 were re-allotted to a motley assortment of other types of aircraft.

Evidently the proposed Darracq contract did not survive long enough to have serial numbers allocated, perhaps because the firm had just been asked to build a further batch of 120 F.E.8s. Possibly to compensate for the loss of Darracq output, the initial contract placed with the Whitehead company (87/A/1101) was enlarged to 100 aircraft, A6150-A6249. It seems that no further approaches to other contractors were made, and the RFC's Pups were produced only by the Standard and Whitehead companies.

J.A.Whitehead, who had formed Whitehead Aircraft Ltd in May 1915, was a publicity-conscious, thrusting entrepreneur. Work had started in the former drill hall in Townshend Road on 19th May 1915, and his company's production contracts that preceded the Pup orders had been one for six B.E.2bs and another for 100 Maurice Farman Shorthorns. He built large new works at Feltham, in which the components made at Richmond were assembled. Unfortunately for historians, Whitehead chose to call the Pups built by his company 'Whitehead Fighting Scouts', and this piece of arrogance has led to some confusion over the years.

The first Whitehead-built Pup, A6150, was with the AID at Farnborough, presumably to undergo acceptance inspection, on 27th January 1917; shortly afterwards it went to the Central Flying School. Its batch successor, A6151, was in the AID's

The first Whitehead-built Pup, A6150, had an adjustable tailplane. On 27th January 1917 it was at the Royal Aircraft Factory, Farnborough, probably for inspection by the AID, and in February it was at Central Flying School, where this photograph was taken.

hands on 28th January, and was allocated initially to No.66 Squadron; on 27th March this was amended to a less specific allocation to the Expeditionary Force, but evidently it was damaged and was with DAE.2a Repair Section on 14th April. It did join No.66 Squadron in due course, as did at least 26 others from the same batch at one time or another.

The 100th Whitehead-built Pup was delivered in June 1917, but supplementary orders were placed in May and July, following British Requisitions Nos.9l, 110 and 128. The last order on Whitehead was for 200 Pups: these had been asked for by British Requisition No.203, dated 3rd October 1917, and an order was placed, prior to formal contract, on 12th October. All Whitehead Pups up to C1550 were delivered under Contract No.87/A/1101; the final 200 under Contract No. A.S.29677 were numbered D4011-D4210, and the 750th and last Whitehead-built aircraft was delivered in the last week of May 1918.

Production at the Coventry works of the Standard company continued until mid-October 1918, when the 600th Pup built under Contract No. A.S.11541/1 was completed, bringing the total of Standard-built aircraft to 850. Pups delivered against the later orders from both contractors were intended to be used on training duties, for the Pup made an excellent - though, some argued, too forgiving - fighter trainer.

In the early days of the Pup's operational service forecasts and statistics of output were studied with concern. A conference held on 9th February 1917 concluded that a monthly output of 80 would be required. The most that Sopwith had managed up to that time was ten per week, Beardmore two per week, Standard about five and Whitehead was only starting. The

Sopwith company hoped to maintain their output at about ten per week, but the outlook was uncertain: although the Camel was in prospect and Sopwith were bringing it into production, it was still an unknown quantity.

By December 1917 production of Pups was increasing, and apparently meeting predictions: of the 90 Pups promised for delivery in that month 86 had been delivered by 22nd December. Output reached its peak in the first quarter of 1918, when 500 Pups were delivered, 156 from Standard and 344 from Whitehead. By that time, of course, virtually all were destined to go to training units.

D4196 was one of the last Pups to be built by the Whitehead company, and by the time of its delivery in early April 1918 newly-built Pups were primarily intended for training units. The markings worn by D4196 suggest that it may have been an aircraft of No.34 Training Depot Station, Scampton.

Bearing the date 18th November 1917, this photograph shows Pups in production in the Coventry works of the Standard Motor Co. At centre right are B6083, B6088 and B6089; identifiable at left are B6085, B6087 and (presumably) B6086. Of these, B6085-B6088 were delivered to the RNAS for training purposes and were at Chingford early in January 1918. By that time B6089 was with No.30 Training Squadron, RFC, at Tern Hill, and was later used by No.6 Training Squadron, Australian Flying Corps. According to official statistics, accepted deliveries from Standard under Contract No. A.S.11541 had reached a total of 166 by 17th November 1917, the day preceding the date of this photograph.   (Bruce Robertson)

When Capt Vyvyan RN wrote to Capt Lambe RN on 14th February 1917, the RNAS had 23 Pups at Dunkerque and six ready for delivery at Brooklands. It was hoped that a further 12 would be delivered over the next two weeks, but in a cautionary note Vyvyan warned that delays in Pup deliveries might occur because of the efforts being made to reduce the aircraft's tail-heaviness (see page 82). He quoted estimates of 16 Pup deliveries to Dunkerque in each of the five months March to July 1917, with eight expected in August.

The RNAS was perhaps less concerned than the RFC over the production of Pups specifically, for that Service was also receiving Sopwith Triplanes for its fighting squadrons, and in the spring of 1917 the numbers of Triplanes in Naval squadrons and in prospect exceeded those of Pups. On 1st April there were with the Naval squadrons 37 Pups and 46 Triplanes; in the Depot

Delivered late in September 1918, C514 went to the Pool of Pilots, RAF Manston. In addition to its narrow white band marking, it bore the name Prince, perhaps bestowed by its occupant, Captain S. Andersen, DFC.

there were respectively 18 and 11; to be delivered from the Sopwith company expectations were for 13 Pups and 15 Triplanes. A month later the squadrons had 41 Pups and 52 Triplanes, while the Depot held, again respectively, 19 and 22. Additionally, assorted Nieuport scouts were in Naval service on 1st May 1917, 18 with squadrons, seven, in the Depot, and 48 expected. Over the two weeks 1st to 15th August 1917, the entire RNAS strength of Pups comprised 141 in commission; six were deleted, and 15 more allotted for the remainder of August.

RFC requirements in February 1917 aimed at providing for two Pup squadrons already in France, two more to come, and training units. With 61 Pups available on 1st February 1917, the specified need was for 35 deliveries in February and 50 in each of the three following months. The total of 185 required for the four months was matched almost exactly by the combined output of Standard and Whitehead for that period, namely 183.

Because RNAS squadrons were operating with the RFC (in succession to Naval Eight, No.3 Squadron, RNAS, equipped with Pups, was attached to the RFC from 1st February to 15th June 1917) it was necessary for some RFC Pups to go to these Naval units, and some RNAS pilots found themselves flying aircraft supplied against RFC contracts. The first such Pup was the ill-starred first production aircraft built by the Standard company, A626. As already recorded in pages 50-51, this Pup had been tested at CFS between 12th and 21st October 1916; shortly afterwards it was sent to France, arriving at No.2 Aircraft Depot, Candas, on 4th November. Thus it got to France nearly a week earlier than the copy of the official CFS Test Report on its performance that had been sent to RFC Headquarters. A626 did not tarry at No.2 AD, for it was sent that same day to No.70 Squadron, RFC, then equipped with Sopwith 1½ Strutters. By 28th December 1916, A626 was in 'B' Flight of No.8 (Naval) Squadron, but on 4th January 1917, while flown by FSL J.C.Croft, it was forced

Captured A626 was sent to Adlershof for testing and examination. This is one of the German official photographs taken there. It is interesting to note that the aircraft had been fitted with wheel covers for this purpose, whereas it had had none when captured. (A.E.Ferko)

down by *Leutnant* Friedrich Mallinckrodt of *Jasta* 10 and landed intact. Inevitably, it aroused the keen interest of its captors, and was taken to Adlershof for examination and testing. Thus a complete and airworthy specimen of one of the latest British fighter types was obliged to reveal its qualities to its enemies within weeks of its entry into the arena.

At least 167 of the Pups built to RFC orders saw service with, or were earmarked for, RNAS units. The great majority of these were used by training stations, but nine are known to have gone to operational Naval squadrons. It appears that these inter-Service allocations were not regarded as official transfers.

On 31st October 1918, with the Armistice less than two weeks away, the Royal Air Force had on charge a total of 877 Pups (in the official list still, at that late date, resolutely identified as Sopwith Scouts) and ten Sopwith 990las (but see also page 125).

The first Pup to fall into German hands intact, A626 was the first to have been built by the Standard Motor Co. Here it is seen on 4th January 1917, after FSL J.C.Croft of No.8 (Naval) Squadron had been forced down by Leutnant Friedrich Mallinckrodt near Bapaume.

Chapter 9

Pup Engines

The standard power unit for the Pup was the 80hp Le Rhône 9C rotary engine, but a number of the early production aircraft built for the RNAS had the 80hp Clerget 7Z. As noted on page 45 it was originally intended that 9496-9497 should have the 100hp Gnome Monosoupape, but this was amended in June 1916 to specify the 80hp Clerget; at that time the Clerget 7Z was also specified as the engine to be fitted to the 50 Pups that were to be numbered 9901-9950.

A change to the 80hp Le Rhône might have been decided upon when the contract for 9901-9950 was eventually allocated (in July 1916) to Beardmore. This decision might have been forced by considerations of engine availability: initially only 26 80hp Clergets had been ordered from unidentified French manufacturers, and all had been delivered by March 1916. A contract for 100 of these seven-cylinder Clergets had been placed with Gwynnes Ltd, of Hammersmith, whose deliveries started in January 1916 but ceased in May 1917, when only 47 engines had been delivered. The balance of 53 were cancelled, possibly to allow the firm to concentrate on production of the Clerget 9Z and 9B, of which they eventually delivered 1,750. Production of the 80hp Clerget was taken up by Gordon Watney & Co Ltd, of Weybridge, whose deliveries started in August 1917.

An 80hp Le Rhône engine in a Pup, with the cowling off.

When Pup production was starting in 1916, however, it might well have been considered that too few 80hp Clergets would be available to meet the need. In the event, 9496-9497 were fitted with the 80hp Clerget, as were 9901-9909 and 9911 of the Beardmore batch, but all the other 40 aircraft, 9910 and 9912-9950, initially had the 80hp Le Rhône. Similarly, although it had been intended to fit the Clerget engine to 9898-9900, by November 1916 a decision to change to the Le Rhône had evidently been taken, and these three Pups were delivered with that engine.

As late as March 1918 the official monthly list, imposingly titled *His Majesty's Naval Aircraft, built, building and under repair*, was still proclaiming that the 30 Pups of the second Beardmore batch, N6430-N6459, had the 80hp Clerget, whereas it appears that they were in fact fitted with the 80hp Le Rhône.*

The fact that so many RNAS operational Pups had the Le Rhône engine suggests a change of opinion in the Air Department of the Admiralty. In 1915, when the first Bristol Scouts were being delivered to the RNAS and RFC, the Air Department had insisted on having only the 80hp Gnome for RNAS Scouts, for it was officially considered that that engine was more reliable than the Le Rhône and therefore better suited to the over-sea operations that the Navy's Bristol Scouts might be called upon to undertake. The RNAS Pups, especially in their Type 9901a shipboard form, were even more likely to have to operate over water, yet their Le Rhône engines were apparently perfectly acceptable by 1917.

As far as is known, all the Pups flown in France by RFC Squadrons Nos.46, 54 and 66 had the 80hp Le Rhône engine; so also had those that were used at the Scout School attached to No.2 Aircraft Depot at Candas.

That the 80hp Le Rhône was highly regarded by RFC pilots was made clear by Oliver Stewart. In his book *The Clouds Remember* he wrote:

'In the make-up of the Pup was the almost perfect engine - certainly the finest rotary engine ever made - the 80hp Le Rhône. This was a sweet-running entirely amiable engine capable of an excellent horse-power rendering and able to withstand harsh treatment when the occasion arose.

'The present writer, when flying an 80hp Le Rhône Sopwith Pup, was attacked by five German aeroplanes when he had been isolated from his patrol a long way over the lines. He was forced to abandon heroics and to run for the lines, turning every time he was attacked to bring answering fire to bear. On that occasion

__Note:__ At the end of March 1918, N6436 was being re-assembled at Cranwell for training purposes, with an 80hp Gnome, and N6439 and N6453 were engineless at that date. The others then still in service or known to have had the 80hp Le Rhône were N6431-N6435, N6438, N6440-N6444, N6446, N6447, N6449, N6451, N6452 and N6457.

The 80hp Le Rhône engine, cowled and with propeller on, in a Beardmore-built Pup at RNAS Walmer.   *(Chaz Bowyer)*

the 80hp Le Rhône was frequently forced up by means of what are now given the grandiose title of "power dives", but which were then called "shoving the nose down", to fantastic revolutions per minute. But the engine did not falter or give up, and when the aeroplane reached home it was running just as well as when it set out. If I can return in some measure now the service given me by that 80hp Le Rhône, it would be base ingratitude not to take the chance.'

Meeting the growing production need for more 80hp Le Rhône engines must have been perceived as a problem early in 1916: indeed, it might have been awareness of the general scarceness of the engine that led to the early installations of the 80hp Clerget mentioned above. In 1915 the British flying services acquired only 100 Le Rhône 9C engines, all from French makers; in 1916 253 were received, 142 from French sources and 111 from W.H.Allen, Son & Co Ltd, of Bedford, who had made their first delivery in May 1916.

At least some other Le Rhônes must have been delivered installed in French-built aircraft; but rotary engines had to be changed relatively often, and the prospect of large-scale production of the Pup must have posed a threat to both maintenance and output. The RFC's allocation of French-built 80hp Le Rhônes for the second quarter of 1916 was a meagre 21 engines.

Deliveries made in 1917 dropped to a mere 158 engines, only 28 of which were produced by W.H.Allen, who were obviously concentrating on the 110hp Le Rhône 9J, of which they delivered no fewer than 540 that year. On 22nd June 1917, Allen's were given an order for 400 Le Rhône 9C engines plus 100 sets of spares, and on 1st November 1917, a further 500 engines were ordered from the same manufacturer. In all, 1,200 engines of the 80hp type were ordered from Allen's, but their total deliveries up to December 1918 amounted to only 339.

An early order initiated on 18th May 1917, was placed with Gordon Watney & Co Ltd, of Weybridge, for 200 Le Rhônes. Curiously, although no Le Rhône was delivered from this contractor, Watney produced 300 examples of the 80hp Clerget, 60 in 1917 and 240 in 1918, out of 553 ordered. Of orders totalling 550 the Daimler Co Ltd, of Coventry, made 349 Le Rhônes in 1918; although 400 were ordered from Peter Hooker none was delivered; but F.W.Berwick & Co Ltd, of

Park Royal, starting in March 1918, delivered 400 of the 500 that had been ordered from them. The total wartime production of the 80hp Le Rhône by British manufacturers therefore amounted to only 1,088 engines. With 1,241 received from French makers, the grand total of 80hp Le Rhônes received by the British Services was 2,329.

Use of this excellent little engine was by no means confined to the Sopwith Pup, for it also powered the Bristol Scout, Morane-Saulnier Parasols of Types L, LA and P (M.S.24 version), Avro 504 variants, and other less numerous types.

Nevertheless, it is clear that the substantial increase in production of the 80hp Le Rhône in 1918 (total deliveries for the year were 1,818, whereas the total for the three preceding years was only 511) was largely intended to provide engines for Pups, for the aircraft was by then an important training type. This is confirmed by the paragraph relating to the 80hp Clerget in the first official *Statement of Engines*, dated 15th March 1918:

> '*80hp Clerget. Non-standard training engine*
> 'This engine is utilised only in the Sopwith Scout to cover the shortage of 80hp Le Rhônes, and, while provision of spares necessary to keep serviceable the number of engines produced is required, the use of this engine will die out when 80 Le Rhônes are available in sufficient quantities, which should be the case, on anticipated deliveries, by June, after which date the 80 Clerget will probably be allowed to die out.'

Of the Le Rhône 9C itself the *Statement of Engines* said:

> '*80hp Le Rhône. Standard training engine*
> 'This engine is being utilised in the Sopwith Scout, and will also be fitted to a proportion of Avros. Provision for spares and repair facilities must be provided to keep serviceable all engines produced.'

The second *Statement of Engines*, dated 5th June 1918, gave the 80hp Clerget a partial reprieve:

> 'This engine is utilised only in the Sopwith Scout, mainly in the Middle East Brigade, and provision of spares necessary to keep serviceable the number of engines produced is required.'

This was perhaps a somewhat belated catching-up with the note on the Pup itself that had appeared in the fourth *Statement of Aeroplanes*, dated 23rd February 1918:

'*Sopwith Scout. Obsolete Service Machine;
Standard Training Machine*

'Large numbers of these machines will continue to be delivered for Training purposes up to June 1918, and heavy provision for spares should therefore be made. Two Squadrons of these machines (fitted with 100hp Monosoupape) will also require to be maintained for Home Defence for several months and supplies of any special spares necessitated by the fitting of this engine must be available. Training machines in this country will be fitted with the 80hp Le Rhône or 80hp Gnome, those in the Middle East Brigade with 80hp Clerget. All special spares necessitated by the use of these various engines must be provided.'

This official concern for the two Home Defence squadrons, Nos.61 and 112, was well-intentioned, but the former unit had replaced its Pups with S.E.5s as in January 1918, and No.112 Squadron was about to receive the first of its Sopwith Camels that were to replace its Pups. Apparently No.112's re-equipment was substantially complete by mid-May 1918, yet the next *Statement of Aeroplanes*, dated 9th May 1918, still maintained (of the Pup) that:

'One squadron of these machines (fitted with 100 Monosoupape) will also require to be maintained for Home Defence for several months....'

From which it would appear that inter-departmental communications left something to be desired.

As earlier noted (see page 45) it had initially been intended to fit the 100hp Gnome Monosoupape engine to the two Sopwith-built pre-batch Pups 9496-9497, and it seems probable that at least some installation/design work to that end was undertaken in the spring of 1916. It is also probable that recourse to that engine was had a year later in an attempt to improve the performance of the Pup for regular operational use in France, for its combat shortcomings at lower altitudes placed it at a severe disadvantage when it was compelled to compete with German fighters that had twice the power of the Pup's Le Rhône 9C.

Numerically, the Monosoupape was no more plentiful than the 80hp Le Rhône: only 310 (of a total of 356 ordered) were received from French makers, mostly in 1915 and 1916; in England, Vickers made 19 in 1914-15; and the only substantial supplier was Peter Hooker Ltd, of Walthamstow. The first Hooker-built Monosoupape was delivered in February 1915, and supplementary contracts led to expanding output: 125 in 1915, 437 in 1916, 697 in 1917, and 910 in 1918. These totalled 2,169, just over half of the 4,115 that had been ordered from the company. Orders were placed with Brazil, Straker & Co Ltd (for 500), and with the Laycock company (for 1,000), but neither firm had delivered an engine before the war ended.

What was probably the first installation of a 100hp Monosoupape in a Pup was made in A653, and at the time can only have been a logical attempt to improve the Pup's performance. The aircraft went to Martlesham Heath on 15th April 1917 to undergo performance trials, wherein its speed was recorded as 101.5mph at 10,000ft and 94.5mph at 15,000ft; the times of climb to these heights were, respectively, 13mins and 26mins 54 secs; while the absolute ceiling was approximately 20,000ft; endurance was calculated to be about 1¾hrs at full speed at 10,000ft.

A copy of the performance report (No. M.95) was sent to RFC Headquarters on 3rd May 1917. There, Brig Gen Brooke-Popham wrote on it, evidently for Maj-Gen Trenchard's attention: 'The climb is no better than with the 80hp Le Rhône, and the speed at 10,000ft is less.'

To which Trenchard added witheringly 'It would be'; and that seemed to put paid to any idea of using the Monosoupape-engined Pup in France. Perhaps in thus dismissing the Pup, both Brooke-Popham and Trenchard retained unhappy memories of earlier operational experience of the 100hp Monosoupape, but in fact Brooke-Popham was somewhat less than fair in his comment. While he was right about the speed at 10,000ft (but only by 0.5mph), the Monosoupape Pup took 1min 25secs less than the 80hp version to reach that altitude, and 3mins 10sec less to climb to 15,000ft.

A653 was subsequently fitted with a revised engine cowling, a sketchy-looking affair that was extensively cut away under the engine. When again tested on 24th May 1917 the speed at 10,000ft was 104mph, and the climb to that height was reduced to 12mins 25secs. The Vickers gun was also markedly offset to port.

The dry weight of the Monosoupape engine was 303lb, that of the 80hp Le Rhône only 268lb. Nevertheless, the

Three views of A653 with its modified installation of a 100hp Gnome Monosoupape engine. The cowling was so much cut away that it was little more than an oil shield, and there was a Rotherham wind-driven petrol pump on the rear starboard centre-section strut. A653 had initially been allocated to No.43 Reserve Squadron on 22nd December 1916, but went instead to London Colney for No.54 Squadron. On 10th January 1917 its allocation was again revised to one of wastage replacement in France but, presumably after sustaining damage, it was with DAE2a Repair Section on 27th February, a circumstance that might have led to the experimental installation of the Monosoupape. A653's tests at Martlesham Heath in mid-April are mentioned in the text and in August 1917 it joined the newly-formed No.61 (Home Defence) Squadron at Rochford, where it crashed on 6th October 1917.

Two views of the installation of the 100hp Gnome Monosoupape in Pups under construction in the Whitehead factory. The characteristic cowling was cut away, had seven stiffening ribs riveted on externally and was liberally slotted.

Martlesham test report noted that A653 was slightly tail heavy. The Rigging Instructions for the Pup required the tailplane to be rigged with 2½ degrees of incidence when the Monosoupape was fitted; the corresponding value for the Le Rhône installation was 1½ degrees. Perhaps this increase in tailplane incidence was a consequence of the official trials of A653, and there can be little doubt that it was applied to all the Monosoupape-powered Pups that were used by some Home Defence squadrons later in 1917.

Photographic evidence suggests that some of the Monosoupape Pups were completed with that engine at the Whitehead works, but others were modified to have it after delivery. The installation had a characteristic cowling, cut away at the bottom and liberally slotted. An armament advantage on operational Monosoupape-powered Pups was the use of the Constantinesco gun-synchronising mechanism on the Vickers gun, an installation that must have given a much greater rate of fire than was possible with the purely mechanical Scarff-Dibovski interrupter gear.

Pup fuselages lined up at the Whitehead factory, minus their wings etc.

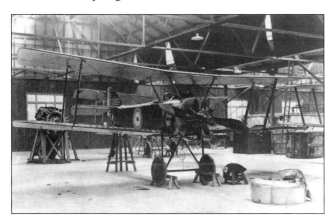

Three views of B5292 being assembled in the Whitehead factory, before and after applying the cowling to the Monosoupape engine.

Preparing to start the engine of a Monosoupape-powered Pup.

A number of Monosoupape Pups found their way to training units; several went to the School of Special Flying at Gosport, and at least one figured in an escapade of the sort that gave that historic unit the unique blend of skill and notoriety that was encouraged by its creator and Commanding Officer, Robert Smith-Barry.

In spite of Trenchard's indifference towards the Monosoupape Pup, it appears that consideration was given to sending this variant to France. On 8th August 1917, Section T.1.B sent to RFC Headquarters copies of drawings for the Constantinesco synchronising gear on the Pup with the 100hp Monosoupape engine. As far as is known, no such Pup ever went to the RFC in France.

According to an official RNAS Disposition of Aircraft list recording station and squadron states as at 30th March 1918, there was at Hendon Aircraft Acceptance Park a Naval Pup in course of erection with a 100hp Monosoupape engine. This was N6173, and its intended duty was enigmatically given as 'Service'. Also at Hendon AAP on that date were two other Pups with that engine, B6073 and B6074, designated for 'Special Service'. N6173 went to France, and was recorded as on the strength of the Expeditionary Force on 30th June 1918. It was flown to Lympne on 31st July and returned to Marquise next day, but crashed on arrival there and was written off.

In 1917 a further attempt to improve the Pup's performance was made by installing a 110hp Le Rhône 9J engine. This excellent power unit delivered 131hp at 1,300 rpm and weighed 336lb dry, thus 33lb heavier than the Monosoupape and 68lb heavier than the Le Rhône 9C. The earliest known Pup installation of the 110hp Le Rhône was made in A6220, possibly by the 6th Wing's Aeroplane Repair Section at Dover. This had been completed before 11th

September 1917, on which date a report on the aircraft was submitted by the Officer Commanding No.40 Training Squadron, Croydon:

'When I received the machine from ARS, 6th Wing, at Dover, I was informed that no alteration had been made to the normal rigging of the 80 Le Rhône Sopwith. It was fitted with a 110 Le Rhône De Havilland 5 propeller.*

'On testing it at Dover I found that the revolutions on the ground were 1,275 rpm and the rpm would have been 1,500 in the air flying level, so that the engine had to be throttled down. [Normal maximum rpm for the 110hp Le Rhône were 1,350] The machine flew perfectly true laterally and fore and aft, except for a slight tendency to be tail heavy.

'I brought the machine to Croydon Aerodrome and this morning had a propeller taken off a 130hp Clerget Sopwith Camel and fitted.** This propeller gave 1,175 rpm on the ground and 1,300 in the air flying level.

'I tested the machine again this morning at Croydon and obtained the following results:

A climb of 4,000ft in 3 mins 50 secs

A speed at 5,000ft of 110mph shown by the air speed indicator, with the engine giving 1,300 rpm.

'I found the machine to be very much inclined to put its nose down on right-hand turns, but this can be overcome by a liberal use of reverse rudder.

'The machine stalled at 45mph but stalled straight - as is the case with the 80 Le Rhône - in a gentle stall, but showed a slight tendency to put the right wing down in a steep stall.

---

* ***Note:*** *For the D.H.5 three different types of propeller were officially listed:*

Type A.B.644	-	*diameter 2,590mm, pitch 2,650mm*
Type 1708	-	*diameter 2,590mm, pitch 2,360mm*
Type L.P.710c	-	*diameter 2,740mm, pitch 2,120mm*

Not known what was fitted to A6220, could have been an L.P.710c.

** ***Note:*** *As with the D.H.5, there were for the Camel three types of propeller for the 130hp Clerget 9B, viz:*

Type A.D.644	-	*diameter 2,590mm, pitch 2,650mm*
Type L.P.2850	-	*diameter 2,590mm, pitch 2,270mm*
Type L.P.2850M	-	*diameter 2,590mm, pitch 2,270mm*

B5259 was one of the very few Pups to have the 110hp Le Rhône 9J engine. Here it is seen at London Colney, fitted with a small head fairing and armed with a Lewis gun on the centre section, perhaps on the type of mounting employed by Home Defence Pup squadrons. Originally allocated to the RFC in France, B5259 was re-allocated to Training Division, but in a further revision was again allocated to the RFC with the Expeditionary Force in France on 9th November 1917, but it soon returned from France Its engine cowling, necessarily of greater diameter than standard, must have been hand-made, for its segmented appearance indicates that it was built up without any attempt to work in double curvature.   *(RAF Museum)*

'The machine is difficult to land down as when it comes to the position of having its wheels about a foot off the ground and the tail low, and has lost flying speed, pulling back the stick does not bring the tail down as it should do, and the weight of the engine tries to pull the nose down, with the result that the machine drops straight on to its wheels, and rather hard. I am inclined to think that this will result in a good many buckled undercarriages, as the undercarriage of this machine is rather light.

'I should be very interested to have an explanation of the reason why the machine is not nose heavy with no alteration in the rigging, which I should have expected, owing to the extra weight of the engine, and also why the propeller gives so many more revolutions than it does with the 130 Clerget which gives, with the same propeller, just under 1,100 rpm on the ground and about 1,175 in the air flying level.'

It is doubtful whether the understandably mystified CO of No.40 Training Squadron was ever given an explanation of the longitudinal-trim phenomenon that he described, but it is clear that it was hoped to use the 110hp Pup operationally. That Trenchard had reservations about this combination is reflected in the note he sent to Maj-Gen Brancker on 25th September 1917, after he had studied the report on A6220:

'If this machine is to be adopted, I think it is essential that the wings should be made stronger. The machine would also be improved by:

(1)   Having a balanced rudder in place of the present rudder and fin, the new rudder to be about one-third larger than the present one.
(2)   Shortening the elevator by about 4 inches.'

Trenchard had heeded the views of RFC Pup pilots, who found that the standard Pup gathered speed rapidly in a dive, and had to be eased out it with care: the fear of wing failure was very real, though it often had to be put aside in the heat of combat.

On the previous day, 24th September 1917, the Air Board had sent to Headquarters copies of Alteration Sheet No.668 relating to Gun Actuating Gear, 80 and 110hp Le Rhône Sopwith Pup. On 26th September Brooke-Popham wrote to DAE asking for 'drawings and all necessary details regarding the fitting of 110hp Le Rhônes in the Sopwith Pups'. and enquiring whether the necessary parts and fittings were available. The Director of Equipment wrote to the GOC RFC on 3rd October advising that the drawings were

being sent that day by hand, and that Supplies had been asked to have twelve cowlings made at once.

At the 182nd Meeting of the Progress & Allocation Committee on 26th September 1917, Brancker stated that the Pup with 110hp Le Rhône

'... was flying very well and the performance was considered better than the Camel, but General Salmond had expressed the opinion that the wings should be made stronger, and this was a matter for the Technical Department to consider.'

On 5th October the Committee was informed that:

'The Technical Department had investigated the matter as far as it was possible without a sand test, and they did not consider it would be safe,'

It was stated that Pups were already flying with the 110hp Le Rhône, but it was decided to allot a Pup to the Technical Department for appropriate sand-loading tests.

Apart from A6220, it is known that B5259, B5908 and B5941 were fitted with the 110hp engine. The only example known to have gone to France was B5908, which was put through a performance test at No.1 Aircraft Depot, St.Omer, on 11th October 1917. Its propeller was a Type P.3012, the standard type for use with the 100hp Gnome Monosoupape engine in both the Pup and the Bristol Scout. Good climbing times were obtained, but only the uncorrected ASI readings of speed were recorded, making comparison with other, corrected, performance reports valueless. The test of B5908 was, moreover, curtailed and incomplete, because the pilot (Capt Waller) became unwell and had to return; nevertheless, he reported that:

'... the torque is slightly more noticeable in this than with the 80hp Le Rhône, but the machine seems to handle in exactly the same manner'.

This Pup, B5908, was probably the only example with the 110hp engine to go to a squadron. It went to No.66 Squadron, RFC, on 14th October 1917 but stayed only three days, returning to No.1 AD on 17th October. Apparently it was kept in France for some time, for the date of its return flight to England was 11th March 1918.

For the structural tests requested by the Technical Department., B5941was sent to Farnborough. The Royal Aircraft Factory produced three reports (BA 170, BA 184 and BA 202), of which no copies have yet been found, but their essential conclusion was communicated to the DAE by T.l.M on 2nd November 1917:

In its basic form the 80hp Clerget installation had a plain full-circular cowling, as seen on this Pup at an Egyptian training unit.

Although the 80hp Clerget was specifically regarded as an alternative engine for Pups in the Middle East, it was fitted to some aircraft of home-based training units. In some cases the engine had the cowling normally fitted to the Monosoupape version, as on this Pup of No.83 Squadron at Narborough

Sopwith Pup – Sand Test

'The test on the above machine has shown that the load factor is now 6.6 as compared with the previous proof load figure of 7.95.

'In the opinion of this Department, the above load factor is not sufficient to warrant the installation of the 110hp Le Rhône in this machine.'

Four days later, DDE sent a copy of this report to RFC Headquarters and intimated that the fitting of the 110hp Le Rhône in the Pup was to be abandoned.

As already mentioned, many Pups of training units had the 80hp Gnome or 80hp Clerget engine. The former was a thoroughly well-known power unit that needed no new evaluation. It seems that the first installation in a Pup was made at the Southern Aircraft Repair Depot, Farnborough, in May 1917, and that it was passed straight into training service without official performance tests. The 80hp Clerget was not, in practice, exclusively confined to the training squadrons of the Middle East Brigade. Both of these engines were also used in some of the Pups used for training purposes by the RNAS, and by early 1918 small numbers of that Service's training Pups had been fitted with the 60hp Le Rhône 7B. Most of these were at Cranwell, one at Redcar, by the end of March 1918; at least four (B5929, B5979, B5988 and B6076) had previously had the 80hp Gnome engine.

This somewhat desperate-seeming replacement might have been made for want of 80hp Gnomes, for that engine was probably becoming relatively scarce by 1918. Apart from 12 engines of the type made in 1914 by the Sopwith company, only the Daimler Co Ltd, of Coventry produced the 80hp Gnome in Britain. Daimler output started in December 1914, and the company's orders for the engine finally totalled 1,030. Production was never spectacular: the nine delivered in 1914 were followed by 204 in 1915, 405 in 1916 and 349 in 1917. With the total at 967 Daimler production ceased in December 1917, the last 63 being cancelled. Only 143 were received from French manufacturers in 1914-15.

The little 60hp Le Rhône was scarcer still: French makers supplied to Britain only 80 in 1915 and 34 in 1916, a total of 114. The engine was so light (176lb) that the Pups that were fitted with it must have been uncomfortably tail-heavy unless ballasted.

Above: This trainee pilot at Montrose is a Frenchman named Delapena, and he has obligingly stood to one side to reveal the Clerget installation in this Pup, which had a Monosoupape-type cowling.
Below: A Standard-built Pup with the 80hp Gnome engine.

Chapter 10

Pup Armament

The idea of mounting a fixed machine-gun on a tractor aeroplane, regulated by a synchronising mechanism to fire through the propeller's plane of rotation, was not new at the time of the Pup's appearance. The earliest known patent for such a mechanism was the German DRP Nr 276396 (*Abfeuerungsvorrichtung für Schusswaffen auf Flugzeugen*), for which the Swiss engineer Franz Schneider (at that time an employee of the German *Luft-Verkehrs-Gesellschaft*, better known as the LVG) applied on 15th July 1913. Various other similar devices were proposed or patented before the 1914-18 war started, notably a mechanism designed by Raymond Saulnier that underwent firing trials in Paris in the spring of 1914 but, frustrated by too many hang-fire rounds in the ammunition, was abandoned on the outbreak of war.

In what appeared to be an extraordinary aberration on the part of the German authorities, who probably placed no value on Schneider's invention at that time, details of his patent were published in the German periodical *Flugsport* on 30th September 1914, some eight weeks into the war. There can be little doubt that it would be seen by Anthony Fokker and would give him the inspiration to produce a similar mechanism. What eventually emerged in April 1915 as the first Fokker interrupter gear was the work of three German engineers employed by Fokker: Luebbe, Heber and Leimberger.

Although the way ahead had been indicated, briefly but clearly, by Roland Garros in his Morane-Saulnier Type L parasol monoplane with its deflector propeller, it was really the Fokker monoplane with its synchronised gun that brought a greatly sharpened intensity to air combat in the summer of 1915. Germany's opponents had to match this development, and to win time to create their own mechanisms were obliged to resort to inconvenient overwing or oblique gun-mountings, or to retain and even develop pusher aircraft with their inherent disadvantages of performance and configuration.

The Sopwith Pup came along just in time to be fitted with a mechanical synchronising gear that enabled it to have a single fixed Vickers gun firing through the plane of revolution of its propeller. The standard interrupter mechanism on the Pup with the 80hp Le Rhône engine was the Scarff-Dibovski gear, but it was soon learned from combat experience that this had shortcomings.

By its nature, use of the Scarff-Dibovski mechanism meant that the gun's rate of fire was determined by engine speed. The Pup gathered speed relatively quickly in a steep dive, and the lightness of its structure imposed a limit on the diving speed from which safe recovery could be quickly effected: this meant that pilots had to throttle back in a dive, thus slowing down their gun's rate of fire just when maximum weight of fire was needed.

Another drawback of the Vickers/Scarff installation was its dependence on a firing lever placed under the rear of the gun: as installed, this lever had to be depressed by hand to fire the gun. The physical management of aircraft, engine and gun in a diving attack must have adversely affected pilots' concentration precisely when it had to be at its most acute. At least in No.66 Squadron RFC an attempt was made to put the firing control within easier reach by fitting to the gun's firing lever a lanyard or wire with a ring attached. In his book *Sopwith Scout 7509*, P.G.Taylor wrote that he 'let go of the firing cord'; and 'I pulled the gun ring as the Hun came in'.

The early production Pups armed with the Vickers gun had perforce to rely on the webbing ammunition belt of the time.

This photograph of the cockpit area of A6174 of No.54 Squadron, RFC (see also photograph on page 69),gives a general impression of the installation of the Vickers gun. The cover of the ammunition belt feed channel is open. This Pup still had the original Sopwith windscreen when captured: it must have created difficulties for the pilot in using the Aldis optical sight mounted to port of the gun.

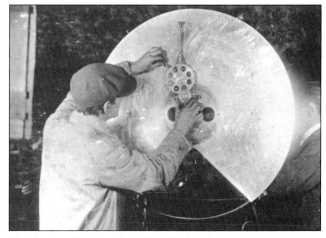

The drive mechanism of the Scarff-Dibovski synchronising gear on a Pup.

In No.3 (Naval) Squadron protective padding on the rear end of the Vickers gun replaced the Sopwith windscreen; the Aldis sight, although close to the gun, was not obscured. FSL J.A.Glen perches on the cockpit decking of N6183, named "MILDRED H". (Chaz Bowyer)

This belt was stowed in a box to starboard of the gun and wound off on to a large drum; the drum was rotated as necessary by the tension of a wire cable attached to an elastic cord that was taken along the port upper longeron all the way aft to pass over a pulley attached to the sternpost then forward again along the upper starboard longeron to an eyebolt by the top spacer behind the cockpit. There was a suitably disposed chute to catch empty cartridge cases which it discharged to port. The entire installation would have won the approval of the late Mr W.Heath Robinson.

Early in 1917, the belt-feed for the Vickers gun was markedly improved by the introduction of disintegrating-link belts. This made it possible for rounds of ammunition to be formed into belts that progressively broke up as the gun was fired, thus doing away with the cumbersome webbing belt and all of its problems. Although it now seems astonishing, the use of disintegrating-link belts in Pups apparently did not immediately lead to redesign of the belt box, and certainly did not bring about the removal of the redundant winding-off drum.

With the disintegrating belt the Pup could accommodate only 350 rounds in its belt box, whereas previously 500 rounds had been carried. On 27th February 1917 Major K.K.Horn, OC No.54 Squadron, RFC, sent to the OC 14th Wing a report on several matters concerning his squadron's aircraft. His first point therein concerned the amount of ammunition to be carried:

FSL Lloyd Breadner, also of No.3 (Naval) Squadron in N6181, "HMA HAPPY". On this aircraft the Aldis sight was supplemented by a gate-form sight on the gun, and windscreen panels were fitted either side. *(Chaz Bowyer)*

A somewhat similar view of the cockpit of A6194 of No.66 Squadron, RFC (see also photograph on page 68), which also still had its windscreen when captured. Here, however, the Aldis sight is better placed, and the part of the cockpit opening under the gun has been faired over to reduce draught. A ring and wire or lanyard attached to the firing lever can just be distinguished in the cockpit. (A.E.Ferko)

On FSL J.A.Shaw's "JULIA" (N6442) of RNAS Walmer a larger one-piece windscreen straddled the gun. which had the same gate-form foresight on the gun (see also photograph on page 174). (Chaz Bowyer)

'(1) The present type of ammunition box, now that disintegrating links are used instead of the web belt, only holds 350 rounds. Could the size of the box be increased, as I do not consider this number sufficient; 500 would be a suitable number.

(2) As disintegrating links are used, could machines be fitted with a chute on the left-hand side for empty links; this has at present to be fitted after machines arrive at Squadrons from Aircraft Depots?

(3) Machines at present turn up without sights. Could these be fitted before machines are delivered to squadrons? No.2 AD have now been lent a set of Aldis Sight fittings and also have a drawing of the Ring Sight.'

Fourth Brigade sent Major Horn's report to RFC Headquarters on 28th February 1917. Brooke-Popham replied on 3rd March saying that the question of an enlarged ammunition box of 500-round capacity was being taken up with the Aircraft Depots, and that these Depots were being instructed to fit a chute to carry away empty links. Unfortunately, he was unable to be so directly helpful in the vital matter of sights:

'At the present moment there are not sufficient Aldis Sights in this country to fit these before the machines are issued, and Ring Sights are being obtained from England also. The fittings for the sights are being obtained from England, and as soon as they are available will be fitted before issue. In the meantime they must be made by the Squadron.'

Clearly, self-reliance, self-help and an ability to make bricks without straw were essential qualities in the RFC early in 1917.

At that stage of the war, increasing production of airframes often led to bottlenecks and shortages of ancillary equipment, and No.54 Squadron was not alone in its difficulties. Perhaps less obvious is the nature of the growing burdens thrown on the Aircraft Depots and squadron workshops, whose personnel were obliged to make good production shortfalls and non-deliveries of such components as sight fittings, often with inadequate resources of material and equipment.

On 9th March, No.2 Aircraft Depot replied to Brooke-Popham's enquiry, opining that a 500-round ammunition box could be installed provided the unwanted belt drum was removed. The AD went on to say that a 'new type of articulated belt chute has been made and fitted to Sopwith Scout A6167',

At left is B2162, aircraft 'N' of No.66 Squadron, RFC, with the overwing Lewis gun installation developed by the squadron. This Pup went to No.66 Squadron from No.1 Aircraft Depot on 24 July 1917, and was still on strength at 30th September. At right is a D.H.5.

B1768 also had the supplementary Lewis gun, but that did not save it from being shot down on 30th September 1917; its pilot, Lt J.W.Boumphrey, was made PoW. Initially allocated to the Expeditionary Force on 20th June 1917, B1768 went to No.66 Squadron from No.1 AD on 22nd August. (A.E.Ferko)

a Whitehead-built Pup that had only recently arrived at No.2 AD and was later to go to No.54 Squadron.

Brooke-Popham promptly approved No.2 AD's design for the chute concerned; he also took the precaution of checking with Fifth Brigade whether the Naval Squadrons used the disintegrating belt and, if so, whether they retained the winding-off drum. Confirmation came on 14th March that the disintegrating belt was always used on both Pups and Triplanes; while on 19th March ADAE informed RFC Headquarters that arrangements were being made to have all Pups fitted with the belt chute at the earliest possible date.

Late in March, No.54 Squadron reported difficulties with the aluminium belt box: with use, the mouth of the container became deformed, causing cross feeds. The Squadron found that the fitting of an additional guide roller helped by keeping the belt clear of the aluminium mouth.

****

The Pup had to begin its fighting career on the Western Front against the opposition of Albatros and Halberstadt fighters that were not only faster but had two fixed and synchronised machine-guns; consequently it was always at a disadvantage, in terms of hitting power, once combat had been joined. Pups could best survive if the combat were at an altitude at which they could exploit their superior manoeuvrability, in the absence of more aleatory favourable factors.

Nothing could have been more natural or understandable than pilots' desire for improved, and preferably increased, armament. With such contemporary examples as the various Nieuport Scout types in widespread use, it is not surprising that attempts were made to mount a Lewis gun on the Pup's centre section, where it was not only an additional weapon but one that did not have its rate of fire retarded by an interrupter gear. This second-gun installation was persevered with by No.66 Squadron, and won the official approval of RFC Headquarters. On 8th September 1917, Brooke-Popham wrote to the 9th Wing:

'.....Lewis guns may be fitted to all Sopwith Scouts of No.66 Squadron. The work must be carried out by the squadron, and machines must not be out of action to effect the alteration if they are likely to be required for work.'

A drawing of the 'Lewis gun mounting for Sopwith Scout as designed and used by No.66 Squadron' was sent to RFC Headquarters by the 9th Wing on 22nd September.

Pups of No.66 Squadron known to have had the overwing Lewis gun were B1768, B2162, B2168, B2176, B2182, B2185

This RNAS Pup had a supplementary Lewis gun on the centre section; the weapon had only a 47-round magazine. The Sopwith windscreen had been replaced by padding on the gun in the same manner as on other RNAS Pups. The officer is FSL W.H.Chisham.

The Beardmore-built Type 9901a Pup of No.2 Wing RNAS that had a Vickers gun installed to make it a two-gun fighter. It was used by 'C' Squadron at Imbros.

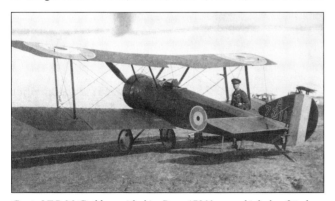

Capt J.T.B.McCudden with his Pup A7311 on which he fitted an overwing Lewis gun in May 1917 while he was serving at Joyce Green as a fighting instructor. He flew this Pup in defensive sorties against German bombers on 13th June and 7th July 1917. A7311 probably saw later service at one of the schools of air fighting and gunnery at Turnberry, for it was reported at East Fortune 21st-23rd October 1917, en route from London Colney to Ayr.

Another Beardmore-built Type 9901a with a Vickers-gun installation, but in this instance it was the only weapon. This photograph was taken at RNAS Walmer. (Chaz Bowyer)

and B2221, all of which were with the squadron at the end of September 1917 (though B1768 was brought down, damaged, on 30th September).

This supplementary armament was also adopted by at least some pilots of No.54 Squadron at about that time. Capt G.A.Hyde, MC, who was then commander of 'A' Flight, left this note in an article *(Ten months with Fifty-four)* published in the December 1937 issue of *Popular Flying:*

> 'One or two of us tried the expedient of fitting a Lewis gun on the top plane to supplement our armament, but we quickly abandoned the idea as we found that it weakened the centre section besides making the Pup heavy on the controls.'

One of No.54 Squadron's Pups that had an overwing Lewis gun was A6238, which was tested on 11th October 1917 by Capt R.M.Charley, who apparently experienced no handling problems. In his log-book he annotated the entry of this flight: 'Pulled machine about in air and seemed all right'. A6238 survived to be flown back to England on 10th January 1918.

It seems probable that No.66 Squadron might have had similar experiences with the overwing Lewis gun, but in

Vickers gun with Constantinesco C.C. hydraulic synchronising system, with Type B trigger motor, on a Whitehead-built Pup.

November 1917 the squadron was withdrawn from the front to be re-equipped with Camels. Thereafter it was transferred to the Italian front and remained there until the war ended.

Some RNAS Pups were also fitted with an overwing Lewis gun on the standard centre section, but probably suffered the same difficulties and disadvantages as those experienced by the RFC. Somewhat more practical was the weapon installation on a Sopwith 9901a of No.2 Wing, RNAS, in the Aegean (probably N6432 or N6433). In this case the Vickers was the added gun: the normal tripod-mounted, upward-firing Lewis gun was retained, while the Vickers was installed as on the standard Sopwith 9901 Pup.

A few months before these generally short-lived additions of overwing Lewis guns were made in the various operational squadrons, at least one individual installation had been made in May 1917. Its originator was Capt J.T.B.McCudden, MC, MM, who had received his Pup, A7311, on 1st May while he was serving as a fighting instructor in England. In his book *Five Years in the RFC* he recorded the matter:

> 'As soon as I arrived at Joyce Green I had a Lewis gun fitted on the top plane of my Pup and so that it fired just above the propeller. I fitted a Lewis gun on the top plane instead of a Vickers shooting through the propeller, because the Lewis could shoot forward and upwards as well, for I could pull the near end of it down and shoot vertically above me. This, of course, would enable me to engage a Hun who had the superior advantage of height. I made myself a rough sight of wire and rings and beads, and very soon the machine was ready to wage war with great skill.'

His object, notwithstanding his instructional posting, was to be able to attack any German aircraft that might attempt to bomb south-east England. He did not have long to wait, for on 13th June 1917, a large formation of 18 Gothas attacked London in daylight. Hastening from Croydon, whither he had gone to lecture, McCudden returned to Joyce Green, armed his Pup, and set off in pursuit of the enemy. He had only three 47-round magazines for his Lewis gun, and his belated take-off

A Beardmore built Type 9901a Pup, showing the aperture-type centre section and gun tripod that externally distinguished this Naval version of the Pup.

Type 9901a Pup of No.2 Wing RNAS Great Yarmouth, with Lewis gun on the tripod.   *(Peter Liddle)*

prevented him from reaching an advantageous firing position. Twenty miles out to sea and still 500ft below the Gothas, he fired all his 141 rounds, which provoked some retaliatory fire, but achieved nothing. He had a similar lack of success on 7th July, despite being in a much more favourable position, when the Gothas again attacked London in daylight.

Towards the end of its service on the Western Front the Pup was required to carry bombs. One of the earliest specific bombing attacks by Pups was apparently enough to persuade the official historian (H.A.Jones) to take a somewhat extreme view of the exercise. In *The War in the Air*, Vol. IV, page 198, he wrote:

'At the beginning of October [1917] night bombing became an added duty of the single-seater fighters. As an experiment Sopwith Pups of No.66 Squadron, carrying 25lb bombs, were sent at dusk to attack German aerodromes. The first attempt, on the 1st of October, was made abortive by a thick mist, but next evening three Pup pilots reached the aerodromes at Cruyshautem and Waereghem, north-east of Courtrai, and successfully bombed them from a low height: at the latter aerodrome a hangar was hit and set on fire.'

The official history makes no mention of the hazardous business that still awaited those Pup pilots - that of landing their lightly loaded and lightly built aircraft on their own darkling aerodrome at Estrée Blanche.

Pups were also required to carry bombs for tactical purposes, but this may have been more theoretical than real, if No.54 Squadron's attitude to this practice was typical. To quote G.A.Hyde again:

'Later on the powers that be decreed that Pups should be fitted with bomb racks! So we turned ourselves into a bombing squadron and carried twenty-pound eggs whenever we crossed the lines. The idea was to annoy brother Boche as much as possible. Since we had no sights by which to tell where we were aiming these missiles, and since we hardly ever crossed below 10,000ft we had no means of knowing whether the Boche was annoyed or not. We certainly were. We got rid of the bombs as quickly as possible, and devoutly hoped that they did not fall in our own trenches.'

As the Pup was then close to the end of its operational career in France the squadrons did not have to overload their aircraft with bombs for long, but the practice of requiring

fighter aircraft to carry bombs continued after the Pup had been succeeded by later types. With the increasing employment of fighters as ground-attack aircraft, the carrying of bombs became even more unpopular with their pilots.

The best installation of the single Vickers gun in Pups must have been that of the Home Defence Pups that had the 100hp Gnome Monosoupape engine (see Chapter 15). These were equipped with the Constantinesco hydraulic synchronising system, which was markedly superior to any of the contemporary mechanical gears.

It has been stated that at least some Pups used on Home Defence duties had an overwing Lewis gun to supplement the Vickers. Such installations seem not to have been recorded photographically, but it is likely that they would be short-lived. In its Home Defence role the Pup had to operate as a day interceptor fighter, with high rate of climb essential; but the additional weight and drag of the gun must have been enough of an impediment to prevent such Pups from intercepting (or, more probably, overtaking) the enemies that they were supposed to destroy with their increased armament.

From the outset, the RNAS wanted alternative forms of armament to be carried by its Pups. The Royal Navy was understandably concerned about the threat posed to its many ships by German airships; consequently its air service tried to provide appropriate armament on a proportion of its fighter aircraft.

On the Pup this included an installation of a Lewis gun mounted on a tripod and arranged to fire upwards through

This Pup of RNAS Great Yarmouth is believed to be 9905, which was built as a Type 9901 Pup and therefore did not have the aperture-type centre section. When photographed it had a Lewis gun mounted on the centre section, and in its cockpit was Lt G.W.R.Fane, who flew this Pup in the early hours of 17th June 1917, in vain pursuit of the night-raiding Zeppelin L.42. The engine efflux through the cowling vents is also visible in this photograph.   *(Chaz Bowyer)*

an aperture in the centre section, which had to be redesigned structurally to provide adequate internal cross-bracing. RNAS Pups built or equipped in this way came to be separately identified as Type 9901a; less visibly they had, or could be fitted with, emergency flotation gear in the form of internal air bags.

At the end of March 1918 there were on charge 32 Pups listed as Sopwith Type 9901a. Of these, 30 were Beardmore-built, ten from the initial batch 9901-9950 and 20 from N6430-N6459; the remaining two were B6011 and B6012, presumably RFC-pattern Pups that had either been fitted with the Type 9901a's form of centre section for RNAS purposes, or, more probably, had had the central cut-out made that was recommended as a cure for tail-heaviness and were mistakenly identified as Type 9901a by RNAS personnel. It is unlikely that they would have had the provision for emergency flotation gear found on true Type 9901a Pups.

It appears that, of the first Beardmore batch of Pups, 9909-9949 were basically Type 9901a, for official lists state that 9909-9950 were 'fitted with alternative Lewis gun and rockets' (but 9950 was extensively modified to become the prototype Beardmore W.B.III - see Chapter 20). Similarly annotated was the second batch of Beardmore-built Pups, N6430-N6459; and all of these 72 Beardmore-built aircraft were fitted with, or equipped to take, standard air-bags to serve as emergency flotation gear. There can be little doubt that this last-mentioned feature was peculiar to the Type 9901a, and that all the Pups of that type were built by Beardmore.

The rocket installation was initially intended for Le Prieur Aerial Torpedoes, possibly the best-known of the armament inventions of Lieut Y.P.G le Prieur, a French naval officer. These were, of course, intended for use against enemy airships and observation balloons. The launching tubes were mounted on the interplane struts of biplanes; the Pup could have up to eight such tubes. They, like the supplementary Lewis guns of Home Defence Pups, must have had an adverse effect on performance.

An RNAS overwing mounting for a Lewis gun. It was apparently a two-position mounting that enabled the gun to be lowered for upward firing or changing magazines.

Two views of the cockpit of an RNAS Pup that had an overwing-mounted Lewis gun. The tray fitted under the gun's magazine was probably intended to facilitate the changing of magazines in the full forced of the slipstream, always a tricky and hazardous operation. Six additional 47-round magazines are stowed within the cockpit. The object to the left of the windscreen is the rear sight for Le Prieur rockets, and the aircraft's control column has a plain broom-handle' top, surmounted by the ignition bllp-switch.

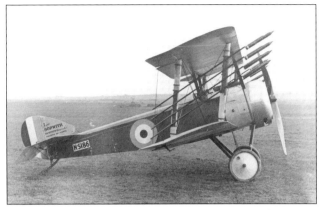

Taken at Eastchurch and dated 25th October 1916, these photographs of N5186 record what must have been a test installation of the rocket armament fitted to some Beardmore 9901a Pups. This Sopwith-built Pup was at Eastchurch by 17th October 1916, when it was flown by Harry Busteed, presumably before the rocket gear was fitted. By 2nd November it was in Reserve at the Dunkerque Depot, and a week later was on. the strength of the RNAS Detached Squadron that became Naval Eight, where it was in 'C' Flight. It was transferred to No.3 (Naval) Squadron in February 1917, being sent, after a crash, to the Depot for repair on 22nd February and a month later was with No.4 (Naval) Squadron. Reported 'wrecked' on 10th April, it was recommended for deletion on 27th April, and was finally struck off on 28th April 1917.

Photographed at East Fortune, to which station it had been delivered on 28th January 1917, No 9914 had the rocket installation fitted. It had been test-flown and officially accepted on 20th January, was sent to East Fortune for HMS Manxman, and was still on that station's strength on 2nd June, 1917. The protective aluminium sheeting on the lower wings in line with the rockets can be seen and the aircraft had an adjustable tailplane.

Three rocket-equipped Beardmore-built Pups at the firm's aerodrome at Inchinnan.

Two more rocket-equipped Beardmore-built Pups at East Fortune. The aircraft at left is 9919, which had been accepted on 5th February 1917 and was delivered to East Fortune on 8th February. On the nearer Pup the aperture in the centre section has been elongated. (K.M.Molson)

A detail view of a rocket-equipped Pup, in which can be seen the large circular foresight for use with rockets. This sight was evidently stayed to the forward centre-section bracing wire. which reflects great confidence in the smoothness of the 80hp Le Rhone's running. The retention of the Lewis gun's tripod must have been something of an obstruction to aiming the rockets.   (K.M.Molson)

RNAS Gunnery Memorandum No.92 of 16th December 1916 advised that:

'The Le Prieur Rockets are generally slow at getting off and do not appear to keep well and should therefore be used for practice.

'The Brock Immediate Rocket is half the size and weight, and leaves very quickly. These latter should be reserved for actual attack.

'Present rockets with 20° elevation carry about 500 yards. Future rockets now in the experimental stage will carry 1,000 yards.

'It is proposed to use only Brock rockets.'

Pup 9910 on Vindex's hoist at an unknown date and without rocket tubes. Test-flown and accepted on 26th December 1916, this Pup was still on the ship's strength a year later, but on and from 5th January 1918 was hangared at Martlesham Heath for Felixstowe.

Under tow to Vindex, Pup 9927 was conveyed in a whaler to which were outrigged a pair of Short floats. The aircraft has a single rocket tube on the interplane struts. Accepted on 27th February 1917, No.9927 was delivered to Felixstowe for Vindex on 17th March 1917.

The rear-sight for rockets was a simple affair somewhat resembling a watchmaker's glass. The bracket within the arc of the windscreen carried a clip to hold down an overwing Lewis gun in the lowered position.

Special sights were fitted on rocket-armed Pups; these are seen in the accompanying illustrations. The fore sight was essentially a fairly large ring, its size being 'such as to cover the diameter of a Zeppelin at a distance of 200 yards'. With these sights the rocket tubes were set at an upward angle to the line of sight: 15 degrees for Brock's Immediate Rockets, 17 degrees for Le Prieur rockets. To protect the lower wings against the rockets' efflux a sheet of 26-gauge aluminium sheet about 2ft wide was fitted on the upper surface of the wings in line with the rockets.

The first of the Beardmore-built 9901as, 9910 and 9911, were not officially accepted until 26th December 1916; 9909 and 9912 came later, on 9th January 1917. What may have been a trial installation of the rocket armament had been made two months earlier in N5186, a standard Sopwith-built Type 9901 Pup that retained its Vickers gun. This Pup was at Eastchurch on 17th October 1916, and it was flown that day by Sqn Cdr Harry Busteed; he logged this 16-minute flight at 3,000ft as 'local test', but made no mention of unusual armament. Probably the rocket installation was made after Busteed's flight, for the accompanying photographs of N5186 with its rocket armament were dated 25th October 1916.

Pups 9910 and 9911 were earmarked for delivery to HMS *Vindex*, but it is not known whether they had rocket gear installed at that or any later time. The performance penalty that the rockets and their tubes exacted is probably reflected in the case of 9926 and 9927, also of HMS *Vindex* (they had been delivered to Felixstowe for *Vindex* on 18th March 1917), which when photographed had only one rocket tube on each side.

As far as is known, no rocket-armed Pup ever fired its missiles in anger; certainly no enemy airship or balloon was destroyed by one.

Delivered on the same date, 9926 is here seen on Vindex's hoist. It, too, had only one rocket tube on the struts each side.

Chapter 11

Teething Troubles and Modifications

All new types of aircraft had their problems during operational service, especially in the early stages, and the Pup was no exception. Some of the suggested modifications listed in official reports and communications have already been mentioned in preceding pages, but other problems and deficiencies arose in service.

Prompt action had evidently been taken to fit stronger centre-section struts following the adverse observations in the RNAS report of 29th November 1916, for on 8th December the Air Department wrote to the Senior Officer, RNAS Dunkerque:

'With reference to your communication concerning the centre plane struts of the 80hp Sopwith machines. Arrangements have already been made to strengthen these up and to send spare struts out for all machines which have already been delivered. These are being hastened in order that early delivery may be given.'

Apparently it took a little longer for this modification to percolate through the ambages of the War Office. Not until 1st January 1917 did one of DAE's staff write to the GOC, RFC, to inform him that

'...It has been decided to increase the size of the centre-section strut on the 80hp Le Rhône Sopwith to the dimensions shown on the attached drawings.'

It took even longer for this modification to be applied to production aircraft built by the Standard company, for as late as 27th February 1917, Major K.K.Horn, OC No.54 Squadron, concluded his submission to the OC 14th Wing (see also page 70) with this paragraph:

'In England the War Office sent up a blueprint of a stronger centre section strut. We had machines fitted with these before coming overseas, but none of the new machines delivered have them. I consider these struts essential, as cases have occurred of the old type breaking.'

Major Horn's report was forwarded to RFC Headquarters by 4th Brigade on 28th February, and was answered by Brooke-Popham on 3rd March. Horn must have had mixed feelings about the response to his understandable concern about the centre-section struts, for it ran:

'The Depot have been instructed to indent for the larger size struts, and these will be fitted on all overhauled machines, but new machines coming out from England with the old struts will not be altered by the Depots before issue to squadrons.'

There seemed to be no established procedure for telling the RFC in France about structural modifications being incorporated in production aircraft. As already recorded on page 47, early production Pups had a variable-incidence

tailplane, but it became evident in January 1917 that this was being replaced by a fixed tailplane in later aircraft. On 12th January 1917, Mjr M. Spicer, OC 5th Army Aircraft Park at Puchevillers, had visited No.8 (Naval) Squadron at Vert Galant and reported to the OC No.2 Aircraft Depot, Candas:

'Rather more than half their machines at present are fitted with variable incidence on the tailplane and the necessary fin; the remainder of the machines have the fixed tailplane.

'As the Navy Supply Depot seem to be unable to supply the necessary spares for the fixed tailplane, I am altering two fins of the movable type to fit the fixed tailplanes; I am also altering one tailplane of the movable type to the fixed type.

'I am unable to alter more, at present, as I can only obtain one set of fittings from a tailplane damaged beyond repair.

'I should suggest that you carried a small supply of these fixed tailplane spares, as the Navy inform me that they are under the impression that the tailplanes with the variable incidence are being given up, and showed me two machines in which the gear operating the variable incidence had been cut out.'

Pups' tails, variable or otherwise, were by no means the only problem with which RFC Headquarters, stores and repair organisations had to grapple in early 1917, but the somewhat fortuitous discovery of a major modification in the RFC's newest fighter aircraft, with its implications for spares availability and maintenance levels, must have been exasperating. Immediately, on 13th January, the OC No.2 Aircraft Depot wrote to Headquarters, sending a copy of Major Spicer's report and observing (with commendable restraint) that it had not been realised that two types of tailplane existed.

This was equally unknown to anyone at Headquarters, whence, on 14th January, a terse memorandum was sent to DAE:

'With reference to tailplanes for 80hp Le Rhône Sopwith Scouts, will you please say which tailplane is to be standard, i.e. (1) the tailplane with variable incidence, or (2) the fixed tailplane.

'I have already asked that spares for the above should be sent out as soon as possible as at present none are available.'

Not until 30th January did A/ADAE reply, informing Headquarters that the fixed tailplane was standard, and that every endeavour was being made to expedite the delivery of spares.

Spares in general were obviously scarce at that time. A644, one of No.54 Squadron's original Pups, crashed on 6th February, and authority was given for it to be struck off as a source of spares; this was duly done at No.2 AD on 13th February.

The fixed tailplane installation that was standard on the large majority of Pups. This one, C1479, was built by Whitehead and was probably delivered late in January 1918.

The suspect undercarriage sockets caused damage that was not confined to themselves, for when they broke they were torn away from the engine-mounting backplate. This necessitated the replacement of the backplate, and by February 1917 this had led to a shortage of backplates. That same month also saw delays in deliveries of spare ailerons, fins and tailplanes, owing to a shortage of steel tubing.

Another modification about which the War Office had not told RFC Headquarters was the availability of a stronger undercarriage. Again Brooke-Popham assailed DAE in a communication dated 27th June 1917:

> 'It is understood that a stronger form of undercarriage is in use in England for Sopwith Scouts that are intended for training purposes.
>
> 'Will you please say whether four Sopwith Scouts with this special undercarriage can be sent out here or else whether four complete sets of undercarriages can be sent out to put on some of the Sopwith Scouts we now have.'

Eventually some of these stronger undercarriages reached France by early September 1917; on the 5th of that month Brooke-Popham instructed No.1 AD to send No.2 AD '... all of the new type strengthened undercarriages for Sopwith Scouts that they have recently received. These are to be used for the Sopwith Scouts in the School' (i.e., the Scout School attached to No.2 AD). Official papers do not specify the nature of the strengthening of the undercarriage, but it was probably provided by the use of heavier-gauge steel in the V-struts.

Standards of quality control and inspection in the production factories were alarmingly poor. This was particularly detrimental to an aircraft of such light construction as the Pup. As early as 4th March 1917, Brooke-Popham advised DAE that the average life of the mainplanes on Pups was about 40 flying hours, 'after which they become so soggy that they have to be replaced'. He warned that, although Aircraft Parks and Depots would do as much overhaul as possible, DAE '.... must be prepared for a large demand for these planes at the rate of some ten sets per squadron per month'.

Reaction came in the form of a missive from DGMA to Brooke-Popham: this, in effect, accepted the situation, promised that enough replacement mainplanes would be sent to France, and advised the maintenance of a surplus reserve stock, which would also be supplied on receipt of the appropriate official demand. There was no indication that anything would be done to ensure that the replacement wings would be any better or more durable than the defective components they were to replace.

Ever the conscientious pragmatist, Brooke-Popham made further enquiries, writing to the Fourth and Fifth Brigades on 11th March 1917, enquiring whether the problem of soggy wings was peculiar to the products of any one manufacturer. Unfortunately this proved unproductive: No.3 (Naval) Squadron (which had been attached to the RFC from 1st February 1917 had kept no relevant records; No.54 Squadron, RFC, confirmed that the planes of their Sopwith Pups had a very short life, but as the squadron had had nothing but Standard-built Pups no comparisons could be made. On 16th March Brooke-Popham told DAE that the structural problem seemed not to be peculiar to any one maker's products, and that the fault was probably attributable 'to the extremely light construction of the planes themselves'.

Matters were not helped by the discovery of faulty workmanship in some wing panels. On 30th April 1917, Second Brigade wrote to RFC Headquarters about two Sopwith Pup mainplanes that had been sent on the previous day from No.46 Squadron to the 2nd AAP for repair:

> 'On examination these planes are found to be of very inferior workmanship, and OC 2nd AAP is not proceeding with their repair until the receipt of further instructions.

'The defects are as follows:

(1) The main spars do not appear to be of the proper dimensions for the fittings, which are in consequence bent.

(2) Some of the bolts used are apparently too short for the thickness of the spars, and the wood has been roughly cut away to allow the nuts to go on.

(3) The cross bracing wires are all very slack as a result of bad rigging, and in some cases the wire has been drawn through the ferrule half an inch.

(4) In the case of the main spar, two holes have been drilled, apparently in the wrong place and plugged with wood.'

On 8th May 1917, Second Brigade again wrote to Headquarters, forwarding a report from Major P.Babington, OC No.6 Squadron, RFC, on the same general theme. His blunt comments on the structural work were:

'The quality of workmanship in the planes fitted to the single-seater Sopwith is extremely low. In two cases I have opened up planes which are very badly put together, and very little trouble seems to have been taken in their inspection as they are all stamped with the AID mark.

'As the ribs in these planes are few and far between it would seem to be essential that the workmanship should be of the best seeing that the machine is capable of a high rate of speed and is dived steeply frequently.'

It is not known whether RFC Headquarters took specific action at that time, but matters did not improve. On 22nd September 1917 the 4th AAP reported to Fourth Brigade that a number of Pup mainplanes recently received from No.1 Aircraft Depot had no aileron fittings or control pulleys; the lower-wing panels had no picketing rings, and no holes had been formed for those bracing wires that had to pass through the wings. The splicing of the aileron control cables was badly done, and the fabric was 'not stitched on to the ribs, but fastened to them with two or three copper tacks'.

Fourth Brigade passed this report to Headquarters, where Brooke-Popham took the matter up instantly with the War Office. On 24th September, No.1 AD reported that it had in stock several Pup wings with fabric that had been tacked, not stitched. Acceptance of wings from the contractor concerned was stopped, and the Aircraft Depots were instructed to stitch and tape all Pup wings that had these defects. It was established that the defective wings had been made by the Wessex Aircraft Company, an obscure sub-contractor to the Sopwith company; nevertheless it is possible that blame might have attached to an AID inspector with the firm for it was found that: 'The tacking of the fabric was sanctioned by local Examiners in Charge without reference to Headquarters'.

A file note dated 12th October 1917 stated that on all wings made by the Sopwith, Standard and Whitehead companies the fabric was sewn to the ribs.

Other faults arose, either from incorrect and possibly out-of-date drawings, or from misinterpretation of working drawings by contractors. On 7th March 1917, Brooke-Popham advised DAE that on Pups made by the Standard company the interplane struts were 1½in longer than those on Sopwith-built Pups; this, of course, meant that the Rafwires of the interplane bracing were also of different dimensions. Even though the Standard company was understood to have brought its strut dimensions into line with Sopwith's, the problem of spares remained as long as both types were in service. On 7th April

A particular detail visible in this excellent German photograph of a captured Pup is the securing safety hinge on the rear periphery of the engine cowling, roughly level with the top of the elliptical access panel.

1917, No.2 AD reported that the rear interplane struts on Whitehead and Beardmore Pups were ½in longer than their counterparts on Sopwith and Standard Pups.

Later in April Lt-Col Robert Loraine, MC, then commanding the 14th Wing, advised Fourth Brigade that the OC No.54 Squadron had reported,

'... that his spare front engine bearers (which he thinks are made by Standard works) are ⅜in too large for a Sopwith Scout built by the Whitehead company.

'It is probable that other spares for the machines are not interchangeable.

'No.54 Squadron have 12 Standard-built machines and 6 Whitehead-built machines, and their spares are believed to be Standard made.

'If they could have casualties replaced by Standard-built machines as far as possible it would minimise the loss of efficiency consequent on the spares not being interchangeable.'

Another deficiency on early Whitehead Pups was that they had only single control cables to the rudder. This arose because the Sopwith drawing supplied to Whitehead showed only the original single-cable arrangement. Brooke-Popham advised DAE on 16th April 1917, and instructed both ADs, Fourth Brigade and 9th Wing that squadrons were to fit double cables to all Whitehead Pups already issued, and the AIDs were to modify all other aircraft before issue. Some three weeks later (on 7th May) the vigilant Brooke-Popham informed DAE that nine Pups (A6164, A6168, A6189-A6192, A6194, A6195 and A6204) had recently been received with single rudder cables. The reply of 12th May advised him that Whitehead Pups from A6218 onwards would have the double cables. Evidently early Standard Pups also lacked the duplicated cables, for the same reply stated that the first Standard-built Pup with double cables would be A668.

By the end of May 1917, No.46 Squadron had on its strength Pups built by Sopwith, Standard and Whitehead. On 29th May, 2nd Brigade reported to Headquarters that the squadron found that the following parts were not interchangeable on its aircraft: engine cowlings, engine bearer plates, undercarriage struts and sockets, interplane struts, streamline wires and tailplanes (perhaps the matter of fixed and movable tailplanes had still not been resolved). Additionally, French and English magneto and pump gear wheels were not interchangeable, and the various types of pump needed different tachometer drives. Life must have been something of a nightmare for RFC equipment officers and Stores personnel.

Further potentially dangerous problems arose with engine cowlings. The Pup had the essentially sensible and practical fixing that was the subject of Sopwith patent No.127,847 and had been employed on the 1½ Strutter: the periphery of the circular engine-mounting frame had a groove into which fitted the correspondingly grooved trailing edge of the annular engine cowling. With the cowling in position, a cable was fitted round the groove and was tightened by a turnbuckle, thus compressing the cowling into the groove of the mounting frame and securing it. That, at least, was the theory, but just as 1½ Strutter pilots had had cowlings come adrift in flight, so did their Pup confrères find that cowlings could come off. No.70 Squadron designed safety clips for the engine cowlings of its 1½ Strutters, and by March 1917 similar clips were being fitted to Pups. Late in April, however, No.46 Squadron reported that two of its Pups had shed their cowlings in flight; one aircraft had been completely wrecked as a consequence, the other damaged. It was the squadron's view that the groove on the engine-mounting frame was not deep enough, and they had therefore fitted two bolts on each side through the cowling and backplate. Second Brigade sent the full text of the squadron's report to RFC Headquarters on 27th April, supporting the unit's suggestion that the additional bolts should be fitted at ADs before aircraft were issued.

The outcome of all this was that thereafter two safety hinges were fitted to Pup engine-mounting backplates at about the 2 o'clock and 10 o'clock positions, the forward leaf of each hinge being secured to the cowling by a butterfly nut.

Pilot comfort was not of a high order in any military aircraft of the 1914-18 war, and the modifications that were made on the Pup to improve the lot of its occupant were few and simple. No pilot of above-average stature could expect to be adequately accommodated in the Pup's tiny cockpit, and even pilots of average build found it difficult to install themselves when fully attired in leather coat and sheepskin boots. Enlarging the cockpit opening provided a modest easement, and apparently was being taken up officially, presumably with contractors, early in May 1917. For Pups already in France, RFC Headquarters wrote to both ADs on 5th May 1917:

'It is found that the pilot's cockpit is too small to allow comfort when seated in it. A portion cut out from one of these cockpits is forwarded to you under separate cover. Please remove the same amount as this from all Sopwith Scouts when overhauled by you.'

The same communication also required the ADs to extend, by 6 in, the plywood foot rests under the rudder bar to prevent the pilot's heels from becoming jammed under the rudder bar.

In March 1917, No.54 Squadron reported that the spruce bearers for the pilot's seat were weak: if they failed, the seat fell on to and jammed the elevator cables. The squadron recommended the use of ash bearers, and late in April Alteration Sheet No.27 called for the substitution of ash for spruce in the seat bearers.

No-one, it seems, liked the Sopwith windscreen. Although neatly mounted on the rear of the Vickers gun, its position and protective padding obscured critical parts of the pilot's field of view. It tended to become misted by oil ejected by the engine and, padded frame notwithstanding, could obviously cause facial injury and disfigurement in a crash.

Typical of the feelings and reactions of many Pup pilots were those expressed by the late Sir Gordon Taylor in his book *Sopwith Scout 7309*. In the spring of 1917 he was a pilot in No.46 Squadron, RFC; writing of the time following his early operational experience on the Pup, he recalled:

'It was then that I modified the windscreen on my aircraft. It was a clumsy affair, heavily padded around a small area of triplex glass behind the machine-gun. Though the padding offered some protection to the pilot's face in a crash, it allowed the airstream to howl into the cockpit, and it also partially obscured the view at the most critical time when closing with an enemy aircraft. So I took it off, faired in the top cowl behind the engine, and fitted a rounded screen which gave an unobstructed view and a draught-free cockpit.... I am convinced that the improved visibility of the new screen saved my life on many occasions in the coming months.'

Taylor's surgery on his Pup may have inspired (or might have merely followed) a squadron modification, for on 14th May 1917, the OC No.66 Squadron reported that his unit had successfully replaced the Sopwith windscreen with a standard Avro windscreen, which had 'proved to be far more efficient'. No.46 Squadron made rather more of a meal of the business, having devised a Triplex screen made in two parts, fitted close up to the sides of the gun; it was necessary to cut away some 4in of the top decking to fit the new screen. It was claimed that it gave satisfactory protection to the pilot, but reduced accessibility of the gun mechanism. A substantial pad was mounted on the rear of the Vickers gun.

In RNAS squadrons the Sopwith windscreen was usually discarded, the gun was well padded, and windscreens of local creation were fitted. When a divided screen was fitted it was usually well forward, leaving clear access to the gun's mechanism.

Although the Pup's flying qualities were excellent and won the affectionate and enthusiastic approbation of all who flew it, it was, at least in its early days, tail-heavy in flight. This fact makes it all the more remarkable that an early modification had been the removal of what should have been a corrective trimming device, the adjustable tailplane.

Despite the observation in the RNAS report of 29th November 1916 (see page 50) that 'No advantage appears to be derived from the adjustable tailplane', that Service had evidently told the Sopwith company about the Pup's tail-heaviness early in 1917. In a letter, dated 14th February 1917, to Capt C.L.Lambe, RN, Senior Officer RNAS Dover, Capt A.Vyvyan of the Admiralty Air Department gave a modest forecast of availability and estimated deliveries of Pups for use at Dunkerque, and added this note:

'A delay has occurred with these due to your reporting to Sopwith that they were tail heavy, and he has altered the stagger ¼-inch.'

It seems that this rigging modification, if it was in fact made, was not passed on to the RFC. Perhaps it was a first thought that might have led to the building of eight RNAS Pups (N6184, N6186-N6192) with stagger reduced from the normal 18in to 15in (and perhaps the ¼-inch alteration quoted by Captain Vyvyan was a misreading of '3-4 inches'). All were used, at one time or another from early March 1917, by operational squadrons in France; but this experiment was not repeated or developed: indeed, on 15th March 1917, ADAE assured RFC Headquarters that 'This experiment was not continued'. If any specific assessment of one of this octet was made, the report thereon has yet to be discovered.

Nevertheless, some alteration of the stagger was being seriously considered two months later. At the 62nd meeting of the Progress & Allocation Committee held on 5th May 1917, Capt Wheatley RN '... said he had got the drawings of the alterations to the stagger, and they have been sent to the firms making the machines, who had been asked to say when they could introduce the modifications. Whether such a modification was pursued further, at that time or later, is unknown, but it seems not to have been adopted for RFC Pups.

On 10th April 1917 RFC Headquarters had sent a telegram to DGMA:

'Reference tail heaviness of Sopwith Scouts this trouble has been accentuated owing to the fact that the longerons are now made of ash instead of spruce. Propose to get over this by increasing the incidence of tailplane lowering trailing edge by half inch or raising leading edge by half inch. Does Sopwith consider this will affect fore-and-aft stability of the machine in any way?'

The reply, also sent as a telegram, was less helpful than it might have been:

'Sopwith anticipates that proposed alteration of incidence of tailplane of Sopwith Scouts would affect stability but is uncertain as to amount of such effect. He considers the proposal worth trying.'

This, however, was soon followed on 16th April by a note from ADAE:

'I am directed to inform you that the alteration in incidence of the tailplane of the Sopwith Scout proposed by you has been carefully investigated. It is considered that the proposal is undesirable.

'The tailplane of the Sopwith Scout, 80 Le Rhône, has now about 1 degree more incidence than the main plane. It being of large area compared with the elevators there is a great danger of the machine being uncontrollable in a nose dive if this angle is further increased.

'A safer proposal as a temporary measure is to use a piece of elastic to take the weight off the pilot's arms. Another alternative is to cut a portion out of the top centre plane. A hole about 10-12 inches wide from the front edge of the rear spar over a distance of about 12-14 inches forward has been found to eliminate the tail heaviness. The actual effect of this hole upon the performance of the machine at a height is not definitely known.'

It has seemed worthwhile to quote these exchanges verbatim and at length, not least because they testify to the trusting innocence with which necessary modifications were empirically approached; they also reflect the dangerous limitations of aeronautical knowledge and understanding at the time.

Perhaps by mid-1917 RFC Headquarters had become accustomed (possibly even resigned) to official decisions and

A Pup that had a small cut-out made in its centre section, presumably to alleviate tail heaviness., was A7345, an aircraft of No.1 Training Squadron, Gosport, that had an 80hp Gnome engine (see also photograph on page 139). Here it is seen at Beaulieu, presumably as a visitor, on 11th June 1917. It was later with No.28 Squadron at Yatesbury, where it crashed on 19th August 1917, killing 2/Lt F.George.

developments that strained credulity, but Brooke-Popham could not - and did not - fail to react to the notification dated 27th June 1917 that he had received from T.1.B. On 4th July he wrote to DAE:

'Reference your 275/3005/5/T.1.B of the 27th ult. forwarding two copies of alteration No.330, relating to the increasing of the angle of incidence of the tail planes of Sopwith Scouts. In view of your letter No.275/3005/5/A.D.(M) dated 16th April 1917, which stated that it was considered undesirable to increase the incidence of the tailplane of these machines, will you please say whether experiments have been carried out in England since your letter of April quoted above, which have proved conclusively that this alteration is entirely satisfactory.'

Ten days later DAE confirmed, without explanation, that experiments had been carried out and had proved that the modification was 'perfectly satisfactory'.

Perhaps this change of official opinion had come about following the testing, in May 1917, of Pup A653 fitted with a 100hp Gnome Monosoupape engine. The official rigging notes on the Pup stated that the Monosoupape version had to have 2½ degrees of incidence on its tailplane, whereas the Pup with the 80hp Le Rhône had only 1½ degrees. No known reference describes any effect, beneficial or detrimental, of this increased tail incidence in Monosoupape-powered Pups.

However that may be, it appears that the rigging of tailplane incidence ceased to be an issue, but there is photographic evidence that at least some RFC Pups had the recommended aperture made in their centre sections. Those RNAS Type 9901a Pups built with the centre section that allowed the use of an upward-firing Lewis gun already had such an aperture, of course, a fact that might have provided the initial inspiration to try a similarly placed cut-out as a palliative on other Pups.

Perhaps, too, the decision to increase the tailplane

incidence on the standard 80hp Pup was taken in preference to altering the angle of the thrust line. On 27th April 1917, eleven days after ADAE had ruled against increasing the incidence, the ever-vigilant Brooke-Popham had written to the Controller of the Technical Department:

'I understand from Major Mead that the Sopwith Company are now altering the angle at which the engine is put into the 80hp Scout so as to reduce the tail-heaviness of the machine. '

'I further understand that all that is necessary to make the alteration are new diagonal struts for holding the centralising collar.

'May a dozen pairs of these struts be sent out at once, please, followed by further supplies as soon as they are available.

'I think Colonel Beatty knows all about it.'

It is not known whether that request ever received any written reply. Unfortunately none seems to have survived.

It appears that the RNAS, after its initial approach to the Sopwith company early in 1917, was less concerned than the RFC about the Pup's tail-heaviness. The matter had been discussed by the Progress & Allocation Committee at several of its meetings early in May 1917. The minutes of this body's meeting of 3rd May recorded that:

'The tail-heaviness of this machine was again discussed and it was reported from Dunkirk that the machine was only tail heavy when full of ammunition, and therefore no action had been taken to overcome this. It was decided to take no action pending further reports.'

Finally, early in August 1917, a simplified method of increasing the tailplane incidence was adopted; this used a form of shackle plate, and was fitted to all new Pups sent from Britain to the RFC in France.

Monosoupape-powered Pups were supposed to have greater incidence on their tailplanes, so it is surprising to see this one with a centre-section aperture This aircraft is B1755 of the Armament Experimental Station, Orfordness, later mentioned on page 148.   (R.G.Moulton)

Chapter 12

In Squadron Service

The equipping of RNAS units and of No.4 Squadron, RFC, has been touched upon in Chapter 7 and some early combat successes have been mentioned. In No.1 Wing, RNAS, 'C' Squadron had received its first Pup by 20th July 1916, but had only a fleeting acquaintance with it, for the aircraft was 9496, destined to join No.3 Wing at Luxeuil (see page 45). The prototype, 3691, was briefly on 'C' Squadron's strength in late August, but the unit's first true allocations appear to have been N5180 and N5182, which were on strength by 7th September 1916. These were followed the next week by N5183 and N5184, but many changes took place at that period between the various RNAS units at Dunkerque, and allocations seemed to be readily variable.

By 9th November, 'C' Squadron had been redesignated No.3 (Naval) Squadron and had lost all its Pups to the new Detached Squadron that became No.8 (Naval), but three weeks later No.3 Naval had begun to rebuild its Pup strength with 9898, N5185 and N5199, and it appears that N5187, N5188, N5195 and N5198 were also added at about that time.

On 1st February 1917, Naval Eight, about to be re-equipped with Sopwith Triplanes, handed over 21 Pups to No.3 (Naval)*, which then replaced No.8 as the Naval fighter squadron with the 22nd Wing, RFC, initially operating from Bertangles. Commanded by a Canadian, Sqn Cdr R.H.Mulock, Naval Three initially had no fewer than six Canadian pilots. It proved to be an outstandingly efficient squadron and a potent fighting unit: during the 4½ months of its attachment to the RFC its balance sheet of victories and losses was impressively favourable. The official historian wrote glowingly of the squadron:

'No.3 (Naval) Squadron south of the main battle area whose "Pups" were involved in some of the fiercest of the fighting before the battle of Arras, suffered no casualty in action. On the other hand, the losses they inflicted were such as to cause the enemy pilots to avoid them in the air whenever they could. On the 6th of April five Sopwith "Pups", led by Flight Commander T C Vernon, while escorting a bombing formation of B.E.s, attacked four Halberstadts which were manoeuvring to dive on the bombers. All four Halberstadts were shot down, two of them in Bourlon Wood, and the bombing raid was completed without further interference.' *(The War in the Air, Vol. III, P.338)*

* **Note:** *According to one official record. No.3 (Naval) Squadron had no Pups on its strength on 1st February 1917, but did have 21 on 15th February. These were: in 'A' Flight, 9898, 9900, N5185, N5188, N6160, N6178 and N6179; in 'B' Flight, 9899, N5194, N5199, N6165, N6169 and N6175, plus N5183 under repair; and in 'C' Flight, N5181, N5196, N5197, N6172, N6174 and N6186, plus N5186 under repair.*

The victorious pilots and their Pups were FSL J.S.T.Fall (A6158), FSL F.C.Armstrong (N6178), FSL A.W.Carter (N6160) and Flt Lt L.S.Breadner (N5199).

An outstanding example of the quality of Naval Three's Canadian pilots and of the Pup's capabilities in combat when flown with skill and determination was provided on 11th April 1917 by FSL Fall, who was again flying A6158 as part of an escort to five B.E.2cs and 2ds intent on bombing Cambrai. The narrative of his combat report was deservedly reproduced in *The War in the Air*, Vol. I, pp.347-348:

Several of the earliest RNAS Pups that had serial numbers in the prefixless ranges acquired spurious N prefixes as time went by. One such was 9900, seen here in some distress, which was with 'C' Squadron at Dunkerque on 28th December 1916. It was formally allocated to No.3 (Naval) Squadron on 29th January 1917, but was struck off that unit's strength on 15th February after a crash (perhaps the incident recorded here). After repair it was at Walmer on 1st June, but moved to Dover three days later. It was deleted on 19th October due to wear and tear.

N6178 went to No.3 (Naval) Squadron on 15th February 1917. It was frequently flown by FSL F.C.Armstrong, who on 6th April 1917 drove down a Halberstadt over Bourlon Wood for his first combat victory, and shared in the similar defeat of an Albatros D.II on 12th April. On 2nd May he again had a part share, with FSLs A.T.Whealy and E.Pierce, in the destruction of an Albatros two-seater; four days later, Armstrong and FSL H.S.Kerby defeated an Albatros D.III. By July 1917, N6178 was with No.11 (Naval) Squadron; on 16th August it was at the Dunkerque Depot, and it went to Dover on 11th October.

Flt Cdr T.C.Vernon, No.3 (Naval) Squadron, in N6179. His victory on 4th March 1917 was over an Albatros D.II, which he drove down out of control near Archiet-le-Grand.   (Chaz Bowyer)

In No.3 (Naval) Squadron, N6205 bore the name "BETTY" and a diagonal white band. This Pup was in 'C' Flight of the squadron by 19th April 1917, and three victories had been claimed by Flt Sub-Lt J.S.T.Fall by the time he damaged it at Marieux on 11th May 1917. After repair by the Aircraft Depot at Dunkirk it was flown back to England, where at the end of the year it was fitted at Grain with deck landing gear.   (via Philip Jarrett)

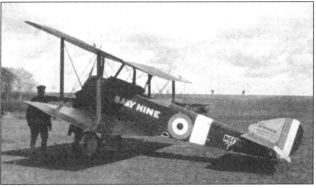

Here also photographed at Marieux in March 1917, N6179 went to No.3 (Naval) Squadron on 15th February; with the pet name "BABY MINE" it was in 'B' Flight by 8th March, and by 12th April had been transferred to 'C' Flight. It was involved in successful combats on 4th March (Flt Cdr T.C.Vernon), two on 23rd April (FSL A.W.Carter), and another on 29th April (Carter again); it was also flown by FSL J.J.Malone. It was reported at Dover on 9th May, and was with the Seaplane Defence Flight at Dunkerque by 3rd July. N6179 returned to Dover on 12th October; in November it was with the Instructional Flight at Manston, and at the end of March 1918 was still on the strength of the RNAS War School there.   (Frank Cheesman)

Distinctively marked with white bars on the centre section, fuselage decking and sides, and white elevators, N6181 was in 'B' Flight of No.3 (Naval) Squadron by 15th March 1917. Named "HMA HAPPY", it was regularly flown by Flt Cdr L.S.Breadner, seen in the cockpit (and on pages 69 and 85). In this Pup he destroyed an Albatros two-seater and an Albatros D.II on 11th April 1917; on 23rd April was credited with both the defeat of a Gotha G.IV (which was captured) and with driving down an Albatros D.III; another Albatros D.III was sent down out of control on 29th April. N6181 was recorded at Dover on 8th May 1917, but was reported to be completely wrecked on 6th July. It was deleted on 15th September 1917.   (K.M.Molson)

Combat success apparently eluded N6183 until 23rd May 1917, when FSL J.A.Glen sent an Albatros D.III down out of control; four days later he destroyed another Albatros D.III; and on 7th July, yet again in N6183, he destroyed an unidentified seaplane off Ostend. This Pup had been at the Depot in Dunkerque on 16th April 1917, before going to No.3 (Naval) Squadron, in which unit, named "MILDRED H", it stayed at least until 12th July. By 14th August it was with No.11 (Naval) Squadron, but, wrecked on that date, was returned to the Depot. Its deletion was recommended on 20th August and was implemented five days later.

'When B.E.s were attacked at Cambrai I attacked H.A. head on at about 8,000 feet. I saw many tracers go into his engine as we closed on one another, I half looped to one side of him, and then the H.A. dived with a large trail of blue smoke. I dived after him down to about 4,000 feet and fired about fifty rounds when he went down absolutely out of control. I watched him spinning down to about 1,000 feet, the trail of smoke increasing. I was immediately attacked by three more Albatros which drove me down to about 200 feet. We were firing at one another whenever possible, when at last I got into a good position and I attacked one from above and from the right. I closed on him, turning in behind him and got so close to him that the pilot's head filled the small ring in the Aldis sight. I saw three tracers actually go into the pilot's head; the H.A. then simply heeled over and went into the ground. The other two machines cleared off. I saw two other H.A. spinning down out of control and while fighting saw two B.E.'s being attacked by H.A. Having lost sight of all the other machines and being so low, I decided to fly home at about that height (200 feet). A company of German cavalry going east along a small road halted and fired on me; also several machine guns opened fire. After flying west for about five minutes I was again attacked by a Halberstadt single-seater and as he closed on me I rocked my machine until he was within fifty yards. I side-looped over him and fired a short burst at him. He seemed to clear off, and then attacked me again; these operations were repeated several times with a slight variation in the way I looped over him, until within about five minutes of crossing the lines (flying against a strong wind), when he was about 150 yards behind me, I looped straight over him and coming out of the loop I dived at him and fired a good, long burst. I saw nearly all the tracers go into the pilot's back, just on the edge of the cockpit. He immediately dived straight into the ground. I then went over German trenches filled with soldiers, and I was fired on by machine-guns, rifles, and small field guns, in or out of range. There was a lot of small artillery firing and many shells bursting in and about the German trenches, somewhere in the vicinity of the Cambrai-Arras road. I saw many small companies of infantry and cavalry of about ten to fifty in each going east along small roads. I noticed no convoys or movement of artillery. I landed at the first aerodrome I saw, No.35 Squadron, RFC [Savy]. My machine was badly shot about.'

Despite this inclusion of Fall's account of his action in the official history it has remained virtually unknown; overshadowed. perhaps. by later combats fought in aircraft that were more powerful and better armed. Yet, viewed against its time and circumstances, it was a Homeric achievement and one of the outstanding single-handed air fights of the war. Not only was Fall's Pup lightly armed with a single slow-firing gun, but it was well below the altitudes where its height-holding abilities would have given it a measure of advantage; above all, it was opposed by Albatros and Halberstadt scouts with twice the armament and twice the horse power of the Pup. Although enemy superiority in performance and numbers enabled the three Albatroses to drive Fall down from 4,000ft to 200ft, the Pup's manoeuvrability gave him the killing advantage at a critical moment.. And after all that hard fighting Fall was still able to make and record observations of enemy troop movements and traffic. Few DSCs were better merited than his*, awarded for this gallant action.

Naval Three returned to No.4 Wing, RNAS, in the Dunkerque Command on 15th June 1917, its return being marked by a letter of warm commendation written by Maj-Gen Trenchard to the Senior Officer, RNAS Dunkerque. This stated that:

'Eighty enemy aircraft were accounted for, which, with only the loss of 12 machines, alone shows the efficiency of the squadron as a fighting unit.'

Despite the distinction of that letter's signatory the 'Eighty enemy aircraft accounted for' was a considerable overstatement; but unquestionably the pilots of Naval Three acquitted themselves brilliantly while attached to the RFC. They continued to do so, but by mid-July 1917 their Pups had been replaced by Camels; as at 19th July only two Pups remained on the squadron's strength.

No.9 (Naval) Squadron had, on its formation, begun to receive Pups early in February 1917. On the 8th of that month it had N6163 and N6164, but a month later still had only one Flight of Pups. By 29th March the squadron had 11 Pups and 3 Nieuports, the Pups being 9916, N6168, N6177, N6193 and N6196 in 'A' Flight; N6167, N6189 and N6199 in 'B' Flight;

---

* **Note:** *In 1944-45, Gp Capt J.S.T.Fall, DSC, AFC, RAF, commanded No.33 Service Flying Training School, RAF Carberry, Manitoba, Canada, where the author [JMB] (then regrettably ignorant of his CO's distinguished fighting career) was serving as an instructor. Group Capt Fall died on 1st December 1988.*

Flt Cdr J.S.T.Fall, DSC, protagonist in the combat of 11th April 1917, for which he was awarded his DSC. This photograph was taken while he was a member of No.3 (Naval) Squadron. Behind him is N6181, Breadner's "HMA HAPPY" (also see photograph on page 84). (via W.J.Cumming)

A6158, the Whitehead-built Pup that was Fall's mount on 11th April 1917. He had earlier destroyed a Halberstadt D.II over Bourlon Wood, flying this Pup, on 6th April. The aircraft had been with the AID at Farnborough when it was officially allocated to the Expeditionary Force on 19th February 1917, and it was in 'B' Flight of No.3 (Naval) Squadron by 11th March. It was lost on 14th May 1917, when FSL W.R.Walker was shot down by Oberleutnant H Lorenz of Jasta 33, Walker being made PoW.

No.4 (Naval) Squadron had Pups for little more than three months. Some, probably flight-commanders' aircraft, bore names, as seen in this photograph. N6185 was "ANZAC"; 9899 (marked N9899) was "DO-DO". N6185 was with the squadron by 22nd March 1917; it was lost near Zeebrugge on 10th May 1917 while being flown by Flt Lt C.J.Moir. On 26th April, flying N6185, he had driven down an Albatros D.V out of control near Dixmude.

and N6188, N6191 and N6192 plus the Nieuports in 'C' Flight. Changes occurred frequently, however: a week later 'B' Flight's aircraft were 9928, N6184, N6199 and N6201.

By 31st May 1917, shortly before No.9 (Naval) began its attachment to the RFC (officially from 15th June) in preparation for the Battle of Ypres, only 'C' Flight still had Pups (9916, N6188, N6191, N6192 and N6193); the other two Flights had Triplanes.

Among No.9 (Naval) Squadron's early duties had been the interception of German bombers intent on, or returning from, raiding targets in south-eastern England. On 25th May some of its Pups, and at least one Triplane. with other Pups from No.4 (Naval), attacked the Gotha formation that had bombed Folkestone. In the combat one Gotha was shot into the sea and

another sent down, apparently out of control; but so confused was the fighting that these successes could not be specifically credited to any pilot or either squadron. Nevertheless, in the records of No.4 (Naval) Squadron the destruction, on that date, of 'one large twin-engined biplane, unknown' near Westende was attributed to FSL A.J.Chadwick. No.9 (Naval) credited FSL O.C.Le Boutillier, flying Triplane N5459, with a Gotha sent down out of control off Ostende.

Naval Nine's Pups played little part in the squadron's attachment to the RFC, for that duty had scarcely begun when the Pups were replaced by Triplanes.

The use of the Pup in No.4 (Naval) Squadron was also short-lived. The unit had been officially formed at Coudekerque on 31st December 1916, re-activating the number of one of the earliest RNAS units that had changed its designation to No.4 Wing in August 1915. The new No.4 (Naval) Squadron initially had Sopwith 1½ Strutters, but progressively changed over to Pups with the duty of escorting RNAS bombers and providing a form of air cover for Naval units. Its first Pup might have been N5184, which was with the squadron by 8th March 1917. Not until 3rd May did Naval Four list three Flights: 'A' with N6185, N6177, N6198 and N6475; 'B' with 9899, N6187, N6200 and N6478; and 'C' with N5196, N6168, N6190, N6196 and N6462. Five weeks later the squadron had seven Pups and five Camels; on 14th June, 'A' Flight had four Pups and three Camels, 'B' Flight three and four, respectively, and 'C' Flight five and two, again respectively. By 19th July No.4 (Naval) had only two Pups left (probably N6176 and N6476), and was otherwise an all-Camel unit.

Between 25th April and the end of May 1917, No.4 (Naval) Squadron recorded 14 combat successes against enemy aeroplanes and one kite balloon. The first of all these, one unidentified aircraft claimed destroyed at Bruges,

No.9899 had seen quite a lot of use before it went to No.4 (Naval) Squadron. By 14th December 1916 it was with 'C' Squadron of No.1 Wing. It was struck off that unit's strength on 16th February 1917, following a crash, joining No.4 (Naval) Squadron on 21st February. On 26th April FSL A.J.Chadwick drove down an Albatros D.III out of control. Various other victories included one on 6th June by FSL G.W.Hemming who defeated and drove down two Albatros D.Vs near Dixmude. On 6th October 1917 it went to Dover. When photographed, its Vickers gun had been stripped of its outer casing, and the fin, tailplane and elevators were coloured., possibly blue.

had been attributed to the same FSL Chadwick who was the putative conqueror of the Gotha on 25th May.

Other RNAS fighter squadrons of the Dunkerque area that had Pups were Nos.11 and 12 (Naval) Squadrons. On 24th May 1917, No.11 had 9898, 9915, N6167 and N6184, but fluctuations in its strength suggest that it might have been robbed, as occasion demanded, to keep other units up to strength. By 14th June it had only N6167 and N6199, but by 12th July it had grown to a two-flight unit, 'A' Flight having 9899, N6168, N6188, N6192 and N6477; while 'B' Flight had N6184, N6187, N6190, N6199 and N6209. No.11's first Camel (B3785) had arrived by 2nd August, and by 6th September 1917 it had only one Pup, N6180, the rest of its strength being Camels.

It seems that No. 2 (Naval) Squadron never was an all-Pup unit. An early record of its aircraft dated 14th June 1917 lists three Pups (9898, N5188 and N5196) as the equipment of 'A' Flight; while 'B' Flight had two Triplanes, N500 and N504; and 'C' Flight apparently had only one aircraft, the Camel prototype N517. On 19th July, No.2 (Naval) had seven Pups and five Triplanes; by 13th September it had seven Pups and nine Triplanes (the Pups including B1816, B1817 and B1818); at 1st November the squadron still had ten Pups with its nine Triplanes; but by 6th December. 'A' and 'B' Flights had Triplanes, while 'C' Flight had a solitary Camel, N5651.

Although No.2 (Naval) Squadron had been the last RNAS unit of the Dunkerque component of the Dover-Dunkerque Command to relinquish its Pups, it was run close by the Seaplane Defence Flight. This was formed at Dunkerque in June 1917 to provide protection for the RNAS seaplanes operating over coastal waters in that area, and as at 19th July it had five Pups (9929, N6171, N6179, N6203 and N6478).

By 2nd August its strength had risen to ten Pups, but, like so many contemporary RNAS units at Dunkerque at that time, its numbers fluctuated: three weeks later it had only five Pups, and on 6th September its strength was five Pups and six Camels. On 18th October it had 14 Bentley Camels and only three Pups (B1819, B1820 and B1821).

By that date there were no Pups left in the RNAS Depot at Dunkerque. In the two preceding weeks a total of 26 (9899, 9900, 9916, 9929, N6160, N6162, N6166, N6168, N6171, N6174, N6178, N6179, N6188, N6190, N6192, N6196, N6206, N6209, N6435, N6436, N6459, N6465, N6467, N6469, N6478, N6479) had been transferred to Dover and N5191, N6161 and N6194 were listed 'for deletion'.

One of the RNAS's most successful fighter pilots, Robert A Little, was an Australian member of No.8 (Naval) Squadron. He had earlier driven down a Fokker monoplane while flying Bristol Scout No.3043 on 9th July 1916, and in Naval Eight he was initially allotted Pup N5182 on 14th November 1916; apparently the aircraft bore the name *Lady Maud*. On 23rd November he shot down a German two-seater in flames, and in N5182 he had further victories on 3rd December 1916 and 7th January 1917; but from 7th April, following Naval Eight's re-equipment, he flew Triplanes and soon became one of the greatest exponents of that type. While in England, officially being rested from operational flying, he nevertheless made two sorties against raiding Gothas on 12th and 22nd August 1917. On these occasions he was again in a Pup, 9947 of RNAS Walmer, but he did not manage to join combat. After returning to France he moved on to Camels, and his total of combat victories stood at 47 when he met his death in somewhat mysterious circumstances on 27th May 1918.

Another Pup of No.4 (Naval) Squadron was N6200. Bearing the name "BOBS", it was in 'B' Flight of the squadron by 12th April 1917, and was flown by FSL A.M.Shook, who is at left in this photograph. On 24th April Shook sent down a Fokker D.II out of control; on 9th May he shared in the defeat of a two-seater near Ghistelles; and on 12th May he destroyed an enemy seaplane off Zeebrugge. N6200 was at Dover on 22nd July, and was officially transferred there on 9th August. By 29th September 1917 it was at Manston, where it served as an aircraft of the RNAS War School; on 30th March 1918 it was still on Manston's strength, though engineless and unserviceable at that date.

Chapter 13

With the RNAS in the Aegean

A few Pups saw operational use in the Aegean area and Macedonia. The Beardmore-built Sopwith Type 9901 Pups 9941 and 9942 made their acceptance flights at Inchinnan on 4th and 10th April 1917 respectively. The former was delivered packed, presumably for shipment overseas; 9942 was officially delivered on 11th April, and was at Port Victoria eight days later. Both were sent to Mudros, and on 1st February 1918 were on the strength of 'G' Flight of No.2 Wing, RNAS. They had been followed by two further Beardmore-built Pups, both of Type 990la: N6432 had been test-flown and accepted on 2nd May 1917, N6433 five days later: both were delivered to Mudros. On 1st February 1918, N6432 was with 9941 and 9942 in 'G' Flight, where their duties doubtless included escorting the five Henry Farman F.27s of that Flight. Earlier they had escorted the D.H.4s of 'C' Squadron RNAS, on bombing missions. N6433 was said to be at 'Base' on 1st February 1918.

Also with No.2 Wing were two Sopwith-built Type 9901 Pups, N6470 and N6471; these were listed as 'Greek Training'

aircraft. Their duties must have included the training of Greek pilots for 'Z' (Greek) Squadron, RNAS. A gallant and experienced Greek naval pilot, Lt Cdr Aristides Moraitinis*, had already gained one victory on one of the Pups on 3rd August 1917, when he drove down a German seaplane near Kavella.

Another Pup combat action occurred on 30th September 1917, when Flt Lt P K Fowler, flying from Imbros, attacked a German two-seat seaplane that had been driven away from Imbros by a Camel and the RNAS's solitary Sopwith Triplane in the Aegean area.

After the Armistice the four Pups N6432, N6433, N6470 and N6471 were handed over to the Greek government together with many other RAF aircraft of various types.

---

* **_Note:_** *Lt Cdr Moraitinis had learned to fly at Eleusis under Sqn Cdr Collyns Pizey, RN, and had taken his Royal Aero Club Aviator's Certificate (No.1087) there on a Sopwith pusher seaplane on 22nd September 1914.*

N6433, one of No.2 (Naval) Wing's few Pups, in flight over inhospitable terrain in the Aegean area. See also page 56 for another photograph of this aircraft.

(W.Evans)

Chapter 14

With the RFC in France

The RFC never had more than three Pup squadrons on the Western Front. The beginnings of No.54 Squadron's participation have been described in pages 51-52 but it had to wait for nearly three months before it was joined in the Field by No.66 Squadron, the second RFC unit to have the Pup. No.66 had been formed on 30th June 1916 at Filton, and had operated as a training unit for some seven months. Its first Pups arrived early in February 1917, among them A663 and A665 on 5th February, and by 24th February the squadron had received eleven Pups. It was officially agreed that No.66 should go to France with only 12 aircraft, the balance to be supplied later, and the squadron arrived in France on 17th March to become a unit in the RFC's 9th Wing.

It arrived in time to participate in the Battle of Arras, the air offensive for which opened on 4th April 1917. The Pups provided escorts for bomber and reconnaissance aircraft, several of their missions leading to hard-fought combats with enemy fighters. For involvement in the Battle of Messines (7th-14th June 1917) No.66 Squadron moved north to Liettres (Estrée Blanche).

While the squadron was there, Captain J.T.B.McCudden was attached to it for three weeks in July 1917 for a refresher course to keep him up to date with operational developments: at the time he was serving as a fighting instructor at Joyce Green. His gallant attempts to attack raiding Gothas in his Pup on 13th June and 7th July have been recounted on pages 72-73 and at the time of his attachment to No.66 Squadron he needed no instruction or familiarisation on the unit's Pups. He made his first flight with No.66 on 13th July 1917, flying B1775, and during his brief attachment flew at least eleven other Pups (A6190, A6210, A6216, B1710, B1746, B1756, B1760, B1762, B1767, B1782 and B1797).

Although McCudden had several combats with No.66 Squadron he had no substantial success. Of one thing he was in no doubt and that was the exemplary manoeuvrability of the Pup, This comes out clearly from the relevant pages of his book *Five Years in the RFC* :

'Of course down at 10,000 and 12,000ft the [Albatros] V-strutter absolutely waltzed round us for speed and climb, but at 16,000ft the average Albatros Scout began to find its ceiling just where the Pup was still speedy and controllable.' ....

'The old Hun came lumbering round, and although he started above, he was now below, after having done one half-turn to my full turn. I now dived on the Hun, who was painted, a dirty dull green, and opened fire from 100ft above. I got my sights on him beautifully when the damned gun stopped, and I had to pull out, but I saw that I had hit the Hun badly and Major Henderson now had a shot at him.'......................

'I was most pleased, however, to prove to myself that when it came to manoeuvring the Sopwith Scout would turn twice to an Albatros's once. In fact, very

A674, built by Standard, was allocated to the Expeditionary Force on 10th January, 1917, but this was cancelled-two days later. Here it is seen at Filton, where No.66 Squadron, RFC, then mobilising, received its first Pups in February 1917; the squadron used A674 for training purposes for some time.

(The late C.H.Barnes)

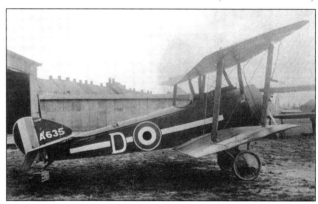

A635 was first allocated to No.54 Squadron on 15th November 1916; it arrived at No.1 Aircraft Depot, St.Omer, on 12th December and was issued to No.54 Squadron on 12th January 1917. It was back at No.1 AD on 12th May 1917, and subsequently went to No.66 Squadron. in whose markings it is seen here in a German photograph taken after its capture on 12th October 1917. On that date 2/Lt M Newcomb was shot down.

(Egon Krueger)

An earlier captive Pup of No.66 Squadron was the Whitehead-built A6194. It had been allocated to the Expeditionary Force on 18th April 1917, and went to the squadron from No.2 AD, Candas, on 20th May. It lasted four days: on 24th May, while being flown by Capt L.H.Smith, it was forced to land in enemy territory.

Although A7302 was allocated to No.66 Squadron, it did not go to France with that unit. *(RAF Museum)*

Inscribed "PUNJAB 12 KASHMIR" as a presentation aircraft, probably before leaving England for France, B1778 was allocated to the Expeditionary Force while still at Coventry Aircraft Acceptance Park on 26th June 1917. It went to No.66 Squadron from No.1 AD on 22nd August, but crashed on 4th September 1917, while being flown by 2/Lt D.H.Houston and was struck off squadron strength.

Another Pup that was used by No.66 Squadron was A6210. On 2nd June 1917, while it was at Lympne, it was officially allocated to the Expeditionary Force. It went from No.1 AD to No.66 Squadron on 22nd July 1917, and was one of the squadron's Pups that were flown by James McCudden during his attachment to the unit.

many Pup pilots have blessed their machine for its handiness, when they have been a long way behind the Hun lines, and have been at a disadvantage in other ways.'

A remarkable operation of a very different kind was a low-level reconnaissance of the German long-range gun, situated at Leugenboom, that had shelled Dunkerque repeatedly. This was undertaken by 2/Lt H.K.Boyson of No.66 Squadron in September 1917, who, according to A.J.Insall, 'came down to below tree-top level to scrutinise the emplacement and brought back a detailed description of it'. Evidently Boyson's Pup had no camera (though-some Pups at training units were so equipped for training purposes); certainly he received no decoration for his daring and valuable exploit, which must have been one of the last missions on which a Sopwith Scout truly performed as a scout.

Mention of No.66 Squadron's modest attempt at night bombing in early October 1917 has already been made on page 73. By that time the squadron's re-equipment with Camels was approaching; once in possession of its new mounts the unit was sent to operate on the Italian front, and moved there on 22nd November 1917.

The RFC's third Pup squadron, No.46, had initially gone to France on 20th October 1916 as a Corps squadron equipped with Nieuport 12 and 20 two-seaters. A change of function transformed it into a single-seat fighter squadron, and its re-equipment with Sopwith Pups began in April 1917. Pups known to have been on squadron strength before the end of April 1917 were A665, A7325, A7327, A7331, A7332, A7334, A7337, A7344 and A7348; others delivered on 2nd May were A6164, A6188 and A7347.

An eminently human account of operational flying on the Pups of No.46 Squadron was provided by the late Air Vice-Marshal Arthur Gould Lee, MC, in his book *Open Cockpit* (Jarrolds, 1969). He first flew a Pup on 24th April 1917, in No.40 Training Squadron at Port Meadow (Oxford), and with

Some single-seat fighters were used for photographic reconnaissance during the war, and at least one Pup was fitted with a camera at a training unit in Britain. The installation was wholly external and beyond the pilot's reach; the camera was a Williamson with windmill drive to the plate-changing mechanism.
(Chaz Bowyer)

A7325, aircraft '1' in No.46 Squadron, RFC. Standing in front of the aircraft in the front view is Lt C.J.Marchant; his Pup then had bi-colour wheel covers. A7325 was initially allocated to the Expeditionary Force on 20th March 1917, and was with No 46 Squadron in the following months.

(Frank Cheesman)

all of 19 hours' flying time on the type, went to France on 16th May. Six days later he joined No.46 Squadron, a matter of only a few weeks after the squadron's conversion to Pups. Of his introduction to the aircraft he wrote:

'At last, on April 24th, I did my first solo on a Pup, and at once realised that all the machines I had flown till now were indeed just machines, even the Avro. For the Pup was a dream to fly, so light on the control, so effortless to handle, so sweet and amenable. and so eagerly manoeuvrable that you found yourself doing every kind of stunt without a thought - loops, sideslip landings, tail slides, rolls, spins. And she was just as manoeuvrable up high, at 15,000ft and above.'

His later, informed, observations about the Pup, its advantages and its shortcomings give a sobering impression of what it meant to fly such an aircraft in combat, delightful flying machine though it was.

'Pups get the top patrols, because at those heights their light wing-loading confers the advantage over every other fighter, including the Albatros, and so, despite the cold and rare air, I admit I prefer to meet Huns at 17,000ft upwards, for then we no longer fight at a disadvantage...............

'At 8,000[ft] the Pup is completely outclassed by the Albatros. You can't get away, you've got to fight it out with one gun against two.' ....

'In 46 Squadron, we did not have a really lethal aeroplane, for though the Pup had been an effective fighter, a year or more before, it had long since been left behind by the Albatros D.III.

'What saved us from being shot down in droves like B.E.s and R.E.s and F.E.8s and D.H.2s and Sopwith and Nieuport two-seaters was the Pup's agility at all heights, which made us a difficult target in a dog-fight, and which even gave us a chance to twist in behind an inexperienced Hun and shoot him down. But once engaged in a fight we couldn't withdraw, for the Pup was slower than every German fighter by a good margin. ....

'Even during my first flights on Pups during training days. I realised what a likeable plane she was, so gentle and responsive yet so spirited, so eager to co-operate, as though, she were a living thing. In England, I was always told to handle her with care, for her structure was fragile, she could easily break up under stress, but now I knew differently. After my vertical 12,000ft dive with racing engine I knew that, though she did not enjoy such discourtesies, she would stand anything bar sheer ham-fisted clumsiness.'

'So docile a creature was meant to be flown for fun, not for killing, and in France she was never a Hun-

getter like the Camel I was to fly later ... Yet despite her deficiencies for aggressive fighting, the Pup, at all heights, could be as evasive as a butterfly...'

The first Camel to go to No.46 Squadron arrived on 7th November 1917. Others followed in ones and twos, and soon the squadron was an all-Camel unit. No.54 Squadron, although the first Pup squadron in the RFC, had to wait until December 1917 to make the change to the Pup's more bellicose descendant, but with its conversion to Camels the operational career of the Pup on the Western Front came to an end.

To the last, however, the Pup's ability to hold its height and retain its agility at high altitude remained an asset. In the period that preceded the Battle of Cambrai, much was done to deny the enemy fore-warning of the attack, which began, without even a preliminary artillery barrage, on the morning

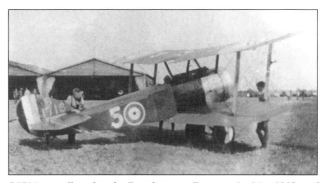

B1716 was allotted to the Expeditionary Force on 1st May 1917, and went to No.46 Squadron from No.1 AD on 16th May. Flying this Pup on 2nd June, 2/Lt F.B.Barager, in company with Capt R.Plenty, sent an Albatros D.III down out of control west of Menia. When photographed, B1716 had bi-colour wheel covers, its individual numeral was painted, on each upper mainplane, and there was a circular marking (perhaps small roundel) painted on the centre section. (RAF Museum)

B1802, here wearing No.46 Squadron's marking of two white bars on the rear fuselage, has its gun tested at the stop butts at Izel-le-Hameau. It had been allocated to No.46 Squadron on 12th July 1917, while still at Coventry AAP. On 24th September 1917, flown by Lt C.W.Odell, it had a share in the destruction of a DFW two-seater. B1802 was flown back to England on 8th December 1917. (Frank Cheesman)

of 20th November 1917. Of the measures taken to drive off enemy reconnaissance aircraft, the official historian wrote:

'Occasional distant sweeps were also made by large formations of Bristol Fighters. Sopwith Pups and D.H.5s, disposed in stepped layers, the Pups about 15,000ft, the Bristols 3,000ft lower, and the D.H.5s 3,000ft lower again. The formations were planned so that each type of aeroplane was used at the altitude to which it was best suited with each type complementary to the other.'   *(The War in the Air, Vol. IV, p.232)*

In one of the hangars at Izel-le-Hameau stand A7348, normally flown by Capt R.Heath., and another Pup, possibly A6202; the latter has a skull-and-crossbones device painted on the wheel cover. A7348 was allocated to the Expeditionary Force on 16th April 1917, and was with No.46 Squadron by 23rd April. When the squadron flew to England on 10th July for its brief Home Defence detachment, A7348 suffered engine failure in mid-Channel, had to ditch, and was lost. Its unfortunate pilot was 2/Lt C.Courtneidge (brother of the famous actress, Cicely), who was rescued.   *(Frank Cheesman)*

Captain R.Heath, 'B' Flight Commander in No.46 Squadron, with his Pup, presumably A7348 but with the numeral applied in different style, The Sopwith windscreen has been replaced by padding on the Vickers gun. Captain Heath was transferred to Home Establishment in mid-June 1917, after intensive service with No. 46 Squadron.   *(Frank Cheesman)*

B1704 was only briefly with No.46 Squadron. It was allocated to the Expeditionary Force from Coventry AAP on 9th April 1917, and was with No.46 Squadron by 25th May. It was reported as a new arrival in No 54 Squadron on 13th June; on 15th July, flown by 2/Lt C.G.Wood, it shared with B1759 and B1761 the destruction of an Albatros D.V. On 22nd August, again flown by 2/Lt C.G.Wood, it destroyed another Albatros D.V near Middelkerke.

The Pups concerned must have been those of No.46 Squadron, which was the only Pup unit in III Brigade, and were therefore in the last days of their operational employment. Although the stratified disposition of aircraft types recognised the Pup's remarkable capability, such formations had drawbacks, as Arthur Gould Lee has made clear:

'But the difficulty about these large groups of machine was that they couldn't be tactically handled in combat, for there was no way of control other than rocking wings, waving arms and firing Very lights, and these were only practicable before the action started. The result was that when two large formations of a dozen or more in each side tried to fight, they couldn't. They became two separate flocks of planes wheeling, climbing, diving, rushing forward to fire a burst then withdrawing, half-engaging then disengaging, singly or in pairs or even threes, but never in my experience to date wholly intermingling in one big battle.'   *(Open Cockpit. P.113)*

The need, at that time, for such complex formations soon passed; and Camels replaced Pups, only to find themselves caught up in murderous ground-attack work.

Usually flown by 2/Lt Norman H.Dimmock (hence the name "NORMIE" on its side), B1727 was allocated to the Expeditionary Force while it was at the Southern Aircraft Repair Depot, Farnborough, on 10th May 1917. It was sent to No.46 Squadron from No.2 AD, Candas, on 24th June. Dimmock returned to Home Establishment in October, but B1727 fought on. Flown by 2/Lt J.H.Cooper on 28th October 1917, it shared in the defeat of an Albatros D.V.

A673 was something of a veteran by the time it reached No.46 Squadron. First allocated to the E.F. on 10th January 1917, it was with No.54 Squadron by 24th February, on which date Captain R.Oxspring flew it to destroy a German two-seater near Bapaume; and on 4th June L.F.J.Morse drove down another unidentified two-seater near Bellicourt. Later with No. 46 Squadron, A673 was shot down in combat with Jasta 12 on 16th September 1917, the victory being credited to Leutnant Schobinger (though Arthur Gould Lee attributes it to Leutnant Jörke). Its pilot, 2/Lt L.M.Shadwell, was made PoW, and the Germans recovered the Pup more or less intact, as seen here.   *(The late A.E.Ferko)*

Another of No.46 Squadron's Pups that fell into enemy hands was B1795. Lt A.F.Bird had the misfortune to encounter Manfred von Richtofen on 3rd September 1917, and became his 61st victim. The aircraft fell near Bousbecque, and Bird was made PoW. Sitting on B1795's fuselage are Manfred von Richthofen and Anthony Fokker; standing at left is Leutnant Möhnike. B1795 had been allocated to the Expeditionary Force from Lympne on 4th July 1917, and was later re-allocated to No.46 Squadron on 18th July. *(Egon Krueger)*

A group of officers of No.46 Squadron, summer 1917. From left; unknown, Captain R Heath, unknown, Joske, Luxmore, Marchant, unknown, McDonald (?.), Barager (?). *(Frank Cheesman)*

Chapter 15

Home Defence

German bombing attacks on Britain during 1915 and 1916 had been made, with few exceptions, by airships during the hours of darkness. Such daylight attacks as were attempted were mostly hit-and-run ventures made by one or two aeroplanes or float seaplanes at or near the limit of their range. The most audacious and enterprising of these was the daylight attack on London on 28th November 1916, when an LVG C.IV captained by Leutnant Walther Ilges and piloted by Deck-Offizier Paul Brandt flew from Mariakerke and dropped six bombs on central London

This raid was accomplished unopposed. Of all the 21 defending sorties made against the LVG, only one (a Bristol Scout D of RNAS Dover) was airborne before Ilges dropped his bombs at 11.50 hours. By that time the Bristol had been airborne a mere five minutes; while the next British aircraft to get into the air, a laughably optimistic Short 184 seaplane, rose from Dover's waters at noon. No other would-be defender took off before 13.00 hours, by which time Ilges and Brandt were well on their homeward way. No British aircraft so much as saw them.

All of that should have told Britain's home-defence organisation something, but early in 1917 the strength of the RFC's Home Defence units was in fact reduced, and some quite extraordinary decisions were taken. The German daylight attack on Folkestone, delivered on 25th May 1917 by 21 Gothas, jolted General Headquarters Home Forces. Of the 77 Home Defence sorties flown from RNAS and RFC aerodromes, nine were made by Sopwith Pups from Dover, Grain, Manstone and Walmer, two by Sopwith Triplanes, and one by a Camel. The RFC squadrons could field only a miscellany of B.E.2cs, 2ds, 2es, 12s and 12as, none of which had the remotest hope of catching a Gotha, plus an odd R.E.8, D.H.5 and Vickers E.S.l.

The Gothas' bombs killed 95 and injured 195 of Folkestone's citizens. On 5th June the German raiders returned to bomb Sheerness, and again the defensive units of south-east England had no palpable success against them. From RNAS Dunkerque three Pups of No.4 (Naval) and seven Pups and Triplanes of No.9 (Naval) Squadron attacked the Gothas and

A6230 was a Pup of No.63 Training Squadron, Joyce Green (where the original of this photograph was taken by Capt J.T.B.MCudden). On 7th July 1917, 2/Lt W.G.Salmon flew this aircraft to attack the Gotha formation that attacked London on that day, although he engaged the enemy he was shot down and killed.

(RAF Museum)

Another training unit Pup that flew as a Home Defence fighter was A6228, then on the strength of No.40 Training Squadron, Croydon. It made at least four defensive sorties against German bombing formations: on 4th and 7th July, and on 12th and 22nd August 1917. Its pilot on 7th July was 2/Lt R.F.W.Martin, who managed to fire on one of the Gothas. (RAF Museum)

claimed to have destroyed two of them, also driving down, out of control, four other German aircraft of which three were described as Albatros D.IIIs.

On 13th June London was bombed in daylight by 18 Gothas; on 4th July Harwich and Felixstowe were attacked; three days later the German bombers returned to London. In these three attacks a total of 236 people were killed: public outrage was vehemently expressed.

The available Home Defence forces included a number of Pups at RNAS aerodromes and with Reserve Squadrons of the RFC: James McCudden's home-defence sorties from Joyce Green have been recounted on pages 72-73. The defending squadrons had been strengthened only to a modest extent, and too large a proportion of their aircraft still consisted of types that had virtually no hope of intercepting enemy bombers, and

little combat effectiveness if contact could have been made.

On 20th June 1917, the Cabinet War Policy Committee decided that the home-defence forces must be supplemented by fighter squadrons drawn from the Western Front. Next day No.56 Squadron, RFC, flew its S.E.5s to England, and No.66 Squadron took its Pups to Calais where, it was hoped, it would be able to intercept enemy formations over the Channel. Haig and Trenchard had agreed, reluctantly, to the detachment of these squadrons, and had stipulated that they must be back on the Western Front by 5th July.

No.66 Squadron put up 17 Pups (A6191, A6197, A6198, A6205, A6215, B1703, B1710, B1724, B1725, B1731, B1744, B1746, B1747, B1756, B1757, B1758, B1762) on the occasion of the raid on 4th July 1917, but a lapse in communications delayed until 08.10hrs the squadron's order to patrol, and by

Although Pups of Home Defence units were not considered suitable for night operations, B5307 was equipped with navigation lights and had night-flying markings. It served with No.61 Squadron at Rochford between at least December 1917 and February 1918, possibly as a practice machine, being fitted with a Monosoupape engine.

Pups of No.61 (Home Defence) Squadron lined up on Rochford aerodrome in October 1917. Fourth from the right is B5905, which has an overwing Lewis gun; other Pups that can be identified are B2222, B1812 and B1764. The last-named had earlier (July) been with No.37 (Home Defence) Squadron, and after its service with No.61 Squadron it was used by No.6 Training Squadron, Australian Flying Corps.

the time the Pups were airborne the Gothas had already traversed the patrol area and were crossing the Belgian coast. No.66 Squadron rejoined the BEF next day without having fired a shot at any Gotha.

With the Gothas' raid on London of 7th July coming less than 48 hours after the return of squadrons Nos.56 and 66 to the BEF, further reinforcement of the Home Defence forces was desperately needed. A modest number of Pups had been added to the strength of Home Defence Group, but these had been allotted to Squadrons Nos.37 and 50 instead of being used to equip a homogeneous squadron. The Cabinet met on 7th and 9th July, and decided that the RFC in France must again provide fighter aircraft to help protect the homeland. This brought about the transfer of No.46 Squadron from Bruay to Sutton's Farm on 10th July: their 19 Pups that were flown to England that day were A648, A6155, A6188, A6200, A6206, A7327, A7333, A7335, A7336, A7346, A7347, A7348, B1701, B1716, B1719, B1727, B1754, B1766 and B1777. One, A7348 flown by Lt C.Courtneidge, suffered engine failure in mid-Channel and had to ditch. This formation was led from France to England by Mjr L.A.Tilney, OC, No.40 Sqn, flying a Nieuport Scout, B1684.

Under its Commanding Officer, Major Philip Babington, MC, No.46 Squadron. maintained an exemplary standard of serviceability and reading; this is lucidly and eloquently described by Arthur Gould Lee in his book *No Parachute*, Part Five.

During its sojourn at Sutton's Farm No.46 flew on defensive patrols on 22nd July and 8th, 12th, 14th, 18th and 22nd August 1917, but the required rigorous adherence to designated patrol beats laid down by Home Defence Group denied the squadron any opportunity to engage enemy raiders. On 30th August 1917, No.46 Squadron flew back to France and to a new aerodrome at Ste.Marie-Cappel.

Replacements, comparable at least in terms of aircraft type, were being formed. On 30th July 1917, No.112 Squadron was formed at Throwley; three days later, on 2nd August, No.61 Squadron formed at Rochford; both new units had Sopwith Pups. When Home Defence Group was upgraded to Brigade status on 28th August 1917, these two new Pup squadrons, together with Nos.44 and 78 Squadrons, constituted the Eastern Wing, which consisted of day-fighter squadrons.

Although a few night sorties had been flown on Pups by RFC and RNAS pilots, the type never became a recognised

B5904 was an aircraft of No.6l (Home Defence) Squadron at Rochford. It had the standard armament with an Avro-type windscreen.

B5905, identified in the photograph on page 96, had the refinement of a head fairing behind the cockpit. The Gnome Monosoupape engine had an objectionable habit of throwing off cylinders and that is what appears to have happened here: two cylinders are missing, the cowling has been destroyed, and the engine has torn itself out of its mounting.

Like B5905 in the preceding illustration, B1806 had its fin painted white. This Pup was with No.61 Squadron in August 1917, and in it 2/Lt J.S.Wood succeeded in attacking a Gotha of the raiding force that bombed Southend on 12th August. Although he fired all his ammunition he scored no significant hit. B1806 was also used by No.112 (Home Defence) Squadron, as seen here.

night fighter in the Home Defence Brigade. For all its remarkable controllability, its light wing loading made it sensitive to any turbulence and wind, consequently landing it on a darkened aerodrome slightly out of wind could result in landing mishaps. Evidently Brig-Gen T.C.R.Higgins, the Officer Commanding Home Defence Brigade, regarded the Pup, for whatever reason, as impossible to fly at night, and said so in a report dated 10th January 1918, in which, *inter alia*, he sought re-equipment of No.112 Squadron.

On 7th July 1917, one of the Pups of No.37 Squadron that took off to attack the raiding Gothas was A653. It will be recalled (see page 62) that this Pup was tested at Martlesham Heath in April 1917, fitted with a 100hp Monosoupape engine. By 7th July A653 was with 'B' Flight of No.37 Squadron at Stow Maries, when it was flown by Capt C.A.Ridley against the Gotha formation. Its armament had been increased by the installation of an overwing Lewis gun on the centre section, but this addition reduced the Pup's performance significantly. By 12th August, A653 was with No.61 Squadron at Rochford.

To what extent, if any, A653's Monosoupape installation influenced the general use of that engine in Home Defence Pups is not known. Although the performance of A653 did not indicate a significant all-round improvement over the standard 80hp Pup, some advantage must have been seen in the Monosoupape version. Perhaps it was hoped that its extra power would enable the aircraft to carry an overwing Lewis gun without incurring too great a penalty in performance: it appears that some Home Defence Pups, like A653, had such a Lewis gun installation but photographic confirmation has yet to be found.

One major armament improvement made on the Monosoupape Pup was the introduction of the Constantinesco gun-synchronising system, as mentioned on page 64. This alone would have excited the envy of RFC pilots on the Western Front, who had long considered themselves hard done by in aircraft terms: first by the lateness of equipment with Pups in Squadrons Nos.46 and 66 - many months after the RNAS squadrons. and only when the type was obsolescent - and in the summer of 1917 when it was learned, belatedly, by the RFC in France that numbers of early-production Camels had been allotted to Home Defence Group instead of going

to the squadrons in France, where there was a daily - indeed hourly - need for more effective fighters.

The Pups of the new Home Defence squadrons, Nos.61 and 112, participated in the defensive action against the Gotha force that bombed Southend on 12th August 1917. No.61 Squadron put up 15 Pups, and No.112 contributed nine. Not surprisingly, with the raiding Gothas virtually over their aerodrome at Rochford, No.61's pilots had most of the action, but it was largely futile pursuit rather than hand-to-hand combat over the target. Although the Pups chased the Gothas many miles out to sea, their pilots were mostly frustrated by guns jamming and engine problems.

Only one of No.112 Squadron's Pups succeeded in engaging the Gothas, but Capt S.H.Pratt in B1773 suffered a gun jam after firing 50 rounds without result. Many - too many - other pilots of other units were denied success by refractory guns. One who was luckier was FSL H.S.Kerby of RNAS Walmer, flying Pup N6440. He attacked the main German formation, but spotted a lone Gotha straggling some 4,000ft lower, dived on it and shot it down into the sea.

Like Fall (see page 83), Kerby was a Canadian. For his victory over the Gotha he was awarded the DSC; and his action makes an interesting comparison with the prolonged and hectic combat for which Fall received the same decoration. Ten days later (22nd August), Kerby was again in action on N6440 against Gothas, and shared in shooting down one of them: part of the credit for its destruction probably belonged to Flt Cdr G.E.Hervey, flying Pup N6191 of RNAS Dover, who had also fired on it; and perhaps to Flt Lt A.F.Brandon, who, in a Camel (B3923) of RNAS Manstone, had attacked a Gotha and apparently registered hits on it.

Against this German raid No.61 Squadron, RFC, flew eighteen Pup sorties, No.112 Squadron eleven, but their prescribed patrol lines were too far from the area of action for them to be able to engage the Gothas. That was their Pups' last real chance of combat, for thereafter the Gothas attacked by night: by December 1917 No.61 Squadron had re-equipped with S.E.5as, and Brig-Gen Higgins' request of 10th January 1918 that No.112 Squadron be re-equipped was met by replacing the Pups with Camels some weeks later.

The six Pups of 'B' Flight, No.112 (Home Defence) Squadron lined up (apparently cross-wind) at Throwley in the autumn of 1917. The three nearest Pups can be identified as B1803 ('5'), B2210 ('7') and B2194 ('3'). B1803 was also used by No.198 (Night) Training Squadron at Rochford, and in early 1918 was reported with No.3 Training Squadron, Shoreham.
(Frank Cheesman)

Chapter 16

A Pup manqué

An intriguing little mystery concerns a Pup that was lent to the French authorities late in 1916 for evaluation. The French had formed a high opinion of the Sopwith 1½ Strutter, of which type the RNAS had transferred no fewer than 71 two-seaters and 12 single-seater bomber variants to the French government by January 1917; additionally, six Sopwith-built 1½ Strutters had been supplied to France direct without receiving British serial numbers. Thereafter, the type was built in large numbers by several French contractors and was extensively used by French *escadrilles*.

It is not known whether the French formally asked for or were offered a specimen of the Pup, but the following letter of 31st January 1917 confirms that one was sent. The letter, addressed to Capt Acton, RN, of the British Aviation Supplies Depot, Paris, was signed by Col Regnier, the French Minister for War:

'During the last quarter of 1916 the British Naval Aviation was kind enough to put at my disposal a Sopwith single-seat triplane [sic] for 80hp Le Rhône, for examination and study.

'As a result of these studies it has been decided that it would not be suitable for the French Aviation to organize the manufacture of machines of this type at the present time.

'Consequently, should the British Admiralty or War Office be able to use the model machine which has been put at my disposal I should be glad if you would let me know and I will despatch it at once to the destination you desire.

'I have the honour to request that you will transmit my best thanks to the Admiralty for their kindness in putting this machine at my disposal.'

The description of the aircraft as a triplane was incorrect. Although the lending of the Pup had been a purely Naval exercise, Regnier's offer was made known to the RFC, though initially represented as a triplane. On 12th February 1917, Brooke-Popham wrote to the BASD. ' .... we do not want this Sopwith triplane with the 80hp Le Rhône'. Two days later he again declined the aircraft in a further note to the BASD: '.... we do not require this machine although it has been found to be a biplane instead of a triplane'.

Presumably that second communication, dated 14th February 1917, had been despatched before Capt Lord Robert Innes-Ker of the BASD telephoned Brooke-Popham that day concerning a further letter from Col

Regnier dated 10th February, from which it had been learned that there was indeed and additionally a 130hp Clerget Sopwith triplane that the French were offering to return.

In itself this was puzzling, for some 16 or more Sopwith Triplanes had been supplied to France direct from the Sopwith company and apparently against a French order, plus three or four RNAS Triplanes; and it is not clear why only this single specimen was offered. Several ex-French Sopwith Triplanes were indeed returned to the RNAS: perhaps the offered one was the last remaining in French hands at the time, though the date seems early.

Capt Acton, RN, had already shown willingness to accept the Sopwith Triplane, and Capt Lord Innes-Ker's telephone message sufficed to change Brooke-Popham's mind, for he wrote on 15th February:

'.... we do require the machine referred to .... discovered to be an ordinary 80hp Sopwith Scout .... we are ready to take both triplanes,* particularly the Sopwith'.

At that time it was still expected that Sopwith Triplanes would be produced for the RFC as well as the RNAS; only on 26th February 1917 was the well-known Triplane/Spad 7 exchange finally settled.

Eventually, on 6th March 1917, RFC Headquarters were informed that Capt Acton had received a telegram from the Air Board to the effect that both the Pup and the Sopwith Triplane were to be sent to Dunkerque, doubtless the RNAS Depot there.

Two days earlier, on 4th March 1917, Pup N6170 of No.3 (Naval) Squadron had been reported missing with its pilot, Lt H.R.Wambolt. In the *Weekly Returns of machines at Wings, Squadrons and Depot on RNAS Dunkirk charge* for 5th April it was recorded that N6170 was 'awaiting survey or decision' and that 'This number has been given to another Pup'; and indeed in its return of 12th April, a week later, No.3 (Naval) Squadron recorded that a Pup numbered N6170 was on the strength of its 'B' Flight.

Nothing in earlier correspondence concerning the Pup that had been lent to the French suggested that it had a British serial number - which, of course, does not

---

* ***Note:*** *The other was the Nieuport triplane N1388, which became A6686.*

necessarily mean that it did not, but it was unusual at the time and in such circumstances for individual aircraft not to be identified by their serial numbers where these were known. It might be relevant to note that when Sopwith Triplanes that had been delivered to the French government, direct and with unofficial numbers (F1 to at least F16 are believed to have been used), were subsequently transferred to the RNAS, they were allotted British Naval serial numbers in the special series that started at N500. There were four such: N524 and N541-N543. Triplanes originally built for the RNAS, delivered with RNAS serial numbers, but transferred to the French government, retained or reverted to their original RNAS identities on return to that Service. Examples were N5384 and N5387.

No official record or listing yet found includes any reference, in either category, to any numbered Pup lent to or received from the French government. The circumstances and chronology recounted above suggest that there might have been a link between the ex-French Pup and the seemingly arbitrary re-allocation of the serial number of the lost N6170 to 'another Pup' for which no previous identity or source was recorded.

Although the chronology of the foregoing speculation holds together reasonably well, an alternative explanation of the re-allocation of the serial number N6170 might lie in the enterprising activities of RNAS engineering personnel at Dunkerque. Wg Capt C.L.Lambe pursued a policy that aimed at having spare aircraft available to provide prompt replacements in the RNAS squadrons. A salvage crew was kept on constant standby and went out to recover crashed aircraft with minimum delay. On return to the Depot at Dunkerque all the re-usable components from a wreck were set aside to form a reserve from which were built up 'new' aircraft as availability and opportunity allowed. As and when appropriate, serial numbers were cut from wrecks, preserved and re-applied to composite rebuilds.

This was not essentially different from the reconstruction of damaged RFC aircraft, or their rebuilding from salvage, in Aircraft Depots and Aeroplane Repair Depots; but the RNAS did not have any formal system for renumbering such rebuilt aircraft: no special blocks of serial numbers were set aside for such purposes. Hence it is equally possible that the second Pup to bear the number N6170 might have been a rebuild from salvaged components. The nature and duration of such reincarnation as might have been contrived remain uncertain: although a Pup numbered N6170 was reported 'wrecked' in No.1 (Naval) Squadron on 1st May 1917, was recommended for deletion on 14th May, and was duly deleted on 19th May, the daily returns for RNAS Dover Aeroplanes in early June 1917 include an N6170, ostensibly serviceable.

Oliver Stewart's first Pup in No.54 Squadron., A6156, is seen here with his basic monogram on centre section, fuselage sides and top decking. Built by Whitehead, it had first been reported with the AID at Farnborough an 16th February 1917, at which date it had already been allocated to the RFC in France. Then photographed, it had the variable-incidence tailplane, and an Aldis sight was mounted close to the port side of the Vickers gun. In the summer of 1917 this Pup was reconstructed at No.1 Aircraft Depot, St.Omer, and was re-issued to No.54 Squadron on 23rd August 1917. It was still with the squadron on 24th September, when Capt F.J.Morse claimed an Albatros D at Mannekensvaere. A6156 was reported at No.1 Aeroplane Supply Depot, on 4th January 1918. (Jean Devaux)

FSL G.G.Simpson of No.8 (Naval) Squadron on his Pup N5185, named "BINKY II" (the first "BINKY" had been a Nieuport 21, and "BINKY III" was Sopwith Triplane N5449 of No.8 (Naval) Squadron). When Naval Eight handed over its Pups to No.3 (Naval) Squadron in February 1918, "BINKY II" was inherited by FSL L.H. ('Tich') Rochford. (Via Frank Cheesman)

Chapter 17

To the Sea in Ships

It has already been noted that the Royal Navy's concern about the threat to its ships posed by Germany's rigid airships prompted the creation of the Admiralty Type 9901a Pup, with its upward-firing Lewis gun or battery of rockets (see pages 74-76). A potential defence against airships had been demonstrated on 3rd November 1915, when Flt Cdr Bernard Fowler successfully flew a Bristol Scout C from a tiny flight deck built on to HMS *Vindex*, an early seaplane carrier, while the ship was under way at sea. In so doing he made history: for the first time, a military aeroplane with standard wheel undercarriage had taken off from the flying deck of a carrier vessel specifically intended to launch aircraft in this way. The Royal Navy had a certain amount of experience in flying-off from ships, for it had started to do so as early as 2nd May 1912, using special trackways rather than decks proper.

Nine months later, Fowler's achievement had an operational sequel. On 2nd August 1916 HMS *Vindex* was at sea on anti-Zeppelin patrol with her escort of four destroyers and a light cruiser (HMS *Conquest*) when the Zeppelin *L.17* was sighted. Flt Lt C.T.Freeman took off from *Vindex* in Bristol Scout D No.8953, armed only with two containers of Ranken Darts, and eventually succeeded in climbing higher than the airship. He made three attacking runs over the *L.17*, on the third of which he thought that one of his missiles had struck the airship. If it did, it failed to ignite, and the *L.17* flew on; Freeman, having no landing-on deck available to him, had to ditch his aircraft. He was saved by the Belgian steamer *Anvers*, but his Bristol Scout was lost.

The flying-off deck on *Vindex* had a maximum length of 65ft. The Bristol Scout had its tail supported on a Tail Guide Trestle that overhung the aft end of the flying deck; even so, it must be doubtful whether the available effective take-off deck length could have been much more than 50ft,

Fowler got off in 46ft, measured from the standing position of his Bristol Scout's wheels.

At that time all ships that could carry aeroplanes had the conventional full-beam configuration of bridge and superstructure with funnel(s) placed roughly amidships: such miniature flying decks as could be fitted therefore had to be mounted forward of these structural features. This not only limited the length of the flying deck but also appeared to rule out any possibility of landing-on.

Perhaps Fowler's and Freeman's flights did enough to convince official minds that the operation of suitable single-seaters from such deck-equipped carriers was feasible. Early in 1917 the Grand Fleet Committee on Air Requirements*, prepared a Report dated 5th February 1917, which was submitted to Admiral Sir David Beatty, Commander-in-Chief Grand Fleet. In paragraph 11 thereof, headed *Anti-Zeppelin Machines*, the Committee stated:

'The Baby Sopwith seaplane at present supplied to the Carriers is admirably suited for this work, but it is recommended that it should be replaced by Sopwith Pup Aeroplanes in the *Campania* and *Manxman* as this will greatly increase the number of occasions when the Anti-Zeppelin type can be flown from the decks of these ships ....'

'27. ... it appears to the Committee essential that the Grand Fleet should be in a position to attack Zeppelins. Machines are now available of a type which has proved successful on shore for this purpose and it only remains to arrange to carry them in the Fleet.'

* **Note:** *This resoundingly-named body consisted of three Naval officers: Rear-Admiral Sir Hugh Evan-Thomas, Capt C.M. de Bartolomé and Flag Commander W.A.Egerton.*

HMS Vindex, which provided the take-off deck for several of the most significant 'firsts' in naval aviation history. Here she is bound for the raid on Hoya, Schleswig-Holstein, on 24th March 1916.

One of Vindex's Pups being lowered on to the after end of her flying deck: this may have been another stage in the operation of hoisting 9926 seen in the photograph on page 76.

Although this photograph might seem to suggest that transporting aircraft aboard Vindex could be alarmingly alfresco at times, it is more probable that it represents an in-harbour situation, for the two Pups do not appear to be secured. The mainplanes of one, resting on their leading edges, have been 'boxed' with jury struts to preserve their rigging while detached. These Pups are unidentified, but the nearer appears to be either N6457 or N6458. This photograph illustrates clearly the limitations of Vindex's tiny flying-off deck.   (RAF Museum)

This report reached Admiral Beatty while he was awaiting an Admiralty reply to his letter of 21st January 1917, in which he had asked to be informed about the policy that the Admiralty intended to pursue in relation to the RNAS, and pressed for development of 'the use of naval aircraft for fleet purposes in every possible respect'. He continued:

'At present the following vessels are attached to the Grand Fleet:

Ship	Speed	Seaplanes carried	Remarks
Campania	18 knots	5 large 6 small	Launching platform
Manxman	16 knots	4 large 4 small	Ditto for small only
Engadine	18 knots	2 large 2 small	No platform

'*Engadine* cannot be counted on to be of any use except in the smoothest water.

'*Manxman*'s value is greatly reduced owing to lack of speed, and small radius of action.

'These are the only vessels available at present for aircraft service, all of which are of very doubtful value, for various causes.

'It is understood that a new seaplane carrier is under construction. I request that I may be informed of her details and probable date of completion.'

The Admiralty reply was dated 14th February 1917, and did not comment on Beatty's assessments of his three carriers; it did, however, tell him:

'The details of new Seaplane Carrier *Argus* are as follows:

Speed - 21 knots. Size - about that of *Campania*
Machines carried -   8 Reconnaissance
                            6 Anti-Zepp.
                            4 Torpedo, if required
               Total 18

'All machines to fly from the Ship's deck. It is further hoped that Reconnaissance machines will be able to alight on the Ship, experiments now being carried out at Port Victoria being most promising. In this case, aeroplanes would be used for Reconnaissance.'

While awaiting the above reply, Beatty sent a copy of the Report of the Grand Fleet Committee on Air Requirements to the Admiralty on 7th February 1917. In his covering letter of that date he included the following paragraphs:

'The provision of efficient anti-Zeppelin machines and suitable ships to carry them I regard as most important; these machines give promise of an effective reply to the German Zeppelins employed on naval scouting duties and should largely reduce the latter's usefulness.

'At the same time, I am not prepared to sacrifice the gun armament of light-cruisers in order to use them as seaplane carriers: the Grand Fleet is by no means over strong in this class of ship when the recent additions to the enemy's fleet are taken into account...................

'Every effort should be made, however, to render the *Furious* an effective seaplane carrier, as although I am of opinion that the right policy is to employ non-fighting ships for this purpose, I am informed that the *Argus* cannot be expected to join the fleet until the end of the year, and it is most desirable that more seaplanes should be available for operations in the near future.'

As far as this history of the Sopwith Pup is concerned, the significant recommendation was the specifying of the Pup as a replacement for the Sopwith Baby: its implications and consequences were to be profound and far-reaching in the full context of ship-borne aircraft and deck flying. It is also noteworthy that the Admiralty expected that aeroplanes would be able to land on ships' decks at sea.

The Grand Fleet Committee's recommendation that Pups should replace Baby seaplanes might have been based on some experience, for the two Beardmore-built Pups 9910 and 9911 had been officially accepted on 26th December 1916. They were thereafter delivered under allocation to HMS *Vindex*, but apparently did not immediately go to that ship. Admiral Beatty clearly recognised the value of shipborne aircraft. Rather lower in the Navy's rank structure was an officer who was equally convinced, but who also held a strong belief that the Pup should replace the Baby because it was the only aircraft that could hope to climb high enough and fast enough to be able to attack a Zeppelin at its ceiling. He was Frederick Joseph Rutland, DSC, AM, RN, who on 31st May 1916 had been the pilot of HMS *Engadine*'s Short 184 No.8359, the only aircraft of any type to play a part in the Battle of Jutland.

Rutland had been appointed to *Manxman* before she was commissioned in December 1916; he was her Senior Flying Officer, and was in charge of the earliest trials in flying seaplanes from her 60ft flying deck early in 1917. He cannot have approached these trials with much enthusiasm or confidence, for three weeks before the Battle of Jutland he had put forward-proposals for the construction of aircraft carriers from which aeroplanes, rather than seaplanes, would operate, flying from flush decks at least 600ft in length and 60ft in beam. For such a ship he specified a speed of 35 knots.

It is not known whether Rutland had heard anything of the proposals of Flt Cdr H.A.Williamson, RN. As early as the summer of 1915 Williamson had concluded that naval aviation would be most efficiently conducted by using wheeled aircraft operating from an uninterrupted flying deck on a specially constructed ship. Most significant - and historic - of all was his proposal of '... the drastic measure of moving all upper deck essentials over to one side of the ship'. He provided three-dimensional expression of this most fundamental idea by making a model of a ship having a flat upper deck and '... on the starboard side a streamlined structure to contain the navigating bridge, searchlights, etc, above which rose a mast and funnels.' Thus Williamson* defined the essentials of later generations of aircraft carriers: the pity is that his ideas were not immediately taken up, instead of reliance being placed on the desultory, hasty and inadequate adaptations of unsuitable ships that appeared during the 1914-18 war.

---

* **_Note:_** *As a matter of historical fact, the basic concept of an aircraft-carrying ship, with continuous flat and wide flight deck, below-deck stowage for its aircraft (for which was envisaged wing-folding to save space), and lifts to move them on to and from the deck, was first enunciated as early as 1909 by the great French engineer and inventor Clement Ader in his book* L'Aviation Militaire. *Regrettably, in more recent times and in relation to his pioneering work in aviation during the last decade of the 19th century, Ader's reputation has been undeservedly traduced; but his ideas of 1909 are a matter of record and cannot be controverted.*

Flt Cdr F.J.Rutland, DSC, RN, the first and greatest of the pioneering practitioners of naval deck flying, in whom were combined, to an exceptional degree, penetrating vision, ingenuity, courage, and brilliant piloting skill and judgement.   *(Fleet Air Arm Museum)*

HMS Manxman, from which Rutland and his pilots did much early deck flying.   *(Fleet Air Arm Museum)*

But Rutland's immediate concern was with *Manxman*. She was a conversion of a small coal-burning passenger steamer of only 2,174 tons that had belonged to the Midland Railway and provided the Isle of Man service; as such, with her miniature flying deck she fell grotesquely short of the kind of carrier vessel proposed by Williamson and advocated by Rutland. The ship carried four Sopwith Baby seaplanes in her forward hangar, and four Short 184 seaplanes in the after hangar.

Seaplanes were flown from forward flying decks by placing their floats on wheeled dollies that were arrested at the end of the take-off run or dropped on becoming airborne. Initial trials of flying-off Sopwith Babies from *Manxman* were conducted in the Firth of Forth in January 1917, and demonstrated the difficulties and dangers of such deck take-offs. Rutland stopped the flying and demanded Pups to replace the Babies. His demand probably preceded the report of the Grand Fleet Committee on Air Requirements by a matter of days.

Whether by coincidence or as a result of the report, two Beardmore-built Pups (9913 and 9914) were earmarked for *Manxman,* and to that end were delivered to East Fortune on 12th February 1917. By 18th March Nos. 9921, 9926 and 9927 had been delivered to Felixstowe for *Vindex*; on 13th April 9943 and 9944 were delivered to East Fortune for *Manxman*, being followed late in April by 9945 and on 4th May by N6430 and N6431. Early in June 1917, 9931-9934 were with *Campania*, awaiting erection; and before the end of that month N6443, N6444, N6455 and N6456 had been delivered to Turnhouse for *Manxman*; N6457 and N6458 had been delivered to Felixstowe for *Vindex*; and N6448 and N6449 had gone to East Fortune, almost certainly for shipboard use.

Rutland and his pilots in *Manxman* explored the Pup's short take-off capabilities in repeated tests. In most flights the aircraft became airborne after a run of 35-40 feet, but Rutland was convinced that it could be done in less than 20 feet, and personally proved that this was possible. To prove his point and to convince his pilots, he had an additional elevated platform built on to the after end of the flying deck of *Manxman*: this structure was 1ft high and apparently 20ft long. Rutland made the first flight from this platform, and subsequently it was found, in a series of flights, that the longest run taken was 18½ feet, the shortest 16½ feet.

When Admiral Sir David Beatty wrote to the Admiralty on 7th February 1917, submitting the Report of the Grand Fleet Committee on Air Requirements, he made it clear that, anxious though he was to have anti-Zeppelin aircraft with the Fleet, he was '... not prepared to sacrifice the gun armament of light cruisers in order to use them as seaplane carriers'. At that time it must have seemed that flying decks had to be at least as big and enveloping as those on *Campania*. *Manxman* and *Vindex*, and indeed such decks would be essential if, as Beatty saw it, the aircraft had to be seaplanes, but Rutland's work on *Manxman*'s minuscule flight platform demonstrated that much smaller structures could suffice to get a lightly loaded aeroplane like the Pup into the air.

In view of his unique experience and skill, Rutland served as technical adviser to the Aircraft Committee of the First Battle-Cruiser Squadron at Rosyth. At about the time when he had developed the short take-off technique, the Committee met to discuss, *inter alia*, a design for a flying-off deck to be fitted to the light cruiser *Yarmouth*. This had been designed by Lt Cdr C.H.B.Gowan, the ship's gunnery officer. His proposal was for a deck 45ft long; when in place it would inhibit the forward gun, but could within a few minutes be removed sufficiently for the gun to fire.

Rutland astonished the Committee by stating that he was prepared to fly off a deck only 15ft long. He invited the Committee to come to sea in *Manxman*, and proved his claim to them on the spot. Admiralty approval was sought and readily granted for a flying-off platform of appropriate dimensions to be made and fitted to *Yarmouth* at Rosyth.

After a remarkable adventure that started on 29th April 1917, which included a fruitless Zeppelin mission in one of *Manxman*'s Pups (No.9918), at the end of which he had no choice but to ditch just off the Danish coast, Rutland returned to Britain via Sweden in June. By that time the flying-off platform had been made and installed on *Yarmouth*; although the task had been completed some weeks earlier, flight trials were postponed until Rutland returned from his Scandinavian excursion. (According to Desmond Young's biography, *Rutland of Jutland* (Cassell, 1963), 'The view of the pilots was that it was a crackbrained scheme anyway and that if Rutland had faith in it he had better be the first to try it.')

In his specifications for a flying-off deck Rutland had

If the trough installation made on Manxman and opposed by Rutland was similar to this structure on HMS Pegasus it becomes clear why he wanted none of it.

Just how hair-raising a Pup's deck take-off in any breath of crosswind could be is graphically demonstrated here as Flt Cdr R.E.Penny becomes obliquely airborne on 1st December 1917 from a trough-fitted trackway aboard HMS Renown. At such lateral angles the risk that the one running wheel would foul its trough must have been considerable, and indeed on this occasion the Pup (N6448) went into the water. (Fleet Air Arm Museum)

never asked for more than a plain platform built to the dimensions that he recommended. He was understandably nonplussed to find that the deck had been built with two parallel troughs for an aircraft's wheels to run in. These had been fitted, on the instructions of the Admiralty (presumably the Air Department thereof), but Rutland was opposed to their use. It took a certain amount of ingenuity to persuade the Admiralty to agree to the removal of the troughs, but eventually reason was seen, and they were taken off.

Parenthetically, it may be observed that take-off troughs were by no means abandoned. Experiments in their use were under way at Grain in September 1917, and various trough installations were made in several ships. Of *Yarmouth*'s platform Rutland himself reported on 29th June 1917:

'The Flying Deck is so constructed that the machine has a run of 19ft 3in measured from the centre of the wheels; this being 3ft longer than the maximum that I stated would be required, thus allowing for small errors on the part of the pilot when getting off.

'The original Deck had two troughs for the wheels to run in, so designed that if a wide-type chassis were used, the wheels would be just clear of the outside cheek of the trough, and if a narrower type were used, the wheels would just clear the inside cheek ....

'I consider that the Flying Deck is very strong and

well designed and, with the abolition of the troughs, and slightly extra width, it would be suitable for any ship of the *Yarmouth* class, and in my opinion these should be fitted without delay.

'I am informed that the object of the troughs is to enable the machine to rise from Light Cruisers of the *Cassandra* class, where it is considered impossible to fit a deck.'

A preliminary flight was made by Rutland from *Manxman* on 27th June 1917. It is possible that the take-off platform might have been shortened, or at least so arranged that the length available was reduced, as may be seen in Rutland's own report:

'An experimental flight was carried out in *Manxman* on 27th June, the day preceding the flight from HMS *Yarmouth*, more for interest sake.

'The conditions were as follows:
Weather. Clouds detached - light airs. Sea smooth, Ship creating an air speed of 19 knots.

'A piece of deck was built up 15ft 6in. long and 1ft high from flying deck proper of *Manxman*.

'I flew from this deck under the above conditions.

'The machine's wheels left the deck almost immediately after releasing, the ship having a big list to port.'

Rutland's take-off from HMS Yarmouth on 28th June 1917. It is believed that the Pup is N6431.   *(Imperial War Museum)*

Rutland's report of his flight from *Yarmouth*'s flying deck was entirely a matter-of-fact account:

'On 28th June I made a flight from the deck of HMS *Yarmouth*.

'Weather conditions: Wind about 5 knots. Clouds detached. Sea smooth.

'The Captain of HMS *Yarmouth* was requested to regulate his speed so that an air speed of 25 knots was maintained.

'The wind fluctuated slightly so that at the moment of flying an air speed of 26 knots was showing on the air-speed indicators (two were used).

'The machine left the deck at an angle of about 4 degrees, and went straight up at this angle.

'The wheels were chalked, and from observation and chalk marks on the deck. it was found that the machine actually left the deck 4ft 6in from the end, making a total run of 14ft 9in.

'In both flights the machine was fully loaded as for Zeppelin attacks, i.e., Lewis gun, two 97-round trays of ammunition, 12 Verys lights, and Verys pistol.'

The take-off run was further proof of Rutland's extraordinary skill as a pilot, and of the accuracy of his predictions and claims as to the Pup's capabilities. His aircraft was N6431, a Beardmore-built Type 9901a.

Evidently the Navy's high command agreed with Rutland's recommendation that greater use should be made of flying-off platforms on warships, At a conference between Admiral Sir David Beatty, C-in-C Grand Fleet. and Rear-Admiral Lionel Halsey, Third Sea Lord, held on 17th August 1917, Beatty,

'stated he wished one Light Cruiser in each Light Cruiser Squadron to have a flying-off deck for an anti-Zeppelin machine. The ships selected were:

1st	Light Cruiser Squadron	- *Caledon*
2nd	Light Cruiser Squadron	- *Dublin*
3rd	Light Cruiser Squadron	- *Yarmouth*
6th	Light Cruiser Squadron	- *Cassandra*

'This policy is to be extended to other Light Cruisers if found to be very successful and desirable.'

Spectacular success came a mere four days later in the action of Lt Bernard Arthur Smart on 21st August 1917. He was aboard *Yarmouth* as pilot of her Pup, N6430, when the Zeppelin *L.23* was sighted, and he found himself making his first take-off from the ship's flying-off deck with intent to kill. In his own account,* written to his mother a few days after the action, he said '….that the lively little plane rose like a bird without using even the 16ft run of the platform'. Smart succeeded in climbing until he was well above the German airship; diving to gain enough speed to overtake his target, he opened fire at 250 yards. His first burst was too high; correcting his aim, he fired again, and his shots ignited the Zeppelin, which fell, an incandescent mass, into the sea below.

Smart, too, was obliged to come down on the sea, having no landing area available to him. His Pup was fitted with inflatable air bags within the fuselage and was not in imminent danger of sinking, but he did not have long to wait until boats from HMS *Prince* picked him up. The engine and machine-gun from N6430 were salvaged, but the sea-soaked airframe was abandoned. Smart was appointed to the DSO for his action.

Flt Cdr W.G.Moore, DSC, RN, made a less productive and more uncomfortable sortie on a Pup (N6450), from HMS *Furious* on 11th September 1917. At 0725 that morning he was sent off from the ship in fruitless pursuit of a Zeppelin that had been sighted from the bridge at 06.56. Moore saw nothing of it, despite a protracted search, and was lucky to sight the ships of the British Naval force just in time to ditch within reach of them at 08.35. He was rescued by HMS *Mystic*, which destroyed the remains of his Pup at 08.49**.

---

* **Note:** *For the full text thereof, see 'Zeppelin', by R.L.Rimell, (Conway Maritime Press. 1984), pages 194-6.*
** **Note:** *Moore gave an amusing and graphic account of this mission and its waterlogged end in his book 'Early Bird', (Putnam, 1963).*

Flt Lt B.A.Smart, DSO, who, as a Flight Sub-Lieutenant flying Pup N6430 from Yarmouth's flying platform destroyed the Zeppelin L.23 on 21st August 1917. (Fleet Air Arm Museum)

Appreciably more hazardous than the deck troughs was this installation, made early in August 1917 on Pup 9922 at Grain by that station's Experimental Depot. As explained in the text, the underwing tandem wheels were deeply grooved to run on parallel rails, and the interplane struts were visibly more substantial than standard.

Other ideas for getting anti-Zeppelin fighters airborne from warships were devised and tried at Port Victoria and the Isle of Grain. The troughs that Rutland had so sensibly discarded from *Yarmouth* were not immediately abandoned; experiments in their use continued into 1918 at Grain, on *Vindex* and on *Pegasus*, but they were not adopted for general use.

The Beardmore-built Type 9901a Pup No.9922 was used in trials of a hair-raising method of take-off from a ship. To the underside of each lower mainplane of the Pup, directly under the interplane struts (which were of more substantial dimensions than the standard struts), was attached a framework that provided bearings for two deeply grooved wheels

These three frames are taken from a film of a take-off made by 9922 from a trackway of trestle-borne rails on the dummy deck at the Isle of Grain, evidently on 16th August 1917. They show:
(a) the port underwing wheels in place on their rail;
(b) the Pup being pushed manually along the trackway: as in (a), the main landing wheels can be seen to be clear of the deck;
(c) the aircraft, with pilot in the cockpit and engine running, just starting its take-off run.

(Imperial War Museum)

arranged in tandem; these wheels were about 8 inches in diameter and their centres were approximately 3ft apart. The wheels were to run along two parallel rails of alarmingly small cross-section and, as the illustrations show, this was successfully tested at Grain. It is not clear how such a trackway could be mounted on the ship in a suitable position, elevated sufficiently to allow the aircraft to clear all parts of the ship. It was probably hoped that such a structure would be relatively easy to erect and dismantle without seriously impeding the use of the ship's armament.

The date of the trials is not known, but the Pup had been thus modified in August 1917, and at least one take-off was safely accomplished and filmed. Nevertheless, one can only wonder why time and effort were expended on such a scheme. the operational perils and difficulties of which were so terrifyingly obvious. No.9922 was still wearing its underwing tandem wheels early in September 1917, when it was photographed at Grain with its landing wheels in troughs on the circular experimental deck.

Experiments in catapult launching of aircraft were conducted at Hendon. The Admiralty Air Department had considered the use of catapults in 1914, but had shelved the idea; it was taken up again in 1917, when a catapult made by Messrs Waygood Otis to the design of R.F.Carey was installed at Hendon. What was described as 'a modified Avro aeroplane', was successfully launched piloted by Flt Cdr R.E.Penny, who had volunteered to pilot the aircraft. At least seven Avros, designated 504H, were converted for catapult launching, presumably to provide training in the technique.

Two Beardmore-built Pups, 9948 and 9949, were delivered to Hendon in May 1917 direct from the Beardmore works. specifically for catapult experiments. No.9948 arrived on 16th May and No.9949 on, or shortly before, 24th May. The former was not reported as ready for testing until 30th May, at which time instructions for the erection of 9949 were still awaited. By

3rd June, 9948 was flying: it made occasional local flights, as on 5th June, when it was flown by Wg Cdr A.M.Longmore, and on 9th June by Flt Cdr E.H.Dunning. On 9th June the fuselage of 9949 was sent to the Waygood Otis works; four days later it was reported that its wings had been sent to the Central Supply Depot at White City, yet on 14th June they were reported to be at the Isle of Grain. On that day 9949's fuselage returned to Hendon.

It is believed that 9948 undertook some form of catapult test at Hendon on 24th June 1917. Evidently it was decided to discontinue the use of Pups in the catapult trials: on 13th August, Hendon reported that the catapult gear was being removed from 9949; a week later the removal of this gear from 9948 was similarly reported. By 1st September, 9948 had been badly damaged, and on that date 9949 was sent off by rail, bound for East Fortune, where it arrived on 8th September. A week later it was transferred to Donibristle, and by 29th September it was aboard HMS *Nairana*. Two weeks later, by 13th October, 9949 was allotted to HMS *Furious* for deck-landing trials, but the ship was at that time undergoing extensive modification at Newcastle (see page 112), and this Pup was again reported to be at Donibristle as at 29th December 1917. It later took part, to its detriment, in the flying experiments on *Furious* (see page 119); at one time it had a deck gear skid undercarriage. No.9949 remained in use, continuing to fly in deck-flying trials on HMS *Argus* as late as November 1919. Its stablemate 9948 was still at East Fortune on 30th March 1918, designated for service with carriers, but did not survive until the war ended.

As for the catapult trials, the Admiralty had decided in June 1917 to transfer work on the contemporary Armstrong catapult to shipboard - specifically to the installation on the steam hopper *Slinger* - but three Avro 504Hs were officially allocated to Hendon for catapult experiments on 24th September 1917, and were still there at the end of March 1918.

On 1st September 1917, Harry Busteed flew 9922, 'testing troughs off deck'. Dated 7th September,1917, this photograph shows the Pup with its landing wheels in troughs and its tailskid supported on a Tail Guide Trestle. All of this furniture is set up on the dummy deck at Grain.

Chapter 18

Gun-turret Platforms

Successful though Smart's *Yarmouth*-launched mission had been, the fixed flying-off deck made it essential that the ship steam into wind for the launching of the aircraft. This not only imposed obvious limitations but could also expose the launching ship to danger and reduce the overall formation strength of the squadron of ships. It ruled out completely any possibility of using similar fixed platforms on battleships and battle-cruisers.

An ingenious solution to the problem was proposed by Lt Cdr C.H.B.Gowan, who had been *Yarmouth*'s gunnery officer at the time of Rutland's experiments. This was to use one of a ship's gun turrets as a turntable: a flying-off platform mounted on top of the turret could be trained into the 'felt' wind, enabling an aeroplane to be launched without obliging the ship to alter course.

To test Gowan's idea, a platform was built on to 'B' Turret of the battle cruiser HMS *Repulse*; it had a downward slope over the gun barrels. On 1st October 1917, Sqn Cdr F.J.Rutland made a successful take-off in Pup N6453 while *Repulse* was steaming at 24kts; the turret was trained at 42 degrees on the starboard bow, and the 'felt' wind of 31.5mph (27.36kts) was ample to ensure a ready take-off. The platform was transferred aft to 'Y' Turret and installed to face over the tail of the turret; and on 9th October, with the turret on a starboard bearing of 63 degrees, Rutland again made a faultless take-off. Gowan's idea was convincingly vindicated, Rutland's skill was again

demonstrated, and the way was clear for the Navy's larger ships to be provided with anti-Zeppelin fighter aircraft.

This was one of the subjects discussed at a meeting between the Deputy First Sea Lord and the Commander-in-Chief: Beatty's views were set down in a memorandum that was discussed by the Operations Committee of the Board of Admiralty. All of this must have happened shortly after Admiralty policy on Aircraft in Ships had been set out in a letter to Admiral Beatty dated 25th September 1917, which had adumbrated a number of progressive developments, and on the subject of anti-Zeppelin fighters had said:

'The 30 fighting machines though probably sufficient to deal with Zeppelins and any "heavier than air" craft at present carried with the-High Sea Fleet may not fulfil requirements in the future, and it is therefore proposed by the Admiralty to increase the number of fighters by fitting as many additional Cruisers and light Cruisers as possible on the lines of the *Glorious* and *Yarmouth*. The Commander-in-Chief's opinion on this point is required and if the proposal is concurred in the Commander-in-Chief is requested to select the vessels to be fitted.

'NOTE: Up to the present it is not certain to what extent Seaplanes or Aeroplanes are being carried with the High Sea Fleet.'

Type 9901a Pup N6453 on 'B' Turret of HMS Repulse.

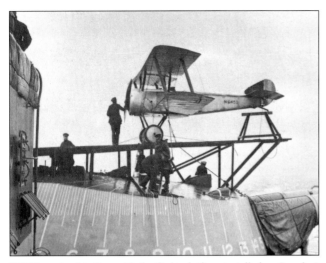

N6453 again, this time with the flight platform installed on Repulse's 'Y' Turret and facing over the tail of the turret.

N6443 on the turret platform of HMS Tiger. In this case the Tail Guide Trestle has an extended rail.

Now, however, the success of the *Repulse* turret trials opened up new possibilities, and on 17th October 1917 it was decided that:

'(i)   All light cruisers and battle cruisers should carry fighting aeroplanes, provided their gun armament, was not interfered with.

'(ii)   That the *Furious* should be fitted with an after landing deck, 300 feet in length, with such modification of the ship's structure as was entailed thereby.

'(iii) That the *Courageous* and *Glorious* should not be fitted in the same manner as the *Furious*, but should remain unaltered.

'(iv)   That it was unnecessary at that time to determine whether the *Argus* should be used exclusively as a torpedo-plane carrier.'

(The War in the Air, Vol. IV, pp.30-31)

Work on the fitting of turret platforms on battle cruisers was put in hand at once, and by early 1918 nine battle cruisers (*Australia, Indomitable, Inflexible, Lion, New Zealand, Princess Royal, Renown, Repulse* and *Tiger*) and two large light cruisers (*Glorious* and *Courageous*) had been equipped; rotatable platforms had also been designed as replacements for fixed platforms on light cruisers. The first such ship to have a revolving platform was HMAS *Sydney*, and the *Birkenhead, Chatham, Melbourne* and *Southampton* soon followed. Ironically, *Yarmouth* did not receive her new platform until June 1918, HMS *Dublin* not until August 1918.

Not many of these various warships had Pups, for they had been largely replaced by 2F.1 Camels by the time the platforms were completed. In practice, difficulties arose when fighter aircraft had to be carried to sea lashed to their platforms and the supporting guns had to be fired: the concussive and blast effects were such that the lightly built 2F.1 Camels were all but shaken

An early experiment in deck landing at Grain, in which 9497 (now marked N9497) was fitted with an arrester hook and a skeletal propeller guard to prevent damage by the system of arrester ropes or cables,. This photograph bears no date, but must have been contemporary (c.March 1917) with photographs on page 116.

HMS Furious in her initial configuration, with only a forward flying deck and her after 18-inch gun still in place.   (via P.H.T.Green)

to pieces and were certainly rendered unairworthy. Even without this near-seismic problem, it was difficult to protect the aircraft adequately against wind and water.

All such platform-launched fighters, when operating with the Fleet at sea and beyond reach of land, had no alternative but to ditch when their mission ended. It has been stated many times that the cost of a complete Pup was roughly equal to that of a single shell for one of the big guns, and for a time at least it was held that, especially if the prize were the destruction of a Zeppelin, ship-launched Pups were expendable. This line of thinking apparently overlooked the fact that shells were not reusable, whereas if an aircraft could be safely landed on a suitable ship it could serve its fleet again - as could, incomparably more importantly, its pilot; for the pilots of ditched and unseaworthy aeroplanes could not with certainty count on being rescued uninjured. Shells, on the other hand, were not manned.

The fact that the Royal Navy was at one time prepared to accept that its ship-launched fighters would have to ditch should not be interpreted as indicating that it was indifferent to the question of deck landings: the reverse was the case.

When Flt Cdr H.A.Williamson drew up his proposals for an aircraft carrier (see page 103), he conceived the ship to be a true floating aerodrome, capable of landing-on her aircraft after flight. To this end he included in his design a system of arrester/retaining wires arranged fore and aft on the deck and stretched over an inclined ramp. Trials of this scheme were conducted at Grain about the turn of the year 1915/1916, but the experiments were not further pursued because at that time the Navy had no ship capable of providing a suitable flight deck.

On 9th August 1916, Rear Admiral F.C.T.Tudor, Third Sea Lord, sent to the Director of Air Services a paper setting out proposals for the design and armament of aircraft capable of attacking Zeppelins. The matter was discussed at a conference, following which Rear Admiral Tudor set out a summary, dated 1st September 1916, of the principal requirements: these were for heavier and more destructive armament, most of it of a size and nature that could not have been carried and deployed by any aircraft then capable of taking off at sea.

However, Tudor's initial paper of 9th August 1916 had been, to some extent, inspired by Lt Freeman's attempt of 2nd August to attack the Zeppelin *L.17* in his *Vindex*-launched Bristol Scout (see page 101), and he had evidently recognised the potential of carrier-borne aeroplanes as anti-Zeppelin aircraft. Tudor must have been aware of the ideas and proposals for aircraft carriers that had been put forward a year earlier by Flt Cdr Williamson, and he had recognised that such ships offered the possibility of landing-on their aircraft.

Rear Admiral Tudor therefore ordered the resumption of the RNAS's experiments in deck landing, and work began without delay. On 19th September 1916, an Avro 504 fitted

with a rigid hook was tested at the Isle of Grain; flown by Flt Lt M.E.A.Wright, its landings were made into an arrangement of three arrester ropes. These had a 30lb sandbag at each end, were set up 20ft apart, and were supported 6in from the ground.

It is interesting to note that the purpose of the ropes was to arrest the aircraft's landing run. The landings were, of course, made on the aerodrome at Grain, where there was no ship's motion, nor was there any turbulence created by the ship's superstructure. The tests were nevertheless regarded as encouraging, and it was requested that a wooden deck 200ft square should be built at a cost of about £800 to permit better practice and training in landing on a ship. This was approved on 3rd October 1916 by the Third Sea Lord (Rear Admiral Tudor), with the sensible amendment suggested, by Rear Admiral C.L.Vaughan-Lee, Director of Air Services, that the deck be circular and 210ft in diameter.

This deck was in use by mid-February 1917, and from then until the Armistice the men of Port Victoria and the Isle of Grain worked unremittingly on many devices intended to improve deck flying. The earliest recorded deck-landing experiment looked like a continuation of the trials of September 1916, using an Avro 504C (No.1485) fitted with a hinged hook that engaged transverse ropes supported 2ft above the deck surface and weighted at their extremities by sandbags.

A few weeks later similar landings were made by the Pup 9497, which had been fitted with a light frame to protect the propeller, and an inadequate-looking hook hinged to the lower longerons in perilously fragile fashion and pulled down by a length of rubber bungee cord. It will be recalled that No.9497 had been allocated to Grain for deck-flying experiments as early as 4th September 1916 and had been delivered to Port Victoria on 1st November 1916.

It and several other Pups* gave yeoman service at Grain in trying out the various devices and techniques that were explored there in developing practical deck flying. They were also used in ditching experiments, the design and development of emergency flotation gear, and occasionally as Home Defence fighters. In all of these activities 9497 participated, although its part in Home Defence was confined to one sortie flown by Flt Lt C.T.Freeman on 13th June 1917.

__Note:__ There were 18 Pups at Grain Experimental Depot on 3rd January 1918: 9497, 9898, 9912, 9922, 9939, N6167, N6176, N6203, N6468, B2217, B5939, B5940, B5968-5970 and B6002-B6004. At that date B2217, B5939, B5940, B5968-B5970 and B6002-B6004 were without engines; all the others had 80hp Le Rhônes. All had been allocated to Grain for use in deck-flying experiments, the majority of them on 4th and 7th December 1917.

Connections between Grain and HMS *Furious* were strong and virtually continuous until the war ended, for the ship was the only vessel that could provide the conditions that enabled RNAS pilots to put into practice some of the ideas and inventions that originated at the experimental station, *Furious* had been designed to be a fast battle-cruiser with primary armament of two 18-inch guns, one forward and the other aft. As early as 14th July 1916, while *Furious* was under construction, an Admiralty letter informed the Commander-in-Chief Grand Fleet that it was ' ... hoped to arrange for Seaplanes to be carried in *Courageous*, *Glorious* and *Furious*, if this can be done without delaying considerably the completion of the ships'.

By March 1917, *Furious* had been modified to carry two seaplanes and a portable flying-off platform, but at a meeting held on 13th March it was decided that the ship's aircraft capacity should be greatly increased by removing the forward 18in gun, its mounting turret and some upper-deck armour, to permit the fitting of a large (228ft x 50ft) flying deck forward of the bridge and superstructure. At that time *Furious* was still regarded primarily as a seaplane carrier, and when she was commissioned in June 1917 under Capt Wilmot S.Nicholson, RN, her aircraft complement was three Short 184 seaplanes and five Sopwith Type 9901a Pups. These can only have been N6450-N6454, which were delivered from Beardmores direct to Messrs Armstrong at Newcastle, in whose yard *Furious* was converted. These five Type 9901a Pups were accepted between 6th and 15th June 1917. In overall charge of the flying from *Furious* was Sqn Cdr E.H.Dunning; his senior flying officer

Flt Lt (later Squadron Commander) Edwin Harris Dunning, DSC, who, with his skilful landings on Furious, bade fair to equal the talents and accomplishments of Rutland, but was cruelly denied further opportunities.   *(Fleet Air Arm Museum)*

Pups were put aboard Furious by placing them on a crude catamaran-form raft consisting of two Wight seaplane floats connected by a framework of timbers; the aircraft were then towed out to the carrier. Here the subject is N6451.   *(Fleet Air Arm Museum)*

N6453, the Pup on which Sqn Cdr Dunning made his first successful landing on Furious's forward deck, is here seen on Smoogroo airfield, which provided a local land base for the aircraft of ships anchored in Scapa Flow.   *(Fleet Air Arm Museum)*

An early attempt by Dunning to land on Furious's deck, possibly his first successful landing, made on 2nd August.1917. N6453 was without armament on this occasion, and was distinguished by an unpainted patch of new fabric on the outboard end of the lower starboard aileron. It had no grab-toggles at any point. Although the Pup is well forward above the deck it was probably stationary, or nearly so, in relation to the ship, and one officer is reaching up to grasp the trailing edge of the port lower wing.

was Flt Cdr W.G.Moore, who provided an informative account of the early days aboard the carrier in his book *Early Bird*. On joining the Fleet, *Furious* sailed from Newcastle, where she had been converted, to Scapa Flow. Geoffrey Moore recounts how the ship's pilots were able to practise take-offs with the ship at anchor; they landed at a small airfield hastily established at Smoogroo Bay.

Another of the pilots was FSL W.F.Dickson (later Marshal of the Royal Air Force Sir William Dickson, GCB, KBE, DSO, AFC), who recalled, in a BBC recorded interview in 1975:

> 'Now when *Furious* was in harbour at Scapa Flow we used to practise flying from a small airfield called Smoogroo, and when we flew alongside our ship and waved to our friends aboard we had this idea: couldn't we possibly somehow land back on this rather splendid flying-off deck; we explored the possibilities of it; of coming up alongside and rolling our wheels along the deck.' (Quoted by Alan Johnson in his book *Fly Navy*, David & Charles, 1981)

Attempts to perform this considerable feat were made by Sqn Cdr E.H.Dunning, DSC. He succeeded on his first approach, made on 2nd August 1917, with *Furious* making 26 knots into a 21-knot wind, thus giving a 47-knot airstream over the deck. Dunning approached along the port side of the ship crabbed to starboard until he was centred over the deck, and cut his engine. The Pup was seized manually by a deck party of other pilots who, according to Geoffrey Moore (who was one of them), '...had some difficulty hauling the aircraft down squarely on to the deck and holding it in the wind, but we did so and the aircraft was secured without damage and Dunning stepped out.'

It is extremely doubtful whether precision flying of this particular kind could have been contemplated on any other type of aircraft at that time. The Pup's exceptional controllability, responsiveness and lack of vices could be exploited by a pilot of Dunning's skill to achieve this remarkable result.

Five days later Dunning made a second landing on *Furious*' deck, but it was a gustier day, the deck party were unable to prevent his Pup from being blown backwards, and the elevators struck the coaming of the hatch of the below-deck hangar, sustaining damage that grounded the aircraft. This did not satisfy Dunning. Geoffrey Moore was sitting in N6452, waiting his turn to make a flight and landing, but Dunning ordered him out of his Pup and took it over for a further run.

A good muster of some of HMS Furious' ship's company gathered round N6453 as Dunning eased himself out of the cockpit. These men had witnessed history being made.

On 7th August 1917 Dunning again landed on Furious's deck. This time N6453 had its Lewis gun in position, and grab-ropes had been fitted under the lower wings and fuselage to ease the task of the deck party, who in effect had to do what the various systems of arrester/securing gear were intended to do. Geoffrey Moore, who was one of those involved, identified the officers in this photograph as (left to right) Langton, W.F.Dickson, A.N.Gallehawk, R.K.Thyne, F.M.Fox, R.D.G.Sibley, W.D.Jackson and Moore himself.

Dunning's touch-down in N6452. which he had taken over from Geoffrey Moore after N6453 had sustained elevator damage. This photograph shows how far forward on the deck the Pup was: it also suggests that the aircraft might have been held down had Dunning not decided to try again. N6452 had no gun fitted.

With its engine choked and unresponsive, N6452 plunges over the starboard side.

One of the deck party who was present at all of Dunning's flights was P/O Walter O.Porter, who kept a diary at the time. His relevant entries were:

'2nd August 1917 Pentland Firth for sight setting.
                           6453 Pilot Sq. Com. Dunning
                           alighted on deck 11.10am.
3rd August   Changed Lang prop to original prop
                           and sent 6450 off deck. Cleaning
                           engine and taking off cowling 6453.
6th August   Cleaned engine of 6453, worked very
                           hard, had it finished by dinner time.
                           New W.O. in charge now.
                           Tested engine of 6452.
7th August   Drained petrol out of 6453 and 6452.
                           Fixing cowling to 6453 during dinner
                           hour. Sq Com Dunning left deck
                           1.30pm and landed 2pm. Skidded
                           backwards into hatch coaming and
                           damaged tail, afterwards took 6452
                           and made three attempts, last one
                           ending fatally.'

It is not clear whether the 'three attempts' recorded by P/O Porter were full circuits and approaches or merely three essays at touching down. Whatever the circumstances, on Dunning's final attempt he arrived slightly too high over the deck and touched down too far forward: he waved away the handling party and, intending to go round again, opened-up the engine; but it choked, the aircraft stalled and fell over the starboard side of the ship. The impact stunned Dunning, and by the time *Furious* had managed to heave to and get a boat away he had drowned.

This tragedy led to a ban on further attempts to land on the flying deck; no further landings were made, but FSL W.D.Jackson and Flt Lt F.M.Fox made

The wreckage of N6452, about to be hoisted aboard Furious.

Such was the force of the impact that stunned Dunning that the engine cowling was virtually moulded round the Le Rhône. Despite the nature of the trials, it is clear that N6452 did not have the underwing flotation bags fitted.

A Pup on the forward deck of Furious, its attitude suggesting that its tailskid is on a Tail Guide Trestle. In the foreground is a captive take-off dolly used by seaplanes when flying off the deck.

Two Pups on Furious's flying deck, their wheels straddling the fore-and-aft slot in which the seaplane dolly ran. The palisade structures were wind-breaks that could be raised when necessary.

Sqn Cdr Busteed, a strongly motivating personality in the evolution of deck-flying techniques, in N6453 on Furious, apparently holding the Pup in flying attitude simply by use of the elevators in the slipstream: the aircraft is being restrained by lines attached to the underwing picketing points. This photograph is dated 27th August 1917, three weeks after Dunning's fatal accident, yet the tip of the lower starboard aileron remains unpainted.

Elegant in form but of questionable strength, this early arrester hook had been fitted to 9497 by 8th March 1917, the date of this RNAS Grain photograph. The hook is virtually identical with the one that had been tested on the Avro 504C No.1485 two weeks earlier,

Arrester hook lowered, 9497 crosses the perimeter of the circular deck at Grain. This photograph bears the date 16th March 1917.

The sandbag-weighted arrester ropes were raised above the deck surface on the wooden supports seen in the foreground of this breezy photograph, also dated 16th March 1917, which captures the moment when 9497's hook engaged the first rope. With the arresting ropes at such a height above the deck the need for the propeller guard on the Pup is evident.

Understandably, first thoughts on the fitting of skids in place of wheels were that some form of springing should be retained. This resulted in the relatively complex arrangement seen here on (it is believed) 9922; it retained the V-struts of the wheel undercarriage. This photograph is dated 24th September 1917, at which time the aircraft had an articulated arrester hook pivoted on a pylon under the centre of gravity.

This detail view provides a clearer impression of the skid undercarriage, the arrester hook, and its inverted-pyramid mounting. (Philip Jarrett)

experimental landing approaches on 11th October 1917; Jackson flew N6449 and made five runs over the flying deck. When Sqn Cdr F.J.Rutland was appointed to *Furious* as Dunning's successor he, too, tried similar approaches, in one of which he touched down on the deck and flew off again.

A more constructive consequence of Dunning's death was a proposal to fit *Furious* with an aft deck for landing-on her aircraft. This was opposed by her Commander, Capt Wilmot Nicholson, who, in a telegram dated 12th September 1917, pointed out that such a deck, located abaft the funnel and superstructure would suffer from eddy currents of air that would make-landing-on hazardous, and that it would be very difficult to transfer aircraft forward from the landing-on deck to the flying-off deck. He also recorded the further objection that the inevitable removal of the after armament would deprive the ship of any conventional offensive capability.

Capt Nicholson's representations were not accepted, and *Furious* returned to Newcastle for her second major alteration. An Admiralty letter to Beatty dated 25th September 1917, claimed that 'a landing deck of over 400 feet in length would be obtained while the only structures above it liable to cause air disturbances are the fore bridge, fore mast and funnel, which lend themselves to streamlining'. In reality, the modified *Furious* had a landing deck only 284ft long, and her upperworks had no streamlining. This being so, even greater importance attached to suitable arrester/securing gear.

RNAS Grain had resumed its experimental work on deck landing in September 1916, and by 8th March 1917 Pup 9497 had been fitted with its arrester hook; it was making arrested landings on the dummy deck on 16th March, relying on transverse arrester ropes rigged 15ft apart and attached to sandbags. Results showed that such end-weighted ropes had to be hooked dead centre, otherwise the aircraft slewed to the side of the shorter length of rope: if reproduced on a ship's deck such a reaction might send the aircraft overboard.

Modifications and variations of systems of hooks, ropes, wires and cables were tried; in particular, longitudinal wires were adopted to minimise the likelihood of an arrested aircraft going over the side. These wires were anchored at deck-surface level aft, converging from 1 foot to 4 inches in spacing, and

The same Pup with a rigid-skid undercarriage, in a photograph dated 6th December 1917.

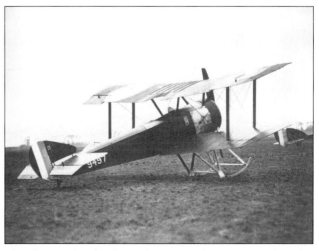

This photograph, of 18th March 1918, is of 9497 (its serial number restored to N-less correctness) with a rigid-skid undercarriage. Retaining horns are fitted to each skid just ahead of the bases of the V-struts.

their forward ends were secured to the top of a braking ramp that sloped up to a height of 14 inches.

A remarkable departure, on both Pups and 1½ Strutters, was the substitution of wooden skids for wheels in the undercarriage. It was reasoned that skids offered more braking friction on touchdown than wheels, and they had the additional advantage of more readily allowing securing horns to be fitted: these, once trapped under the fore-and-aft wires, provided a secure restraint that could hold the aircraft on the deck.

One of the earliest skid-undercarriage installations - perhaps even the first - was made on the Beardmore-built Pup 9922. In July 1917 this Pup was flown by Harry Busteed, who noted in his log-book: 'Testing landing on skids: entirely satisfactory.' That skid undercarriage may have been the one seen in the accompanying photograph, which bore the date 24th September 1917. It was quite an elaborate affair, for it retained the basic V-struts, half-axles and rubber shock-cord of the wheel undercarriage. The skids were attached to the

half-axles as direct replacements for the wheels; their various struts formed complex and drag-producing structure, but the whole provided springing for the skids.

This Pup also had a single-arm arrester hook the engaging end of which was large and articulated. The upper end of the hook arm was pivoted to an inverted pyramid of struts so positioned that the pivot point lay more or less vertically in line with the aircraft's centre of gravity, and some to ten inches below the underside of the fuselage. The inverted pyramid looked impossibly frail, and the skids had no securing horns to engage fore-and-aft wires.

By 9th November 1917, 9922 had been fitted with a rigid-skid undercarriage. In this the abandonment of any form of shock absorber resulted in a lighter and less complex structure. The basic V-struts were increased in length sufficiently to retain the normal ground angle of the Pup, and a third strut on each side secured the forward ends of the skids. A similar undercarriage had been fitted to 9497 by 22nd December, when it was flown by Busteed. By mid-March 1918 the skids on 9497 had been fitted with simple horns just ahead of the base of the main V-strut.

In that month *Furious* returned to the Fleet with her 284 x 70ft landing-on deck fitted, and retaining her funnel, foremast and conning-tower structure centrally: narrow gangways connected the after deck to the forward in a less-than-satisfactory attempt to provide a means of transferring aircraft from one deck to the other. In a letter written late in December 1917 but probably not despatched until 2nd January 1918, the Admiralty requested Sir W.G.Armstrong, Whitworth & Co Ltd to install in *Furious* a form of arrester gear designed. by that firm. Perhaps the necessary design and experimental work had still to be undertaken, for the first arrester gear fitted to the ship was the system of fore-and-aft wire cables with forward ramp

HMS Furious after her reconstruction with a landing-on deck abaft the superstructure, showing the connecting gangways between the forward and after decks: these were supposed to facilitate the transfer forward of aircraft that had landed on the after deck. The two aircraft visible, one with wings off, the other fully rigged, are Sopwith 1½ Strutters.

Clearly visible in this photograph of HMS Furious, immediately abaft the funnel, is the structure supporting the rope mantlet seen in the photographs that follow.
(J.Blenky)

Dated 25th March 1918, these three photographs show the unfortunate conclusion of a landing on Furious by 9949. Whatever horns its skids had must have been torn off; consequently the aircraft overran the braking ramp and was forcibly arrested by the rope safety mantlet. No.9949 was one of the two Beardmore-built Pups that had earlier been sent to Hendon for experiments in launching by catapult.

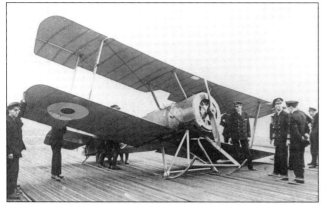

The skid undercarriage did not take kindly to side loads. In this, case the aircraft had only the same retaining horns as 9497 illustrated on page 117, but arrival on Furious's deck was more fraught than alighting on the dummy deck at Grain. As can be seen, the closely spaced fore-and-aft wires greatly impeded movement by deck personnel.

Epitomising Geoffrey Moore's description of skid Pups 'dropping on the deck like shot partridges.', C214 had evidently overshot the braking ramp with greater force than 9949 and suffered an undercarriage collapse in consequence. This Pup was at RNAS East Fortune on 11th January 1918, and was still on the strength of that station in March 1918; this photograph is one of several that bore the date 3rd April 1918 but probably recorded events occurring a few days earlier.

Dated 15 April 1918, this photograph records a landing by Lt W.F. Dickson, RAF, on Furious's after deck. It illustrates how the fore-and-aft wires were supported on skittle-shaped wooden supports.

Dickson's Pup after its landing. Its arrangement, of two sets of horns on each skid, supplemented by a V-form horn mounted centrally on the rear spreader bar, had been devised and tested at Grain late in March 1918.

Similarly equipped was N6438, flown to a successful landing on 15th April 1918 by Capt A.N.Gallehawk, RAF.

N6438 had poorer luck next day. The note that accompanied the original of this photograph ran 'Machine running along deck towards ropes. (Taken at 10 yards)'. Evidently the photographer had great faith in the protective capabilities of Furious's rope mantlet.

And the landing run ended in this untidy fashion, the Pup's inscription "EXCUSE ME" a mutely ironic commentary on its legless posture.

The undercarriage of Capt W.R.D. Acland's aircraft had three V-form horns under the rear spreader bar of its undercarriage.

Capt W.R.D. Acland's landing concluded faultlessly with his Pup neatly secured at the forward end of the braking ramp. It was to remain there for some time, it seems, for its engine had been covered when this photograph (dated 19th April 1918) was taken.   (RAF Museum)

In the wartime experimental work on deck-flying techniques and equipment no individual aircraft did more than N6190, one of the eight Pups that had reduced stagger of 15 inches. Already a veteran of operational service with No.4 (Naval) Squadron, April - May 1917, and No.11 (Naval) Squadron, July 1917, it had been transferred to Dover on 11th October, and was with the War School at Manstone by 20th October. Administratively, it was apparently still on Manstone's strength at the end of March 1918 although it was physically at Grain. This photograph, taken at Grain, is dated 14th March 1918; in it, N6190 is seen with two sets of horns on each of its skids, and it may have been used in experimental trials of this arrangement.

that had been developed at Grain under the direction of Sqn Cdr Harry Busteed.

Once *Furious* was back with the Fleet, no time was lost in starting a series of landing-practice flights. Her Commander, Capt Nicholson, had pointed out in his telegram of 12th September (see page 117) that the turbulence created by the ship's funnel and superstructure would make landing-on an aft-positioned deck hazardous. One of the pilots in the tests was Geoffrey Moors; that he and his colleagues shared Nicholson's opinion was made clear in *Early Bird*, pp.121-2:

'All this [arrester gear] looked good, but it was immediately clear to us pilots, sensitive as we were to airflow and to the fickle behaviour of the wind, that landing was not going to be easy.

'The Naval constructors seemed to have overlooked the fact that when a ship is steaming at thirty knots into a wind, the air currents behind all the superstructure - bridge, mainmast, and funnel - lying amidships created a backwash. There were eddies of air there, following along with the ship, and the hot gases from the funnel did not help either. We had a big net spread abaft the funnel so that we did not fly into it. This net was subsequently replaced by vertical ropes, but that wasn't the real trouble. The trouble was that directly we got over the stern of the ship our air speed, on which we depended for keeping us airborne, diminished because the air was going with us, and we just dropped on the deck like shot partridges.

'A lot of machines did land safely, but a lot of them got broken up on landing, and it was generally decided that, after all, that was not a very clever arrangement.

This was the end of deck-landing experiments for the time being. We were fed up with them.'

The accompanying photographs graphically confirm that the attrition rate was high. The victims of the aft-deck turbulence even included Sqn Cdr Rutland, whose Pup was blown across the deck, turned upside down when its skids struck the bulwark, and fell over the side: it was saved from falling into the sea by a sparking plug of its engine catching in a countersunk rivet hole. Rutland narrowly escaped serious injury by leaping out of the aircraft just before it ended up inverted; he plunged some 55ft into the sea with the ship making 28 knots and was rescued. His report of the incident was dated 28th March 1918; it concluded:

'I am of the opinion that the funnel gases are the cause of the trouble experienced, observing that practically no bumps were felt with an air speed of 20 knots in harbour. I consider that the question of eliminating these funnel gases should be gone into very closely.

'It appears to be very difficult, if not impossible, to land without drift: the skids will not stand drift neither will the present arresting gear allow machine to land with drift.'

With *Furious'* landing-on deck virtually proved unusable, and doubt cast on the advisability of using skid undercarriages, Grain carried on testing modifications and new forms of arrester gear. The *Furious* trials had demonstrated conclusively that arrester gear, in dealing with lightly loaded aircraft, had to be as effective in holding them down as in stopping their landing run.

The skid undercarriage of N6190: two pairs of horns on each skid, none under the spreader bar. Photograph taken 16th March 1918.

Another photograph dated 16th March 1918. In it N6190 is seen in the ideal position of final arrest on the experimental deck at Grain. the horns on its skids neatly and securely under the arrester wires, and the aircraft at the 'forward' end of the braking ramp. It was this system that was tried out on Furious.

A closer look at N6190's skid undercarriage on the ramp at Grain.

Landings on Grain's deck were not always so neatly placed nor so safely concluded as N6190's demonstration piece. In this case one of Grain's other Pups has gone over the side of the ramp and broken its undercarriage. The markings on the aircraft's mainplanes are unusual. This photograph is dated 10th September 1918.

Dated 10th September 1918, these two photographs depict the 'Hayrake and Comb' gear at Grains: the aircraft to which it was fitted was probably the long-suffering N6190. The first photograph is a three-quarter rear view of the arresting members before the test; the second is a front view with the 'rakes'/'combs' in the braking position.

Several attempts were made to use transverse wires, or a combination of fore-and-aft and transverse wires. An early transverse-wire arrangement known as the Sliding Cage was probably tested before the *Furious* trials were held; it proved to be prone to jamming, and several modifications failed to make it acceptable. It was intended both to arrest and to hold down the aircraft.

N6190 again, this time fitted with an arrester hook for experiments with a combination of fore-and-aft and transverse wires. The forward extensions to the skids had been fitted at an earlier date, presumably to protect the propeller in other experiments with transverse wires. This photograph is dated 13th September 1918, but unfortunately does not identify the gear by any specific name.

The fore-and-aft wire arrangement was tried next; subsequently transverse ropes with sandbags were added, and many trial landings were made. In the course of these, more than one type of hook was tried, and their installations varied. This scheme was abandoned, primarily because it took too long to rig the deck.

A so-called Friction Hook attached to the tailskid was tried late in July 1918, but, being so far aft, it accentuated the Pup's tendency to swerve across the deck; it also necessitated a very slow approach and tail-down landing. It, too, was abandoned.

The bucolically named Hayrake and Comb Gear of September 1918 was one of Grain's more bizarre devices. Its essential principle can be seen in the relevant photographs; in these it can also be seen that the landing skids were fitted with forward extensions. This was a wise addition for the 'hayrakes' had too abrupt an arresting action and, being so far below the Pup's centre of gravity, then tended to turn the aircraft over on its nose.

A system that seemed promising was the Sillars Gear. It was one of several suggestions sent to Grain from the Fleet, and was devised by ERA James Sillars of HMS *Iron Duke*. This combined fore-and-aft wires with sliding transverse ropes that were attached to rings running on diverging fore-and-aft wires spaced 30ft apart at the threshold and 60ft apart forward. When hooked and carried forward by the landing aircraft, these sliding ropes were quickly braked to a standstill by the divergence of their guide wires. This gear was repeatedly tested from August 1918 and was considered to be most suitable for aircraft with wheel undercarriages fitted with horns on the spreader bar.

With the same date, this photograph provides a close-up of N6190's hook at the time, engaged on one of the transverse wires. It also illustrates the rigging reminder, painted on above the serial number, that N6190 had non-standard stagger.

A week later, 20th September 1918, N6190 photographed after a hook-arrested landing on Grain's deck apparently devoid of fore-and-aft wires.

Grain's Threaded Axle Gear fitted to a skid Pup, here seen before use. The central wheel on the axle obviously had to be ineffective and maintained contact with the deck surface to be able to drive the braking jaws inwards.

After a properly executed - and securely held - landing the rotation of the wheel caused the jaws to travel inwards along the oppositely threaded halves of the axle, with increasing frictional pressure against the fore-and-aft cables. These photographs are dated 27th September 1918.

When applied to a wheel undercarriage, the Threaded Axle Gear needed no central driving wheel, and stood a slightly better chance of being effectively driven after initial touch-down. These 'before and after' photographs, taken at Grain, are dated 16th October 1918.

Almost as outlandish as the Hayrake and Comb Gear was the Threaded Axle Gear of late September 1918, the principle of which can be seen in the photographs that illustrate it. This was tried on a skid Pup, but work on a version for a wheel undercarriage was also initiated. Also tried at this time yet again on a long-suffering skid Pup, was the Eccentric Roller Gear, another friction-brake mechanism. A surviving photograph conveys no clear idea of the fittings involved.

Although the Armstrong Whitworth arrester gear* had, in effect been ordered off the drawing board for *Furious* in January 1918, it was late October before Grain was able to try out a test installation on a straight planked runway. The gear was another,

but different, combination of longitudinal and transverse wires, and the test Pup was the seemingly indestructible N6190, one of the eight built with 15 inches of stagger. It was tried on skids on the Armstrong Whitworth Gear on 28th October 1918, when its port skid was broken and its arrester hook damaged. Next it was tried again, this time with a wheel undercarriage and propeller guard, and its hook pivoted further aft.

** **Note:** The Armstrong-Whitworth gear was the subject of British Patent No.131,398, applied for on 24th June 1918. It was jointly in the names of the company and Lt Cdr Louis John le Mesurier, RN.*

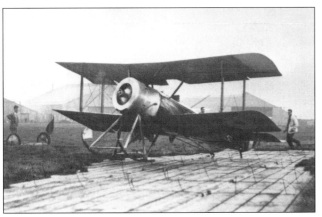

Tests of the Armstrong Whitworth arrester gear, evidently a wholly transverse wire system, were conducted on a special small deck at Grain. On the left N6190 on skids has touched down but is slewing to the right after the engagement of its hook. On the right a presumably later arrival has resulted in the collapse of the port skid structure and damage to the V-shaped hook frame. Both photographs are dated 28th October 1918.

The undercarriage of the Pup flown in the Argus trials by Lt Col R.B.Davies, VC, DSO, RAF, also in a photograph dated 23rd October 1918. Five of the nine horns have engaged wires. Conspicuously present is the frontal hydrovane, primarily fitted to prevent nosing over in the event of ditching, but doubling duty as a propeller guard.

This Pup was one of the first aircraft to undertake flying trials aboard HMS Argus late in 1918. Here a Pup flown by Lt A.R.Arnold, DSO, DFC, RAF, is about to touch down. The fore-and-aft wires are raised between two narrow ramps, and the aircraft has an array of nine V-form horns under its spreader bar. The date of this photograph is 23rd October 1918.

Yet the ever-resilient N6190 tried again next day. Here it is again. on 29th October1918, now on wheels and equipped with a propeller guard, touching down just in front of the first arrester wire of the Armstrong-Whitworth rig. Again the Pup slewed, but apparently sustained no damage.

Again the Pup slewed, but apparently sustained no damage.

permit of landing being made upon it....

'Its disadvantages are, considerable weight - about 180 tons for a deck 200ft by 60ft - great cost and time of construction and the fact that it must be built into the ship.'

The world's first purpose-designed aircraft carrier, HMS *Argus* (14,450 tons), was launched in December 1917 and commenced trials in September 1918. She had a full-length (567ft) flush deck wholly without obstruction or superstructure, and her intended complement of aircraft was to be eight reconnaissance, six anti-Zeppelin and four torpedo carriers. By late 1918, of course, her operational anti-Zeppelin aircraft would have been 2F.1 Camels, but in her early deck-landing trials at least one Pup was used. The Pup flights were made some time after the last of three sequences of trial landings flown on 24th and 26th September and 1st October, but on or before 23rd/24th October 1918. The earlier trials had apparently been flown by 1½ Strutters with wheel undercarriages. In like fashion the Pup flown by Lt-Col R.B.Davies, VC, DSO, and Lt A.R.Arnold, DSO, DFC, had wheels, and under its undercarriage spreader-bar were fitted no fewer than nine V-form horns to engage the fore-and-aft wires of *Argus'* arrester gear. Ahead of the wheels was mounted a curved hydrovane that doubled duty as an airscrew guard.

Pup with extensions on its skids and a ski on its hook, on the section of magnetic deck that reached Grain shortly before the Armistice. This photograph bears the date 31 October 1918.

On 31st October 1918, a Pup with steel-shod skids and a steel ski on its arrester hook was photographed on a section of magnetic deck. Evidently this was to be the next brainwave to be tried, but, as Grain lamented in a report:

'The holding-down ability of the deck can be measured but no exact arresting figures can be obtained as the small section of deck (20ft by 10ft) sent here does not

Chapter 19

Other Naval Experiments

In addition to the enormous amount of work that the Pup did in deck-landing experiments, the type was also used in several other fields of experimentation in Naval flying. The use of air-bags as emergency flotation gear on aircraft that had to fly over stretches of sea had been seen before the outbreak of war. Although the RNAS was not the original inventor of such equipment it did a great deal to develop it and to devise standard flotation gear for several different types of aircraft.

Leading much of the early work was Harry Busteed, who first turned his attention to the question while he was in command of RNAS Eastchurch. Early in March 1917 he took over command of Port Victoria Repair Depot, and shortly afterwards he began experimenting with air bags on Sopwith Pups. Initially he used the Beardmore-built 9901a, the type-eponymous Pup that he had received at Eastchurch.

As it was hoped to produce a form of flotation gear that would keep the ditched aircraft floating level instead of adopting the inevitable nose-down attitude produced by air-bags within the rear fuselage, the original idea was to fit spanwise air-bags along the underside of the lower wings at the leading edge. Stowed, they were folded flat against the wing surface, held in place by a long flap of fabric fixed along the leading edge and secured to the front spar by clips that could be released simultaneously by the pilot when inflation was required. This was provided by compressed air from a standard starting bottle via suitable injectors; when inflated the bags were tubular with domed ends. Each was 9ft 6in long and 16in in diameter when inflated; their volume was then 12.25 cuft. It was recognised that the wheel undercarriage would 'trip up' the aircraft on striking the water, so a jettisonable undercarriage was made and fitted. This was in course of installation on 1st May 1917, and its air-bags were being fitted three days later.

The first trial, made by Busteed himself on 12th May, was not an unqualified success. The undercarriage was dropped without trouble, but when the Pup struck the sea the covering of the fuselage underside was ripped off, and the inrush of water brought the aircraft into a nose-down attitude. Busteed himself recorded the result tersely:

'Testing drop chassis and landing in water. Air bags blew satisfactorily but machine had tendency to turn over on its nose in water.'

His Pup was retrieved, repaired and modified: between the attachment points of the undercarriage a planing surface of stiff plywood was mounted below the fuselage and a small duralumin hydrovane was attached to the tailskid, mounted at a negative angle in the hope that it would, if adequately immersed, hold the tail down. These remedies were effective: the next attempt, early in June, and several subsequent trials, were successful.

The wear and tear on the subject aircraft was considerable. After each test it was stripped and recovered, but it was stated that the Pup sustained no structural damage on any of its ditchings. The engine was stripped down and overhauled after the first two trials, 'but thereafter it was found sufficient to wash it out thoroughly with paraffin, inject copious castor oil, and then give it a short run.'

How many true Pups were fitted with the underwing Mk.I air-bags is not known, but in mid-July 1917 the Technical Committee of the Department of Aeronautical Supplies reported that '24 sets of wings for Sopwith Pups complete with the special air bag attachments are now in hand at Messrs Beardmore's, and when complete will be sent to those ships or stations where Pups are being used at present without air-bags.' Of the Pups built by Beardmore, 16 of the first batch (9901-9950) and all 30 of the second batch (N6430-N6459) were fitted for airbags. These flotation bags were also fitted to Beardmore S.B.3Ds and can be seen stowed in the photograph on page 132. A tail bag, designated Mk.II, was also made for the Pup, evidently for installation in the rear fuselage. This was also cylindrical with domed ends; it was 6ft 6in long and 12 inches in diameter, with a volume of 4.6 cu ft. Each Mark 1 bag weighed 4lb 3½oz, the Mark II a mere 1lb 10½oz. The production form of bag was made of 2-ply D fabric proofed to Specification 7/2.

Alternative fuselage-mounted bags of greater capacity were also developed at Grain. These were designated Mk.IV and existed in five sizes diminishing to conform to the tapering of an aircraft fuselage. Each was box-shaped with slight taper of depth and width; a suitable combination of sizes could fill much of the internal space within the rear fuselage. Photographs suggest that four bags (presumably the Mk IVb, IVc, IVd and IVe) were used on the Type 9901a Pup and the Beardmore S.B.3D; these weighed a total of 6lb 3½oz. Flotation tests in a hybrid Pup/S.B.3 airframe were undertaken late in April 1917, a date that suggests that at least part of the test airframe might have been contributed by the prototype S.B.3, No.9950, for the first production S.B.3 did not fly until late June.

From these trials pioneered by the Pups came a whole range of airbags of various shapes and sizes for many other types of aircraft: D.H.4, Handley Page 0/100, P.V. N50 and Grain Griffin, Sopwith 1½ Strutter and 2F.1 Camel, Voisin biplane, Hanriot HD-3, F.E.2b, D.H.6, D.H.9A, Vickers Vimy and others. Grain flotation gear was also tried out on American DH-4s after the war.

As at 7th November 1918, the Royal Air Force had in commission on naval duties 18 Pups and 10 Ship's Pups (with the formation of the new Service the RNAS designations of Type 9901 and Type 9901a had generally been dropped). Despite earlier antipathy towards the designation 'Pup', the former were listed as 'Sopwith Pup'. the latter, cumbrously, as 'Sopwith Pup, converted to ship aeroplane'. Fifteen Pups (C217, C1502, C1503, C1516-C1518, C1523, C1532, C1533, C1535, C1537-C1541) were at Turnhouse, and it seems that the five at Mudros (9942, N6432, N6433, N6470 and N6471) were all regarded as standard Type 9901 Pups, whereas N6432 and N6433 had earlier been listed as Type 9901a by the RNAS. The 10 'Ship's Pups' still in commission on 7th November 1918 were 9931, 9932 and 9944 at Smoogroo, 9949 and N6456 at Donibristle, and 9940, 9943, N6431, N6439 and N6455 at Turnhouse.

After the Armistice, experimental work at Grain did not stop completely, and several Pups, including B2217 (which in January 1918 had had an 80hp Clerget engine) remained in use. Early in 1920 both it and B5940 took part in trials of the

Overhead Landing Gear, Grain Type Mk.I. Initially seen (with almost surreal optimism) as yet another method of bringing aircraft on board ship, this required pilots to fly their aircraft on to an overhead wire cable by engaging a rigidly mounted overwing hook in a loop that was free to run along the cable. In the shipboard installation the loop-bearing cable was to be stretched between two booms carried outboard. Presumably (one hopes) this was only to be attempted with calm seas and light winds, but even in such conditions only an aircraft as docile and controllable as the Pup could conceivably hope to come anywhere near success. Nevertheless, it seems that Camels were also tried, at least on the Grain fixed-cable rig.

In the trials at Grain, the Pups had a very large cut-out made in the centre section to give the pilot a clear view of his aircraft's hook, the loop and the cable. The landing cable itself was apparently supported by four tall poles braced by guys; between each 'end' pair of poles ran transverse cables, to the mid-points of which the landing cable was anchored. Thus the pilot had to aim to fly between one end pair of poles and perform a kind of conjuring trick in engaging the hook in the loop at the moment of entering the rig.

On 2nd March, 1920 Harry Busteed logged a flight on B2217 as 'practice at landing on single wire (overhead)'. Two days later he made two similar flights on a Camel and one on a Pup, and at least four further Pup flights late in April. Against 15th June 1920, he recorded 'Single wire landing trials, Gerrard [possibly F/O J.Gerard] gets on but doesn't know'. Perhaps this refers to the aircraft seen in these two illustrations, which were dated 14th June 1920. In these, a biggish loop appears to be caught on the aircraft's hook: if events were as noted by Busteed, the Pup would probably be moving under some power up to the far end of the cable, where the loop could have broken away from the cable: such a sudden check to the aircraft's movement would have effectively stalled it and recovery would have been impossible. Busteed logged two more 'Wire practice' flights on a Camel on 21st June, but, as far as is known, no attempt was ever made to try the technique on a ship at sea. It was, however, regarded as a possible method of returning aeroplanes to airships.

At least two Pups were used in experiments on Parachute dropping late in 1917. These trials were flown at Cranwell; 9938 took part in them on 28th October and N6472 on 12th December 1917.

Dated 14th June.1920, these two photographs record the dishevelled end of an attempt to 'land' Pup B5940 on the Overhead Landing Gear, Grain Type Mk.I, as mentioned in the text. The poles in the background were the main supports of the cable system; the close-up photograph depicts the hook installation on the Pup's centre section, which has a large cut-out between the spars to enlarge the pilot's field of view. On the hook itself is an elliptical loop, which may have been the cable-borne receiver of the aircraft's hook.

Chapter 20

Beardmore W.B.III (S.B.3D, S.B.3F)

When the Pup was introduced to shipboard flying, the vessels from which it was to operate were small, and such hangar accommodation as they had was cramped and inadequate. At the time and in the circumstances, the wing-folding capability of contemporary carrier-borne Short seaplanes was clearly advantageous. The Sopwith company, too, had adapted the Schneider/Baby seaplane for on-board stowage by making the rear fuselage detachable.

With active consideration being given to the shipboard use of the Pup, the desirability of reducing its dimensions for stowage must have been readily perceived. This could only have been confirmed by practical examination of the physical implications of the early proposal to allocate the Beardmore-built Pups 9910 and 9911 to *Vindex*. Precisely when, where and to whom the inspiration to modify the Pup to fold occurred is not clear. It might have originated in the Air Department of the Admiralty, but its execution was entrusted to the Beardmore company, whose aviation department was headed by G.Tilghman Richards. The modified aircraft was given the Beardmore type designation W.B.III.

In January 1955 Mr Richards wrote, in a letter to the author:

'The W.B.III was simply a re-design of the Sopwith Pup as a folding, flotation scout; there was no pretence that it was a true Beardmore creation, and it was always referred to at Dalmuir as the "Folding Pup".'

The first modified aircraft was 9950, which should have been the last Pup of the initial Beardmore production batch 9901-9950. It was apparently so numbered out of sequence, for it was delivered by rail to the Design Flight at Eastchurch on 2nd February 1917, whereas 9949 was not test-flown and accepted until 15th May 1917. Harry Busteed recorded in his log-book that he flew 9950 at Eastchurch on 7th February 1917, noting 'Folder' against the entry, and the official performance trials report on the aircraft was dated 8th February 1917.

Virtually everything that could have been done to make the Pup fold into the smallest possible volume was in fact done. The revision of the airframe aimed at producing the least complicated folding geometry: this meant that the wings had

With the ponderous Beardmore W.B.I single-engine bomber behind them stand A.Dukinfield Jones (in flying helmet) and G.Tilghman Richards. Jones was the Beardmore company's test pilot, and test flew virtually all of the Pups and S.B.3Ds built by Beardmore. Richards was the head of the firm's aviation department, and designed the W.B.I, II, IV, V and subsequent post-Armistice Beardmore aircraft. The precise extent of his involvement in modifying the Pup to S.B.3D form has never been defined.

Four aspects of 9950, the Beardmore W.B.III prototype, under construction in the factory. In these photographs, details of the interplane bracing, undercarriage folding and air-bag installation are visible.

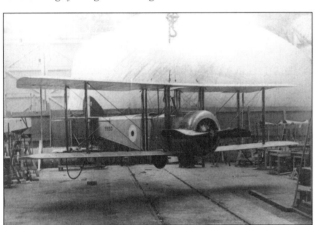

zero stagger, and folded rearwards to lie along the fuselage sides: to accommodate them the fuselage was lengthened to ensure that the interplane struts and inter-aileron links cleared the tailplanewhen the mainplanes were fully folded.

The centre section was reduced in width, and small stub wings were fitted to secure the lower mainplanes. Full-gap interplane struts connected the centre section to these stub wings, replacing the more conventional form of centre-section struts; similar full-gap struts were fitted between the inboard ends of the mainplanes to preserve the bracing truss when folded. Despite the mechanical complexities that wing-folding must have created, the ailerons were shaft-operated much as on contemporary Nieuports: the Beardmore company, as contractors for the Nieuport 12, were familiar with the method. Upper and lower ailerons were linked by strut-like connecting members.

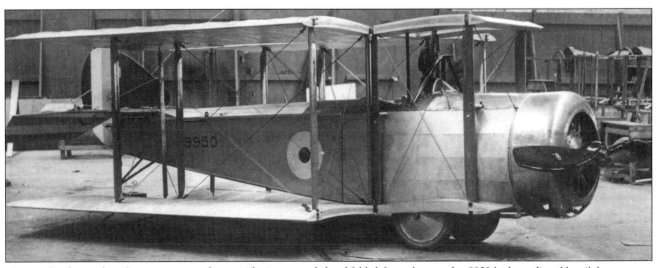

The completed aircraft, its Lewis gun mounted, seen with wings extended and folded. It can be seen that 9950 had an adjustable tailplane.

Dated 28th April 1917, two months before the first production W.B.III was test-flown and accepted, this photograph is one of several that show immersion tests at Grain using a seemingly hybrid Pup/W.B.III airframe with Mk.I underwing and Mk.IV in-fuselage air bags. W.B.III wings without stagger are attached to the fuselage via a centre section supported on seemingly conventional Pup struts. The upper and lower ailerons have faired connecting members as on the W.B.III. The conclusion that at least some of these components came from 9950 appears inescapable.

The undercarriage, too, was designed to fold. It was so articulated that in the folded position only half of each wheel protruded from the underside of the fuselage. To provide the requisite ground clearance for the extremities of the wings in the folded position a greatly heightened tailskid was fitted, mounted on a pylon.

Armament consisted of an upward-firing Lewis gun on a tripod mounting immediately ahead of the cockpit. It had initially been intended to fit rocket-launching equipment: an early data table indicates that the aircraft's weight would be increased by 79lb when rockets were carried. An adjustable tailplane was retained on 9950.

9950 made a forced landing at All Hallows, Isle of Grain, on 10th March 1917, while being flown by Flt Lt P.A.Johnston, and by 1st April 1917 was reported to be under repair in the Experimental Constructive Department at Grain. The possibility that 9950 might have provided at least some of the hybrid airframe used in preliminary tests of Mk.IV air-bags has been mentioned on page 125. Grain's Daily Report of 16th

The Beardmore assembly shop. Components of W.B.IIIs surround the airframe of a Beardmore W.B.V; the fuselage of a second W.B.V is visible beyond, and to its left stands an unpainted Sopwith 2F.1 Camel.
(Angus Mackay Collection, via University of Glasgow)

Two views of a Beardmore W.B.II mounted on the fixed forecastle platform of a warship, being prepared for launching.

April 1917 recorded that 9950 was 'awaiting water test', but on the following wing day stated that it was being dismantled. Its engine was installed in the Pup 9922 on 1st May and the station's Daily Reports suggest that the dismantling process progressed in slow time. Not until 27th May was the aircraft unequivocally recorded as dismantled, it being recorded as officially deleted on 19th June 1917.

The Beardmore company designation W.B.III found no official use in the RNAS, which knew the production aircraft as the S.B.3D ('S.B.' signifying Sopwith-Beardmore). One hundred were ordered, initially by a Provisional Order dated 19th May 1917, under Contract No. A.S.775/17: these took up the serial numbers N6100-N6129 (which had originally been allotted for Pups to be built by Beardmore under Contract No. A.S.14757 dated 12th February 1917) and N6680-N6749.

N6100 was test-flown by A.Dukinfield Jones on 25th June 1917, and officially accepted next day. It has been stated that the first production W.B.IIIs were delivered with the folding undercarriage and were known, if only briefly, as the S.B.3F ('F' signifying Folding). Indeed they might have been, but it seems likely that they were soon modified to have a non-folding but jettisonable undercarriage. Presumably the production S.B.3F's undercarriage was as narrow in track as that of the prototype, which had proved to be very unsteady on the ground in any wind, and had to be supplemented by outboard skids under the lower wings to provide a measure of protection to the wing structure. Official RNAS lists named all the Beardmore W.B.IIIs in service as S.B.3Ds ('D' denoting Dropping Undercarriage).

Similarly, it seems that few production aircraft retained the interplane struts at the inboard ends of the mainplane panels; instead, a simple jury strut was inserted between upper and lower front spars when the wings were folded. A few of the early W.B.IIIs had a cut-out in the centre section, and a tripod

N6100, the first production W.B.III, after modification to S.B.3D form, with non-folding undercarriage overwing Lewis gun, inboard interplane struts removed, and revised aileron control system. These were the modifications completed on this aircraft on 23th October,1917. When first built, it had been test-flown on 25th June 1917 and accepted next day. It was with, or allocated to, HMS Cassandra in December 1917 going to Donibristle on 21st March 1918 and then to HMS Nairana.

Two views of N6101, still retaining the inboard-end interplane struts on its wing panels, faired links between upper and lower ailerons, and the wingtip skids necessitated by the narrow track of the original folding undercarriage. This last, however, has been replaced by a non-folding jettisonable structure of normal track. N6101 was test-flown and officially accepted on 6th July 1917. As an S.B.3D, N6101 was at East Fortune without an engine early in January 1918. When photographed, it bore its company type number W.B.III on the fin. It was eventually deleted in March 1918.

on the fuselage for an upward-firing Lewis gun. At an early stage this was replaced by an overwing mounting for the gun, slightly offset to starboard, and the cut-out was abandoned.

At the same time the method of actuating the ailerons was modified, the shaft system being replaced by cables. Similarly, cables replaced the earlier connecting links between upper and lower ailerons. Although the prototype W.B.III had had an adjustable tailplane the production aircraft had a fixed tail unit.

Most of these modifications were the outcome of decisions taken in the summer of 1917. By 14th July it had been decided '… that the 30 of these machines on order from Messrs Beardmore shall be fitted with the dropping chassis, which means a relief of about 50lb weight when the machine gets away and drops its chassis, and also a considerable decrease in head resistance.' and that seems to be a clear indication that N6100-N6129 were indeed all modified to become S.B.3Ds.

The alterations to the aileron system were probably the subject of a Class 1 Modification required by T.1.N Section; on 1st September 1917 it was reported that this would cause more delay than had been expected. Additionally it had been found that the structural strength of the S.B.3D was inadequate, and corrective action, combined with the aileron modifications, would set back deliveries by about a month. In mitigation, it was opined that 'The alterations which have been asked for should, however, simplify construction and should not therefore affect the total number of machines to be delivered before the end of the year.'

It seems that the early production of the S.B.3D was subject to other retarding factors. As early as 23rd June 1917, two days before the first production aircraft was test-flown, a report of the Department of Aeronautical Supplies stated:

'Messrs Beardmore have been instructed by the Admiralty to concentrate their efforts on rigid airships, and deliveries of folding Scouts are beginning to fall behind as a result thereof. Enquiry

It would be interesting to know how N6117 achieved this remarkable posture. Whether the cause was aeronautical or meteorological, the mishap occurred at Grain in November 1917; nevertheless, N6117 was still listed on Grain's strength on 5th January 1918. It had initially been test-flown and accepted at Dalmuir on 5th October 1917. An interesting feature of this photograph is its revelation of the underwing flotation bag in its stowed position under the leading edge of the port wing.

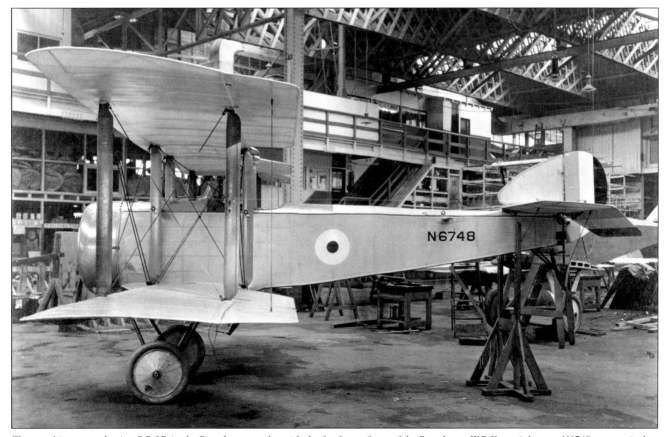

The penultimate production S.B.3D in the Beardmore works, with the fuselage of one of the Beardmore W.B.Vs at right rear. N6748 was engineless when photographed, and may have been delivered in that condition. On 30th March 1918 it was in store, without engine, at Killingholme; and on 7th November 1918 it was at Renfrew, still with no engine.

HMS Nairana also received, and flew, S.B.3Ds. Her small flying deck with its steeply inclined ramp is clearly revealed in this aerial view.

HMS Pegasus was probably the first ship to embark an S.B.3D. Her flying deck can be seen forward; the large structure aft was her hangar for seaplanes.

has been made of the manufacturers as to whether they can continue to give delivery of these machines.'

But continue they did: the second production aircraft, N6101, was test-flown and accepted on 6th July, and was followed on 10th July by N6102 and N6103. A delay of a month followed because (so it was said) a consignment of Le Rhône engines had been aboard a ship that had been sunk in the Channel, and deliveries of engines for the S.B.3Ds were interrupted. However that might have been, N6104 did not fly until 10th August 1917, but N6105-N6110 were all completed and flown in that month. Up to N6127 had been accepted by 23rd October, and deliveries of the initial batch of 30 had been made before the end of October 1917.

Test-flight and acceptance dates are not known for the earliest S.B.3Ds in the second batch, but deliveries clearly followed in unbroken sequence after N6129. It is known that N6683 was flown on 3rd November 1917, and accepted three days later; N6701 was flown and accepted on 10th December. Deliveries ended in February 1918, having been made in these numbers:

1917: June - 1; July – 4; August – 7; September – 2; October – 17; November – 26; December – 26.

1918: January – 14; February - 3

It seems likely that N6702-N6707 and N6709-N6733 went straight into store at Killingholme. N6708 went to Grain, and was there on 5th January 1918, fitted with the 80hp Le Rhône from N6117, and by the end of March N6708 it was at Rosyth.

The aircraft which went to Killingholme were all were reported to be there, without engines, on 11th January 1918, and by 30th March N6734-N6748 had joined them. At that last date there were 46 S.B.3Ds in Reserve at Killingholme; in service elsewhere were another 40.

The standard power unit for the S.B.3D was the 80hp Le Rhône 9C, which was fitted to most production aircraft that were flown. Whether those that went into store were ever engined is doubtful. There were a few exceptions, but the only known alternative engine was the 80hp Clerget 7Z, which was fitted to N6125-N6127, N6683 and N6684.

Lack of engines doubtless presented problems. As at 29th December 1917, although the following S.B.3Ds were reported to be in course of erection at Rosyth, all were without engines at the time: N6118, N6124, N6128, N6682, N6688, N6690, N6696, N6697, N6699 and N6700. Also reported engineless at that time was N6102 at Turnhouse.

The first S.B.3D to go to a ship was probably N6104, which was delivered to HMS *Pegasus*; so, in their turn, were N6106 and N6107; at later dates N6126, N6681 and N6692 were allocated to that carrier. Delivered to *Nairana* were N6105, N6108 and N6110; by 15th January 1918, N6687 was on *Nairana*'s strength. N6109 was delivered to East Fortune by rail on 10th October 1917 and was held there for HMS *Manxman*; it is not known whether this S.B.3D was ever put aboard the ship.

Most of the other S.B.3Ds went, at one time or another, to Fleet Bases or Depots at Scapa Flow, Rosyth. Donibristle, Turnhouse and East Fortune, and probably provided aircraft for

An S.B.3D on Nairana's ramp, being prepared for take-off. Its Lewis gun is in place, the pilot has what appears to be a form of optical gun-sight, and the stowed underwing flotation bags are visible. The oil staining on the fuselage fabric suggests that this S.B.3D had done a fair amount of flying.

An S.B.3D on Nairana, seen at an angle that reveals the cross-member between the upper ends of the forward undercarriage struts. Also noteworthy is the appreciable drop that awaited the aircraft on leaving the ramp. Dimly discernible in the hangar under the ramp is a Sopwith 2F.1 Camel, the type that rendered the S.B.3D obsolete.

Just how jarring that drop from the ramp could be is dramatically illustrated by the sudden - and full - deflection of the wheels of this S.B.3D on its take-off run. This photograph reveals the offset position of the Lewis gun.

An S.B.3D lifting off from HMS Nairana.

other ships. Some went to HMS *Furious*, as was recalled by Geoffrey Moore in *Early Bird*:

'The Sopwith Pups were very light little fighter aircraft, very controllable and pleasant to fly. Some we had in *Furious* were modified by Beardmore's to fold for passing down a hatch and stowing between decks. This folding rather spoiled their performance and handiness; to make them fold conveniently they reduced some of the wing stagger, consequently they did not handle quite as nicely as the standard series. I used to give little exhibitions of aerobatics for the entertainment of the fleet, but was never really happy when doing this in a "folder" on account of some lack of response in the controls and I was always wondering whether, if subjected to exceptional strain, they would "fold" in the air!'

Moore had performed an early trial ditching of an S.B.3D from Grain. In a letter to the author, dated 8th August 1961, he recalled:

'I have just reminded Busteed of a thing I did for him. Dropped the undercarriage of a Pup on the foreshore of Sheerness harbour and then ditched the Pup (a folder), which had a hydrovane and inflatable air bags.'

The hydrovane mentioned by Moore must have been part of the work done by Grain's Experimental Constructive Department late in July 1917. The ECD's summary of work for the week ending 28th July 1917 mentioned, *inter alia,* that 'Two Beardmore folding "Pups" have arrived, and have been flown. They are now being fitted with planing boards, prior to trials of landing on water.'

At that date the two S.B.3Ds in question can only have

On this occasion, N6129 took off from Nairana with its gun at full elevation; the optical gun-sight is at the right of the aircraft's windscreen. This S.B.3D was at Donibristle on 29th December 1917; although marked 'for deletion' at Houton on 30th March 1918, it was still listed as being at Smoogroo on 7th November 1918.

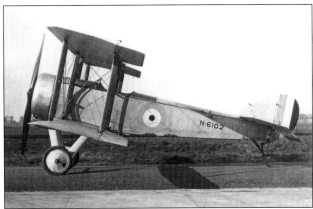

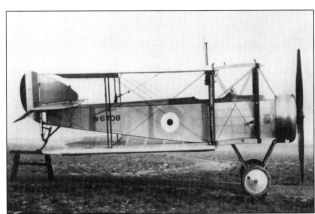

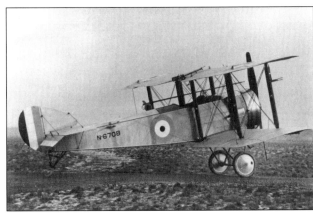

Three views of the S.B.3D N6102 at Grain; the photographs are dated 19th October 1917. The fairings on the undercarriage emphasise its geometry, particularly in the frontal aspect. Test-flown and accepted on 11th July 1917, N6102 was delivered to Grain. By late December it was at Donibristle, and on 30th March 1918 was at Turnhouse without an engine. There it apparently remained until the war ended.

Another S.B.3D that went to Grain was N6708. These three photographs are dated 3rd January 1918, and show the aircraft with a boom-mounted pressure head for its air-speed indicator. At about that date N6708 received the engine from N6117 (seen upended on page 131). It had spells in HMS Nairana and was eventually deleted in August 1918.

These two photographs (dated 18th January 1918) record N6708's involvement in acceleration tests at Grain. They show Grain's experimental deck being used for take-off measurements, in contrast to its more frequent use as an arrester-gear test surface.

On HMS Repulse's trough-equipped trackway the S.B.3D N6115 stands with wings folded and secured at several points, late in 1917. This aircraft was with HMS Nairana at the end of December 1917, and apparently spent a few days aboard HMS Princess Royal before going to Donibristle by 11th January 1918. It was still at Donibristle, but unserviceable, at 30th March, and deleted in August 1918.   (Fleet Air Arm Museum)

been N6102 and N6103. Both had been test-flown and accepted on 10th July 1917, and were subsequently sent direct to Grain, having been officially allocated to that Station on 20th June. As the accompanying illustrations show, N6102 was later fitted with a jettisonable undercarriage that had fairings fitted to the legs of the V-struts. In this form it was photographed at Grain on 10th October 1917; no hydrovane can be seen in the photographs, but the aircraft did have the revised wing structure and aileron system.

Although only about 40 S.B.3Ds had been delivered by mid-November 1917 it seems that a spares problem was perceived. In that month N6104-N6108 and N6110 were reduced for spares at Rosyth, which seems strange in the light of the fact that Beardmore had a contract to the value of £10,047 6s 0d for spares for S.B.3Ds.

Few allocations of S.B.3Ds to warships are known. N6115 was put aboard the battle cruiser *Renown* late in 1917, evidently to take off from an arrangement of troughs laid out on the fo'c'sle. Not surprisingly, this was not a success, and by early 1918 *Renown* had been fitted with a turret-mounted platform, N6115 was subsequently in *Nairana* late in December 1917 and, perhaps only briefly, in the battle-cruiser *Princess Royal*. The light cruiser *Cassandra* had N6100 on 21st March 1918; nine days later the aircraft had returned to Donibristle and its place aboard *Cassandra* had been taken by N6128.

Although Beardmore S.B.3Ds were flown from *Nairana* and *Pegasus* it seems that the type was never involved in any operational action. By 9th May 1918, its inclusion in the official *Statement of Aeroplanes, Ship Aeroplanes and Seaplanes* was under the heading *S.B.3D: Obsolete Service Ship Fighter Aeroplane*, and ran: 'No further deliveries of this machine or its spares are required, there being only 81 of this type still left in service.' The S.B.3D and the Type 9901a Pup had, of course, been superseded in service by the Sopwith 2F.1 Camel.

The next *Statement*, dated 16th August 1918, was similarly worded, but indicated that the number of S.B.3Ds still in

service had dropped to 70; and the *Statement* of 26th October reported a further reduction to only 56. The official statistical table dated 31st October 1918, published as Appendix XLI to *The War in the Air*, records a total of 55: of these, 18 were in store and 37 under the heading *Grand Fleet and Northern Patrol*. Those in store were at Renfrew without engines; they were N6724, N6731-N6734 and N6737-N6749. Potentially for use by the Fleet there were at Smoogroo N6139, N6685, N6686, N6693, N6698 and N6701; at Donibristle, N6682, N6692, N6696, N6702, N6705-N6707, N6710, N6713-N6715; at Rosyth, N6700, N6703, N6709, N6711 and N6712; and Turnhouse held, fitted with engines, N6102, N6716, N6717 and N6719, plus 11 without engines, namely N6718, N6720-N6723 and N6725-N6730.

The S.B.3D was finally declared 'obsolete for all purposes' in Air Ministry Order No.896 of 7th August 1919, in company with the Sopwith Pup, Camel, Triplane and Baby, and many other contemporary types.

Sopwith Pup – Seaplane Proposal

In the Department of Aeronautical Supplies Report No.18 for the week ending 7th July 1917, there appeared this item under the heading *Seaplanes*:

'Various new designs have been considered and the question of the conversion of Sopwith Pups into Seaplanes is being considered. Satisfactory seaworthiness trials have been carried out in connection [sic] therewith.'

A sensible reason underlying that proposal is hard to discern. Perhaps the idea was to enable the Pup to alight on the water and be retrieved rather than ditching and almost certainly being lost; but one wonders whether it was realised that putting floats on a Pup (if that, is what in fact was proposed) would so diminish its performance that it could have no hope of getting anywhere near an airship fast enough to be effective. And what could a Pup seaplane have done that could not have been done by the existing Sopwith Baby seaplanes?

Chapter 21

Pups in Training

Inevitably, the Sopwith Pup was widely used in training units of the RFC, RNAS and RAF. Many embryo fighter pilots first made their acquaintance of the little aircraft in the Reserve (later Training) Squadrons, at the RFC's Scout School attached to No.2 Aircraft Depot, Candas, or at the RNAS War School at Manston. Some of those who survived their operational tours in France renewed that acquaintance on returning to training stations as instructors: experienced, much more assured as pilots, and better qualified to appreciate the Pup's qualities as a flying machine.

First impressions did not always inspire love at first sight. P.G.Taylor's introduction to single-seat scouts had been on the exquisite little Bristol Scout, a type that should have been more efficiently armed and might then have made a name for itself as a fighter; but it has always been - unfairly, one feels - overshadowed by the more numerous Pup. In *Sopwith Scout 7309*, Taylor wrote thus of his first impressions of the Pup A651 of No.43 Reserve Squadron. Ternhill, which he flew in January 1917:

'As it turned out, my first experience of the "Pup" was disappointing. In the air I found it compared unfavourably with the Bristol. Though it was light enough on controls there seemed to be a noticeable lag, a kind of sponginess which left me sadly out of touch after the instant sensitivity of the Bristol. I came down out of the air that day disillusioned and depressed. All the high elation of flying scouts had gone. If this is to be my mount, I didn't think much of it...................

'But in the Services it is usually necessary to accept the inevitable and even make the best of it. With no escape from the Sopwith Pup possible, I began to look at it with as open a mind as possible. It must have *something* in its favour, some exploitable quality upon which I could concentrate in order to make the best use of it as a weapon. So during my first week at Tern Hill I flew the Pup whenever possible, trying to come to terms with it. I made twenty flights, and gradually a change came in our relationship. I began to sit more

B1705 was, in May 1917, with No.43 Reserve Squadron, RFC, Ternhill, where P.G.Taylor had first flown a Pup a few months earlier. By the summer of 1917, B1705 was at Lilbourne, where it was flown by pilots of Service Squadrons Nos.73 and 84, which were then mobilising.

A single photograph cannot do justice to any aircraft painted in an individualistic colour scheme, such as that of B2192 of No.1 School of Special Flying, Gosport around August 1917. This Monosoupape-powered Pup was, according to Gosport lore, painted in black and white stripes, and had associations with Harold Balfour and Leslie Foot.

comfortably in the seat to feel more relaxed and more sympathetic. It seemed flimsy after the Bristol Scout, and as light as a leaf on the wind; but I began to accept the differences and finally to feel that the whole thing was just as secure as the Bristol had been. She was an ugly little craft, squat and top-heavy looking, but she was undeniably nimble and seemed to welcome whatever aerobatics I chose to put her through.

'I avoided looping her, largely on account of disquieting rumours about her structural strength. It was said that if you looped a Sopwith Pup her wings would come off, also that she would not stand up to a really tight spin. I knew that one day I would have to perform both these manoeuvres – if I was ever to fight in the Pup I would have to be able to throw her around with complete confidence. But I never saw a single person loop or spin the Pup, and for the moment I shelved the problem, leaving it as just another worry to niggle at the back of my mind.'

That beauty is in the eye of the beholder is a commonplace, one that apparently embraced the aesthetics of aircraft such as the Pup. In contrast to Taylor's somewhat jaundiced opinion was the reaction of John McGavock Grider, the American diarist of *War Birds*, who was enraptured by his first encounter on 25th November 1917, at Thetford:

'Today I saw my first scout machine, a Sopwith Pup. It's the prettiest little thing I ever laid my eyes on. I am going to fly one if I live long enough. They aren't as big as a minute and are as pretty and slick as a thoroughbred horse. Tiny little things, just big enough for one man and a machine-gun.'

Grider eventually flew a Pup at London Colney on 8th February 1918. He had relatively little flying time to his credit, but he survived the experience. His diary note of 9th February was somewhat less ecstatic than his earlier reaction:

'I got off in a Pup yesterday. Gosh, what a thrill! They are not so different, but they are so quick and sensitive that they will crash taking off or landing before you know what they are going to do. I didn't bust anything, but I pancaked like the devil landing.'

Initially, the Pups that were flown on training duties were used to provide experience on type for pilots destined for operational Pup squadrons, but the aircraft's good flying qualities led to its progressively widening use in advanced flying training. As it was such a joy to fly, it was greatly favoured by instructors as personal aircraft, nowhere more than at No.1 School of Special Flying at Gosport.

The late Lord Balfour of Inchrye, PC, MC, was (as Capt H.H.Balfour, MC) in 1917 an instructor at Gosport. In a letter published in *Flight* of 9th April 1954, he reminisced:

'... in 1917 a few Pups were gloriously (even if inefficiently) re-engined by being fitted with 100hp "Mono" Gnome motors.

'Each flight commander at Gosport School of Special Flying under the late Colonel Smith-Barry had one allotted to him as a private plaything to let off steam on. One day Major Bell-Irving, MC, and I fetched two from Farnborough. The "clock" could be got to 100mph with nose held down, hedge hopping. On arrival at Gosport, Bell-Irving did a climbing turn, stalled and spun, badly crashing his legs and ankles.'
[Duncan Bell-Irving's crash, in B805, occurred on 13th August 1917.]

In his book *An Airman Marches*, Lord Balfour recorded that his Pup was 'gaily coloured and kept in a spotless, condition', and described an amusing incident when it was borrowed by Capt W.G.Barker (later Col Barker, VC, DSO, MC), who flew it at roof-top height over Piccadilly Circus in London.

Personal colour schemes of varying degrees of exuberance

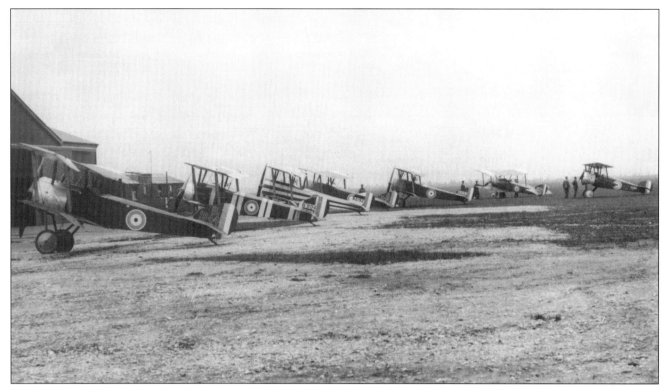

Some of Gosport's Pups and one Camel paying a visit to Beaulieu. The five nearest Pups are, from left to right, B1844, B804, B2192, B1849 and B2193; and the print bears the date 7th September 1917.

found expression on some of the Pups of RFC training units, as did individual names applied by their 'owners' (as distinct from the inscriptions on presentation aircraft). Such outward and visible signs denoted affection, respect, perhaps even devotion, to the little Sopwith. One instructor, whose appreciation came of long flying experience and of many combats in the Pup's predecessor, the 1½ Strutter, and in its successor the Camel, was the late Wg Cdr Norman Macmillan, OBE, MC, AFC. He had first flown a Pup (A659) at Central Flying School early in 1917; after his long operational stint in No.45 Squadron, he returned to England and to instructional duties with No.34 Training Squadron, initially at Ternhill, then later at Chattis Hill, near Stockbridge. There he was allocated a Pup for his own use, as he recalled in his book *Into the Blue*:

'About mid-May [1918] the Sopwith Pup became finally obsolete as a Service type and senior instructors were allowed to have those which were available in the Group, and were granted permission to use them to fly on leave in lieu of travelling by

train. The one allotted to me was a perfect little beauty. There never was, and never can be, a nicer aeroplane to fly than the Sopwith Pup. Stable, sweet on controls, light in weight, and with an engine (the 80 horsepower Le Rhône nine-cylinder rotary) which ran like a sewing machine, she was the realisation of my mental picture of what flying ought to be, for she positively glided through the air.'

Popular though the Pup was, there were some who felt that, in the context of training future fighter pilots, it was too gentle and forgiving: certainly it could not have provided any foretaste of the waspish and wilful Camel that many of the trainees would have to fly later in their training and in operational units. An extraordinary example of the Pup's docility and resilience was described by the late Wg Cdr Louis Strange, DSO, OBE, MC, DFC and Bar, in his book *Recollections of an Airman*. The place was Central Flying School, to which Strange had been posted as an instructor in April 1917:

B6116 at the Central Flying School in early 1918. It is painted in the standard colour scheme, but appears to have a replacement aileron on the upper starboard wing as the roundel segment does not match the remainder.

This Central Flying School Pup, coyly concealing its identity, was painted white overall and had a camera gun on the decking ahead of the cockpit Its engine was the standard 80hp Le Rhone, but it had a cutaway cowling. This was probably the 'private' aircraft of a senior instructor.

C280 had reached RNAS Manston by March 1918; it was listed by the RNAS War School at that station as a 'final training' aircraft.
(Alan Greening via Aeroplane Monthly)

Painted on B6121's flank fairing panel is a quasi-heraldic device emblematising No.1 School of Aeronautics, Reading. The outline of a hand beside the roundel is the more personal marking of the occupant of the cockpit, Lt S Keith Jopp, who had earlier lost a hand in a flying, accident.

A7317 with No.17 Training Squadron, Port Meadow in mid-1917.
(via Frank Cheesman)

Another view of A7345 (see also photograph on page 81) of No.1 Training Squadron, Gosport, photographed while visiting Beaulieu on 11th June 1917. This 80hp Gnome Pup was flown on 6th June 1917 by Lt-Col (later Group Captain) G.I.Carmichael who, long before P.G.Taylor wrote 'Sopwith Scout 7309', annotated his entry of the flight in his log-book: 'Very nice. Glides 45-50. Like a leaf.'

'I remember one very curious incident, which is an absolute fact. One day, when I was standing on the North Tarmac, I saw a Sopwith Pup go into a half-roll and then stay upside down with its engine and propeller stopped. The machine glided down straight into the wind from a height of 2,500 feet; in fact, I should have called it quite a stately landing if only it had been the right way up, but I expected a horrid crash when it descended on the downward slope of the hill by the golf course.

'To my surprise, the machine just turned over the right way up. It appeared undamaged, but my amazement increased when I saw the pilot emerge, swing the propeller, get in, and fly off again. I jumped into the nearest machine, climbed up and signalled him to go down and land again, which he did quite safely, and when I got down myself, I found that his machine was really undamaged except for a few splinters on the leading edge of the top plane.

'When I asked the pilot what on earth he meant by flying the machine straight off again after landing upside down, he merely looked at me in blank astonishment. Subsequently he told me that the last thing he remembered was starting to try a roll, after which he knew nothing more until he woke up to find himself sitting in the machine on the golf course. As it was forbidden to land there, he promptly started his engine and took off again!'

Official records confirm that this remarkable incident occurred on 4th September 1917; because the pilot (2/Lt C.S.Dickinson) was uninjured he was not named on the casualty report, but his aircraft was, by a minor coincidence, A659, the Pup that had given Norman Macmillan his introduction to the type some months earlier. By September 1917 it had acquired an 80hp Clerget engine, and was in 'C' Flight at Central Flying School.

No aircraft, not even a Pup, could have survived such an arrival completely unscathed. Even if the propeller had stopped in a horizontal position the rolling over of the aircraft must, in the absence of some unbelievably sympathetically contoured and providentially located bunker on the golf course to have

done at least some damage to the engine cowling which, even if it did not actually impede the engine's rotation, can hardly have escaped the notice of the pilot when he swung the propeller to re-start his engine.

The casualty report did not detail damage to the Pup, but it was signed by Louis Strange himself, who recorded:

'Glided down upside down and hit ground in that position. Apparently no effort was made to right the machine from the upside-down position.'

Sadly, some people were killed on Pups at training units; indeed, on 5th September 1917, the day after A659's inverted escapade, its numerical predecessor, A658, crashed at CFS, killing 2/Lt J.G.O'Giollagain. It, too, had an 80hp Clerget. And yet, although no comparative statistics are available, deaths of trainee pilots in Pups must have been many fewer than those caused by the fiery and unforgiving Camel. Therein, perhaps, lies the paradox of why some instructors considered the Pup to be ill-suited to training duties: its docility and viceless tractability gave to inexperienced trainees a false impression of ease and safety in flying that was too often brusquely shattered by later and more homicidally inclined types.

By the autumn of 1918 it had been decided that the Avro 504K was to be the RFC's standard training aircraft, and was to supersede all other training types, the Pup included. The seventh *Statement of Aeroplanes*, dated 26th October 1918, reflected this decision in its paragraph on the Pup:

Sopwith Scout
Obsolete Service and Training Machine

'The provision of spares for this machine should be carefully examined as its use is dying out as a training machine in this country. There are also a considerable number of machines in store, and outstanding requisitions for spares should be cut down and use made of machines in store when spares are required or machines should be replaced.'

With the Armistice only a little more than two weeks away there must have been little call for that instruction to be invoked.

Here photographed at Brooklands, B2152 had initially been allocated to the Expeditionary Force on 30th April 1917, but an amendment on 9th May changed its destination to Training Brigade. Another change of allocation to the Expeditionary Force again, occurred on 14th May, but finally on 17th May the allocation to Training Brigade was reinstated. The aircraft was used by No.56 Training Squadron, London Colney from June 1917, later going to No.3 Training Squadron, Shoreham.

C242 was at one time with No.7 Training Squadron, Netheravon. It is not known when it acquired the dazzling harlequin colour scheme (presumably in red, white and blue), seen in these photographs and it also had a small monogram in the white lozenge on the fuselage side at about roundel position. This appears to consist of the letters 'C' and 'S' entwined in a central letter 'A', but its significance is not known. The aircraft had an 80hp Gnome engine when photographed. C242 was one of the few Pups to come on to the British Civil Register in the post-Armistice period, becoming G-EBFJ.

Most training units adopted some form of unit marking in the later stages of the war, but up to the time of writing these have never been analysed, systematically identified or catalogued. Here C287 of No.18 Training Squadron, Montrose, wears a broad band, possibly red, sidelined in white and with the letter 'C' superimposed.

When photographed B2196 had a camera-gun fitted, a dark (perhaps red) band painted round its rear fuselage and dark-coloured streamers tied to its interplane struts. It is known that this Pup was with No.55 Training Squadron, Yatesbury, in the summer of 1917.

The markings of C215 were more probably personal than unit-related: the stripes, struts and wheel covers were most probably white, and tonal values suggest that the fuselage and tail unit might have been blue, and that the lozenge marking on the centre section might have been white and blue. It is believed that C215 was with the School of Special Flying at Gosport, when photographed. It had also served at Eastbourne.

B9440 was very much of No.63 Training Squadron at Joyce Green, for it was assembled from spares by that unit and received its serial number on 13th August 1917. How long it stayed with No.63 Training Squadron is uncertain, for it was reported with No.65 Training Squadron at Sedgeford in September 1917.

Used by Nos.6 and 8 Training Squadrons, Australian Flying Corps, at Minchinhampton and Leighterton respectively, D4170 proclaimed its Australian association by an emu painted on a dark (red?) band on the fuselage. Its overall finish was apparently white. (Colin Owers)

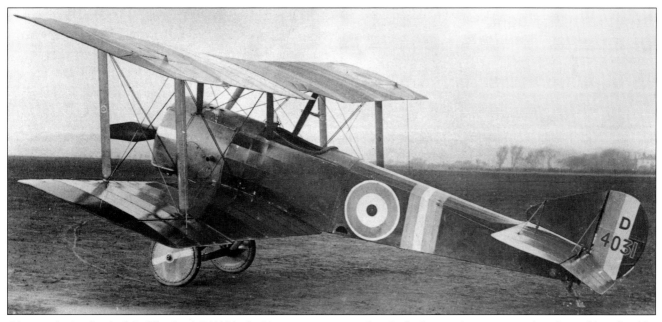

A late-production Pup built by Whitehead, D4031 had a Monosoupape-type cowling. Its fuselage marking appears to have been a blue-white-blue band; the wheel covers similarly appear to have been blue with a white line across a diameter, and there was a white stripe across the chord of the engine cowling. This aircraft was reported to be of No.3 Training Depot Station, Lopcombe Corner. (Frank Cheesman)

Also of No.3 Training Depot Station, Lopcombe Corner, but with an all-white finish, was B5253. It was known on the unit as Major Cogan's Pup, presumably Major F.J.L.Cogan.

Training aircraft at Scampton were marked with a broad coloured band, with white outlines, on the fuselage: it appears that different Flights or Squadrons of No.34 Training Depot Station were distinguishes by the colour of the band and B2243 was of that unit, and had evidently had several replacements of mainplanes or ailerons.

A627, the second production Pup built by the Standard Motor Company, had initially been allocated to the Expeditionary Force on 13th September 1916, and it went to No.54 Squadron on 22nd October 1916, some two weeks in advance of its formal specific allocation to the squadron on 8th November. At a later date A627 turned to training duties, and here it is seen with a marking that suggests a Scampton location, probably No.81 Squadron, and an idiosyncratic presentation of its serial number.   (RAF Museum)

C273 had a white-edged blue band and the rare refinement of a head fairing behind the cockpit. It was flown by Nos.85 and 87 Squadrons at Hounslow.   (L.A.Rogers)

C414 was an aircraft No.103 at No.4 (Auxiliary) School of Aerial Gunnery at Marske in 1918.

Training Squadrons Nos.22 and 23 were both located at Aboukir (then referred to as Abu Qir), and there can be little doubt that pooling of available aircraft was freely practised. C1493 was not alone among the station's aircraft in having its serial number repainted in larger-than-standard numerals.   (Trevor Foreman)

A more exotically painted Pup in Egypt. As its serial number has been painted over it cannot be positively identified, but it was one of the eight numbered B6041 to B6048. Of these, B6043, B6044 and B6046 were used by No.5 Fighting School at Heliopolis, B6047 by No.19 Training Depot Station, El Rimal, and B6048 by No.195 Training Squadron, which was redesignated No.19 TDS in July 1918.
                                                              (RAF Museum)

A Pup of a training unit with mounting blocks for a camera-gun just to port of the windscreen. Although the camera-gun was thus offset, the Aldis optical sight was mounted on the centre line. In the side view can be seen the safety hinge-fitted over the retaining cable of the engine cowling (see page 80). Visible in the rear view is the small aluminium tread plate on the rear spar of the port lower wing to enable the pilot to get into his cramped cockpit.

Service squadrons used Pups while working up to operational effectiveness. B1788 was the first Pup to be delivered to No.64 Squadron at Sedgeford for such employment, in June 1917.

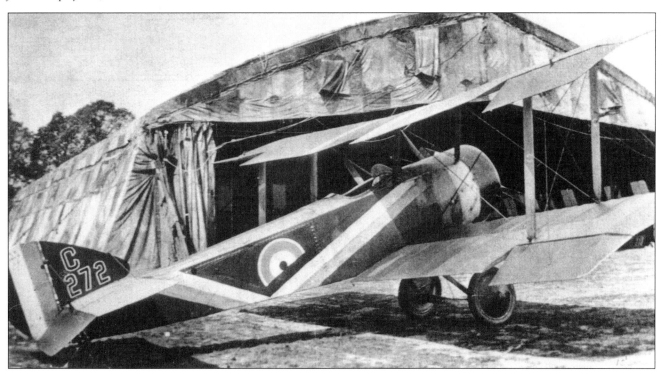

Another of No.64 Squadron's Pups at Sedgeford was C272, its bright markings suggesting that it may have been a fighting instructor's aircraft (and that this photograph might have been taken at a later date and with a different unit). It had white chordwise stripes along the outer ribs of its centre section. a white tailplane, and wide V in tricolour stripes on the fuselage. (Chaz Bowyer)

B5932 was used by No.73 Squadron during its mobilisation period at Lilbourne, then later by No.54 Training Squadron at Castle Bromwich.

At Scampton, among No.8l Squadron's practice aircraft in April 1918 was Pup B6124, "MUMMY".

Probably employed as a practice aircraft, B2218 in October 1918 was with No.506 Flight at Owthorne, a unit of No.251 Squadron, equipped with D.H.6s for anti-submarine patrol. In this photograph B2218 is seen at Killingholme.

B6065 had additional markings on its upper wing; there appears to be a large 101 on the port, an equally large 'S' or '5' on the starboard. The cockpit opening looks unusually long, and the windscreen is large.

(K.M.Molson)

B4128 was one of several Pups that were reconstructed from salvage and/or spares by No.2 (Northern) Aircraft Repair Depot at Coal Aston, near Sheffield. In addition to its striped paint scheme, it bore a representation of a pennant over the number 19; on the fuselage side at the cockpit is the hypocoristic inscription "ICKLE POOP".

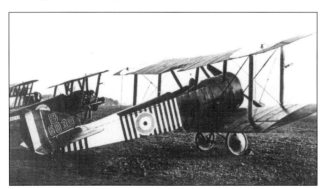

B6039 had distinctive markings on its fuselage. The presence of the Camel B9242 suggests that this photograph might have been taken at Shawbury, whilst with No.10 Training Squadron.

C231 had a Monosoupape-type engine cowling but probably an 80hp engine therein. In addition to its star marking it had white wheel covers. It was used by Nos.90 and 95 Squadrons at North Shotwick.

Another training-unit Pup whose unit and location remain unknown was this patriotically marked specimen, on which even the inner wheel covers and the propeller had been decorated. This might well have been painted in the post-Armistice period. (via K.M.Molson)

Why, when, and by whom this much modified Pup was created at Catterick is not known; nor is it known whether it was ever flown. The lack of an engine cowling suggests that it might have been intended to serve as a taxying trainer, and the inadequately mounted rudimentary skids on the undercarriage provide a hint of confirmation. The shortened mainplanes have been fitted with inversely tapered ailerons; these with their overhanging horn balance areas might have been inspired by the ailerons of the Fokker D.VII. (Trevor Henshaw)

Chapter 22

Experimental Flying

The deck-flying experiments in which Pups played such a vital part have been described earlier. These were by far the most important and far-reaching experiments in which Pups were used, for they were a fundamental component of the work that led directly to the entire practice of carrier-borne aviation. Every major idea or technique in that field over the years has been devised, pioneered or developed by aviators and engineers of Britain's Royal Navy from the earliest days. The years of the 1914-18 war saw a remarkable manifestation of brilliant ideas, bold thinking and daring innovation, in all of which Pups of the RNAS and RAF figured conspicuously.

In other experimental endeavours, Pups were used less extensively than succeeding types. The Armament Experimental Station at Orfordness had B1717 (80hp Le Rhône) and B1755 (100hp Monosoupape), which were occasionally flown to observe experiments with other types of aircraft or to make weather tests. B1755 was used in some air-to-ground firing tests, and was

evidently a good aircraft: Capt R.M.Charley, who had over 400 hours of operational flying on the Pups of No.54 Squadron, RFC, flew B1755 for the first time on 22nd March 1918, and noted in his log-book: 'Very nice machine; almost as good as Camel or S.E.5'. He flew both Pups at Orfordness from time to time, and it seems that by 13th July 1919 B1717 had been painted in one of the experimental camouflage schemes devised at Orfordness. In comparison with a camouflaged Salamander the Pup scheme was better, in Charley's opinion. On 20th September 1918, he flew a Pup from Orfordness to Hendon, recording the aircraft as C9924, which, properly, was a Bristol F.2B. His Pup might have been the Beardmore-built 9924, which had been on the strength of RNAS Hendon at the end of March 1918.

Orfordness used a Monosoupape-powered Pup, possibly B1755, in firing trials of three different types of K.N.17, Mk.VII, S.A. ball-ammunition to determine suitability for use in Vickers guns regulated by interrupter gears. The Pup had the Constantinesco C.C.

B1755, photographed at Orfordness, where it was one of the fleet of assorted aircraft that were employed by the Armament Experimental Station there on various tasks (see also photograph on page 82).
(R.G.Moulton)

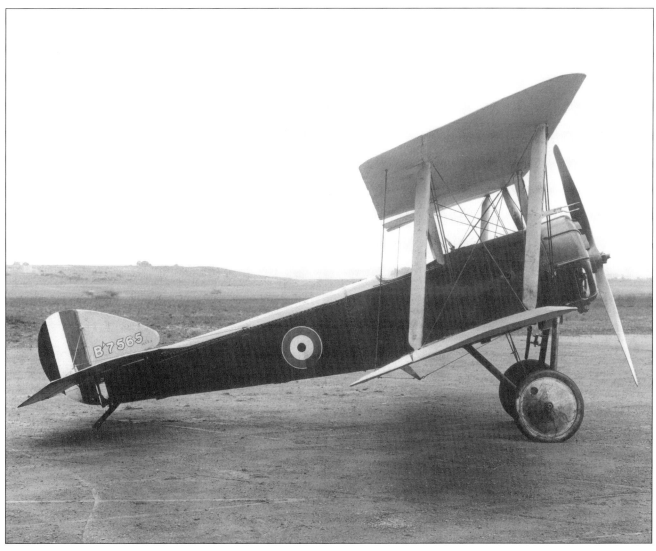

The Royal Aircraft Establishment's last surviving Pup, which had an 80p Le Rhone engine in a Monosoupape cowling, and a Rotherham petrol pump on the port forward undercarriage leg. This photograph of B7565 is dated 3rd July 1923. (RAE, Crown copyright)

synchronising gear, and the in-flight firing was done at a height of 10,000ft.

At Orfordness, a Pup was used in air-firing tests of missiles that were recorded as Capt Wynne's rockets. This seemed a somewhat unlikely event, for early ground-firing tests of five such rockets, conducted on 22nd and 24th May 1917, had been by no means promising. In firing at an 8 cu ft balloon at a range of only 25 yards only the fourth rocket struck and destroyed the balloon: two missed it completely, and the other two exploded (and, said Report B/74, 'might have set a machine on fire'). A sixth rocket 'was found to have nothing inside it beyond an electric igniter'.

Nevertheless, the air-firing tests were flown on 19th October 1917; perhaps by that time the rockets had been modified in some unspecified way. Two sorties were flown; eight rockets were fired on each. The rockets were aimed by using an Aldis gun-sight, and were fired from tubes on the Pup's interplane struts, mounted at an angle of elevation 7-8 degrees above the line of sight. They were fired at a ground target 10ft square from a height of 1,200ft to 1,500ft, the Pup diving at an angle of about 45 degrees and a speed of 120-135mph. The rockets were fired in pairs, but on each flight one rocket proved defective.

Results varied widely and the weapons must have been unpredictable. On the first flight, four shots were correct in range, but lateral error varied from 6 yards left to 100 yards left; on the second, three shots were correct

laterally, but range error was anything from 50 yards short to 50 yards over. Yet it was optimistically concluded that: 'From these trials it appears that with practice and careful adjustment of the angle between the rocket tubes and the gun sights considerable accuracy can be obtained'. Nevertheless, the Wynne rockets were never heard of again.

The Orfordness Pup B1717 survived the Armistice for a time. On 15th May 1919, it arrived at Farnborough, and apparently remained there until 6th October, when it left for Waddon. At that date, that destination probably was the end of the line for B1717, for the Pup was one of many types of aircraft that were officially decreed to be obsolete for all purposes under Air Ministry Order No.896 of 7th August 1919.

Farnborough's Royal Aircraft Establishment retained Pup B7565 at least until 1923. It had been used, on 23rd September 1919 in the testing of the Gravity Ground Indicator, evidently a primitive aid to blind landing and perhaps related to the Palethorpe Skid and the Noakes Ground Indicator, both of which were tested on S.E.5as in, respectively, 1919 and 1920. B7565 was present at Hendon in the Royal Air Force Pageant on 24th June 1922, when it was damaged. Repaired, it soldiered on well into 1923 as the last Pup in official service in Britain, and made its last recorded flight on 27th June 1923. It was one of many Pups that had the combination of an 80hp Le Rhône engine and the type of cowling usually associated with the Monosoupape.

Chapter 23

Pups of the British post-Armistice Civil Register

Despite its affectionate popularity among RFC, RNAS and RAF pilots during the war, private owners did not flock to buy redundant Pups after the Armistice, and only eight came on to the British civil register in the post-war years. There might have been at least one more, for Norman Macmillan badly wanted to keep his (presumably B5314), as he recalled in *Into the Blue*:

> 'I tried to buy my own pet Pup, but could not agree a price with the official Disposal Board. They had no second-hand terms. Every Pup was priced at £250. I pointed out that mine had flown a great many hours. It made no difference to the bureaucratic mind. The answer was that I could have a brand new one for the same price, but if I wanted one that had flown as much as mine, well, that was my own choice, not theirs, I refused to buy on such uncommercial terms. I flew

her last on 14th June 1919, and later learned that she had "been reduced to produce, or, in other words, broken up.'

Six Pups were initially registered in 1920 by the Aircraft Disposal Co as *G-EAVF* and *G-EAVV to G-EAVZ*. Of these, *G-EAVV* (ex-C440), *G-EAVY* (ex-C438) and *G-EAVZ* (ex-C540) were scrapped in 1921 by the ADC and apparently never sold to any individual owners. Also scrapped in 1921 were *G-EAVF*, which had been owned by M.E.Tanner, and *G-EAVX* (ex-B1807). The latter had been registered by A.R.M.Rickards, but unfortunately was damaged in the 1921 Aerial Derby while being flown by D.L.Forestier-Walker and was scrapped on 21st July 1921.

G-EAVW had been C312 and, in its civil guise, belonged to Flt Lt Tryggve Gran, a Norwegian serving in the Royal Air Force. On 30th July 1914, he had made an outstanding flight from Cruden Bay in Scotland to Kleppe, near Stavanger in Norway. His aircraft then was a Blériot monoplane, but his achievement, occurring virtually on the eve of war, excited little attention despite the fact that it was the first crossing of the North Sea to be made by an aeroplane. During the war he served as a pilot in the RFC, notably as a member of Home Defence Squadrons Nos.39 and 44, in which he flew B.E.12s, B.E.12as and S.E.5as. In 1919 Gran was one of a syndicate who entered the Handley Page V/1500 F7140 in the *Daily Mail* Transatlantic Flight contest; he was to have been the aircraft's navigator on the flight, but the Vickers Vimy crewed by Alcock and Brown won the contest, whereafter the V/1500 attempted a non-stop flight from Harbour Grace in Newfoundland to New York as an alternative.

B1807 seen in its Service days, when it was a Monosoupape-powered Pup of No.112 (Home Defence) Squadron. On 12th August 1917, flown by 2/Lt J.G.Goodyear, it was one of nine of the squadron's Pups that took off from Throwley to attack the formation of Gothas that bombed Southend on that day. After the Armistice it survived to come on to the British civil register as G-EAVX.

In its Service days Gran's Sopwith Pup had been-equipped for night-flying, so it is possible that he might have become acquainted with the type, if not C312 specifically, at a night-flying unit. While he owned it, as *G-EAVW*, it was based at Andover.

G-EBAZ (ex-C1524) was first owned by Herbert ('Bill') Sykes, who had had long and intimate experience of Pups, for he had been the Whitehead company test-pilot. Appropriately, C1524 had been built by Whitehead. Sykes kept it at Erith in 1922, but in the following year sold it to P.T.Capon.

Formerly C242, sometime of No.7 Training Squadron, Netheravon, and possessor of an eye-catching harlequin paint scheme (see page 141), *G-EBFJ* was owned by J.T.Norquay, and survived until 1924.

Central figure in this group is Major Tryggve Gran, post-war owner of C312 in its civil identity as G-EAVW, Here he is seen in the cockpit of the Handley Page V/1500 F7140 with (left) Major H.G.Brackley, DSO, DSC, and (right) Vice-Admiral Mark Kerr. These three were the team who were to have attempted the Atlantic crossing in the V/1500 in 1919.

At left, in helmet and goggles is Herbert Sykes, the Whitehead company's wartime test pilot and post-war owner of the civil-registered Pup G-EBAZ. Here he is seen with the Martinsyde two-seat biplane (100 hp Anzani) that he flew frequently in 1916. On it he flew for at least one wartime film, hence presence of the cameraman in this photograph.

G-EBAZ, probably after Herbert Sykes had parted with it. At right is C.P.B.Ogilvie, at one time a collector of early aircraft.

(via the late E.J.Arnsby)

Perhaps symbolising the constellation Canis Minor, C312 was armed and equipped for night flying, with navigation lights near each lower wingtip and on the decking just abaft the cockpit. The roundels on the mainplane have no white circles; those on the fuselage have been replaced by a stylised smiling sun. This Pup was used by No.189 (Night) Training Squadron, Sutton's Farm, and became G-EAVW post-war.

Chapter 24

The Pup
in Australia

The Australian Central Flying School at Point Cook near Melbourne, remote as it was from the theatres of war, had difficulty in keeping abreast of flying-training developments, not least because it lacked adequate modern aircraft. This was not for want of effort on the part of its Commanding Officer, Capt E. Harrison; and in 1918 he sought a number of B.E.2ds for use as trainers. Because the B.E.2d was then long out of production he was offered Avro 504Ks, and eventually he recommended that Avros and twelve Bristol Scouts should be ordered. The CFS had had first-hand experience of the Bristol Scout D, having received 8976 in September 1916.

But the little Bristol, too, was no longer in production; hence the cable that was sent to the Australian High Commissioner in London on 4th October 1918 advised that the CFS would accept 20 Avros with 80hp Le Rhône engines, and continued: 'Suggest latest machines replace Bristol Scouts, would prefer 12 Sopwith Pups with 80hp Le Rhône engines.' With the approval of the British Air Board these aircraft, plus spares and supporting equipment, were officially ordered.

They did not leave Britain's shores until after the Armistice; the Pups were shipped in three consignments: two in the SS *Somali*, eight in the SS *Bakara*, and the remaining two in the SS *Barambah*. The expected arrival dates of the ships were, respectively, 10th, 13th and 18th February 1919. The twelve Pups had the British serial numbers C521 to C532 and for a time after their arrival in Australia they retained these identities. Records of their earliest employment are incomplete, but it is known that C529 and C532, which had been transported by the SS *Barambah*, and were probably the last to arrive, had been unpacked and were ready for inspection by 29th April 1919. All were used at Point Cook. On 8th April 1920, C529 was struck off strength, but the circumstances of its deletion remain unknown.

The remaining eleven were transferred to No.1 FTS, Laverton, on 31st March 1921, and by 3rd October 1921 they were allotted Australian serial numbers in the Royal Australian Air Force's numbering system. The Pups became *A4-1* to *A4-11*, matching the numerical sequence of their original British numbers. On 29th March 1922, approval was given to the conversion of *A4-5*, *A4-7* and *A4-11* to components as a source of spares for the other eight aircraft. Following a crash (late July or early August 1922), authority to strike off *A4-8*

Two of the twelve Pups that were purchased by the Australian government in October 1918, photographed at the Australian Central Flying School, Point Cook. (*Colin Owers*)

A4-9, originally C530, fitted with a Thornton-Pickard camera gun.

C526 (later numbered A4-6) after a landing mishap at Point Cook. (*Colin Owers*)

Early in its civil career in Australia, G-AUCK (ex-C476) stands in front of the Pratt brothers' hangar at Geelong in 1922.   (Colin Owers)

was sought on 23rd August; and a similar fate befell *A4-4*, its conversion to components after a crash being approved on 13th February 1925. Another crash subject was *A4-10*, which suffered on 13th February 1923, this eventually becoming a ground instructional airframe.

As at 30th June 1925, Point Cook recorded that it had six Pups: five of them were in the repair depot, though one of the five was reported to be serviceable. At the RAAF Pageant presented at Flemington racecourse in December 1924, three Pups demonstrated their agility by chasing gas-filled balloons in a way that no other aircraft could match.

That event may have been the Pup's last public appearance in RAAF service, for the type was withdrawn in 1925. Towards the end of 1922 the question of providing Royal Australian Navy light cruisers with aircraft more manageable than the available Fairey IIID was examined. In the discussion of the matter the names of the Pup and Camel came up as possible subjects for conversion to seaplanes but were almost immediately dismissed as unsuitable (which they undoubtedly were).

Also to Australia went C476, though its purchasers had not originally intended to use it there. The brothers Percy and Charles Pratt were New Zealanders who, shortly after the Armistice and in Egypt, formed a partnership with the intention of introducing civil aviation to their native land. Through the RAF aircraft disposals organisation at Heliopolis they acquired four aircraft: two D.H.6s, an Avro 504K with a Monosoupape engine, and the Pup C476, which had an 80hp Clerget. Late in 1919 these were shipped from Alexandria bound for Wellington, via Melbourne and Sydney. Charles Pratt sailed with the aircraft in the SS *Cooee*; Percy went on ahead to make the necessary arrangements to set up an airfield, hangar accommodation and basic service in New Zealand.

A protracted shipping strike in Australia kept the SS *Cooee* port-bound at Melbourne for so long that the Pratt brothers decided to abandon their original idea and set up in business in Victoria instead. This they did at Geelong. On 27th December

1920, Charlie Pratt flew the Pup in the Victorian Aero Club's first aerial derby but failed to gain a place. With the advent of Australia's Air Navigation Regulations in 1921 the Pup acquired the civil registration *G-AUCK* on 28th June. By 1927 the aircraft was lying dismantled in the Pratt brothers' hangar and was struck off the civil register, though it later became *VH-UCK*, on 14th July 1931.

Apparently *VH-UCK* remained in store for several years, though a letter published in the December 1937 issue of the British-aviation monthly *Popular Flying* suggests that the Pup was flying at about that time. The letter came from one George Bennett, who wrote from Geelong West:

'The machines at present on our aerodrome are a Moth and a Westland Widgeon; others not in flying condition, but practically new [sic], are an Avro, a Sopwith Pup and a D.H.6. The Pup is complete with Clerget engine; our instructor once won a race on it here but was disqualified for low flying.'

In 1939 a proposal to install a Genet Major radial engine in the aircraft was submitted to the Department of Civil Aviation for approval. Drawings of the proposed installation were provided by John Lawrence Roche, who, in partnership with Harry Moss, bought the Pup from the Pratts. Evidently the partners thought the Pup tricky to handle, especially on touch-down, when they regarded it as 'a fierce ground-looper'. (It has to be said that, even though the term 'ground-loop' was unknown in 1917-18, no pilot of that period even mentioned this phenomenon as a fault or characteristic of the wartime Pup.) Be that as it may, Roche and Moss blamed this proclivity of their Pup on the combination of wheels with very small-section tyres, separately sprung half-axles, and an inadequate rudder.

Photographic evidence indicates that the installation of the Genet engine came first: according to Harry Moss it was an 80hp Genet II 'from a wrecked Blackburn Bluebird' (though just which Bluebird that might have been is far from clear). Its

Progressive stages in the modification of VH-UCK after the fitting of an Armstrong-Siddeley Genet radial engine. The original installation was clean, being helped by the neat spinner, but ruined the aircraft's proportions. The Pup became a two-seater with a fuel tank added to the centre section; the height of the undercarriage was reduced, but the original wheels. fin and rudder were retained for a time. (via Colin Owers)

The aesthetics of VH-UCK suffered further from the addition of doughnut wheels and an enlarged, horn-balanced rudder. (via Colin Owers)

World War II brought a camouflage scheme and a tricolour fin flash. When photographed it had evidently reverted to single-seat for a time.

(via Colin Owers)

mounting was extended well forward, and the installation was neatly cowled; there was a pointed spinner on the propeller. Undercarriage height was reduced, and the fuselage fuel tank was replaced by a 15-gallon tank, allegedly of Avro origin, in the centre section; this allowed a small second cockpit to be made; at this stage the Sopwith fin and rudder were retained.

To cure the aircraft's ground-looping tendencies, doughnut-tyred wheels on a one-piece axle were fitted, and a larger, horn-balanced rudder replaced the original, the fin being modified to suit. Harry Moss has stated that this rudder had originally belonged to a wrecked Short Scion, but no Scion ever had a rudder of the form fitted to *VH-UCK*.

After all these modifications, whatever ground-looping proclivities, the aircraft might have had were apparently cured, for Moss wrote that thereafter 'it was a smooth little thing to fly and the looping nonsense was a thing of the past'. Maybe so, but by then the Pup had been reduced to a grotesque caricature of itself; not so much a Pup as a mongrel.

It might have been still flying early in 1944. In *The Aeroplane* of 14th April 1944, there appeared a letter from G.R.Harris of Victoria. in which he reported that he had recently seen 'several interesting aircraft flying' there:

> 'The most surprising one was a Sopwith Pup. I am not certain of it being a Pup, but it was definitely a Sopwith as the makers' plate was still attached to the instrument panel. It had a five-cylinder radial motor, which I am told was a Whirlwind V. I could not find any plate on the motor, so was unable to confirm this. It had a Genet Major airscrew and two BTH magnetos on the front of the crankcase ..... The machine itself is civil registered as *VH-UCK* and was both flown in and flown away after repainting.'

Bearing in mind wartime (i.e., World War II) difficulties and delays, one cannot now know how long before 14th April Mr Harris had written that letter; nor can one know the date of '*UCK*'s departure that he witnessed. Perhaps it was at about the time when the erstwhile Pup had its Certificate of Airworthiness renewed on 17th August 1943. Amazingly, at that date it was recorded that the airframe had flown only 20 hours.

In December 1943 *VH-UCK* had been sold to W. Stillard of Deniliquin, NSW. What it did thereafter is not known, but it did not survive for long. On 4th September 1945, Stillard wrote to the Department of Civil Aviation that the aircraft had been broken up and burnt: it was rumoured that it had been accidentally damaged, but it is certain that the long career of *VH-UCK* had come to an end.

****

John Hopton has very kindly provided this detailed account of the Australian Pups:

GENERAL HISTORY

All of the thirteen examples of the Sopwith Pup delivered to Australia were from a batch of 350 aircraft (C201 to C550) subcontracted by the Standard Motor Co., Ltd. at their Coventry works, against Contract no. A.S.11541/17 of 20th August 1917.

The Military Aircraft

The origin of the twelve Pups acquired for use at the Central Flying School (CFS) dates from September/October 1917. Almost a year later, the Department of Defence (DoD) began moves to modernise the equipment at the CFS. A "shopping list" was generated on 27th August 1918, which was immediately cabled to the Australian High Commissioner in London for execution. The prime purpose of this exercise was to order 20 examples of the Avro 504J fitted with the 100hp Gnome Monosoupape B2 engine, 12 examples of the Bristol Scout fitted with a Le Rhône engine quoted as being of 90hp, and quantities of spares and other equipment. As Indent No. 413, this list was sent on to the Air Ministry's Director of Aircraft Equipment on 4th September 1918.

Immediately a problem appeared, this being the unavailability of Bristol Scout aircraft. The Air Ministry advised that "Bristol Scout machines have not been in manufacture for more than a year now, and the use of these machines for training purposes has been abandoned." It was also advised that supply problems with Monosoupape engine spares made it impossible to send same, and that the current version of the 504, fitted with the 80hp Le Rhône, was available if acceptable in place of the Monosoupape-engined version. These facts were communicated to the DoD on 23rd September 1918.

After discussion, it was decided to accept the lower-powered 504s and to order Sopwith Pups as replacements for the Bristol Scouts as originally ordered, all to be fitted with the 80hp Le Rhône 9C. On 2nd October 1918 the Secretary, DoD was advised of this modified order which was, in turn forwarded to London on the 4th and immediately passed on to the Air Board.

The 8th November saw the despatch of a cablegram to London enquiring the status of the order. This was replied to on the 19th indicating that some aircraft were ready for despatch and were waiting on space becoming available on board shipping bound for Australia, and that a quantity of spares and 12 engines were due to be shipped on the *Takada*. This cablegram also requested a formal order number be advised. This latter was so advised as "Order Victoria No. 1163" on the 28th, and London was asked to inform DoD of the approximate cost of the order. An overview of all proceedings to date in regard to this order was set down in a memo dated 9th December 1918, which was surface-mailed and not received by DoD until 8th February 1919 It was not until after this documentation had arrived that the order itself was formally generated on the 12th, and - for reasons unknown at present - it was not until 17th April that it was forwarded for transmission to London.

Shipped on S.S. *Takada*

In the event, the items loaded on *Takada* comprised a considerable amount of spares and instructional material, and the engines were not loaded, perhaps due to the vessel departing earlier than had been expected. These latter were eventually shipped on *Euripides*, departing England on 21st February 1919, whereas *Takada* had departed on 23rd November 1918.

Shipped on S.S. *Barambah*

Two Pups (C529 & C532), two 504Ks (E3743 & E3744), accompanied by 10 engines and a large quantity of spares and equipment arrived on this vessel, which had departed England on 24th December 1918 and docked at Port Melbourne in March 1919. Amongst the material received were 32 spare propellers which were, unfortunately, of the wrong type. These were type T.1708 intended for fitment to the 110hp Le Rhône 9J, being of a different pitch and diameter, and as such useless for the lower-powered engines shipped to Australia. Indicating their invoiced cost to be £560, the O.C. of the Aircraft Repair Section (ARS), Capt. A.E.Geere, recommended their return to England.

In his advice, Geere also noted that "Sopwith Scout No. C.529 is damaged, in that the leading edge of the tail plane is broken in three places. This is not a very serious defect, as it can be quite easily repaired." The Pups from *Barambah* were officially received at Point Cook on 26th April 1919.

Shipped on S.S. *Berrima*

The shipment on *Berrima* was comprised almost entirely of the remaining 18 504K aircraft (E3741, E3742, E3744 to

E3850 & H2171 to H2180). Nearly all of these machines had, due to poor packaging, been seriously damaged, and Geere advised HQ "The question of damage to the Avro machines has been duly dealt with by a Board of Officers whose findings and recommendations will be forwarded to you."

Shipping papers have not been found for the remaining ten Pups, but it is known that two were shipped on *Somali* and eight on *Bakara*.

Use of the Pup

There is not a lot of public record covering the use of the Pup. One early flight, comprising four 504Ks and three Pups, was attempted on 12th June 1919 to the Victorian country centre of Ballarat. However, the elements were not favourable, and the flight was little less than disaster, as described in the Melbourne "*Argus*" over the next two days, as :-

> *Precis* : of seven aircraft departing Point Cook, only one - a "Pup" - reached its destination Ballarat, due to poor weather conditions. It was flown by Captain Huxley, MC, who is attached to the staff of the Aviation School. Of the three Pups, two turned back after fighting strong north winds of 30 to 40 m.p.h. and having doubts about their fuel supplies.
>
> Captain Huxley, M.C., the only one of seven military aviators who left Point Cook on Thursday for Ballarat to reach his destination, returned to the flying school (13th.). The weather was ideal and the journey of approximately 60 miles was accomplished in 35 minutes. That conditions were unfavourable on Thursday is indicated by the fact that the time occupied by Captain Huxley on the forward journey was one hour fifty minutes.

The Last Military Pup

On 31st May 1930, the Secretary of the Treasury approved the free issue of an S.E.5a (possibly A2-27) and a Pup aircraft (thought to be either A4-1 or A4-10) to the East Sydney Technical College. The aircraft had been nominally on charge to No.3 Squadron at Richmond, N.S.W., and had been housed since about 1926 in the Drill Hall at Paddington, NSW. For reasons at present unknown, but thought to be the possibility of more modern aircraft being available for instructional work, the C.O., No.3 Sqn. requested the disposal of these two items in a letter to HQ on 11th March 1930. No reply forthcoming, a second letter was sent, on 3rd April 1930. This too yielded no reply, and in an effort to spur things along, a third letter was sent on 17th April, this time enclosing a letter from the College requesting the donation of the aircraft. This effort at last stirred those in authority into action, and the matter was considered on Air Board Agenda 1391, the Air Board approving disposal to the college on 27th May 1930, this leading to formal Treasury approval as noted. The College, in a letter to the Department on 18th June 1930, expressed appreciation for the gift of the two obsolete air frames. At present, details of their delivery to the College, the use they were put to, and their ultimate disposal, are unknown.

The Civil Aircraft

Charles Daniel Pratt, a New Zealander, enlisted as a member of the 11th Mounted Rifles and had been sent to Egypt in 1916. He was one of the few New Zealanders who were able to undertake flying training at Heliopolis, in 1917. Prior to his embarkation, he purchased from local disposal stocks four virtually new aircraft, these being the 504K E3432, two D.H.6 aircraft C1972 and C7625, and the Pup C476. These were crated then delivered by rail to Port Said, where they were trans-shipped by lighter to the ship on which he and his companions were to travel home to New Zealand. Eventually the ship arrived at Port Melbourne, Victoria, on this homeward voyage, and the circumstances Pratt found himself in changed his plans forever.

He had intended to set himself up in the aviation business on return home to New Zealand, but at this particular time the port of Melbourne was in the midst of both an influenza epidemic and a waterfront strike. Ship-bound for some time, Pratt soon made contact with local aviators. As his finances were dwindling and the prospect of the ship continuing its voyage in the near future were uncertain, he decided to make an effort and to set about the business of establishing an operation in the new field of aviation, in or around the Melbourne area. The author was privileged to be one of a fascinated audience who once listened to Pratt describe in his modest way how he set about solving some of the problems he encountered, once having decided upon his course of action. One night, early in May 1919, he and the ship's Captain rigged one of the on-board derricks and unloaded a crated D.H.6 onto South Wharf. Over the ensuing days, he assembled and rigged the aircraft (C1972), and then - dodging various impediments in his path on the wharf - Pratt flew the machine away. His initial destination was R.G.Carey's landing ground, approximately half-a-mile away, where he landed successfully.

For a short period he conducted joy-flight operations from the sand-flats at the end of the Port Melbourne pier, and then transferred his activities to the Belmont Common at Geelong, some 40 miles to the south. While all of this was going on, the ship suddenly sailed for Sydney, taking with it Pratt's brother and cousin, and his remaining three aircraft. These latter were off-loaded in Sydney, and being "military aircraft", were transported to the arsenal. The family members continued on to New Zealand, where their affairs were placed in order before they returned to Geelong to aid and abet Charlie in his activities. The aircraft, after some debate with military authorities, were released from the arsenal and railed to Geelong. Pratt had erected a hangar at Belmont Common, and soon all four machines were assembled and carrying out a fairly modest business for Pratt's small operation, which went by the name of the "Geelong Air Service."

C476 was assembled and test flown at Belmont Common, probably in July, 1919; at this time the airframe had a total time of 0.30hrs and the 80hp Clerget 7Z engine 0.35hrs. Pratt flew the aircraft sparingly, and entered it in the Ideal Homes Exhibition-sponsored local races in 1921 and 1922. Once the Civil Aviation Branch [CAB] became established and were able to ascertain which aircraft would come under their control, Pratt's aircraft were all allotted civil registrations, in May 1922. The Pup was allocated *G-AUCK*, and as such was issued with Certificate of Registration No.24 on 12th July 1921, back-dated to 28th June 1921, marked as "pending" and valid for 12 months in the "tourist" class. It was not until 29th December 1921 that Pratt applied for a Certificate of Airworthiness, and after satisfactory test-flights late in March, 1922, CofA No.53 was issued to *G-AUCK* on 7th April 1922.

Pratt last flew the Pup on 24th June 1923, at which time it had achieved a total time on the airframe of 10.05hrs, with 10.35hrs on the engine; soon after it was dismantled and stored in various buildings about the aerodrome. It was kept on the civil register until early in 1931, when an annual registration fee was imposed by the CAB, an act which Pratt declined to countenance. It was cancelled from the register on 14th July 1931. As with all other Australian civil aircraft, *G-AUCK* was

required to be re-marked as *VH-UCK* within a 12-month period from 28th March 1929. It is considered that this was not carried out, allowing the situation of the aircraft at that time.

Pratt's Pup lingered in obscurity for some years, adorning the hangars. The bunting-draped fuselage was towed through Geelong on the May-day Parade in 1924, but otherwise it just gathered dust. Pratt was certainly wishing to dispose of it by November 1927, but it was not until some ten years had passed that a prospective buyer, one Arthur Bone of Geelong, made enquiries of the Civil Aviation Board on 4th June 1937 regarding re- registration of the aircraft - converted to two-seat configuration and fitted with a Genet Major engine!

Nothing much happened until early 1939, by which time Jack Roche, owner of the Renown Press, had taken over the project. The Department of Civil Aviation (DCA) were not particularly happy with the idea of putting the old Pup back on the register, but did not rule out the plan entirely; their one serious prohibition was to rule that it could not be converted to two-seat form. Roche, working with engineer Harry Moss, carried out the conversion at Geelong. The Genet Major [No. AS.38] had been installed early in 1939, using an identical mount system to the Avro Avian; the engine was, in fact, from the Avian II *VH-UGA*. By mid-June, the Pup had been re-covered and registration applied, and four months later, on Saturday 14th October, Roche carried out taxying tests and a test flight. On the 19th was granted permission to fly the Pup to Essendon for inspection. Roche flew the machine to Coode Island late in January, 1940 and made flights on the following week-ends, including a return trip to Geelong on 11th February. Roche was in "hot-water" with the authorities for a period due to these several illegal flights, but all was sorted out eventually. By 13th May 1940 the airframe had accumulated a grand total of 13.00 hours.

On 21st May 1941 the Pup was formally re-registered to John Lawrence Roche of Carnegie, Vic,. and a valid CofA issued. This latter lapsed in May 1942, and was renewed on 18th August. Interestingly, Roche had not given up on the idea of conversion to two-seat form. In June 1943 he applied again to carry this out, but the DCA would not give permission. The CofA lapsed on 17th August, and, after renewal on 6th November, Roche then applied to the DCA for permission to sell the Pup to Wallace O.Stillard of Deniliquin, NSW on the 30th. This sale was approved on 4th December and the transfer of ownership formalised on the 31st. Stillard, proprietor of the Sportsman's Arms Hotel at Deniliquin, flew the machine irregularly, and allowed the C of A to expire on 5th November 1944 by which time the airframe had a grand total of 50.15 hours.

One A.G.P.Williams, of Urana, NSW evinced some interest in acquiring the Pup in mid-May 1945, but nothing came of this. On 4th September 1945 Stillard advised the DCA that "The aircraft has been dismantled and the motor and propeller sold a few days ago to Mr. H.Hayback of Yarrawonga for use in a motor boat, and will not be used again in the above aircraft as this machine has been broken up." To his letter, Stillard added the postscript that "This machine was not crashed but owing to its age decided to sell engine and burn the rest as it is useless to anyone." Stillard's comment that the aircraft had been "dismantled" is true, although not in the usual sense! The aircraft had been parked beside the farmhouse, and late one night had been lifted into the air by a "willy-willy" (a local mini-tornado) and deposited with some force on the roof - instant dismantling! For many years, rumours abounded that the aircraft was still to be seen in and around the Yarrawonga district, but its remains were recorded on the local dump in the early fifties - and these only fragments.

Chapter 25

In Other Lands

The Pup was not exported in any great quantity, but the following details are known of use by other countries, apart from Australia (see Chapter 24). Information on individual aircraft, where available, may be found in Appendices 14 and 15.

Belgium

Belgium was interested in the type. Under British Requisition No.153, against the date of 31st July 1917, 'six Sopwith Scout machines, with spares, for Belgian Government' were sought; at that time no contractor was named. On 19th October 1917, under B.R.153, Contract No. A.S.24542 was attributed to the Sopwith Company, more specifically for 'six Sopwith Single-seater 80hp Le Rhône Scouts for Belgian Government'. This confirmed beyond doubt that the aircraft concerned were Pups. These administrative exercises followed events belatedly, for it is known that some Pups had been in Belgian hands and service at Calais-Beaumarais by late May 1917.

It is known that at least four Pups, with Belgian numbers *SB1* to *SB4,* saw some service with the *Aviation militaire belge.* These may have been the four Pups that were with the Belgian l^e *Escadrille* in 1917; one of the pilots who flew them occasionally was Willy Coppens (the late Baron Coppens de Houthulst). The Pup was also used, obviously as a secondary type, by the 5^e *Escadrille*; and it has been reported that two or three were employed as advanced trainers by a Belgian unit (possibly a counterpart of the RFC's Scout School) based at Calais-Beaumarais, where the instructor was Lt Albert van Cotthem.

France

The brief association of one anonymous Pup with the French wartime authorities has already been recorded in pages 99-100. As far as is known, no other example of the Pup was evaluated by the French.

Greece

In the Aegean war zone, Pups of 'C' Squadron, RNAS, were occasionally flown by Greek pilots of 'Z' Squadron. When hostilities ended, the four surviving Pups (N6432, N6433, N6470 and N6471) were transferred to the Greek government. The first two were Beardmore-built Type 9901a Pups; as at 1st February 1918, N6432, together with 9941 and 9942, was on the strength of 'G' Flight, No.2 Wing, RNAS. N6433 was then under repair at Mudros, while N6470 and N6471 were designated as Greek Training Aircraft. By 1st October, 9941 was no longer listed, 9942 was under repair, N6432 was at Marsh aerodrome, and N6433, N6470 and N6471 were annotated 'Greek Training'. No Greek serial numbers appear to have been allocated.

One of the six Pups delivered to the Aviation militaire belge in 1917.   *(Guy Destrebecq)*

A Belgian Pup bearing the comet emblem of the 5ᵉ Escadrille. It is believed that this photograph was taken at Calais-Beaumarais, where the maintenance and aircraft depot of the Aviation militaire belge was situated. *(Guy Destrebecq)*

C386 in Japanese service. but still wearing its British serial number on its rudder.

A Pup on a flying-off platform on a Japanese battleship.

One of the Japanese Pups that came on to the Japanese civil register was J-TETV, which was re-registered as Mizuta Special J-HUXY after receiving some modifications. This may be the scene after T.Miya crashed into a bank when landing in a small field after a goodwill flight at his place of birth, Wakanatsu City in the Fukuoka prefecture on 14th October 1922 or 3rd December 1922. *(Noburu Jyoko)*

The former N6164 of No.9 Squadron, RNAS after repair and assimilation into the Dutch Luchtvaart Afdeling in 1917.   *(F.Gerdessen)*

Japan

Japan had received specimens of several types of British aircraft during the 1914-18 war, and in 1919 the Japanese government acquired Pups (C481-C499, C503-C509, C533-538, C1496, D4144-4152, D4155, D4156, D4160, D4161, D4163, D4165, D4168 and D4169) and two Beardmore S.B.3Ds (N6735 and N6736); the latter two went to Japan in the late summer of 1918. Although the initiative for the importation of these aircraft apparently came from the Japanese army, Pups were also flown by Japanese naval aviators. The army gave its Pups the designation Type S⇐ Model 3 Fighter, and used the type to equip the 1, 2 and 4 *Hikodaitai* (air battalions). Some were sent to Vladivostok to join the Japanese Expeditionary Force in Siberia in the 'intervention' of 1918-22, but what, if anything, they did is unknown. It has been reported that at least one Japanese Navy Pup, *JN125*, was used in flying-off experiments, perhaps in connection with the gun-turret-platform flights made by Gloucestershire Sparrowhawks from Japanese capital ships. It may have been the Pup seen in the illustration opposite. The Pup's tractability inspired a mild form of aerobatic record setting in 1921. Capt Ozeki performed 405 consecutive loops on C505, but this was surpassed by Capt Kawaida, who completed 456 loops, flying D4165. Some of these Pups later had Japanese civil registrations, known examples being detailed in Appendix 15. A Japanese two-seat conversion of the Pup was at least designed, possibly as the two-seat trainer version that has been attributed to the Japanese navy.

Netherlands

The Dutch *Luchtvaart Afdeling* acquired a Pup on 1st March 1917, when N6164 of No.9 (Naval) Squadron, flown by Flt Lt F.V.Branford, came down in Dutch territory near Cadzand. It overturned on landing and sustained some damage; its engine was also damaged and took in some sea water. Dutch personnel repaired the Pup; although the structural work had been completed by 17th April 1917, its engine could not be persuaded to run satisfactorily. By 23rd April the engine from a Nieuport (perhaps the Nieuport 11 No.3981 of No.1 Wing.

RNAS, interned on 26th February 1917) was substituted, and on 26th April the Pup was flown satisfactorily.

On 23rd May this Pup was flown in comparative trials with the native Trompenburg V.1, and proved to be appreciably faster and to have a very much better rate of climb. As early as 3rd March 1917, Director Wynmalen of the Trompenburg company had stated that he would prefer to build the Nieuport rather than the Pup: the results of the comparative trials should have made him change his mind, but did not; and Trompenburg built Nieuport 11 copies that were not officially accepted until October 1918. Even then, they were considered unsafe and were never used. It seems there was at one time a proposal to build Pups also, but this came to naught.

Pup N6164 was eventually purchased, on 23rd September 1917, *by the Luchtvaart Afdeling* for £1,700 - which suggests that the Admiralty made, on paper at least, a profit on the transaction. The officially listed price of the Pup airframe was £710 18s 0d, of its 80hp Le Rhône £620, giving a total of £1,330 18s 0d, to which should be added the price of Vickers gun and other more minor details. Nevertheless, these accessories were unlikely to have cost the difference of £369 2s 0d. In Dutch service N6164 was first numbered *LA-41*, but in 1918 was renumbered as *S212*.

Russia

Another singleton that went to foreign parts was N6204, which was given to the Russian government in 1917, but its activities (if any) and fate have yet to be discovered.

United States of America

A United States Navy document of uncertain age and origin, entitled Serial List of Designating Numbers of Naval Aircraft, includes two named as Sopwith Pups, to which the numbers A5655 and A5656 were allotted. The authenticity of this identification is impaired by the attribution of 130hp Clerget engines to the aircraft; and as A5658 and A5659 were Camels the possibility that the so-called Pups might in truth have been Camels cannot be excluded.

Chapter 26

The Sopwith Type STI.2 Dove

A post-war adaptation of the Pup was the Type STI.2 Dove. It was publicised in 1919 as a 'Sporting two-seater', though possibly a little underpowered with only a wartime 80p Le Rhône 9C engine to carry two occupants seated in tandem. The overall length was little different compared with the Pup but the wings, which were of reduced area, were swept back to adjust the centre of gravity so as to compensate for the extra occupant.

It was claimed that, when fitted with dual control, it would be particularly suitable for instructing pilots who have passed preliminary tests, before placing them on high-powered single-seaters, this presumably referring at that time to military aircraft.

On 10th May 1919, Major W.G.Barker VC flew Dove c/n W/O 2714 to Hounslow, with a young Prince of Wales (later King Edward VIII and afterwards the Duke of Windsor) as a passenger. The aircraft at that time only carried the name 'DOVE' in capital letters on the fuselage, but was about to become *K-122* and later *G-EACM*. It was sold in Canada about a year later, becoming *G-CAAY* with Bishop-Barker Aeroplanes Ltd of Toronto.

When displayed at the 1920 Olympia Show the Dove was described:

'Petrol is fed by gravity, thus eliminating all pressure troubles. Both pilot and passenger are comfortably situated, possessing very good visibility. The low landing speed, together with the extra strong landing chassis, enables it to alight on or get away from very small fields. Fuel is carried for a period of two-and-a-half hours at a cruising speed of 85mph, and an adjustable tailplane allows of the machine being flown with the maximum comfort.'

Retaining the rotary engine of the Pup was a disadvantage, this type of engine soon proving to be out of favour with post-war private owners, who much preferred the new post-war stationary engines then beginning to become available for light civil aircraft.

A total of 18 Doves is believed to have been completed, though not all can be accounted for. A few were exported to Sweden and Australia.

A newly-built Sopwith Dove, probably the prototype, at Brooklands in April 1919. In the background can be seen the famous banked motor racing circuit, part of which still survives.

(via Philip Jarrett)

On 19th March 1919 the Australian Government announced that it would award £10,000 to the first Australian airman to fly from England to Australia in 720 consecutive hours [= 30 days] before midnight on 31st December 1920. H.J.L.('Bert') Hinkler, who had been a mechanic at Sopwith's Kingston Skating Rink works before joining the RNAS, still as a mechanic, entered a Dove, but after a rival team decided to make an immediate start in a twin-engined Blackburn Kangaroo it was decided that all attempts should be postponed until September 1919 to allow time for participants to make proper preparations. Various conditions were imposed, including one that competitors be enrolled in the Australian Air Force in order that none of them should be financially prejudiced by the delay. The conditions were unacceptable to Hinkler, and he withdrew. In the event Vickers Vimy G-EAOU departed on 12th November and arrived at Darwin on 10th December, having covered 11,060 miles in 135 hours 55 minutes flying time and 28 elapsed days, the pilots, Ross Smith and Keith Smith, both being knighted.

Four Doves as well as two Sopwith Gnus arrived in Australia in 1919, being imported by the Larkin-Sopwith Aviation Co of Australasia Ltd, which had been registered in London with a capital of £31,500 with the object of assisting aerial transport companies in the formation and maintenance of their passenger services. W/O 3004/2 (ex K-168, G-EAHP) arrived at Melbourne in SS Demosthenes on 13th October 1919. After being test flown at Glenhuntly, Victoria, it made its first public appearance twelve days later at the Henley Regatta Day when Captain J.Larkin flew at nine o'clock in the evening with it lit up across the full span of its wings and with the fuselage outlined in green lights. At an air display on 26th December at Epsom Racecourse, Victoria, Captain A.W.Vigers flew in mock combat with Capt R.King in a Gnu, and later flew in air races. This Dove was later sold to Aerial Transport of South Australia (ATDSA) and afterwards to Dudley Angas, Hill River Station, Clare, South Australia. It eventually crashed on 17th August 1920 during an attempted flight between Glenelg, Adelaide and Melbourne. A replacement Dove arrived in Australia on 3rd September 1920 and was painted in a black and white check colour scheme, to be operated by what had now become the Larkin-Sopwith Aircraft Supply Co Ltd, but with the demise of the parent Sopwith company the name was changed in July 1921 to the Larkin Supply Co Ltd.

In April 1933, in a liquidation sale of the assets of the General Aircraft Co Ltd of Sydney, VH-UDN was sold for £60.

The sole survivor is G-EBKY, which was eventually converted to Pup standard, and can be seen flying at Old Warden during the summer months.

Specifications

Wing span: 24 ft 9½ in. Length: 19 ft 4 in. Height: 8 ft 6 in.
Wing area: 211¼ square feet.
Maximum speed: 100 mph. Time to 5,000 ft: 7½ min.
Range: 250 miles.
Weight empty: 1,065 lbs.
All-up weight: 1,430 lbs (certificated weight 1,350 lbs).

Production and use

18 aircraft stated to have been built, known works order numbers and registrations etc being as follows:

W/O 2714 — Regd K-122 20.5.19 to The Sopwith Aviation Co, Brooklands. Used by Major Barker VC to fly HRH Prince of Wales at Hounslow 10.5.19; CofA issued 19.5.19. Regd G-EACM [CofR 65] 8.19 to same owner. Sold abroad 5.20, almost certainly to Bishop-Barker Aeroplanes Ltd., Toronto, registration G-CAAY issued 23.6.20, CofR C42. Sold to A.S.Highstone, Sault St Marie, Ontario 1921. DBR in accident at Sault St Marie, 1921. [c/n '33937' quoted in Canadian Register]

W/O 2769/1 — K-133/G-EACU, 7.8.19, Sopwith Aviation Co., Brooklands; to Lt Olof Enderlein, Hägernäs, Sweden. Imported 1.23, test flown 7.2.23, regd probably 5.5.23 as S-AFAA, known to have used ski undercarriage. Sold to Gustaf Lundström 4.25, last inspected 18.7.28, to Svensk Filmindustri about 12.28 for use as wind generator

W/O 2769/2 — K-148/G-EAFI, 30.6.19, Sopwith Aviation Co., Brooklands; reportedly cancelled on delivery 'to Norway' 10.21, no evidence; to H.Carlsson/NLR, Sweden; sold to Oskar Bladh, Stockholm as S-AYAA; [c/n quoted as '4212']; Regd 5.8.24, cancelled 31.12.26

W/O 3004/1 — K-157/G-EAGA, 14.8.19, Sopwith Aviation Co., Brooklands; sold abroad 9.19

W/O 3004/2 — K-168/G-EAHP, 11.9.19, Sopwith Aviation Co., Brooklands; sold abroad 9.19; Arrived Melbourne in SS Demosthenes 3.10.19; Crashed 17.8.20

W/O 3004/3 — G-EAJI, 30.9.19, Sopwith Aviation and Engineering Co. Ltd., Brooklands; sold abroad 8.20, believed to E.O.Cudmore, Melbourne as G-AUDN 6.21, later VH-UDN, dbr 3.34

W/O 3004/4 — G-EAJJ, 26.4.20, Sopwith Aviation and Engineering Co. Ltd., Brooklands; to Larkin Supply Co., Melbourne 3.20, to G-AUJJ 6.21; scrapped 6.25

W/O 3004/5 — G-EAKH, 17.4.20, Sopwith Aviation Co., Brooklands; to Larkin Supply Co., Melbourne 3.20, to G-AUKH 6.21; scrapped 6.28

W/O 3004/6 — G-EAKT, 17.4.20, Sopwith Aviation Co., Brooklands; sold abroad 3.20, believed to A.L.Long, Hobart, Tasmania as G-AUDP; crashed before registration

W/O 3004/7 to 13 unidentified Doves?

W/O 3004/14 — G-EBKY registered 27.3.25 to D.L.Hollis Williams; C. of A. 12.4.27; C.H.Lowe-Wylde, West Malling 9.30; w.f.u. 12.33; Restored to R.O. Shuttleworth, Old Warden 7.37 and converted to Sopwith Pup (q.v.)

Swedish reports show two unidentified Doves arriving on 28.1.21 and 18.2.21, owned by NLR/Carlsson; the first crashed at Sundsvall 28.2.21, the second at Tierp 26.2.21. These may be from the gap W/O 3004/7-13, or one could have been W/O 2769/2

Chapter 27

Envoy

In Rupert Brooke's verse 'The little dog died when he'd had his day', but Sopwith's Pup has lived on far beyond the end of the war into which it was born, and at the time of writing is by no means extinct. So enduring is the reputation of the Pup, and so strong its aesthetic appeal, that many reproductions were made and flown decades after the true production aircraft plied the martial trade for which they were created. The first such latter-day Pup was the aircraft built at Calgary, Alberta, in 1955 by S.N.Green, faithfully conforming to the makers' drawings. Others, of varying degrees of structural and geometrical authenticity, followed over the years; a few of them embodied enough identifiable original components to reclaim true wartime identities.

These brought airworthy Pups, or near-Pups, into the hands of pilots who had advantages and experience far beyond anything available to or attainable by those who were the Pup's true contemporaries: pilots who had access to techniques of testing and refinements of assessment that were undreamed of in 1917-18. Two post World War II pilots who have left handling appraisements were the late Air Commodore Allen Wheeler, OBE, and the late Neil Williams. Their articles appeared 23 years apart: Allen Wheeler's 'Immortal thoroughbred' was published in *Flight* magazine of 20th July 1950, Neil Williams' 'Sopwith Pup' in *Pilot* in July 1975. By coincidence, the aircraft that was the subject of these commentaries was the modified Sopwith Dove, originally *G-EBKY* and a two-seater, that was extensively modified by Richard Shuttleworth shortly before the 1939-45 war; after its rebuilding it closely resembled a Pup, and has been maintained in flying condition by the Shuttleworth Trust. Until the autumn of 1983 it had a variable-incidence tailplane, non-standard fin and rudder of increased area, a higher than standard tailskid, tapered interplane struts and - something no self-respecting Pup ever had - underwing skids to protect the lower wing-tips against grounding. Precisely how comparable its handling qualities were to those of a standard Pup fastidiously rigged by skilled contemporary riggers can never be known.

Allen Wheeler was, at the time of writing his *Flight* article, OC Experimental Flying at the Royal Aircraft Establishment, Farnborough; he was a pilot of exceptional experience and outstandingly well qualified to assess the Pup. Apart from his long RAF experience, his association with the early aircraft in the Shuttleworth Collection had brought him an intimate knowledge of the characteristics of such aeroplanes.

For him the Shuttleworth aircraft reflected many of the charms of the Pup:

'The take-off is quite straightforward, there being practically no swing. Such as there is, is easily almost unconsciously corrected by rudder. The only surprise at take-off is to find oneself in the air so soon. The next impression, on getting into the air, is that the aircraft is very unstable fore and aft and that somebody has forgotten to connect up the elevators - until one finds that the elevators are, in fact, so light at slow speeds that one has some difficulty in feeling them at all. The ailerons, on the contrary, are very nice indeed at low speeds, but tend to become spongy at normal operating speeds of between 100mph and 140mph. The rudder is effective and pleasantly light.

'So far as manoeuvrability goes the Pup is a joy to fly, but the ailerons are definitely spongy at high speed and give the impression that it would not be easy to do a slow roll; in fact I believe the few people who were able to achieve good slow rolls on the Pup managed it by pushing the stick hard over until it touched their knees (which it does all too soon), and then tucking it under the knee and pushing it the rest of the way across the cockpit.

'The aircraft is, as one would expect of a 1914-18 fighter, fully aerobatic. The gyroscopic action one experiences with other heavy rotaries is almost entirely absent with the 80hp Le Rhône, presumably because the engine is very light and the Pup's rudder and elevators are particularly effective. The best climbing speed is between 65 and 70mph, with the engine doing about 1,140 rpm, i.e., full engine speed on the climb.

'Looping is a very straightforward manoeuvre indeed. One dives to about 115mph, then pulls the stick gently back; the force necessary to do so can easily be applied with the little finger. There is a very slight tendency to swing as one passes over the top of the loop, but it is corrected almost unconsciously with the rudder. The amazing thing about the loop, both from the pilot's point of view and from that of anyone who watches it nowadays, is that the loop itself is of such small dimensions that one hardly realises what has happened. This is very different from the loops performed by modern fighters, which usually include some 5,000ft of altitude and may be a mile-and-a-half or two miles in diameter.

'The Pup stalls in very much the same way as all the more aged biplanes, that is to say, much more suddenly than a modern aircraft, but perfectly controllably and with little loss of height. Recovery from an ordinary stall is immediate. ....

'Taken all round, the Pup is a delightful little aircraft to fly, with one of the smoothest-running engines one could ever experience even today, excluding only jets. It has no vices and is, in fact, extremely easy to handle, but, and this is an important "but" one has to land it, not just push it on the ground as one does with so many modern aircraft. Moreover, one has to "handle" the engine, and not merely open the throttle as one does today.'

Neil Williams was one of the leading aerobatic and display pilots of his day; as such, he had much experience of aircraft specially built or modified for that form of epideictic flying, with exceptionally responsive and powerful controls, and adequately powered withal. He took a less than enthusiastic view of the Dove-Pup convert, especially of the sensitivity of its 80hp Le Rhône engine:

'We try some turns: to the right she is pleasant and well-harmonised, but to the left she feels clumsy and needs a lot of rudder. Certainly she is not "sweet on the controls", nor particularly sensitive either, unless one considers the deterioration in pitch stability with power "sensitive". It is only in turns to the right that she begins to approach the sort of handling that one has come to expect in a classical modern type.

'With more confidence that we now have the engine under control we try a loop. We press forward on the stick and note that the tail-heaviness increases as we accelerate to 105mph which gives 1,200rpm. The slipstream really hammers around the windshield and tugs hard at our goggles - one wonders how they used to fight and sight their single gun in the bitter cold at 20,000 feet [sic] in 1916. The ailerons are heavy at this speed as we release some of the forward pressure. The nose arcs upwards and we need fast and accurate footwork to keep straight. The view upwards is good because of the slot in the centre section of the top wing. Over the top with the aircraft back in trim, but we need full left rudder to keep straight against the enormous gyroscopic forces. As we dive out we close the fine adjustment we don't want high rpm or 'G' as this is a very precious aeroplane.

'As we fly around the circuit we note that the roll rate is poor and the ailerons are heavy even at moderate speeds. It is only too easy to fly with crossed controls, and the rudder is ridiculously light. The Pup can turn quite tightly, too, maybe a little tighter than a Tiger Moth. As the bank approaches the vertical one is again aware of the strong tendency to yaw to the right.'

Was he, one wonders, really writing about the same aeroplane as Allen Wheeler?

The aircraft may not have reproduced with total authenticity the qualities of a true Pup, but, with great respect, one ventures the opinion that here it was not the aircraft but the pilot who was different - different from those of 1917-18 most markedly in training, in period, in knowledge, in awareness, in long-practised skill, and - dare one say? - in perception. In July 1973, when Neil Williams' faintly patronising article was published, aviation was 55 years older than it was in the Pup's day; in particular, one notes his comparison with 'a classical modern type'. Pilots of 1973 were not only incomparably better educated and trained (in the aeronautical sense), but also immeasurably more disposed to take for granted aviation in general and aircraft handling in particular. Long gone was the sense of exultant wonder at participating in a newly-discovered near-miracle; gone too, alas, the rapture of flying an aircraft that provided at that time a dazzling and captivating revelation of what man-controlled flight could be. Such, in its time and to its contemporary pilots, was the Sopwith Pup.

It was for those pilots, and as one of them, that the late Major Oliver Stewart, MC, AFC, spoke with unassailable authenticity and authority when he summed up the Pup as:

'The perfect flying machine. This is the term which the Sopwith triplane nearly fulfilled and which the Sopwith Pup did fulfil. As a military aircraft it had certain shortcomings, but as a flying machine - a machine which gave a high return in speed and climb for a given expenditure of horse-power, which had well-balanced, powerful controls, which was stable enough but not too stable, which was sensitive enough without being too sensitive, and which obeyed its pilot in a way that eventually secured his lasting admiration and affection - the Sopwith Pup was and still is without superior.'

(*The Clouds Remember*)

Above: The instrument panel of a Pup. At top left is the tachometer; next to it, under the magneto switch, is the watch; central is the compass, with the lateral clinometer directly under it; at top right is the air-speed indicator (here graduated in knots); and at bottom right the altimeter. At bottom left is the crank handle of the winding-off drum for the ammunition belt.
Right: The cockpit of a Whitehead-built Pup, with yet another arrangement of the instruments and equipment. A refinement is the inboard chute for spent cases and discarded links, fitted centrally and curving to starboard to discharge under the aircraft.

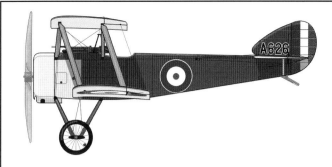

Sopwith Pup:
A626 of No.8(N) Sqn., Captured by the Germans
on 4 January 1917.

Sopwith Pup:
N6171/P, "Black Arrow" of No.3(N) Sqn., RNAS
in March 1917. Pilot F/Sub-Lt. E. Pierce.

Sopwith Pup:
N6200, "Bobs" of No.4(N) Sqn., RNAS, Bray Dunes,
in April 1917.

Sopwith Pup:
A7334/2 of No.46 Sqn., RFC, Boisdinghem,
in April 1917. Flown by 2/Lt. F.L. Luxmoore.

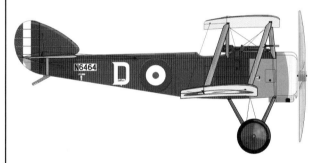

Sopwith Pup:
N6464/D of No.3(N) Sqn., RNAS, flown by F/Sub-Lt. J.
Bampfylde Daniell. Shot down by Vzfw Reissinger of Jasta 12,
near Heynecourt on11 May 1917, Daniell becoming a POW.

Sopwith Pup:
N6442 "Julia" of the Walmer Defence Flight
in June 1917.

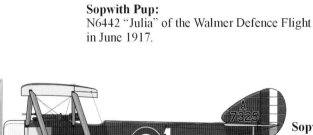

Sopwith Pup:
A7325/1 of No.46 Sqn., RFC, flown by Capt. S.H. Pratt,
circa mid-1917.

Sopwith Pup:
N6475/9 of No.11(N) Sqn., RNAS, Hondschoote,
Belgium in July1917.

Sopwith Pup:
N6203/6, "Mina" of the Seaplane Defence Flight, RNAS,
St. Pol, France in July 1917. Flown by F/Sub-Lt. L.H. Slatter.

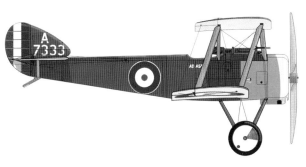

Sopwith Pup:
A7333, "Ad Astra" of No.46 Sqn., RFC,
Sutton's Farm, July-August 1917.

Sopwith Pup:
B1778, "Punjab 12 Kashmir", served with No.66 Sqn.,
RFC in August 1917.

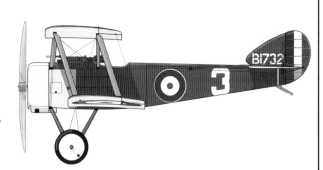

Sopwith Pup:
B1732/3 of No.66 Sqn., RFC. Flown by 2/Lt. P.A. O'Brien.
Shot down by Ltn. Dannhuber of Jasta 26, on 17 August 1917.

Sopwith Pup:
N6452 flown by Sqn. Cdr. E. H. Dunning from HMS *Furious*,
on 7 August 1917. Sadly the aircraft ditched and Dunning
was drowned.

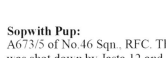

Sopwith Pup:
A673/5 of No.46 Sqn., RFC. The pilot 2/Lt. M. Shadwell
was shot down by Jasta 12 and captured on 16 September 1917.

Sopwith Pup:
B1768/D of No.66 Sqn., RFC. The pilot Lt. J.W. Boumphrey
was shot down and captured on 30 September 1917.

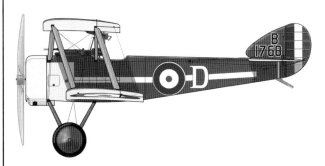

Sopwith Pup:
A7344/3 of No.54 Sqn., RFC. The pilot 2/Lt. P. Norton
was shot down and captured on 13 October 1917.

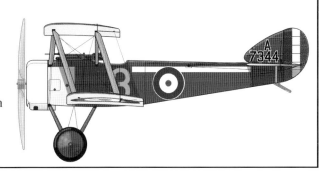

M.D. Howley 2002

Sopwith Pup:
B1803/5, of No.112 (Home Defence) Sqn., RFC, Throwley, late-1917. Flown by 2/Lt. A.B. Garnons-Williams, formerly South Wales Borderers, hence the fuselage badge.

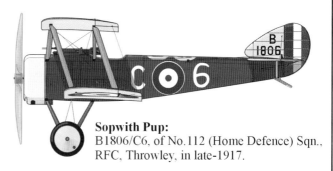

Sopwith Pup:
B1806/C6, of No.112 (Home Defence) Sqn., RFC, Throwley, in late-1917.

Sopwith Pup:
A7317, of the Central Flying School, Upavon, flown by Lt. F.P. Fullard in 1917.

Sopwith Pup:
B1719/4 of No.46 Sqn., RFC, Sutton's Farm, flown by 2/Lt. R.M. Ferrie in 1917.

Sopwith Pup:
A635/D of No.66 Sqn. RFC, captured by the Germans on 12 October 1917. 2/Lt. M. Newcomb POW.

Sopwith Pup:
B2192, Monosoupape-powered, flown by Capt. H. Balfour of the School of Special Flying, Gosport, circa 1917.

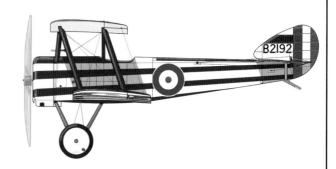

Sopwith Pup:
B5307 of No.61 (Home Defence) Sqn., RFC, night-flying from Rochford in January 1918.

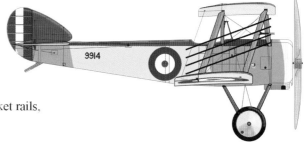

Sopwith Pup:
9914 of the RNAS fitted with rocket rails, in 1917.

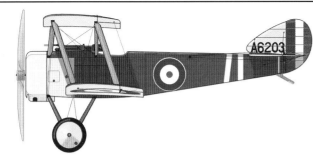

Sopwith Pup:
A6203 of an unknown RFC Sqn., North Shotwick in 1918.

Sopwith Pup:
B5307/8B of No.61 (Home Defence) Sqn.,
RFC, Rochford,circa January 1918.

Sopwith Pup:
B5385/6 of No.3 Training Sqn., RFC, Shoreham
in January 1918.

Sopwith Pup:
B7525 of No.60 Training Sqn.,
RFC, Scampton, in March 1918.

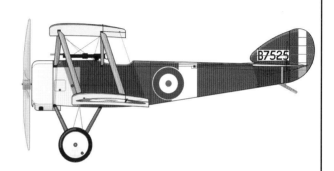

Sopwith Pup:
N6192/AC of No.11(N) Sqn. RNAS, St.Pol, France
on 15 August 1917.

Sopwith Pup:
C417 of No.3 Fighting School, Bircham Newton
flown by Capt. J. Michness, 16 September 1918.

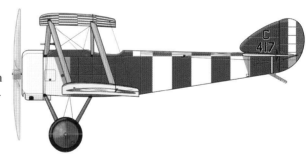

Sopwith Pup:
B1807/A7 of "A" Flight, No.76 (Home Defence) Sqn., RAF,
Copmanthorpe, in 1918.

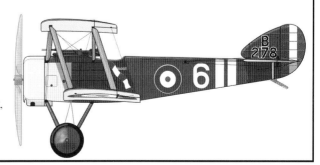

Sopwith Pup:
B2178/6, "Madge" of No.112 Sqn., RFC, Throwley,
in February 1918. Flown by "Bunny" Newton.

M.D. Howley 2002

Sopwith Pup:
B7575 of No.26 Training Depot Station, RAF Edzell, in
September 1918. Checks are probably black and white.

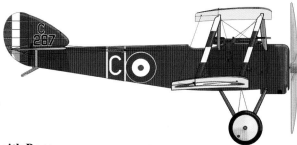

Sopwith Pup:
C287/C of No.18 Training Squadron,
RAF, Montrose circa June 1918.

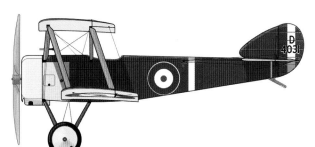

Sopwith Pup:
D4031 of No.2 Training Depot Station, RAF,
Gullane circa July 1918.

Sopwith Pup:
N6438, "Excuse me!" Of the RAF
undertaking trials on HMS *Furious*
in April 1918.

Sopwith Pup:
C312 of No.189 (Night) Training Squadron, RAF,
Sutton's Farm in 1918. Fuselage design possibly red,
white and blue.

Sopwith Pup:
C354 possibly of No.44 Sqn., RAF,
Hainault Farm, in 1918.

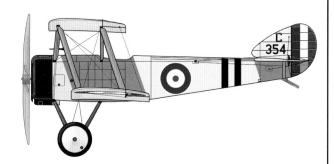

Sopwith Pup:
N6161 of No.3(N) Sqn., RNAS, shot down near Blankenbergh
on 1 February 1917. F/Sub-Lt. G.L.Elliott made POW.
Re-marked in German insignia. Roundels possibly
overpainted in green.

Beardmore WBIII:
The second production aircraft, based at
RNAS East Fortune from July 1917.

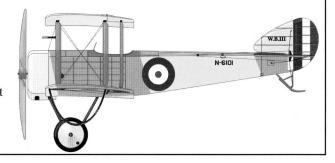

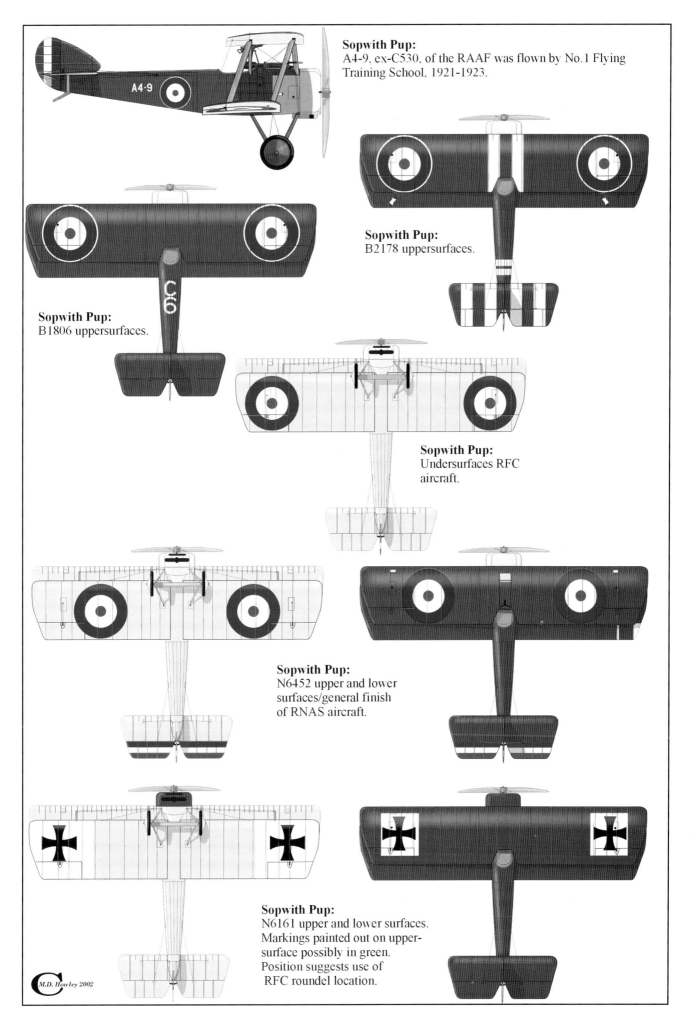

Sopwith Pup:
A4-9, ex-C530, of the RAAF was flown by No.1 Flying Training School, 1921-1923.

Sopwith Pup:
B2178 uppersurfaces.

Sopwith Pup:
B1806 uppersurfaces.

Sopwith Pup:
Undersurfaces RFC aircraft.

Sopwith Pup:
N6452 upper and lower surfaces/general finish of RNAS aircraft.

Sopwith Pup:
N6161 upper and lower surfaces. Markings painted out on uppersurface possibly in green. Position suggests use of RFC roundel location.

M.D. Howley 2002

Pup G-EKBY, a converted Sopwith Dove owned by the Shuttleworth Trust, seen here at Upavon in June 1962 carrying the mark 'N5180'.

(James Halley)

American-built Pup replica 'N5192', seen here at Porterville in September 1973. *(Ron J Bulinski)*

Pup replica G-BIAU seen here at Cranfield in June 1983, marked 'N6452'. (A.J.Ward)

Pup replica G-BZND, marked 'N5199' is seen here on a farm airstrip in Hampshire during 2001. Fitted with a 90hp 5-cylinder Salmson engine, it had not yet flown at the time of writing. (Brendan Goddard)

B1777 was a presentation aircraft, "BRITISH GUIANA No.2", that bore the additional name "CHU CHIN CHOW" after a contemporary musical stage show, bestowed on it by Lt A.S.G.Lee, who took it over at No.1 AD, St.Omer on 10th July 1917, having just survived a crash in A6202. He immediately flew it to England with his squadron to take up Home Defence duties at Sutton's Farm. Back in France, on B1777, he destroyed an Albatros D.V on 4th September 1917 and had 'out of control' successes on 11th, 22nd and 30th September, and on 11th October. Although B1777 was crashed by another pilot in mid-October 1917, it was evidently repaired, for it was flown back to England on 19th November 1917.

(L.A.Rogers)

B5906 of No.46 (HD) Squadron at Hainault Farm was named "IMPIKOFF" and also bore the numeral 5 on its sides and centre section. Here it is seen beside a Sopwith Comic night-fighter conversion of a Camel; overhead is a B.E.2e. This Pup had neither navigation lights nor armament when photographed. By late 1918 it was serving with No.36 (HD) Squadron at Usworth.

Presented by Mr H.E.Arnhold of Shanghai, C305 bore the name "THE ORIOLE", for a time at least. It was delivered in February 1918 and served with both No.189 (Night) Training Squadron at Sutton's Farm and No.44 (HD) Squadron, North Weald.

For obvious reasons, girls' names were popular embellishments on many aircraft of all nationalities. The personnel of RNAS Walmer included a signwriter with a distinctive style of lettering seen here on this unidentified Pup named "AILEEN", with FSL W.A.Chisam (see photograph on page 69).

(Chaz Bowyer)

C305 in service with No.189 (Night) Training Squadron. Its navigation lights and star-scattered decor (perhaps applied by the same hand that embellished C312 - see photograph on page 151) confirm its nocturnal employment, which must have come appreciably later than the belief that the Pup could not be flown safely at night. Its presentation name has been supplanted by an emblem of a sword and scabbard crossed, and an access panel has been formed in the fuselage side where a roundel would normally have appeared.

The same hand had painted the name "JULIA" on N6442, here photographed when with the Defence Flight at Walmer. This Type 9901a Pup was armed with a synchronised Vickers gun. and was flown by FSL J.A.Shaw (see photograph on page 69). Flying N6442, he flew home defence sorties against the German bombing raids of 5th, 13th and 16th June and 7th and 22nd July 1917. N6442 was then new, having arrived at Walmer only on 3rd June 1917. By December it was at the East Fortune Naval Flying School, and was still there as a 'practice' aircraft on 30th March 1918.

Postscript

Recollections of an Airman

The following account was written in the early eighties by (Lt) Russell Smith,
and is now held by the Royal Air Force Museum (ref B1172), which very kindly agreed to its reproduction here.

THIS IS A TRUE ACCOUNT OF A W.W.1 FLYING EXPERIENCE

Truth can be stranger than fiction

Early in November 1916, eighteen specially selected Royal Flying Corps pilots began to assemble at Castle Bromwich aerodrome in the English Midlands to join a new squadron, No.54, which was being formed to receive the first RFC allotment of machines of a new aircraft design, the "Sopwith Scout", best known as the "Sopwith Pup". This tractor biplane, a single-seater fighter, was powered by an 80hp Le Rhône rotary engine having a two-bladed, laminated-wood propeller. The armament was one Vickers machine-gun mounted in a fixed position on the top and centre line of the fuselage between the engine and the pilot. When firing, the gun mechanism was activated by a timing device intended to prevent the bullets from striking the revolving blades of the propeller. Unfortunately, vibration sometimes altered the adjustment so that the bullets struck the blades. To avoid this, another mechanism was substituted which interrupted the normal rapid fire of the gun whenever a revolving blade was in the way and this proved successful. The gun sights assisted the pilot to aim the gun by flying the aircraft directly at a still target, or the correct distance ahead of a moving target.

The maximum speed of the aircraft was about 110mph flying level near the ground, but the speed diminished proportionately as the air became thinner at greater altitudes. Manoeuvrability of the machine rapidly decreased above 13,000 feet. On a test flight in January 1917, a maximum of 18,000 feet was registered on the altimeter when the plane was on the verge of stalling. That was the maximum ceiling of that machine. Without oxygen (and we carried none), one became very depressed in this situation and to linger was dangerous.

A full tank carried enough petrol for about 2½ hours, including starting the engine, testing revolutions, taking off, climbing to 12,000 feet, completing the mission and returning. After engaging hostile aircraft, I once ran out of petrol on the way home but, fortunately, had no head-wind and had sufficient altitude to glide the rest of the way and landed safely. There was danger of forgetting this fuel limitation in the heat of the battle.

At full strength, the squadron had three flights, each with a flight commander and five other pilots, but in France we were seldom operational at full strength because of the lack of serviceable aircraft.

Our pilots were drawn from Britain and the rest of the Commonwealth. Some had all of their service in the RFC but most had previous service with regiments before being seconded to the RFC and so were fully trained regimental officers before they learned to fly.

When the last plane arrived, we were ready and, on 22nd December 1916, the Squadron set out to fly to France via London.

On the way, I found that my compass was faulty and landed at Hendon near London to get it replaced but had no success either there or at London Colney, where I flew two days later, after which I carried on to Folkestone on the south-east coast on the same day. Being Christmas Eve, nothing could be done immediately so I stayed there but succeeded in arranging with Farnborough Air Station to forward a new compass by motor cycle to be installed at Lympne landing place. At noon on 26th December I did half an hour's engine test but, at 5,000 feet, could not see the French coast because of poor visibility. After landing and reporting, I then flew to Lympne. As the new compass had not arrived after a reasonable time, they promised to send another by a different motor cyclist. Ultimately the second compass arrived safely, was installed satisfactorily and, on 30th December 1916, I crossed the Channel and landed at St.Omer as required.

I had to face two tricky situations, one when leaving England and the other landing in France. When taking off for France I had a few anxious moments. After passing the point of no return, the engine faltered (probably too rich a mixture) and this could have been disastrous had I not been able to correct the trouble immediately. By holding the wheels on the ground as long as possible, the machine gained flying speed and was air-borne just before we passed over the edge of the cliff and the shore-line below. After climbing steadily for some time, and attaining a good safe altitude, I still could not distinguish anything definite on the ground in France, and then realised that the whole country was covered by a low-lying thick layer of cloud. Elsewhere, it was a bright sunny day. Then I noticed that the coastline of France was clearly outlined by the beach which was visible outside the low clouds. Obviously I would have to go down very low and, if possible, fly below the clouds to find St.Omer.

I had never been in France but I had a map and could see Cap Gris Nez on the ground; I soon found that I could fly under the low clouds so I was able to locate the aerodrome without difficulty.

Before landing I saw that a squadron of artillery observation machines were trying to land in a strong wind and some of the pilots were having difficulty. Some touched the ground too soon, bounced and damaged a wing or turned over. One crashed against a pole beside the runway. I waited until they all got down and were out of the way before I attempted to land. I then flew low over the runway to attract attention to me. Fortunately, they knew what to do for a light, fast, plane such as mine and sent out pairs of mechanics at suitable intervals in line facing the wind leaving a space between the individuals in the pairs, wide enough to allow a machine to land between them. I came in as slowly as possible keeping the tail-plane up in flying position by means of the engine until near enough to one of the pairs for the men to rush in from either side and grab the wing tips. In this way they prevented the aircraft from rising from the ground in the strong wind when the tail-plane dropped down.

Because of bad weather, I could not proceed until 7th January 1917 when I flew to Bertangles aerodrome, near Amiens, where I rejoined my Squadron. The weather continued to be damp and cold and flying was limited, but we did have a chance to get more familiar with our new aircraft and the surrounding country from the air. On 10th February, we moved to Chipilly, a forward aerodrome nearer the frontlines, and were engaged in offensive patrols or the escort of machines taking photographs.

On 14th April 1917 at 6 o'clock in the morning, our flight left on an offensive patrol between Cambrai and St. Quentin at 12,000 feet. We came upon hostile aircraft and drove them down. As my tracer bullets appeared to be hitting the target without causing any apparent damage, unfortunately I stayed in the power dive too long. When I pulled out, I'd lost contact with the flight. I started to regain altitude keeping a sharp lookout all around especially above me, but there was no one close. I soon spotted three aircraft in "V" formation, below and behind, coming up from the east to attack. I carried on, watching them and looking for any others. When those below me got closer, I was convinced by their speed and peculiar markings, that they belonged to "Richthofen's Travelling Circus" and, a few years ago, I received reliable confirmation that the "Circus" was operating in that area at that time. When I estimated that my machine would have come into their gun sights as they climbed, and, before they started to fire, I turned quickly and dived on the leader on a collision course firing continuously. The two outside planes fanned outward in climbing turns and the leader soon pushed his nose down and passed under me. I started evasive action - and then my engine misfired and I knew I had run out of fuel. Without the engine there was only one defence. I closed the throttle and put the machine into a tight, vertical spin intending to come out of it at a low altitude and land. There was no indication that my attackers were following me down and I didn't see them again. It may be they thought they had finished me.

When in a small plane, spinning in a tight corkscrew motion, one seems to be in the centre of a huge bowl of which the horizon is the brim and the whole earth, as far as one can see, forms the bowl which is turning about a point directly below, at the same speed and in the opposite direction from that in which the plane is spinning. When near the ground, I abandoned the spin and glided west taking evasive action against possible-ground fire. When the throttle was opened, the engine started but only for a moment; the tank was empty. I could see trenches but no occupants and thought I was near the front lines but couldn't determine on which side, or if I was in no-man's-land. I was surprised that there were not more shell holes. Right in front of me, the ground appeared level so I touched down as slowly as possible in a tail-down stall-landing and was out of the cockpit before the plane had stopped running. The aircraft was intact; it just lacked fuel. Without a moment's delay I started to run, or scramble as quickly as possible in full flying, kit, to the nearest shell hole and was about to jump in when I saw that it was half full of water. Continuing to another hole further from the plane, I found it dry, clean and still warm from the explosion of the shell which created it. Artillery was ranging on my machine and the ground around me shook continually from the near misses. When the bombardment slackened, there was the noise of a rifle bullet passing over my head. After one or two more bullets, I suspected a sniper was busy. It was still early in the morning and I thought of the long day ahead of me. I don't know if I slept. In fact I don't remember anything more until I regained consciousness in the late afternoon when I found myself kneeling in the bottom of the shell hole with my head and shoulders slowly swaying from side to side. I was still wearing my fleece-lined, sheep-skin, hip flying boots, my heavy wool-lined leather coat and my leather flying helmet. I felt hot and removed the helmet and found it soaked with blood where it had covered my right ear. The bleeding, which had stopped, began again so I jammed the helmet back in place and pressed the fur-lining against the wound before I began to black out again. As the bleeding stopped, I soon was able to see again and noticed a chunk of damp clay as large as my head lying beside me and, embedded in it, a metal shell splinter with only a small, sharp, jagged point protruding slightly. Could this chunk of clay and splinter have been hurled from a nearby shell burst and fallen on the side of my head as I lay on my side? I thought so. I now had a very pressing problem. Should I wait for darkness to try to get medical aid and risk being too weak from loss of blood; or, should I make a dash for it now while I still had the strength, and risk being shot? I decided to go at once. I crawled up the side of the shell hole and out on top; nothing happened, so I started to run with my head and shoulders as low as possible. Glancing back to the right toward the place I had left the plane, I saw wreckage only; to the left I saw a body in German uniform lying on the parapet of a communication trench, (the sniper); and looking straight ahead I saw a "tin hat" slowly rising above the parapet of a trench some distance in front of me. The tin hat stopped, leaving only enough space below the brim for the wearer to see me. Then two more hats came up, one on either side, and stopped. That was a wonderful sight, for they were not German helmets. I raised my hands above my head and struggled forward. When I reached the parapet, they were still in the same position and the soldiers reached out and pulled me into the trench.

They were men of the Newfoundland Regiment, and my arrival in the morning had subjected their battalion to very heavy fire and I'm afraid I was not very popular: They told me that they had shot the sniper. One of them took me back to a first-aid station in the old wine cellar under the ruins of the mansion at Monchy-le-Preux. Here the medical officer and several wounded soldiers had been cut off from communication with the battalion for three days. The M.O. decided not to disturb my helmet and, at dusk, a couple of men took me further back to a forward dressing station in an old German "Pill Box" where an ambulance was expected. On the way, a German scout-plane flying very low passed over us where we had flopped beside the path. In the fading light, I could see many dead horses scattered across the valley and was told they were the mounts of the Lord Strathcona Horse slain in a cavalry charge over open country - probably the last such charge in history. The transport had arrived at the Pill Box and, being a walking case, I sat with the driver on the way to the hospital in the City of Albert. After my wound was dressed, I became a stretcher case and was transferred to a hospital train bound for the Coast. I don't remember much of the journey after that and believe I was delirious during the night. From the train, we were put on board a hospital ship and, in the morning, transferred to an English hospital-train for London where I was sent to Lady Montgarret's Hospital in her house in Cadogan Gardens.

With no complications, my head wound healed quickly. In less than eight weeks, I had recovered, passed a board and was flying again in England regularly.

In retrospect, after more than sixty years, I think that to get from the Somme River Valley in France including air combat over hostile country, a forced landing in no-man's-land, a head wound from shell fire after several hours in a shell hole, a miraculous escape to our front lines, first-aid in a French hospital, evacuation across France, the English Channel and Southern England to a London hospital, all in thirty-six hours, filled with stress and tensions, must be regarded as an almost incredible experience.

Appendix 1

Specifications

Structure

The Pup airframe was typical of its period. It was constructed predominantly of wood, cross-braced by wire, and mostly covered with fabric.

Fuselage

Although the earliest Pups had spruce longerons, ash was soon substituted. These members were 1⅛in square from the nose of the fuselage over the forward five bracing bays; they tapered to 15/16in square over the sixth and seventh bays, and further tapered to ⅞in square to the sternpost. All spacers were of spruce, spindled out: verticals 1, 2 and 4 were 1⅛in square in section. 3 was 2in x 1⅛in, 5 was 1⅛inch square, 6 was l inch square, 7 and 8 were 15/16in square, the ninth ⅞in square, and the sternpost was a piece of 18-gauge mild steel tubing, of ⅞in outside diameter. Transverse spacers were tapered from their centres to their extremities.

The top decking was built up of formers made of ⅛in birch three-ply, supporting five stringers of ¼in x ⅜in spruce. At and immediately behind the cockpit opening the decking was covered with plywood, the remainder with fabric; the covering ahead of the cockpit was of 22-gauge aluminium sheet. as were the side panels. Cross-bracing in the three front side bays was of 10-gauge and 12-gauge steel wire; the remainder of the bracing in the sides and in plan was of 14-gauge wire throughout, with the exception of the 12-gauge transverse bracing in the foremost bay.

Mainplanes

Each mainplane panel had two spruce spars separated by four compression struts, of which the outermost was a ¾in diameter tube of 20-gauge duralumin; the others were of spruce, The full-chord ribs were also of spruce, but the riblets were of 3/16in birch three-ply; the wingtips were formed of ⅜in diameter 20-gauge mild-steel tubing, and the trailing edges were of Accles & Pollock No.121 Section 22-gauge flattened steel tubing.

The mainplanes were secured to their centre sections by long, specially formed rods pushed through the inward projections of the mainplane spar ends. which fitted into box ends of the centre-section spars. Interplane and incidence bracing was by streamline-section wires.

Tail unit

In the tailplane the main spar was of spruce, the rear of ⅞in diameter 22-gauge mild steel tubing. as was the spar of the elevators. The leading edge was a light spruce member, and the ribs were built up as mere formers. Wingtip profiles and elevator trailing edges were of Accles & Pollock No.121 Section; the elevator ribs, of ⅜in x 20-gauge steel tubing, were brazed to the trailing edge and the elevator spar. Similarly the fin and rudder assembly was wholly made of steel tubing: rudder post and sternpost were of ⅞in x 22-gauge tubing, profiles of fin and rudder of Accles & Pollock No.121 22-gauge section, and the rudder rib of 22-gauge tubing; all joints were brazed.

The details of the design are well illustrated in the drawings prepared by the Southern Aircraft Repair Depot, Farnborough.

Weights of components (a transcription of an incomplete list dated 1st October 1917)

One Aileron	4 lb
Rudder	3 lb
Centre plane	22 lb
Tailplane and elevators,	21 lb
Lower plane without ailerons	32 lb
Top plane	30 lb
Tank	37 lb
Armour seat	9 lb
Cushion	3 lb
2 wheels	30 lb
Axle	4 lb
Two V Tubes for undercarriage	17½ lb
4 interplane struts	10 lb
4 half struts	2 lb

Appendix 2

Power

80hp Le Rhône 9C –
Nine-cylinder air-cooled rotary engine

Diameter	945 mm (37.2 in)
Bore	105 mm (4.13 in)
Stroke	140 mm (5.51 in)
Compression ratio	4.5 to 1
Weight dry	268 lb
Normal output	90hp at 1,250 rpm
Maximum output	92hp at 1,300 rpm at ground level
Fuel consumption	60 pts per hour
Oil consumption	10.2 pts per hour
Normal running speed	1,250 rpm

Propeller :
  British & Colonial P.43
      Diameter   2600 mm (8 ft 6.36 in)
      Pitch   2,360 mm (7 ft 8.91 in)
  Or Lang L.P.1020A
      Diameter   2,600 mm (8 ft 6.36 in)
      Pitch   2,430 mm (7 ft 11.67 in)
  Or Integrale I.P.C.2360
      Diameter   2,500 mm (8 ft 2.43 in)
      Pitch   2,400 mm (7 ft 10.49 in)
All were wooden two-blade right-hand tractor airscrews.

80hp Clerget 7Z –
Seven-cylinder air-cooled rotary engine

Diameter	915 mm (36.02 in)
Bore	120 mm (4.72 in)
Stroke	150 mm (5.91 in)
Compression ratio	4.3 to 1
Weight dry	234 lb
Normal output	82hp at 1,200 rpm.
Fuel consumption	53 pts per hour
Oil consumption	11.6 pts per hour
Normal running speed	1,200 rpm
Propeller:	as for 80hp Le Rhône

80hp Gnome Lambda –
Seven-cylinder air-cooled rotary engine

Diameter	930 mm (36.61 in)
Bore	124 mm (4.88 in)
Stroke	140 mm (5.51 in)
Compression ratio	3.75 to 1
Weight dry	212 lb
Normal output	65 hp at 1,150 rpm
Maximum output	67.5hp at 1,250 rpm
Fuel consumption	53 pts per hour
Oil consumption	11.7 pts per hour
Normal running speed	1,150rpm

Propeller:
  British & Colonial P.3000
      (wooden two-blade right-hand tractor)
          Diameter   2500 mm (8 ft 2.43 in)
          Pitch   2200 mm (7 ft 2.61 in)

100hp Gnome Monosoupape B-2 –
Nine-cylinder air-cooled rotary engine

Diameter	980 mm (38.58 in)
Bore	110 mm (4.33 in) (5.91 in)
Stroke	150 mm (5.91 in)
Compression ratio	4.85 to 1
Weight dry	303 lb
Normal output	113hp at 1,250 rpm
Fuel consumption	94 pts per hour
Oil consumption	17.1 pts per hour
Normal running speed	1,250 rpm

Propeller :
  British & Colonial P.3012
      (wooden two-blade right-hand tractor)
          Diameter   2,550 mm (8 ft 4.39 in)
          Pitch   2,310 mm (7 ft 6.94 in)

110hp Le Rhone 9J –
Nine-cylinder air-cooled rotary engine

Diameter	1,005 mm (39.57 in)
Bore	112 mm (4.4 in)
Stroke	170 mm (6.69 in)
Compression ratio	4.83 to 1
Weight dry	336 lb
Normal output	131hp at 1,300 rpm
Fuel consumption	87 pts per hour
Oil consumption	10.9 pts per hour
Normal running speed	1,300 rpm

Propeller:
  Lang L.P.710c
      (wooden two-blade right-hand tractor)
          Diameter   2,740 mm (8 ft 11.87 in)
          Pitch   2,120 mm (6 ft 11.46 in)

60hp Le Rhône 7B –
Seven-cylinder air-cooled rotary engine

Bore	105 mm (4.13 in)
Stroke	140 mm (5.51 in)
Weight	176 lb
Fuel consumption	36 pts per hour
Oil Consumption	8 pts per hour
Normal running speed	1,100 rpm

Pups known to have had alternative engines

The large majority of Pups had and retained the standard power unit, the 80hp Le Rhône 9C. Those aircraft listed below are known to have had, at one time or another, alternative engines. Doubtless there were others.

<u>80hp Clerget</u>
9496, 9497, 9898-9900, 9901-9909, 9911, 9949 (as at 30.3.18), A658-A660, B1785, B2166, B2217, B5288, B5334, B5345, B5907, B5939, B5990, B6010 (later), B6016, B6026, B6057, B6058, B6092, B6141, B6144, B7529, C258, C476, C1540, D4106.

<u>130hp Clerget</u>
B1809 (later).

<u>80hp Gnome</u>
9907, 9928, A6225 A7345, B1788, B1825, B2164, B2183, B2202-B2204, B2208, B2211, B2226, B2239, B2247, B5255, B5355, B5928, B5929 (January 1918, later 60hp Le Rhône), B5942, B5948, B5949, B5950, B5857, B5979 (January 1918, later 60hp Le Rhône), B5980, B5988 (January 1918, later 60hp Le Rhône), B5989, B5991, B5992 (December 1917; converted to 80hp Le Rhône by 11.1.18), B5993 (December 1917; converted to 80hp Le Rhône by 11.1.18), B5994 (December 1917; converted to 80hp Le Rhône by 11.1.18), B6001 B5992 (December 1917; converted to 80hp Le Rhône by 11.1.18), B6010 (converted to 80hp Le Rhône by 16.3.18), B6013 (January 1918, later 60hp Le Rhône.), B6014, B6021-6024*, B6031-B6034, B6049- B6051, B6075 (January 1918, converted to 80hp Le Rhône by 30.3.18), B6076 (January 1918, later 60hp Le Rhône), B6095, B6096, B6099, B6139, B6143, B6145, B6149, B7481, B8821, B9440, C202, C208, C238, C241, C242, C8654, D4030, E9996, N5181, N5188, N5195, N5197, N6160, N6168, N6169, N6171, N6177, N6179, N6188, N6189, N6192, N6195, N6196, N6196-N6198, N6201, N6202, N6209, N6436, N6465, N6467,N6475, N6477.

*   *B6023 had 80hp Gnome as at 5.1.18;*
    converted to 60hp Le Rhône by 30.3.18

<u>100hp Gnome Monosoupape</u>
A638, A653, A6244, A6249, B735, B803-B805, B849, B877, B1755, B1763, B1764, B1773, B1803, B1806, B1807, B1809, B1812, B2163, B2192, B2210, B2222, B2233, B2246, B5289, B5292, B5296, B5303, B5307, B5320, B5327, B5363, B5369, B5387, B5400, B5904-B5906, B5933, B5937, B5953, B5995, B6017, B6018, B6023 (ex 80hp Gnome), B6073, B6074, B6100, B6139, B7500, D4013, N6173.

<u>60hp Le Rhône</u>
9925 (by 30.3.18), 9935, B5929 (by March 1918, previously 80hp Gnome), B5978 (March 1918), B5979 (by March 1918, previously 80hp Gnome), B5988 (by March 1918, previously 80hp Gnome), B6013 (by March 1918, previously 80hp Gnome), B6023 (by February 1918, previously 80hp Gnome), B6052, B6061, B6064, B6076 (by March 1918, previously 80hp Gnome), C205, C238, C259.

<u>Beardmore S.B.3Ds with 80hp Clerget</u>
N6125-N6127, N6683, N6684.

<u>Beardmore S.B.3Ds with 100hp Gnome Monosoupape</u>
N6103 (later).

100hp Gnome-Monosoupape.

80hp Gnome.

80hp Clerget.

80hp Le Rhône.

Appendix 3

Dimensions

SS Tabloid:

Span 25ft 6in.	Length 20ft 4in.	Height 8ft 5in.
Chord 5ft ½in.	Gap 4ft 6in.	Stagger 12in.
Dihedral ldeg 30min.	Incidence 1deg.	

Span of tail 8ft 3in over elevators (9ft 2in on SS3)
Propeller diameter 8ft 2in.   Wheel track 4ft 9in.
Areas: Wings, upper 128.3sq ft; lower 113 sq ft; total 241.3sq ft.
Ailerons (RNAS late Tabloids only) 28sq ft.
Tailplane 11.8 sq ft.   Elevators 11.8sq ft.
Fin (production Tabloid) 1.8sq ft.
Rudder, prototype 7 sq ft. production 4.27sq ft.

Sparrow:

Span 26ft 9in.	Length 19ft.
Chord 5ft 1½in.	Gap 4ft 4⅞in. Stagger 18in.
Dihedral 4 degrees.	Incidence 1deg 30min.

Propeller diameter 2400mm (7ft 10½in.), pitch 1800mm. (5ft 10.9in).
Wheel track 4ft 4⅞in.

Pup:

Span 26ft 6in.	Length 19ft 3¾in.	Height 8ft 10½in.
Chord 5ft 1½in.	Gap 4ft 4⅞in.	Stagger 18in. (15in on N6184 & N6186-N6192 only).
Dihedral 3 degrees.	Incidence 1deg 30in.	

Span of tail 10ft 1in.
Incidence of tailplane: 1deg. 30min with 80hp Le Rhône.
                             2deg. 30min. with Monosoupape.
Wheel track 4ft 7in.   Tyres 700 x 75mm.
Areas: Wings 254 sq ft.
Ailerons, each 5.5 sq ft, total 22 sq ft.
Tailplane 23 sq ft.   Elevators 11.8 sq ft.
Fin 3.5 sq ft.   Rudder 4.5 sq ft.
Tankage :   Petrol 19¼ gallons; oil 4¼ gallons.

Beardmore S.B.3D:

Span 25ft 3in (folded 10ft 6in). Length 19ft 6in.   Height 8ft 6in. (S.B.3F folded, 6ft).
Chord 5ft 1½in.   Gap 4ft 5in.   Stagger nil.
Incidence 1deg 30min.
Span of tail 10ft 1in.   Tyres 700 x 75mm.
Areas: Wings 236ft.
Ailerons, each 5.5 sq ft, total 22sq ft
Tailplane 23 sq ft.   Elevators 11.8sq ft.
Fin 3.3sq ft.   Rudder 4.2sq ft.

These data probably relate to the prototype, 9950.

Appendix 4

Official Rigging Notes

(80 H.P. LE RHÔNE or 100 H.P. MONOSOUPAPE)

MANUFACTURERS' ORDER OF ERECTION.

1. Fuselage assembled and trued up.
2. Tail Skid fitted.
3. Fairing, Dashboard, and Deck fitted.
4. Controls fitted in front of Fuselage.
5. Undercarriage fitted.
6. Machine erected and trued up in Flying Position, with Main Planes and Empennage in skeleton.
7. Controls loosely connected.
8. Main Planes and Empennage dismantled.
9. Petrol Tanks fitted.
10. Fuselage covered and doped.
11. Engine Mounted and Engine Accessories and Controls fitted.
12. Gun Magazine and Shoots fitted.
13. Press Plate at bottom of first bay fitted.
14. Oil Tank fitted.
15. Gun and Actuating Gear fitted.
16. Centre Section fitted (after being covered and doped).
17. Wheels and Shock Absorbers fitted on Undercarriage.
18. Cowling fitted.
19. Main Planes and Empennage fitted (after being covered and doped).
20. Controls connected up and adjusted.

TRUING UP FUSELAGE.

The Side Struts are numbered from front to rear.

With Fuselage true and in Flying Position, the Top Longerons and Top Transverse Struts are horizontal throughout. Place the Fuselage on two trestles, one being placed under the first bay and the other under the ninth bay.

Trammel and adjust the Internal Cross Bracing Wires until the diagonals in the transverse sections through Nos.1 and 8 Side Struts are respectively equal.

Mark points on Nos.1 to 8 Side Struts 14¾″ vertically below the upper surface of the Top Longerons. These points will be in the horizontal plane through the Thrust Line when the Fuselage is true.

Lightly clamp a straightedge transversely across No.1 Side Struts, so that the marked points coincide with the *upper edge.*

Lightly clamp a straightedge transversely across No.8 Side Struts, so that the marked points coincide with the *lower edge,* on account of these points being close to the Bottom Longerons.

On each straightedge mark a point midway between each pair of Side Struts, and mark two other points, one on each side, of the mid point and about 1′ 6″ from it.

From these points stretch two lines *outside* the Fuselage, one on each side, from the *upper edge* of the front straightedge to the *lower edge* of the rear straightedge.

Pack up the Fuselage until the upper edge of the front straightedge and the lower edge of the rear straightedge are on the same horizontal line when viewed from the side. Check by spirit level and long straightedge.

The upper edge of the front straightedge, the lower edge of the rear straightedge and the two side lines are now in the *horizontal plane* through the Thrust Line.

Stretch a centre line from the Sternpost Lower Socket to the *middle point* of the front straightedge. This line will be *inside* the Fuselage.

Mark the mid points of all Top and Bottom Transverse Struts.

By means of light frames attached to the trestles stretch a longitudinal line beneath the Fuselage and about 1′ 6″ *below* it.

This line is accurately centred in position by means of plumb lines dropped from a plug in the upper socket of the sternpost and from a centre point of the front straightedge.

This lower stretched line, the *internal* stretched line, and the mid points of the Top and Bottom Transverse Struts will all be in the *vertical plane* through the Thrust Line when the Fuselage is true.

To true up proceed as follows: -

(a) Adjust Internal Cross Bracing Wires so that corresponding diagonals are equal at each Transverse Section. (Transverse Sections 1 and 8 were trued up before the straightedges were attached.) Check by trammel.

(b) Adjust Top and Bottom Cross Bracing Wires until all the mid points on the Top and Bottom Transverse Struts are in line with the *Internal* and *Lower* stretched lines. Check by dropping a plumb line from the mid point of each of the Top Transverse Struts. This plumb line should just touch both stretched lines, and also the mid point of the Bottom Transverse Strut in the same Transverse Section.

(c) Adjust Side Bracing Wires on both sides until the marked points on all Side Struts are in line with the two *outer* stretched lines and all Side Struts are vertical. Check the marked points by sighting them in between the two *outer* stretched lines.

TRUING UP THE UNDERCARRIAGE.

The Undercarriage should be symmetrical about the vertical, centre line of the Machine.

Adjust the Undercarriage Cross Bracing Wires until the diagonals between corresponding gauge points on the Front Undercarriage Struts are equal. Check by trammel.

The axle is jointed at the centre. Adjust the Centre Vertical Bracing Wire until the two portions of the axle are in line. Check by straightedge.

The axle should be at right angles to the longitudinal centre line of the Machine. Check by taking measurements from the lower socket of the Sternpost to the Axle End Collar of the Undercarriage Wheels. These measurements should be the same on both sides.

PLACING MACHINE IN FLYING POSITION.

Before truing up the Centre Section and attaching the Main Planes it is necessary to get the Machine in Flying Position.

To do this, block up the Machine under the Undercarriage Struts and support the Tail on a trestle placed near the Sternpost.

The Machine is in Flying Position when the Top Longerons are level transversely and longitudinally. The Spars at the bottom of the Fuselage also will be level transversely.

Level transversely by spirit level and straightedge placed across the Top Longerons, and make any adjustments by packing blocks under the Undercarriage Struts.

Level longitudinally by spirit level placed on the Top Longerons, and make adjustments by raising or lowering the Tail.

TRUING UP CENTRE SECTION.

The Centre Section should be symmetrical about the vertical centre line of the Machine when viewed from the front.

Adjust transversely by Centre Section Front Cross Bracing Wires until corresponding diagonals are equal. Check by trammel.

Adjust longitudinally by Centre Section Side Bracing Wires until correct Incidence and Stagger are obtained.

The Stagger of the Centre Section is 18″. This can be adjusted *after* the Lower Main Planes have been fitted.

Check by dropping plumb lines from the Leading Edge of the Centre Section. The fore and aft horizontal distance of the Leading Edge of the Lower Main Planes from the plumb lines should be 18″.

ATTACHING THE MAIN PLANES.

Place the Lower Main Planes in position and insert the Securing Rod on each side from the *rear*.

Push the latter Rod well in, and secure it to the *Ribs* at the roots of the Main Planes by nuts and bolts,
    not forgetting to insert the *Splitpins*.

Loosely connect the Landing Wires.

Lift the Upper Main Planes in position, insert the Securing Rods from the *front*, and after pushing the Rods well in,
    secure the front of the Rods to the Leading Edges of the Main Planes.

Loosely connect Flying and Incidence Wires.

TRUING UP MAIN PLANES.

Drop plumb lines from four points, two each side, from the Leading Edge of the Upper Main Planes. True up until

(a) All plumb lines are in line viewed from the side.

(b) The Leading Edges are of the Lower Main Planes are symmetrical about the centre line of Machine. Check by taking measurements from Bottom Sockets of Front Outer Struts to Rudderpost and Propeller Boss. Corresponding measurements should be the same on both sides.

(c) The Dihedral of the Main Planes is 3°. Adjust by Front Landing Wires and check by Abney level and straightedge along the Front Spar.

(d) The *Stagger* of the ain Planes is 18″ throughout. Adjust by Incidence Wires and check by measuring the fore and aft horizontal distances from the Leading Edge of the Lower Main Planes to the plumb lines dropped from the Leading Edge of the Upper Main Planes.

(c) The *Incidence* is 1½° throughout. Adjust by Incidence, Rear Landing, and Rear Flying Wires, and check by Abney level and straightedge, taking care to place the latter from Leading Edge to Trailing Edge at Ribs.

(f) There is no "Wash in" or "Wash out".

FIXING THE EMPENNAGE.

Bolt the Tail Plane in position and connect the Tail Plan Bracing Wires.

True up the Tail Plane to be level transversely.

Check by spirit level along the Front Spar.

Check for Tail Plane being square with Machine by taking measurements from Tops of Side Struts No.7 to lateral extremities of Hinged Tube of Tail Plane and to outer Hinges of Elevator.

These measurements should be the same on both sides.

The Incidence of the Tail Plane is 1½° for 80 H.P. Le Rhöne and 2½° for 100 H.P. Monosoupape. Check by using a straightedge with two small blocks attached. These blocks must be of such dimensions that when one is on the Front Spar and the other on the Hinged Tube of the Tail Plane the *upper edge* of the straightedge is parallel to the fore and aft centre line of the Tail Plane.

The Incidence can be measured by an Abney level over the straightedge with Machine in Flying Position.

Bolt the Fin in position.

Hinge the Rudder to the Sternpost and Fin, not forgetting to insert the Split-pins; similarly hinge the Elevators to the Tail Plane Hinged Tube.

CONTROLS.

Connect up the Controls and adjust them so that

(a) With the Pilot's Control Stick vertical there is no droop oneither the Ailerons or the Elevators.

(b) The Rudder and Tail Skid should point directly fore and aft and be square with Machine when the Rudder Bar is square in Fuselage.

LIST OF PRINCIPAL DIMENSIONS.

Span of Upper Main Planes	approx. 28′ 6″
Span of Lower Main Planes	approx. 26′ 6″
Chord of Upper Main Planes	5′ 1½″
Chord of Lower Main Planes	5′ 1½″
Incidence of Upper Main Planes	1½″
Incidence of Lower Main Planes	1½″
Stagger	18″
Dihedral, Upper Main Planes	3°
Dihedral, Lower Main Planes	3°
Overall Length	19′ 3¾″
Height	9′ 3¾″
Incidence of Tail Plane (80 H.P. Le Rhône)	1½°
Incidence of Tail Plane (100 H.P. Monosoupape)	2½°
Droop of Ailerons (with Pilot's Control Stick vertical)	Nil
Droop of Elevators (with Pilot's Control Stick vertical)	Nil

POINTS TO OBSERVE WHEN OVERHAULING MACHINE.

See that the Leading Edges of the Main Planes are symmetrical about centre line of Machine.

Check the Stagger.

Examine the Bracing Wires for length and tautness in the Centre Section, and see that the Split-pins are in position, and that all Lock Nuts are tight.

Check the Dihedral.

Check the Incidence.

See that the Interplane Struts are straight.

Examine all Main Plane Bracing Wires for length and tautness, and see that all Split-pins are in position.

Examine all Controls, Control Pulleys and Cables, see that they work freely, and that Turnbuckles on Cables are locked.

Examine Tail Plane and see that it is set correctly and is square with Machine, that Tail Plane Bracing Wires are correct both as to tautness and length, that all Split-pins are in position, and that Lock Nuts are tight.

Examine Rudder and Fin and see that they are set straight and square with Machine.

See that there is no Droop on Ailerons and Elevators.

Examine Undercarriage and Skid.

Examine Tank Mountings and Connections.

Examine Engine Mounting, Engine Controls, and Engine, Accessories.

SOPWITH PUP
(100H.P. GNOME MONOSOUPAPE)

Fig.1 – Machine in Flying Position

SOPWITH PUP
(80H.P. LE RHÔNE & 100H.P. GNOME MONOSOUPAPE)

Fig.2 – Machine in Flying Position

SOPWITH PUP
(80H.P. LE RHÔNE & 100H.P. GNOME MONOSOUPAPE)

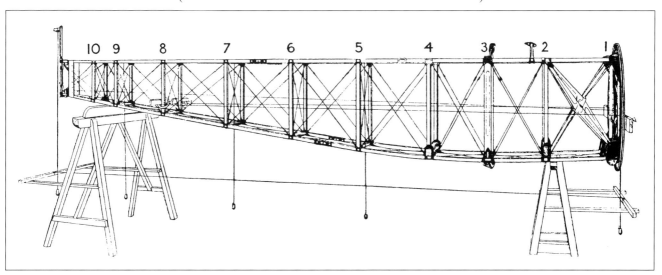

Fig.3 – Truing up Fuselage

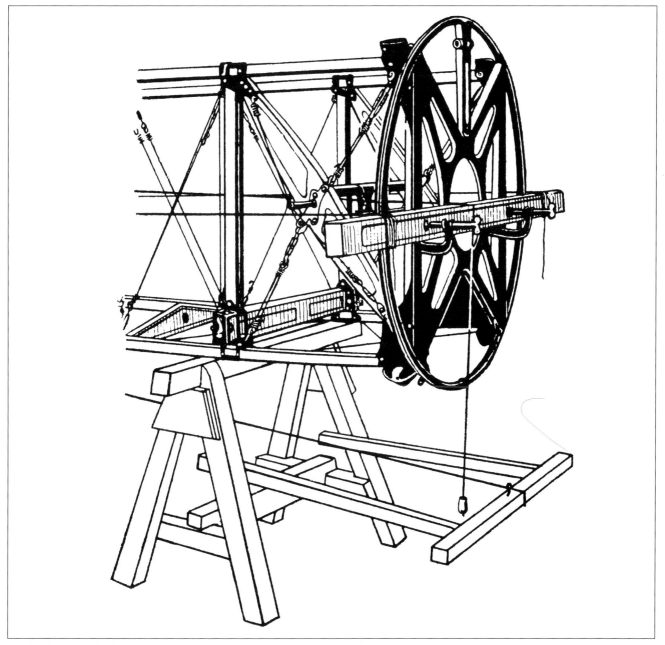

Fig.4 – Truing up Fuselage

SOPWITH PUP
(100H.P. GNOME MONOSOUPAPE)

Fig.5 – Centre Section and Undercarriage

SOPWITH PUP
(80H.P. LE RHÔNE & 100H.P. GNOME MONOSOUPAPE)

Fig.6 – Empennage

SOPWITH PUP
(80H.P. LE RHÔNE & 100H.P. GNOME MONOSOUPAPE)

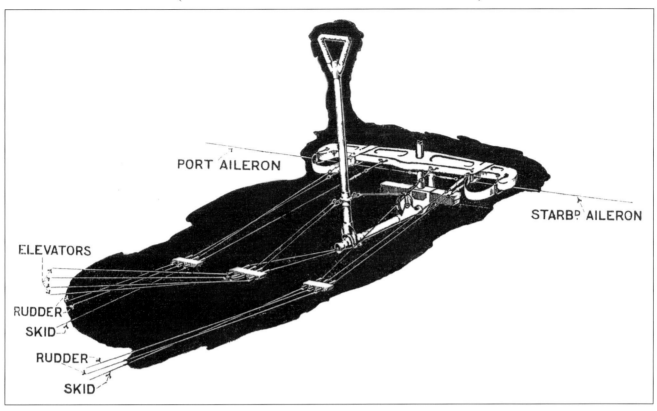

Fig.7 – Control Diagram

SOPWITH PUP
(80H.P. LE RHÔNE & 100H.P. GNOME MONOSOUPAPE)

Fig.8 – Control Diagram

SOPWITH PUP
(80H.P. LE RHÔNE & 100H.P. GNOME MONOSOUPAPE)

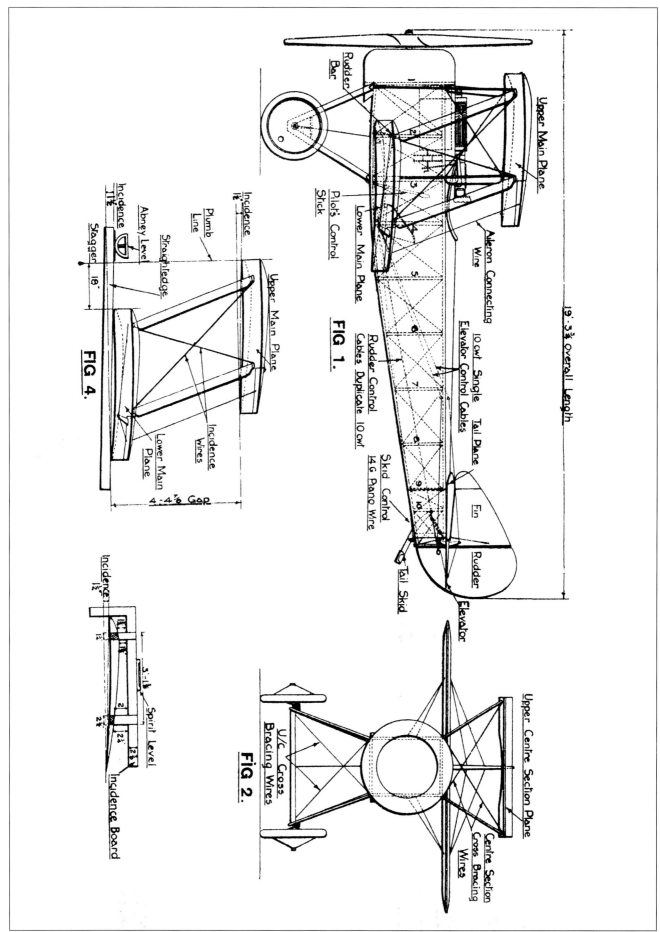

Fig.9 – Rigging Diagrams 1, 2, 4

SOPWITH PUP
(100H.P. GNOME MONOSOUPAPE)

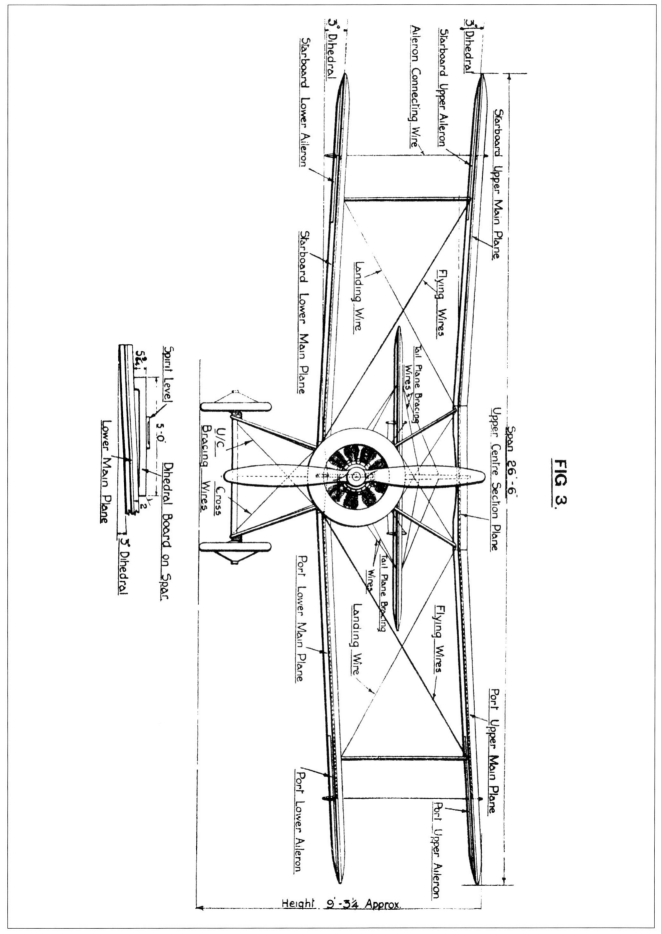

Fig.10 – Rigging Diagram 3

SOPWITH PUP

(80H.P. LE RHÔNE & 100H.P. GNOME MONOSOUPAPE)

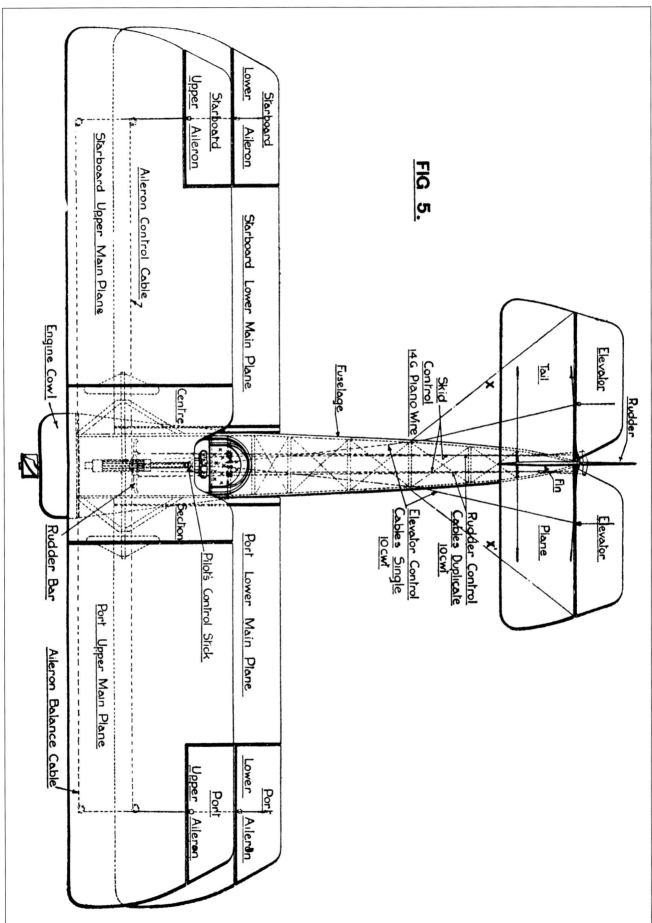

Fig.11 – Rigging Diagram 5

Table of RAF Wire Sizes

(80h.p. Le Rhône & 100h.p. Gnome Monosoupape)

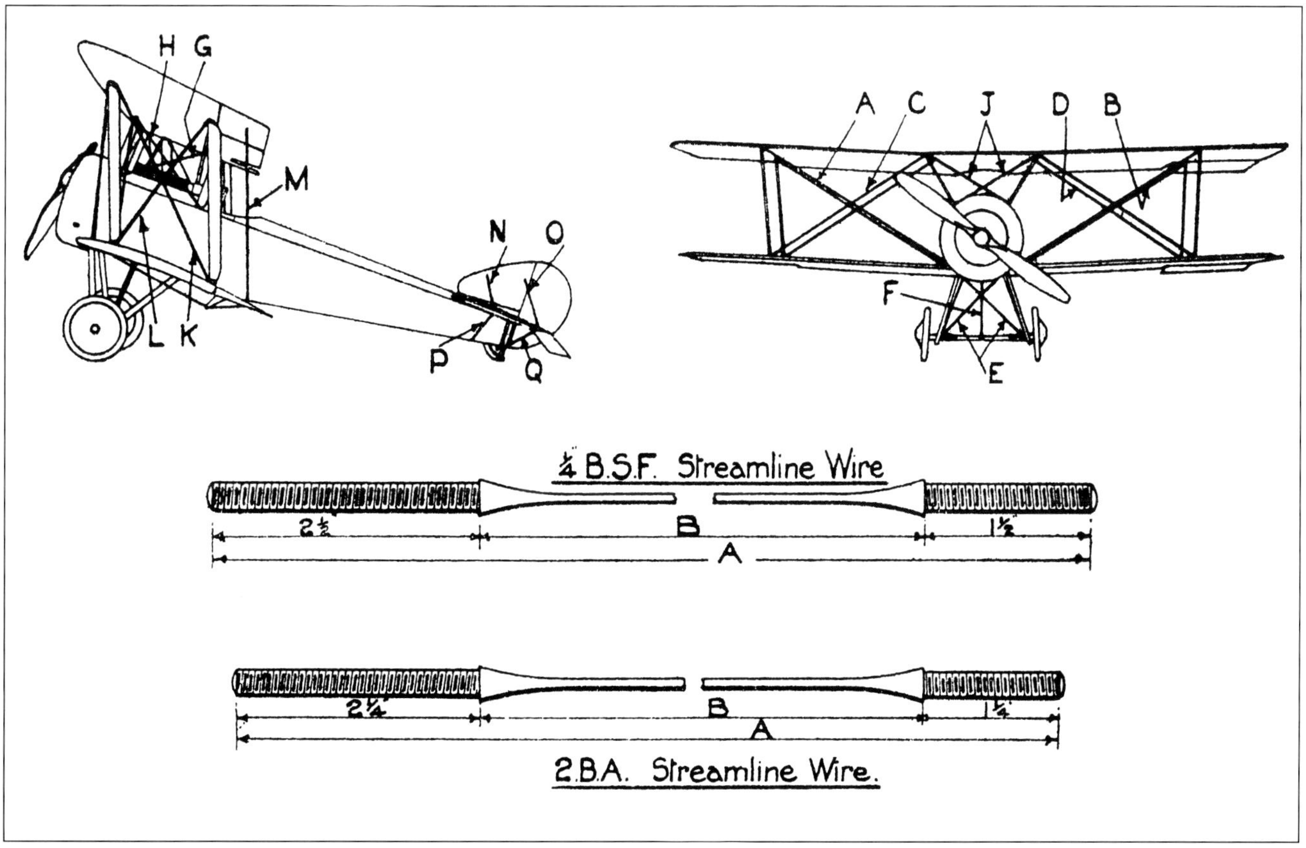

Fig.12 – RAF Wire Lengths

Index Letter On Machine	Description	No. Off	Size	Admiralty Lengths	Sopwith Lengths	
					A	B
A	Front Flying Wires	4	¼-in B.S.F.		9ft 2¾in	8ft 10¾in
B	Rear Flying Wires	4	ditto		9ft 2¾in	8ft 10¾in
C	Front Landing Wire	2	ditto		7ft 8¾in	7ft 4¾in
D	Rear Landing Wire	2	ditto		7ft 8¾in	7ft 4¾in
E	Undercarriage Cross Bracing Wire	2	ditto		3ft 9in	3ft 5in
F	Undercarriage Centre	1	ditto	2ft 5in	2ft 8in	2ft 4in
G	Centre Section Side Bracing (Short)	2	2 B.A.	3ft 4¼in	3ft 6¾in	3ft 3¼in
H	Centre Section Side Bracing Long)	2	ditto	3ft 4¼in	3ft 7¼in	3ft 3¾in
J	Front Centre Section Cross Bracing	2	ditto	3ft 4¼in	3ft 6¾in	3ft 3¼in
K	Incidence Wire (Long)	2	ditto	5ft 8in	5ft 10½in	5ft 7in
L	Incidence Wire (Short)	2	ditto	3ft 11¼in	4ft 1¾in	3ft 10¼in
M	Aileron Connecting Wires	2	ditto	4ft 3in	4ft 5½in	4ft 2in
N	Tail Plane Bracing Wire (Top Front)	2	ditto	2ft 9½in	3ft 0in	2ft 8½in
O	Tail Plane Bracing Wire (Top Rear)	2	ditto	2ft 11in	3ft 1½in	2ft 10in
P	Tail Plane Bracing Wire (Bottom Front)	2	ditto	2ft 4¾in	2ft 7¼in	2ft 3¾in
Q	Tail Plane Bracing Wire (Bottom Front)	2	ditto	2ft 10in	3ft 0¼in	2ft 9in

Appendix 5

Armament

One fixed 0.303in Vickers belt-fed machine-gun with 500 rounds; on the standard Le Rhône-powered Pup this gun had the Scarff-Dibovski interrupter mechanism; with the 100p Gnome Monosoupape engine the Constantinesco C.C. Fire Control Timing Gear was fitted. Ring-and-Bead and Aldis optical sights. At a late stage, some RFC Pups had additionally a 0.303in Lewis gun on an overwing mounting; in France, some were equipped with bomb carriers for 25lb bombs.

On the Admiralty Type 9901a Pup the standard basic armament was one 0.303in Lewis machine-gun with three 97-round magazines, mounted on a tripod ahead of the cockpit at an upward angle, its line of fire through the aperture in the centre section. Alternatively, up to eight rockets were carried on the interplane struts, four on each side.

The Beardmore S.B.3D had a single Lewis gun. On a few of the earliest aircraft this was on a tripod mounting and fired upwards, as on the Type 9901a Pup; but most S.B.3Ds had the gun on an overwing mounting on the centre section, slightly to starboard of centre and firing forwards over the propeller.

Front view of a rocket-equipped Pup, possibly 9917 of East Fortune in May 1917. Standing in front are FSL Ash (left) and FSL Cooper.
(via Frank Cheesman)

Appendix 6

Weights and Performance

Sopwith Pup

Aircraft	3691		9906	A626	A653 with original cowling	A653 with modified cowling	A6220	B5908
Engine	80hp Le Rhône		80hp Clerget	80hp Le Rhône	100hp Gnome Monosoupape		110-hp Le Rhône	110-hp Le Rhône
Airscrew	Lang -		-	L.P.1020	Vickers 57		L.P.710c	P.3012
Date of trial	27.3.16, 29.3.16	-	12.16	21.10.16	April 1917	May 1917	11.9.17	October 1917
Weights (1b)								
Empty	-	-	820	787	856	856	-	-
Fuel & oil	-	-	-	178	181	181	-	-
Military load	-	-	-	80	80	80	-	-
Pilot		-	-	180	180	180	-	-
Loaded	1,099	-	1,114	1,225	1,297	1,297	-	-
Max speed (mph) at height								
Ground level	Average speed (no height stated): 101.9	108	-	113.3	-	-	-	-
400ft		-	107*	-	-	-	-	-
5,000ft			-	105	-	-	110*	100*
6,000ft		-	91*	-	-	-	-	-
6,500ft		110	-	-	105	107	-	-
10,000ft		106	-	102	101.5	104	87*	90*
15,000ft		-	-	85*	94.5	100	-	80
Climb to	Min/sec	M s	M s	M s	M s	M s	M s	M s
1,000ft	0 53	- -	- -	1 05	0 55	0 55	- -	- -
3,000ft	- -	- -	2 30	3 30	2 54	2 54	- -	- -
4,000ft	4 00	- -	- -	- -	- -	4 00	3 50	- -
5,000ft	5 10	4 59	- -	6 25	5 12	5 12	- -	4 -
6,000ft	6 30	- -	6 05	8 15	6 30	6 30	- -	- -
10,000ft	13 10	12 29	- -	16 25	13 00	12 25	8 55	9 00
15,000ft	25 00	- -	- -	32 40	26 54	23 24	- -	18 00
18,000ft	- -	- -	- -	- -	- -	- -	25 00	- -
Service ceiling (ft)	-	-	-	17,500	18,000	18,500	-	-
Endurance (hrs)	4	-	-	3	1¾	1¾	-	-

* The recorded figures in these cases are of indicated airspeed and are therefore not directly comparable to the other, corrected, figures in this table.

Beardmore S.B.3

Aircraft	9950	Production with undercarriage	Production without undercarriage	N6102	–
Date	8.2.17	15.8.17	15.8.17	3.9.17	12.1.18
Weights (lb):					
Empty	828	865	844	849	890
Fuel & oil	181	165	165	165	164
Military load	49	36	36	36	55
Pilot	180	180	180	180	180
Loaded	1238	1246	1225	1230	1289
Speed in mph at					
2,000ft	-	82	-	90	-
6,500ft	-	-	-	85	98
10,000ft	90	-	80 at 9,000ft	79	91
Climb to	Min/sec	Min/sec	Min/sec	Min/sec	Min/sec
2000ft	2 00	-	-	2 50	-
6,500ft	8 00	16 00	13 00	10 40	12 10
10,000ft	14 15	-	24 45	20 25	24 20
Ceiling (ft)	16,000	-	13,800	16,000	12,400
Endurance (hrs)	3	-	-	2¾	91

Two views of S.B.3D N6115 being hoisted on board HMS Renown in November 1917.   *(H.H.Dannreuther / FAA Museum)*

Appendix 7

Four-man Procedure for Erecting Pups

With a gang of 4 men. No 1 man is gang leader.
It is assumed that the fuselage reached the Park with the centre section and u/c fitted;
otherwise fit u/c, [and] the centre section.
Carry on as follows:

Nos.1 & 2	Set fuselage in flying position, with sand bag on skid.
No.1	taking his position in Pilot's seat and directing
No.3	to adjust chocks & trestles.
No.1	Then checks centre section for alignments, and
No.2	checks fuselage.
Nos.1 & 2	Take root incidence.
Nos.3 & 4	proceed to sort and lay out the struts, wires and planes in convenient positions near fuselage, examining them whilst doing so, and to fix clips on ailerons to keep them in position and prevent aileron controls drawing through.
Nos.1 2 3 &4	are now ready to erect machine.
No.1	enters front landing wire in top trunnion P.S.
No.2	enters rear landing wire in top trunnion P.S.
Nos.3 & 4	lift P.S. lower plane into position.
No.4	retaining hold of plane at tip.
No.1	connects up front landing wire to bottom trunnion.
No.2	connects up rear landing wire to bottom trunnion.
No.3	meanwhile connects and secures the bottom plane connecting rod.
Nos.1 2 3 & 4	then proceed to connect up S.S. bottom plane in the same manner as port side.
Nos.1 & 2	pull up landing wires, Port, then Starboard side on front spar to the correct dihedral then pull up landing wires on rear spars to give correct incidence at tips according to incidence at roots.
Nos.3 & 4	then hand P.S. top plane up to 1 & 2 men.
No.1	takes root of plane and enters connecting rod and secures same whilst No.2 holds tip of plane.
No.3	fixes front strut and
No 4	the rear strut.
Nos.1 2 3 & 4	then proceed to connect up starboard top plane in the same manner.
Nos.3 & 4	then proceed to fix tail plane, fin and rudder, each man connecting, truing up and locking his respective side.
No.1	connects upper aileron controls and removes aileron supporting clips, then adjusts and locks aileron.
No.2	fits and adjusts stagger wires for correct stagger on Port and Starboard sides; then proceeds to fit and adjust all flying wires.
No.1	fixes gap wires, Port and Starboard, adjusts and locks same then connects, adjusts and finally locks lower aileron centre.
No.1	then assists No.2 to check dihedral and incidence with Abney level on top and bottom planes, also lock flying wires. Any variation in the dihedral from what it should be suggests something wrong with spars, the strut lengths, the bedding of the struts themselves or the centre section.
Nos.1 2 3 & 4	having finished the above
Nos.3 & 4	go all round the moving parts and grease same; finally fixing all inspection covers and lacing fuselage cover.
No.1	Assisted by No.2 now inspects the Machine, paying particular attention to the parts he has not rigged himself. The machine is now complete.

Appendix 8

Production and Serial Numbers

Contractors: The Sopwith Aviation Co Ltd, Canbury Park Road, Kingston-upon-Thames, Surrey;
                    William Beardmore & Co Ltd, Dalmuir, Dunbartonshire;
                    The Standard Motor Co Ltd, Cash's Lane, Coventry, Warwickshire;
                    Whitehead Aircraft Ltd, Townshend Road, Richmond, Surrey,

A contract (No.7/A/885) allotted to the Wells Aviation Co Ltd, Elystan Street, Chelsea, London, was cancelled before production could start.

Contracts and Serial Numbers

Contractor	Contract No.	Quantity	Serial numbers
Sopwith	C.P.109458/16	1	5691
	C.P.109545/16	2	9496 - 9497
	C.P.120390/16	3	9898 - 9900
	C.P.119901/16	20	N5180 - N5199
	C.P.100785/16	50	N6160 - N6209
	C.P.102622/17	20	N6460 - N6479
	C.P.102622/17	70	C3707 - C3776
			(delivered as spares)
	A.S.24542	6	Belgian numbers, SBl - SB4 known
Beardmore	C.P.117318/16	50	9901 - 9950
	A.S.14757	30	N6430 - N6459
Standard	87/A/461	50	A626 - A675
	87/A/461	50	A7301 - A7350
	87/A/461	150	B1701 - B1850
	A.S.11541	250	B5901 - B6150
	A.S.11541	350	C201 - C550
Whitehead	87/A/1101	100	A6150 - A6249
	87/A/1101	100	B2151 - B2250
	87/A/1101	150	B5251 - B5400
	87/A/1101	100	B7481 - B7580
	87/A/1101	100	C1451 - C1550
	A.S.29677	200	D4011 - D4210
	(87/A/1101)		
Wells	87/A/885	(100)	(A5138 - A5237)
Beardmore	A.S.775/17	30	N6100 - N6129
	A.S.775/17	70	N6680 - N6749

Other serial numbers

A8732 - A8737:   Allotted probably in December 1916, for the renumbering of RNAS Pups N5193, N5194, N5190, N5183, N5182 and N5192 to be taken over by the RFC; later cancelled because the transfers were not made.

N503:   Allotted for a Type 9901 Pup for which a 110hp Clerget 9Z engine was specified. Confirmation that such an aircraft was ever built has yet to be found.

Appendix 9

Reconstructed Pups

B735, B803 B805, B849:	by No.1 (Southern) Aircraft Repair Depot, Farnborough
B1499:	by 7th Wing Aeroplane Repair Section, Norwich 12.12.17
B4082, B4124, B4126, B4131, B4136, B4141, B4158:	by No.2 (Northern) ARD, Coal Aston
B7752, B8064:	by No.1 (Southern) ARD, Farnborough
B8784-B8786:	by 6th Wing ARS, Folkestone 28.1.18
B8795:	by 26th Wing ARS, Thetford 13.2.18
B8801:	by 7th Wing ARS, Norwich 14.2.18
B8821:	by 26th Wing ARS, Thetford, 2.18
B8829:	by 7th Wing ARS, Norwich 20.3.16
B9440:	by No. 63 Training Squadron, Joyce Green 13.8.17
B9455:	by 6th Wing ARS, Folkestone 1.9.17
B9931:	by 6th Wing ARS, Folkestone 25.10.17
C3500-C3503:	by 6th Wing ARS, Folkestone 21.1.18
C4295:	by 7th Wing ARS, Norwich 11.1.18
C8653:	by 18th Wing ARS, Northolt/Hounslow 17.12.17
C8654:	by 7th Wing ARS, Norwich 17.12.17
C9990-C9991:	No.7 Training Depot Station ARS, Feltwell 25.3.18
C9993:	by 26th Wing ARS Thetford 2.4.18
E9996:	7th Wing ARS, Norwich 30.4.18
F321:	by No.2 (Northern) ARD, Coal Aston
F4220:	by 33rd Wing ARS, Salisbury 5.7.18

Two photographs of a stripped Pup fuselage, believed to be that of one of the few Pups that were used by Belgian units. These bear the date 3rd April 1918 and were taken at Calais-Beaumarais.

(AELR Museum)

Appendix 10

Notes on Individual Pups and S.B.3Ds

These notes are not complete. There is no single official record, or group of records, that provides the component details for a uniformly systematic and comprehensive compilation of this kind. What follows is a synthesis from official files, individual log books, published works and correspondence. The reader is reminded that some official records are inconsistent or inaccurate. For example, under the stress of operational demands the entering up of some unit records and individual log books might have been delayed, and some dates wrongly recorded in consequence. It goes without saying that typing and transcription errors in such documents are an ever-present but not always detectable hazard.

Dates given, unless specifically of dispatch or departure, are generally representative, signifying only that an aircraft is believed to have been at that time with the unit or at the place named. It appears that dates of official allocations were sometimes recorded before the aircraft concerned were completed or delivered.

Such combat successes as are quoted are what were claimed: It is not known how many were fully confirmed, nor is it at all certain that quoted identifications of enemy types were correct.

Manstone/Manston. For unexplained reasons, the RNAS generally (though not invariably) chose to spell the place name as Manstone, in particular in its printed weekly lists of *Disposition of Aircraft*. To the RAF the aerodrome was, and still is, Manston.

Ship names are printed in italics.

Another view of captured Pup N6161 (also see page 55), lost by No.3 Naval Squadron on 18th January 1917.   *(via Mick Davis)*

Appendix 11

RFC Pups used by, or allocated to, the RNAS

A626, A6158

B1816-1825, B2173, B2181, B2183, B2202- B2204, B2208, B2211-2213, B2217, B2218, B2226, B5928, B5930, B5938-B5940, B5948-B5950, B5958-B5960, B5968-B5970, B5978-B5980, B5988-B5994, B6011-B6014, B6021-B6024, B6031-B6034, B6049-B6052, B6061-B6064, B6073-B6076, B6085-B6088, B6096-B6100, B6143, B6146, B6149

C202, C205, C208, C211, C214, C217, C220, C223, C226, C229, C232, C235, C238, C239, C241, C244, C247, C250, C253, C256, C259, C262, C265, C268, C269, C271, C274, C277, C280, C283, C286, C289, C292, C295, C298, C301, C304, C307, C310, C313, C314, C316, C317,C319, C320, C322, C325, C326, C331-C334, C336, C338, C340, C342-C345, C350-C355, C357, C359, C361, C1502, C1503, C1508, C1516-C1518, C1523, C1532, C1533, C1535, C1537, C1541

N6203 was named "MINA" by Flt Sub-Lt L.H.Slatter whilst with the Seaplane Defence Flight at St. Pol in July 1917. It had earlier served with 'C' Flt of No.3 Naval Squadron, with which victories were claimed on 21st and 29th April by Flt Sub-Lt H.S.Broad. *(via Frank Cheesman)*

Appendix 12

Named Pups

Presentation Pups

B1777	British Guiana No.2
A6174	Canada
B1760	Capetown No.1 (succeeded B.E.2c 2653)
B1839	Citizens of the Town & District of Thana
B1775	Gold Coast Aborigines No.2
B1834	Gold Coast Aborigines No.2 (succeeded B1775)
B5296	Gold Coast Aborigines No.2 (succeeded B1834)
C282	Gold Coast Aborigines No.2 (succeeded B5296)
A6234	Johannesburg No.1
C306	Liverpool Overseas Club
B1778	Punjab No.12 Kashmir
B1779	Rewa Fiji
B1780	Rhodesia No.1 (succeeded B.E.2e A3053)
C305	The Oriole

Other named Pups

A7333	Ad Astra (in No.46 Squadron)
?	Aileen
N6185	Anzac (in No.4 (Naval) Squadron)

N6179	Baby Mine (in No3 (Naval) Squadron)
N6205	Betty (in No.3 (Naval) Squadron)
N5185	Binky II (in No.3 (Naval) Squadron)
N6171	Black Arrow (in No.3 (Naval) Squadron)
N6207	Black Bess (in No.3 (Naval) Squadron)
N6172	Black Tulip (in No.3 (Naval) Squadron)
B5253	Bluebird (in No.3 Training Depot Station)
N6200	Bobs (in No.4 (Naval) Squadron)
B1777	Chu Chin Chow (British Guiana No.2) (in No. 46 Squadron RFC)
9899	Do-Do (in No.4 (Naval) Squadron)
N6438	Excuse me! (at RNAS Donibristle)
N6474	Excuse me! (in No.3 (Naval) Squadron)
N6195	Gab….. (in No.3 (Naval) Squadron) [full name not known]
N6181	Happy (in No.3 (Naval) Squadron)
B4128	Ickle Poop (in School of Special Flying?)
B5906	Impikoff (in No.44 HD Squadron)
?	I Wonder (RNAS)

B1820, named "JOHNNIE WALKER" after the Scotch whisky of that name, served as a training machine at RNASTE Vendôme (later No.205 Training Depot Station) from December 1917 until being wrecked when the engine failed on take-off on 29th July 1918.

The first letter of the name on this photograph of N5187 is partially hidden by a wing strut, but could be either "TICKIE" and "VICKIE" N5187 whilst serving with No.8 (Naval) Squadron between December 1916 and February 1917. It subsequently served with Nos.3 and 4 (Naval) Squadrons before being wrecked in April 1917.

"WIND-UP" of the Walmer Defence Flight. Seated in the cockpit is believed to be the future Lady Ellwood.

B1820	Johnnie Walker (at Vendôme)
N6442	Julia (in Walmer Defence Flight)
N5182	Lady Maud (in No.8 (Naval) Squadron)
B2178	Madge (in No.112 HD Squadron)
N6183	Mildred H (in No.3 (Naval) Squadron)
N6203	Mina (in Seaplane Defence Flight)
B5259	Monkey (in No.56 Training Squadron)
B6124	Mummy (in No.81 Squadron)
B1727	Normie (in No.46 Squadron RFC)
?	OS III (No.54 Squadron RFC – Captain Oliver Stewart's aircraft)
D4185	Pelusium
C514	Prince (in Pool of Pilots)
?	Retreat (various parrot and animal motifs on fuselage and tail surfaces)
9496	The Pup
N5187	Tickie or Vickie (in No.8 (Naval) Squadron?)
B5910	Umpikof (in No.112 (HD) Squadron)
B1802	Will o' the Wisp (in No.46 Squadron RFC)
?	Wind-up (in Walmer Defence Flight)
A648	Yes (in No.54 Squadron RFC)

A rather indistinct photograph of an apparently unserialled Pup with the name "RETREAT" on the fin. The fin and fuselage carry various designs which seem to include a parrot and a cat.

Appendix 13

Individual Pup Histories

1 SOPWITH PUP (ADMIRALTY TYPE 9901) ordered on Contract number C.P.109458/16, numbered 3691 & built Kingston-on-Thames. (80hp Le Rhône)

3691   Prototype. Passed by Sopwith Experimental Department 9.2.16; CFS Upavon trials 3.16 (speed 27.3.16; climb 29.3.16); Deld Chingford 10.5.16 (visited Grain 16.5.16); Grain 25.5.16; Chingford via Dover to AD Dunkirk for service trials 28.5.16 (F/L LH Hardstaff); 5 Flt 'A' Sqdn 5 (Naval) Wing Coudekerque 1.6.16 to at least 2.6.16 (recorded on strength in early April, presumably in anticipation); AD Dunkirk repair from mid 6.16; Sopwith Fighter Flt/5 Flt 'A' Sqdn 5 (Naval) Wing Coudekerque 22.6.16 ('ready'); Composite Flt/6 Flt 'A' Sqdn 5 (Naval) Wing by 29.6.16; Scouts Flt/2 Flt 'A' Sqdn 1 (Naval) Wing Furnes 10.7.16; AD Dunkirk repair by 27.7.16 - @17.8.16; 'C' Sqdn 1 (Naval) Wing St.Pol by 31.8.16; AD Dunkirk repair by 7.9.16; Sopwith single-seater Flt 'C' Sqdn 1 (Naval) Wing St.Pol by 21.9.16; LVG C out of control nr Ghistelles 15.30 24.9.16 (FSL SJ Goble); AD Dunkirk repair 24.9.16 (repair then in reserve); Tested 2.11.16 (presumably after modification to production standard); 'C' Sqdn 1 (Naval) Wing 4.11.16; D Flt 'B' Sqdn 1 (Naval) Wing 9.11.16 (briefly re-designated Detached Sqdn with 22nd Wing

RFC); 8 (N) Sqdn (coded 'B') 16.11.16; Halberstadt shot down Bapaume, shared with N5197 26.12.16 (FSL NE Woods); 3 (N) Sqdn 3.2.17; AD Dunkirk 10.2.17 (repair); Aircraft Park Dover 30.4.17; Enemy aircraft patrol, left 18.20, attacked Gothas, shot up and went into spin but recovered 25.5.17 (FSL RFS Leslie); Anti-Gotha patrol, left 07.38 4.7.17; Aircraft Park Dover, for another station by 10.17; CSD White City W/E 8.12.17; Deleted 21.12.17 and to USA for Lady Drogheda's exhibition of British armaments; RNAS/RAF Manston (date unknown); Thence to Agricultural Hall, for preservation as museum exhibit 13.9.18, but evidently not preserved and eventually scrapped

2 SOPWITH PUP PROTOTYPES (became ADMIRALTY 9901 TYPE) ordered under Contract number C.P.109545/16, numbered 9496 and 9497 and built Kingston-on-Thames. (80hp Clerget)

9496   Officially accepted Brooklands for 3N Wing 10.7.16; Deld Chingford 9.7.16 (sic); Aircraft Park Dover 19.7.16; AD Dunkirk and on to 'C' Sqdn 1 (Naval) Wing 20.7.16; Villacoublay 17.8.16; 3 Wing Luxeuil by 25.8.16; Named 'THE PUP'; Surveyed (for deletion) 6.4.17

9497   Allotted Grain for landing experiments 4.9.16; Flown at

9497 landing on a dummy deck at Grain around January 1917 after being fitted by Beardmore with an experimental arrester gear and airscrew guard. It had been marked "N9497" in error at Port Victoria Repair Station.   *(via Philip Jarrett)*

Beardmore airfield, Inchinnan 5.10.16 & 13.10.16; Deld Grain 27.10.16 (extensive and varied use for deck-landing experiments); Port Victoria Repair Station, tested for Admiralty trials, slightly damaged 31.10.16 (Dukinfield Jones); Put forward 12.16 for modifications by Beardmore; Experimental arrester gear and airscrew guard 22.12.16; Tested after erection 24.12.16 (S/Cdr HM Cave-Brown-Cave); Tested on dummy deck at Grain; Flown off deck 10.1.17 (S/Cdr HM Cave-Brown-Cave); Put forward 1.17 for Sopwith to dismantle and pack for Beardmore; Marked "N9497" in error at Port Victoria Repair Station 2.17; Renamed Experimental Constructive Dept, Grain 26.2.17; 3 deck landings 28.2.17 (F/L CT Freeman); 2 landings on experimental deck 5.3.17 (F/L CT Freeman); 2 deck landings 15.3.17 (S/Cdr HR Busteed then F/L CT Freeman); 2 deck landings 16.3.17 (F/L CT Freeman); 2 deck landings 18.3.17 (F/L EH Dunning then F/L CT Freeman); Deck landings 21.4.17, 1.5.17 & 26.5.17 (all F/L CT Freeman); Anti-Gotha patrol, left 11.50, landed 13.00 13.6.17 (F/L CT Freeman); Steel tipped skids, horns on undercarriage, tail hook 6.17; Deck landing rail trials 20.7.17; Deck landing trials with skids in troughs 7.9.17; Skid test on deck 6.12.17; Experimental Armament Dept, Grain by 2.18 (80hp Le Rhône); Skid test on deck 14.3.18; Stalled on dummy deck 16.3.18; Deck landing skids by 3.18; Still EAD Grain 6.18

3 SOPWITH PUP (ADMIRALTY 9901 TYPE) pre-production aircraft ordered under Contract number C.P.120390/16, numbered 9898 to 9900 and built Kingston-on-Thames. Deld from Brooklands. Put forward week ending 1.9.16 for French Government but not taken up. (80hp Clerget)

9898   Deld Aircraft Park Dover 25.11.16; AD Dunkirk 28.11.16; 3 (N) Sqdn 30.11.16 (listed on Sqdn strength in anticipation 23.11.16); AD Dunkirk to 'A' Flt 8 (N) Sqdn 20.12.16; 'A' Flt 3 (N) Sqdn 3.2.17; Roland driven down, shared with N5188 13.45 16.2.17 (FSL JA Glen); Halberstadt DII out of control nr Menencourt 11.45 4.3.17; 2-str out of control Vaux (confirmed) 10.30 17.3.17; 2-str in flames Ervillers 11.00 17.3.17 (all FSL JJ Malone Can); Blown over on landing 4.17; To AD Dunkirk W/E 12.4.17 (mainplanes, engine & propeller replaced); 11 (N) Sqdn 19.5.17; 12 (N) Sqdn 13.6.17; Driven down on sands by rain, retd aerodrome, crashed on landing 14.8.17 (FSL SA Hamilton-Bowyer); Repaired by 21.8.17; Aircraft Park Dover 23.11.17; Allotted Grain for experiments 7.12.17; Experimental Constructive Dept, Grain 15.12.17 to at least 6.18 (experiments, fitted 80hp Le Rhône)

9899   Deld Aircraft Park Dover 6.12.16; AD Dunkirk 11.12.16; 3 (N) Sqdn 11.12.16; 'C' Sqdn 1 (Naval) Wing by 14.12.16; AD Dunkirk by 23.12.16 (repair); by road to 'B' Flt 8 (N) Sqdn, arr 24.1.17; 'B' Flt 3 (N) Sqdn 3.2.17; Crashed on landing 14.2.17 (FSL JA Glen); AD Dunkirk 15.2.17 (repair); 'B' Flt 4 (N) Sqdn (named "DO-DO") 21.3.17; Albatros D.III out of control nr Steenbrugge, south of Bruges 15.30 26.4.17 (FSL AJ Chadwick); Siemens-Schuckert DI crashed in sea 5m east of Zeebrugge 07.20, own aircraft shot up 12.5.17 (FSL AJ Enstone); Forced landed on beach 20.5.17 (F/Cdr AM Shook) (flying next day); 2 white Albatros D.V out of control 5m north-east of Dixmude 16.00 6.6.17 (FSL GW Hemming); Marked as "N9899" 6.17; 11 (N) Sqdn 7.6.17; 4 (N) Sqdn 12.6.17 (temp attd); 11 (N) Sqdn 4.7.17; Albatros, probably 2-str out of control south of Middelkerke 18.45 17.7.17 (FSL HF Airey); Ran into

ditch on landing 14.8.17 (FSL HF Airey); still 11 (N) Sqdn by 16.8.17; AD Dunkirk by 23.8.17 to at least 27.9.17; Aircraft Park Dover by 6.10.17; Surveyed 16.10.17; Deleted 19.10.17 Wear and tear

9900   Listed on Dunkirk strength, presumably in anticipation 7.9.16; Deld AD Dunkirk 12.16; by road to 3 (N) Sqdn, arr 29.1.17; Crashed landing Cormont on aerial gunnery course 14.2.17; AD Dunkirk 15.2.17 (repair); 9 (N) Sqdn 3.3.17 to at least 9.3.17; Aircraft Park Dover from/by 14.3.17 (repair and overhaul for Dunkirk); AD Dunkirk 19.4.17; 3 (N) Sqdn Marieux 4.17; Aircraft Park Dover 9.5.17; Walmer 9.5.17; Enemy aircraft patrol 1.6.17 (FSL WM Lusby); Dover 4.6.17; HD sortie against Gotha bombing Sheerness, left 18.20, landed 19.30 5.6.17; Wings and propeller damaged 8.6.17; AD Dunkirk 23.6.17; Seaplane Defence Flt 11.7.17; 12 (N) Sqdn 15.7.17 to at least 26.8.17; AD Dunkirk by 30.8.17 to at least 6.9.17; Aircraft Park Dover by 13.9.17; Surveyed 16.10.17; Deleted 19.10.17 Wear & tear

50 SOPWITH PUP (ADMIRALTY 9901 TYPE) ordered 7.6.16 (updated W/E 3.11.16) under Cont Nos C.P.117318/16 & A.S.11764/17 from Sir William Beardmore & Co Ltd, numbered 9901 to 9950 and built Dalmuir. Fitted with alternative Lewis gun and/or Le Prieur Aerial Torpedo (i.e. rocket) armament from 9909 onwards. 16 aircraft fitted with airbags. First flights usually at Inchinnan airfield by A.Dukinfield Jones. (9901-9909 & 9911 80hp Clerget; 9910 & 9912-9959 80hp Le Rhône)

9901   (Serial number used as Admiralty Type number for Pup). (80hp Clerget No.573, propeller No.616) FF 26.9.16; Accepted 16.10.16; Deld in crate to Design Flt Eastchurch 1.11.16; Flown 6.11.16 (by Dukinfield Jones, S/Cdr HR Busteed & F/L PA Johnston); Flown 14.11.16, 11.12.16 & 2.1.17 (S/Cdr HR Busteed); Undercarriage collapsed landing 5.1.17 (S/Cdr HR Busteed); Experimental Constructive Dept, Grain 18.3.17; Tested with air bags inflated 18.4.17 (S/Cdr HR Busteed); Ditching experiments 5.17; Emergency flotation experiments 17.6.17; Anchored for 6 hours with airbags for flotation tests 23.6.17; Fitted with jettisonable undercarriage mid-1917; Flown from HMS *Manxman* to HMS *Yarmouth* in Firth of Forth 28.6.17 (S/Cdr FJ Rutland); Detachable chassis repaired after sea landing 12.8.17; With N6440 shot down GoIV No.663, 1 of 10 Gothas, into sea 1m off Margate 22.8.17 (F/Cdr GE Hervey); NFT

9902   (80hp Clerget No.578, propeller No.624) FF 23.10.16; Accepted 8.11.16; FF Grain 23.10.16 (A Dukinfield Jones); Officially accepted 8.11.16; RNASTE Cranwell 14.11.16; Wrecked 24.7.17; Crashed and damaged 6.2.18 (pilot unhurt); Surveyed 25.2.18 wrecked; Deleted 13.3.18

9903   (80hp Clerget No.576, propeller No.606) FF & accepted 9.11.16; Deld RNASTE Cranwell 27.11.16; Crashed and badly damaged Cranwell 1.3.18 (pilot unhurt); Still u/s at Cranwell 30.3.18; Became 201/202 TDS Cranwell 1.4.18

9904   (80hp Clerget No.571, propeller No.736) Put forward to fit rocket gear 10.16; Beardmore to fit to fly off deck 11.16 (NTU?); FF & accepted 21.11.16; Presumably dismantled for transport; Deld Gt Yarmouth for erection 2.12.16; Accepted 15.12.16 (Dukinfield Jones); Enemy aircraft patrol 9.3.17 (F/L E Cadbury); Anti-Zeppelin patrols 26.3.17, 24.5.17 (left 04.00) & 17.6.17 (left 15.20) (all F/L E Cadbury); U/s at Yarmouth 30.3.18; Became 490 Flt Gt Yarmouth 25.5.18; Burgh Castle by 6.18; Enemy aircraft patrol, engine failure, forced landed

Two naval officers fooling about around the wreckage of 9905 after it came to grief while landing at Great Yarmouth, possibly on 27th June 1917 at the hands of Flt Lt G.W.R.Fane.
(via Frank Cheesman)

Gt Yarmouth 8.6.18; Covehithe by 25.6.18; Crashed on landing, wrecked 29.6.18 (pilot unhurt)

9905   (80hp Clerget No.1031, propeller No.749, later 80hp Le Rhône?) Put forward to fit rocket gear 10.16; Beardmore to fit to fly off deck 11.16 (NTU?); FF & accepted 22.11.16; Presumably dismantled for transport; Deld Gt Yarmouth for erection by 7.12.16; Accepted 15.12.16 (Dukinfield Jones); Enemy aircraft patrols 30.3.17 & 4.4.17 (both F/L GWR Fane); Martlesham Heath 8.4.17; Gt Yarmouth 20.4.17; Anti-Zeppelin patrol, left 03.20, returned 04.05 17.6.17 (F/L GWR Fane); Overturned landing 27.6.17 (F/L GWR Fane); Enemy aircraft patrol 5.9.17 (F/L GWR Fane); Became 490 Flt Gt Yarmouth 25.5.18; Burgh Castle by 6.18; Covehithe by 25.6.18; Engine failure, forced landed in sea and sank 5.7.18 (pilot unhurt)

9906   (80hp Clerget No.1032, propeller No.748) FF 3.12.16; Accepted Dalmuir 7.12.16; Deld Manston 12.12.16; overseas 23.1.17; 3 Wing Luxeuil by 23.2.17; Fighting patrol, transparent celluloid covering of centre section ruptured in air reducing speed and climb 25.2.17 (F/Cdr C Draper); Reported to need extensive repairs 30.3.17; Surveyed Luxeuil 2.4.17; Deleted 4.17

9907   (80hp Clerget No.1030, propeller No.769, later 80hp Gnome) FF 3.12.16; Accepted 7.12.16; Despatched to Manston 5.1.17, arrived 7.1.17; Westgate 10.1.17 (repair); Manston 13.2.17; Anti-Gotha patrols, left 16.55, landed 18.22, left again 18.25, landed 19.40 25.5.17; Anti-Gotha patrol, left 18.05, landed 19.05 5.6.17 (all FSL JE Scott); Anti-Gotha patrol, left 10.45, damaged landing Aldeburgh 12.20 13.6.17 (FSL RH Daly); Anti-Gotha patrol, left 07.40, landed 09.10 4.7.17; Anti-Gotha patrols, left 09.27, landed 11.15, left again 11.22, landed 13.25 7.7.17; Anti-Gotha patrol 08.55, landed 10.02 22.7.17 (all FSL CH Fitzherbert); For deletion 2.18; To Greenwich less engine W/E 16.2.18 (presumed for ground instructional use)

9908   (80hp Clerget No.1033, propeller No.770) FF, but damaged landing 7.12.16 (F/L Allen); Flown again & accepted 16.1.17; Despatched to RNASTE Cranwell for erection 16.1.17, arrived 24.1.17; Lost, forced landed in

field, hit hedge and crashed beyond repair 4.9.17 (FSL SD Culley); Surveyed 22.9.17; Deleted 8.10.17 wrecked

9909   (80hp Le Rhône No.7994, propeller No.777) FF 9.1.17; Accepted 16.1.17; Despatched to RNASTE Cranwell for erection, arrived 26.1.17; Deleted 28.7.17

9910   (80hp Le Rhône No.7993, propeller No.785) (Fitted rocket armament) FF & accepted 26.12.16; Earmarked and despatched for HMS *Vindex*, but deld Felixstowe and to Trimley for erection 10.1.17; Flown 13.1.17; Levington NLG 3.2.17; Martlesham Heath 20.2.17; Gt Yarmouth for visit, but engine failure and stayed 8.4.17; Hostile seaplane patrol 16.4.17 (F/L GWR Fane); CSD White City 6.2.18; Surveyed 18.3.18; Deleted 27.3.18 Damaged beyond repair

9911   (80hp Clerget No.1036, propeller No.834) later 80hp Le Rhône?) (Fitted rocket armament) FF & accepted 26.12.16; Earmarked and despatched for HMS *Vindex*, but deld Felixstowe and to Trimley for erection 10.1.17; Felixstowe 16.1.17; Trimley 17.1.17; Levington NLG 3.2.17; Martlesham Heath 20.2.17; Gt Yarmouth 26.4.17; Martlesham Heath 28.4.17 (held for HMS *Vindex*); Damaged landing 14.6.17 (F/L FN Halstead); [HMS *Vindex*, converted to 80hp Clerget W/E 2.11.17]; HMS *Vindex* @19.1.18; still at Martlesham Heath 23.2.18; War School RNAS Manston by 23.2.18; Deleted W/E 23.3.18

9912   (80hp Le Rhône No.8070, propeller No.814) (Fitted rocket armament) FF & accepted 9.1.17; Deld Port Victoria Repair Station, Grain 23.1.17; Renamed Experimental Constructive Dept, Grain 26.2.17; 2 deck landing experiments 4.4.17; War Flt Grain 15.5.17; Anti-Gotha patrol, left 17.28, landed 19.30 25.5.17; Anti-Gotha patrols, landed 10.15, left again 10.25, landed 11.19 7.7.17; Anti-Gotha patrols, returned, then left again 17.50, chased Gothas but gun problems, landed 19.20 12.8.17 (all F/L CT Freeman); Experimental Dept Grain by 29.12.17 (deck landing experiments); Rosyth (via Cranwell & Lincoln) 23.3.18; Retd Grain by 1.4.18; Hendon 10.8.18; Retd Grain 11.8.18

9913   (80hp Le Rhône No.8144, propeller No.778) (Fitted rocket armament) FF & accepted 19.1.17; Packed for transport; Deld East Fortune by rail for HMS

Squadron Commander F.J.Rutland flying a rocket-armed Pup, probably 9918, off the deck of HMS Manxman in the Spring of 1917.

(IWM Q.65602)

Manxman 26.1.17; Tested by *Manxman* pilot 13.2.17 & 15.2.17; Totally wrecked in HMS *Manxman* 26.2.17; Deleted 15.3.17

9914   (80hp Le Rhône No.7996, propeller No.747) (Fitted rocket armament) FF & accepted 20.1.17; Deld East Fortune for HMS *Manxman* 28.1.17; Flown 22.2.17; HMS *Manxman* 26.2.17; Damaged by 1.3.17; East Fortune 28.3.17 (u/s); Repaired; East Fortune for HMS *Manxman* 13.5.17; Fleet Practice Station Turnhouse 8.6.17; Crashed on take-off 3.7.17; Deleted 7.8.17

9915   (80hp Le Rhône No.8224, propeller No.826) FF & accepted 29.1.17; Deld Aircraft Park Dover 7.2.17; AD Dunkirk 10.2.17; 9 (N) Sqdn 14.2.17; Forced landed in dense fog, struck hill, lost undercarriage and propeller nr Suresnil 14.2.17 (FSL CD Crundall); AD Dunkirk 15.2.17 (repair); 11 (N) Sqdn 23.5.17; Crashed on landing 26.5.17 (FSL TR Swinburne); AD Dunkirk by 31.5.17 (repair); Aircraft Park Dover 13.6.17 (officially transferred from Dunkirk to Dover 9.8.17); Walmer 28.9.17; To East Fortune Naval Flying School W/E 10.11.17; Deleted W/E 6.4.18

9916   (80hp Le Rhône No.7997, propeller No.747) (Fitted rocket armament) FF & accepted 29.1.17; Deld Aircraft Park Dover 7.2.17; AD Dunkirk 8.2.17; 9 (N) Sqdn 11.2.17 (in 'A' Flt by 26.4.17); 2-str shot down into sea off Middelkerke shared with N5188 20.30 2.5.17; 2-str out of control Ostende shared with N6188 & N6193 14.15 31.5.17 (now in 'C' Flt); Crashed Steenwerck 3.6.17 (all FSL HF Stackard); AD Dunkirk by 7.6.17; Aircraft Park Dover 13.6.17; AD Dunkirk 28.6.17; Seaplane Defence Flt 4.7.17; 'B' Flt 12 (N) Sqdn 15.7.17; AD Dunkirk W/E 30.8.17; Aircraft Park Dover W/E 13.9.17 (officially transferred from Dunkirk to Dover 11.10.17); Deleted W/E 1.12.17

9917   (80hp Le Rhône No.100134, propeller No.863) FF & accepted 3.2.17; Deld East Fortune 10.2.17; HMS *Manxman* 9.3.17; Badly damaged 29.4.17; HMS *Manxman* 6.6.17; Fleet Aeroplane Depot Turnhouse 29.6.17; Rosyth 7.9.17; Donibristle 15.9.17 (possibly in HMS *Nairana* 9.17); Rosyth 16.10.17; Fleet Aeroplane Depot Turnhouse W/E 21.3.18 (being erected 31.3.18); Deleted W/E 11.7.18

9918   (80hp Le Rhône No.100136, propeller No.864) (Fitted rocket armament) FF & accepted 3.2.17; Deld East Fortune 10.2.17; HMS *Manxman* 28.2.17; Lost at sea 29.4.17 (F/Cdr FJ Rutland - presume later recovered); Deleted 12.5.17

9919   (80hp Le Rhône No.8071, propeller No.865)) FF & accepted 5.2.17; Deld East Fortune 8.2.17; HMS *Manxman* 9.3.17; Badly damaged 29.4.17; Deleted 14.5.17

9920   (80hp Le Rhône No.8139, propeller No.815) (Fitted rocket armament);) FF & accepted 5.2.17; Deld East Fortune 8.2.17; HMS *Manxman* 28.2.17; Lost at sea 29.4.17 (pilot picked by HMS *Patrician*); Deleted 12.5.17

9921   (80hp Le Rhône No.8138, propeller No.812) FF & accepted 13.2.17; Deld Felixstowe for HMS *Vindex* 27.2.17; Martlesham Heath 2.3.17; Engine failure, forced landed Eye, taken to Pulham Airship Station, then retd Martlesham Heath 11.3.17 (F/L MJG Day); Main spars reported warped 15.6.17; HMS *Vindex* 23.6.17; War School RNAS Manston 19.1.18; To Controller of Technical Development for use at Grain; Experimental Dept Grain, crashed on landing Eastbourne, slightly damaged 23.3.18 (pilot unhurt); still at Eastbourne for CTD by 6.4.18

9922   (80hp Le Rhône No.8222, propeller No.829) (Fitted rocket armament) Allotted Grain for "launching trials" 24.1.17; FF & accepted 15.2.17; Deld Experimental Constructive Dept, Grain 5.3.17; Deck landing trials 28.3.17 (F/Cdr LP Openshaw & F/L CT Freeman) & 29.3.17 (F/Cdr LP Openshaw); Anti-Gotha patrol, left 18.05, closed on Gotha but engine trouble, returned, landed 18.52 25.5.17 (S/Cdr HR Busteed); Much experimental deck flying at Grain; Fitting deck landing hook and sprung skids by 14.7.17; Tested deck landing

9928 was mis-painted as "N9928". It joined No.9 (Naval) Squadron in France and is seen here after overturning in a ploughed fields, possibly on 22nd May 1917 at the hands of Flt Sub-Lt J.W.Pinder. It was subsequently repaired at the Aircraft Depot Dunkirk and then flown back to England where it joined the War School at RNAS Manston.   *(via Philip Jarrett)*

skids 20.7.17 & 23.7.17 x 2 (S/Cdr HR Busteed); Emergency landing in sea on skid test flight 30.7.17 (S/Cdr HR Busteed); Rail-launching test 16.8.17 [see pages 107-108]; Tested with rigid skids 9.11.17 (S/Cdr HR Busteed); Manston to Experimental Constructive & Armament Dept, Grain W/E 23.2.18; Launching trials 3.18; Listed as fully serviceable at Grain 30.3.18, but deleted W/E 1.4.18

9923   (80hp Le Rhône No.8074, propeller No.848) FF & accepted 15.2.17; Deld RNASTE Cranwell 2.3.17 to at least 4.17; Freiston by 6.17; Retd Cranwell by 9.17; Crashed, completely wrecked Cranwell South 14.1.18 (pilot unhurt); Surveyed 25.2.18; Deleted 13.3.18 Wear & tear

9924   (80hp Le Rhône No.8257, propeller No.835) (Fitted rocket armament) FF & accepted 21.2.17; Deld RNASTE Cranwell 2.3.17; Hendon 14.5.17 (under repair to at least 6.6.17, then used by 2 AAP Comm Flt); Enemy aircraft patrol, landed Fairlop, then retd Hendon 3.10.17 (F/L MA Simpson); Used at Hendon by Air Dept officers for visiting RFC (later RAF) stations by 1.18 to at least 4.19

9925   (80hp Le Rhône No.8283, propeller No.836) FF & accepted 23.2.17; Deld RNASTE Cranwell 7.3.17; Wrecked 18.7.17; Engine failure on take-off, swerved and blown over 18.10.17 (FSL AC Sharwood); Overturned landing, slightly damaged 31.12.17 (pilot unhurt); Crashed, slightly damaged Waddington 16.2.18 (pilot unhurt); Crashed, badly damaged, Cranwell South 14.3.18 (pilot unhurt); Fitted 60hp Le Rhône but u/s by 30.3.18; Became 201/202 TDS Cranwell 1.4.18

9926   (80hp Le Rhône No.8153, propeller No.845) (Fitted rocket armament) FF & accepted 26.2.17; Packed for transportation, and deld Felixstowe by rail for HMS *Vindex* 17.3.17; HMS *Vindex* 14.4.17; Lost at sea, retd later 28.9.17 (F/L WB Foster); Surveyed 29.9.17; Deleted 8.10.17

9927   (80hp Le Rhône No.8215, propeller No.854) FF & accepted 27.2.17; Packed for transportation, and deld Felixstowe by rail for HMS *Vindex* 17.3.17; Hangared and erected Martlesham Heath 30.3.17; HMS *Vindex* 4.4.17; Lost at sea whilst chasing a Zeppelin 25.9.17 (F/Cdr BD Kilner killed); Surveyed 29.9.17; Deleted 8.10.17

9928   (80hp Le Rhône No.8216, propeller No.861) (Fitted

rocket armament) FF & accepted 26.2.17; Despatched to Dover 5.3.17 (arr 17.3.17) (mispainted as "N9928"); AD Dunkirk 28.3.17; 9 (N) Sqdn 4.4.17 (still as "N9928" initially); Fired at 2-str which landed just over Dutch frontier down the coast (FSL E Pierce); Crashed on landing 22.5.17 (FSL JW Pinder); AD Dunkirk W/E 14.6.17; Aircraft Park Dover 3.7.17 (officially transferred from Dunkirk to Dover 9.8.17); War School RNAS Manston for erection 14.10.17 (marked 'C' and now fitted 80hp Gnome); Deleted W/E 2.3.18

9929   (80hp Le Rhône No.100287, propeller No.879) FF & accepted 27.2.17; Despatched to Dover 5.3.17 (arrived 17.3.17); AD Dunkirk 21.3.17; 4 (N) Sqdn 28.3.17; Forced landed and damaged nr Bergues 23.4.17 (FSL EOA Andrews); AD Dunkirk by 26.4.17; Aircraft Park Dover 2.5.17 (repair, then to War Flt, Dover); Anti-Gotha patrol, left 18.20, landed 19.15 5.6.17; Anti-Gotha patrol, left 11.09, landed 12.15 13.6.17; AD Dunkirk 23.6.17; Seaplane Defence Flt 3.7.17; AD Dunkirk 4.8.17 to at least 23.8.17; 12 (N) Sqdn from/by 25.8.17 to at least 3.9.17; AD Dunkirk by 6.9.17; Aircraft Park Dover W/E 4.10.17 (officially transferred from Dunkirk to Dover 18.10.17); Surveyed 16.10.17; Deleted 19.10.17 Wear & tear

9930   (80hp Le Rhône No.100280, propeller No.852) (Fitted rocket armament) FF & accepted 8.3.17; Despatched to Killingholme for erection 18.4.17; Redcar Naval Flying School 25.5.17; Martlesham Heath for HMS *Vindex* 12.6.17; HMS *Vindex* 23.6.17; Houton Bay by 29.12.17; War School RNAS Manston by 23.3.18; Deleted 25.3.18

9931   (80hp Le Rhône No.100291, propeller No.855) (Converted to 9901a Ships Pup) FF & accepted 8.3.17; Despatched to Killingholme for erection 18.4.17; Scapa by rail for *Campania* 30.4.17; HMS *Campania* for erection 8.5.17; Scapa/Houton Bay W/E 13.10.17 to at least 8.12.17; HMS *Campania* by 12.17; HMAS *Sydney* 11.12.17 to at least 19.1.18; HMS *Dublin* 1.18; Houton Bay for overhaul W/E 2.2.18; Scapa W/E 25.5.18; Smoogroo W/E 18.7.18; Scapa W/E 28.11.18; Smoogroo W/E 12.12.18; Scapa W/E 19.12.18; Smoogroo W/E 31.12.18; Disposed W/E 16.1.19

9932   (80hp Le Rhône No.100265, propeller No.883)

(Converted to 9901a Ships Pup) FF & accepted 8.3.17; Despatched Killingholme for erection 18.4.17; Scapa by rail for *Campania* 30.4.17; HMS *Campania* for erection 8.5.17 to at least 15.7.17 (last mention there); [Not Scapa or HMS *Yarmouth* by 29.9.17]; HMS *Yarmouth* to Scapa for overhaul W/E 3.11.17; HMS *Yarmouth* by 23.11.17; Scapa to HMAS *Sydney* 7.12.17; HMS *Yarmouth* by 14-21.12.17; Houton Bay Reserve by 29.12.17; Scapa W/E 18.5.18; Smoogroo W/E 11.7.18; Scapa W/E 12.12.18 to at least 30.1.19

9933   (80hp Le Rhône No.100260, propeller No.909) (Fitted with skid undercarriage and upward firing Lewis gun) FF & accepted 14.3.17; Despatched Killingholme for erection 18.4.17; Scapa by rail for erection 30.4.17; HMS *Campania* for erection 8.5.17 to at least 15.7.17 (last mention in records)

9934   (80hp Le Rhône No.100266, propeller No.884) (Fitted rocket armament) FF & accepted 14.3.17; Deld Killingholme for erection 18.4.17; HMS *Campania* for erection 8.5.17 (also on HMS *Tiger*, dates unknown); Surveyed 20.9.17; Deleted 24.9.17 wrecked

9935   (80hp Le Rhône No.100261, propeller No.892) FF & accepted 14.3.17; Deld Killingholme for erection 18.4.17; To RNASTE Cranwell 20.4.17 (arr 21.4.17); Wrecked 15.6.17; Repaired; Still Cranwell 19.10.17; Freiston by 11.17; RNASTE Cranwell by 1.18 (now 60hp Le Rhône); Crashed and wrecked Cranwell South 24.1.18 (pilot unhurt); Visited HMS *Eagle* 10.3.18; Freiston 14.3.18; Engine failure, crashed and badly damaged nr aerodrome 20.3.18 (pilot unhurt); For deletion by 30.3.18; Became 201/202 TDS Cranwell 1.4.18

9936   (80hp Le Rhône No.100281, propeller No.911) (Fitted rocket armament) FF & accepted 29.3.17; Deld Killingholme for erection 18.4.17; To 'B' Flt Cranwell 20.4.17 (arr 21.4.17); Wrecked 18.7.17; Crashed Cranwell South 16.2.18 (pilot unhurt); Became 201/202 TDS Cranwell 1.4.18

9937   (80hp Le Rhône No.100288, propeller No.919) FF & accepted 29.3.17; Deld Killingholme for erection 24.4.17; D Flt Cranwell 24.4.17; Deleted 5.12.17 on becoming ground instructional airframe

9938   (80hp Le Rhône No.100283, propeller No.875) (Fitted rocket armament) FF & accepted 29.3.17; Deld Killingholme for erection 18.4.17; RNASTE Cranwell 24.4.17; Parachute dropping experiments 28.10.17; At Freiston 11.17 to at least 12.17; Deleted W/E 22.2.18

9939   (80hp Le Rhône No.100290, propeller No.951) FF & accepted 29.3.17; Deld Killingholme for erection 19.4.17; Allotted Grain for landing experiments 11.5.17; Experimental Constructive Dept, Grain 22.5.17 (engine trials); Repair undercarriage 23.6.17; Still in use for deck landing and arrester gear trials 7.19

9940   (80hp Le Rhône No.100293, propeller No.953) (Fitted rocket armament) FF & accepted 30.3.17; Deld Killingholme for erection 18.4.17; Allotted War Flt Grain 21.5.17 (arr 25.5.17 via Huntingdon & Chingford); Anti-Gotha patrol, left 18.25, landed 19.20 5.6.17 (F/Cdr RDG Sibley); Anti-Gotha patrol, left 11.05 attacked Gothas over Southend, shot up but chased them out to sea, crashed on landing Manston 12.34 13.6.17 (F/L FM Fox); Converted to 9901a Ships Pup; East Fortune by rail 14.9.17; Donibristle 22.9.17; HMS *Furious* by lighter 25.9.17; East Fortune 14.11.17; 'F' Sqdn East Fortune Naval Flying School by 4.12.17; Donibristle 11.1.18; Fleet Aeroplane Depot Turnhouse W/E 21.2.18 (Depot Flight from W/E 22.3.18); HMS *Furious* W/E 20.4.18; Fleet Aeroplane Depot Turnhouse W/E 11.7.18;

Seen here with No.2 (Naval) Wing at Thasos, 9941 had been shipped to the Aegean in mid 1917, serving at Stavros and then Marsh Aerodrome before joining 'G' Squadron of No.2 (Naval) Wing at Mudros early 3.18. The parent unit became No.62 (Naval) Wing on 1st April 1918, and 9941 was last recorded at the Repair Base at Mudros in June 1918.
(via Frank Cheesman)

Donibristle W/E 15.8.18; Fleet Aeroplane Depot Turnhouse W/E 19.9.18 to at least 30.1.19

9941   (80hp Le Rhône No.100294, propeller No.931) FF & accepted 4.4.17; Packed and shipped to Aegean; Stavros by 28-29.10.17; Marsh Aerodrome by 1.2.18; 'G' Sqdn 2 (Naval) Wing Mudros by 3.18; Became 'G' Sqdn 62 (Naval) Wing Mudros 1.4.18 to at least 5.18; Repair Base Mudros by 6.18

9942   (80hp Le Rhône No.100250, propeller No.950) (Fitted rocket armament) FF & accepted 10.4.17; Deld 11.4.17; At Port Victoria by 19.4.17; Packed and shipped to Aegean; Stavros 23.11.17; Imbros (Kephalo Bay) by 1.12.17; Marsh Aerodrome by 1-20.1.18; 'C' Sqdn 2 (Naval) Wing Mudros; 'G' Sqdn 2 (Naval) Wing Mudros by 3.18; Became 'G' Sqdn 62 (Naval) Wing Mudros 1.4.18 to at least 5.18; 'F' Sqdn 2 (Naval) Wing Amberkoj by 6.18; Repair Base Mudros by 10.18 to at least 11.18

9943   (80hp Le Rhône No.100262, propeller No.932) FF & accepted 11.4.17; Deld East Fortune for HMS *Manxman* 13.4.17; HMS *Manxman* 3.5.17; Fleet Aeroplane Depot Turnhouse 4.5.17; HMS *Manxman* 29.6.17; undercarriage, propeller and wings damaged 3.7.17; Fleet Aeroplane Depot Turnhouse 3.7.17; HMS *Manxman* 19.7.17; Rosyth 7.9.17; Converted to 9901a Ships Pup; Fleet Aeroplane Depot Turnhouse to HMS *Furious* by lighter for erection 12.9.17; East Fortune 14.11.17 (with 'F' Sqdn Naval Flying School there by 21.12.17); Donibristle 11.1.18; Fleet Aeroplane Depot Turnhouse W/E 21.2.18; Depot Flt Turnhouse W/E 22.3.18; Fleet Aeroplane Depot Turnhouse W/E 30.3.18 to at least 30.1.19

9944   (80hp Le Rhône No.100267, propeller No.914) (Fitted rocket armament) FF & accepted 12.4.17; Deld East Fortune for HMS *Manxman* 13.4.17; HMS *Manxman* 3.5.17; Turnhouse 7.5.17; HMS *Manxman* 13.5.17 to at least 15.7.17; Attd HMS *Yarmouth* 7.17 (for 10 days); HMS *Manxman* 19.7.17 (overhaul); Turnhouse by 7.8.17; HMS *Pegasus* by transport 1.9.17 to at least 2.9.17; HMS *Manxman* 9.17; HMS *Pegasus* 7.9.17; HMS *Repulse* W/E 14.12.17; Rosyth W/E 20.12.17 to at least 11.1.18; HMS *Pegasus* by 3-10.1.18; Rosyth to HMS *Pegasus* W/E 10.1.18; HMS *Tiger* W/E 17.1.18; Houton Bay overhaul 2.2.18 (for HMS *Southampton* by 9.3.18); Scapa W/E 18.5.18; Smoogroo W/E 11.7.18; HMS *Vindictive* 26.10.18 to at least 29.10.18; Smoogroo 10.18; HMS *Vindictive* 1.11.18 ('aeroplane practice' with or from *Vindictive* 14.11.18);

Smoogroo 14.11.18; HMS *Vindictive* W/E 21.11.18; Turnhouse 25.11.18; HMS *Vindictive* 11.18 to at least 30.1.19 (experimental work)

9945 (80hp Le Rhône No.100269, propeller No.886) FF 16.4.17; Accepted 23.4.17; Deld East Fortune for HMS *Manxman* 28.4.17; HMS *Manxman* 11.5.17; Rosyth 7.9.17; Donibristle by 5.10.17; HMS *Nairana* by 10.17; Donibristle by 11.17; HMS *Nairana* 8.11.17; HMS *Repulse* W/E 8.11.17; Donibristle W/E 15.11.17; Rosyth W/E 23.11.17; Donibristle to HMS *Nairana* W/E 27.11.17; Rosyth by 29.12.17; to Fleet Aeroplane Depot Turnhouse W/E 21.2.18; Deleted W/E 10.10.18 but selected for preservation; A minute dated 23.10.18 stated 9945 would be dispatched from the Turnhouse Depot to the Agricultural Hall, Islington "in about a fortnight's time"

9946 (80hp Le Rhône No.100258, propeller No.877) (Fitted rocket armament) FF & accepted 24.4.17; Deld RNASTE Cranwell 5.5.17 (for deck practice); Wrecked 27.7.17; Tested after repair 13.8.17; Converted to 9901a Ships Pup; East Fortune Naval Flying School by rail for carriers 22.9.17 to at least 30.3.18 (probably with 'F' Sqdn there); Reported as damaged but repairable 6.1.18; Became 208 TDS East Fortune 1.4.18; Became Grand Fleet School of Aerial Fighting & Gunnery East Fortune 19.7.18; Spun in from 2,000 ft 24.7.18 (2/Lt FA Cash killed)

9947 (80hp Le Rhône No.100272, propeller No.918) FF & accepted 24.4.17; Deld Aircraft Park Dover by rail for Walmer 4.5.17; Defence Flt Walmer 7.5.17; Anti-Gotha patrol, left 17.30, landed 18.20 25.5.17 (FSL WH Chisam); Anti-Gotha patrol, left 18.30, landed 19.20 25.5.17; Anti-Gotha patrol, left 18.25, landed 19.25 5.6.17; Anti-Gotha patrol, left 11.20, landed 13.14 13.6.17; Anti-Gotha patrol, left 09.30, landed 11.35 7.7.17 (all F/L S Kemball); Anti-Gotha patrol, left 08.40, landed 10.35 22.7.17 (FSL WM Lusby); Anti-Gotha patrol, left 18.20, landed 20.40 12.8.17 (F/L RA Little); Anti-Gotha patrol, left 10.35, landed Dunkirk 22.8.17 (F/L RA Little); 2 Enemy aircraft patrols 3.9.17 (FSL MR Kingsford); Enemy aircraft patrol 15.9.17 (F/L RA Little); Aircraft Park Dover 6.10.17; To Donibristle 10.17; Converted to Type 9901a Ships Pup; Rosyth W/E 13.12.17; HMS *Nairana* W/E 14.12.17; HMS *Renown* W/E 21.12.17;

Standard-built A628 was initially allocated to the Expeditionary Force, but before it could be delivered it was re-allocated for trials with the Experimental Station at Orfordness. However, on arrival from the Southern Aircraft Depot, Farnborough, on 6th November 1916 it went up on its nose. Note that the fin serial number has been painted as "A.628". (via Frank Cheeseman)

Donibristle W/E 21.12.17; HMS *Nairana* W/E 28.12.17; Crashed & completely wrecked by 11.1.18; Rosyth W/E 18.1.18; To Walmer 7.7.18 to at least 30.1.19

9948 (80hp Le Rhône No.100249, propeller No.895) (Converted to 9901a Ships Pup) (Fitted rocket armament?) FF & accepted 2.5.17; Deld Hendon for erection 16.5.17 (launching tests with catapult of Carey design); Ready for flight tests 30.5.17; Removing catapult gear 20.8.17; Badly damaged 1.9.17; East Fortune Naval Flying School by rail 1.10.17 (probably for 'F' Flt); U/s by 30.3.18, but still at East Fortune to at least 5.18 (for carriers)

9949 (80hp Le Rhône No.100255, propeller No.1214) (Converted to 9901a Ships Pup) FF & accepted 15.5.17; Fuselage deld Hendon 24.5.17 (catapult launching experiments with 9948); Fuselage sent to Otis Works 9.6.17; Wings to Central Supply Depot 13.6.17; Fuselage & wings retd Hendon 14.6.17 (wings at Grain); Removing catapult gear 13.8.17; East Fortune by rail 1.9.17 (arrived 8.9.17); Donibristle 15.9.17; HMS *Nairana* by 29.9.17; HMS *Furious* by 13.10.17 (deck landing experiments with skid undercarriage); Donibristle by 27.10.17; HMS *Nairana* 8.11.17; HMS *Nairana* to Donibristle W/E 8.11.17; Rosyth W/E 13.12.17; HMS *Nairana* W/E 14.12.17; Rosyth W/E 20.12.17; HMS *Nairana* to HMS *Renown* W/E 20.12.17; HMS *Nairana* to Donibristle W/E 28.12.17; Rosyth W/E 5.1.18; Turnhouse W/E 9.3.18; Rosyth 3.18; Depot Flight Turnhouse W/E 22.3.18; HMS *Furious* by 3.18; Damaged during deck-landing trials 25.3.18 [see photos on page 119]; 80hp Clerget by 30.3.18; Rosyth W/E 28.3.18; Turnhouse W/E 4.4.18; Donibristle W/E 31.10.18; HMS *Argus* W/E 21.11.18; Turnhouse W/E 12.12.18 to at least 30.1.19; HMS *Argus* by 11.19 (deck landing experiments with skid undercarriage)

9950 Converted to Beardmore W.B.III (SB3F) prototype. Deld Design Flt Eastchurch by rail for tests 2.2.17; Tested 7.2.17 (S/Cdr HR Busteed); Forced landed All Hallows, Isle of Grain 10.3.17 (F/L PA Johnston); Experimental Constructive Dept, Grain 12.3.17 (repair); Reported 'awaiting water test' 16.4.17 (possibly used in flotation tests of air-bag installation late 4.17); Dismantling commenced 17.4.17, apparently completed by 27.5.17; Deleted 19.6.17

50 SOPWITH PUP ordered 22.5.16 under Contract number 87/A/461 from Standard Motor Co Ltd, Coventry and numbered A626 to A675. (80hp Le Rhône 9C unless stated otherwise)

A626 Tested Radford Aerodrome, Coventry 27.9.16; Allotted to Test Sqdn CFS Upavon 11.10.16, test flown there 12-21.10.16; England to ARS 2 AD and on to 70 Sqdn 4.11.16; ARS 2 AD to 8 (N) Sqdn 10.11.16; 2-str shot down 26.12.16 (FSL JC Croft); Left on OP 14.30, last seen in combat with 7 enemy aircraft nr Bapaume around 15.15, shot down north of Rheims 4.1.17 (FSL JC Croft PoW) [Aircraft captured, believed shot down Neuchatel, north of Rheims, by Ltn F Mallinckrodt, Jasta 10]; Recommended for deletion 11.1.17

A627 At Coventry, allotted to Expeditionary Force 13.9.16; Deld 54 Sqdn Castle Bromwich 22.10.16, its first Pup; Not to France with Sqdn 12.16; 81 Sqdn Scampton by 9-29.9.17; Mis-painted at some stage as "627^A"

A628 At Standard works 28.10.16; Allotted to Expeditionary Force 31.10.16; At SAD Farnborough, allotted to Expeditionary Force; Reallotted to Experimental Station Orfordness for trials, went on nose on arrival 6.11.16

A629 At Standard works, allotted to Expeditionary Force

28.10.16; Crashed and repaired at SAD Farnborough; Allotted 54 Sqdn Castle Bromwich 8.11.16

A630 (Engine No.35042/WD2543) At Standard works 28.10.16; Allotted to Expeditionary Force 2.11.16; At SAD Farnborough allotted 54 Sqdn 8.11.16; Deld 54 Sqdn Castle Bromwich by 11.16; To France with Sqdn via ARS 1 AD 24.12.16; Left 08.40, F.E.2 escort, last seen going down on its back after combat 3-4m south-west of St.Quentin 25.3.17 (2/Lt NA Phillips killed) [claimed nr Gissecourt by Ltn F Mallinckrodt, Jasta 20]; Wreckage traced, to ARS 2 AD, SOC 12.4.17 NWR

A631 At Standard works allotted to Expeditionary Force 3.11.16; Allotted to 54 Sqdn 8.11.16; Allocation cancelled and sent to SAD Farnborough; Tested to destruction at Royal Aircraft Factory Farnborough

A632 At Standard works, allotted to Expeditionary Force 3.11.16; Again allotted to Expeditionary Force 6.11.16; Reallotted to 54 Sqdn 8.11.16; At 30.12.16, 54 Sqdn aircraft in England awaiting orders to proceed overseas; At London Colney 10.1.17, reallotted from 54 Sqdn to Expeditionary Force for "wastage"; At SAD Farnborough 26.1.17, allotment to Expeditionary Force cancelled now on charge to DAE.2a Repair section; Allotted to 66 Sqdn 23.2.17 but not to France with Sqdn 3.17; 65 Sqdn Wye by 13.8.17

A633 (Le Rhône 35068/WD2369) Deld SAD Farnborough 9.11.16; 54 Sqdn Castle Bromwich 26.11.16; To France with Sqdn via ARS 1 AD 24.12.16; 54 Sqdn by 14.1.17; Left 10.33 on reconnaissance escort duty, FTR, attacked by 2 enemy aircraft over St Quentin, last seen going down in spin 4.3.17 (Capt A Lees wounded PoW) [claimed near St.Quentin by Ltn G Schlenker, Jasta 3]

A634 Allotted to 54 Sqdn Castle Bromwich 10.11.16, and with Sqdn by 6.1.17; To France with Sqdn via ARS 1 AD 26.12.16; Undercarriage collapsed when taxying after landing after escorting F.E.2s 24.3.17 (Lt O Stewart); ARS 2 AD 25.3.17; SOC 31.5.17 NWR

A635 Allotted to 54 Sqdn Castle Bromwich 15.11.16 and arrived there by 30.11.16; England to ARS 1 AD 12.12.16; Reallotted from 54 Sqdn to Expeditionary Force for 54 Sqdn "wastage" 23.12.16; ARS 1 AD to 54 Sqdn 12.1.17; Albatros D.II out of control north of Peronne 10.30 and 2-str forced to land Maricourt (captured) 10.50 25.1.17 (Capt A Lees); ARS 2 AD 12.5.17; 46 Sqdn 5.7.17; ARS 1 AD 13.7.17; 66 Sqdn (coded 'D') 30.9.17; Offensive patrol, last seen with formation at 12,000ft over Ypres, shot down Rolliemolenhoek by Ltn T Quandt, Jasta 36 12.15, captured intact 12.10.17 (2/Lt M Newcomb PoW)

A636 Allotted to 54 Sqdn Castle Bromwich 15.11.16 and with Sqdn by 6.1.17; To France with Sqdn 24.12.16; Kite balloon destroyed east of Vendeville, shared with A668, A672 & A673 & A6166 5.4.17 (Lt MDG Scott); Damaged 14.4.17 (Lt MDG Scott); ARS 2 AD 15.4.17; SOC 27.17 NWR

A637 Allotted 54 Sqdn Castle Bromwich 15.11.16 and with Sqdn by 24.11.16; To France with Sqdn via ARS 1 AD 24.12.16; 2-str out of control Peronne 08.00 2.4.17 (Lt OM Sutton); Casualty Report 25.4.17 says had crashed twice, been rebuilt, now slow and soggy and unfit for further service in the field; ARS 2 AD 27.4.17; ARS 1 AD 10.7.17; 54 Sqdn 13.7.17; Left on OP 19.30, on return crashed on landing, pilot unable to see the ground 23.7.17 (2/Lt DF Lawson); ARS 1 AD 25.7.17; SOC 27.7.17

A638 (100hp Gnome Monosoupape No.20371) Allotted 54 Sqdn Castle Bromwich 24.11.16, but possibly reallotted; 'B' Flt 50 HD Sqdn Throwley, Anti-Gotha patrol, landed 08.43 4.7.17 (Lt RW le Gallais); 112 HD Sqdn Throwley

30.7.17; Anti-Gotha patrol, left 17.24, landed 19.20 12.8.17; Anti-Gotha patrol, left 10.20, landed 11.52 22.8.17 (both Lt RW le Gallais); Port wing broke off in spin at 900ft 15.9.17 (Lt RW le Gallais killed)

A639 Allotted 54 Sqdn Castle Bromwich 24.11.16; To France with Sqdn via ARS 1 AD 24.12.16; Albatros C last seen in nose dive Falvy-Croix 14.20-14.35 11.2.17 (Capt WV Strugnell); Taking off from forced landing, propeller struck a stake and burst as soon as the aircraft was in the air, forced landed 2.4.17 (Capt WV Strugnell OK); SOC 54 Sqdn and the RFC in the field 2.4.17

A640 Ternhill to 54 Sqdn Castle Bromwich, but foggy, engine failure, forced landed, crashed turning to avoid hill, damaged undercarriage, propeller and one wing 27.11.16 (2/Lt RM Charley unhurt); To France with Sqdn via ARS 1 AD 24.12.16; Engine failed on return from Offensive patrol, forced landed and crashed in ploughed field 30.1.17 (2/Lt E Hamilton); ARS 2 AD 10.2.17; 54 Sqdn 1.5.17; Albatros C crashed nr Walincourt, shared with A6165, A6168, A6183, A7306, A7330 18.40 11.5.17 (2/Lt MB Cole); Albatros D out of control east of St Emile, shared with A6172, A6183, A7330, B1730 & B2151 06.45 3.6.17 (2/Lt JW Sheridan); Turned on nose on landing 16.6.17 (2/Lt JW Sheridan); ARS 2 AD 17.6.17; SOC 5.7.17

A641 Allotted 54 Sqdn Castle Bromwich 29.11.16; With 54 Sqdn by 3.12.16; At 30.12.16 a 54 Sqdn aircraft in England awaiting orders to proceed overseas; Not with 54 Sqdn by 13.1.17

A642 (Le Rhône 2286/WD5825) Allotted 54 Sqdn Castle Bromwich 29.11.16; To France with Sqdn via ARS 1 AD 24.12.16; 2-str forced to land Villers-au-Flos 13.50 11.2.17 (2/Lt JV Fairbairn): Left 11.15 on F.E. escort duty, FTR, last seen over Cambrai 14.2.17 (2/Lt JV Fairbairn PoW wounded, to Holland 15.4.18) [forced to land nr Cambrai by Ltn G Schlenker, Jasta 3 12.45; Eterpigny, south of Peronne per Germans]

A643 Allotted 54 Sqdn Castle Bromwich 3.12.16; Stalled on turn, crashed 4.12.16 (2/Lt HE Startin injured)

A644 Allotted 54 Sqdn Castle Bromwich 3.12.16; To France with Sqdn via ARS 1 AD 24.12.16; Returning from the Aerial School of Gunnery at Cormont, the engine failed at a height of 600ft, forced landed in small field, lost undercarriage on wire fence 15.1.17 (2/Lt JV Fairbairn); ARS 2 AD 6.2.17; SOC 13.2.17

A645 (Le Rhône 35053/WD2554) Allotted 54 Sqdn Castle Bromwich 4.12.16; With Sqdn by 10.12.16; To France with Sqdn via ARS 1 AD 24.12.16; Crashed on telephone wires Abbeville 15.1.17 (2/Lt RM Charley); Repaired by 22.1.17; Left 11.40 on F.E. escort duty, FTR, last seen in combat Grevillers-Rocquigny 15.2.17 (2/Lt E Hamilton killed) [shot down in combat nr Grevillers [Sapignies-Douchy] by Ltn Frh E von Stenglin, Jasta 1]

A646 Allotted 54 Sqdn 9.12.16; 1 AAP Coventry to 54 Sqdn Castle Bromwich 9.12.16; At 30.12.16, 54 Sqdn aircraft in England awaiting orders proceed overseas; ARS 1 AD 2.1.17 accommodated for 54 Sqdn; At Sqdn 5.1.17; Just after landing from F.E.2 escort, turned over by gust of wind 24.3.17 (2/Lt RM Foster); ARS 2 AD 25.3.17; SOC 8.4.17 NWR

A647 Allotted 54 Sqdn Castle Bromwich 10.12.16; To France with Sqdn via ARS 1 AD 24.12.16; Escorting F.E.2s to Bapaume, shot up in combat, forced landed La Houssoye 15.2.17 (2/Lt NA Phillips unhurt); SOC 54 Sqdn and RFC in the field 15.2.17

A648 Allotted to 54 Sqdn Castle Bromwich 15.12.16 and delivered same day (Coded '13' and named "YES"); To France with Sqdn 26.12.16; Casualty Report 24.4.17

says unfit for further service; ARS 2 AD 27.4.17; 46 Sqdn ('F') 5.7.17; Flown back to England (Sutton's Farm) for HD detachment with Sqdn 10.7.17 and back to France 30.8.17 but on landing collided with B1766 (Lt AF Bird); ARS 1 AD 2.9.17; SOC 26.9.17

A649   Allotted 54 Sqdn Castle Bromwich 15.12.16; To France with Sqdn via ARS 1 AD 24.12.16; 2-str out of control 3m east of Roye, shared with A669 & 2/Lt JW Sheridan 11.35 17.3.17 (Lt GA Hyde); Returning from escort duty attacked by Albatros D.III which was sent out of control Walincourt 07.30 30.4.17 (Lt GA Hyde MC); ARS 2 AD 6.5.17; ARS 1 AD 11.7.17; 54 Sqdn 28.7.17; Albatros out of control, shared with B1792 12.8.17 (2/Lt FW Gibbes); Left 05.00 on Offensive patrol, damaged in combat with 3 enemy aircraft 19.8.17 (2/Lt FW Gibbes); ARS 1 AD 21.8.17; SOC 22.8.17; Flown back to England?; 40 TS Croydon by 8.17

A650   (Engine No.WD2518) Allotted 54 Sqdn Castle Bromwich 15.12.16; At 30.12.16 54 Sqdn aircraft in England awaiting orders to proceed overseas; Not listed as a 54 Sqdn aircraft by 13.1.17; Allotted to 66 Sqdn Filton 23.2.17 but not to France with Sqdn 3.18; 40 RS Port Meadow by 26.4.17; 40 TS to Croydon 1.6.17 (HD); Anti-Gotha patrol, left 17.19, landed 19.15 12.8.17 (2/Lt JF Bremner); Anti-Gotha patrol, left 11.00, landed 11.45 22.8.17 (Lt NO Vinter); Broke up in air, crashed Wallington 18.10.17 (2/Lt TW George killed)

A651   Allotted 54 Sqdn Castle Bromwich 18.12.16 but re-allotted; 43 RS Ternhill by 24.1.17; 'B' Flt 37 HD Sqdn Stow Maries, Anti-Gotha patrol, left 07.29, landed 09.20 4.7.17 (Capt CA Ridley); 34TS Ternhill

A652   Allotted 54 Sqdn Castle Bromwich 18.12.16; To France with Sqdn via ARS 1 AD 24.12.16; 2-str in spinning dive, RH top plane came off Courcelles 14.10 27.1.17; 2-str in vertical dive Le Transloy 10.45 13.2.17 (both 2/Lt FN Hudson); On landing turned over by strong wind 24.3.17 (Lt GA Hyde MC); ARS 2 AD 26.3.17; SOC 8.4.17 NWR

A653   (100hp Gnome Monosoupape B-2; Engine No.30754/WD11827 when crashed) Allotted 43 RS Ternhill 22.12.16 but re-allotted; 54 Sqdn by 12.16

(Vickers gun on upper port longeron); At London Colney 10.1.17 reallotted from 54 Sqdn to Expeditionary Force for "wastage"; At SAD 27.2.17, allotment to Expeditionary Force cancelled, now on charge to DAE.2a Repair Section (fitted with 100hp Gnome Monosoupape B-2 (No.30754/WD11827), and Vickers gun offset to port); CFS Upavon by 4.17; Testing Squadron, Martlesham Heath from 15.4.17 to at least 5.17 (performance trials); 'B' Flt 37 HD Sqdn Stow Maries, anti-Gotha patrol, left 09.30, attacked Gothas east of Girdler lightship, own aircraft shot up, landed safely 11.44 7.7.17 (Capt CA Ridley OK); 61 HD Sqdn Rochford (coded 'B-8') 2.8.17; Anti-Gotha patrol, left 17.25, landed 18.59 12.8.17; Anti-Gotha patrol, left 10.24, landed 11.29 22.8.17 (both 2/Lt G Howe); On flight to test gun collided with an Avro 504 B3112 at low altitude, wrecked 6.10.17 (Lt JD Belgrave slight concussion)

A654   (Engine No.519/WD2930) Allotted 54 Sqdn Castle Bromwich 20.12.16 (Sqdn moved 22.12.16); Joined 54 Sqdn at London Colney 26.12.16; At London Colney re-allotted from 54 Sqdn to Expeditionary Force for "wastage" 10.1.17; England to ARS 1 AD 15.1.17; 54 Sqdn 23.1.17; Left 11.40 escorting F.E.2s, left formation in combat, shot down by AA Ligny-Tilloy, claimed by 1 Army Flak 15.2.17 (Capt CLM Scott killed)

A655   Allotted 43 RS Ternhill 12.16; With 43 RS Ternhill by 28.1.17

A656   Allotted 43 RS Ternhill 24.12.16; With 43 RS Ternhill by 23.1.17

A657   Allotted 43 RS Ternhill 2.1.17; 102 Sqdn to 30.10.17

A658   (80hp Clerget No.1039/WD2279) Flown to CFS Upavon by 2/Lt M Kay 23.1.17 (used by 'B' Sqdn); Crashed cause unknown but a wing was presumed to have collapsed in mid-air 5.9.17 (2/Lt JG O'Giollagain killed)

A659   (80hp Clerget No.557/WD5987) CFS Upavon by 26.2.17 (used by 'C' Sqdn, later 'B' Sqdn); On second solo flight in a Pup glided down upside down and hit the ground in that position, no effort was made to right the machine 4.9.17 (2/Lt CS Dickinson injured)

A660   (80hp Clerget) Flown to CFS Upavon by 2/Lt M Kay

Another Standard-built Pup, A650, with Whitehead-built A6187 in the background, both of No.40 Training Squadron, which moved from Port Meadown to Croydon on 1st June 1917. Although from the same batch as A628, the fin serial number has been painted as "A'650". It survived until 18th October 1917 when it broke up in the air and crashed at Wallington, 2/Lt T.W.George being killed.   *(J.M.Bruce/G.S.Leslie collection)*

24.1.17 (with 'B' Sqdn by 20.6.17); Mid-air collision 11.3.18 (2/Lt HD Coldwell killed)

A661   At 1 AAP Coventry 11.1.17, allotted to Expeditionary Force; England to ARS 1 AD 9.2.17; 54 Sqdn 13.2.17; Enemy aircraft damaged 2.4.17 (Capt R Oxspring); Left 06.30, OP for XV Corps, shot up in combat 14.4.17 (Lt RN Smith wounded); SOC 54 Sqdn and the RFC in the field 14.4.17

A662   At 1 AAP Coventry 11.1.17, allotted to Expeditionary Force; Allotment cancelled; At SAD 20.1.17, now on charge to DAE.2a Repair Section (presume crashed); 66 Sqdn Filton by 22.2.17; Not to France with Sqdn 17.3.17; 63 TS Joyce Green by 20-25.8.17; 74 Sqdn London Colney by 31.8.17; 3 TS Shoreham to 18th Wing ARS Hounslow 23.12.17; SOC 4.1.18

A663   At 1 AAP Coventry 11.1.17, allotted to Expeditionary Force for "F" Replacement Sqdn but reallotted to 66 Sqdn Filton 13.1.17; Joined 66 Sqdn 5.2.17; To France with Sqdn 17.3.17; Albatros C in vertical dive 08.00 23.4.17; Albatros C in vertical dive Vitry 16.30 23.4.17 (both Capt JO Andrews); Engine failure, forced landed, crashed on aerodrome 5.5.17 (2/Lt RM Marsh injured); ARS 2 AD by 1.6.17; SOC 20.6.17

A664   (Engine No.1209/WD7980) At 1 AAP Coventry 10.1.17, allotted to Expeditionary Force for "F" Replacement Sqdn but reallotted to 66 Sqdn Filton 13.1.17; Arr 66 Sqdn 3.2.17; Flying from Coventry to Farnborough, FL nr Oxford 26.2.17 (2/Lt Angus Bell-Irving); Not to France with Sqdn 17.3.17; At 21st Wing ARS Rendcomb 27.3.17 reallotted from 66 Sqdn to Expeditionary Force as "wastage"; ARS 1 AD to ARS 2 AD 2.5.17; 66 Sqdn by 10.5.17; Shot down east of lines on OP to Boiry-Lens 12.5.17 (Lt JR Robertson killed) [Claimed by Obltn A Rt von Tutschek, Jasta 12, Baralle-Marquion 10.50]

A665   At 1 AAP Coventry 11.1.17, allotted to Expeditionary Force for "F" Replacement Sqdn but reallotted, to 66 Sqdn Filton 31.1.17; Not to France with Sqdn 17.3.17; At (S)ARD Farnborough 27.3.17, reallotted from 66 Sqdn to Expeditionary Force as "wastage"; England to ARS 1 AD 28.3.17; 'A' Flt 46 Sqdn 20.4.17; Patrol, shot down in combat, FL nr Kemmel 17.45 23.5.17 (2/Lt JP Stephen DoW) [Ltn K Schafer, Jasta 28 claimed Pup at Wytschaete-Bogen 18.45 German time - the first 46 Sqdn Pup casualty]

A666   Deld 'B' Sqdn CFS Upavon by 2/Lt M Kay 29.1.17 to at least 31.5.17

A667   66 Sqdn Filton from 23.2.17 but not to France with Sqdn 17.3.17

A668   At 1 AAP Coventry 12.1.17, allotted to Expeditionary Force; ARS 2 AD to 54 Sqdn 15.2.17; Kite balloon destroyed east of Vendeville, shared with A636, A672 & A673 & A6166 5.4.17 (Capt RGH Pixley); In a fight lasting about 15 minutes which started at 9,000ft and went down to 50 ft 2-str crashed into a house at either Lesdain or Seranvillers 15.00-15.15, returning at ground level was attacked by 3 enemy aircraft and came under heavy ground fire, shortly after crossing the lines the bottom port wing buckled up, the aircraft turned upside down and fell to the ground from about 50ft, crashed into shell hole, 10.5.17 (Capt RGH Pixley slightly injured); SOC 54 Sqdn and the RFC in the field 11.5.17

A669   At 1 AAP Coventry 12.1.17, allotted to Expeditionary Force; ARS 2 AD to 54 Sqdn 15.2.17; 2-str out of control smoking east of Roye 11.35 17.3.17 (2/Lt NA Phillips) [shared with by Lt GA Hyde/A649, 2/Lt JW Sheridan, and Capt RGH Pixley, the combat report does not give serials]; Lost way, landed to enquire whereabouts, the

pilot got some civilians to hold the machine whilst he started the propeller but the moment the engine fired they ran away with the result that the machine stood on its nose then fell over on its back 24.4.17 (2/Lt JW Sheridan); ARS 2 AD 28.4.17; SOC 1.5.17 NWR

A670   At 1 AAP Coventry 12.1.17, allotted to Expeditionary Force; ARS 2 AD to 66 Sqdn 24.3.17; Offensive patrol, damaged in forced landing 24.4.17 (2/Lt RM Marsh); ARS 2 AD; SOC 15.9.17

A671   At 1 AAP Coventry 10.1.17 allotted to Expeditionary Force; ARS 2 AD to 54 Sqdn 15.2.17; Left 10.38 4.3.17 escorting F.E.s engine cut out at 12,000ft over St Quentin, managed to glide back and crashed our side of the lines (Lt MDG Scott OK); SOC 54 Sqdn and RFC in the field 5.3.17

A672   At 1 AAP Coventry 10.1.17, allotted to Expeditionary Force; ARS 2 AD to 54 Sqdn 26.2.17; Kite balloon destroyed east of Vendeville, shared with A636, A668, A673 & A6166 5.4.17; Scout in spin out of control and another in steep dive, fate unknown Premont 07.10 26.4.17 (both 2/Lt RM Charley); ARS 2 AD 15.6.17 (time expired); ARS 1 AD 3.9.17; 66 Sqdn 5.9.17; Choked engine on take off, crashed 11.9.17 (2/Lt DH Houston); ARS 1 AD 12.9.17; SOC 16.9.17

A673   (Engine No.100240/WD7915) At 1 AAP Coventry 10.1.17, allotted to Expeditionary Force to be shipped to 2 AD; ARS 2 AD to 54 Sqdn 24.2.17 but had to return due to fog, arrived 25.2.17; 2-str wing came off and crashed Bapaume 12.30 11.3.17; Kite balloon destroyed east of Vendeville, shared with A636, A668, A672 & A6166 5.4.17 (both Capt R Oxspring MC); Scout out of control Premont 07.10 26.4.17; 2-str out of control Belicourt 06.25 4.6.17 (both Lt FJ Morse); Casualty Report 12.6.17 says unfit for further service in the field; ARS 2 AD 16.6.17; 46 Sqdn (coded '5') 9.9.17; Left 12.15 on Offensive Patrol, last seen in combat with 7 enemy aircraft 16.9.17 (2/Lt LM Shadwell PoW) [shot down Ecourt St.Quentin by Vzfw R Jörke, Jasta 12 14.00 BUT Ltn V Schobinger, Jasta 12 claimed Pup south-west of Lecluse 14.20]

A674   At 1 AAP Coventry 10.1.17, allotted to Expeditionary Force to be shipped to 2 AD but this cancelled 12.1.17; To 66 Sqdn Filton 5.2.17; Not to France with Sqdn 17.3.17; 63 TS Joyce Green by 8.17

A675   At 1 AAP Coventry 10.1.17, allotted to Expeditionary Force to be shipped to 2 AD but this cancelled 12.1.17; 66 Sqdn Filton 5.2.17; To France with Sqdn 17.3.17; Crashed on landing 22.3.17 (Lt TH Wickett), flying again 25.3.17; Forced landed Pozières, landed in shell hole 8.4.17 (Lt TH Wickett); SOC 8.4.17 Wrecked

100 SOPWITH PUP ordered 28.9.16 under Contract number 87/A/885 from Wells Aviation Co Ltd, London and numbered A5138 to A5237. Order cancelled 2.10.16 and numbers reallotted

100 SOPWITH PUP ordered 18.10.16 under Contract number 87/A/1101 from Whitehead Aircraft Ltd, Richmond, Surrey and numbered A6150 to A6249. Fitted with "adjustable empennage". (Ordered with 80hp Le Rhône 9C but some fitted with alternative engines)

A6150   At Farnborough by 27.1.17 to at least 2.17 for tests; CFS Upavon by 2.17; Propeller hit tail of 1½ Strutter (Lt AP Long) in flight 23.3.18 (2/Lt P Sellars killed)

A6151   At Farnborough by 28.1.17; 66 Sqdn Filton 3.2.17; Undercarriage damaged landing 7.2.17 (2/Lt RM Marsh); ARS 21st Wing Rendcomb 10.2.17; 66 Sqdn 23.2.17; Not to France with Sqdn 17.3.17; At Croydon 27.3.17, reallotted from 66 Sqdn to Expeditionary Force; At (S)ARD Farnborough 14.4.17, allotment to Expeditionary Force cancelled now on charge to DAE.2a Repair Section

A6152   At Farnborough by 3.2.17; to 66 Sqdn Filton 8.2.17; To France with Sqdn via ARS 1 AD 17.3.17; Escort to Lens-Brebières-Lecluse, badly shot up in combat 24.4.17 (2/Lt CC Morley OK); ARS 2 AD, SOC 31.5.17 NWR

A6153   At Farnborough by 8.2.17; to 66 Sqdn Filton 13.2.17; Not to France with Sqdn 17.3.17; 'B' Flt 50 HD Sqdn Throwley, Anti-Gotha patrol, left 08.05, retd with engine trouble 08.20 4.7.17 (2/Lt NF Perris); 112 HD Sqdn Throwley 30.7.17; Anti-Gotha patrol, left 17.25, retd 18.20, left again 18.23, landed 19.08 12.8.17; Anti-Gotha patrol, left 10.20, landed 11.53 22.8.17 (both Capt C Sutton)

A6154   At Farnborough by 14.2.17; With AID Farnborough 16.2.17, allotted to Expeditionary Force; To France by air 3.17; ARS 1 AD to ARS 2 AD 4.3.17; 66 Sqdn 25.3.17; Offensive patrol, forced landed in soft ground, damaged 8.5.17; At ARS 2 AD 1.6.17; SOC 20.6.17

A6155   At Farnborough by 11.2.17; to 66 Sqdn Filton 13.2.17; To France with Sqdn via ARS 1 AD 17.3.17; Halberstadt out of control 8.4.17 (Lt AJ Lucas); Offensive patrol, bad landing, hit hangar 3.5.17 (Lt AJ Lucas died of injuries 16.5.17); ARS 2 AD, SOC 31.5.17 NWR

A6156   At AID Farnborough 16.2.17, allotted to Expeditionary Force; England to ARS 1 AD 27.2.17; ARS 2 AD 4.3.17; 54 Sqdn 25.3.17; Albatros D.III crashed St.Quentin 08.00 6.4.17 (Lt O Stewart); Scout out of control Premont 07.10 26.4.17 (Lt SG Rome MC); Albatros D.III apparently out of control Premont 08.00 24.5.17; 3 Albatros D.III crashed south-west of Cambrai, shared with A6165, A6167, A6183 & A6192 12.00 6.6.17 (all Lt O Stewart) [the Combat Report says that combat was with a large formation of enemy aircraft, each of the 5 pilots claimed a victory but in the close range fighting it was impossible to follow an enemy aircraft down, 2 were seen to crash by other pilots and 1 by our artillery]; Casualty Report 12.6.17 says unfit for further service in the field; ARS 1 AD 19.6.17; 54 Sqdn 23.8.17; Albatros D Mannekensvaere 12.40 24.9.17 (Capt FJ Morse); Report 9.11.17 says unfit for further service in the field; Rep Pk 1 ASD 12.11.17; 1 AI to Rep Pk 1 ASD 11.1.18

A6157   (Engine No.1655/WD612) At AID Farnborough 1.5.17, allotted to Expeditionary Force; ARS 1 AD to 'B' Flt 46 Sqdn (coded '6') 6.6.17; Left 09.10 on OP Polygon Wood, in combat with 10 enemy aircraft, shot down south of Roulers by Ofstr M Müller, Jasta 28 11.45 7.6.17 (Lt AP Mitchell PoW wounded)

A6158   At Farnborough by 17.2.17; At AID Farnborough 19.2.17, allotted to Expeditionary Force; England to ARS 1 AD 4.3.17; 3 (N) Sqdn 11.3.17; Halberstadt D.II out of control Bourlon Wood 10.20 6.4.17 (FSL JST Fall); Albatros out of control, Albatros D.II crashed & Halberstadt crashed Cambrai 08.45, then badly shot up, forced landed Savy 11.4.17 (FSL JST Fall OK); 2 AD Candas by 19.4.17; 3 (N) Sqdn (marked 'WB') 3.5.17; Offensive patrol, left 10.20, last seen Ecourt St.Quentin, shot down by Obltn H Lorenz, Jasta 33 12.25 14.5.17 (FSL WR Walker PoW) [combat south of Estrées per Germans]

A6159   At Farnborough by 26.2.17; To 66 Sqdn Filton 3.17; To France with Sqdn via ARS 1 AD 17.3.17; landed cross wind and turned over 14.4.17 (2/Lt GRE Hayter); ARS 2 AD by 1.6.17; 46 Sqdn 7.10.17; 2 ASD 16.11.17 (exchanged for a Camel); 2 AI to Rec Pk and on to England 24.1.18; 6 TS AFC Ternhill; 'B' Flt 5 TS AFC Shawbury

A6160   At AID Farnborough 24.2.17, reallotted from 66 Sqdn to

Expeditionary Force; England to ARS 1 AD 4.3.17; 3 (N) Sqdn 11.3.17; Halberstadt DIII out of control Bourlon Wood 10.20 6.4.17 (FSL AW Carter); Shot down in combat nr Elincourt by Ltn K Schneider, Jasta 5 10.30 29.4.17 (FSL SL Bennett killed)

A6161   At AID Farnborough by 15.3.17 allotted Expeditionary Force; At 66 Sqdn Filton 3.2.17; To France with Sqdn 17.3.17; Forced landed Abbeville 8.4.17, dismantled (2/Lt AG Robertson); ARS 2 AD by 1.6.17; SOC 4.8.17

A6162   At AID Farnborough by 15.3.17 allotted Expeditionary Force; England to ARS 1 AD 24.3.17; 66 Sqdn 30.3.17; Lost bearings and landed at Havre 7.4.17, left on 8.4.17 but forced landed Houchin with engine failure, completely wrecked (2/Lt RM Marsh OK); ARS 2 AD, SOC 27.4.17 NWR

A6163   At Farnborough by 2.3.17; 66 Sqdn Filton; At ARS 1 AD 24.3.17 "accommodated for 66 Sqdn" To Sqdn 25.3.17; Practice flight, wings folded up at 50ft, crashed 27.3.17 (Lt S Stretton killed); SOC 27.3.17 Wrecked

A6164   At Farnborough 21.3.17, allotted to Expeditionary Force; To France by air 4.17; ARS 1 AD to 46 Sqdn 2.5.17; Practice flight, engine cut landing, crashed on nose, damaged 13.5.17; ARS 1 AD 15.5.17; SOC 18.5.17 NWR

A6165   At makers Richmond 22.2.17, allotted to Expeditionary Force, to be shipped to 2 AD ARS; 2 AD to 54 Sqdn 27.3.17; Shot up in combat with enemy aircraft south of Lagnicourt 6.4.17 (2/Lt RM Foster); ARS 2 AD 6.4.17; 54 Sqdn 27.4.17; Albatros C crashed nr Walincourt, shared with A640, A6168, A6183, A7306 & A7330 18.40 11.5.17 (Mjr CE Sutcliffe); 3 Albatros D crashed south-west of Cambrai, shared with A6156, A6167, A6183 & A6192 12.00 6.6.17 (2/Lt AL Macfarlane) [the Combat Report says combat was with a large formation of enemy aircraft, each of the five pilots claimed a victory but in the close fighting it was impossible to follow enemy aircraft down, 2 were seen to crash by other pilots and 1 by our artillery]; ARS 1 AD and on to ARS 2 AD 27.6.17 (time expired); 2 AD (later 2 ASD) Scout School, Candas 29.6.17; 2 AI 5.2.18; Rec Pk 18.2.18; Flown back to England 27.2.18

A6166   At makers Richmond 22.2.17, allotted to Expeditionary Force, to be shipped to 2 AD; ARS 2 AD to 54 Sqdn 27.3.17; Kite balloon destroyed east of Vendeville, shared with A636, A668, A672 & A673 5.4.17; 2-str out of control Le Catelet 07.30 6.4.17 (both Capt FN Hudson MC); Casualty Report 12.6.17 says unfit for further service in the field; ARS 2 AD 15.6.17; ARS 1 AD 3.9.17; 66 Sqdn 5.9.17; ARS 1 AD 15.10.17 exchanged for Camel; At Rep Pk 1 ASD 7.11.17; 8 AAP Lympne 9.1.18; AES Orfordness 9.1.18; TOC 'C' Flight 4 TDS Hooton Park 22.1.18; 90 Sqdn North Shotwick 5.2.18

A6167   At makers Richmond 22.2.17, allotted to Expeditionary Force, to be shipped to 2 AD; ARS 2 AD to 54 Sqdn 7.4.17; 3 Albatros Ds crashed south-west of Cambrai, shared with A6156, A6165, A6183 & A6192 12.00 6.6.17 (2/Lt RM Foster) [the Combat Report says in combat with a large formation of enemy aircraft, each of the five pilots claimed a victory but in the close range fighting it was impossible to follow an enemy aircraft down, 2 enemy aircraft were seen to crash by other pilots and 1 by our artillery]; Casualty Report dated 20.7.17 complains about performance and recommends return to AD as unfit for further service; ARS 1 AD 21.7.17; 2 AD Scout School, Candas 23.7.17; Crashed on landing 19.9.17 (2/Lt FM Nash), engine installed in Bristol Scout A1759; Still at 2 AD Scout School 31.10.17

A6168   At makers Richmond 22.2.17, allotted to Expeditionary

Force, to be shipped to 2 AD; ARS 2 AD to 54 Sqdn 3.4.17; 2-str out of control Gonnelieu 08.10 14.4.17; White 2-str crashed Seranvillers 15.30 9.5.17 (both 2/Lt MB Cole); Albatros C crashed nr Walincourt shared with A640, A6165, A6183, A7306 & A7330 18.40, then Albatros D crashed in a pond nr Beaurevoir 19.10 11.5.17 (Capt WV Strugnell); 2-str crashed between Sailly and Cambrai 11.00 12.5.17 (2/Lt MB Cole); Escort F.E.s, left 13.30, in combat with 6 enemy aircraft, shot down south-west of Gouzeaucourt/west of Gonnelieu by Ltn Werner Voss, Jasta 5 [14.45 - German time] 26.5.17 (2/Lt MB Cole wounded); SOC 27.5.17 wrecked

A6169   At makers Richmond 6.3.17, allotted to Expeditionary Force; Shipped to France 3.17; ARS 2 AD to 66 Sqdn 16.4.17; Travelling flight, crashed Bellevue 19.5.17 (Capt LA Smith); ARS 2 AD, SOC 31.5.17 NWR

A6170   At makers Richmond 6.3.17, allotted to Expeditionary Force; Shipped to France 3.17; ARS 2 AD to 66 Sqdn 11.4.17; Forced landed Noyon 16.4.17 (2/Lt AG Robertson injured); ARS 2 AD, SOC 20.4.17 NWR

A6171   At makers Richmond 6.3.17, allotted to Expeditionary Force; Shipped to France 3.17; On delivery from ARS 2 AD to 54 Sqdn, engine cut out just as aircraft was coming into the aerodrome, forced landed on road and turned over 28.4.17 (2/Lt JW Sheridan OK); ARS 2 AD 1.5.17; SOC 4.8.17

A6172   (Engine No.35051/WD2552) At makers Richmond 6.3.17, allotted to Expeditionary Force; Shipped to France 3.17; ARS 2 AD to 54 Sqdn 15.4.17; Turned over on landing due to sudden gust of wind 26.4.17 (Lt MDG Scott); ARS 2 AD 28.4.17; 54 Sqdn 2.6.17; Albatros D out of control east of St Emile, shared with A640, A6183, A7330, B1730 & B2151 06.45 3.6.17 (Lt EJY Grevelink); Damaged on the ground by enemy aircraft fire 7.7.17; ARS 1 AD 7.7.17; 54 Sqdn 25.8.17; On 06.15 Offensive patrol, petrol pipe hit in combat, forced landed just behind the Belgian front line in the wire entanglements nr Boitshouke 4.9.17 (Lt K Shelton OK); ARS 1 AD 6.9.17; SOC 26.9.17

A6173   At makers Richmond 6.3.17, allotted to Expeditionary

Force; Shipped to France 3.17; ARS 2 AD to 66 Sqdn 14.4.17; ARS 1 AD 25.6.17; ARS 2 AD 26.6.17; SOC 6.8.17

A6174   (Engine No.35012/WD2513) Presentation aircraft 'Canada'. At makers Richmond 6.3.17, allotted to Expeditionary Force; Shipped to France for 2 AD 3.17; ARS 2 AD to 54 Sqdn (coded 'L') 15.4.17; Escort, chased down in flat spin, but forced landed and opverturned Lesdain, by Ltn Werner Voss, Jasta Boelke 9.5.17 (2/Lt GCT Hadrill PoW)

A6175   (Engine No.2348/WD5897) At makers Richmond 6.3.17, allotted to Expeditionary Force; Shipped to France for 2 AD 3.17; ARS 2 AD to 66 Sqdn (coded '5') 21.4.17; Escort to Solesmes, last seen nr Cambrai, shot down nr Bourlon by Obltn H Lorenz, Jasta 33 24.4.17 (Lt RS Capon PoW wounded)

A6176   At makers Richmond 6.3.17, allotted to Expeditionary Force; Shipped to France 3.17; ARS 2 AD to 66 Sqdn 24.4.17; Test flight, spun after catching slip-stream of another a/c, forced landed, crashed 11.5.17 (2/Lt GRE Hayter); SOC 20.5.17 NWR

A6177   At makers Richmond 7.3.17, allotted to Expeditionary Force; Shipped to France for 2 AD 30.3.17; ARS 2 AD to 66 Sqdn 18.4.17; Albatros C driven down to 200ft and probably crashed Fresnes 08.45 30.4.17; Albatros D.II

A6174 'L' of No.54 Squadron was on escort duty on 9th May 1917 when it was chased down in a flat spin by Ltn Werner Voss of Jasta Boelke. It force landed and overturned at Lesdain, 2/Lt G.C.T.Hadrill being taken prisoner.   *(via Philip Jarrett)*

Lt R.S.Capon in A6175 '5' of No.66 Squadron was taken prisoner when he was shot down near Bourlon by Obltn H Lorenz of Jasta 33 on 24th April 1917.He had been on escort duty to to Solesmes, being last seen near Cambrai.   *(via Frank Cheesman)*

out of control Orchies 14.15 2.5.17 (both Capt JO Andrews); Escort, bad landing, hit tent on aerodrome 4.5.17; At ARS 2 AD by 1.6.17; SOC 6.8.17

A6178   (Engine No.35011/WD2512) At makers Richmond 7.3.17, allotted to Expeditionary Force; Shipped to France for 2 AD 30.3.17; ARS 2 AD to 66 Sqdn 24.4.17; Op to Douai-Brebières, shot down nr Vitry by Ltn Karl Allmenroder, Jasta 11 07.40 10.5.17 (Lt TH Wickett PoW wounded)

A6179   At AID Farnborough 3.4.17, allotted to Expeditionary Force; En route from Lympne to (S)ARD Farnborough 11.4.17, allotment to Expeditionary Force cancelled now on charge to DAE.2a Repair Section

A6180   At AID Farnborough 11.4.17, allotted to Expeditionary Force; At (S)ARD Farnborough 13.4.17, reallotted to Training Brigade; 40 RS Port Meadow by 28.5.17

A6181   At makers Richmond 28.3.17, allotted to Expeditionary Force; Shipped to France 4.17; ARS 2 AD to 66 Sqdn 24.4.17; 2 enemy aircraft out of control Zonnebeke 20.15 4.6.17 (Lt AB Thorne); ARS 1 AD 9.6.17; ARS 2 AD 15.6.17; ARS 1 AD 11.7.17; Offensive patrol, badly shot up 8.6.17 (Lt AB Thorne OK); ARS 1 AD 9.6.17; ARS 2 AD 11.7.17; 66 Sqdn 23.8.17; Offensive patrol, shot up, turned over on landing 24.9.17 (2/Lt WG Heathcote slight cuts); ARS 1 AD 26.9.17; SOC 29.9.17

A6182   At makers Richmond 28.3.17, allotted to Expeditionary Force; Shipped to France 4.17; ARS 2 AD to 66 Sqdn 26.4.17; Forced landed on test flight, completely wrecked 1.6.17 (2/Lt AC White slight cuts); ARS 1 AD 4.6.17; 54 Sqdn 22.8.17; Casualty Report 23.8.17 says on inspection the engine was found to be out of alignment with the fuselage; Returned to ARS 1 AD 25.8.17; 54 Sqdn 26.9.17; OP to Dixmude, hit by AA, believed also shot up, crashed on landing 24.10.17 (2/Lt CG Wood wounded in arm)

A6183   (Engine No.10026) At makers Richmond 28.3.17, allotted to Expeditionary Force; Shipped to France 4.17; ARS 2 AD to 54 Sqdn 27.4.17; Albatros C crashed nr Walincourt, shared with A640, A6165, A6168, A7306 & A7330 06.40 11.5.17 (Lt OM Sutton); In combat over Premont collided with an Albatros D and wing damaged, returned safely but the enemy aircraft was seen to break up 08.10 24.5.17; Albatros D out of control Honnecourt 11.25, shared with A7330 and an Albatros D crashed Gonnelieu 11.30 1.6.17; Albatros D out of control east of St Emile, shared with A640, A6172, A7330, B1730 & B2151 06.45 3.6.17 (Lt OM Sutton); 3 Albatros Ds crashed south-west of Cambrai, shared with A6156, A6165, A6167, A6192 12.00 6.6.17 [the Combat Report says combat was with a large formation of enemy aircraft, each of the 5 pilots claimed a victory but in the close range fighting it was impossible to follow an enemy aircraft down, 2 enemy aircraft were seen to crash by other pilots and 1 by our artillery] (all Lt OM Sutton); Damaged on the ground by enemy aircraft fire, Bray Dunes 7.7.17; ARS 1 AD 7.7.17; 66 Sqdn 14.8.17; FTR from Special Duty flight, bombing enemy aerodrome in the Ypres sector 20.9.17 (2/Lt CHF Nobbs PoW)

A6184   At makers Richmond 28.3.17, allotted to Expeditionary Force; Shipped to France 4.17; ARS 2 AD to 66 Sqdn 24.4.17; Damaged in forced landing nr Arras 26.4.17 (2/Lt CC Morley OK); At ARS 2 AD 1.6.17; ARS 1 AD 13.7.17; 54 Sqdn 25.7.17; Longerons damaged by enemy aircraft fire on 09.15 Offensive patrol, forced landed, crashed 26.8.17 (2/Lt SJ Schooley unhurt); ARS 1 AD 30.8.17; SOC 26.9.17

A6185   At Farnborough by 15.4.17; 40 TS Croydon by 5.6.17; Yatesbury by 7.17; 56 TS London Colney by 13.8.17 to at least 1.18

A6186   At Farnborough by 15.4.17; With AID Farnborough

16.4.17, allotted to Expeditionary Force; England to ARS 1 AD 20.4.17; ARS 2 AD 28.4.17; 66 Sqdn 1.5.17; Albatros D out of control Henin Lietard 19.10 22.5.17 (2/Lt CF Smith); OP to Cambrai, shot down 26.5.17 (2/Lt CF Smith PoW) [Ltn Hochstatter, Jasta 12 at Cagnicourt 08.10 OR Vzfw R Jörke, Jasta 12 at Etaing 08.10?]

A6187   At Farnborough by 15.4.17; 40 RS Port Meadow by 5.17; As 40 TS moved to Croydon 1.6.17 to at least 3.6.17; 56 TS London Colney by 16.7.17 to at least 21.8.17

A6188   At AID Farnborough 19.4.17, allotted to Expeditionary Force; England to ARS 1 AD 22.4.17; 46 Sqdn 2.5.17; Left on OP 18.40, badly shot up, forced landed Dickebush 26.5.17 (2/Lt AG Lee wounded); ARS 1 AD 29.5.17; ARS 2 AD 15.6.17; 46 Sqdn (coded '4') 22.6.17; Flown back to England (Sutton's Farm) for HD detachment with Sqdn 10.7.17; Anti-Gotha patrol, left 17.14, landed 18.35 12.8.17 (Lt EY Hughes); Back to France 30.8.17; DFW 2-str out of control 5.9.17; 2-str out of control south of Scarpe, shared with B1777, B1837 & B1843 10.55 11.9.17; 2-str out of control south of Scarpe River, shared with B1777 & B2191 08.20 21.9.17 (all Lt EY Hughes); Left 06.40 for bombing operation, believed hit by mg fire, forced landed, crashed Ervillers 20.11.17 (Sgt J Leigh wounded then injured); To Rep Pk 2 ASD 21.11.17

A6189   At AID Farnborough 26.4.17, allotted to Expeditionary Force; England to ARS 1 AD 28.4.17; ARS 2 AD to 54 Sqdn 11.5.17; On practice flight wheel broke on landing, machine turned over 1.6.17 (2/Lt LW Osman); ARS 2 AD 3.6.17; SOC 20.6.17

A6190   At AID Farnborough 25.4.17, allotted to Expeditionary Force; England to ARS 1 AD 26.4.17; ARS 2 AD to 66 Sqdn 5.5.17; Albatros out of control 28.5.17 (Lt CC Sharp); Turned over on landing 5.6.17 (2/Lt JW Boumphrey); ARS 1 AD 6.6.17; 66 Sqdn 5.7.17; Albatros D.V OOC Gheluwe 20.15, claim not allowed, credited as driven down 26.7.17 (Lt JTB McCudden); Engine caught fire returning from Offensive patrol, switched off, forced landed, turned on nose 16.8.17 (2/Lt RA Stedman OK); ARS 1 AD 17.8.17; SOC 19.8.17

A6191   At AID Farnborough 25.4.17, allotted to Expeditionary Force; England to ARS 1 AD 28.4.17; ARS 2 AD to 66 Sqdn 5.5.17; Left 08.20 for Anti-Gotha patrol against Gothas raiding Harwich & Felixstowe, landed 09.30 4.7.17 (2/Lt JW Boumphrey); ARS 1 AD 20.7.17; SOC 27.7.17

A6192   At AID Farnborough 30.4.17, allotted to Expeditionary Force; ARS 1 AD to ARS 2 AD 11.5.17; 54 Sqdn 12.5.17; 3 Albatros Ds crashed south-west of Cambrai, shared with A6165, A6156, A6167 & A6183 12.00 6.6.17 (2/Lt MC McGregor) [the combat report says combat was with a large formation of enemy aircraft, each of the 5 pilots claimed a victory but in the close range fighting it was impossible to follow an enemy aircraft down, 2 enemy aircraft were seen to crash by other pilots and 1 by our artillery]; Gun test, stalled at 40ft due to engine failure and crashed 29.6.17 (2/Lt MC McGregor injured); ARS 1 AD 1.7.17; 54 Sqdn 9.9.17; Crashed into another machine on landing 13.11.17 (2/Lt HV Young OK); Rep Pk 1 ASD 14.11.17; SOC 21.11.17

A6193   55 RS Yatesbury by 6.2.17; Became 55 TS Yatesbury 31.5.17; 'B' Flt 28 Sqdn Yatesbury 23.7.17; 17th Wing HQ Beaulieu by 11.9.17

A6194   At makers Richmond 18.4.17, allotted to Expeditionary Force; England to ARS 1 AD in case 30.4.17; ARS 2 AD to 66 Sqdn (coded '4') 20.5.17; OP east of Croiselles-Hermies, forced down Noyelles-sous-Lens by Ltn Haugg

& Ltn Kellein, Fl Abt 48 and captured intact 24.5.17 (Capt LH Smith PoW wounded, escaped to Switzerland 27.12.17) [or possible "Sopwith" down Monchy 08.40 by Ltn J Schmidt, Jasta 3]

A6195   At makers Richmond 18.4.17, allotted to Expeditionary Force; England to ARS 1 AD in case 30.4.17; 46 Sqdn 14.5.17; Patrol, crashed on landing 26.5.17; ARS 1 AD 27.5.17; 66 Sqdn 7.7.17; Crashed and overturned in wheat field nr aerodrome 14.7.17 (2/Lt FG Huxley); ARS 1 AD 15.7.17; SOC 21.7.17

A6196   At makers Richmond 18.4.17, allotted to Expeditionary Force; ARS 1AD by 18.5.17; ARS 2 AD by 1.6.17; 54 Sqdn 6.6.17; Hostile aircraft patrol, turned over on landing 8.6.17 (2/Lt LW Osman); ARS 2 AD 9.6.17; SOC 20.6.17

A6197   At makers Richmond 18.4.17, allotted to Expeditionary Force; ARS 1 AD by 19.5.17; 66 Sqdn 6.6.17; Left Calais 08.20 on Anti-Gotha patrol at Harwich and Felixstowe, landed 09.30 4.7.17 (2/Lt FA Smith); Albatros D out of control Roulers 07.15 4.9.17 (Lt FA Smith); Casualty Report 4.9.17 says return to AD, machine "time expired" and unsuitable for service flying; ARS 1 AD 5.9.17; 66 Sqdn 9.10.17; ARS 1 AD 15.10.17 exchanged for a Camel; ARS 2 AD 21.10.17; 46 Sqdn 22.10.17; Practice flight, bad landing in cross wind, damaged 5.11.17 (2/Lt HNC Robinson); Rep Pk 2 ASD 6.11.17

A6198   At makers Richmond 18.4.18, allotted to Expeditionary Force; ARS 1 AD by 14.5.17; 66 Sqdn 7.6.17; Left 08.20 Anti-Gotha patrol against Gothas raiding Harwich & Felixstowe, landed 10.50 4.7.17 (2/Lt JB Hine); Returning from Offensive patrol, turned over on landing 12.7.17 (2/Lt JB Hine OK); ARS 1 AD 14.7.17; SOC 21.7.17

A6199   At makers Richmond 18.4.17, allotted to Expeditionary Force; Shipped to France without engine 5.17; ARS 2 AD to 54 Sqdn 21.5.17; 2-str destroyed south of Middelkerke, shared with A6211 & B1704 07.30 15.8.17 (2/Lt G Clapham); Casualty Report 16.8.17 says unfit for

further service; ARS 1 AD 18.8.17; SOC 19.8.17

A6200   At makers Richmond 18.4.17, allotted to Expeditionary Force; Shipped to France without engine 5.17; ARS 1 AD by 18.5.17; 46 Sqdn 28.5.17; Albatros D out of control 7.6.17 (Lt RS Asher); With Sqdn to England (Sutton's Farm) for HD detachment 10.7.17; Left 17.14 on Anti-Gotha patrol, landed 18.47 12.8.17 (2/Lt RS Asher); Back to France with Sqdn 30.8.17; Crashed on landing 19.15 5.9.17 (2/Lt DS Smallman); Casualty Report 9.9.17 says machine appreciably slower than other machines in the Sqdn and complete overhaul needed; ARS 2 AD 13.9.17; SOC 19.9.17

A6201   At makers Richmond 18.4.17, allotted to Expeditionary Force; Shipped to France without engine 5.17; ARS 2 AD to 66 Sqdn 27.5.17; Left 08.20 Anti-Gotha patrol against Gothas raiding Harwich & Felixstowe, landed 10.35 4.7.17 (2/Lt SJ Oliver); Offensive patrol, shot down Slypshoek by Vzfw Weber, Jasta 8 16.30 10.8.17 (2/Lt SJ Oliver killed)

A6202   At makers Richmond 18.4.18, allotted to Expeditionary Force; Shipped to France without engine 5.17; ARS 1 AD by 26.5.17; 46 Sqdn 28.5.17; Crashed St.Omer while taking off for HD detachment to England 10.7.17 (2/Lt AG Lee); ARS 1 AD 17.7.17; 54 Sqdn 5.6.17; Offensive patrol, crashed on landing 25.7.17 (2/Lt SJ Schooley slightly injured); ARS 1 AD 27.7.17; SOC 11.8.17

A6203   At AAP Feltham 24-25.4.17, allotted to Expeditionary Force; Shipped to France without engine 5.17; ARS 1AD by 24.5.17; ARS 2 AD by 1.6.17; 54 Sqdn 5.6.17; Albatros D out of control north of Yser to Westende les Bains 13.15 13.7.17 (2/Lt RM Charley); Black and white checked Albatros D in the sea Slype 18.30 5.9.17; Albatros D.III hit but disappeared into mist, regarded as indecisive Slype 09.00 25.9.17 (both Lt RM Charley); Albatros D out of control Lombartzyde 13.45 13.11.17 (Capt RM Charley); Flown back to England 23.12.17; TOC "C" Flight 4 TDS Hooton

A6203 with one of the first-line squadron, possibly No.95 Squadron, working up at North Shotwick in the Spring of 1918.   *(MAP)*

Park 23.1.18; 90 Sqdn North Shotwick 7.2.18; 96 Sqdn North Shotwick 3.4.18; 95 Sqdn North Shotwick to 37th Wing Half ARS North Shotwick 9.4.18; 95 Sqdn North Shotwick 17.5.18 - @24.6.18

A6204   At AAP Feltham 24-25.4.17, allotted to Expeditionary Force; Shipped to France without engine 5.17; ARS 1 AD by 24.5.17; 46 Sqdn 29.5.17; Left 16.45 on OP to Houthulst, shot down nr Ypres 2.6.17 (Lt DR Cameron PoW) [possibly the Sopwith 1-str claimed nr Ypres by FlMl Kunstler MF Ja1]

A6205   At AAP Feltham 24-25.4.17, allotted to Expeditionary Force; Shipped to France without engine 5.17; ARS 2 AD to 66 Sqdn 27.5.17; Left Calais 08.20 for Anti-Gotha patrol against Gothas raiding Harwich & Felixstowe, landed Bekesbourne 4.7.17 (Lt GEC Round); ARS 1 AD 16.7.17; 54 Sqdn 21.7.17; Casualty Report 23.7.17 complains that aircraft received in damaged condition and return to depot requested; ARS 1 AD 24.7.17; 54 Sqdn 8.8.17; Damaged when gale hit hangar which collapsed 28.8.17; ARS 1 AD 30.8.17; SOC 26.9.17

A6206   At AAP Feltham 24-25.4.17, allotted to Expeditionary Force; Shipped to France without engine 5.17; ARS 1 AD to 46 Sqdn 2.6.17; Albatros out of control east of La Bassée 18.20 7.7.17 (Lt K MacDonald); Flown back to England (Sutton's Farm) for HD detachment with Sqdn 10.7.17; Failed to gather speed after pulling out of vertical spin, crashed 25.7.17 (2/Lt FH Eberlin killed); At (S)ARD Farnborough 30.7.17 allotment to Expeditionary Force cancelled, now on charge to E.1 Repair Section

A6207   At AAP Feltham 24-25.4.17, allotted to Expeditionary Force; Shipped to France without engine 5.17; ARS 2 AD to 66 Sqdn 28.5.17; Enemy aircraft driven down Gheluvelt, shared with B1726 20.15 4.6.17 (2/Lt AG Robertson); On offensive patrol, aerial collision with B1745 Roulers, crashed Moorslede, both claimed by Obltn K Mettlich, Jasta 8 14.20 8.6.17 (2/Lt AG Robertson killed)

A6208   At Lympne 15.5.17, allotted to Expeditionary Force; England to ARS 1 AD 7.6.17; 66 Sqdn 8.6.17; On test flight got into a spin and crashed, completely wrecked 25.6.17 (Lt AB Thorne injured); ARS 1 AD SOC 27.6.17

A6209   At Lympne 15.5.17, allotted to Expeditionary Force; England to ARS 1 AD 11.6.17; ARS 2 AD 14.6.17; 54 Sqdn 15.6.17; Left on offensive patrol, on return crashed on landing due to darkness 18.45 22.8.17 (Lt K Shelton); ARS 1 AD 23.8.17; SOC 26.8.17

A6210   At Lympne 2.6.17, allotted to Expeditionary Force; England to ARS 1 AD 11.6.17; ARS 2 AD 13.6.17; 54 Sqdn 16.6.17; Damaged on the ground by enemy aircraft fire 7.7.17; ARS 1 AD 7.7.17; 66 Sqdn 22.7.17; Offensive patrol, on take off tail too high, propeller hit ground 14.8.17 (2/Lt CHF Nobbs); ARS 1 AD 15.8.17; SOC 17.8.17

A6211   At Lympne 15.5.17, allotted to Expeditionary Force; England to ARS 1 AD 14.6.17; 54 Sqdn 19.6.17; 2-str destroyed south of Middelkerke, shared with A6199 & B1704 07.30 15.8.17; Albatros D in the sea north of Middelkerke 11.30 25.9.17 (both Capt O Stewart MC); Casualty Report 5.10.17 says unfit for further service in the field; ARS 1 AD 7.10.17 (time expired); SOC 10.10.17

A6212   En route from Mkrs to Newhaven 12.7.17, allotted to Expeditionary Force; Arr ARS 2 AD in case without engine 14.7.17; ARS 1 AD 5.8.17; 66 Sqdn 8.8.17; Offensive patrol, damaged in combat, forced landed, crashed on landing, La Bellevue 15.8.17 (2/Lt OD Hay wounded); ARS 1 AD 17.8.17; SOC 19.8.17

A6213   No information

A6214   'B' Flt 56 RS London Colney by 5.17; Became 56 TS London Colney 31.5.17 to at least 23.9.17

A6215   At AID Farnborough 21.5.17, allotted to Expeditionary Force; ARS 1 AD to 66 Sqdn 2.6.17; Left Calais 08.20 for Anti-Gotha patrol against Gothas raiding Harwich & Felixstowe, landed Lympne 4.7.17 (2/Lt CC Morley); Test flight near aerodrome, forced landed through magneto trouble 5.7.17 (2/Lt CC Morley OK); ARS 1 AD 6.7.17; 54 Sqdn 10.8.17; In combat 18.8.17 (Capt AL Macfarlane wounded); Albatros D b/u and fell in the sea Middelkerke 11.35 25.9.17, Albatros D.III crashed between Pervyse and Schoorbeke, shared with B1792 14.30 18.10.17 (both 2/Lt ME Gonne); Casualty Report 16.11.17 says unfit for further service in the field; 2 ASD to Rep Pk 1 ASD 18.11.17; Rec Pk 19.11.17; Flown back to England 23.11.17; 28 TS Castle Bromwich, tyre came off 11.1.18 (2/Lt RK Whitney)

A6216   (Engine No.3196/WD625) At AID Farnborough 24.5.17, allotted to Expeditionary Force; ARS 1 AD by 1.6.17; 46 Sqdn 3.6.17; Left 09.45, Offensive patrol, badly damaged in combat, controls shot away, crashed on landing 5.6.17 (2/Lt PW Wilcox OK); ARS 1 AD 6.6.17; 66 Sqdn 8.7.17; OP nr Thielt, last seen at 5,000ft going west north of Dixmude, shot down nr Bixschoote/nr Thielt by Uffz E Schäpe, Jasta 33 08.30 28.7.17 (2/Lt JB Hine PoW)

A6217   At Lympne 2.6.17, allotted to Expeditionary Force; England to ARS 1 AD 12.6.17; 54 Sqdn 7.7.17; Returning from OP engine failed to pick up when coming in to aerodrome, forced landed in cornfield 21.7.17 (2/Lt P Goodbehere); ARS 1 AD 23.7.17; SOC 27.7.17

A6218   11 TS Scampton

A6219   65 Sqdn Wye by 9.8.17

A6220   Experimental installation of 110hp Le Rhône 9J, tested Dover and Croydon by 9.17; 1 (Observers) School of Aerial Gunnery New Romney by 5.18 to at least 11.8.18

A6221   63 TS Joyce Green by 6.17; Crashed on landing, caught by gust 22.7.17 (2/Lt HVL Tubbs)

A6222   73 Sqdn Lilbourne by 9.9.17; 25th Wing ARS Castle Bromwich 22.9.17; 74 Sqdn London Colney by 10.17

A6223   63 TS Joyce Green by 6.17 to at least 7.17

A6224   81 Sqdn Scampton by 5.7.17

A6225   (80hp Gnome) 65 Sqdn Wye by 9.17; Harling Road 21.9.17

A6226   (80hp Gnome No.3853/WD44) 39 HD North Weald by 4.7.17; 81 Sqdn Scampton, cowl came off, pilot did a flat turn and nose dived in, written off 11.7.17 (2/Lt FR Goodearle slightly injured)

A6227   65 Sqdn Wye by 10.7.17

A6228   40 TS Croydon by 3.7.17; Anti-Gotha patrol, left 07.33, landed 08.30 4.7.17 (Sgt Parry); Anti-Gotha patrol, left 09.25, attacked and shot up Gothas over London, landed 11.55 7.7.17 (2/Lt RFW Martin); Anti-Gotha patrol, left 17.18, landed 19.15 12.8.17; Anti-Gotha patrol, left 10.20, landed 11.45 22.8.17 (both Lt AG Taylor); Crashed on landing, undercarriage, right wing and propeller broken 29.9.17 (2/Lt A Koch); Still 40 TS 12.17; Wireless Experimental Establishment Biggin Hill ('C'), crashed

A6229   65 Sqdn Wye by 12.7.17; 94 Sqdn Harling Road 21.9.17 – 10.17

A6230   63 TS Joyce Green, anti-Gotha patrol, shot up by Gotha while attacking a formation, forced landed, crashed nr aerodrome 7.7.17 (2/Lt WG Salmon died of wounds) [claimed by Offstr R Klimke & Obltn Leon, KG13] [several people were arrested at the site for having removed Salmon's goggles and other items]

A6231   63 TS Joyce Green; 65 Sqdn Wye by 7.17; 73 Sqdn Lilbourne by 7.17

Immaculate-looking Whitehead-built A6231 with the serial number painted in white at the bottom of the fin. It is reported to have served at various times with No.63 Training Squadron at Joyce Green, No.65 Squadron at Wye and No.73 Squadron at Lilbourne.   *(via Philip Jarrett)*

A6232   40 TS Croydon by 20.6.17 to at least 1.7.17; Sopwith "6232" flown Folkestone to Dartford 7.7.17 (Capt HM Sison); 18th Wing ARS Hounslow to 74 Sqdn London Colney 10.9.17; WO & SOC 9.11.17

A6233   63 TS Joyce Green by 7.17

A6234   (Presentation aircraft 'Johannesburg No.1'). 63 TS Joyce Green by 6.17 to at least 7.17

A6235   63 TS Joyce Green by 6.17 to at least 7.17; 74 Sqdn London Colney by 7.17 to at least 19.10.17; 3 TS Shoreham to 18th Wing ARS Hounslow 23.12.17; SOC 4.1.18

A6236   94 Sqdn Harling Road by 17.11.17

A6237   No information

A6238   At makers Richmond 1.6.17, allotted to Expeditionary Force; England to ARS 1 AD 29.7.17; 54 Sqdn 31.8.17 (coded '2', with pilot's initials 'HHM' in white on the centre-section); Albatros D.III crashed in flames east of Slype 18.15 16.9.17; Albatros D in flames Middelkerke 11.35 25.9.17 (both 2/Lt HH Maddocks); Still 54 Sqdn 11.10.17; Rep Pk 1 ASD to Rec Pk 12.12.17; 1 AI to Rec Pk 29.12.17; 8 AAP Lympne 10.1.18; Castle Bromwich 21.1.18 (in transit); 'C' Flight 4 TDS Hooton Park 23.1.18; 37th Wing ARS Houton Park 10.3.18; 4 TDS Hooton Park 14.4.18

A6239   At makers Richmond 1.6.17, allotted to Expeditionary Force; Still there 7.7.17 when allotment cancelled; 18th Wing ARS Hounslow to 85 Sqdn Hounslow 20.4.18; 18th Wing ARS Houslow 2.5.18; 41 TDS London Colney 28.7.18

A6240   (Engine No.3642c) At makers Richmond 5.6.17, allotted to Expeditionary Force; England to ARS 1 AD in case without engine 25.6.17; 54 Sqdn 2.7.17; Albatros C in sea north-west of Nieuport 04.10 11.7.17 (Capt FN Hudson MC); Left on special reconnaissance 18.30, FTR, last seen over Bruges heading towards Ostende 13.7.17 (Capt FN Hudson MC PoW) [Credited Ltn G Flecken, Jasta 20]

A6241   At makers Richmond 5.6.17, allotted to Expeditionary Force; England to ARS 2 AD in case without engine 26.6.17; ARS 1 AD 4.9.17; 46 Sqdn 5.9.17; Albatros D which was on A7330's tail out of control Douai 09.30-10.15 21.9.17 (Capt VAH Robeson); ARS 2 ASD 13.12.17 (exchanged for a Camel); 2 AI to 2 ASD Scout School, Candas 19.1.18; 2 AI 5.2.18; Reception Park 26.3.18; Flown back to England 27.3.18

A6242   At makers Richmond 5.6.17, allotted to Expeditionary Force; England to ARS 1 AD in case without engine 27.6.17; 66 Sqdn 6.7.17; Had taken off on patrol when engine trouble developed, crashed attempting to land 26.9.17 (2/Lt JG Warter OK); ARS 1 AD 29.9.17; SOC 30.9.17

A6243   61 HD Sqdn Rochford, left 17.19 on Anti-Gotha patrol, landed 19.20 12.8.17; Left 10.24 on Anti-Gotha patrol, landed 11.28 22.8.17 (both Lt JD Belgrave)

A6244   (100hp Gnome Monosoupape B-2) 37 HD Sqdn, practice flight, crashed due to engine failure Stow Maries 26.7.17 (Capt EWS Cotterill seriously injured)

A6245   61 HD Sqdn Rochford, left 10.25 on Anti-Gotha patrol, landed 11.29 22.8.17 (2/Lt EH Chater); Overturned landing in high wind 14.1.18 (Lt AH Bird); 143 HD Sqdn Detling, SOC 28.7.19

A6246   'B' Flt 37 HD Sqdn Stow Maries, left 08.25 on Anti-Gotha patrol, landed 09.30 22.7.17 (Capt CE Holman); 61 HD Sqdn Rochford 2.8.17; Left 17.23 on Anti-Gotha patrol, landed 18.55 12.8.17 (Capt CE Holman); Left 10.25 on Anti-Gotha patrol, landed 11.25 22.8.17 (Lt LB Blaxland)

A6247   198 (Night) TS Rochford to 90 HD Sqdn Buckminster 13.12.18 to at least 17.12.18; 142 HD Sqdn Detling, crashed & WO 13.9.19

A6248   'B' Flt 37 HD Sqdn Stow Maries, left 08.26 on anti-Gotha patrol, landed 10.11 22.7.17 (2/Lt HA Edwardes); 61 HD Sqdn Rochford 2.8.17; Left 10.24 on anti-Gotha patrol, landed 11.25 22.8.17 (Lt HA Edwardes)

A6249   (100hp Gnome Monosoupape) 61 HD Sqdn Rochford (coded 'C-1'), left 17.23 on Anti-Gotha patrol, landed 19.17 12.8.17; Left 10.22 on Anti-Gotha patrol, landed 11.35 22.8.17 (both Capt EB Mason); 30 TS (AFC) Ternhill by 1.18; 29 TS (AFC) Shawbury; 5th (T) Sqdn AFC; 6th (T) Sqdn AFC

12 SOPWITH PUP to have been renumbered A6681 to A6692

War Office letter ref A DAE (AE2) dated 6.1.17 gave instructions that aircraft 3691, N5181, N5184, N5185 to N5188, N5191, N5196 to N5198, 9898 had been allotted serials A6681 to A6692, and were to be repainted. This was cancelled by letter of 10.1.17, it having been realised that these were RNAS aircraft not RFC property. They were on charge to 8N Sqdn which was at that time attached to the RFC.

50 SOPWITH PUP ordered additionally under Contract number 87/A/461 from Standard Motor Co Ltd, Coventry and numbered A7301 to A7350. (80hp Le Rhône 9C)

A7301   At AAP Coventry 10.1.17, allotted to Expeditionary Force but this cancelled 12.1.17; TOC 66 Sqdn Filton 14.2.17; To France with Sqdn 17.3.17; ARS 1 AD for reconstruction 18.3.17; 66 Sqdn 30.3.17; Wrecked Fienvillers 21.4.17 (2/Lt RS Capon); SOC 21.4.17 Wrecked; Evidently returned to England; 63 TS Joyce Green

A7302   AAP Coventry to 66 Sqdn Filton 8.2.17; Returning from CFS to Filton, Forced landed with engine trouble,brought back by road 27.2.17 (Mjr OT Boyd MC); Not to France with Sqdn 3.17

A7303   (Engine No.WD2192) At AAP Coventry 10.2.17, allotted to Expeditionary Force; To France by air; ARS 1 AD by 1.3.17; ARS 2 AD 4.3.17; 66 Sqdn 24.3.17; Halberstadt out of control Vitry 07.45 22.4.17; Albatros out of control Lecluse 1910 23.4.17 (both Lt JT Collier); Offensive patrol, in combat 4.5.17 (Lt JT Collier wounded); OP to Douai-Brebières, shot down nr Brebières [16.5.17 (2/Lt DJ Sheehan killed)

A7304   At AAP Coventry 16.2.17, allotted to Expeditionary Force; England to ARS 1 AD 4.3.17; ARS 2 AD 11.3.17; 66 Sqdn 14.4.17; Albatros D.III out of control 7.5.17 (2/Lt Angus Bell-Irving); Forced landed, crashed, overturned 13.5.17; At ARS 2 AD 1.6.17; SOC 4.8.17

A7305   At AAP Coventry 20.2.17, allotted to Expeditionary Force but reallotted to 66 Sqdn Filton 24.2.17; To Sqdn 26.2.17; At ARS 1 AD 24.3.17 (accommodated for 66 Sqdn); To Sqdn 25.3.17; Halberstadt out of control damaged 8.4.17 (Lt JT Collier); 2-str driven down Douai 13.4.17 (Capt R Oxspring); Escort to Lens-Brebières-Lecluse, badly shot up in combat 24.4.17 (Capt R Oxspring); At ARS 2 AD 1.6.17; SOC 6.8.17

A7306   At AAP Coventry 12.1.17, allotted to Expeditionary Force; ARS 2 AD to 54 Sqdn 26.2.17; Albatros C in vertical dive Buissy-Inchy 08.15 14.4.17; Albatros D.III

The 'A' prefix has been omitted from the serial number of A7313, which is seen her crashed on its nose, possibly with No.45 Training Squadron at South Carlton, with which it was serving in August 1917.
(via Frank Cheesman)

in spin 6m east of St Quentin 07.10 1.5.17 (both Capt WV Strugnell MC); Black and white scout crashed Seranvillers 15.30 9.5.17; Albatros C crashed nr Walincourt, shared with A640, A6165, A6168, A6183 & A7330 18.40 11.5.17; Albatros C out of control Beaurevoir 06.55 30.5.17 (all Lt EJY Grevelink); Left 10.45 on F.E. escort duty to Anneux, FTR, in combat just south-west of Cambrai, last seen going down on back out of control 6.6.17 (Lt EJY Grevelink) [possibly by Vzfw R Riessinger south of Inchy 13.10 - but see B1730]

A7307   At AAP Coventry 12.1.17, allotted to Expeditionary Force; Shipped to France for 2 AD 2.17; ARS 2 AD to 54 Sqdn 5.3.17; Patrol to St.Quentin, shot up by AA, crashed 11.5.17 (Lt FJ Morse); ARS 2 AD 12.5.17; 54 Sqdn 10.6.17; On practice formation flight, crashed on landing 21.7.17 (Sgt HN Barnard injured); ARS 1 AD 23.7.17; SOC 27.7.17

A7308   (Engine No.100221) At AAP Coventry 12.1.17, allotted to Expeditionary Force; ARS 2 AD to 54 Sqdn 28.2.17; 2-str in flames Roisel, victory shared with Capt WV Strugnell, serial not known 07.45 19.3.17 (Lt EJY Grevelink); Left 07.00 for OP on 4th Army Front, shot down in flames in combat with 3 aircraft of Jasta 6 11.5.17 (2/Lt HC Duxbury killed) [Vzfw F Krebs, Jasta 6, south of Lesdain 08.35]

A7309   At AAP Coventry 12.1.17, allotted to Expeditionary Force; In France with 66 Sqdn (coded '2') 22.3.17; Blown over after landing 24.3.17 (2/Lt TC Luke); Flying again 30.3.17; Albatros forced to land south of Oppy 7.5.17 (2/Lt PG Taylor); Albatros C out of control Gheluvelt 08.00 7.6.17; Albatros C out of control north of Passchendaele 08.20 15.6.17 (All 2/Lt PG Taylor); ARS 1 AD 25.6.17 (time expired); ARS 2 AD 26.6.17; 2 AD (later 2 ASD) Scout School, Candas 27.6.17; Rep Pk 2 ASD 22.3.18; Rep Pk 1 ASD 1.4.18

A7310   (Le Rhône 9J?) 'B' Sqdn CFS Upavon by 5.17 to at least 7.7.17; 34 TS Ternhill by 20.7.17; 'C' Sqdn CFS Upavon by 9.17 to at least 12.3.18

A7311   42 RS Hounslow to 41 TS Doncaster 1917 (Lt JTB McCudden's aircraft, thereafter flown at various training stations); Wyton (6th Wing) to 64 Sqdn Sedgeford 10.5.17; 63 TS Joyce Green, anti-Gotha patrol, left 11.25, landed 13.20 13.6.17; Anti-Gotha patrol, left from Dover 10.00, shot up, damaged, landed safely 11.45 7.7.17 (both Lt JTB McCudden OK); 18th Wing Fighting School London Colney by 24.9.17; To Ayr via East Fortune with 504 A9798 & Pup A7328 21.10.17 (arr 23.10.17) (for 1 SAF?)

A7312   At AAP Coventry 16.2.17, allotted to Expeditionary Force; England to ARS 1 AD 4.3.17; 54 Sqdn 11.3.17; Albatros D.III out of control north-east of St Quentin 19.30 24.4.17 (Capt JC Russell); Offensive patrol, overturned by wind landing, damaged 18.5.17; ARS 2 AD 19.5.17; SOC 20.6.17

A7313   At AAP Coventry 24.2.17; 66 Sqdn Filton 24.2.17; Not to France with Sqdn 3.17; Crashed as 'A' (unit?); 45 TS South Carlton by 21.8.17; Crashed on nose (unit?)

A7314   (Engine No.35090/WD2591) 66 Sqdn Filton by 3.17; To France with Sqdn via ARS 1 AD 17.3.17; Halberstadt out of control 8.4.17; Albatros D forced to land Vitry 0700 30.4.17; Albatros D forced to land and Albatros D driven down Dury 0700-0730 26.5.17 (All Lt CCS Montgomery); OP Houthulst-Roulers-Quesnoy, shot down nr Roulers by Vzfw H Oberländer, Jasta 30 11.45 7.6.17 (2/Lt RM Marsh PoW)

A7315   Allotted to 66 Sqdn Filton 24.2.17; To France with 66 Sqdn (coded '2') via ARS 1 AD 17.3.17; Destroyed Albatros D.III 7.5.17 (Lt PG Taylor); Enemy aircraft out of control 25.5.17 (2/Lt FA Smith); Patrol lined up for

Two views of Standard-built A7327 '1' of 'C' Flight of No.46 Squadron, in which Captain S.W.Pratt claimed four victories in June and July 1917. The white figure '1' was carried both aft of the fuselage roundel and also inboard of the upper wing roundels. Red wheels discs bore a white skull and crossbones, the latter repeated above the centre section. (Cross & Cockade International)

take off when run into by 56 Sqdn S.E.5 A4846 5.6.17 (2/Lt FA Smith); ARS 1 AD 6.6.17; 54 Sqdn 28.7.17; Casualty Report 16.9.17 says unfit for further service in the field; ARS 1 AD 20.9.17; SOC 3.10.17

A7316   Allotted to 66 Sqdn Filton 24.2.17; Ferried from Coventry to Filton, landed downwind, bent axle 1.3.17 (2/Lt EJD Townsend); To France with Sqdn via ARS 1 AD 17.3.17; Cowling came off on test flight, crashed on landing, 24.3.17 (2/Lt DF Cox); At ARS 2 AD 1.6.17; SOC 6.8.17

A7317   66 Sqdn Filton by 2.17; Not to France with Sqdn 3.17; CFS Upavon by 21.4.17 to at least 6.6.17; 17 TS Port Meadow by 7.17 – 9.17; Lilbourne by 14.9.17; 73 Sqdn Lilbourne 15.9.17 to at least 17.11.17; 54 TS Castle Bromwich by 23.4.18 to at least 27.5.18; Flown Eastbourne to Upper Heyford 1.8.18; Tipped on nose at one time

A7318   40 RS Port Meadow by 25.5.17; As 40 TS to Croydon 1.6.18; Anti-Gotha patrol, left 17.21, landed 19.25 12.8.17 (2/Lt AC Hurst); 94 Sqdn Harling Road 10.17

A7319   40 RS Port Meadow by 25.5.17; As 40 TS to Croydon 1.6.17; Anti-Gotha patrol, left 07.33, landed Goldhangar 4.7.17 (Lt Cummings); Broke up in air 9.7.17 (Lt SM Evans killed)

A7320   At AAP Coventry 13.3.17, allotted to Expeditionary Force; England to ARS 1 AD 18.3.17; 66 Sqdn by 5.4.17; Took off slightly cross wind and downhill also got into slipstream of another aircraft, undercarriage collapsed 13.4.17 (2/Lt DF Cox); ARS 2 AD, SOC 9.5.17 NWR

A7321   (Engine No.1564/WD5464) At AAP Coventry 13.3.17, allotted to Expeditionary Force; England to ARS 1 AD 18.3.17; ARS 2 AD 28.3.17; 66 Sqdn 8.4.17; Ran out of fuel, forced landed, ran into barbed wire fence, machine turned over 16.4.17 (Lt TH Wickett OK); At ARS 2 AD 1.6.17; 46 Sqdn 13.9.17; Left on OP 08.55, in combat 09.30-10.30, Albatros D forced to land Jigsaw Wood then FTR, seen by our ground forces to have come down under control Boiry-Notre Dame after combat with 6 or 7 enemy aircraft 21.9.17 (2/Lt RS Asher killed) [shot down by Untoff U Neckel, Jasta 12, south-west of Boiry/east of Monchy Le Preux 09.15 German time?]

A7322   40 RS Port Meadow by 29.5.17; As 40 TS moved to Croydon 1.6.17 to at least 6.8.17

A7323   At AAP Coventry 13.3.17, allotted to Expeditionary Force; England to ARS 1 AD 18.3.17; ARS 2 AD 25.3.17; 66 Sqdn 8.4.17; Collided with Bristol F.2b A7105 at over 2,000ft, forced landed, crashed 30.4.17 (Capt R Oxspring MC injured), the crew of the Bristol were both killed; SOC 30.4.17 Wrecked

A7324   At AAP Coventry 20.3.17, allotted to Expeditionary Force; England to ARS 1 AD 28.3.17; 66 Sqdn 30.3.17; Halberstadt OOC 15.00-17.35 8.4.17 (Capt GW Robarts); ARS 1 AD 25.6.17 (time expired); ARS 2 AD and on to 2 AD Scout School, Candas 27.6.17; ARS 2 AD 31.7.17 (damaged); 2 AD Scout School, Candas to ARS 2 AD 2.9.17; 46 Sqdn 17.9.17; Albatros D crashed Brebières, shared with A7335 10.10 22.9.17 (2/Lt RLM Ferrie); Crashed on landing 16.10.17 (Lt RLM Ferrie), flying again 17.10.17; Albatros D out of control 13.15 28.10.17, shared with B1727 (Lt RLM Ferrie); Rep Pk 2 ASD 12.11.17 (exchanged for a Camel); 8 AAP Lympne 16.12.17; 3 TDS Lopcombe Corner to 18th Wing ARS Hounslow 14.3.18; 27 TS London Colney to 41 TDS London Colney 29.7.18

A7325   At AAP Coventry 20.3.17, allotted to Expeditionary Force; England to ARS 1 AD 29.3.17; 'B' Flt 46 Sqdn (coded '1') 20.4.17; Albatros D.V out of control 5.6.17 (2/Lt NH Dimmock); On gunnery practice flight forced landed in wheat field, overturned, damaged 26.6.17 (2/Lt RLM Ferrie OK); ARS 2 AD 27.6.17; SOC 5.7.17

A7326   (80hp Le Rhône) 43 RS Ternhill by 5.17; 84 Sqdn, entered spinning nose dive, port wing collapsed in high-speed pull-up, crashed 1m north-east of Lilbourne aerodrome 10.8.17 (Lt WA Taylor killed)

A7327   At AAP Coventry 27.3.17, allotted to Expeditionary Force; England to ARS 1 AD 3.4.17; 46 Sqdn (coded '1') 27.4.17 (Capt SW Pratt's aircraft with skull and crossbones on wheels & centre section); Albatros out of control 25.5.17; Albatros D.III out of control 3.6.17; Albatros 2-str seen by our AA to go down with much smoke Ploegsteert 10.50 15.6.17; Albatros D.V "fell like a stone" out of control Lens 19.30 17.6.17 (all Capt SW Pratt); 2-str out of control La Bassée, shared with Lt PW Wilcox 05.55 3.7.17 (Lt KW McDonald); Flown back to England with Sqdn 10.7.17; En route to (S)ARD Farnborough from 46 Sqdn 8.8.17, allotment to Expeditionary Force cancelled, now on charge to E.1 Repair Section

A7328   Flown by Lt Conway from London Colney to Ayr via East Fortune with 504 A9798 & Pup A7311 21.10.17 (arr 23.10.17) (for 1 SAF?)

A7329   At AAP Coventry 21.3.17, allotted to Expeditionary Force; England to ARS 1 AD 28.3.17; 66 Sqdn 31.3.17; Albatros D out of control Lecluse 1910 23.4.17 (2/Lt FW Williams); On OP forced landed nr Gavrelle, completely wrecked 30.4.17 (2/Lt DF Cox) ; SOC 30.4.17 Wrecked

A7330   At AAP Coventry 21.3.17, allotted to Expeditionary Force; England to ARS 1 AD 3.4.17; ARS 2 AD 26.4.17; 54 Sqdn 28.4.17; 2-str crashed Seranvillers 15.30 9.5.17;

A7333, named "AD ASTRA", of No.46 Squadron, after being brought back by Lt S.W.Williams from Penshurst to Sutton's Farm around July-August 1917. Left to right 2/Lt N.H.Dimmock (78 Sqn), Lt F.L.Luxmore (78 Sqn), Lt Marchant's sister and Lt Williams (46 Sqn). Note the circle on top of the centre section.   (via Frank Cheesman)

Albatros C crashed nr Walincourt shared with A640, A6165, A6168 & A7306 18.40 11.5.17; Albatros D.III OOC Honnecourt, shared A6183 11.25 1.6.17; Albatros D out of control east of St Emile, shared with A640, A6172, A6183, B1730 & B2151 0645 3.6.17 (all Lt MDG Scott); Damaged on the ground by enemy aircraft fire 7.7.17; ARS 1 AD 8.7.17; 46 Sqdn 2.9.17; Albatros D.V out of control Douai 0930-10.30 21.9.17 (Lt PWS Bulman); 2 ASD 8.11.17 exchanged for a Camel; Rec Pk 18.11.17; Flown back to England 19.11.17

A7331   At AAP Coventry 27.3.17, reallotted from 66 Sqdn to Expeditionary Force as "wastage"; England to ARS 1 AD 20.4.17; 46 Sqdn 27.4.17; Crashed landing from Offensive patrol, damaged 1.6.17 (2/Lt EH Lascelles injured); ARS 1 AD 2.6.17; 54 Sqdn 24.7.17; Offensive patrol, left 09.10, shot up by AA, damaged 5.9.17 (2/Lt PC Norton unhurt); Casualty Report says aircraft is unfit for further service in the field; ARS 1 AD 6.9.17; SOC 26.9.17

A7332   At AAP Coventry 19.3.17, allotted to Expeditionary Force; England to ARS 1 AD 5.4.17; 'A' Flt 46 Sqdn 20.4.17; Patrol, mid-air collision with R.E.8 over Dickebusch, completely wrecked 16.20 22.5.17 (2/Lt CL Gunnery killed); SOC 22.5.17 Wrecked

A7333   (Engine No.2228/WD7855) At AAP Coventry 24.3.17, allotted to Expeditionary Force; England to ARS 1 AD 5.4.17; 46 Sqdn (named 'AD ASTRA') 14.5.17; Flown back to England (Sutton's Farm) for HD detachment with Sqdn 10.7.17 and back to France 30.8.17; Left on OP to Menin 09.30, shot down in combat, last seen over Linselles 10.30 3.9.17 (Lt SW Williams PoW) ["Sopwith" claimed in combat east of Wervicq 10.30 by Ltn O Fruhner, Jasta 26?] [or Obltn Oskar Freiherr von Boenigk, Jasta 4]

A7334   At 1 AAP Coventry 27.3.17, allotted to Expeditionary Force; England to ARS 1 AD 3.4.17; 46 Sqdn (coded '2') 7.4.17; Albatros D.III crashed Westroosebeke 20.00 4.6.17 (2/Lt FL Luxmoore); ARS 1 AD 24.6.17; 54 Sqdn 7.7.17; Casualty report 27.7.17 says aircraft has been entirely rebuilt after crash and is unfit for further service in the field; ARS 1 AD 28.7.17; Flown back to England 5.8.17; 'B' Flt 28 Sqdn Yatesbury by 15.8.17; 55 TS Yatesbury by 8.17

A7335   At AAP Coventry 26.4.17, allotted to Expeditionary Force; To 46 Sqdn 11.5.17; Flown back to England (Sutton's Farm) for HD detachment 10.7.17; Anti-Gotha patrol, left 17.14, landed 18.47 12.8.17 (Lt CA Brewster-Joske (Aus)); Retd to France with Sqdn 30.8.17; Albatros

D crashed Menin 10.30 3.9.17; 2 Albatros D.V out of control Ecourt St Quentin 13.15 16.9.17; Albatros D.III crashed north of Brebières, shared with A7324 10.10 22.9.17 (all Capt CA Brewster-Joske, Aust); Rep Pk 2 ASD 12.11.17 (exchanged for a Camel); Rec Pk 22.1.18; To Le Crotoy 28.1.18 "for Cap de la Ferriere"; Allotted to HQ Flight 30.1.18; SOC Rep Pk 2 ASD 11.8.18 "from Le Crotoy"

A7336   No information

A7337   At AAP Coventry 27.3.17, allotted to Expeditionary Force; Flown to France 4.17; ARS 1 AD to 46 Sqdn 23.4.17; Flown back to England (Sutton's Farm) for HD detachment 10.7.17; Anti-Gotha patrol 12.8.17 (Lt AW Wilcox); Retd to France with Sqdn 30.8.17; Crashed on take-off 4.9.17 (Lt DS Smallman); ARS 1 AD 6.9.17; SOC 26.9.17

A7338   (80hp Le Rhône) 43 TS Ternhill, stalled, then crashed on top of mess hut at Castle Bromwich 2.7.17 (2/Lt EC Rylands badly shaken)

A7339   At AAP Coventry 26.4.17, allotted to Expeditionary Force; Flown to France 5.17; ARS 2 AD to 54 Sqdn 12.5.17; Propeller broke when running engine up damaging machine 12.7.17 (Capt SH Storey OK); ARS 1 AD 14.7.17; SOC 21.7.17

A7340   (Engine No.35117/WD10966) At AAP Coventry 29.3.17, allotted to Expeditionary Force; Flown to France 4.17; ARS 1 AD to ARS 2 AD 26.4.17; 66 Sqdn 30.4.17; Albatros D.III out of control Marcoing 19.45 24.5.17 (2/Lt FW Williams); OP east of Croiselles-Hermies, shot down by Jasta 33 27.5.17 (Lt SS Hume PoW) [Ltn Heffelink, nr Hamblain OR Offz St Altmeier nr Corbeheim]

A7341   At AAP Coventry 3.4.17, allotted to Expeditionary Force; At (S)ARD Farnborough 25.4.17 allotment to Expeditionary Force cancelled, now on charge to DAE.2a Repair Section; 40 TS Croydon by 20.6.17; Anti-Gotha patrol 12.8.17 (Lt NC Clarke); 64 Sqdn Sedgeford by 15.9.17

A7342   At AAP Coventry 9.4.17, allotted to Expeditionary Force; En route to (S)ARD Farnborough 28.4.17, allotment to Expeditionary Force cancelled now on charge to DAE.2a Repair Section

A7343   'B' Sqdn CFS Upavon by 22.4.17 to at least 22.5.17; 84 Sqdn Lilbourne (flown by Capt AW Beauchamp-Proctor); 73 Sqdn Lilbourne by 16.10.17 to at least 13.12.17; 74 TS Castle Bromwich by 17-28.2.18; 54 TS Castle Bromwich by 15.2.18 to at least 14.3.18

A7344   At AAP Coventry 3.4.17, allotted to Expeditionary Force; England to ARS 1 AD 10.4.17; 46 Sqdn 23.4.17; ARS 1 AD by 1.6.17; ARS 2 AD 12.6.17; 54 Sqdn (coded 'F') 13.6.17; Damaged on the ground by enemy aircraft fire 7.7.17; ARS 1 AD 8.7.17; 54 Sqdn (coded '3') 31.8.17; Albatros D.V out of control nr Ostende 18.45 11.9.17 (Lt RM Charley); OP St.Pierre Capelle-Zarren, in combat east of lines, shot down at Kayem-Beerst by Ltn R Francke, Jasta 8 08.05 [German time?] 13.10.17 (2/Lt PC Norton PoW); Aircraft captured

A7345   (80hp Gnome No.2965/WD3478) 1 TS Gosport by 6.17; 'B' Flt 28 Sqdn Yatesbury, first solo flight in Pup, stalled and nose dived in 19.8.17 (2/Lt F George seriously injured, died of injuries)

A7346   At AAP Coventry 17.4.17, allotted to Expeditionary Force; Flown to France 4.17; At Calais en route to ARS 1 AD 20.4.17; ARS 2 AD 9.5.17; 54 Sqdn 12.5.17; Damaged in combat 2.6.17; ARS 2 AD 2.6.17; 46 Sqdn 5.7.17; Flown back to England (Sutton's Farm) for HD detachment with Sqdn 10.7.17; Left in England

A7347   At AAP Coventry 16.4.17, allotted to Expeditionary Force; England to ARS 1 AD 20.4.17; 46 Sqdn 2.5.17; Albatros D.V out of control 7.7.17 (Lt KW McDonald); Flown back to England (Sutton's Farm) for HD detachment with Sqdn 10.7.17; En route from Sqdn to (S)ARD Farnborough 8.8.17, allotment to Expeditionary Force cancelled now on charge E.1 Repair Section

A7348   (Engine No.2228-5727-7855) At AAP Coventry 16.4.17, allotted to Expeditionary Force; England to ARS 1 AD 22.4.17; 'B' Flt 46 Sqdn (coded '3') 23.4.17; COL 16.5.17 (Lt C Courtneidge); Flying again 18.5.17; Flown back to England (Sutton's Farm) with Sqdn for HD detachment, but lost in English Channel en route 10.7.17 (Lt C Courtneidge rescued)

A7349   40 RS Port Meadow by 26.5.17; Became 40 TS Port Meadow 31.5.17; 40 TS moved to Croydon 1.6.17 to at least 11.17; Damaged undercarriage and prop landing 22.10.17 (2/Lt EC Eaton OK)

A7350   40 RS Port Meadow by 26.5.17; Became 40 TS Port Meadow 31.5.17; 40 TS moved to Croydon 1.6.17; Spun after loop too near ground, stalled then dived in 4.6.17 (2/Lt W Cass killed)

6 SOPWITH PUP (N5193, N5194, N5190, N5183, N5182 & N5192) to have been transferred from Admiralty charge and numbered A8732 to A8737. Not taken over.

1 SOPWITH SCOUT [i.e. PUP] ordered from Sopwith and numbered B331, but cancelled and serial number re-allotted.

1 SOPWITH PUP to have been transferred from Admiralty charge (serial?) and numbered B381. Not taken over.

Rebuilds by 1(S)ARD Farnborough numbered in range B701 to B900, included these Pups.

B735   (100hp Gnome Monosoupape) 37 HD Sqdn Stow Maries by 7.17; 61 HD Sqdn Rochford 24.7.17; Anti-Gotha patrol 12.8.17; Anti-Gotha patrol 22.8.17 (both 2/Lt AH Bird); Raid patrol, Engine failure, forced landed, tyre burst, axle & wing damaged 3.9.17 (Lt AH Bird); Wheel collapsed landing, crashed 29.9.17 (Lt AH Bird); Still 61 HD Sqdn 1.18; 85 Sqdn Hounslow, mid-air collision 18.2.18 (Flt Cdt HK Bulkley USAS killed); SOC 20.2.18

B803   (100hp Gnome Monosoupape) 'B' Flt 28 Sqdn Yatesbury by 31.8.17; 1 TS Gosport by 9.17

B804   (100hp Gnome Monosoupape) 67 TS Shawbury by 12.17; 10 TS Lilbourne by 27.2.18; With 10 TS to Gosport 25.6.18 – 28.8.18

B805   (100hp Gnome Monosoupape B-2, engine No.3081/WD20392) School of Special Flying Gosport, bad flying, crashed 13.8.17 (Capt Alan Duncan Bell-Irving injured)

B849   (100hp Gnome Monosoupape) 36 HD Sqdn Seaton Carew by 6.1.19; 198 (Night) TS Rochford (coded 'A'), crashed

B850   86 Sqdn Northolt by 6.18

B877   (100hp Gnome Monosoupape) 74 Sqdn London Colney, engine choked, hit tree 29.12.17 (Lt E Barlow injured)

1 SOPWITH PUP built from spares by 7th Wing ARS Norwich and allotted serial number B1499 12.12.17

B1499   No information

150 SOPWITH PUP ordered additionally under Contract number 87/A/461 from Standard Motor Co Ltd, Coventry and numbered B1701 to B1850. (80hp Le Rhône 9C)

B1701   At AAP Coventry 17.4.17, allotted to Expeditionary Force; England to ARS 1 AD 28.4.17; 46 Sqdn 24.5.17; Flown back to England (Sutton's Farm) for HD detachment 10.7.17; Anti-Gotha patrol 12.8.17 (Lt AF Bird); Returning to France crashed on landing at ARS 1 AD 30.8.17 (Lt AF Bird OK); 54 Sqdn 14.10.17; Albatros D.III crashed north of Dixmude shared with B1796 13.50 4.11.17 (2/Lt HH Maddocks); Rep Pk 1 ASD by 29.12.17; SOC 6.3.18 destroyed by fire

B1702   At AAP Coventry 17.4.17, allotted to Expeditionary Force; England to ARS 1 AD 24.4.17; ARS 2 AD 28.4.17; 54 Sqdn 9.5.17; ARS 2 AD 20.5.17; SOC 31.5.17 NWR

B1703   At AAP Coventry 17.4.17, allotted to Expeditionary Force; ARS 2 AD to 66 Sqdn 5.5.17; Albatros forced to land on 14.45 OP 7.5.17; Albatros D.III down smoking 06.25-08.15 13.5.17 (both Capt JO Andrews); 2-str out of control 18.25-20.50 23.5.17; 2-str out of control 06.00-08.30 28.5.17 (both 2/Lt TC Luke); 2-str destroyed Gheluvelt 08.00 7.6.17; Anti-Gotha patrol against Gothas raiding Harwich & Felixstowe 4.7.17; Albatros C destroyed nr Lens [Hénin Lietard] 10.35 11.7.17 (all Capt JO Andrews); Offensive patrol, badly shot up, crashed on landing 27.7.17 (2/Lt RA Stedman unhurt); ARS 1 AD 29.7.17; SOC 8.8.17

B1704   At AAP Coventry 9.4.17, allotted to Expeditionary Force; England to ARS 1 AD 28.4.17; 46 Sqdn 25.5.17; Left on patrol 10.30, shot up by mg, damaged landing on airfield 27.5.17 (Capt NS Caudwell wounded); ARS 1 AD 28.5.17; ARS 2 AD 12.6.17; 54 Sqdn 13.6.17; Albatros D.V out of control Slype-Leffringhe shared with B1759 & B1761 09.00 15.7.17; 2-str destroyed south of Middelkerke, shared with A6199 & A6211 07.30 15.8.17; Albatros D.V with black & white stripes on fuselage destroyed Middelkerke 19.00 22.8.17 (all 2/Lt GC Wood); Damaged when gale hit hangar 28.8.17; ARS 1 AD 30.8.17; SOC 26.9.17

B1705   43 RS Ternhill by 5.17, 84 Sqdn Lilbourne by 7.17; 73 Sqdn Lilbourne, WO, SOC 21.9.17

B1706   CFS 'B' Sqdn (later 'A' Sqdn) Upavon by 22.5.17 to at least 22.9.17; 61 TS South Carlton, crashed 4.5.18 (Lt EI Dexter killed)

B1707   CFS 'C' Sqdn Upavon by 22.1.18

B1708   (80hp Le Rhône No.35072/WD2573) 43 TS Ternhill, spinning nose dive, totally wrecked 16.6.17 (2/Lt DF Farrar badly shaken)

B1709   AAP Coventry 24.4.17, allotted to Expeditionary Force; ARS 1 AD to 46 Sqdn 14.5.17; Albatros out of control Houthulst 18.00 2.6.17; Albatros destroyed Wervicq 10.30 7.6.17; Albatros D.V OOC Lens 19.30 17.6.17 (all Lt CA Brewster-Joske); Left on OP 09.10 21.6.17, FTR, last seen at 10.30 over the lines (2/Lt HA Tonks AusFC killed)

B1710   At AAP Coventry 25.4.17, allotted to Expeditionary Force; ARS 2 AD to 66 Sqdn 12.5.17; Anti-Gotha patrol against Gothas raiding Harwich & Felixstowe 4.7.17; Albatros out of control Beuvry 06.20 13.7.17 (both 2/Lt CCS Montgomery); ARS 1 AD "time expired" 12.8.17; 2 AD Scout School, Candas 14.8.17; Last mention 10.12.17

B1711   At AAP Coventry 25.4.17, allotted to Expeditionary Force; En route from Lympne to (S)ARD Farnborough 5.5.17, allotment to Expeditionary Force cancelled, now on charge to AEA Repair Section; 'B' Flt 50 HD Sqdn Throwley, Anti-Gotha patrol 4.7.17; Anti-Gotha patrol 7.7.17 (both 2/Lt NE Chandler); 112 HD Sqdn Throwley 30.7.17; Anti-Gotha patrol 12.8.17 (2/Lt NE Chandler); Anti-Gotha patrol 22.8.17 (2/Lt Cox)

B1712   At AAP Coventry 25.4.17, allotted to Expeditionary Force; ARS 1AD to ARS 2AD 11.5.17; 54 Sqdn 12.5.17; Offensive patrol, overturned by wind landing, damaged 18.5.17; ARS 2 AD 19.5.17; ARS 1 AD 9.9.17; 54 Sqdn 12.9.17; Offensive patrol, bad landing, damaged 4.11.17 (2/Lt A Thompson); Rep Pk 1ASD; SOC 9.11.17

B1713   At AAP Coventry 26.4.17, allotted to Expeditionary Force; ARS 1AD to ARS 2AD 13.5.17; 54 Sqdn 19.5.17; In combat on OP north-east of Nieuport, shot down in steep glide, fell in flood water east of Stuyvenskerke/Middelkerke Lake 06.30-06.45 17.7.17 (2/Lt CT Felton PoW wounded) [Sopwith 1-str claimed 06.30 by Vzfw J Buckler of Jasta 17]

B1714   At AAP Coventry 26.4.17, allotted to Expeditionary Force; En route from Lympne to (S)ARD Farnborough 5.5.17, allotment to Expeditionary Force cancelled now on charge to AE.1 Repair Section; 62 TS Dover, engine failure, forced landed 7.17

B1715   At AAP Coventry 1.5.17, allotted to Expeditionary Force; ARS 2 AD to 66 Sqdn 11.5.17; FTR Offensive patrol, shot down in Busigny area 28.5.17 (Lt RM Roberts PoW) [Sopwith claimed nr Malincourt 12.30 by Ltn W Blume of Jasta 26]

B1716   At AAP Coventry 1.5.17, allotted to Expeditionary Force; ARS 1 AD to 46 Sqdn 16.5.17; Albatros D.III out of control W of Menin, shared with Capt R Plenty 08.55 2.6.17 (2/Lt FB Barager); Flown back to England (Sutton's Farm) for HD detachment with Sqdn 10.7.17; Anti-Gotha patrol, left 17.14, landed 18.50 12.8.17 (2/Lt FB Barager); With Sqdn back to France 30.8.17; Left 09.30 on Southern Offensive patrol, badly shot up in combat Menin 10.30, forced landed La Lovie 3.9.17 (Lt FB Baragar wounded); ARS 1 AD 6.9.17; SOC 26.9.17

B1717   AES Orfordness by 8.17; Anti-Gotha patrol, left 17.35, landed 18.35 12.8.17 (Lt N Howarth); Anti-Gotha patrol, left 10.30 22.8.17 (Lt AJ Francis); Still AES 2.1.18; Anti-Gotha patrol 13.3.18 (Capt RM Charley); Tested after rebuilt (Capt RM Charley); Subject of Orfordness camouflage experiments 13.7.18; Arr RAE Farnborough 15.5.19; Waddon 6.10.19

B1718   No information

B1719   At (S)ARD Farnborough 7.5.17, allotted to Expeditionary Force; Left for France 5.17; ARS 2 AD to 66 Sqdn 11.5.17; OP Houthulst Wood-Roulers-Quesnoy, shot up in combat, crashed on landing 7.6.17 (2/Lt AV Shirley OK); ARS 1 AD 7.6.17; ARS 2 AD 17.6.17; 'B' Flt 46 Sqdn (coded '4') 28.6.17; Flown back to England (Sutton's Farm) for HD detachment 10.7.17; Anti-Gotha patrol, left 17.14 12.8.17 (2/Lt RLM Ferrie); Back to France 30.8.17; Albatros D.V out of control 16.9.17 (Lt RLM Ferrie); Crashed on landing, wrecked 20.10.17 (2/Lt HNC Robinson); ARS 2 AD 22.10.17

B1720   Wireless & Observaters School Brooklands by 19.8.17

B1721   At (S)ARD Farnborough 10.5.17, allotted to Expeditionary Force; Flown to France 5.17; ARS 2 AD to 54 Sqdn (coded '3') 19.5.17; Escorting F.E.s, left 05.45, FTR, reported in combat at 14,000ft with 8 enemy aircraft, chased down east of Hebescourt, captured by Germans 30.5.17 (Lt FW Kantel PoW); [claimed nr Ponchause, east of Beaurevoir by Vzfw C Huller, Jasta 6 08.10 30.5.17]

B1722   Throwley (112 HD Sqdn?) by 5.18

B1723   'B' Flt 37 HD Sqdn Stow Maries, anti-Gotha patrol, left 08.23, hit by British AA over Shoeburyness, cowling shot off, landed 09.42 22.7.17 (Capt CA Ridley); 61 HD Sqdn Rochford 2.8.17; Anti-Gotha patrol, left 17.23, landed 18.55 12.8.17; Anti-Gotha patrol, left 10.24, landed 11.30 22.8.17 (both Capt CA Ridley); Still 61 HD Sqdn 12.17

Standard-built B1717 is seen here with the Aeroplane Experimental Station at Orfordness, from where it carried out anti-Gotha patrols in August 1917 and March 1918. Various trials included camouflage experiments in July 1918. In May 1919 it was transferred to the Royal Aircraft Establishment at Farnborough. In the background is a D.H.5 fitted with an elevated Vickers machine gun. (via Frank Cheesman)

B1724   At AID Farnborough 7.5.17, allotted to Expeditionary Force; Flown to France 5.17; ARS 2 AD to 66 Sqdn 13.5.17; Albatros D.III destroyed west of Houthem 09.00 15.6.17; Anti-Gotha patrol, left 08.20 against Gothas raiding Harwich & Felixstowe, landed 10.40 4.7.17 (both 2/Lt TC Luke); Albatros D.III in flames 18.45-20.55, own aircraft shot up 28.7.17 (2/Lt TC Luke wounded); Casualty Report 30.7.17 says all damage has been repaired but considered unfit for further service in the field, fit for a scout school; ARS 1 AD 30.7.17; 2 AD (later 2 ASD) Scout School, Candas 5.8.17; 2 AI 5.2.18; Rec Pk 26.3.18; 8 AAP Lympne 27.3.18; 143 HD Sqdn Detling, SOC 28.7.19

B1725   At (S)ARD Farnborough 10.5.17, allotted to Expeditionary Force; ARS 2 AD to 66 Sqdn 13.5.17; Scout driven down Henin Lietard 1910 22.5.17 (2/Lt Angus Bell-Irving); Crashed 8.6.17 (Lt Angus Bell-Irving); Anti-Gotha patrol, left 08.20 against Gothas raiding Harwich & Felixstowe, landed Dover 4.7.17 (2/Lt WR Keast); Shot up on OP Langemarck-Bixschoote, crashed 2m north of Dickebusch 7.7.17 (2/Lt WR Keast died of wounds 21.8.17); ARS 1 AD 9.7.17; SOC 10.7.17

B1726   (Engine No.1506/WD7872) At AID Farnborough 7.5.17, allotted to Expeditionary Force; ARS 2 AD to 66 Sqdn 25.5.17; Enemy aircraft driven down 27.5.17; Enemy aircraft driven down Gheluvelt shared with A6207 20.15 4.6.17; Albatros D driven down damaged Lille 17.30 7.6.17 (all Capt JD Latta MC); OP Roulers, damaged in combat, crashed Voormezeele 8.6.17 (Capt JD Latta wounded) [possible after combat west of Dadizeele 13.15 with Obltn von Voigt, Jasta 8 who claimed a "Nieuport"]; ARS 1 AD 12.6.17; 54 Sqdn 6.7.17; Flying to new aerodrome turned over on landing 16.7.17 (2/Lt TL Tebbit); ARS 1 AD 19.7.17; SOC 23.7.17

B1727   At (S)ARD Farnborough 10.5.17, allotted to Expeditionary Force; England to ARS 1 AD 11.6.17; ARS 2 AD 17.6.17; 46 Sqdn (coded 'N' later '2', named 'NORMIE' by Norman Dimmock) 24.6.17; Flown back to England (Sutton's Park) with Sqdn 10.7.17; Anti-Gotha patrol, left 17.14, landed 18.50 12.8.17 (2/Lt NH Dimmock); Back to France with Sqdn 30.8.17; Offensive patrol, Albatros D.V out of control 13.15 shared with A7324, then forced landed La Couchie, bad landing, wrecked 28.10.17 (2/Lt JH Cooper OK); ARS 2 AD 30.10.17

B1728   At makers 30.4.17, allotted to Expeditionary Force; Shipped to France without engine 5.17; At ARS 1 AD by 19.5.17; 46 Sqdn 8.6.17; On test flight failed to recover from spin 27.6.17 (2/Lt GP Kay seriously injured, died of injuries 29.6.17); ARS 2 AD and SOC 30.6.17

B1729   (Engine No.35021/WD3522) At makers 30.4.17, allotted to Expeditionary Force; Shipped to France without engine 5.17; ARS 1AD by 26.5.17; ARS 2 AD to 54 Sqdn 3.6.17; Left at 06.25 on F.E. escort duty, FTR, attacked by 3 enemy aircraft seen to land safely then machine burst into flames, presumed to have been set on fire by pilot 5.6.17 (2/Lt BG Chalmers PoW) [claimed shot down nr Masnières by Ltn F Kempf, Jasta Boelcke 07.40 German time]

B1730   (Engine No.4907/WD1217) At makers 30.4.17, allotted to Expeditionary Force; Shipped to France without engine 5.17; ARS 2 AD to 54 Sqdn 28.5.17; Albatros D out of control Beaurevoir 07.10 30.5.17; Albatros D out of control east of St Emile, shared with A640, A6172, A6183, A7330 & B2151 06.45 3.6.17 (both Mjr CE Sutcliffe); Left 10.45 on F.E. escort duty to Anneux, in combat just south-west of Cambrai, shot down inverted 6.6.17 (Mjr CE Sutcliffe killed) [unconfirmed claim south-west of Saint-les-Marquion 12.20 by Ltn H Becker, Jasta 12]

B1731   At makers 30.4.17, allotted to Expeditionary Force; At Lympne 9.5.15 reallotted to Training Brigade but this cancelled 14.5.17 and again allotted to Expeditionary Force; 8 AAP Lympne, anti-Gotha patrol 5.6.17 (Lt D Armstrong); ARS 1 AD 6.6.17; 66 Sqdn 8.6.17; Anti-Gotha patrol, left 08.20 against Gothas raiding Harwich & Felixstowe, landed 10.45 4.7.17; Albatros D.V crashed north-east of Ypres 19.55 12.7.17 (both 2/Lt EH Lascelles); On test flight landed cross wind and wrecked undercarriage 24.7.17 (2/Lt FG Huxley); ARS 1 AD 25.7.17; SOC 27.7.17

B1732   (Engine No 100243) At makers 30.4.17, allotted to Expeditionary Force; At Lympne 9.5.17 reallotted to Training Brigade but this cancelled 14.5.17 and again allotted to Expeditionary Force; England to ARS 1 AD and on to ARS 2 AD 9.6.17; 54 Sqdn 15.6.17; On practice flight misjudged landing and stalled 5.7.17 (2/Lt HS Graves); ARS 1 AD 7.7.17; 66 Sqdn (coded '3') 13.8.17; Bombed Marche aerodrome in the dark, 2 Albatros D.V that tried to get off shot down and crashed 05.15 16.8.17 (2/Lt WA Pritt); Offensive patrol, last seen Houthulst Wood-Staden at 12,000ft 17.8.17 (2/Lt PA O'Brien PoW, escaped to UK 21.11.17) [claimed by Ltn X Dannhuber, Jasta 26]

B1733   At makers 30.4.17, allotted to Expeditionary Force; England to ARS 1 AD 11.6.17; 66 Sqdn 7.7.17; Albatros D driven down damaged and Albatros D out of control east of Houthulst Wood 19.30-20.15 17.8.17 (Capt Angus Bell-Irving); Swerved on take off for OP wrecking lower planes and undercarriage 11.10.17 (2/Lt FDC Gore); SOC at ARS 1 AD 15.10.17

B1734   (80hp Le Rhône) 45 TS South Carlton, spinning nose dive 15.6.17 (2/Lt HS Kitson AFC killed)

B1735   48 RS Waddington by 28.5.17; Crashed into a wood (unit?)

B1736   48 RS Waddington, axle bent 27.5.17 (2/Lt JK Campbell); CFS Upavon by 6.17

B1737   74 Sqdn London Colney by 22.8.17; WO & SOC 8.11.17

B1738   56 RS London Colney by 5.17; 40 TS Croydon by 6.17; Anti-Gotha patrol, left 11.45, landed 13.50 13.6.17; Anti-Gotha patrol, left 17.22, landed 19.15 12.8.17 (Lt RM Collingwood); Anti-Gotha patrol, left 10.30, landed 11.35 22.8.17 (Lt TWL Stallibrass)

B1739   (80hp Le Rhône) 'B' Flt 56 TS London Colney by 5.17 to at least 1.18

B1740   62 TS Dover, Anti-Gotha patrol, left 17.37, landed 18.55 12.8.17 (Lt DM Faure); Anti-Gotha patrol, left 23.05, landed 00.05 2/3.9.17

B1741   No information

B1742   (80hp Le Rhône) At AAP Coventry 19.5.17, allotted to Expeditionary Force; England to ARS 1 AD 11.6.17; 54 Sqdn 19.6.17; Engine hit by AA 20.7.17 (2/Lt FW Gibbes); Casualty Report says no longer fit for war flying, fit to cross thre Channel and for school work 21.8.17; To ARS 1 AD and on to ARS 2 AD 22.8.17; 2 AD (later 2 ASD) School, Candas 31.8.17; 8 AAP Lympne 6.1.18; 'C' Flight 4 TDS Hooton Park 24.1.18; 37th Wing Half ARS Hooton Park 20.3.18; 4 TDS Hooton Park, crashed 27.4.18 (Lt VWV Lowrie killed)

B1743   At AAP Coventry 19.5.17, allotted to Expeditionary Force; En route to (N)ARD Coal Aston 6.6.17 allotment to Expeditionary Force cancelled now on charge to E.1 Repair Section; 11 TS Spittlegate by 7.17 to at least 8.17; 4 TDS Hooton Park by 24.1.18

B1744   At AAP Coventry 22.5.17, allotted to Expeditionary Force; England to ARS 1 AD 3.6.17; 66 Sqdn 6.6.17; Left 08.20 on Anti-Gotha patrol from Calais against raiders attacking Harwich and Felixstowe, turned over on landing 10.00 4.7.17 (2/Lt RA Stedman); ARS 1 AD 5.7.17; 54 Sqdn 31.8.17; Test flight, engine cut out ran into a ditch on landing 7.9.17 (2/Lt HH Maddocks); ARS 1 AD 8.9.17; SOC 26.9.17

B1745   At AAP Coventry 22.5.17, allotted to Expeditionary Force; Flown to France 5.17; ARS 1 AD to 66 Sqdn 7.6.17; On Offensive patrol, aerial collision with A6207 Roulers, crashed Moorslede 14.20 8.6.17 (2/Lt AV Shirley killed) [both claimed by Obltn K Mettlich, Jasta 8]

B1746   At AAP Coventry 24.5.17, allotted to Expeditionary Force; England to ARS 1 AD and on to 66 Sqdn 9.6.17; Left Calais 08.20 for Anti-Gotha patrol against Gothas raiding Harwich & Felixstowe, landed 10.40 4.7.17 (Capt CC Sharp); In combat with 3 Aviatik C, one of which glided east, Armentières 16.10 22.7.17 (Capt JTB McCudden); Engine cut out on take off, crashed 7.8.17 (2/Lt OD Hay slight cuts); ARS 1 AD 9.8.17; SOC 10.8.17

B1747   At AAP Coventry 24.5.17, allotted to Expeditionary Force; England to ARS 1 AD and on to 66 Sqdn 9.6.17; Left Calais 08.20 for Anti-Gotha patrol against Gothas raiding Harwich & Felixstowe, landed 10.45 4.7.17 (2/Lt EL Ardley); Anti-Gotha patrol Calais, crashed at 2 AD, completely wrecked 7.7.17 (2/Lt EL Ardley wounded); ARS 2 AD to 46 Sqdn 13.10.17; Left 08.40 for Bourlon Wood, FTR 22.11.17 (2/Lt TL Atkinson PoW)

B1748   45 TS from South Carlton 28.7.17

B1749   45 TS from South Carlton 28.7.17

B1750   27th Wing ARS Waddington to 82 Sqdn Waddington 13.6.17; 27th Wing ARS Waddington 21.6.17; 19th Wing ARS Catterick from 2.11.17

B1751   19th Wing ARS Catterick to 6 TS Catterick from 28.10.17

B1752   Flying Instructor 24th Wing from 16.7.17; Harlaxton

B1753   55 TS Yatesbury by 10.7.17; 'B' Flt 28 Sqdn 23.7.17 to at least 20.8.17

B1754   (Engine No.4435/WD10648) At AAP Coventry 5.6.17, allotted to Expeditionary Force; England to ARS 1 AD 14.6.17; ARS 2 AD 17.6.17; 46 Sqdn 29.6.17; With 46 Sqdn to England (Sutton's Farm) for HD detachment 10.7.17; Retd to France with 46 Sqdn 30.8.17; Left 05.48, Offensive patrol, combat over Menin 06.45 FTR 3.9.17 (Lt KW McDonald PoW died of wounds) [Sopwith claimed 06.30 Wervicq-Tenbrielen by Ltn E Mohnicke, Jasta 11)

B1755   At AAP Coventry 5.6.17, allotted to Expeditionary Force but cancelled; AES Orfordness fitted with 100hp Gnome Monosoupape B-2 by 22.3.18 to at least 25.4.18

B1756   At AAP Coventry 5.6.17, allotted to Expeditionary Force; England to ARS 1 AD 16.6.17; 66 Sqdn 25.6.17; Anti-Gotha patrol against Gothas raiding Harwich and Felixstowe, landed Lympne 4.7.17 (2/Lt DF Cox); ARS 1 AD 20.10.17, exchanged for a Camel; SOC 22.10.17

B1757   At AAP Coventry 5.6.17, allotted to Expeditionary Force; England to ARS 1 AD 16.6.17; 66 Sqdn (coded 'A') 25.6.17; Left Calais 08.20 for Anti-Gotha patrol against Gothas raiding Harwich and Felixstowe, landed 10.40 4.7.17 (2/Lt JM Warnock); Enemy aircraft out of control 28.7.17 (2/Lt PG Taylor); Albatros C crashed in flames 2m NW of Ypres 09.10 20.8.17; Albatros C in vertical dive smoking Eessen 08.00 11.9.17 (both Capt PG Taylor); ARS 1 AD 20.10.17, exchanged for a Camel; 54 Sqdn 6.11.17; Left on OP 08.30, FTR, last seen going

into clouds in control east of Dixmude with 2 enemy aircraft on tail 9.11.17 (2/Lt A Thompson PoW) [Possible Sopwith claimed south of St.Julien 09.40 [German time] by Ltn F Loerzer, Jasta 26]

B1758   At AAP Coventry 5.6.17, allotted to Expeditionary Force; England to ARS 1 AD 21.6.17; 66 Sqdn 25.6.17; Left Calais 08.20 for Anti-Gotha patrol against Gothas raiding Harwich and Felixstowe, landed Lympne 4.7.17 (Capt GW Robarts); OP Langemarck-Bixschoote, in action Zonnebeke, shot up, crashed on landing Bailleul No.1 airfield, 11.20 7.7.17 (Capt GW Robarts wounded); ARS 1 AD 9.7.17; 46 Sqdn 3.9.17; Rep Pk 2 ASD 11.11.17; Rep Pk 1 ASD to 1 AI 6.12.17; Rep Pk 1 ASD to Rec Pk 13.1.18; 8 AAP Lympne 15.2.18; 87 Sqdn Hounslow from 25.2.18; 18th Wing ARS Hounslow 12.3.18; 2 TS Northolt 2.5.18; 56 TS London Colney 25.5.18

B1759   At AAP Coventry 5.6.17, allotted to Expeditionary Force; England to ARS 1 AD 20.6.17 ("wrecked"); 54 Sqdn 7.7.17; Albatros D out of control Slype-Leffringhe, shared with B1704 & B1761 09.00 15.7.17 (Lt FJ Morse); Offensive patrol, shot up in combat 21.8.17 (Lt FJ Morse unhurt); ARS 1 AD 23.8.17; ARS 2 AD 19.9.17; 46 Sqdn 7.10.17; 2 ASD 15.11.17, exchanged for a Camel

B1760   Presentation aircraft 'Capetown No.1'. At AAP Coventry 11.6.17, allotted to Expeditionary Force; England to ARS 1 AD 6.7.17; 66 Sqdn 7.7.17; Albatros D.III out of control smoking north-east of Ypres 19.55 12.7.17; In a fight described as severe, aileron controls shot away 16.7.17 (Lt TV Hunter OK); Flying again 17.7.17; Albatros D.III destroyed Ardoye 14.25-17.30 patrol 27.7.17; Albatros D.III out of control east of Roulers 28.7.18; Albatros D.V out of control north-east of Menin 3.9.17; Albatros D.V out of control smoking north-east of Menin 11.35 3.9.17; Albatros D out of control Roulers 07.15 4.9.17 (All Lt TV Hunter); On test flight engine cut out, forced landed and crashed nr aerodrome 23.9.17 (Capt TPH Bayetto); ARS 1 AD 25.9.17; SOC 26.9.17

B1761   At AAP Coventry 11.6.17, allotted to Expeditionary Force; England to ARS 1 AD 19.6.17; 54 Sqdn 27.6.17; Albatros D out of control Slype-Leffringhe, shared with B1704 & B1759 09.00 15.7.17 (2/Lt AL Macfarlane); Left 05.55 on Offensive patrol, damaged by enemy aircraft fire, tank hit 10.8.17 (2/Lt AL MacFarlane OK); SOC ARS 1 AD 12.8.17

B1762   At AAP Coventry 14.6.17, allotted to Expeditionary Force; England to ARS 1 AD 19.6.17; 66 Sqdn 25.6.17; Left Calais 08.20 on Anti-Gotha patrol against Gothas attacking Harwich and Felixstowe, landed 10.40 4.7.17 (Lt TV Hunter); Albatros D.III destroyed east of Roulers, shared with B2162 18.55-21.00 28.7.17; Aviatik C out of control south-west of Roulers 11.45 21.8.17 (both 2/Lt WA Pritt); Casualty Report 17.9.17 says unfit for further service flying; ARS 1 AD 18.9.17; SOC 3.10.17

B1763   (100hp Gnome Monosoupape) 'B' Flt 50 HD Sqdn Throwley from/by 26.6.17; 112 HD Sqdn Throwley 30.7.17; Left 17.24 on Anti-Gotha patrol 12.8.17; Left 10.17 on Anti-Gotha patrol, landed 12.02 22.8.17 (both 2/Lt IM Davies); 36 HD Sqdn South Ashington, mid-air collision with B1805 13.1.19 (Lt H Croudace killed)

B1764   (100hp Gnome Monosoupape) 'B' Flt 37 HD Sqdn Stow Maries, left 07.30 on Anti-Gotha patrol, retd 07.56 with gun jam 4.7.17 (Lt J Potter); Left 09.29 on Anti-Gotha patrol, attacked Gothas, own aircraft shot up, landed 11.05 7.7.17 (2/Lt GA Thompson); 61 HD Sqdn Rochford ('C4') 2.8.17 to at least 10.17; Left 17.23 on

Anti-Gotha patrol, landed 18.50 12.8.17; Left 10.22 on Anti-Gotha patrol, landed 11.30 22.8.17 (both Sgt WAE Taylor); 6th (T) Sqdn AFC Minchinhampton

B1765 'B' Flt 37 HD Sqdn Stow Maries, left 07.29 on Anti-Gotha patrol, returned 09.21 4.7.17; Left 09.46 on Anti-Gotha patrol, attacked Gothas but gun jammed, landed Hainault and left again, landed 11.47 7.7.17 (both Capt EWS Cotterill); 61 HD Sqdn Rochford 2.8.17; Left 17.23 on Anti-Gotha patrol, landed 18.21 12.8.17; Left 10.24 on Anti-Gotha patrol, landed 11.24 22.8.17 (both 2/Lt HA Blain)

B1766 At makers 20.6.17, reallotted from Inspector of Stores Depots to Expeditionary Force; England to ARS 1 AD in case without engine 26.6.17; 46 Sqdn 10.7.17; Flown back to England (Sutton's Farm) for HD detachment with Sqdn 10.7.17; Left 17.14 on Anti-Gotha patrol, landed 18.50 12.8.17 (2/Lt LM Shadwell); Back to France, while stationery, hit by A648 which was landing 30.8.17; Practice flight, crashed on landing 7.9.17 (2/Lt HNC Robinson OK); ARS 2 AD 7.9.17; SOC 15.9.17

B1767 At makers 20.6.17, reallotted from Inspector of Stores Depots to Expeditionary Force; England to ARS 2 AD in case without engine 28.6.17; ARS 1 AD 10.7.17; 66 Sqdn 20.7.17; Enemy aircraft out of control 28.7.17 (2/Lt JW Boumphrey); FTR from special patrol along the Belgian coast, last seen landing east of Ostende with engine trouble 22.8.17 (2/Lt EH Garland PoW)

B1768 (Engine No.2393/WD5972) At makers 20.6.17, reallotted from Inspector of Stores Depots to Expeditionary Force; England to ARS 1 AD in case without engine 29.6.17; 66 Sqdn (coded 'D') 22.8.17; FTR from 10.00 Offensive patrol, last seen in slow spin over Gheluwe 30.9.17 (Lt JW Boumphrey PoW) [Sopwith 1-seater claimed in combat Wambeke 11.55 by Obltn H Auffarth, Jasta 18, or Sopwith claimed in combat St.Marguerite 11.50 by Ltn R Runge, Jasta 18?]

B1769 'B' Flt 50 HD Sqdn Throwley, left 07.43 on Anti-Gotha patrol, retd 08.22 with engine trouble 4.7.17 (2/Lt NF Perris); 112 HD Sqdn Throwley 30.7.17; Left 17.25 on Anti-Gotha patrol, returned 18.59 12.8.17; Left 10.21 on Anti-Gotha patrol, retd with petrol feed trouble 11.35 22.8.17 (both 2/Lt S Cockerell); 188 (Night) TS Throwley to 75 HD Sqdn North Weald 23.9.18; SOC 24.4.19

B1770 At makers 20.6.17; reallotted from Inspector of Stores Depots to Expeditionary Force; England to ARS 2 AD in case without engine 28.6.17; ARS 1 AD 10.7.17; 54 Sqdn 21.7.17; Returning from Offensive patrol, crashed on landing 25.7.17 (Sgt EF Smith); ARS 1 AD 27.7.17; SOC 1.8.17

B1771 'B' Flt 37 HD Sqdn Stow Maries by 6.17; Left 09.28 on Anti-Gotha patrol 4.7.17; Left 07.29 on Anti-Gotha patrol, attacked 22 enemy aircraft at 13,000ft over Billericay, returned 09.21 7.7.17 (both Capt EB Mason); 61 HD Sqdn Rochford, left 17.18 for Anti-Gotha patrol, landed 19.00 12.8.17; Left 10.25 for Anti-Gotha patrol, landed 11.39 22.8.17 (both Lt LF Hutcheon)

B1772 (100hp Gnome Monosoupape) 112 HD Sqdn Throwley by 2.8.17; Left 10.20 for Anti-Gotha patrol, landed 11.45 22.8.17 (Capt Thomas); Still 112 HD Sqdn Throwley 19.4.18 to at least11.6.18; 188 (Night) TS East Retford to 75 HD Sqdn North Weald 27.9.18; SOC 24.4.19

B1773 (100hp Gnome Monosoupape No.8070) 112 HD Sqdn Throwley by 12.17; Left 17.25 for Anti-Gotha patrol, retd 17.30 with engine trouble then took off again 17.35, landed 19.17 12.8.17 (Capt SH Pratt); On gunnery practice crashed Herne Bay 31.8.17 (Capt SH Pratt seriously injured)

B1774 61 HD Sqdn Rochford, left 17.23 for Anti-Gotha patrol, landed 19.50 12.8.17; Left 10.26 for Anti-Gotha patrol, landed 11.33 22.8.17 (both 2/Lt EE Turner); 86 Sqdn Northolt, WO 27.2.18

B1775 (Engine No 100246) Presentation aircraft 'Gold Coast Aborigines No.2'. At AAP Coventry 23.6.17, allotted to Expeditionary Force; England to ARS 1 AD 11.7.17; 66 Sqdn 14.7.17; FTR Offensive patrol, seen to dive on enemy aircraft north-west of Roulers 21.8.17 (2/Lt WR Keast killed) [Sopwith claimed in combat Ypres-Fresenberg by Ltn E Hess, Jasta 28]

B1776 (Engine No WD15609) At AAP Coventry 23.6.17, allotted to Expeditionary Force; At (N)ARD Coal Aston 24.7.17, allotment to Expeditionary Force cancelled now on charge to E.1 Repair Section; Still at (N)ARD Coal Aston 20.8.17, allotted to 46 Sqdn Sutton's Farm but reallotted to Expeditionary Force 31.8.17; England to ARS 1 AD 14.9.17; 54 Sqdn 20.9.17; Left 10.40, shot up in combat with enemy aircraft, crashed on landing 25.9.17 (2/Lt N Clark (Aus?) OK) [Sopwith claimed south of Langemarck by Ltn H Kroll, Jasta 24]; ARS 1 AD 29.9.17; SOC 30.9.17

B1777 Presentation aircraft 'British Guiana No.2'. At AAP Coventry 26.6.17, allotted to Expeditionary Force; England to ARS 1 AD 3.7.18; 'C' Flt 46 Sqdn (coded '4', later 'X', named 'CHU CHIN CHOW') 10.7.17 (collected by Lt AS Lee as replacement for A6202); Flown back to England (Sutton's Farm) for HD detachment 10.7.17; Left 17.14 for Anti-Gotha patrol, landed 18.40 12.8.17 (Lt AS Lee); Back to France 30.8.17; Albatros D which had been diving on an R.E.8, sent down out of control Polygon Wood 17.00 4.9.17; 2-str out of control south of Scarpe shared with A6188, B1837 & B1843 10.55 11.9.17; 2-str out of control south of Scarpe shared with A6188 & B2191 08.20 21.9.17; Albatros D.V out of control Sailly-en-Ostrevent 22.9.17; DFW C out of control Vitry 16.35 30.9.17 (all Lt AS Lee); 2 ASD 8.11.17, exchanged for a Camel; Rep Pk 1 ASD 15.11.17; Flown back to England 19.11.17; 42 TDS Hounslow to Artillery & Infantry School Worthy Down 10.8.18

B1778 Presentation aircraft 'Punjab 12 Kashmir'. At AAP Coventry 26.6.17, allotted to Expeditionary Force; AAP Lympne to ARS 1 AD 5.7.17; 66 Sqdn 22.8.17; On practice formation flight overturned on landing 4.9.17 (2/Lt DH Houston OK); ARS 1 AD 5.9.17; SOC 26.9.17

B1779 Presentation aircraft 'Rewa Fiji'. At AAP Coventry 27.6.17, allotted to Expeditionary Force; England to ARS 1 AD 5.7.17; 54 Sqdn 7.7.17; On Offensive patrol, forced landed nr Furnes, crashed 24.7.17 (2/Lt SJ Schooley); ARS 1 AD 26.7.17; SOC 27.7.17

B1780 Presentation aircraft 'Rhodesia No.1'. At AAP Coventry 29.6.17, allotted to Expeditionary Force; England to ARS 1 AD 3.7.17; 54 Sqdn 14.7.17; Left 04.20 for OP east of Nieuport, damaged by AA, forced landed on the sands by Bray Dunes, turned on nose 16.7.17 (Capt SH Storey unhurt); ARS 1 AD and SOC 19.7.17

B1781 At makers 20.6.17, reallotted from Inspector of Stores Depots to Expeditionary Force; England to ARS 1 AD 3.7.17 in case without engine; 66 Sqdn 11.7.17; On test flight landed cross wind and turned on nose 24.7.17 (2/Lt ATW Lindsay); SOC ARS 1 AD 27.7.17

B1782 At makers 20.6.17, reallotted from Inspector of Stores Depots to Expeditionary Force; England to ARS 2 AD in case without engine 9.7.17; ARS 1 AD 18.8.17; 54 Sqdn 22.8.17; Left 13.45, OP to St.Pierre Capelle-Houthulst, in combat east of lines, collided with

B1834 nr Beerst, 22.10.17 (2/Lt G Cowie killed) [both credited west of Beerst 15.25 [German time] by Ltn H Max von Müller, Jasta 28]

B1783   At makers 20.6.17, reallotted from Inspector of Stores Depots to Expeditionary Force; Shipped to ARS 1 AD without engine 5.7.17; 54 Sqdn 16.7.17; Offensive patrol, turned over by wind on landing 17.8.17 (2/Lt G Clapham); ARS 1 AD 19.8.17; SOC 21.8.17

B1784   At makers 20.6.17, reallotted from Inspector of Stores Depots to Expeditionary Force; England to ARS 2 AD in case without engine 9.7.17; ARS 1 AD 31.7.17; 54 Sqdn 22.8.17 to at least 16.11.17; At Rec Pk 22.12.17; Retd UK; 7 TDS Feltwell, hit top of marquee landing, crashed 6.7.18 (Lt F Hotrum seriously injured)

B1785   (80hp Clerget) 30th Wing HQ, spun in on landing Turnhouse 23.7.17 (2/Lt BA Taylor injured); 2 ASD to 1 ASD 6.12.17

B1786   64 Sqdn Sedgeford from 6.17 to at least 1.9.17

B1787   64 Sqdn Sedgeford from 6.17; Practice flight, engine failure, spun in, completely wrecked 3.9.17 (2/Lt FBH Anderson died of injuries 8.9.17)

B1788   (80hp Gnome No.3977/WD4469) 64 Sqdn Sedgeford from 6.17; On practice flight went into spin, came out of it at 500ft then lost control and spiralled in beside Sedgeford-Docking road 16.30 8.8.17 (2/Lt AL Dean died of injuries 9.8.17)

B1789   64 Sqdn Sedgeford from 6.17 to at least 24.9.17; 7th Wing ARS Norwich to 87 Sqdn Sedgeford 26.11.17 to at least 30.11.17

B1790   At makers 20.6.17, reallotted from Inspector of Stores Depots to Expeditionary Force; England to ARS 1 AD in case without engine 13.7.17; 66 Sqdn 24.7.17; On take off for OP tail too high, propeller hit the ground 27.7.17 (2/Lt ATW Lindsay); ARS 1 AD 29.7.17; SOC 1.8.17

B1791   At makers 20.6.17, allotted to Expeditionary Force; England to ARS 2 AD in case without engine 8.7.17; ARS 1 AD 16.7.17; 54 Sqdn 17.7.17; On practice flight misjudged landing and hit standing corn, turned over 20.7.17 (Sgt HN Barnard); ARS 1 AD 23.7.17; SOC 8.8.17

B1792   At AAP Lympne 3.7.17, allotted to Expeditionary Force; England to ARS 1 AD 13.7.17; 54 Sqdn 20.7.17; Albatros D.III out of control, shared with A649 12.8.17 (Lt GA Hyde MC); Albatros D.V out of control Mannekensvere 12.40 24.9.17; Albatros D.V crashed between Pervyse and Schoorbeke 14.30 18.10.17 (both Lt GA Hyde MC); DFW C gliding down apparently out of control Lombartzyde 13.00 13.11.17 (Capt GA Hyde MC); Casualty Report 16.11.17 says unfit for further service in the field; Time expired 19.11.17; 1 AI to Rep Pk 1 ASD 23.11.17; SOC 24.11.17

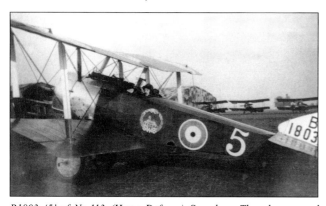

B1803 '5' of No.113 (Home Defence) Squadron, Throwley, around August 1917. The large South Wales Borderers/Egypt badge was applied by 2/Lt A.B.Garnons-Williams, this being his parent regiment.
(via Frank Cheesman)

B1793   At AAP Lympne 4.7.17, allotted to Expeditionary Force; England to ARS 1 AD 13.7.17; 54 Sqdn 17.7.17; Left 13.45, Offensive patrol, damaged in combat with 3 Albatros D.III [1 destroyed?] east of Nieuport 15.25 17.10.17 (Lt K Skelton); SOC ARS 1 AD 26.10.17 [Sopwith claimed south of Nieuport 15.20 by Obltn B Loerzer, Jasta 26]

B1794   At AAP Lympne 4.7.17, allotted to Expeditionary Force; England to ARS 1 AD 24.7.17; 66 Sqdn 31.7.17; Offensive patrol, last seen over Houthulst Wood, FTR 31.8.17 (2/Lt ES Bacon killed) [Claimed by Jasta 6]

B1795   (Engine No.035123) At AAP Lympne 4.7.17, allotted to Expeditionary Force; Still at Lympne 18.7.17 reallotted to 46 Sqdn Sutton's Farm (coded 'Z'); Left 17.14 on Anti-Gotha patrol, landed 19.25 12.8.17 (Mjr P Babington MC); To France with Sqdn 30.8.17; Left 05.45, shot down 06.35 south of Bousbecque by Rittm Frhr Manfred von Richtohofen (his 61st victory), Jagd Geschw 1, 3.9.17 (Lt AF Bird PoW)

B1796   At AAP Lympne 9.7.17, allotted to Expeditionary Force; ARS 1 AD 20.7.17; 54 Sqdn 26.7.17; Albatros D.III crashed north of Dixmude, shared with B1701 13.50 4.11.17 (2/Lt SJ Schooley); Casualty Report 13.11.17 says unfit for further service in the field; Rep Pk 1 ASD 14.11.17 time expired; Rec Pk 16.11.17; Flown back to England 19.11.17; 63 TS Joyce Green to 18th Wing ARS Hounslow 28.8.18; 42 TDS Hounslow to 30 TDS Northolt 17.9.18

B1797   At AAP Lympne 9.7.17, allotted to Expeditionary Force; ARS 1 AD 24.7.17; 66 Sqdn 27.7.17; Enemy aircraft out of control 28.7.17 (2/Lt EL Ardley); On offensive patrol, crashed nr Poperinghe 13.8.17 (Lt EL Ardley injured); ARS 1 AD 15.8.17; SOC 17.8.17

B1798   At makers 4.7.17, allotted to Expeditionary Force; England to ARS 1 AD in case without engine 15.7.17; 66 Sqdn 16.8.17; Crashed on take-off for OP 21.8.17 (2/Lt HB Young); ARS 1 AD 22.8.17; 66 Sqdn 30.9.17; Special patrol, badly shot up, crashed landing 12.10.17 (2/Lt FDC Gore OK); ARS 1 AD 12.10.17; SOC 19.10.17 NWR

B1799   At makers 4.7.17, allotted to Expeditionary Force; England to ARS 1 AD in case without engine 15.7.17; 54 Sqdn 18.8.17; Damaged by enemy aircraft fire on 11.30 OP 11.9.17 (2/Lt G Clapham unhurt); ARS 1 AD 12.9.17; ARS 2 AD 21.10.17; 46 Sqdn 31.10.17; 2 ASD 12.11.17; SOC 13.12.17

B1800   At makers 4.7.17, allotted to Expeditionary Force; England to ARS 2 AD in case without engine 17.7.17; ARS 1 AD 18.8.17; 54 Sqdn 19.8.17; Left 06.45 for OP to St.Capelle-Zarren, in combat east of lines, went down over Zarren 13.10.17 (2/Lt FW Gibbes killed) [Pup claimed south-west of Kokelaere 07.50 by Ltn E Böhme, Jasta 2]

B1801   81 Sqdn Scampton to ARD 28.7.17

B1802   At AAP Coventry 12.7.17, allotted to Expeditionary Force; Coventry to 46 Sqdn Sutton's Farm (coded 'W', named 'Will O' The Wisp') 17.7.17; Left 17.14 for Anti-Gotha patrol, landed 18.40 12.8.17 (Lt C Courtneidge); To France with Sqdn 30.8.17; Albatros C out of control south of Scarpe River, shared with A6188, B1837, B1842 & B1843 09.30 4.9.17 (Lt C Courtneidge); DFW C crashed south of Havrincourt Wood shared with B1829, B1837 & B2191 10.30 24.9.17 (Lt CW Odell); Shot up in combat on OP 30.9.17 (2/Lt E Armitage died of wounds 4.10.17); 2 ASD 16.11.17 (exchanged for a Camel); Flown back to England 8.12.17; 8 AAP Lympne by 10.12.17; 3 TS Shoreham 21.12.17; 3 TDS Lopcombe Corner by 9.5.18

A line-up of training aircraft at Vendôme in 1918. The nearest aircraft are Bristol Scout C 3060, Pup B1820 (named "JOHNNIE WALKER") and Avro 504 B8634 then six more 504s.
(via Philip Jarrett)

B1803   (100hp Gnome Monosoupape) 112 HD Sqdn Throwley (coded '5', with South Wales Borderers/Egypt badge beneath cockpit), left 10.20 for Anti-Gotha patrol, retd with engine trouble 11.45 22.8.17 (2/Lt JWR Thompson); 3 TS Shoreham by 1.18; 198 (Night) TS Rochford by 11.9.18, SOC 2.4.19
NB The South Wales Borders badge was applied by 2/Lt A.B.Garnons-Williams, being his parent regiment

B1804   87 Sqdn Hounslow by 12.17; 85 Sqdn Hounslow to 87 Sqdn Hounslow 28.2.18; 85 Sqdn 20.3.18; 92 Sqdn Tangmere 4.4.18; 93 Sqdn Tangmere 7.5.18; 60th Wing to 5(E)ARD Henlow 30.7.18

B1805   (80hp Le Rhône) 61 HD Sqdn Rochford by 2.18 to at least 3.18; 36 HD Sqdn Usworth, mid-air collision with B1763 13.1.19 (Lt F Yorke killed)

B1806   (100hp Gnome Monosoupape) 61 HD Sqdn Rochford by 8.17; Left 17.23 for Anti-Gotha patrol, landed 19.17 12.8.17 (2/Lt JS Wood); Left 10.22 for Anti-Gotha patrol, landed 11.25 22.8.17 (Capt SE Starey); 112 HD Sqdn Throwley (coded 'C-6') late 1917; 61 HD Sqdn Rochford by 6.18

B1807   (100hp Gnome Monosoupape) 112 HD Sqdn Throwley, left 17.40 for Anti-Gotha patrol, landed 19.07 12.8.17 (2/Lt JG Goodyear); Left 10.20 for Anti-Gotha patrol, landed 12.06 22.8.17 (2/Lt NE Chandler); 36 HD Sqdn; 198 (Night) TS Rochford to 76 HD Sqdn (coded 'A7') 18.9.18; 39 Sqdn North Weald Bassett to Southern Area 16.8.19; Became *G-EAVX*, regd by Aircraft Disposal Co, owned by A.R.M.Rickards; Crashed & WO 16.7.21

B1808   61 HD Sqdn Rochford by 2.8.17; Left 10.22 for Anti-Gotha patrol, landed 11.30 22.8.17 (Capt HC Stroud); Forced landed on Southend Pier during balloon practice, crashed on rail and shorted electric railway line, WO 19.10.17 (pilot OK)

B1809   (100hp Gnome Monosoupape No.30559/WD8106 later 130hp Clerget) 61 HD Sqdn Rochford by 8.17; Left 17.23 for Anti-Gotha patrol, landed 19.11 12.8.17 (Capt HC Stroud); Left 10.23 for Anti-Gotha patrol, landed 11.40 22.8.17 (2/Lt JS Wood); Engine failed, turned towards aerodrome but went into flat spin 31.8.17 (2/Lt JS Wood seriously injured)

B1810   61 HD Sqdn Rochford; 112 HD Sqdn Throwley, left 17.25 for Anti-Gotha patrol, retd with gun trouble 18.15, took off again 18.30, landed 19.17 12.8.17 (2/Lt JWR Thompson)

B1811   61 HD Sqdn Rochford, left 17.19 for Anti-Gotha patrol, landed 19.10 12.8.17; Left 10.23 for Anti-Gotha patrol, landed 11.40 22.8.17 (both 2/Lt P Thompson)

B1812   (100hp Gnome Monosoupape) 61 HD Sqdn Rochford by 9.17 to at least 12.17; 87 Sqdn Hounslow by 29.1.18

B1813   43 TS Ternhill by 24.7.17; 95 Sqdn North Shotwick to 37th Wing Half ARS North Shotwick 10.4.18

B1814   At AAP Coventry 17.7.17; Allotted to 46 Sqdn Sutton's Farm but reallotted Expeditionary Force 20.7.17; England to ARS 1 AD 23.7.17; 54 Sqdn 24.7.17; Ran into ditch on landing 27.7.17 (2/Lt K Shelton); ARS 1 AD 29.7.17; SOC 1.8.17

B1815   1 (Observers) School of Aerial Gunnery New Romney by 5.18 to at least 6.18

B1816   Deld Aircraft Park Dover without engine 20.7.17; AD Dunkirk 10.8.17; 11 (N) Sqdn by 14.8.17; AD Dunkirk 31.8.17; 'C' Flt 12 (N) Sqdn from/by 4.9.17; Wrecked 12.9.17; AD Dunkirk 19.9.17; Surveyed 22.9.17; Deleted 27.9.17 Damaged beyond repair

B1817   Deld Aircraft Park Dover without engine 20.7.17; AD Dunkirk 9.8.17; 11 (N) Sqdn by 14.8.17; AD Dunkirk 31.8.17; 'C' Flt 12 (N) Sqdn from/by 4.9.17 to at least 22.11.17; 2 ASD to BAC Paris by transport 11.12.17; RNASTE Vendôme (by rail via Abbeville) W/E 29.11.17 (sic) to at least 30.3.18 (still there, but u/s and engineless)

B1818   Deld Aircraft Park Dover without engine 20.7.17; AD Dunkirk 11.8.17; 11 (N) Sqdn by 16.8.17; AD Dunkirk 31.8.17; 'C' Flt 12 (N) Sqdn from/by 4.9.17 to at least 22.11.17; 2 ASD to BAC Paris by transport 11.12.17; RNASTE Vendôme (by rail via Abbeville) W/E 29.11.17 (sic) to at least 31.3.18 (still there, but u/s and engineless)

B1819   Deld Aircraft Park Dover without engine 22.7.17; AD Dunkirk 11.8.17; Seaplane Defence Sqdn 5.9.17; Aircraft Park Dover 22.10.17; Hendon W/E 3.11.17; RNASTE Cranwell W/E 10.11.17; Surveyed 21.11.17; Deleted 5.12.17 Damaged beyond repair

B1820   Deld Aircraft Park Dover without engine 22.7.17; AD Dunkirk 11.8.17; Seaplane Defence Sqdn 15.8.17; 12 (N) Sqdn 16.11.17; RNASTE Vendôme W/E 6.12.17; Became 205 TDS Vendôme (named *"JOHNNIE WALKER"*) 1.4.18; Went on nose landing, slightly damaged 23.6.18 (Flt Cdt RB Mumford unhurt); Engine failure on take-off, swerved, hit 504J B8635 outside Bessonneau hangar, wrecked 29.7.18 (2/Lt JAVM Robert unhurt); Deleted 15.8.18 but still reported there 11.18

B1821   Deld Aircraft Park Dover without engine 22.7.17; AD Dunkirk 16.8.17; Seaplane Defence Sqdn 5.9.17; Aircraft Park Dover 27.10.17; Eastchurch 5.1.18; Eastbourne Naval Flying School W/E 19.1.18; Crashed on landing 8.6.18 (pilot unhurt)

B1822   Deld Aircraft Park Dover without engine 25.7.17; Walmer Defence Flt 30.9.17; Aircraft Park Dover 5.11.17; East Fortune Naval Flying School by 10.11.17 to at least 30.3.18; Crashed on landing 9.12.17 (FSL AC Sharwood); Still there 30.3.18, but u/s and engineless; Became 208 TDS East Fortune 1.4.18

B1823   Deld Aircraft Park Dover without engine 25.7.17; AD Dunkirk 16.8.17; Walmer Defence Flt 29.9.17; East Fortune Naval Flying School u/s by 10.11.17; Apparently serviceable 6.1.18; Deleted 9.2.18 u/s

B1824   (80hp Le Rhône) Deld RNASTE Cranwell store 24.7.17; Collided FSL Wood in B.E.2e outside 'G' Flight hangar 12.9.17 (FSL HLP Lester); Surveyed 14.9.17; Deleted 8.10.17 wrecked

B1825   (80hp Gnome) Deld RNASTE Cranwell store 25.7.17; Became 201/202 TDS Cranwell 1.4.18; 208 TDS East Fortune W/E 6.4.18

B1826   (80hp Le Rhône No.234/WD6181) At 6 SD Ascot 30.7.17, allotted to Expeditionary Force; England to ARS 1 AD in case without engine 8.8.17; 66 Sqdn 5.9.17; FTR from OP [in Roulers area?] 24.9.17 (Lt D Moir Paton killed) [Sopwith claimed in combat north-west of Dixmude 13.00 German time by Obltn B Loerzer, Jasta 26]

B1827   At 6 SD Ascot 30.7.17, allotted to Expeditionary Force; England to ARS 1 AD in case without engine 10.8.17; ARS 2 AD 18.9.17; 46 Sqdn 20.9.17; Aviatik C crashed Pelves shared with B1828, B2186 11.50 25.9.17 (Lt PWS Bulman); 2 ASD 13.12.17 (exchanged for a Camel); 2 ASD Scout School, Candas 21.12.17 (for storage only); 2 AI 5.2.18; Rep Pk 2 ASD 9.2.18; 2 AI 18.2.18; 2 ASD to England via Rec Pk 27.4.18; Tested at 1 (S)ARD Farnborough 11.5.18

B1828   At 6 SD Ascot 30.7.17, allotted to Expeditionary Force; England to ARS 1 AD in case without engine 7.8.17; 46 Sqdn 4.9.17; Albatros D.V crashed nr Douai 09.30-10.15 21.9.17; Aviatik C crashed Pelves, shared with B1827 & B2186 11.50 25.9.17 (both 2/Lt PW Wilcox); Practice flight, crashed and wrecked 11.30 10.11.17 (2/Lt AJ Ballantyne died of injuries); Rep Pk 2 ASD 11.11.17; SOC

B1829   At 6 SD Ascot 30.7.17, allotted to Expeditionary Force; England to ARS 1 AD in case without engine 8.8.17; 46 Sqdn 6.9.17; DFW C crashed south-east of Havrincourt Wood shared with B1802, B1837 & B2191 10.30 24.9.17 (2/Lt E Armitage); Offensive patrol, after combat crashed in a trench nr Wailly with engine failure 30.9.17 (2/Lt CW Odell); ARS 2 AD 2.10.17; SOC 8.10.17

B1830   At 6 SD Ascot 30.7.17, allotted to Expeditionary Force; England to ARS 1 AD in case without engine 9.8.17; 66 Sqdn 20.9.17; Offensive patrol, last seen with formation at 12,000ft over Ypres 12.15 12.10.17 (2/Lt RWB Matthewson PoW) [possibly the Sopwith 1-str claimed in combat north-west of Moorslede 11.15 by Ltn H von Häebler, Jasta 36]

B1831   At 6 SD Ascot 30.7.17, allotted to Expeditionary Force; England to ARS 1 AD in case without engine 7.8.17; 66 Sqdn 3.9.17; Practice flight, landed 1m south-east of Armentières, wrecked 5.9.17 (Lt J Fitzgerald slight injuries); ARS 1 AD 7.9.17; SOC 26.9.17

B1832   England to ARS 1 AD 25.8.17, allotted to Expeditionary Force 28.8.17; 66 Sqdn 4.9.17; ARS 1 AD 15.10.17 exchanged for a Camel; ARS 2 AD 21.10.17; At 2 ASD Scout School, Candas by 31.12.17; Rep Pk 2 ASD 22.3.18; Rep Pk 1 ASD 1.4.18

B1833   At AAP Lympne 21.9.17, allotted to Expeditionary Force; England to ARS 1 AD 25.9.17; 100 Sqdn 29.9.17; Left behind on Sqdn move 10.17; ARS 1 AD 5.10.17; Became Rep Pk 1 ASD 1.11.17; Rec Pk 13.1.18; Flown back to England 25.1.18; 5th (T) Sqdn AFC Minchinhampton; 6th (T) Sqdn AFC Minchinhampton

B1834   Presentation aircraft 'Gold Coast Aborigines No.2' (succeeded B1775). At AAP Lympne 21.9.17, allotted to Expeditionary Force; ARS 1 AD 27.9.17; 54 Sqdn 14.10.17; Left 13.45, OP to Keyem, in combat east of lines, collided with B1782 nr Beerst 22.10.17 (2/Lt P Goodbehere PoW) [both credited to Ltn Max von Müller, Jasta 28 who claimed them as Camels]

B1835   8 AAP Lympne to ARS 1 AD 30.8.17; ARS 1 AD to 66 Sqdn 1.9.17; On 06.15 OP, forced landed nr Bailleul, crashed 7.10.17 (2/Lt GL Dore wounded in leg); ARS 1 AD 7.10.17; SOC 14.10.17

B1836   At 8 AAP Lympne 21.9.17, allotted to Expeditionary Force; ARS 1 AD 28.9.17; 66 Sqdn 30.9.17; Offensive patrol, last seen with formation at 12,000ft over Ypres 12.10.17 (2/Lt AW Nasmyth killed) [Sopwith 1-seater claimed in combat Westroosebeke 11.15 by Ltn H Hoyer, Jasta 36]

B1839 of No.64 Squadron, inscribed 'Presented by the Citizens of the Town & District of Thana, being inspected after overturning during working up at Sedgeford in September 1917. The squadron left for France the following month equipped with D.H.5s. *(Don Neate/)*

B1837   At AAP Coventry 31.7.17, allotted to Expeditionary Force; To 46 Sqdn Sutton's Farm 8.17; Anti-Gotha patrol 12.8.17 (2/Lt E Armitage); To France with Sqdn 30.8.17; Albatros C out of control south of Scarpe River, shared with A6188, B1802, B1842 & B1843 09.30 4.9.17 (2/Lt E Armitage); 2-str out of control south of Scarpe shared with A6188, B1777 & B1843 10.55 11.9.17 (Lt E Armitage); DFW C crashed south-east of Havrincourt Wood shared with B1802, B1829 & B2191 10.30 24.9.17 (Lt C Courtneidge); On test flight misjudged landing and crashed 29.9.17 (2/Lt EY Hughes OK); 2 AD 1.10.17; SOC 8.10.17

B1838   (80hp Le Rhône No.35132/WD10981) At AAP Coventry 4.8.17 allotted to Expeditionary Force; England to ARS 1 AD 9.8.17; 66 Sqdn 13.8.17; Offensive patrol, shot down, last seen fighting low down over Menin-Roulers road around 07.15 4.9.17 (Lt SA Harper MC PoW wounded) [claimed by Ltn E von Stapenhorst, Jasta 11]

B1839   Presentation aircraft inscribed 'Presented by the Citizens of the Town & District of Thana'. At AAP Coventry 1.8.17, allotted to Expeditionary Force but reallotted to Training Brigade 8.8.17; 64 Sqdn, crashed Sedgeford, overturned 9.17; SOC 28.9.17

B1840   81 Sqdn Scampton by 5.18

B1841   At makers 27.7.17, allotted 46 Sqdn; To 46 Sqdn Sutton's Farm 8.17; Anti-Gotha patrol 12.8.17 (2/Lt GE Thomson); To France with Sqdn 30.8.17; Crashed on landing Le Hameau 18.9.17 (2/Lt DS Smallman injured); ARS 2 AD 20.9.17; SOC 26.9.17

B1842   At makers 27.7.17, allotted to 46 Sqdn Sutton's Farm; Anti-Gotha patrol 12.8.17 (2/Lt CW Odell); To France with Sqdn 30.8.17; Albatros C out of control south of Scarpe River, shared with A6188, B1802, B1837 & B1843 09.30 4.9.17 (2/Lt CW Odell); Damaged in combat 5.9.17 (2/Lt CW Odell OK – claimed by Ltn Werner Voss, Jasta 10); ARS 1 AD 6.9.17; SOC 26.9.17

B1843   At makers 27.7.17, allotted 46 Sqdn; To 46 Sqdn Sutton's Farm 8.17; Anti-Gotha patrol 12.8.17 (Capt MDG Scott); To France with Sqdn 30.8.17; Albatros C out of control south of Scarpe River, shared with A6188, B1802, B1837 & B1842 09.30 4.9.17; Albatros D crashed also 2-str out of control south of Scarpe, the latter shared with A6188, B1777 & B1837 10.55 11.9.17 (Capt MDG Scott); Wrecked on take off when undercarriage strut gave way 18.9.17 (Capt MDG Scott OK); ARS 19.9.17; SOC 22.9.17

B1844   School of Special Flying, Gosport by 9.8.17 to at least 7.9.17; 62 Sqdn Rendcomb by 30.10.17; 10 TS Shawbury by 18.12.17; 67 TS Shawbury by 3.18; 67 TS moved to North Shotwick 1.4.18; 37th Wing Half ARS North Shotwick 2.4.18

B1845   CFS 'D' Sqdn Upavon, crashed while looping at 100ft 3.5.18 (2/Lt CJ Ford killed)

B1846   At AAP Coventry 4.8.17; allotted to Expeditionary Force; England to ARS 1 AD 9.8.17; 66 Sqdn 11.8.17; Crashed on take off from forced landing 23.8.17 (2/Lt TJ McInnes); ARS 1 AD 24.8.17; SOC 26.8.17

B1847   18th Wing Fighting School London Colney by 28.9.17

B1848   198 (Night) TS Rochford to 19.3.19

B1849   (80hp Clerget No.1126/WD11128) Gosport by 9.17; 10 TS Lilbourne (coded 'B') by 4.18 to at least 17.6.18; Prop accident 6.5.18 (Cpl Mech EC Dean slightly injured)

B1850   67 TS Shawbury to 4 TDS Hooton Park 14.12.17 to at least 17.12.17; 10 TS Shawbury by 18.12.17; With 10 TS to Gosport 25.6.18

100 SOPWITH PUP ordered 4.17 additionally under Contract number 87/A/1101 from Whitehead Aircraft Ltd, Richmond, Surrey and numbered B2151 to B2250. (Ordered with 80hp Le Rhône 9C but some fitted with 80hp Gnome Lambda)

B2151   (80hp Le Rhône No.100224) At makers Feltham 30.4.17; allotted to Expeditionary Force; To France without engine 5.17; ARS 1AD by 26.5.17; ARS 2 AD to 54 Sqdn 31.5.17; Albatros D out of control east of St Emile, shared with A640, A6172, A6183, A7330 & B1730 0.645 3.6.17 (Capt RGH Pixley MC); Left 05.00 as part of escort to FEs, in combat with enemy aircraft Le Catelat, shot down Auben-en-Bois by Ltn Werner Voss, Jasta 5 07.10 4.6.17 (Capt RGH Pixley MC killed)

B2152   At makers Feltham 30.4.17, allotted to Expeditionary Force; En route to Lympne 9.5.17, reallotted to Training Brigade; Further reallotted to Expeditionary Force 14.5.17, but again realloted to Training Brigade 17.5.17; 56 TS London Colney by 6.17 to at least 11.17; Landed Queniborough, Leics LG, sun in eyes, prop hit ridge, went on nose 21.9.17 (2/Lt WFG Marsh unhurt); 3 TS Shoreham to 18th Wing ARS Hounslow 23.12.17; SOC 4.1.18

B2153   At makers Feltham 30.4.17, allotted to Expeditionary Force; En route to Lympne 9.5.17, reallotted to Training Brigade; Further reallotted to Expeditionary Force 14.5.17, but again reallotted to Training Brigade 17.5.17; 56 RS London Colney by 5.17; 40 RS Croydon by 10.6.17; Bumpy weather, bent axle landing 24.6.17 (2/Lt RE Taylor)

B2154   (Gnome) At makers Feltham 30.4.17, allotted to Expeditionary Force; En route to Lympne 9.5.17, reallotted to Training Brigade; Further reallotted to Expeditionary Force 14.5.17, but again reallotted to Training Brigade 17.5.17; 56 TS London Colney by 20.6.17 to at least 11.17 (now 110hp Le Rhône); 85 Sqdn to 18th Wing ARS Hounslow 23.12.17; SOC 4.1.18

B2155   At makers 5.6.17, allotted to Expeditionary Force; England to ARS 1 AD in case without engine 20.6.17; 54 Sqdn 7.7.17; On travelling flight to new aerodrome, turned over on landing 16.7.17 (2/Lt CG Wood); ARS 1 AD 19.7.17; SOC 23.7.17

B2156   At makers 5.6.17, allotted to Expeditionary Force; England to ARS 2 AD in case without engine 20.6.17; ARS 1 AD 10.7.17; 54 Sqdn 16.7.17; On 09.15s OP damaged by shrapnel from an AA shell 21.8.17 (2/Lt TL Tebbit unhurt); ARS 1 AD and SOC 23.8.17

B2157   61 HD Sqdn Rochford, Anti-Gotha patrol 12.8.17; Anti-Gotha patrol 22.8.17 (both Lt JT Collier); 29th TS (AFC) Shawbury; 5th (T) Sqdn AFC Minchinhampton; 6th (T) Sqdn AFC Minchinhampton

B2158   112 HD Sqdn Throwley, Anti-Gotha patrol, retd with engine trouble 12.8.17 (2/Lt AJ Arkell); Anti-Gotha patrol 22.8.17 (2/Lt AJ Arkell)

B2159   61 HD Sqdn Rochford, Anti-Gotha patrol 12.8.17; Anti-Gotha patrol 22.8.17 (both Capt CB Cooke); Northolt 19.1.18; 86 Sqdn Northolt by 12.3.18; WO 19.3.18

B2160   En route to ARS 1 AD via Newhaven 6.7.17, allotted to Expeditionary Force; Arr ARS 1 AD in case without engine 13.7.17; 54 Sqdn 26.7.17; Offensive patrol, on landing turned over in cornfield 7.8.17 (Sgt EF Smith); ARS 1 AD 9.8.17; SOC 10.8.17

B2161   En route to France via Newhaven 6.7.17; Arr ARS 2 AD in case without engine 10.7.17; ARS 1 AD 31.7.17; 54 Sqdn 15.8.17; Left 06.45, OP to St.Pierre Capelle-Zarren, in combat east of lines, went down over Zarren 13.10.17 (2/Lt JHR Salter killed) [Sopwith 1-str claimed 07.55 [German time?] at Praet Bosch by Lt H Klein, Jasta 10]

The remains of B2180 'G' of No.46 Squadron after being shot down by Ltn W Ewers of Jasta 12, 11th October 1917. It was piloted by an American, 2/Lt A.A.Allen, who was killed, his aircraft being last seen in combat over Marquion.   *(via Frank Cheesman)*

B2162   En route to France via Newhaven 9.7.17; Arr ARS 1 AD in case without engine 13.7.17; 66 Sqdn (coded 'N') 24.7.17 (fitted Lewis gun on centre section); Albatros D.III destroyed east of Roulers, shared with B1762 28.7.17 (2/Lt FG Huxley); Albatros D out of control Roulers 0715 4.9.17 (2/Lt WA Pritt MC); On 10.00 OP, Albatros destroyed, then crashed 30.9.17 (2/Lt WA Pritt, MC); ARS 1 AD 1.10.17; SOC 5.10.17

B2163   (Gnome Monosoupape) 74 Sqdn London Colney by 14.9.17; 18th Wing ARS Hounslow 23.12.17; SOC 4.1.18

B2164   (80hp Gnome later 80hp Le Rhône No.59813) 81 Sqdn Scampton, stalled at 50ft, crashed 20.11.17 (pilot injured); 'C' Flt CFS Upavon, stalled on left hand turn 23.1.18 (Sgt JN Temple slightly injured); 37 TDS Yatesbury, hit tree 20.9.18 (Lt GA Gowler injured)

B2165   65 Sqdn Wye by 15.8.17; 94 Sqdn Harling Road by 10.17 to at least 2.11.17

B2166   (80hp Clerget) 81 Sqdn Scampton by 20.8.17; Stalled at 50ft, crashed 20.11.17 (2/Lt JT Rymer slightly injured)

B2167   At makers 5.9.17, allotted to Expeditionary Force; England to ARS 1 AD in case without engine 16.9.17; 66 Sqdn (coded 'L') 24.9.17; ARS 1 AD 15.10.17 (exchanged for a Camel) SOC 18.10.17

B2168   At makers 5.9.17, allotted to Expeditionary Force; England to ARS 1 AD in case without engine 16.9.17; 66 Sqdn 23.9.17 (fitted Lewis gun on centre section); Left on OP 10.00, Albatros down smoking Menin 12.00, own aircraft damaged, forced landed Kemmel 30.9.17 (Capt TPH Bayetto wounded); ARS 1 AD 1.10.17; SOC 5.10.17

B2169   'B' Sqdn CFS Upavon late 1917/early 1918

B2170   (80hp Le Rhône) 'B' Sqdn CFS Upavon by 30.6.17 to at least 31.8.17

B2171   (80hp Le Rhône No.1048/WD8021) 'B' Sqdn CFS Upavon, climbing turn, then stalled and spun in 30.8.17 (2/Lt HW Evans died of injuries)

B2172   No information

B2173   (80hp Le Rhône No.8283) Deld RNASTE Cranwell for erection 10.9.17; Crashed and badly damaged Cranwell South 10.3.18 (pilot unhurt); Fully serviceable by 30.3.18; Became 201/202 TDS Cranwell 1.4.18

B2174   En route from makers to Newhaven 5.9.17, allotted to Expeditionary Force without engine; ARS 1 AD to 66 Sqdn 14.10.17; ARS 1 AD 19.10.17 (exchanged for a Camel); 54 Sqdn 31.10.17; Rep Pk 1 ASD to Rec Pk 28.12.17; Flown back to England 23.1.18

B2175   'B' Sqdn CFS Upavon by 4.7.17

B2176   En route from makers to Newhaven 9.7.17, allotted to Expeditionary Force; England to ARS 1 AD in case without engine 14.7.17; 66 Sqdn 28.7.17 (fitted Lewis gun on centre section); 2 Albatros D.III driven down, one apparently out of control Houthulst Wood 19.45 17.8.17; Albatros D forced to land Ypres-Menin road 19.35 21.8.17 (all 2/Lt EH Lascelles); ARS 1 AD 15.10.17; ARS 2 AD 24.10.17 (exchanged for a Camel) ; SOC 2.1.18

B2177   (80hp Le Rhône No.35121/WD10970) En route from makers to Newhaven 9.7.17, allotted to Expeditionary Force; England to ARS 2 AD in case without engine 13.7.17; ARS 1 AD 31.7.17; 66 Sqdn (coded '3') 18.8.17; Offensive patrol, seen to dive on enemy aircraft north-west of Roulers 21.8.17 (2/Lt PH Raney killed) [believed Sopwith 1-str claimed east of Ypres by Ltn E Weiss, Jasta 28]

B2178   112 HD Sqdn Throwley (coded '6', named 'MADGE'), cowl blown off, forced landed, hit fence, crashed 18.2.18 (pilot injured)

B2179   En route from makers to Newhaven 9.7.17.allotted to Expeditionary Force; Wye by 8.17 [65 Sqdn?]; 28 TS Castle Bromwich by 27.12.17

B2180   En route from makers to Newhaven 9.7.17, allotted to Expeditionary Force; England to ARS 1 AD in case without engine 15.7.17; 46 Sqdn (coded 'G') 3.9.17; Crashed on landing 16.35 5.9.17 (2/Lt DS Smallman); Left on DOP Bourlon Wood 15.25, last seen in combat over Marquion 11.10.17 (2/Lt AA Allen USA killed) [claimed in combat Sains-les-Marquion 16.45 by Ltn W Ewers, Jasta 12]

B2181   (80hp Le Rhône) Deld RNASTE Cranwell 18.9.17; Collided with B2208 and slightly damaged 16.2.18 (pilot unhurt); Serviceable by 30.3.18; Became 201/202 TDS Cranwell 1.4.18; Became 56 TDS Cranwell 27.7.18 to at least 11.18

B2182 En route from makers to Newhaven 12.7.17, allotted to Expeditionary Force; England to ARS 2 AD in case without engine 14.7.17; ARS 1 AD 5.8.17; 66 Sqdn 22.8.17 (fitted Lewis gun on centre section); ARS 1 AD 15.10.17 (exchanged for a Camel); ARS 2 AD 24.10.17; 46 Sqdn 22.11.17; 2 ASD 13.12.17 (exchanged for a Camel); 2 AI to 2 ASD Scout School, Candas 19.1.18; 2 AI 5.2.18; Rec Pk 18.2.18; Flown back to England 21.2.18; 74 TS Castle Bromwich by 17.3.18

B2183 (80hp Le Rhône) Deld RNASTE Cranwell 18.9.17; Became 201/202 TDS Cranwell 1.4.18 to at least 5.18

B2184 At 6 SD Ascot 30.7.17, allotted to Expeditionary Force; England to ARS 1AD in case without engine 9.8.17; ARS 2 AD 23.9.17; ARS 1 AD 29.9.17; 66 Sqdn 2.10.17; ARS 1 AD 20.10.17 (exchanged for a Camel); At Rep Pk 1 ASD 29.12.17; Rec Pk 9.1.18; Flown back to England 13.1.18; 10 TDS Harling Road by 18.10.18

B2185 (80hp Le Rhône No.35040/WD2541) 56 TS London Colnet by 9-18.6.17; En route from makers to Newhaven 12.7.17, allotted to Expeditionary Force; England to ARS 2AD in case without engine 14.7.17; ARS 1 AD 31.7.17; 66 Sqdn 16.8.17; (fitted Lewis gun on centre section); FTR from 10.00 Offensive patrol, spun in south of Gheluwe 30.9.17 (2/Lt JG Warter killed) [Sopwith claimed in combat Ploegsteert Wood 11.55 by Ltn J Veltjens, Jasta 18 or Sopwith claimed in combat Deulemont 11.50 by Obltn R Bertholt, Jasta 18?]

B2186 At 6 SD Ascot 30.7.17, allotted to Expeditionary Force; England to ARS 1 AD in case without engine 9.8.17; ARS 2 AD 20.9.17; 46 Sqdn 21.9.17; Aviatik C crashed Pelves shared with B1827 & B1828 11.50 25.9.17 (2/Lt EG Thomson); Left 06.40, bombing operation to Havrincourt, shot up, crashed on landing 08.40 20.11.17 (2/Lt EG Thomson unhurt); Rep Pk 2 ASD 20.11.17

B2187 At 6 SD Ascot 30.7.17, allotted to Expeditionary Force; England to ARS 1 AD in case without engine 9.8.17; ARS 2 AD 18.9.17; 46 Sqdn 19.9.17; 2 ASD 15.11.17 (exchanged for a Camel); Flown back to England 8.12.17; Erecting Park 8 AAP Lympne to 87 Sqdn 25.12.17; 85 Sqdn Hounslow, WO 7.3.18

B2188 At 6 SD Ascot 30.7.17, allotted to Expeditionary Force; England to ARS 1 AD in case without engine 11.8.17; 101 Sqdn 29.9.17; Special Duty Flight, 54th Wing 10.2.18: On delivery to 'I' Flt, crashed on landing St.André 10.6.18 (Capt AF Lindo OK); Rep Pk 1 AD 11.6.18 (attd 58 Sqdn); SOC 15.6.18 NWR

B2189 At 6 SD Ascot 30.7.17, allotted to Expeditionary Force; England to ARS 1 AD in case without engine 8.8.17; 66 Sqdn 25.9.17; Special mission, forced landed Treizennes, undercarriage wrecked 1.10.17 (2/Lt R Erskine); ARS 1 AD 3.10.17; SOC 7.10.17

B2190 At makers Feltham 30.6.17, allotted to Expeditionary Force; At AID Farnborough 20.7.17, now on charge to E.1 Repair Section and to go to (S)ARD Farnborough

B2191 At 6 SD Ascot 30.7.17, allotted to Expeditionary Force; England to ARS 1AD in case without engine 9.8.17; ARS 2 AD and on to 46 Sqdn 19.9.17; LVG C out of control south of Scarpe shared with A6188, B1837 & B1843 10.55 11.9.17; Albatros D out of control south of Scarpe, shared with A6188 & B1777 08.20 21.9.17; DFW C crashed SE Havrincourt wood, shared with B1802, B1829 & B1837 10.30 24.9.17; 2 Albatros D.V out of control Vitry 16.30-16.35 30.9.17 (all Capt MDG Scott); Albatros D crashed nr Cambrai 09.10 1.12.17 (Lt EY Hughes); 2 ASD 13.12.17 (exchanged for a Camel); 2AI to Rec Pk and on to England 24.1.18; 10 TS Lilbourne by 18.2.18; With 10 TS to Gosport 25.6.18 – 27.9.18

B2192 (100hp Gnome Monosoupape B-2) School of Special Flying Gosport by 8.17 (Capt HH Balfour, horizontal black & white stripes on fuselage and wings, also flown by Capt EL Foot MC); 62 Sqdn Rendcomb by 6.10.17; 43 TS Ternhill, engine failure during formation flying, forced landed nr a/f 15.3.18 (2/Lt FJ Wolno)

B2193 School of Special Flying, Gosport by 6.9.17

B2194 112 HD Sqdn Throwley (coded '3'), left 10.21 for Anti-Gotha patrol, landed 12.05 22.8.17 (Lt JS Poole); 29 TS AFC Shawbury 1917; 198 (Night) TS Rochford, crashed on landing Eastbourne 23.3.18 (pilot OK); 37 HD Sqdn Stow Maries to 61 HD Sqdn Rochford 11.3.19; 37 HD Sqdn Stow Maries 24.5.19; WO 16.8.19

B2195 112 HD Sqdn Throwley, left for Anti-Gotha patrol 10.20, landed 11.45 22.8.17 (Lt CRW Knight)

B2196 'B' Flt 28 Sqdn Yatesbury by 10.8.17; 55 TS Yatesbury by 8.17; 98 Sqdn Old Sarum to 103 Sqdn Old Sarum 14.1.18

B2197 (80hp Le Rhône No.35054/WD2555) At makers Feltham 25.7.17, allotted to Expeditionary Force; England to ARS 1AD 5.8.17; 66 Sqdn 22.8.17; Shot down, last seen fighting low down over the Menin-Roulers road around 07.15 4.9.17 (Capt CC Sharp PoW wounded) [believed shot down south of Ypres 09.45 by Vzfw K Wusthoff, Jasta 4]

B2198 63 TS Joyce Green by 13.8.17; 46 Sqdn by 10.17; 94 Sqdn Harling Road by 6.12.17

B2199 65 Sqdn Wye by 8.17; 94 Sqdn Harling Road by 10.17; Crashed in hedge (unit'?); Crashed in field (unit'?)

B2200 CFS 'C' Sqdn Upavon by 16.1.18

B2201 84 Sqdn Lilbourne by 7.17

B2202 (80hp Gnome) Deld RNASTE Cranwell without engine W/E 5.9.17; U/s at 30.3.18; Became 201/202 TDS Cranwell 1.4.18; 211 TDS Portholme Meadow by 6.6.18; 188 (Night) TS Throwley

B2203 (80hp Gnome) Deld RNASTE Cranwell without engine W/E 5.9.17; Crashed and damaged propeller and undercarriage 11.1.18 (pilot unhurt); Crashed and damaged axle, Cranwell South 26.3.18 (pilot unhurt); Became 201/202 TDS Cranwell 1.4.18; Crashed and damaged 4.4.18 (pilot unhurt); 74 TS Castle Bromwich 2.6.18 to at least 13.6.18; 32 TDS Montrose from 17.7.18

B2204 (80hp Gnome) Deld RNASTE Cranwell without engine 11.9.17; Engine failure, forced landed, undamaged, Ballisford 13.3.18 (pilot unhurt); Became 201/202 TDS Cranwell 1.4.18

B2205 Deld RNASTE Cranwell without engine W/E 5.9.17; Surveyed 27.11.17; Deleted 6.12.17 wrecked

B2206 6 TS Montrose to 32 TDS Montrose 15.7.18; Flown Beaulieu to Hendon 29.7.18; Once coded '16' (training aircraft)

B2207 (80hp Clerget) 36 TS Montrose by 1.18; 30th Wing ARS Montrose to 36 TS Montrose 16.5.18; 30th Wing ARS Montrose 22.5.18; 36 TS Montrose 4.6.18; 30th Wing ARS Montrose 19.6.18; 6 TS Montrose 11.7.18; 32 TDS Montrose 15.7.18

B2208 (80hp Gnome) Deld 'G' (Experimental) Flt Cranwell by road W/E 5.9.17; Collided with B2181 and completely wrecked 16.2.18 (pilot unhurt); Surveyed 25.2.18; Deleted 13.3.18

B2209 188 (Night) TS Throwley to 76 HD Sqdn 27.9.18; SOC 24.4.19

B2210 (100hp Gnome Monosoupape) 112 HD Sqdn Throwley (coded '7') by autumn 1917 to at least 3.18

B2211 (80hp Gnome) Deld RNASTE Cranwell for erection 11.9.17; Crashed on aerodrome and badly damaged 1.3.18 (pilot unhurt); Fully serviceable by 30.3.18; Became 201/202 TDS Cranwell 1.4.18; 208 TDS East Fortune W/E 6.4.18; Grand Fleet School of Aerial Fighting & Gunnery Leuchars by 7.19 to at least 8.19

B2221 after emerging from the production line in the Whitehead factory at Richmond, Surrey in September 1917. The firm proudly advertised them in both 'Flight' and 'The Aeroplane' magazines as "Whitehead Fighting Scouts". The aircraft shows the consistent factory finish of Cellon Scheme B as applied to these aircraft.
(via Philip Jarrett)

B2212   (80hp Le Rhône) Deld RNAS Manston War Flt (coded '6') W/E 15.9.17; U/c broke taxying after landing 29.1.18 (PFO JL Allison); Experimental Constructive & Armament Dept, Grain W/E 23.2.18 (experiments); Eastbourne (for Grain) 23.3.18

B2213   (80hp Le Rhône) RNAS Manston War Flt W/E 15.9.17; 206 TDS Eastbourne 25.4.18; Became 50 TDS Eastbourne 15.7.18; 157 Sqdn Upper Heyford 1.8.18; Tank on fire, flew into ground, burnt out 4.8.18 (Lt WC Williams injured)

B2214   56 TS London Colney by 18.11.17; Crashed 21.12.17; SOC

B2215   3 TDS Lopcombe Corner by 31.10.17

B2216   61 HD Sqdn Rochford by 11.6.18; 198 (Night) TS Rochford to 75 HD Sqdn North Weald 30.11.18; SOC 20.4.19

B2217   Deld Killingholme store 15.9.17; Experimental Constructive Dept, Grain 16.12.17 (Experiments) (80hp Clerget No.5709 by 12.1.18, serviceable with 80hp Le Rhône by 30.3.18); Rosyth 23.3.18 (via Cranwell and Lincoln); retd Experimental Constructive Dept, Grain (via Cranwell) 3.4.18; Northolt by 5.18; Hendon 14.5.18; Salisbury 18.5.18; Stonehenge to Grain (via Hendon) 19.5.18; Hendon 4.6.18; Grain 5.6.18; Hendon by 4.7.18; Grain by/to 2.20 (W/Cdr HR Busteed's aircraft); Crashed during practice landing on single wire overhead [presumably with Grain experimental overwing hook] 2.3.20 (W/Cdr HR Busteed); Pulham (cable landing experiments)

B2218   61 TS South Carlton by 25.5.18; 506 Flt 251 Sqdn Owthorne by 10.18 to at least 6.11.18 (white fin with spitting cat)

B2219   91 Sqdn Chattis Hill from 27.10.17

B2220   At 7 AAP Kenley 1.9.17, allotted to Expeditionary Force; England to ARS 1 AD 14.9.17; 66 Sqdn 26.9.17; Test flight, damaged landing 15.10.17 (2/Lt TJ McInnis); ARS 1 AD 16.10.17; SOC 18.10.17

B2221   At 7 AAP Kenley 5.9.17, allotted to Expeditionary Force; England to ARS 1 AD 15.9.17; 66 Sqdn 18.9.17 (fitted Lewis gun on centre section); ARS 1 AD 20.10.17 (exchanged for a Camel); SOC 22.10.17

B2222   (100hp Gnome Monosoupape) 61 HD Sqdn Rochford by 10.17

B2223   (80hp Le Rhône) At makers 5.9.17, allotted to Expeditionary Force; England to ARS 1 AD in case without engine 17.9.17; Became Rep Pk 1 ASD 1.11.17; 54 Sqdn 18.11.17; Rep Pk 1 ASD to Rec Pk 28.12.17; Flown back to England 4.1.18; 94 Sqdn Harling Road from 19.1.18; To 26th Wing ARS Thetford, undercarriage collapsed on landing 28.5.18 (Mjr AJ Capel unhurt)

B2224   At makers 5.9.17, allotted to Expeditionary Force; England to ARS 1 AD in case without engine 17.9.17; Became Rep Pk 1 ASD 1.11.17 to at least 11.11.17

B2225   No information

B2226   (80hp Le Rhône) Deld RNASTE Cranwell for erection 11.9.17; Became 201/202 TDS Cranwell 1.4.18

B2227   34 TDS Scampton by 10.18 to at least 7.12.18

B2228   39 TS South Carlton by 15.5.18

B2229   'D' & 'C' Sqdns CFS Upavon by 2.1.18 to at least 9.3.18

B2230   7th Wing ARS Norwich to 87 Sqdn Sedgeford 26.11.17; 87 Sqdn to Hounslow 19.12.17; Crashed nr airfield 31.12.17 (Lt EL Smithers); SOC 4.1.18

B2231   81 Sqdn Scampton by 1.10.17; 1 AAP Coventry to Catterick 8.3.18

B2232   Flown from Farnborough to 'B' Sqdn CFS Upavon by Lt J Oliver 13.9.17; Chattis Hill 14.9.17

B2233   (100hp Gnome Monosoupape B-2) 56 TS London Colney by 9.17; Wheel broke landing, overturned 26.10.17 (2/Lt JA Aldridge); Caught fire in air, forced landed, burnt out 8.3.18 (2/Lt P McAllen slightly injured); SOC 9.3.18

B2234   56 TS London Colney by 9.17; 18th Wing ARS Hounslow 6.11.17

B2235   34 TDS Scampton by 13.10.18

B2236   (80hp Gnome) 42 TS Wye, engine trouble at 100ft, stalled into trees 14.2.18 (2/Lt WS Wheeler injured)

B2237   (80hp Le Rhône No.5498/WD10864) CFS Upavon by 12.17; Caught fire in the air, dived in 26.2.18 (2/Lt WT Galbraith killed)

B2238   CFS Upavon by 12.17 – 1.18; 3 TDS Lopcombe Corner by 15.5.18

B2239   (80hp Gnome) 1 TS Beaulieu, choked engine, crashed 9.12.17 (2/Lt JW Savignac injured)

B2240   CFS 'C' & 'A' Sqdns by 6.12.17 to at least 11.18

B2241   No information

A line-up of Pups of No.61 (Home Defence) Squadron at Rochford in October 1917. Aircraft identifiable, from right to left, are B2222, B1812, B1764 'C4' and B5905, the latter with a Lewis gun on the centre section.
(J.M.Bruce/G.S.Leslie collection)

B2242   6 TS Montrose, crashed 13.11.17 (2/Lt RB Esdaile killed)

B2243   54 TS Eastbourne by 7.18 (error for B2245?); 34 TDS Scampton by 12.10.18

B2244   54 TS Harlaxton by 27.10.17 to at least 4.11.17

B2245   10 TS Shawbury by 14.12.17; 74 TS Castle Bromwich by 25.2.18 to at least 24.4.18; 54 TS Castle Bromwich, moved to Eastbourne 6.7.18

B2246   (100hp Gnome Monosoupape B-2) 54 TS Harlaxton, spinning nose dive from 200ft, possibly due to damage to aircraft 7.12.17 (2/Lt JR Falck killed)

B2247   (80hp Gnome) 73 TS Turnhouse, lost propeller, spiralled in 19.10.17 (2/Lt PA Anderson killed)

B2248   87 Sqdn Sedgeford by 15-17.10.17; 7th Wing ARS to 94 Sqdn Harling Road 12.12.17

B2249   53 Sqdn by 3.18 [unlikely?]

B2250   87 Sqdn Sedgeford by 13.10.17 to at least 6.12.17

200 rebuilds at 2(N)ARD Coal Aston numbered B4001 to B4200, included these Pups

B4100   60 TDS Aboukir by 12.18; Unknown Middle East unit (coded'B'), crashed

B4121   58 TS Suez by 26.9.18
         [Probably incorrect as this serial was issued to an F.K.]

B4123   43 TDS Chattis Hill by 1.19

B4124   (80hp Le Rhône 9C) Issued for training W/E 13.5.18; 30th Wing ARS Montrose to 6 TS Montrose by 13.5.18; WO & SOC 27.5.18

B4125   Issued for Expeditionary Force W/E 27.5.18 (NTU?); 143 HD Sqdn Detling, SOC 28.7.19

B4126   (80hp Le Rhône 9C) Issued for training W/E 15.4.18; 45 TS South Carlton, stalled on turn, spun in 2.6.18 (2/Lt KW Allman killed)

B4127   Issued for training W/E 6.5.18

B4128   (80hp Le Rhône 9C) School of Special Flying Gosport [or TS in 19th Wing, Catterick?] (named "ICKLE POOP" with black and yellow or orange vertical fuselage stripes)

B4129   (80hp Le Rhône 9C) Issued for training W/E 10.6.18

B4130   (80hp Le Rhône 9C) Issued for training W/E 10.6.18; School for Marine Operational Pilots, Dover by 26.12.18

B4131   Issued for training W/E 13.5.18

B4132   (80hp Le Rhône 9C) Issued for training W/E 10.6.18;

B4135   Issued for training W/E 20.5.18; 2 TDS Gullane to ARS Gullane 18.6.18

B4136   (80hp Le Rhône 9C) Issued for training W/E 10.6.18; 47 TDS Doncaster, mid-air collision, crashed 3.10.18 (2/Lt CH Alvord seriously injured)

B4137   (80hp Le Rhône 9C) Issued for training W/E 10.6.18; Deld 6 TS Montrose 12.6.18; ARS Gullane 20.6.18

B4138   Issued for Expeditionary Force W/E 27.5.18 (NTU?)

B4139   (80hp Le Rhône 9C) Issued for Midland Area W/E 24.6.18; 51 TDS North Shotwick, mid-air collision with 504K E1719 11.8.18 (2/Lt JC Thomson seriously injured)

B4140   (80hp Le Rhône 9C) Issued for training W/E 10.6.18

B4141   (80hp Le Rhône 9C) Issued for training W/E 13.5.18; 30th Wing ARS Montrose to 6 TS Montrose by 15.5.18; WO & SOC 5.7.18

B4158   (80hp Le Rhône 9C) Issued for training W/E 10.6.18; 1 Sqdn CAF 1918; 42 TDS Hounslow to 41 TDS London Colney 16.8.18

B4159   (80hp Le Rhône 9C) Issued for Expeditionary Force W/E 27.5.18 (NTU?); 4 TDS Hooton Park, spun in Eastham, Cheshire 16.7.18 (2/Lt LP Waite killed)

B4181   (80hp Le Rhône 9C) Issued for NE Area W/E 1.7.18; 38 TDS Tadcaster, spun in 12.11.18 (Capt ST Edwards died of injuries)

B4189   (80hp Le Rhône 9C) 27 TS London Colney by 17-20.6.18

B4195   5th (T) Sqdn AFC Minchinhampton

B4196   27 TS London Colney by 19-24.6.18 [BUT possible clash with S.E.5a serial]
         [Also reported with 29 TS Shawbury]

BIPLANE FIGHTERS ordered 5.7.17 additionally under Contract number 87/A/1101 from Whitehead Aircraft Ltd, Richmond, Surrey and numbered B5251 to B5400. (Ordered with 80hp Le Rhône but some fitted with alternative engines)

B5251   87 Sqdn Sedgeford by 13.10.17 to at least 18.11.17

B5252   87 Sqdn Sedgeford by 23.10.17 to at least 23.11.17; 40 TS Croydon by 11.17; Crashed 21.1.18 (Lt VM Yeates)

B5253   1 (S)ARD Farnborough to 3 TDS Lopcombe Corner 29.10.17 to at least 1.11.17 (Major FJL Cogan's aircraft, named "BLUEBIRD", white fuselage)

B5254   1 (S)ARD Farnborough to 3 TDS Lopcombe Corner 29.10.17

B5255   (80hp Gnome No.4-30/1439/WD166) 93 Sqdn Chattis Hill by 11.11.17; 92 Sqdn Chattis Hill, spun in after take-off 24.2.18 (2/Lt WR Elson seriously injured)

B5256   87 Sqdn Sedgeford by 22.11.17

B5257   Night roundels, no gun; 3 TDS Lopcombe Corner by 11-12.11.17

B5258   No information

B5259   (110hp Le Rhône 9J) Reallotted from Training Division to Expeditionary Force 9.11.17, aircraft then in France; At Rep Pk 1 ASD by 11.11.17; Retd to England; 56 TS London Colney, HD aircraft (named "MONKEY") (overwing Lewis gun on centre section)

B5260   (80hp Clerget) Scampton to 6 TS Catterick (via 19th Wing ARS) 30.10.17; 6 TS moved to Montrose 24.11.17 to at least 12.17; 18 TS Montrose by 4.18; 30th Wing ARS to 36 TS Montrose 27.4.18; 30th Wing ARS Montrose 9.5.18; 18 TS Montrose to 30th Wing ARS Montrose 30.5.18; 2 TDS Gullane 26.6.18

B5261-2 No information

B5263   At makers 8.10.17, allotted to Expeditionary Force, to be shipped without engine to 1 AD via Newhaven; At Rep Pk 1 ASD by 11.11.17

B5264   No information

B5265   21st Wing to 91 Sqdn Chattis Hill 29.10.17

B5266   No information

B5267   3 TDS Lopcombe Corner by 28.10.17; CFS 'D' Sqdn Upavon by 7.11.17 to at least 3.18

B5268   No information

B5269   21st Wing to 92 Sqdn Chattis Hill 29.10.17; With 92 Sqdn to Tangmere 17.3.18; Mid-air collision at 30ft with 92 Sqdn 504 B986, crashed 7.4.18 (2/Lt VR Craggie killed)

B5270   21st Wing to 92 Sqdn Chattis Hill 29.10.17

B5271   42 TS Wye by 22.3.18; CFS Upavon by 30.5.18; 43 TDS Chattis Hill by 10.18; Spun in from low height while landing 14.11.18 (2/Lt R Leask injured)

B5272   43 TS Chattis Hill by 6.18

B5273   No information

B5274   73 TS Turnhouse by 11.11.17; Tested at 30th Wing ARS Turnhouse 14.1.18; 73 TS Turnhouse by 2.18

B5275   (80hp Clerget) 73 TS Turnhouse by 13.10.17 to at least 2.11.17; 6 TS Montrose to 30th Wing ARS Montrose 14.4.18; 18 TS Montrose by 10.5.18; 30th Wing ARS Montrose 17.5.18; WO & SOC 16.6.18
         BUT 54 TS Castle Bromwich by 24.4.18

B5276   73 TS Turnhouse by 10.10.17 to at least 2.11.17; 43 TDS Chattis Hill, crashed on landing 14.11.18

B5277   30th Wing ARS Turnhouse to 18 TS Montrose 29.10.17

B5278   (80hp Clerget) 30th Wing ARS Turnhouse to 18 TS Montrose 1.11.17; 36 TS Montrose by 1.18; 30th Wing

B5279   ARS Montrose to 36 TS 9.4.18 to at least 9.5.18; 30th Wing ARS Montrose 13.5.18; 36 TS Montrose 25.5.18; 30th Wing ARS Montrose 4.6.18; 18 TS Montrose 3.7.18; 30th Wing ARS Montrose 5.7.18

B5279   30th Wing ARS Turnhouse by 10.17; 18 TS Montrose 1.11.17

B5280   No information

B5281   56 TS London Colney by 10.17 to at least 1.18

B5282   61 TS South Carlton by 12.5.18

B5283   34 TS Ternhill by 3.1.18

B5284   56 TS London Colney by 26.3.18; Rolled at 200ft, then spun in 4.6.18 (Lt BW Meadway killed); WO 10.6.18

B5285   74 Sqdn London Colney by 22.12.17; 85 Sqdn Hounslow 28.2.18; 93 Sqdn Tangmere from 3.4.18;18th Wing ARS Hounslow 19.4.18; 42 TS Wye 27.5.18 (allocation cancelled); 86 Sqdn Northolt 16.6.18

B5286   18th Wing ARS Hounslow to 26th Wing 6.11.17

B5287   89 Sqdn Harling Road by 11.17 to at least 12.17; 1 Fighting School Turnberry

B5288   (80hp Clerget) 18th Wing ARS Hounslow to 6th Wing 2.11.17; 56 TS London Colney to 63 TS Joyce Green 3.11.17; 42 TS Wye, engined choked on take-off, crashed 22.5.18 (2/Lt FHH Biddle died of injuries)

B5289   (100hp Gnome Monosoupape) 18th Wing ARS Hounslow to 26th Wing 6.11.17; 94 Sqdn Harling Road by 19.11.17 to at least 17.12.17

B5290   18th Wing ARS Hounslow to 74 Sqdn London Colney 4.11.17

B5291   93 Sqdn Chattis Hill 13-21.2.18; 29 TDS Beaulieu by 7.18; 28 TDS Weston-on-the-Green by 1-2.8.18

B5292   (100hp Gnome Monosoupape B-2) Fitted modified cowling; 93 Sqdn Chattis Hill by 10.4.18

B5293   34 TS Ternhill by 10.12.17

B5294   No information

B5295   10 TS Shawbury by 8.2.18 – 11.3.18

B5296   (100hp Gnome Monosoupape No.30347/WD4068) Presentation aircraft 'Gold Coast Aborigines No.2' (succeeded B1834). 112 HD Sqdn Throwley, vertical nose dive, crashed 3.1.18 (Lt LH Jull killed)

B5297   93 Sqdn Chattis Hill by 23.1.18; 93 Sqdn moved to Tangmere 18.3.18; 157 Sqdn Upper Heyford 24.7.18

B5298   No information

B5299   No information

B5300   No information

B5301   Deld Brooklands to CFS 'D' Sqdn Upavon 27.1.18 to at least 3.2.18

B5302   3 TDS Lopcombe Corner by 19.5.18

B5303   (100hp Gnome Monosoupape B-2 No.6009/B456/ WD4248) 92 Sqdn Chattis Hill by 11.1.18; Spun in out of control, wrecked, Stockbridge 13.1.18 (2/Lt AW Blackie injured)

B5304   37 HD Sqdn Stow Maries to 37 HD Sqdn Goldhangar 19.7.18; 198 (Night) TS Rochford to 19.3.19

B5305   No information

B5306   (80hp Le Rhône) 85 Sqdn Hounslow to 26th Wing 22.1.18; 89 Sqdn Harling Road, flew into ground 21.4.18 (2/Lt WEH Blyth died of injuries 22.4.18) BUT 29 TDS Beaulieu by 25.9.18

B5307   (100hp Gnome Monosoupape) 61 HD Sqdn Rochford (coded 'B-8') by 12.17 to at least 2.18; Engine failure, forced landed, overturned 28.1.18 (Lt AH Bird)

B5308   No information

B5309   No information

B5310   70 TS Beaulieu by 1.18; 3 TDS Lopcombe Corner by 16.2.18; 70 TS Beaulieu by 8.5.18; 28 TDS Weston-on-the-Green by 10.8.18

B5311   Stockbridge by 28.12.17 [3 TDS Lopcombe Corner?]; 92 Sqdn Chattis Hill by 28.1.18; 70 TS Beaulieu by 13.4.18

B5312   (80hp Le Rhône) 65 TS Dover, dived in sea and sank 12.4.18 (2/Lt FS Greatwood drowned)

B5313   74 Sqdn London Colney by 22.12.17; 87 Sqdn Hounslow 28.2.18; Crashed on landing 12.3.18 (Lt Atkins); 18th Wing ARS Hounslow 15.3.18; WO 1.4.18

B5314   CFS 'C' Sqdn Upavon by 28.1.18 to at least 28.2.18; 40 TS Croydon 1918; 34 TS Chattis Hill by 5.18; Became 43 TDS Chattis Hill 15.7.18 until unit disbanded 15.5.19 (coded 'C', Capt N Macmillan's personal aircraft)

B5315-6   No information

B5317   CFS 'D' Sqdn Upavon by 5.1.18

B5318   No information

B5319   45 TS South Carlton 1918

B5320   (Gnome Monosoupape) ARS to CFS 'A' Sqdn Upavon by 5.1.18 to at least 3.5.18

B5321   CFS 'C' Sqdn Upavon by 5.1.18; 42 TS Wye by 3.18

B5322   11 TS Scampton by 12.5.18

B5323   (100hp Gnome Monosoupape B-2) 42 TS Wye, out of control, hit ground in dive 27.1.18 (2/Lt SV Layton injured)

B5324   87 Sqdn Sedgeford by 9.12.17; 87 Sqdn moved to Hounslow 19.12.17; 18th Wing ARS Hounslow 8.3.18; 92 Sqdn Tangmere 26.4.18; 41 TDS London Colney, WO 30.7.18

B5325   86 Sqdn Northolt from 12.5.18

B5326   (Gnome) CFS 'C' & 'A' Sqdns Upavon by 13-14.2.18; 3 TDS Lopcombe Corner by 9.5.18

B5327   (100hp Gnome Monosoupape) 11 TDS Boscombe Down by 10.18

B5328   No information

B5329   (80hp Clerget) 6 TS Montrose by 1.18; 30th Wing ARS Montrose to 6 TS Montrose 15.4.18; 30th Wing ARS Montrose 22.4.18; 6 TS Montrose to 30th Wing ARS Montrose 13.5.18; 18 TS Montrose 13.6.18; 30th Wing ARS Montrose 18.6.18

B5330   1 TS Beaulieu by 9.4.18

B5331   28 TS Castle Bromwich by 7-14.1.18; 37th Wing Half ARS North Shotwick to 95 Sqdn North Shotwick 29.3.18; 37th Wing Half ARS North Shotwick to 95 Sqdn North Shotwick 1.5.18

B5332   (80hp Le Rhône) 73 Sqdn Lilbourne by 12.17; 54 TS Castle Bromwich by 27.1.18 to at least 17.5.18; 42 TDS Hounslow to 205 TDS Vendôme 15.8.18

B5333   18th Wing ARS Hounslow to 86 Sqdn Northolt 18.12.17 until squadron disbanded 4.7.18; 1 Sqdn CAF

B5334   (80hp Clerget) 54 TS Castle Bromwich, tested 25.1.18

B5335   10 TS Shawbury, crashed on landing 17.12.17 (2/Lt JK Shook)

B5336   18th Wing ARS Hounslow to 3 TS Shoreham 22.12.17

B5337   11 TDs Old Sarum

B5338   18th Wing ARS Hounslow to 3 TS Shoreham 22.12.17; WO & SOC 30.12.17

B5339   No information

B5340   Lilbourne

B5341   Lilbourne; 10 TS Shawbury, flew Harlaxton to Leicester, Engine failure, crashed 15.12.17 (2/Lt JK Shook OK)

B5342   No information

B5343   coded '3' at one time (unit unknown)

B5344   18th Wing ARS Hounslow to 3 TS Shoreham (coded '3') 22.12.17

B5345   (80hp Clerget) 60 TS Scampton by 3.18; Pilot fainted, out of control, spun in 8.6.18 (Lt FG Marsh seriously injured)

B5346   No information

B5347   74 Sqdn London Colney to 56 TS London Colney 15.3.18; WO 17.4.18

B5348   86 Sqdn Northolt from 11.1.18 until squadron disbanded 4.7.18

B5374, probably with No.7 Training Depot Station at Feltwell in the autumn of 1917 has two white bands around the rear fuselage.

(Cross & Cockade International)

B5349 30th Wing ARS Turnhouse by 1.1.18 to at least 2.2.18; 18 TS Montrose to 32 TDS Montrose 15.4.18; 2 TDS Gullane to ARS Gullane 2.6.18; 2 TDS Gullane to ARS Gullane 16.7.18; WO & SOC 6.8.18

B5350 18 TS Montrose to 32 TDS Montrose 15.4.18; 2 TDS Gullane to ARS Gullane 17.6.18; 2 TDS Gullane 24.6.18

B5351 (80hp Clerget) 28 TS Castle Bromwich by 27.1.18; 30th Wing ARS Montrose to 36 TS Montrose 16.4.18; 30th Wing ARS Montrose 5.5.18; 36 TS Montrose 16.5.18; WO & SOC 22.5.18
BUT 25 TS Thetford by 9.5.18

B5352 (80hp Le Rhône) Scampton by 31.5.18; 34 TDS Scampton 4.7.18; Bad flying, hit tree, wrecked 12.11.18 (2/Lt KB Bannister slightly injured)

B5353 87 Sqdn Hounslow from 4.1.18; Crashed on take-off 13.1.18 (2/Lt Lees); 85 Sqdn Hunslow from 19.4.18; 18th Wing ARS London Colney 26.4.18; 27 TS London Colney 21.6.18

B5354 18th Wing ARS Hounslow to 85 Sqdn Hounslow 18.12.17; 18th Wing ARS 9.1.18; 74 Sqdn London Colney to 85 Sqdn Hounslow 8.3.18; 30 TDS London Colney, WO 7.9.18

B5355 (80hp Gnome No.28367/WD3369) 87 Sqdn Hounslow; Into spin when foot jammed in rudder bar during a loop, crashed 12.2.18 (2/Lt JH Hargreaves injured)

B5356 (80hp Le Rhône) 86 Sqdn Northolt from 11.1.18; Wheels struck rising ground, overturned 2.5.18 (2/Lt LW Savidge seriously injured); WOC 4.5.18

B5357-8 No information

B5359 45 TS South Carlton by 11.5.18

B5360 (80hp Le Rhône) 87 Sqdn Hounslow by 1.18; 91 Sqdn Tangmere from 28.3.18; Believed pilot fainted in air, crashed 27.5.18 (2/Lt AT Wyman died of injuries); WO 2.6.18

B5361 Deld ARS Beaulieu 30.11.17 (arr on/by 14.12.17)

B5362 Deld ARS Beaulieu 30.11.17 (arr on/by 14.12.17); 11 TDS Old Sarum by 30.4.18 to at least 1.5.18

B5363 (100hp Gnome Monosoupape B-2) 94 Sqdn Harling Road by 19.1.18; Crashed, tested after repair 8.2.18; Forced landed 19.2.18 to at least 28.2.18; Tested after re-engined with Gnome 9.3.18 to at least 12.3.18

B5364 CFS Upavon by 11.17

B5365 CFS 'C' Sqdn Upavon by 23.12.17 to at least 14.3.18; Caught by wind taxying, overturned 24.1.18 (2/Lt WE Gilbert OK); 43 TDS Chattis Hill, tested 24.1.19

B5366 73 Sqdn Lilbourne by 12.17

B5367 CFS 'A' & 'C' Sqdns Upavon by 11.1.18 to at least 28.2.18

B5368 94 Sqdn Harling Road by 28.12.17 to at least 19.1.18

B5369 (Gnome Monosoupape) 94 Sqdn Harling Road by 22.1.18; Tested after re-engined with Le Rhône 26.3.18 to at least 13.5.18

B5370 40 TS Croydon by 24.12.17; Crashed & WO 1918

B5371-3 No information

B5374 7 TDS Feltwell by 16.7.18 to at least 6.9.18; At 10 TDS Harling Road 15.10.18 (perhaps visiting only)

B5375 7 TDS Feltwell by 15.7.18

B5376 85 Sqdn Hounslow from 2.1.18; 87 Sqdn Hounslow 1.18; 91 Sqdn Tangmere from 19.4.18; 50 TDS Eastbourne by 10.18 to at least 11.18

B5377 No information

B5378 1 ASD, test, left 15.50, wing folded at 2,000ft, crashed, caught fire 3.2.18 (2/Lt THS Crosby killed)

B5379 Tested at 30th Wing ARS Turnhouse 12.1.18; 73 TS Turnhouse by 1.18; 18 TS Montrose to 2 TDS West Fenton 15.4.18

B5380 74 Sqdn London Colney from 8.1.18; 86 Sqdn Northolt, WO 27.6.18

B5381 10 TS Lilbourne (coded 'A') by 8.4.18 to at least 17.6.18, and probably with 10 TS to Gosport 25.6.18

B5382 3 TDS Lopcombe Corner (coded '2') from 27.1.18 to at least 5.5.18; Undercarriage ripped (unit/date?)

B5383 85 Sqdn Hounslow from 8.1.18; 94 Sqdn Harling Road to 7 TDS Feltwell 19.7.18

B5384   18th Wing ARS Hounslow to 87 Sqdn Hounslow 31.12.17; WO 1.3.18

B5385   (Le Rhône) 3 TS Shoreham (coded '6') from 23.1.18; Crashed on landing Shoreham 1.18; 3 TDS Lopcombe Corner by 8.5.18

B5386   56 TS London Colney by 14.1.18; Went on nose 5.18; WO 29.5.18

B5387   (100hp Gnome Monosoupape B-2) CFS 'C' Sqdn Upavon (coded 'D') by 23-27.2.18; 43 TS Chattis Hill by 6.18

B5388   No information

B5389   18th Wing ARS Hounslow to 87 Sqdn Hounslow 31.12.17; Blown over landing, crashed 24.1.18 (Lt HAR Biziou); Cable lost in air, forced landed downwind, crashed on aerodrome 27.2.18 (Lt HAR Biziou); 85 Sqdn Hounslow, WO 13.4.18

B5390   10 TS Shawbury by 2.18; South-Eastern Area Flying Instructors School, Shoreham by 9.18

B5391   56 TDS Cranwell by 10.18 to at least 11.18

B5392-3 No information

B5394   tested at 30th Wing ARS Turnhouse 7.1.18

B5395-6 No information

B5397   (80hp Le Rhône No.WD2589) 65 TS Dover, engine failure, forced landed, hit tree, dived in 30.1.18 (2/Lt FS Greatwood injured)

B5398   No information

B5399   67 TS Shawbury by 1.18; 67 TS moved to North Shotwick 1.4.18; 37th Wing Half ARS North Shotwick 21.5.18; 67 TS North Shotwick, mid-air collision, crashed 9.7.18 (2/Lt HE Bray killed); Wreckage to 37th Wing Half ARS Shotwick 10.7.18

B5400   (100hp Gnome Monosoupape B-2) 67 TS Shawbury by 1.18; Pilot fainted, hit tree, crashed 25.1.18 (2/Lt GA Welsh injured); Repaired; 67 TS moved to North Shotwick 1.4.18

250 SOPWITH PUP ordered 13.7.17 under Contract number AS.11541/17 from Standard Motor Co Ltd, Coventry and numbered B5901 to B6150. (Ordered with 80hp Le Rhône 9C but some fitted with alternative engines)

B5901   72 Sqdn Netheravon by 12-27.10.17; Tested at ARS Beaulieu 28.2.18; 70 TS Beaulieu by 3.18 to at least 2.5.18

B5902   5 TDS Easton-on-the-Hill by 5.18; 31 TDS Fowlmere by 5.12.18

B5903   72 Sqdn Netheravon by 28.10.17; 87 Sqdn Hounslow by 7.1.18; Crashed Isleworth 16.2.18 (2/Lt Bruce injured)

B5904   (100hp Gnome Monosoupape B-2) 61 HD Sqdn Rochford (coded 'A-1') by 9.17

B5905   (100hp Gnome Monosoupape B-2) 61 HD Sqdn Rochford (coded 'A-2') by 9.17 - 10.17 (fitted Lewis gun on centre section); Rochford by 5.6.18; 198 (Night) TS Rochford to 36 HD Sqdn 16.10.18 to at least 24.12.18

B5906   (100hp Gnome Monosoupape B-2, No.35154/WD28939) 44 HD Sqdn Hainault Farm 1918 (coded '5', named 'IMPIKOFF', red & white stripes); 36 HD Sqdn Usworth, prop accident 29.11.18 (Lt JG Bertrand injured); Still 36 HD Sqdn 28.12.18

B5907   (80hp Clerget No.WD11204) 60 TS Scampton, hit 504 on ground when landing, crashed 29.5.18 (2/Lt LG Cartwright slightly injured); 198 (Night) TS Rochford to 189 (Night) TS Sutton's Farm 6.9.18; 198 (Night) TS Rochford to 37 HD Sqdn 22.11.18; 61 HD Sqdn 11.3.19; SOC 11.4.19

B5908   (110hp Le Rhône 9J) At (S)ARD Farnborough 6.10.17, allotted to Expeditionary Force; Flown to France 10.17; Tested at ARS 1 AD 11.10.17; ARS 1 AD to 66 Sqdn 14.10.17; ARS 1 AD 17.10.17; Became Rep Pk 1 ASD

1.11.17; Flown back to England 11.3.18 (Apparently the only Pup with the 110hp Le Rhône to go to an operational unit)

B5909   No information

B5910   112 HD Sqdn Throwley (named 'UMPIKOF') by 2.4.18; Crashed 19.4.18 (2/Lt OL Frampton)

B5911   At makers 25.8.17, allotted to Expeditionary Force; England to ARS 1 AD in case without engine 4.9.17; 54 Sqdn 9.9.17; Returning from OP choked the engine just outside the aerodrome and crashed 12.10.17 (2/Lt N Clark); ARS 1 AD 14.10.17; SOC 17.10.17 NWR

B5912   At makers 25.8.17, allotted to Expeditionary Force; England to ARS 1 AD in case without engine 6.9.17; 66 Sqdn 12.10.17; ARS 1 AD 19.10.17 (exchanged for a Camel); 54 Sqdn 23.10.17; Flown back to England 12.12.17; 30 TS AFC Minchinhampton; 6 TS AFC Minchinhampton

B5913   At makers 25.8.17, allotted to Expeditionary Force; England to ARS 1 AD 9.9.17; 54 Sqdn 10.9.17; Rep Pk 1 ASD by 28.12.17; Rec Pk and on to England 4.1.18; 1 TS Beaulieu by 1.4.18

B5914   At makers 25.8.17, allotted to Expeditionary Force; England to ARS 1 AD in case without engine 4.9.17; 66 Sqdn 11.9.17; On special duty flight, forced landed Fruges, crashed 1.10.17 (2/Lt DH Houston OK); ARS 1 AD 3.10.17; SOC 7.10.17

B5915   At makers 25.8.17, allotted to Expeditionary Force; England to ARS 1 AD in case without engine 6.9.17; 66 Sqdn 1.10.17; ARS 1 AD 20.10.17 (exchanged for a Camel); Rec Pk to 8 AAP Lympne 4.1.18

B5916   At makers 25.8.17, allotted to Expeditionary Force; England to ARS 1 AD in case without engine 6.9.17; 66 Sqdn 14.10.17; ARS 1 AD 20.10.17 (exchanged for a Camel); 54 Sqdn 25.10.17; Left 13.45, OP to St.Pierre Cappelle-Zarren-Houthulst Wood, shot up by AA fire, forced landed, crashed Lampernisse 27.10.17 (2/Lt A Thompson unhurt); ARS 1 AD 30.10.17

B5917   At makers 25.8.17, allotted to Expeditionary Force; England to ARS 1 AD in case without engine 6.9.17; 66 Sqdn 2.10.17; ARS 1 AD 19.10.17 (exchanged for a Camel); 54 Sqdn 23.10.17; Casualty Report 2.11.17 says part of top longeron had been shot through by AA fire, on dismantling the fuselage was found to be badly trued up, there were other constructional defects; Rep Pk 1 ASD 2.11.17; SOC 9.11.17

B5918   At makers 25.8.17, allotted to Expeditionary Force; England to ARS 1 AD in case without engine 8.9.17; 54 Sqdn 8.10.17; Left 06.45, OP to St.Pierre Capelle-Zarren, in combat east of lines, fell out of control nr Zarren 13.10.17 (2/Lt WW Vick PoW) [Sopwith 1-str claimed in combat Bouvekerke 08.00 by Vzfw H Körner, Jasta 8 or Unconfirmed "Pup" claimed east of Dixmude 08.00 by Ltn A Heldmann, Jasta 10?]

B5919   (80hp Le Rhône No.2973/WD15607) At makers 25.8.17, allotted to Expeditionary Force; England to ARS 1 AD in case without engine 8.9.17; 54 Sqdn 14.10.17; Rep Pk 1 ASD to Rec Pk 4.1.18; Flown back to England 4.1.18; 17th Wing Beaulieu, lost in fog, stalled avoiding tree, spun in 23.1.18 (2/Lt M Corrie injured)

B5920   At makers 25.8.17, allotted to Expeditionary Force; England to ARS 1 AD in case without engine 10.9.17; 54 Sqdn 13.10.17; 8 AAP Lympne 16.12.17; 86 Sqdn Northolt by 4.18; WO 14.6.18

B5921   At makers 25.8.17, allotted to Expeditionary Force; England to ARS 1 AD in case without engine 8.9.17; 54 Sqdn 18.10.17 to at least 16.11.17; Rep Pk 1 ASD to Rec Pk 28.12.17; 8 AAP Lympne 29.12.17; 4 TDS Hooton Park from 25.1.18

B5922   At makers 25.8.17, allotted to Expeditionary Force; England to ARS 1 AD in case without engine 12.9.17; ARS 2 AD 21.10.17; 46 Sqdn 22.11.17; Rep Pk 2 ASD 13.12.17; 2 AI to 2 ASD Scout School, Candas 19.1.18; 2 AI 5.2.18; Rec Pk 23.2.18; 8 AAP Lympne 26.2.18; Worthy Down 17.3.18

B5923   At makers 25.8.17, allotted to Expeditionary Force; England to ARS 1 AD in case without engine 8.9.17; Rep Pk 1 ASD to 54 Sqdn 12.11.17; Rec Pk to 8 AAP Lympne 8.3.18; 42 TDS Hounslow to 2 Group 16.8.18

B5924   At makers 25.8.17, allotted to Expeditionary Force; England to ARS 1 AD in case without engine 11.9.17; Rep Pk 1 ASD to 54 Sqdn 14.11.17; To Rep Pk 1 ASD, on practice flight, pilot overshooting, opened up engine too late, flew into observation tower 9.3.18 (Lt Bradshaw badly injured); SOC 11.3.18

B5925   At makers 25.8.17, allotted to Expeditionary Force; England to ARS 1 AD in case without engine 11.9.17; Became Rep Pk 1 ASD 1.11.17; 54 Sqdn 14.11.17; Rep Pk 1 ASD to 1 AI 10.12.17; Rec Pk 22.12.17; 8 AAP Lympne to 89 Sqdn Harling Road 19.1.18

B5926   At makers 25.8.17, allotted to Expeditionary Force; England to ARS 1 AD in case without engine 12.9.17; Rep Pk 1 ASD to 54 Sqdn 11.11.17 to at least 18.11.17; Rep Pk 1 ASD by 22.12.17; Rec Pk 9.1.18; 8 AAP Lympne 13.1.18

B5927   61 HD Sqdn Rochford by 10.18; SOC 11.4.19

B5928   (80hp Gnome Lambda) Deld RNASTE Cranwell 11.9.17; Listed as u/s and engineless 30.3.18; Became 201/202 TDS Cranwell 1.4.18

B5929   (80hp Gnome Lambda, later 60hp Le Rhône) Deld RNASTE Cranwell 11.9.17; Crashed & badly damaged Cranwell South 19.3.18 (pilot unhurt); Fully serviceable by 30.3.18; Became 201/202 TDS Cranwell 1.4.18; 'G' (Experimental) Flt Cranwell, propeller accident 3.6.18 (3AM LF Baker killed)

B5930   Deld Aircraft Park Dover W/E 29.9.17; War School RNAS Manston W/E 3.11.17; Engineless at 29.12.17; Serviceable by 11.1.18; U/s and engineless again 30.3.18; To Eastbourne but crashed on landing 17.6.18 (pilot unhurt)

B5931   No information

B5932   73 Sqdn Lilbourne by 10.17 to at least 7.11.17 (white band afte of fuselage roundel); 54 TS Castle Bromwich by 5-25.4.18; 42 TDS Hounslow to 41 TDS London Colney 16.8.18

B5933   (Gnome Monosoupape) 'A' Sqdn CFS Upavon by 5.1.18; Low spin, crashed 7.1.18 (Lt GW Calverley killed)

B5934   No information

B5935   3 TDS Lopcombe Corner by 19.11.17

B5936   'C' Sqdn CFS Upavon by 7.12.17; Spun in at low height 1.4.18 (2/Lt WG Carmichael injured)

B5937   (100hp Gnome Monosoupape B-2 No.30825/WD20396) 'D' Sqdn Upavon CFS, steep turn landing, crashed 4.1.18 (2/Lt L Francis injured)

B5938   Deld Aircraft Park Dover W/E 29.9.17; War School RNAS Manston W/E 3.11.17; Engineless at 29.12.17 & 30.3.18; Became Pool of Pilots Manston 1.4.18; Eastbourne to Manston 22.5.18

B5939   Deld Killingholme store for erection 15.9.17; Allotted Experimental Constructive Dept, Grain for experiments, arrived 15.12.17 (80hp Clerget No.573 by 12.1.18); Engineless by 30.3.18; Test Depot, Grain to Grain W/E 1.6.18; Grain from 7.19 (deck landing and arrester gear); Pulham (cable landing experiments)

B5940   Deld Killingholme store for erection 15.9.17; Allotted Experimental Constructive Dept, Grain for experiments 4.12.17 (arrived 22.12.17); Engineless at 12.1.18 & 30.3.18; Still Experimental Constructive Dept, Grain 11.19 (fitted overwing hook to centre section for overhead "landing" wires 19.4.19)

B5941   (110hp Le Rhône 9J) Farnborough c.9.17 to at least 11.17 (subjected to sand loading tests of mainplanes)

B5942   (80hp Gnome) 56 TS London Colney by 22.11.17; Flat spin at 150ft, crashed 13.2.18 (Lt B Ingram injured)

B5943   71 Sqdn Castle Bromwich 1917; 28 TS Castle Bromwich by 11.1.18; Failed to flatten out of dive on ground target, went straight in with engine full on 22.4.18 (Sgt HJ Birtles killed)

B5944   43 TDS Chattis Hill by 7.18

B5945-7 No information

B5948   (80hp Gnome) Deld RNASTE Cranwell for erection 25.9.17; Both airframe & engine u/s by 30.3.18; Became 201/202 TDS Cranwell 1.4.18

B5949   (80hp Gnome) Deld RNASTE Cranwell for erection 18.9.17; Became 201/202 TDS Cranwell 1.4.18; Pulham (cable landing experiments)

B5950   (80hp Gnome) Deld RNASTE Cranwell for erection 25.9.17; Airframe u/s by 30.3.18; Became 201/202 TDS Cranwell 1.4.18

B5951   No information

B5952   89 Sqdn Harling Road, spun too near ground, dived in 14.1.18 (2/Lt FH Patten killed)

B5953   (100hp Gnome Monosoupape B-2) 88 Sqdn Harling Road, forced landed, crashed 4.1.18 (2/Lt JJ Magill injured)

B5954   No information

B5955   88 Sqdn Harling Road; 89 Sqdn Harling Road, spinning nose dive, crashed 22.10.17 (pilot injured); SOC 25.10.17

B5956   73 Sqdn Lilbourne by 10.17; 28 TS Castle Bromwich by 12-13.1.18

B5957   (80hp Gnome) 73 Sqdn Lilbourne by 28.10.17 to at least 25.12.17; 28 TS Castle Bromwich by 12.1.18; Mid-air collision 23.1.18 (2/Lt RG Hall killed)

B5958   Deld Aircraft Park Dover W/E 29.9.17; War School RNAS Manston W/E 3.11.17; Became Pool of Pilots Manston 1.4.18 to at least 12.5.18; 206 TDS Eastbourne by 21.5.18

B5959   Deld Aircraft Park Dover W/E 29.9.17; War School RNAS Manston W/E 3.11.17; U/s and engineless by 30.3.18; Deleted W/E 30.3.18

B5960   Deld Aircraft Park Dover W/E 29.9.17; War School RNAS Manston W/E 3.11.17; Became Pool of Pilots Manston 1.4.18; 6th Wing 27.7.18

B5961   72 Sqdn Netheravon by 27.10.17?; Unidentified TS (white bar through roundel, and fuselage diamond)

B5962   8 AAP Lympne, tested 5.1.18

B5963   No information

B5964   93 Sqdn Chattis Hill by 17.11.17; 1 TS Beaulieu by 24.4.18

B5965   73 Sqdn Lilbourne by 23.10.17 to at least 15.12.17; 74 TS Tadcaster to 32 TDS Montrose by 21.7.18; 30th Wing ARS Montrose 22.7.18; WO & SOC 9.8.18

B5966   28 TS Castle Bromwich; 73 Sqdn Lilbourne by 6.11.17

B5967   1 (S)ARD Farnborough to 3 TDS Lopcombe Corner 29.10.17 to at least 11.11.17; CFS 'C' Sqdn Upavon by 29.12.17 to at least 16.7.18

B5968   Deld Killingholme store for erection by 10.17 [not there 29.9.17]; Allotted Experimental Constructive Dept, Grain for experiments 4.12.17 (arrived 13.12.17); Engineless and under repair by 5.1.18 to at least 1.4.18

B5969   Deld Killingholme store for erection W/E 6.10.17; Allotted Experimental Constructive Dept, Grain for experiments 4.12.17 (arrived 13.12.17); Engineless and under repair by 5.1.18 to at least 1.4.18

B5970   Deld Killingholme store for erection W/E 6.10.17;
         Allotted Experimental Constructive Dept, Grain 4.12.17
         (arrived 22.12.17); Engineless by 5.1.18 & 30.3.18;
         Hendon 17.5.18; Grain 18.5.18; Hendon 6.6.18;
         Yarmouth 4.7.18; Hendon 7.18; Norwich 1.8.18; Hendon
         8.18; To Leighterton 10.8.18 (probably only visiting)

B5971   At or en route to 6 SD Ascot 5.10.17, allotted to
         Expeditionary Force, to be packed and shipped to 1 AD
         via Newhaven; At Rep Pk 1 ASD 11.11.17

B5972   (80hp Le Rhône) At or en route to 6 SD Ascot 5.10.17,
         allotted to Expeditionary Force, to be packed and
         shipped to 1 AD via Newhaven; At Rep Pk 1 ASD
         11.11.17; To 2 ASD but forced landed Fruges en route
         2.12.17 (Capt RF Jenyns); 1 AI 8.12.17; Rec Pk
         22.12.17; 8 AAP Lympne England 4.1.18; ARS Hooton
         Park to "C" Flight 4 TDS Hooton Park 25.1.18; Loud
         report heard, pilot believed fainted or lost control, dived
         into river 27.1.18 (2/Lt RDG Brendel killed)

B5973   At or en route to 6 SD Ascot 5.10.17, allotted to
         Expeditionary Force, to be packed and shipped without
         engine to 1 AD via Newhaven; At Rep Pk 1 ASD
         11.11.17

B5974   At or en route to 6 SD Ascot 5.10.17, allotted to
         Expeditionary Force, to be packed and shipped to 1 AD
         via Newhaven; At Rep Pk 1 ASD 11.11.17; Left for
         repair at 2 ASD, but forced landed Fruges en route
         4.12.17 (Capt RF Jenyns); 1 AI 8.12.17; Rec Pk
         22.12.17; 8 AAP Lympne 11.3.18; 73 TS Beaulieu by
         1.4.18; 1 TS Beaulieu by 22.4.18; 70 TS Beaulieu by
         10.5.18

B5975   At makers 28.9.17, allotted to Expeditionary Force, to be
         shipped without engine to 1 AD via Newhaven; England
         to ARS 1 AD 14.10.17 in case without engine; Became
         Rep Pk 1 ASD 1.11.17 to at least 21.11.17

B5976   At makers 28.9.17, allotted to Expeditionary Force, to be
         shipped without to 1 AD via Newhaven; England to ARS
         1 AD in case without engine 14.10.17; Rep Pk 1ASD
         11.11.17

B5977   At makers 28.9.17, allotted to Expeditionary Force, to be
         shipped without engine to 1 AD via Newhaven; England
         to ARS 1 AD in case without engine 15.10.17; Rep Pk
         1ASD 11.11.17

B5978   (80hp Le Rhône, later 60hp Le Rhône by 30.3.18) Deld
         RNASTE Cranwell 9.10.17; Crashed and undercarriage
         smashed, Cranwell South 14.1.18 (pilot unhurt);
         Overturned landing, slightly damaged 27.2.18 (pilot
         unhurt); Became 201/202 TDS Cranwell 1.4.18

B5979   (80hp Le Rhône, later 60hp Le Rhône by 5.1.18) Deld
         RNASTE Cranwell 9.10.17; Crashed and wrecked,
         Cranwell South 6.1.18 (pilot unhurt); Became 201/202
         TDS Cranwell 1.4.18

B5980   (80hp Gnome) Deld RNASTE Cranwell 10.17; Tyre
         burst landing in snowstorm 26.11.17 (FSL LH Pearson);
         Completely destroyed by engine fire 11.3.18; Surveyed
         12.3.18; Deleted 16.3.18

B5981   At makers 28.9.17, allotted to Expeditionary Force, to be
         shipped to 1 AD via Newhaven; England to ARS 1 AD in
         case without engine 15.10.17

B5982   At makers 28.9.17, allotted to Expeditionary Force, to be
         shipped without engine to 1 AD via Newhaven; At Rep
         Pk 1 ASD by 11.11.17

B5983   At makers 28.9.17, allotted to Expeditionary Force, to be
         shipped to 1 AD via Newhaven; England to ARS 1 AD in
         case without engine 14.10.17; 2 AI to 2 ASD Scout
         School, Candas 19.1.18; 2 AI 5.2.18; Rec Pk and on to 8
         AAP Lympne 23.2.18

B5984   At makers 28.9.17, allotted to Expeditionary Force, to be
         shipped to 1 AD via Newhaven; England to ARS 1 AD in
         case without engine 14.10.17

B5985   At makers 28.9.17, allotted to Expeditionary Force, to be
         shipped to 1 AD via Newhaven; England to ARS 1 AD in
         case without engine 15.10.17

B5986   At makers 28.9.17, allotted to Expeditionary Force, to be
         shipped without engine to 1 AD via Newhaven 10.17

B5987   At makers 28.9.17, allotted to Expeditionary Force, to be
         shipped to 1 AD via Newhaven; England to ARS 1 AD in
         case without engine 15.10.17; SOC 30.1.18 NWR

B5988   (80hp Gnome, later 60hp Le Rhône by 30.3.18) Deld
         RNASTE Cranwell (coded '1') W/E 12.10.17; To
         Freiston by 3.18; Became School of Aerial Fighting &
         Bomb Dropping Freiston 1.4.18; Forced landed in
         marshes, propeller and undercarriage damaged 1.4.18
         (pilot unhurt); Became 4 School of Aerial Fighting &
         Gunnery Freiston 6.5.18 to at least 11.5.18

B5989   (80hp Gnome by 5.1.18) Deld RNASTE Cranwell for
         erection W/E 20.10.17; Became 201/202 TDS Cranwell
         1.4.18

B5990   (80hp Clerget by 5.1.18) Deld RNASTE Cranwell W/E
         12.10.17; Became 201/202 TDS Cranwell 1.4.18; 55 TS
         Lilbourne by 4.18

B5991   (80hp Gnome by 29.12.17, later 80hp Le Rhône by
         11.1.18) Deld War School RNAS Manston W/E 6.10.17;
         U/s and engineless by 30.3.18; Became Pool of Pilots
         Manston 1.4.18; 206 TDS Eastbourne by 21.6.18

B5992   (80hp Gnome by 29.12.17, later 80hp Le Rhône by
         11.1.18; 80hp Le Rhône No 5455/WD7985 when
         crashed) Deld War School RNAS Manston W/E 6.10.17;
         Became Pool of Pilots Manston 1.4.18; Mid-air collision
         with B9931 17.7.18 (Sgt EH Sayers killed)

B5993   (80hp Gnome by 29.12.17, later 80hp Le Rhône by
         11.1.18) Deld War School RNAS Manston W/E 6.10.17;
         Deleted W/E 30.3.18

B5994   (80hp Gnome by 29.12.17, later 80hp Le Rhône by
         11.1.18) Deld War School RNAS Manston W/E 6.10.17;
         Became Pool of Pilots Manston 1.4.18; 206 TDS
         Eastbourne 16.5.18; Engine failure, crashed
         Groombridge, nr Tunbridge Wells 17.5.18 (pilot unhurt)

B5995   (100hp Gnome Monosoupape B-2) 21st Wing to 3 TDS
         Lopcombe Corner 29.10.17; Choked engine on turn,
         sideslipped in 28.11.17 (2/Lt KH Wallace injured)

B5996   No information
B5997   No information
B5998   'B' Sqdn CFS Upavon by 12.17 to at least 1.18
B5999   No information
B6000   No information
B6001   (80hp Gnome by 29.12.17, later 80hp Le Rhône by
         30.3.18) Deld War School RNAS Manston by road
         19.10.17; Ground looped, overturned 4.12.17 (FSL GD
         Smith); Became Pool of Pilots Manston 1.4.18; 206 TDS
         Eastbourne 8.5.18 to at least 7.18; 4 FS Freiston (date
         unknown)

B6002   Deld Killingholme store by road W/E 2.11.17; Allotted
         Experimental Constructive Dept, Grain for experiments
         4.12.17 (arrived 15.12.17); At Grain to at least 7.18

B6003   Deld Killingholme store by road W/E 2.11.17; Allotted
         Experimental Constructive Dept, Grain for experiments
         4.12.17 (arrived 22.12.17); Hendon 12.6.18; Test Depot,
         Grain 24.7.18 (experiments & deck landing trials);
         Centre section reported loose 8.11.20 (flown 571 hours)

B6004   Deld Killingholme store by road W/E 2.11.17; Allotted
         Experimental Constructive Dept, Grain 4.12.17 (arrived
         22.12.17); Serviceable but without engine by 30.3.18;
         Still at Grain 25.5.18

B6005   No information
B6006   56 TS London Colney (all-white) by 22.11.17 to at least
         29.1.18
B6007   56 TS London Colney by 22.11.17 to at least 4.1.18

B6008   18th Wing ARS Hounslow to 26th Wing 6.11.17; 89 Sqdn Harling Road by 11.17 to at least 12.17; 2 FS Marske 11.18

B6009   16 TDS Amriya, SOC 14.8.18

B6010   (80hp Gnome, later 80hp Le Rhône by 16.3.18, later 80hp Clerget) 18th Wing ARS Hounslow to 26th Wing 6.11.17; 89 Sqdn Harling Road to 94 Sqdn Harling Road 5.2.18 to at least 12.2.18; Tested after re-engined with Le Rhône 16.3.18 to at least 19.3.18; 35 TDS Duxford, hit by R.E.8 B5141 on ground 6.8.18 (Lt L Brown injured) [In photo, swastika on wheel disc, white band aft of roundel]

B6011   (Converted to 9901a Ships Pup) Deld Rosyth W/E 9.11.17; Donibristle W/E 30.11.17; Rosyth W/E 5.1.18; Engineless at 11.1.18; Donibristle 1.2.18; Fleet Aeroplane Depot Turnhouse W/E 21.2.18; Deleted W/E 25.5.18

B6012   (Converted to 9901a Ships Pup) (80hp Le Rhône No.6627 by 11.1.18); Deld Rosyth by road W/E 9.11.17; Donibristle W/E 22.11.17; Rosyth W/E 5.1.18; Donibristle W/E 8.2.18; Rosyth W/E 16.3.18; Fleet Practice Station Turnhouse W/E 21.3.18; U/s and engineless by 30.3.18; Mid-air collision with 1½ Strutter 9894 over Firth of Forth, crashed 4.9.18 (2/Lt HA Sutherland, Canadian, killed); Deleted W/E 19.9.18

B6013   (80hp Gnome by 5.1.18, later 60hp Le Rhône by 30.3.18) Deld RNASTE Cranwell W/E 1.11.17; Became 201/202 TDS Cranwell 1.4.18

B6014   (80hp Gnome by 5.1.18) Deld RNASTE Cranwell W/E 1.11.17; Crashed, damaged 25.2.18 (pilot unhurt); Forced landed, overturned 2m from aerodrome 25.3.18 (pilot unhurt); Under repair 30.3.18; Became 201/202 TDS Cranwell 1.4.18

B6015   70 TS Beaulieu by 1.18 to at least 5.18

B6016   (80hp Clerget No.1108/WD11110) 79 Sqdn Beaulieu by 12.17; Tested at ARS Beaulieu 10.3.18; 73 TS Beaulieu, engine failure, forced landed, port wing hit tree, crashed 28.3.18 (Lt ER Cavanagh injured)

B6017   (100hp Gnome Monosoupape B-2) 3 TDS Lopcombe Corner, crashed 2.1.18 (2/Lt VR Pauline)

B6018   (100hp Gnome Monosoupape B-2) 88 Sqdn Harling Road, out of control in spin, dived in 4.12.17 (2/Lt SG Page injured); 207 TDS Chingford by 5.18

B6019   (100hp Gnome Monosoupape B-2 No.30744/WD11817) 92 Sqdn Chattis Hill, collapsed in air, spun in, wrecked 6.12.17 (2/Lt D Barnett injured)

B6020   18 TS Montrose by 7.18

B6021   (80hp Gnome by 5.1.18, later 80hp Le Rhône No.53066/WD48772); Deld RNASTE Cranwell for erection W/E 1.11.17; Crashed and slightly damaged 5.3.18 (pilot unhurt); Blown over on take-off, slightly damaged, Cranwell South 9.3.18 (Sub-Lt FS Bowles unhurt); U/s at 30.3.18; Became 201/202 TDS Cranwell 1.4.18; School of Aerial Fighting & Bomb Dropping Freiston, collided at 100ft with B.E.2e B3716, crashed River Witham outfall [then with Gunnery School, Freiston] 26.4.18 (2/Lt NV Grimsditch slightly injured)

B6022   (80hp Gnome by 5.1.18) Deld RNASTE Cranwell W/E 1.11.17; Crashed, badly damaged 22.3.18 (pilot unhurt); U/s at 30.3.18

B6023   (80hp Gnome by 5.1.18, to 60hp Le Rhône 2.18) Deld RNASTE Cranwell for erection W/E 1.11.17; Became 201/202 TDS Cranwell 1.4.18

B6024   (80hp Gnome by 5.1.18) Deld RNASTE Cranwell for erection 1.11.17; U/s at 30.3.18

B6025   43 TDS Chattis Hill, tested 4.12.18 to at least 1.19

B6026   (80hp Clerget) 7 TDS Feltwell, stunting too low, spun in 11.6.18 (2/Lt JW Cox killed)

B6027-9   No information

B6030   No information

B6031   (80hp Gnome by 5.1.18) Deld RNASTE Cranwell W/E 3.11.17; Crashed, wrecked Cranwell South 3.1.18 (pilot unhurt); Surveyed 3.1.18; Deleted 17.1.18

B6032   (80hp Gnome by 5.1.18) Deld RNASTE Cranwell W/E 1.11.17; Crashed, slightly damaged, Cranwell South 28.2.18 (pilot unhurt); U/s at 30.3.18; Became 201/202 TDS Cranwell 1.4.18

B6033   (80hp Gnome by 5.1.18) Deld RNASTE Cranwell W/E 1.11.17; Became 201/202 TDS Cranwell 1.4.18

B6034   (80hp Gnome by 5.1.18) Deld RNASTE Cranwell W/E 1.11.17; Crashed, undercarriage damaged, Cranwell South 22.1.18 (pilot unhurt); Serviceable at 30.3.18; Became 201/202 TDS Cranwell 1.4.18; 1 FS Ayr by 10.6.18

B6035   1 AAP to 4 TDS Hooton Park by 19.12.17; 37th Wing Half ARS Hooton Park 14.3.18; 4 TDS Hooton Park 11.5.18 to at least 7.8.18

B6036   Deld 'C' Flt 4 TDS Hooton Park 12.12.17; ARS Hooton Park 23.1.18; 4 TDS Hooton Park 14.2.18; 37th Wing Half ARS Hooton Park 28.2.18; 4 TDS Hooton Park to 22.3.18; 37th Wing Half ARS North Shotwick 5.5.18

B6037   No information

B6038   10 TS Shawbury by 4.1.18; Stalled on turn at 100ft, spun in, wrecked 18.2.18 (2/Lt JH Batten killed)

B6039   43 TS Ternhill by 12.17 (striped fuselage); 10 TS Shawbury by 21.1.18; 37th Wing Half ARS Hooton Park to 4 TDS Hooton Park 1.6.18

B6040   73 Sqdn Lilbourne by 24-25.12.17; 43 TS Ternhill by 2.18 to at least 3.18; MAEE by 1920 (overhead launching gear tests); Pulham (cable landing experiments)

B6041   22 TS Aboukir by 7.18; 58 TS Suez by 5.10.18; 5 Fighting School Heliopolis, WO 21.3.19

B6042   22 TS Aboukir by 7.18; School of Aerial Gunnery Aboukir by 9.18; Disbanded into 5 Fighting School Heliopolis 5.9.18; Stalled at 20ft coming in to land, pancaked and overturned 18.9.18 (2/Lt EH Rossington); Repaired on station; Whilst taking off struck civilian on road 21.10.18 (2/Lt VE Davis); to ARS; WO 23.10.18

B6043   School of Aerial Gunnery Aboukir by 9.18; Disbanded into 5 Fighting School Heliopolis 5.9.18; Crashed on take off 4.10.18 (Flt Cdt HJ Gambling); To ARS; WO 29.3.19

B6044   School of Aerial Fighting, Heliopolis by 21.3.18; Became 5 Fighting School Heliopolis 5.9.18; 58 TS Suez by 7.10.18; Artillery Observation School Almaza, WO 4.6.19

B6045   School of Aerial Fighting, Heliopolis crashed, error of judgement 15.3.18 (Lt M Curtis-Beale killed)

B6046   School of Aerial Fighting, Heliopolis by 30.3.18 to at least 2.4.18; 22 TS Aboukir by 7.18; 19 DS El Rimal by 11.18; 5 Fighting School Heliopolis by 2.1.19; WO 29.3.19

B6047   19 TDS El Rimal by 10.18 to at least 11.18; 18 TDS Ismailia, WO 4.3.19

B6048   195 TS Abu Sueir; Became 19 TDS El Rimal 21.7.18, SOC 1.8.18

B6049   (80hp Gnome No.23746 by 5.1.18) Deld Redcar Naval Flying School for erection W/E 17.11.17; 201/202 TDS Cranwell 26.4.18; North Eastern Area Flying Instructors School Redcar by 8.18; Pulham (cable landing experiments)

B6050   (80hp Gnome No.23771 by 5.1.18) Deld Redcar Naval Flying School for erection W/E 17.11.17; Deleted W/E 19.1.18

B6051   (80hp Gnome No.27459 by 5.1.18) Deld Redcar Naval Flying School for erection W/E 17.11.17; U/s by 30.3.18; 201/202 TDS Cranwell 8.5.18

B6052   (60hp Le Rhône No.3118 5.1.18) Deld Redcar Naval Flying School for erection W/E 17.11.17; Deleted W/E 6.4.18

B6053   Erected in Egypt, FF 15.5.18; 22 TS Aboukir 16.5.18; Making his first flight in a Pup, went into slow right hand spin after restarting engine and crashed from low height 20.5.18 (2/Lt FA Vandenberg killed)

B6054   19 TDS El Rimal by 11.18; WO 28.1.19

B6055   20th Training Wing, WO 16.9.18

B6056   20 TDS Shallufa, WOC 14.11.18

B6057   (80hp Clerget) School of Aerial Fighting Heliopolis, broke up in air, wing collapsed in badly executed manoeuvre 17.8.18 (Sub Lt A Morfopoules killed); SOC 19.8.18 BUT Gosport & Pool Flight by 7.18 to at least 8.18

B6058   (80hp Clerget No.10789/WD11081) 195 TS El Rimal by 7.18; 19 TDS El Rimal 21.7.18; Crashed on landing, cushions fouled control lever, 7.8.18 (2/Lt W Druce injured); SOC 28.8.18

B6059   22 TS Aboukir by 7.18; WO 11.9.18

B6060   20 TDS Amriya, WO 24.2.19

B6061   (60hp Le Rhône No.801 by 11.1.18) Deld RNASTE Cranwell for erection W/E 23.11.17; U/s at 30.3.18; Became 201/202 TDS Cranwell 1.4.18; Became 56 TDS Cranwell 15.7.18; Overturned on take-off, badly damaged 13.10.18 (Flt Cdt HP Bird OK); Still at Cranwell 9.1.19

B6062   (80hp Le Rhône 9C No.100288 by 11.1.18) Deld RNASTE Cranwell for erection W/E 23.11.17; Became 201/202 TDS Cranwell 1.4.18; Became 56 TDS Cranwell 15.7.18 to at least 9.18

B6063   Deld RNASTE Cranwell for erection W/E 23.11.17; Became 201/202 TDS Cranwell 1.4.18; Crashed, slightly damaged 11m north of Heckington 2.4.18 (pilot unhurt); Crashed, Cranwell South 3.4.18 (pilot unhurt); Became 56 TDS Cranwell 15.7.18 to at least 9.18

B6064   (60hp Le Rhône by 30.3.18) Deld RNASTE Cranwell for erection W/E 23.11.17; Became 201/202 TDS Cranwell 1.4.18; Hit on ground by B.E.2c 9966, completely wrecked 3.4.18 (pilot unhurt)

B6065   Unit unknown, but '101' and 'S' (or '5') on upper wings

B6066   No information

B6067   62 TS Hounslow by 9.5.18 to at least 1.6.18; 92 Sqdn

B6068   No information

B6069   65 TS Dover, climbing turn on take-off, stalled, crashed 27.1.18 (2/Lt CC Ivens injured)

B6070   No information

B6071   No information

B6072   Beverley by 16.1.18; 49 TS Tadcaster (?) by 5.18

B6073   (100hp Gnome Monosoupape B-2 No.33196) Deld AAP Hendon for erection W/E 1.11.17, and used by 2 AAP Comm Flt for "Special Service" by Air Department officers to at least 25.5.18

B6074   (100hp Gnome Monosoupape B-2 No.33129) Deld AAP Hendon for erection W/E 1.11.17, and used by 2 AAP Comm Flt for "Special Service" by Air Dept officers to at least 23.2.18; Medical Flt Hendon by 23.4.18 to at least 5.18; 70 TS Beaulieu by 6.18; 29 TS Hendon from 26.7.18

B6075   (80hp Gnome by 5.1.18, later 80hp Le Rhône by 30.3.18) Deld RNASTE Cranwell W/E 30.11.17; Became 201/202 TDS Cranwell 1.4.18; SOC 29.5.18

B6076   (80hp Gnome by 5.1.18, to 60hp Le Rhône 2.18) Deld RNASTE Cranwell W/E 12.12.17; U/s by 30.3.18; Became 201/202 TDS Cranwell 1.4.18

B6077   (80hp Le Rhône) 73 TS Turnhouse by 3.12.17; 36 TS Montrose by 4.18; 30th Wing ARS Montrose to 18 TS Montrose 25.4.18; 30th Wing ARS Montrose 2.5.18; 18 TS Montrose 8.5.18; WO & SOC 16.6.18

B6078   73 TS Turnhouse by 12.17

B6079   Tested at 30th Wing ARS Turnhouse 30.1.18; 36 TS Montrose by 10.6.18; 30th Wing ARS Montrose 19.6.18

B6080   36 TS Montrose by 1.18; 30th Wing ARS Montrose WO & SOC 8.4.18

B6081   (80hp Clerget) 30 Wing ARS Turnhouse to 18 TS Montrose 30.3.18; 30th Wing ARS Montrose 25.5.18; 6 TS Montrose 3.6.18; 30 Wing ARS Montrose 8.6.18; 36

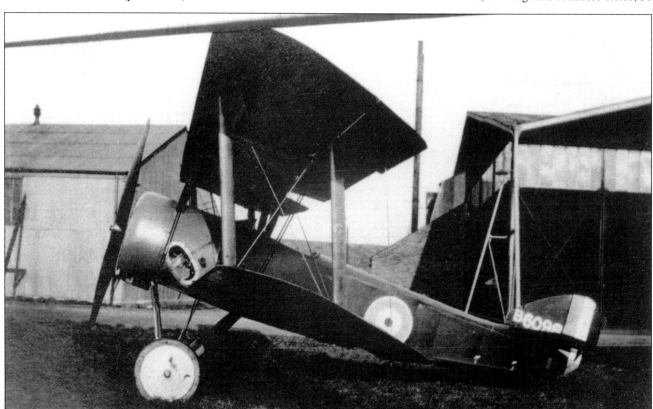

Possibly seen here with No.27 Training Depot Station late in the war, standard-built B6088 was initially a naval machine based at Chingford and Fairlop, and was later with No.62 Training Squadron at Hounslow by June 1918.   *(via Frank Cheesman)*

A factory full of Pups under construction at Coventry by the Standard Motor Company Limited around September 1917. Part of a large order for 250 aircraft to be numbered B5901 to B6150, identifiable in the background are B6104 and B6107. (J.M.Bruce/G.S.Leslie collection)

TS Montrose to 30 Wing ARS Montrose 11.7.18; 32 TDS Montrose by 21.10.18 to at least 13.11.18

B6082 No information

B6083 38 TDS Tadcaster, spinning nose dive 10.8.18 (Flt Cdt AE Yates seriously injured)

B6084 47 TDS Doncasterby 24.9.18, crashed on nose 10.18

B6085 Deld Chingford W/E 8.12.17; No engine 5.1.18; Erected engineless 30.3.18; Became 207 TDS Chingford 1.4.18; 56 TS London Colney 7.6.18; 54 TDS Fairlop, allocated 4 TDS Hooton Park 13.8.18 (allocation cancelled)

B6086 Deld Chingford for erection W/E 8.12.17; No engine 5.1.18; Erected engineless 30.3.18; Became 207 TDS Chingford 1.4.18; 56 TS London Colney 7.6.18; WO 14.8.18

B6087 Deld Chingford for erection W/E 8.12.17; No engine 5.1.18; Erected engineless 30.3.18; Became 207 TDS Chingford 1.4.18; 27 TS London Colney 7.6.18

B6088 (No engine 5.1.18, later fitted 80hp Le Rhône) Deld Chingford for erection W/E 12.12.17; Detd Fairlop 2.18; Retd Chingford by 21.3.18; Became 207 TDS Chingford 1.4.18; 62 TS Hounslow c.6.18; 27 TDS Crail [no date]

B6089 28th Wing ARS Yatesbury to 4 TDS Hooton Park 14.12.17 to at least 17.12.17; 30th TS (AFC) Ternhill by 1.18; Became 6th (T) Sqdn AFC Ternhill 14.1.18; Pilot sick in air, overcome by nausea, unable to control machine, crashed, wrecked 20.1.18 (Lt RJT Forsyth AFC died of injuries 16.2.18)

B6090 67 TS Shawbury to 4 TDS Hooton Park 14.12.17 to at least 17.12.17; 30th TS (AFC) Ternhill; Became 6th (T) Sqdn AFC Ternhill 14.1.18

B6091 67 TS Shawbury to 4 TDS Hooton Park 14.12.17 to at least 17.12.17; 30th TS (AFC) Ternhill; Became 6th (T) Sqdn AFC Ternhill 14.1.18; Wrecked [date unknown]

B6092 (80hp Clerget) 28th Wing ARS Yatesbury to 4 TDS Hooton Park 14.12.17 to at least 17.12.17; 10 TS Shawbury by 4.1.18; 67 TS Shawbury by 2.18; 67 TS moved to North Shotwick 1.4.18; Choked engine, dived in from 35ft 27.5.18 (2/Lt T Whitman injured)

B6093 (80hp Le Rhône No.59703) 40 TS Croydon, stalled on turn, spun in 8.5.18 (2/Lt C Darbyshire injured)

B6094 40 TS Croydon by 23.12.17 to at least 18.1.18

B6095 (80hp Gnome) 94 Sqdn Harling Road by 14.1.18 to at least 30.3.18

B6096 (80hp Gnome No.4457/WD3985) 7th Wing ARS Dover to 3 TS Shoreham 19.12.17; Spun down from 3,000ft when controls jammed by foot, crashed 19.1.18 (2/Lt LH Wright-Meyer severely injured)

B6097 Deld Chingford for erection W/E 12.12.17; No engine at 5.1.18; Being erected engineless 30.3.18; Became 207 TDS Chingford 1.4.18; Became 54 TDS Chingford 20.7.18 (at Fairlop 10.18)

B6098 Deld Chingford for erection W/E 15.12.17; No engine at 5.1.18; Being erected engineless 30.3.18; Became 207 TDS Chingford 1.4.18; Became 54 TDS Chingford 20.7.18 (at Fairlop 10.18)

B6099 (80hp Gnome by 5.1.18) Deld Eastbourne Naval Flying School W/E 15.12.17; Became 206 TDS Eastbourne 1.4.18 to at least 7.4.18

B6100 (100hp Gnome Monosoupape by 5.1.18) Deld Eastbourne Naval Flying School W/E 12.12.17; Became 206 TDS Eastbourne 1.4.18; Crashed on landing, then crashed into by 504A B4316 9.5.18 (pilot unhurt); Flying again by 15.7.18 when became 50 TDS Eastbourne

B6101 School of Aerial Gunnery Aboukir by 1.9.18; Disbanded into 5 Fighting School Heliopolis 5.9.18; Crashed while trying to avoid a collision with an S.E.5 which had landed parallel 28.10.18 (Lt AJ Brewin); 19 TDS El Rimal by 11.18; WO 21.3.19

B6102 'X' AD to 22 TS Aboukir 30.5.18; 19 TDS El Rimal by 7.18; WO 1.12.18

B6103 No information

B6104 (80hp Le Rhône) 30th Wing ARS Montrose to 36 TS Montrose 27.4.18; 30th Wing ARS Montrose, WO & SOC 16.6.18

B6105 (80hp Le Rhône) 30th Wing ARS Turnhouse by 1.1.18; 73 TS Turnhouse by 1.18; 18 TS Montrose to 30th Wing ARS Montrose 8.5.18; 36 TS Montrose 18.5.18; 30th Wing ARS Montrose 18.5.18; 36 TS Montrose 30.5.18; ARS 30th Wing Montrose 2.6.18; 36 TS Montrose 4.6.18; 32 TDS Montrose, turned into wind, crashed 21.7.18 (2/Lt P Frederichsen injured)

B6106 58 TS Suez, SOC 14.8.18

B6107   58 TS Suez by 30.7.18 to at least 5.9.18; Artillery Observation School Almaza, WO 4.6.19

B6108   (80hp Clerget) 22 TS Aboukir by 7.18; 5 Fighting School Heliopolis by 1.18; Bumpy landing cross-wind, went on nose 1.10.18 (Flt Cdt APK Hattersley); ROS; Struck ridge on approach 21.10.18; Wreckage to 'X' AD; WOC 26.10.18

B6109   'X' AD to 19 TDS El Rimal 5.8.18 to at least 10.18; WO at 19 TDS El Rimal 26.2.19

B6110   19 TDS El Rimal, WO 12.3.19

B6111   58 TS Suez, crashed 5.10.18 (2/Lt HS Strange died of injuries 7.10.18)

B6112   195 TS El Rimal by 6.18; 19 TDS El Rimal 21.7.18; Turned on glide near ground, crashed 30.11.18 (Flt Cdt D McWhinnie died of injuries same day); SOC 8.12.18

B6113   'X' AD to 20th Training Wing 10.6.18; 22 TS Aboukir, WOC 30.5.19

B6114   'X' AD to 20th Training Wing 10.6.18; 22 TS Aboukir, WOC 30.5.19

B6115   No information

B6116   CFS 'B' Squadron Upavon by 1.18

B6117   CFS 'C' Squadron Upavon by 21.2.18

B6118   No information

B6119   3 TDS Lopcombe Corner by 9.5.18

B6120   No information

B6121   Flown from 5 School of Military Aeronautics Denham (coded 'G') to 1 School of Military Aeronautics Reading by Lt WLS Keith-Jopp 14.2.18

B6122-3 No information

B6124   81 Sqdn Scampton (named 'MUMMY') by 11.3.18 to at least 29.5.18

B6125   No information

B6126   81 Sqdn Scampton by 5.3.18; 34 TDS Scampton 4.7.18; At Knavesmire (York Racecourse) by 10.18

B6127   (80hp Clerget No.1057/WD11053) 39 TS South Carlton by 11-17.5.18; 46 TS South Carlton, stalled on climbing turn, spun in 2.11.18 (Lt HRS Easom injured)

B6128   11 TS Scampton by 10.5.18; 44 TDS Bicester, propeller accident while starting 10.1.19

B6129   70 TS Beaulieu by 20-21.4.18

B6130   No information

B6131   (80hp Le Rhône No.23099/WD2573) 92 Sqdn Chattis Hill by 30.1.18; 92 Sqdn moved to Tangmere 12.3.18 to at least 5.18; 91 Sqdn Tangmere, prop accident 5.6.18 (Capt SA Flavelle slightly injured)

B6132   No information

B6133   91 Sqdn Tangmere to 86 Sqdn Northolt 10.5.18

B6134-5 No information

B6136   (80hp Le Rhône) 3 TDS Lopcombe Corner, hit ground while flying low 13.10.18 (Lt ID Wood slightly injured)

B6137   No information

B6138   (80hp Le Rhône No.WD45803) 159th US Aero Sqdn, Joyce Green, prop accident 24.4.18 (Pte EM Glean injured); 63 TS Joyce Green to 41 TDS London Colney 30.7.18

B6139   (80hp Gnome) 94 Sqdn Harling Road by 16.3.18 to at least 26.5.18

B6140   (80hp Gnome) 94 Sqdn Harling Road by 28.2.18 to at least 21.5.18; 7 TDS Feltwell to Yarmouth 20.7.18

B6141   (Clerget) 10 TS Shawbury, crashed taxying 24.1.18 (2/Lt JK Shook); 67 TS Shawbury by 27.2.18; 67 TS moved to North Shotwick 1.4.18; 37th Wing half ARS North Shotwick 2.4.18

B6142   67 TS Shawbury by 28.1.18 to at least 4.18; 43 TS Chattis Hill by 6.18

B6143   Deld RNASTE Cranwell for erection W/E 11.1.18; Engineless at 11.1.18; Erecting with 80hp Gnome 30.3.18; Became 201/202 TDS Cranwell 1.4.18

B6144   (80hp Clerget No.1107/WD11109) 67 TS Shawbury by 28.1.18; Forced landed, crashed 29.1.18 (2/Lt R Dolman injured); 95 Sqdn North Shotwick to 37th Wing Half ARS North Shotwick 31.3.18; 95 Sqdn North Shotwick 11.4.18; 37th Wing Half ARS North Shotwick 1.5.18; 95 Sqdn North Shotwick 17.5.18 to at least 20.6.18

B6145   (80hp Le Rhône later 80hp Gnome) 67 TS Shawbury, engine failure, forced landed, crashed 30.1.18 (2/Lt EG Taylor injured); With 67 TS to North Shotwick 1.4.18; 37th Wing Half ARS North Shotwick 13.5.18

B6146   (80hp Le Rhône by 30.3.18) Deld engineless to Coventry W/E 11.1.18; Cranwell W/E 12.1.18; Became 201/202 TDS Cranwell 1.4.18; Became 56 TDS Cranwell 27.7.18 to at least 10.18; BUT (80hp Gnome) 37th Wing ARS Hooton Park to 'C' Flt 4 TDS Hooton Park 26.1.18

B6147   Deld 4 TDS Hooton Park by rail without engine 5.1.18

B6148   (80hp Gnome later 80hp Le Rhône) Deld 'C' Flt 4 TDS Hooton Park by rail without engine 5.1.18; 37th Wing ARS Hooton Park 8.2.18; 4 TDS Hooton Park 8.3.18; 37th Wing Half ARS Hooton Park to 4 TDS Hooton Park 11.5.18; Spun in 2.6.18 (Lt CS Garden USA killed); Wreckage to 37th Wing Half ARS Hooton Park 3.6.18

B6149   Deld RNASTE Cranwell without engine for erection W/E 11.1.18; Serviceable with 80hp Gnome by 30.3.18; Became 201/202 TDS Cranwell 1.4.18

B6150   Deld 4 TDS Hooton Park by rail without engine 5.1.18; 37th Wing Half ARS Hooton Park 18.6.18; 4 TDS Hooton Park 5.7.18

100 SOPWITH PUP ordered 24.7.17 additionally under Contract number 87/A/1101 from Whitehead Aircraft Ltd, Richmond, Surrey and numbered B7481 to B7580. (Possibly all initially placed in store) (Ordered with 80hp Le Rhône 9C but some fitted with alternative engines)

B7481   (80hp Gnome No.2981/WD32556) 85 Sqdn Hounslow from 8.1.18; 87 Sqdn Hounslow by 29.1.18; 93 Sqdn Chattis Hill from 27.3.18; Engine failure, crashed on roof 12.4.18 (Lt TV Brake injured)

B7482   74 Sqdn London Colney to 56 TS London Colney 15.3.18 to at least 8.6.18

B7483   85 Sqdn Hounslow from 8.1.18

B7484   No information

B7485   (80hp Le Rhône) 36 TS Montrose by 1.18; 6 TS Montrose by 12.5.18; Engine failure, forced landed, overturned, broke prop, fin & rudder 18.5.18 (2/Lt AS Compton OK); 30th Wing ARS Montrose to 6 TS Montrose 17.6.18; Mid-air collision with C381 8.7.18 (2/Lt GH Grimshaw killed); 30th Wing ARS Montrose 15.7.18; WO & SOC 16.7.18
        BUT 26 TS Narborough, WO 8.6.18

B7486   (80hp Clerget) 6 TS Montrose to 30th Wing ARS Montrose 3.4.18; 6 TS Montrose 26.4.18; ARS 30th Wing Montrose 2.6.18; WO & SOC 15.6.18;
        BUT 2 TDS West Fenton by 7.18

B7487   74 Sqdn London Colney from 8.1.18; 30th Wing ARS to 6 TS Montrose 3.4.18

B7488   No information

B7489   (80hp Clerget) 30th Wing ARS to 36 TS Montrose 30.3.18; 30th Wing ARS Montrose 17.4.18; 18 TS Montrose 18.5.18; WO & SOC 31.5.18

B7490   (100hp Gnome Monosoupape) 74 Sqdn London Colney from 8.1.18; 1 School of Navigation & Bomb Dropping Stonehenge by 29.8.18 to at least 27.11.18

B7491   (80hp Clerget) 30th Wing ARS Montrose to 18 TS Montrose 20.4.18; 30th Wing ARS Montrose to 18 TS Montrose 22.5.18; 30th Wing ARS Montrose 6.6.18; WO & SOC 16.6.18

B7492   74 Sqdn London Colney to 86 Sqdn Northolt 28.2.18;
         WO 10.3.18

B7493   74 Sqdn London Colney from 8.1.18

B7494   74 Sqdn London Colney from 8.1.18

B7495   (80hp Le Rhône) Tested at 30th Wing ARS Turnhouse
         27.1.18 & 30.1.18; 6 TS Montrose to 30th Wing ARS
         Montrose 3.5.18; 36 TS Montrose 23.5.18; Steep
         landing, crashed 1.6.18 (2/Lt CV Hicks injured); WOC
         8.6.18

B7496   (80hp Clerget) Tested at 30th Wing ARS 27.1.18; 36 TS
         Montrose 6.4.18; 2 TDS West Fenton by 5.18; 30 Wing
         ARS Montrose to 6 TS Montrose 10.6.18; 36 TS
         Montrose to ARS Gullane 3.7.18; 30 Wing ARS
         Montrose to 32 TDS Montrose 16.7.18 - @4.10.18

B7497   No information

B7498   45 TS South Carlton by 9.5.18

B7499   (80hp Le Rhône) 81 Sqdn Scampton by 12-14.2.18

B7500   (100hp Gnome Monosoupape) 61 TS South Carlton by
         14.5.18; Crashed there [date unknown]

B7501   (80hp Le Rhône) 54 TS Castle Bromwich, hit tree,
         crashed 9.4.18 (2/Lt CD James slightly injured)

B7502   81 Sqdn Scampton by 14.2.18 to at least 4.18

B7503   32 TDS Montrose by 6.18

B7504   81 Sqdn Scampton by 4.18 to at least 8.6.18

B7505   61 TS South Carlton by 11.5.18

B7506   (80hp Le Rhône) 6th (T) Sqdn AFC Minchinhampton,
         came badly out of dive, insufficient margin, crashed
         14.8.18 (2/Lt CC Lewis killed)

B7507   6th (T) Sqdn AFC Minchinhampton

B7508   5th (T) Sqdn AFC Minchinhampton

B7509   5th (T) Sqdn AFC Minchinhampton

B7510   43 TS Ternhill by 2.18 to at least 14.3.18

B7511   No information

B7512   54 TS Castle Bromwich by 6.2.18

B7513   (80hp Le Rhône) 95 Sqdn North Shotwick from 23.3.18;
         37th Wing Half ARS North Shotwick 10.5.18; 95 Sqdn
         North Shotwick to 37th Wing Half ARS North Shotwick
         6.6.18; 95 Sqdn North Shotwick by 3-7.7.18; 4 TDS

         Hooton Park, shot up by another aircraft, crashed 6.8.18
         (2/Lt JF Roscoe killed)
         [two white bands in front of tail in photo]

B7514   No information

B7515   (80hp Le Rhône) 74 TS Castle Bromwich by 26.4.18;
         Propeller accident 18.6.18 (2AM G Silcox injured)

B7516   51 TDS North Shotwick by 7.8.18

B7517   43 TS Ternhill by 1.18 to at least 2.18; 1 TS Beaulieu by
         3.18 to 7.18

B7518   55 TS Lilbourne by 3.18 – 4.18; 54 TS Eastbourne by
         7.18

B7519   67 TS Shawbury by 25.1.18; Became 51 TDS North
         Shotwick 15.7.18; Engine failure, forced landed, crashed
         9.8.18 (2/Lt WStC Slater)

B7520   61 TS South Carlton by 21.5.18

B7521-2 No information

B7523   32 TDS Montrose to 30th Wing ARS Montrose 23.7.18;
         26 TDS Edzell by 7.8.18

B7524   No information

B7525   60 TS Scampton by 3.18

B7526   No information

B7527   NARD Greenhill 1918

B7528   (80hp Le Rhône) 30th Wing ARS Montrose to 6 TS
         Montrose 21.4.18; 30th Wing ARS Montrose 31.5.18;
         WO & SOC 16.6.18

B7529   (80hp Clerget) 36 TS Montrose, mid-air collision with 36
         TS Camel B7338, fell out of control 4.4.18 (Lt EW
         Burton AFC killed; SOC 15.4.18

B7530-1 No information

B7532   Flown Lincoln to Hendon 29.5.18

B7533   28 TS Castle Bromwich 1918

B7534   No information

B7535   (80hp Le Rhône) 55 TS Lilbourne, stalled at low height,
         dived in 4.5.18 (2/Lt W Stephenson slightly injured)

B7536-8 No information

B7539   81 Sqdn Scampton by 22.5.18

B7540-1 No information

B7542   11 TS Scampton by 8.5.18

Highly chequered B7575 of No.26 Training Depot Station at Edzell around September 1918. It forced landed on 1st October after engine failure while piloted by Lt B.C.Smith.

(RAF Museum P13088)

B7543	32 TDS Montrose 1918
B7544	No information
B7545	18 TS Montrose by 28.6.18
B7546-9	No information
B7550-2	No information
B7553	74 TS Castle Bromwich by 14-25.3.18
B7554-9	No information
B7560-4	No information
B7565	RAE Farnborough from 7.6.19; Tested with Gravity Ground Indicator 23.9.19; Damaged at Hendon Air Pageant 24.6.22; Last flown 27.6.23
B7566-9	No information
B7570-1	No information
B7572	(80hp Clerget) Arr 30th Wing ARS Montrose 17.6.18; 36 TS Montrose 22.6.18; 2 TDS Gullane 26.6.18
B7573	(80hp Clerget) Arr 30th Wing ARS Montrose 17.6.18; 6 TS Montrose 21.6.18; 32 TDS Montrose 15.7.18; 26 TDS Edzell by 23.9.18
B7574	No information
B7575	(80hp Le Rhône) Arr 30th Wing ARS Montrose 17.6.18; 18 TS Montrose 22.6.18; 32 TDS Montrose 15.7.18; ARS Montrose 21.7.18; 26 TDS Edzell (chequerboard finish overall), engine failure, forced landed 1.10.18 (Lt BC Smith)
B7576	Arr 30th Wing ARS Montrose 17.6.18
B7577-9	No information
B7580	No information

PUP rebuils in range B7731 to B8230 by 1(S)ARD Farnborough under Revised Aeroplane Repair Scheme, included these Pups

B7752	42 TS Wye by 3.4.18 to at least 20.4.18; 18th Wing ARS Hounslow from 24.7.18; 42 TDS Hounslow to 30 TDS Northolt 11.8.18; WO 18.9.18

PUP, various rebuilds from spares and salvage

B8784	By 6th Wing ARS Dover, serial allotted 28.1.18
B8785	By 6th Wing ARS Dover, serial allotted 28.1.18
B8786	By 6th Wing ARS Dover, serial allotted 28.1.18

B8795	By 26th Wing ARS Thetford, serial allotted 13.2.18
B8801	By 7th Wing ARS Norwich, serial allotted 14.2.18
B8821	(80hp Gnome) By 26th Wing ARS Thetford; 56 TDS Cranwell by 10.18
B8829	By 7th Wing ARS Norwich; 94 Sqdn Harling Road by 20.4.18 to at least 25.5.18
B9440	By 63 TS Joyce Green, serial allotted 13.8.17 (painted white with black band forward of tail); 64 Sqdn Sedgeford by 6-24.9.17; 87 Sqdn Sedgeford to 3 (Auxiliary) School of Aerial Gunnery New Romney 15.12.17; Became 1 (Observers) School of Aerial Gunnery New Romney 9.3.18 to at least 6.18
B9455	By 6th Wing ARS Dover, serial allotted 1.9.17
B9931	By 6th Wing ARS Dover, serial allotted 25.10.17; 56 TS London Colney to 6th Wing 2.11.17; 87 Sqdn Hounslow by 31.12.17; 3 TDS Lopcombe Corner, WO 20.3.18; Rebuilt?; Pool of Pilots Manston, mid-air collision with B5992 17.7.18 (Sgt JD Bishop killed)

350 SOPWITH PUP TRACTOR BIPLANE FIGHTERS ordered 20.8.17 under Contract number AS.11541/17 from Standard Motor Co Ltd, Coventry and numbered C201 to C550. (Ordered with 80hp Le Rhône 9C but some fitted with alternative engines)

C201	Deld 4 TDS Hooton Park by rail with engine 8.1.18; RNASTE Cranwell from W/E 20.3.18; Forced landed, undercarriage damaged nr Ancaster 20.3.18 (pilot unhurt); Became 201/202 TDS 1.4.18; 1 TS Beaulieu by 29.3.18 to at least 24.4.18; 70 TS Beaulieu by 31.5.18
C202	(80hp Gnome by 30.3.18) ARS Hooton Park to "C" Flight 4 TDS Hooton Park without engine 5.1.18; Deld RNASTE Cranwell without engine for erection 11.1.18; Being erected 30.3.18; Became 201/202 TDS 1.4.18; 95 Sqdn North Shotwick by 17.4.18
C203	2 Flight Group 4 TDS Hooton Park, left by air 3.2.18; 4 TDS Hooton Park to 37th Wing Half ARS Hooton Park 7.2.18; 4 TDS Hooton Park 26.3.18; 37th Wing Half ARS Hooton Park 3.5.18; 4 TDS Hooton Park 20.5.18; 37th Wing Half ARS Hooton Park 1.6.18

Pup C217 of 'F' Flight of the Naval Flying School can be seen among a motley collection of aircraft in the large airship shed at East Fortune at the mouth of the Firth of Forth. Immediately behind it is C214. There appears to have been some sort of accident as the Camel in the foreground has extensive damage to it starboard wing, and C217 has minor damage to its port wing.

(via Philip Jarrett)

C204   'C' Flight 4 TDS Hooton Park to ARS Hooton Park 23.1.18; 4 TDS Hooton Park 26.1.18; SOC 3.2.18, left by air

C205   (60hp Le Rhône) Deld RNASTE Cranwell without engine for erection 11.1.18; Being erected with 60hp Le Rhône 30.3.18; Became 201/202 TDS 1.4.18

C206   (80hp Gnome) 'C' Flight 4 TDS Hooton Park to ARS Hooton Park 23.1.18; 4 TDS Hooton Park 29.1.18; 37th Wing Half ARS Hooton Park 22.3.18; 4 TDS Hooton Park 3.5.18; 37th Wing Half ARS Hooton Park 19.6.18; 4 TDS Hooton Park 7.7.18

C207   Deld 4 TDS Hooton Park by rail without engine 18.1.18; ARS Hooton Park 23.1.18; 'C' Flight 4 TDS 29.1.18; 37th Wing Half ARS Hooton Park 10.3.18; 4 TDS 11.3.18; 37th Wing Half ARS Hooton Park 23.3.18; 4 TDS Hooton Park 25.3.18

C208   Deld RNASTE Cranwell for erection W/E 18.1.18; Being erected with 80hp Gnome 30.3.18; Became 201/202 TDS 1.4.18

C209   92 Sqdn Tangmere by 5.18; 62 TS Hounslow by 14-15.5.18; WO 27.6.18

C210   40 TS Croydon to 41 TDS London Colney 28.7.18

C211   Deld 'F' Flt East Fortune Naval Flying School 11.1.18; Became 208 TDS East Fortune 1.4.18

C212   (110hp Le Rhône) 42 TDS Hounslow to 30 TDS Northolt 3.9.18; to Pool of Pilots Manston 16.9.18

C213   54 TS Castle Bromwich, mid-air collision with 2/Lt Smith while practising air fighting 20.1.18 (Lt BS Smallman injured)

C214   Deld 'F Flt East Fortune Naval Flying School 11.1.18; Donibristle W/E 21.3.18; HMS *Furious* W/E 21.3.18 (skid undercarriage tests with 9949, flown by W/Cdr HR Busteed); Rosyth 18.3.18; Surveyed 18.3.18 (wrecked); Deleted 27.3.18 Presume brought back on charge; To Turnhouse W/E 4.4.18; Deleted W/E 17.5.18

C215   54 TS Eastbourne by 7.18; Became 5 TDS at Eastbourne 15.7.18 - @9.8.18; School of Special Flying Gosport 1918? (Kiwi insignia below cockpit, striped wings)

C216   10 TS Shawbury by 27.1.18; 67 TS Shawbury by 3.18; 67 TS moved to North Shotwick 1.4.18; 37th Wing Half ARS Shotwick 2.4.18; 37th Wing Half ARS Hooton Park to 4 TDS Hooton Park 17.5.18; 37th Wing Half ARS Hooton Park 6.6.18; 4 TDS Hooton Park 8.7.18

C217   Deld 'F' Flt East Fortune Naval Flying School 19.1.18; Rosyth W/E 21.3.18; U/s at East Fortune 30.3.18; Fleet Aeroplane Depot Turnhouse W/E 4.4.18 to at least 30.1.19

C218   67 TS Shawbury by 27.2.18; 67 TS moved to North Shotwick 1.4.18; 37th Wing Half ARS Shotwick 2.4.18; 51 TDS North Shotwick by 2.8.18; 4 TDS Hooton Park, stalled and dived in 17.10.18 (Flt Cdt DW Patstone injured)

C219   67 TS Shawbury by 25.1.18; 67 TS moved to North Shotwick 1.4.18; 37th Wing Half ARS North Shotwick 6.5.18; 4 TDS Hooton Park by 10.8.18

C220   Deld 'F' East Fortune Naval Flying School W/E 19.1.18; Became 208 TDS East Fortune 1.4.18

C221   29th Wing ARS Shawbury to 6th (T) Sqdn AFC Ternhill; 3.2.18; Forced landed 19.2.18; Pilot lost control, spun in 11.6.17 (2/Lt FT Offer injured)

C222   Deld 4 TDS Hooton Park 17.1.18 by rail without engine; ARS Hooton Park 23.1.18; 'C' Flight 4 TDS 29.1.18; 37th Wing Half ARS Hooton Park 26.3.18; 4 TDS Hooton Park 8.5.18

C223   Deld F Flt Naval Flying School W/E 19.1.18; U/s by 30.3.18; Became 208 TDS East Fortune 1.4.18; To Pool of Pilots Manston 4.18; 206 TDS Eastbourne 25.4.18; Grand Fleet School of Aerial Fighting & Gunnery Leuchars by 21.6.19

C224   Deld 4 TDS Hooton Park by rail 31.1.18; ARS Hooton Park to 90 Sqdn North Shotwick 8.2.18

C225   Deld 'C' Flight 4 TDS Hooton Park by rail 8.2.18; 37th Wingh Half ARS North Shotwick to 95 Sqdn North Shotwick 2.3.18; 37th Wing Half ARS Hooton Park to 4 TDS Hooton Park 8.3.18; 37th Wing Half ARS Hooton Park 23.3.18; 4 TDS Hooton Park to 37th Wing Half ARS Hooton Park 6.5.18; 4 TDS Hooton Park 17.5.18; 37th Wing Half ARS Hooton Park 19.5.18

C226   Deld 'F' Flt East Fortune Naval Flying School W/E 19.1.18; U/s by 30.3.18; Became 208 TDS East Fortune 1.4.18; Goggles forced bad landing, crashed 15.4.18 (Lt SJN Haigh seriously injured)

C227   Deld 'C' Flight 4 TDS Hooton Park 17.1.18 by rail without engine; ARS Hooton Park 23.1.18; 'C' Flight 4 TDS Hooton Park 29.1.18; 37th Wing Half ARS Hooton Park 3.6.18; 4 TDS Hooton Park 8.7.18 to at least 8.8.18

C228   Deld 'C' Flight 4 TDS Hooton Park 17.1.18 by rail without engine; ARS Hooton Park 23.1.18; 'C' flight 4 TDS Hooton Park; 29.1.18; 37th Wing Half ARS Hooton Park 22.3.18;

C229   Deld War School RNAS Manston W/E 25.1.18; Became Pool of Pilots Manston 1.4.18; 206 TDS Eastbourne 5.4.18; Became 50 TDS Eastbourne 15.7.18; Crashed on landing 7.8.18 (pilot unhurt)

C230   90 Sqdn North Shotwick by 2.1.18; 'C' Flight 4 TDS Hooton Park 19.1.18; 90 Sqdn North Shotwick 21.1.18; 37th Wing Half ARS North Shotwick 6.3.18; 90 Sqdn North Shotwick 29.3.18; 37th Wing Half ARS Hooton Park 15.4.18; 4 TDS Hooton Park to 37th Wing Half ARS Hooton Park 21.5.18; 4 TDS Hooton Park 6.18; 37th Wing Half ARS Hooton Park 9.7.18

C231   Deld 'C' Flight 4 TDS Hooton Park 19.1.18; 90 Sqdn North Shotwick 21.1.18; 37th Wing Half ARS North Shotwick 1.3.18; 90 Sqdn North Shotwick 10.3.18; 37th Wing Half ARS Hooton Park to 90 Sqdn North Shotwick 18.5.18; 95 Sqdn North Shotwick to 37th Wing Half ARS North Shotwick 18.6.18

C232   Deld RNASTE Cranwell W/E 9.2.18; Freiston, crashed and badly damaged 22.3.18 (pilot unhurt); U/s at Cranwell 30.3.18

C233   92 Sqdn Chattis Hill by 12.2.18

C234   'C' Flight 4 TDS Hooton Park; Crashed 1.2.18; ARS Hooton Park 1.2.18; 34 TDS Scampton by 17.9.18

C235   Deld RNASTE Cranwell W/E 2.2.18 to at least 20.3.18; 36 HD Sqdn Usworth 6.7.18; Tadcaster to 32 TDS Montrose 12.7.18; 26 TDS Edzell, spinning nose dive, crashed 12.8.18 (2/Lt JA Potts seriously injured); Visited 77 HD Sqdn Penston 9.18

C236   3 TDS Lopcombe Corner by 6.18

C237   56 TS London Colney from 9.2.18; WO 2.4.18

C238   (60hp Le Rhône, later 80hp Gnome by 30.3.18) Deld RNASTE Cranwell W/E 25.1.18; Became 201/202 TDS 1.4.18; Grand Fleet School of Aerial Fighting & Gunnery Leuchars by 3.19

C239   81 Sqdn Scampton by 14.3.18; 208 TDS East Fortune by 6.4.18

C240   Pool of Pilots Manston by 6.18; Shipped to Egypt; 20th Training Wing, WO 9.9.18

C241   Deld RNASTE Cranwell W/E 25.1.18; Being erected with 80hp Gnome 30.3.18; Became 201/202 TDS Cranwell 1.4.18; Became 56 TDS Cranwell 27.7.18 to at least 10.18

C242   (80hp Gnome) FF 27.1.18; 7 TS Netheravon (harlequin diamond patterns overall); Artillery Co-operation School Tilshead by 11.18; Became *G-EBFJ;* Scrapped 1924

C243   No information

C244   Deld War School RNAS Manston W/E 25.1.18; U/s and

C235, seen here with a diamond marking aft of the fuselage roundel, was flown by No.26 Training Depot Station at Edzell until it went into a spinning nose dive and crashed on 12th August 1918, 2/Lt J.A.Potts being seriously injured. (*Don Neate/Cross & Cockade International*)

engineless 30.3.18; Became Pool of Pilots Manston 1.4.18; 2 Fighting School Marske by 16.8.18

C245 Artillery Co-operation School Tilshead by 6.18 to at least 11.18; Crashed on nose (unit?)

C246 Arr 'X' AD ex UK 17.6.18; 19 TDS El Rimal, WO 26.2.19

C247 Deld War School RNAS Manston W/E 23.2.18; Became Pool of Pilots Manston 1.4.18 to at least 6.18; 2 Fighting School Marske by 16.8.18; Shipped to Egypt; 19 TDS El Rimal by 11.18

C248 Arr 'X' AD ex UK 17.6.18; 19 TDS El Rimal by 10.18; 5 Fighting School Heliopolis, WO 9.6.19

C249 Arr 'X' AD ex UK 17.6.18; 19 TDS El Rimal 5.8.18 to at least 11.18; WO at Artillery Observation School Almaza 28.4.19

C250 Deld War School RNAS Manston W/E 16.2.18; Became Pool of Pilots Manston 1.4.18 to at least 6.18; Shipped to Egypt; Arr 'X' AD ex UK 6.18; 19 TDS El Rimal 5.8.18 to at least 11.18

C251 Arr 'X' AD ex UK 17.6.18; 19 TDS El Rimal 5.8.18; Crashed 29.9.18 (Bdr GB Burt killed); WO 20th Training Wing 9.10.18

C252 Arr 'X' AD ex UK 17.6.18

C253 Deld War School RNAS Manston W/E 16.2.18; Became Pool of Pilots Manston 1.4.18; 206 TDS Eastbourne 3.5.18; Became 50 TDS Eastbourne 15.7.18 to at least 1.19

C254 Arr 'X' AD ex UK 17.6.18; 58 TS Suez by 18.8.18; 5 Fighting School Heliopolis, WO 21.3.19

C255 Arr 'X' AD ex UK 17.6.18; 5 Fighting School Heliopolis, WO 21.3.19

C256 Deld War School RNAS Manston W/E 16.2.18; Became Pool of Pilots Manston 1.4.18; 42 TDS Hounslow 27.7.18; 41 TDS London Colney 16.8.18

C257 81 Sqdn Scampton by 5.18; 206 TDS Eastbourne, crashed and wrecked 29.6.18

C258 (80hp Clerget) 46 TDS South Carlton, engine failure at low height, spun in, Lincoln 28.10.18 (2/Lt PC Weaver-Adams killed)

C259 (60hp Le Rhône) Deld RNASTE Cranwell W/E 22.2.18; Became 201/202 TDS Cranwell 1.4.18

C260 No information

C261 39 TS South Carlton by 22.4.18; 61 TS South Carlton by 21.5.18

C262 Deld RNASTE Cranwell W/E 15.2.18; Collided with Camel B5674, crashed, badly damaged Cranwell South 28.2.18 (pilot uninjured); U/s at Cranwell 30.3.18; Became 201/202 TDS Cranwell 1.4.18

C263 11 TDS Old Sarum by 24-28.4.18; School of Aerial Photography; Westland Aircraft Yeovil by 1.19 to at least 6.19; To Westland Aircraft Yeovil 16.1.20 to at least 2.20

C264 3 TDS Lopcombe Corner, spun in Nether Wallop 10.3.18 (Capt CL Bath seriously injured)

C265 (80hp Le Rhône 9C) Deld RNASTE Cranwell W/E 22.2.18; Lost, landed, damaged propeller Hubberts' Bridge 20.3.18 (pilot unhurt); U/s at Cranwell 30.3.18; Became 201/202 TDS 1.4.18 to at least 6.18; Became 56 TDS Cranwell 27.7.18 to at least 10.18

C266 93 Sqdn Tangmere to 157 Sqdn Upper Heyford 24.7.18

C267 74 Sqdn London Colney from 1.3.18; 91 Sqdn Tangmere, looped then rolled, spun in 16.3.18 (Capt MDG Scott died of injuries 17.3.18)

C268 Deld RNASTE Cranwell W/E 8.3.18; School of Aerial Fighting & Bomb Dropping Freiston 1.4.18

C269 18th Wing ARS Hounslow from 25.1.18; 56 TS London Colney 25.2.18 to at least 17.5.18; 91 Sqdn 1918; 41 TDS London Colney to Pilots & Observers AG&FS Leysdown 3.9.18 to at least 2.19

C270 18th Wing ARS Hounslow from 25.1.18; 56 TS London Colney 25.2.18; WO 27.5.18

C271 Deld War School RNAS Manston W/E 2.3.18; Became Pool of Pilots Manston 1.4.18; 2 Fighting School Marske, stalled, spun in, burnt out 16.6.18 (2/Lt FC Turner AFC killed)

C272 64 Sqdn Sedgeford by 10.17; 18th Wing ARS Hounslow from 25.1.18; 4 TDS Hooton Park to 37th Wing ARS Hooton Park 26.3.18; 91 Sqdn Tangmere, from 24.3.18; Mid-air collision with 504 E1663, crashed 7.7.18 (2/Lt J Tyllyer seriously injured)

C273 18th Wing ARS Hounslow from 25.1.18; 85 Sqdn Hounslow 6.3.18; 87 Sqdn Hounslow 1918; 62 TS Hounslow; WO 16.6.18

C274 Deld War School RNAS Manston W/E 23.2.18; Became Pool of Pilots Manston 1.4.18 to at least 6.18

C275 73 TS Turnhouse by 19.10.17; TOC 90 Sqdn North Shotwick 19.2.18; 95 Sqdn North Shotwick 1.3.18; 37th Wing Half ARS North Shotwick 22.3.18; To 95 Sqdn North Shotwick 8.4.18; 4 TDS Hooton Park to 37th Wing Half ARS Hooton Park 8.7.18

C276 Deld 90 Sqdn North Shotwick 16.2.18; 37th Wing Half ARS North Shotwick 24.3.18; 96 Sqdn North Shotwick 16.4.18 - @8.6.18; 37th Wing Half ARS North Shotwick to 90 Sqdn North Shotwick 7.7.18; 37th Wing Half ARS North Shotwick 9.7.18

C277 Deld War School RNAS Manston W/E 23.2.18; Became Pool of Pilots Manston 1.4.18; Stalled at 50ft and nose-dived in 5.7.18 (Lt W Towen seriously injured)

C278 90 Sqdn North Shotwick from 19.2.18; 95 Sqdn North Shotwick 1.3.18; 37th Wing Half ARS North Shotwick 16.3.18; 95 Sqdn North Shotwick 29.3.18; 37th Wing Half ARS North Shotwick 7.5.18; 95 Sqdn North Shotwick, flew into ground while low flying, overturned 12.6.18 (2/Lt HN Hastie died of injuries)

C279 90 Sqdn North Shotwick from 12.3.18; 37th Wing Half ARS North Shotwick 7.4.18; 96 Sqdn North Shotwick 19.5.18; Prop accident 28.6.18 (2/AM H Atha injured)

C280 Deld War School RNAS Manston W/E 2.3.18; Became Pool of Pilots Manston (coded '18') 1.4.18; Eastbourne 17.6.18; 42 TDS Hounslow 27.7.18; 3 TDS Lopcombe Corner 3.8.18

C281 No information

C282 Presentation aircraft 'Gold Coast Aborigines No.2' (succeeded B5246). Tested 1 AAP Coventry, burst tyre landing 26.5.18 (2/Lt GH Drew)

C283 Deld East Fortune Naval Flying School W/E 23.2.18 (used for practice landings); Became 208 TDS East Fortune 1.4.18; Grand Fleet School of Aerial Fighting & Gunnery Leuchars by 5.19

C284 Hendon to 1 School of Navigation & Bomb Dropping, Stonehenge 23.3.18 to at least 30.12.18

C285 (80hp Clerget later 80hp Le Rhône) 30th Wing ARS Montrose to 36 TS Montrose 6.4.18; 30th Wing ARS Montrose 27.4.18; 26 TS Edzell by 6.18; 36 TS Montrose by 9.6.18; 30 Wing ARS Montrose 10.6.18; 32 TDS Montrose 15.7.18; 30 Wing ARS Montrose 18.7.18

C286 Deld East Fortune Naval Flying School W/E 23.2.18 (used for practice landings) Became 208 TDS East Fortune 1.4.18

C287 18 TS Montrose (coded 'C') by 1.6.18; Crashed, WOC 11.6.18

C288 (80hp Clerget) 30th Wing ARS Montrose to 36 TS Montrose 9.4.18; 30th Wing ARS Montrose 13.5.18; 36 TS Montrose 21.6.18; 30th Wing ARS Montrose to 36 TS Montrose 11.7.18; 32 TDS Montrose 15.7.18

C289 Deld East Fortune Naval Flying School W/E 2.3.18 (used for practice landings); Became 208 TDS East Fortune 1.4.18; 1 Fighting School Turnberry, tested 5.9.18

C290 49 TS Catterick by 5.8.18; Engine failurre, crashed 14.8.18 (2/Lt AW Buck slightly injured)

C291 36 HD Sqdn Hylton 1918

C292 Deld East Fortune Naval Flying School W/E 23.2.18 (used for practice landings); Became 208 TDS East Fortune 1.4.18;

C293 70 TS Beaulieu by 7.4.18

C294 70 TS Beaulieu by 26.3.18 to at least 9.5.18

C295 Deld RNASTE Cranwell W/E 8.3.18; Crashed, slightly damaged, Cranwell South 21.3.18 (pilot unhurt); Serviceable by 30.3.18; Became 201/202 TDS Cranwell 1.4.18

C296 17th Wing HQ Beaulieu by 20.3.18

C297 94 Sqdn Harling Road from 26.3.18 to at least 27.4.18

C298 Deld RNASTE Cranwell W/E 8.3.18; Engine failure, forced landed, axle damaged, nr Grantham 20.3.18 (pilot unhurt); U/s 30.3.18; Became 201 TDS Cranwell 1.4.18; Became 56 TDS 15.7.18; Spun in off low turn 9.9.18 (Flt Cdt HG Van der Feen seriously injured)

C299 25 TS Thetford, crashed on landing, std wheel and propeller smashed 1918; 7 TDS Feltwell to 1 TDS Stamford 31.8.18

C300 94 Sqdn Harling Road by 28.2.18; 26th Wing ARS Thetford to 94 Sqdn Harling Road 8.3.18 to at least 19.5.18

C301 Deld Cranwell Workshops 3.18; RNASTE Cranwell 14.3.18; Crashed and damaged 26.3.18 (pilot unhurt); u/s 30.3.18; Became 201/202 TDS 1.4.18 to at least 14.5.18

C302 No information

C303 188 (Night) TS Throwley to 198 (Night) TS Rochford 6.9.18; 36 HD Sqdn 5.10.18; 189 (Night) TS Sutton's Farm

C304 Deld Chingford W/E 11.3.18; Being erected 30.3.18; Became 207 TDS Chingford/Fairlop 1.4.18; Became 54 TDS Chingford/Fairlop 20.7.18 to at least 6.11.18

C305 Presentation aircraft 'THE ORIOLE'. Deld 2.18 for training; 189 (Night) TS Sutton's Farm (stars on fuselage); 44 HD Sqdn North Weald, WO 13.9.19

Seen here at Detling in 1918, Standard-built C321 was probably with No.143 (Home Defence) Squadron.   *(J.M.Bruce/G.S.Leslie collection)*

C306   Presentation aircraft 'Liverpool Overseas Club'. 189 (Night) TS Sutton's Farm to 198 (Night) TS Rochford 6.9.18; 76 HD Sqdn 5.10.18; 36 HD Sqdn 13.10.18

C307   Deld RNASTE Vendôme W/E 30.3.18; Became 205 TDS Vendôme 1.4.18; Engine failure, forced landed, slightly damaged on aerodrome 1.7.18 (PFO SR Pragnell); Crashed 16.9.18 (Lt SJ Fisher unhurt)

C308   189 (Night) TS Sutton's Farm, crashed into River Thames whilst contour flying 7.7.18 (Lt WB Ferguson drowned)

C309   FF 1.4.18; 189 (Night) TS Sutton's Farm to 198 (Night) TS Rochford 6.9.18; 190 (Night) TS Newmarket 11.9.18; Spinning nose dive, crashed 18.9.18 (Capt TJC Martyn seriously injured)

C310   Deld RNASTE Vendôme W/E 30.3.18; Became 205 TDS Vendôme 1.4.18; Badly damaged avoiding another aircraft 8.6.18 (PFO FW Wright unhurt); Machine collapsed after nose put down for loop 30.9.18 (Lt SJ Fisher killed)

C311   1 (Communications) Sqdn Kenley by 25.6.19 to at least 11.7.19

C312   189 (Night) TS Sutton's Farm 1918; Became *G-EAVW*

C313   Deld RNASTE Vendôme W/E 30.3.18; Became 205 TDS Vendôme 1.4.18; Swung landing, badly damaged 24.6.18 (PFO AE Betts unhurt); Crashed 13.8.18 (2/Lt AH Williams); Crashed landing downwind 5.9.18 (Flt Cdt R Coombes-White unhurt)

C314   Allotted to store 15.3.18, amended 18.3.18; Deld 3 AAP Norwich without engine W/E 27.3.18; 206 TDS Eastbourne 4.18; Engine failure diving on target, crashed, damaged 3.7.18 (2/Lt AE Wilson injured)

C315   No information

C316   Deld RNASTE Vendôme W/E 30.3.18; Became 205 TDS Vendôme 1.4.18; Crashed on Wing football ground 17.10.18 (Capt SB Joyce slightly injured)

C317   Allotted to store without engine 15.3.18, amended 18.3.18; Deld I SD 3.18 for naval use

C318   No information

C319   Deld RNASTE Vendôme W/E 30.3.18; Became 205 TDS Vendôme 1.4.18; Crashed on take-off, badly damaged 29.6.18 (PFO AE Betts unhurt); Crashed 13.8.18 (Flt Cdt CSG Davies unhurt)

C320   Allotted to store without engine 15.3.18, amended 18.3.18; Deld 1 SD 3.18; 206 TDS Eastbourne by 8.6.18

C321   Photographed at Detling in 1918 [probably 143 HD Sqdn]

C322   Deld RNASTE Vendôme W/E 30.3.18; Became 205 TDS Vendôme 1.4.18; Went on nose landing, badly damaged 17.6.18 (PFO CM Pinkerton); Hit top wing of Avro on take-off, damaged propeller, overturned landing, badly damaged 18.7.18 (PFO RM Barron slightly injured)

C323   54 TDS Chingford/Fairlop by 17.9.18; 2 AAP Hendon, on delivery hit taxying 504 while taking off, crashed 25.11.18 (Lt RI Stedman slightly injured)

C324   56 TDS Cranwell by 9.18; Fairlop by 10.18; Manston from 6.10.18
        BUT 16 TDS Amriya by 9.18

C325   Deld RNASTE Vendôme late 3.18; Became 205 TDS Vendôme 1.4.18; Drifted landing due to gust of wind, badly damaged 18.5.18 (PFO JJ McLeod & Capt PH Martin unhurt); Caught fire at 3,000ft, pilot thrown out at 150 ft nr Crucheray, burnt out 21.6.18 (PFO WSG Barker killed) BUT 84th Wing Vendôme by 8.8.18; Deleted 10.8.18
        ALSO 56 TDS Cranwell by 5.8.18 to at least 13.9.18

C326   36 HD Sqdn Hylton 1918; 56 TDS Cranwell by 7.9.18 to at least 22.11.18

C327-9 No information

C330   96 Sqdn North Shotwick by 19.5.18

C331   Deld Rosyth by rail W/E 30.3.18; Fleet Aeroplane Depot Turnhouse W/E 11.4.18 to at least 4.5.18; 37th Wing Half ARS North Shotwick to 96 Sqdn North Shotwick 19.5.18

C332   Deld Rosyth by rail W/E 30.3.18; Fleet Aeroplane Depot Turnhouse W/E 11.4.18 to at least 5.18

C333   Deld Rosyth by rail W/E 30.3.18; Fleet Aeroplane Depot Turnhouse W/E 6.4.18; 3 (W) ARD Yate W/E 24.5.18 (No engine)

C334   Deld Rosyth by rail W/E 30.3.18; Fleet Aeroplane Depot Turnhouse W/E 6.4.18 to at least 4.5.18

C335   No information

C336   Deld Rosyth by rail W/E 30.3.18; Fleet Aeroplane Depot Turnhouse W/E 6.4.18; 3 (W) ARD Yate W/E 24.5.18 (No engine)

C337   No information

C338   Deld Rosyth by rail W/E 30.3.18; Fleet Aeroplane Depot Turnhouse W/E 6.4.18; 3 (W) ARD Yate W/E 24.5.18 (No engine)

C339   No information

C340   Allotted Eastchurch by 30.3.18

C341   No information

C342   Allotted Eastchurch by 30.3.18

C343   Allotted Eastchurch by 30.3.18

C344   Allotted Eastchurch by 30.3.18

C345   Allotted Eastchurch by 30.3.18

C346-7 No information

C348   19 TDS El Rimal 1918

C349   19 TDS El Rimal by 11.18

C350   Deld 207 TDS Chingford W/E 6.4.18; 62 TS Hounslow co.6.18

C351   Deld Fleet Aeroplane Depot Turnhouse by rail W/E 11.4.18 to at least 4.5.18

C352   Deld Fleet Aeroplane Depot Turnhouse by rail W/E 11.4.18; 3 (W) ARD Yate 24.5.18 (No engine)

C353   Deld Fleet Aeroplane Depot Turnhouse by rail W/E 11.4.18 to at least 4.5.18

C354   Hainault Farm 1918 (44 Sqdn 'hack' or visiting aircraft) (overall grey with two vertical black bands on rear fuselage)

C355-6 No information

C357   Deld Fleet Aeroplane Depot Turnhouse by rail W/E 11.4.18 to at least 4.5.18

C358   No information

C359   Deld Fleet Aeroplane Depot Turnhouse by rail W/E 11.4.18 to at least 4.5.18

C360   No information

C361   Deld Fleet Aeroplane Depot Turnhouse by rail W/E 11.4.18 to at least 4.7.18

C362   No information

C363   Allotted 207 TDS Chingford by 1.4.18

C364   No information

C365   Allotted 207 TDS Chingford by 1.4.18

C366   No information

C367   Allotted 207 TDS Chingford by 1.4.18; To 62 TS Hounslow c.6.17

C368   Allotted 207 TDS Chingford by 1.4.18; At Fairlop 12.18

C369   Allotted 207 TDS Chingford by 1.4.18; To 62 TS Hounslow c.7.18

C370   Allotted 207 TDS Chingford by 1.4.18 (at Fairlop 4.18)

C371-3 No information

C374   CFS Upavon by 4.18 (painted mainly white)

C375   No information

C376   'B' Sqdn CFS Upavon by 22.5.18

C377-9 No information

C380   No information

C381   30th Wing ARS Montrose to 6 TS Montrose 22.6.18; Mid-air collision with B7485 8.7.18 (2/Lt LM Frederick killed); 30 Wing ARS Montrose 15.7.18; SOC 16.7.18

C354, see here at Hainault Farm in 1918, was possibly a 'hack' of No.44 (Home Defence) Sqdn, though it could have been a visiting aircraft. It was painted overall grey with two vertical black bands on the rear fuselage.   *(via Frank Cheesman)*

C382-7	No information
C388	Arrived 30th Wing ARS Montrose 19.6.18; 32 TDS Montrose 18.7.18
C389	30th Wing ARS Montrose from 3.7.18
C390	18th Wing ARS Hounslow from 15.4.18
C391	42 TDS Hounslow from 10.8.18
C392	42 TDS Hounslow from 10.8.18
C393	42 TDS Hounslow from 10.8.18
C394-9	No information
C400	No information
C401	27 TS London Colney from 4.7.18; Tested 1 AAP Coventry 13.8.18
C402	4 TDS Hooton Park by 6.18; 27 TS London Colney from 4.7.18; 25th Wing Castle Bromwich by 4.19
C403	2 TS Northolt from 4.7.18; 30 TDS Northolt 24.7.18
C404	2 TS Northolt from 4.7.18; 30 TDS Northolt 24.7.18; Tested 1 AAP Coventry 16.8.18; 4 TDS Hooton Park
C405	40 TS Croydon from 24.7.18
C406	56 TDS Cranwell by 9.18
C407	No information
C408	56 TDS Cranwell by 11.18
C409	No information
C410	No information
C411	2 Fighting School Marske by 10.18
C412	Tested 1 AAP Coventry 26.8.18
C413	No information
C414	4 (Auxiliary) School of Aerial Gunnery Marske (coded '103') by 2.18; Became 2 Fighting School Marske 29.5.18 (still coded '103') to at least 10.18
C415	Tested 1 AAP Coventry 26.8.18;
C416	Tested 1 AAP Coventry 26.8.18; To UK TS?
C417	Tested 1 AAP Coventry 24.8.18; To 3 Fighting School Bircham Newton 8.18 to at least 16.9.18 (large blue & white checkers)
C418	Tested 1 AAP Coventry 26.8.18
C419	Tested 1 AAP Coventry 26.8.18
C420	47 TDS Doncaster, mid-air collision 11.9.18 (Lt HL Savage killed)
C421	Tested 1 AAP Coventry 26.8.18
C422	47 TDS Doncaster by 16.9.18; 2 Fighting School Marske by 10.18

C423	1 AAP Coventry, prop accident 26.8.18 (Lt G Hodgson injured); 56 TDS Cranwell by 9.18
C424	56 TDS Cranwell by 9.18 to at least 10.18
C425	No information
C426	UK, prop accident 12.9.18 (1/AM CH Tuckfield injured)
C427	No information
C428	2 Fighting School Marske by 17.9.18
C429	2 Fighting School Marske by 21.9.18
C430	2 Fighting School Marske by 27.9.18
C431	Artillery & Infantry Co-operation School, Worthy Down; 43 TDS Chattis Hill from 11.1.19
C432-7	No information
C438	Became *G-EAVY*
C439	No information
C440	Became *G-EAVV*
C441-9	No information
C450-5	No information
C456	Flown from Gosport to 2 AAP Hendon 3.10.18; Tested 14-17.12.18
C457-9	No information
C460-9	No information
C470-2	No information
C473	Arr 'X' AD ex UK 18.11.18; 20 TDS Amriya 24.11.18; 19 TDS El Rimal 1919; WO at Artillery Observation School Almaza 4.6.19
C474	Arr 'X' AD ex UK 19.10.18; 60 TDS Aboukir 13.12.18; WO at 22 TS Aboukir 9.6.19
C475	Arr 'X' AD ex UK 19.10.18; 60 TDS Aboukir 13.12.18; WO at 22 TS Aboukir 9.6.19
C476	(80hp Clerget) Arr 'X' AD ex UK 18.11.18; 20 TDS Amriya 24.11.18; WO at 16 TDS Amriya 23.10.19 (sic); Purchased in Middle East by C.D.Pratt; Arrived Melbourne c.5.19; Became *G-AUCK* 5.21 and flown by him until 9.23; Sold in Melbourne and fitted Genet, becoming *VH-UCK*; Finally dismantled 21.9.45; Survived until the early fifties; Traces last noted on a tip in northern Victoria 1954
C477	Arr 'X' AD ex UK 4.11.18; 5 Fighting School Heliopolis 13.12.18; AWSP (sic) to 22 TS Aboukir 25.3.19; WO at Artillery Observation School Almaza 4.6.19

C417 of No.3 Fighting School, Sedgeford in September 1918 has large blue and white chequers around the fuselage. It is standing in front of the Aeroplane Repair Section hangar.   *(via Mick Davis)*

C478	Arr 'X' AD ex UK 4.11.18; AWSP to 22 TS Aboukir 25.3.19 to at least 6.19; WO at 80 Sqdn Aboukir 15.8.19
C479	Arr 'X' AD ex UK 4.11.18; WO at 'X' AD 1.5.19
C480	Arr 'X' AD ex UK 4.11.18; AWSP to 22 Sqdn 25.3.19; 22 TS Aboukir by 6.19; 80 Sqdn, crashed, error of judgement 14.7.19 (Capt AJB Tonks died of injuries); WO 30.7.19
C481	to C499 Sold to Japanese Government
C488	To Japanese Army Air Force, used in Japan and on Vladivostok
C489	Flown at Tokorozawa Field
C500-2	No information
C503-9	Sold to Japanese Government
C510-3	No information
C514	Pool of Pilots Manston (named 'PRINCE') 1918 (thin forward sloping white band aft of fuselage roundel, carried across top of fuselage)
C515-9	No information
C520	No information
C521	Allotted to Australian Government 22.10.18; Became *A4-1* 3.10.21
C522	Allotted to Australian Government 22.10.18; Became *A4-2* 3.10.21
C523	Allotted to Australian Government 22.10.18; Became *A4-3* 3.10.21
C524	Allotted to Australian Government 22.10.18; Became *A4-4* 3.10.21
C525	Allotted to Australian Government 22.10.18; Became *A4-5* 3.10.21
C526	Allotted to Australian Government 22.10.18; Became *A4-6* 3.10.21
C527	Allotted to Australian Government 22.10.18; Became A4-7 3.10.21
C528	Allotted to Australian Government 22.10.18; Became *A4-8* 3.10.21
C529	Allotted to Australian Government 22.10.18; Damaged during shipment
C530	Allotted to Australian Government 22.10.18; Became *A4-9* 3.10.21

C531	Allotted to Australian Government 22.10.18; Became *A4-10* 3.10.21
C532	Allotted to Australian Government 22.10.18; Became *A4-11* 3.10.21
C533	to C537 Sold to Japanese Government
C538	No information
C539	Artillery Co-operation Sqdn Tilstock by 11.18
C540	Became *G-EAVZ*
C541-9	No information
C550	No information

100 SOPWITH PUP ordered 20.8.17 additionally under Contract number 87/A/1101 from Whitehead Aircraft Ltd, Richmond, Surrey and numbered C1451 to C1550. (80hp Le Rhône 9C) (Many probably initially to store)

C1451-9	No information
C1460-9	No information
C1470-1	No information
C1472	Armament Experimental Station Orfordness by 3.18 (night camouflage trials)
C1473-9	No information
C1480-9	No information
C1490-1	No information
C1492	Arr 'X' AD ex UK 22.6.18; 19 TDS El Rimal 5.8.18; WO 9.11.18
C1493	Arr 'X' AD ex UK 22.6.18; 20th Training Wing 8.7.18; 23 TS Aboukir; WO at 22 TS Aboukir 30.5.19
C1494	No information
C1495	Arr 'X' AD ex UK 22.6.18; 20th Training Wing 28.7.18; SOC 26.8.18
C1496	Sold to Japanese Government; To Imperial Japanese Navy
C1497-9	No information
C1500-1	No information
C1502	Deld Fleet Aeroplane Depot Turnhouse W/E 11.5.18 to at least 30.1.19
C1503	Deld Fleet Aeroplane Depot Turnhouse W/E 11.5.18 to at least 30.1.19

C1504-7   No information
C1508   Deld Fleet Aeroplane Depot Turnhouse W/E 11.5.18 to at least 30.1.19
C1509   No information
C1510   54 TDS Chingford/Fairlop by 27.8.18; SE Area Flying Instructors School, Shoreham by 10.18
C1511-2   No information
C1513   207 TDS Chingford/Fairlop from/by 31.5.18
C1514   207 TDS Chingford/Fairlop by 3.6.18; Became 54 TDS Chingford/Fairlop 20.7.18; SOC 18.8.18
C1515   54 TDS Fairlop, spun into ground 16.10.18 (2/Lt FW Halliwell severely injured)
C1516   Deld Fleet Aeroplane Depot Turnhouse W/E 11.5.18 to at least 30.1.19
C1517   Deld Fleet Aeroplane Depot Turnhouse W/E 11.5.18: Deleted W/E 19.12.18
C1518   Deld Fleet Aeroplane Depot Turnhouse W/E 11.5.18: Deleted W/E 19.12.18
C1519   Deld 207 TDS Chingford/Fairlop 31.5.18; Became 54 TDS Chingford/Fairlop 20.7.18 (at Fairlop 10.18)
C1520   No information
C1521   No information
C1522   37th Wing Half ARS North Shotwick to 90 Sqdn North Shotwick 19.5.18
C1523   Deld Fleet Aeroplane Depot Turnhouse W/E 11.5.18 to at least 30.1.19
C1524   FF 10.8.18; Boscombe Down to RAE Farnborough 22.8.19; Boscombe Down 12.9.19; Became *G-EBAZ*; Scrapped at Stag Lane
C1525   Deld Fleet Aeroplane Depot Turnhouse W/E 11.5.18 to at least 30.1.19
C1526   42 TDS Hounslow to 41 TDS London Colney 3.9.18
C1527-9   No information
C1530   No information
C1531   96 Sqdn North Shotwick by 26.5.18; 95 Sqdn North Shotwick by 7-8.7.18
C1532   Deld Fleet Aeroplane Depot Turnhouse W/E 11.5.18 to at least 30.1.19
C1533   Deld Fleet Aeroplane Depot Turnhouse W/E 11.5.18 to at least 30.1.19
C1534   No information
C1535   Deld Fleet Aeroplane Depot Turnhouse W/E 11.5.18: Deleted W/E 19.12.18
C1536   Arr 'X' AD ex UK 22.6.18; 20th Training Wing 29.7.18; WO 30.9.18
C1537   Deld Fleet Aeroplane Depot Turnhouse W/E 11.5.18 to at least 30.1.19
C1538   Arr 'X' AD ex UK 22.6.18; 20th Training Wing 8.7.18; WO 11.10.18
C1539   SOC in Egypt 22.8.18
C1540   (80hp Clerget) Arr 'X' AD ex UK 22.6.18; 20th Training Wing 29.7.18; 23 TS Aboukir, prop burst, forced landed, crashed 18.8.18 (Flt Cdt L Marchant seriously injured); WOC 28.8.18
C1541   Deld Fleet Aeroplane Depot Turnhouse W/E 11.5.18 to at least 30.1.19
C1542   No information
C1543   Arr 'X' AD ex UK 10.6.18
C1544-5   No information
C1546   Arr 'X' AD ex UK 6.18; 32nd Training Wing 24.6.18; 58 TS Suez by 28.8.18; Stalled on zoom, crashed 19.12.18 (2/Lt AJP Hall injured); WOC 31.12.18
C1547   FF 8.2.18; Arr 'X' AD ex UK 10.6.18; 32nd Training Wing 24.6.18; 18 TDS El Rimal, rolled, pilot fell out, aircraft crashed and burnt 29.8.18 (Flt Cdt FT Browning killed)
C1548   No information

C1549   Arr 'X' AD ex UK 10.6.18; 32nd Training Wing 24.6.18; 19 TDS El Rimal, WO 26.2.19
C1550   Arr 'X' AD ex UK 10.6.18; 19 TDS El Rimal, WO 26.2.19

4 SOPWITH PUP rebuilds from salvage and spares by 6th Wing ARS Dover and numbered C3500 to C3503, serials allotted 22.1.18.

C3500   (80hp Le Rhône No.WD20007) 6th Wing to 4 TS Northolt 12.7.18; 30 TDS Northolt 15.7.18; Prop accident 29.8.18 (Cpl Mech HC Cornish injured); 42 TDS Hounslow 22.9.18
C3501   No information
C3502   (80hp Le Rhône No.53287/WD36164) 65 TS Dover, hit by 504 while taxiing 27.3.18 (2/Lt CL Grimwood slightly injured)
C3503   42 TS Wye by 22.3.18; Engine failure, forced landed, undercarriage caught wires, crashed 23.3.18 (2/Lt CEF Arthur unhurt)

70 SOPWITH PUP ordered 27.7.17 under Contract number CP.102622/17 from The Sopwith Aviation Co Ltd, Kingston-on-Thames and numbered C3707 to C3776. Delivered as spares only.

1 SOPWITH PUP rebuild from salvage and spares by 30th Wing ARS Montrose, Serial numbered C4295 allotted 11.1.18.

C4295   (80hp Le Rhône) 6 TS Montrose to 36 TS Montrose 27.4.18; 18 TS Montrose by 4.18 - @7.6.18; 32 TDS Montrose by 14.9.18

2 SOPWITH PUP built from salvage and spares numbered C8653 and C8654.

C8653   By 18th Wing ARS Hounslow, serial allotted 17.12.17; 87 Sqdn Hounslow by 2.18
C8654   (80hp Gnome No.426) by 7th Wing ARS Norwich, serial allotted 17.12.17; 94 Sqdn Harling Road by 14.1.18; Forced landed in field, hit tree, crashed, 5m from airfield 22.1.18 (Lt LF Bettinson injured)

3 SOPWITH PUP rebuilds from salvage and spares in the range C9986 to C9999.

C9990   By 7 TDS Half ARS Feltwell, serial allotted 25.3.18
C9991   By 7 TDS Half ARS Feltwell, serial allotted 25.3.18
C9993   By 26th Wing ARS Thetford, serial allotted 2.4.18; 94 Sqdn Harling Road 20.4.18; 7 TDS Feltwell 28.5.18

200 SOPWITH PUP ordered 10.12.17 additionally under Contract number 87/A/1101 from Whitehead Aircraft Ltd, Richmond and numbered D4011 to D4210. (Ordered with 80hp Le Rhône 9C but some fitted with alternative engines) (Some to store)

D4011   Deld 4 TDS Hooton Park 4.6.18; 37th Wing Half ARS North Shotwick 4.6.18; 4 TDS Hooton Park 6.6.18
D4012   Deld 4 TDS Hooton Park 4.6.18; 37th Wing Half ARS North Shotwick 4.6.18; 4 TDS Hooton Park 6.6.18 to at least 10.6.18
D4013   (100hp Gnome Monosoupape) Deld 37th Wing Half ARS North Shotwick 6.6.18; 96 Sqdn 6.6.18; 51 TDS North Shotwick 15.7.18 - @28.7.18 [heavily striped]
D4014   Deld 37th Wing Half ARS North Shotwick 6.6.18; 67 TS North Shotwick 6.6.18; Forced landed, crashed 11.6.18 (Lt R Viall); Became 51 TDS North Shotwick 15.7.18 to at least 4.8.18; Prop accident 31.7.18 (2/AM FJJ Leach seriously injured)

D4015   51 TDS North Shotwick by 27.7.18

D4016   6th Wing to 4 TS Northolt 12.7.18; 50 TDS Eastbourne 1918 (painted white overall)

D4017   63 TS Joyce Green to 41 TDS London Colney 30.7.18

D4018   53 TDS Dover to 30 TDS Northolt 27.7.18; 56 TDS Cranwell; 158 Sqdn Upper Heyford by 11.18

D4019   53 TDS Dover to 41 TDS London Colney 27.7.18

D4020   No information

D4021   1 School of Navigation & Bomb Dropping Stonehemge by 24.8.18 to at least 6.9.18

D4022   1 School of Navigation & Bomb Dropping Stonehemge by 27.9.18 to at least 18.2.19

D4023   Arrived 30th Wing ARS Montrose 20.6.18; 32 TDS Montrose by 7.18; SOC 9.8.18 (written off)

D4024   Arrived 30th Wing ARS Montrose 19.6.18; 18 TS Montrose by 28.6.18; 32 TDS Montrose 15.7.18

D4025   Arrived 30th Wing ARS Montrose 21.6.18; 18 TS Montrose 26.6.18; 32 TDS Montrose by 6.7.18; Conv 80hp Clerget to 80hp Le Rhône 27.7.18; Crashed while low flying 30.7.18 (2/Lt OS Parker seriously injured) ; SOC 9.8.18

D4026   Arrived 30th Wing ARS Montrose 21.6.18; 27 TDS Crail, crashed on landing 22.10.18 (Mjr JD Sheridan slightly injured)

D4027   208 TDS East Fortune by 6.4.18; (80hp Le Rhône) Arrived 30th Wing ARS Montrose 20.6.18; 32 TDS Montrose by 7.18; 2 TDS Gullane 26.7.18; Grand Fleet School of Aerial Fighting & Gunnery East Fortune

D4028   Arrived 30th Wing ARS Montrose 21.6.18; 32 TDS Montrose by 7.18; 2 TDS Gullane 26.7.18; Grand Fleet School of Aerial Fighting & Gunnery East Fortune by 26.7.18

D4029   Arrived ARS Gullane 18.6.18; 2 TDS Gullane 26.6.18; ARS Gullane 11.7.18

D4030   (80hp Le Rhône later 80hp Gnome) Arrived 30th Wing ARS Montrose 20.6.18; 6 TS Montrose by 7.18; 30 Wing ARS Montrose 14.7.18; 32 TDS Montrose 15.7.18; Cross-country flight, heavy mist came up, flew into mountain 25.8.18 (2/Lt JH Hall killed); Wreckage found next day

D4031   Arrived 30th Wing ARS Montrose 19.6.18; 2 TDS Gullane 26.6.18; ARS Gullane 16.7.18; 3 TDS Lopcombe Corner 1918

D4032   Arrived 30th Wing ARS Montrose 21.6.18; 30 Wing ARS Montrose to 6 TS Montrose 11.7.18; 32 TDS Montrose 15.7.18

D4033   Arrived 30th Wing ARS Montrose 20.6.18

D4034   208 TDS East Fortune by 6.4.18; Became Grand Fleet School of Aerial Fighting & Gunnery East Fortune 19.7.18 - @25.7.18

D4035   Arrived ARS Gullane 18.6.18; 36 TS Montrose 26.6.18; ARS Montrose 6.7.18

D4036   Arrived 30th Wing ARS Montrose 20.6.18

D4037   Arrived 30th Wing ARS Montrose 20.6.18; 30 Wing ARS Montrose to 32 TDS Montrose 16.7.18 -@26.9.18

D4038-9 No information

D4040-1 No information

D4042   Recd 'X' AD ex UK 23.9.18

D4043   No information

D4044   No information

D4045   Recd 'X' AD ex UK 10.6.18; 20th Training Wing 8.7.18; WO 20.9.18

D4046   Recd 'X' AD ex UK 10.6.18; 20th Training Wing 26.6.18; WO 30.9.18

D4047   No information

D4048   Recd 'X' AD ex UK 10.6.18; 20th Training Wing 26.6.18; 60 TDS Aboukir by 1.19; WO 5.1.19

D4049   No information

D4050   No information

D4051   Recd 'X' AD ex UK 10.6.18; 20th Training Wing 8.7.18, WO 15.11.18

D4052-5 No information

D4056   Recd 'X' AD ex UK 10.6.18; 22 TS Aboukir by 11.18; WO 28.11.18

D4057-9 No information

D4060-9 No information

D4070-4 No information

D4075   1 TS Beaulieu by 10.4.18; Crashed 26.4.18 (2/Lt ACP Stephens seriously injured)

Painted white overall, D4016 was one of the final production batch of 200 aircraft, built by Whitehead and numbered D4011 to D4210. It is seen here with No.50 Training Depot Station at Eastbourne in 1918.   *(J.M.Bruce/G.S.Leslie collection)*

D4076   70 TS Beaulieu by 4.18 to at least 1.5.18

D4077   70 TS Beaulieu by 4.18 to at least 17.5.18

D4078   40 TS Croydon to 41 TDS London Colney 29.7.18

D4079   Shoreham by 22.4.18; 42 TS Wye, mid-air collision with 504 D4394 25.4.18 (2/Lt AG Levy killed)

D4080   No information

D4081   53 TDS Dover to 42 TDS Hounslow 27.7.18; 41 TDS London Colney 11.8.18

D4082   Recd 'X' AD ex UK 10.10.18; 19 TDS El Rimal by 11.18; 80 Sqdn Aboukir by 8.19; WO 3.10.19

D4083   Recd 'X' AD ex UK 3.10.18; 60 TDS Aboukir 6.1.19

D4084   Recd 'X' AD ex UK 10.10.18; 20 TDS Abu Sueir 6.1.19; 19 TDS El Rimal, crashed 23.3.19; SOC 28.3.19

D4085-9 No information

D4090   No information

D4091   56 TDS Cranwell by 10.18; Overshot landing, crashed into Camel, both aircraft damaged 13.10.18 (HP Bird OK)

D4092   56 TDS Cranwell by 11.18

D4093-4 No information

D4095   56 TDS Cranwell 1918

D4096   No information

D4097   Wireless Experimental Establishment Biggin Hill (coded '1') by 3.18; Became W/T Establishment 2.4.18; To Farnborough 7.12.18

D4098   Recd 'X' AD ex UK 10.8.18; 20th Training Wing 21.8.18; 22 TS Aboukir by 16.9.18; WO 12.4.19

D4099   Recd 'X' AD ex UK 2.9.18; 20 TDS Shallufa 27.9.18; 5 Fighting School Heliopolis, WO 29.3.19

D4100   Recd 'X' AD ex UK 18.8.18; 20th Training Wing 15.9.18; 60 TDS Aboukir by 12.18; 22 TS Aboukir, WO 30.5.19

D4101   Recd 'X' AD ex UK 18.8.18; 20th Training Wing 15.9.18; 5 Fighting School Heliopolis, WO 9.6.19

D4102   Recd 'X' AD ex UK 18.8.18; 20th Training Wing 15.9.18; WO 8.10.18

D4103   Recd 'X' AD ex UK 18.8.18; 20 TDS Shallufa 26.9.18; 58 TS Suez

D4104-5 No information

D4106   (80hp Clerget) 4 TDS Hooton Park by 10.8.18; Mid-air collision 11.8.18 (Flt Cdt WP Lund slightly injured)

D4107   23 TDS Aboukir

D4108   North Shotwick by 2.19

D4109   4 TDS Hooton Park by 10.8.18; Engine failure, stalled and wrecked 22.1.19 (2/Lt FW Bortfield slightly injured)

D4110   No information

D4111   4 TDS Hooton Park by 11.8.18

D4112   No information

D4113   22 TS Aboukir

D4114   Recd 'X' AD ex UK 23.9.18; 'X' AD by 1.19; 60 TDS Aboukir 6.1.19; 22 TS Aboukir, WO 13.6.19

D4115   Recd 'X' AD ex UK 2.9.18; 'X' AD by 2.19; 5 Fighting School Heliopolis 8.2.19; 80 Sqdn Aboukir, WO 3.10.19

D4116   Recd 'X' AD ex UK 25.9.18; 20th Training Wing 25.9.18; 80 Sqdn Aboukir, crashed 10.9.19; Still 80 Sqdn to at least 1.20

D4117   Recd 'X' AD ex UK 25.9.18; 20th Training Wing 25.9.18; 23 TS Aboukir by 10.18; WO 16.10.18

D4118   W/T Experimental Establishment Biggin Hill by 6.18

D4119   W/T Establishment Biggin Hill by 4.6.18; 18th Wing ARS Hounslow from 10.6.18

D4120   Deld 18th Wing ARS Hounslow 10.6.18; 30 TDS London Colney 27.7.18

D4121   Recd 'X' AD ex UK 25.6.18; 38th Training Brigade 15.8.18; 5 Fighting School Heliopolis by 9.18 to at least 29.10.18; Hit by 504 D152, damaged 6.9.18 (pilot OK); Artillery Observation School Almaza, WO 4.6.19

D4122   Recd 'X' AD ex UK 25.6.18; 38th Training Brigade 15.8.18; 5 Fighting School Heliopolis by 11.9.18; Damaged when an R.E.8 ran into it on the ground 14.9.18 (Lt Noel); Repaired on station; On landing ran into stationary Camel D6533 22.9.18 (2/Lt PPW Whelan); During mock combat with B.E.2e B4595 collided at 700ft, both aircraft destroyed by fire 26.9.18 (Cdt/Off N Papastathis); WO 28.9.18

D4123   Recd 'X' AD ex UK 25.6.18; 38th Training Brigade 15.8.18; 5 Fighting School Heliopolis, engine cut out, crashed 27.9.18 (Lt A Homewood); To ARS

D4124   Recd 'X' AD ex UK 25.6.18; 38th Training Brigade 15.8.18; School of Aerial Fighting, Heliopolis 23.8.18; Became 5 Fighting School Heliopolis 5.9.18; WO 29.3.19

D4125   Recd 'X' AD ex UK 25.6.18; School of Aerial Fighting, Heliopolis 23.8.18; Became 5 Fighting School Heliopolis 5.9.18; Engine cut out on take off, into trench and turned over 6.9.18 (Lt WF Knight); Repaired on station; Undershot on landing, hit ditch, went on nose 15.9.18 (Lt A Finlayson); Repaired on station; Damaged in heavy landing 2.10.18 (2/Lt A Laskey); Repaired on station; Forced landed with engine trouble in field, overturned in long grass, Gezira 15.10.18 (Cdt/Off J Tzerachis); To 38th Wing ARS Heliopolis; 5 Fighting School Heliopolis, WO 21.3.19

D4126   Recd 'X' AD ex UK 25.6.18; School of Aerial Fighting, Heliopolis 23.8.18; Became 5 Fighting School Heliopolis 5.9.18; Axle broke, wheel came off 5.9.18 (Lt Scott); Repaired on station; Pilot's leg caught in throttle, half cutting out engine on take off and causing an uncheckable swing to the right 12.10.18 (Lt RJ Winbolt); Repaired on station; Crashed landing cross wind 28.10.18 (Lt Col C Bovill); Repaired on station; Artillery Observation School Almaza, WO 4.6.19

D4127   11 TS Scampton by 8.5.18; Became 34 TDS Scampton 15.7.18

D4128   34 TDS Scampton by 14-21.8.18

D4129   34 TDS Scampton by 10.18

D4130   School for Marine Operational Pilots, Dover by 12.18

D4131-2 No information

D4133   32 TDS Montrose by 5.18

D4134   No information

D4135   Deld 30th Wing ARS Montrose 18.5.18; 36 TS Montrose 19.5.18; 2 TDS Gullane 28.5.18

D4136-9 No information

D4139   37th Wing Half ARS Hooton Park by 5.18; 4 TDS Hooton Park 20.5.18; Broke up in air while pulling out of vertical dive on target when went beyond vertical 27.5.18 (Lt WS Murray killed); SOC 20.6.18 BUT 51 TDS North Shotwick by 30.7.18

D4140   Recd 'X' AD ex UK 25.9.18; 20th Training Wing 25.9.18; 20th Training Wing ARS 25.10.18

D4141   6 TS Montrose by 20.5.18

D4142   5 Fighting School Heliopolis, landing in formation collided with Avro 504 E1632, the Avro swung to the right and the Pup ran straight into it 5.10.18 (Lt J Fisher); To 'X' AD; 20 TDS Aboukir 6.1.19; WO 24.2.19

D4143   28 Sqdn Italy by 5-21.10.18; 34 Sqdn Italy 8.11.18

D4144   to D4150. Sold to Japanese Government; All to Imperial Japanese Navy

D4151   No information

D4152   5 TS AFC Minchinhampton 1918

D4153   5 TS AFC Minchinhampton 1918; 6 TS AFC Minchinhampton 1918

D4154   96 Sqdn North Shotwick by 29.5.18; 37th Wing Half ARS North Shotwick 4.6.18; 1 Fighting School Turnberry by 7.18

D4155   Sold to Japanese Government; To Imperial Japanese Navy

D4156   Sold to Japanese Government; To Imperial Japanese Navy

D4157   5 TS AFC Minchinhampton 1918; 6 TS AFC Minchinhampton 1918

D4158   4 TDS Hooton Park to 37th Wing Half ARS Hooton Park 17.5.18; 158 Sqdn Upper Heyford by 11.18

D4159   5 TS AFC Minchinhampton 1918; 4 TDS Hooton Park, spun in 16.7.18 (2/Lt LP Waite, Canadian, killed)

D4160   Sold to Japanese Government; To Imperial Japanese Navy

D4161   Sold to Japanese Government; To Imperial Japanese Navy

D4162   No information

D4163   Sold to Japanese Government; To Imperial Japanese Navy

D4164   5 TS AFC Minchinhampton 1918; 6 TS AFC Minchinhampton 1918

D4165   Sold to Japanese Government

D4166   37th Wing Half ARS North Shotwick to 95 Sqdn North Shotwick 1.3.18 to at least 28.6.18

D4167   5 TS AFC Minchinhampton 1918; 6 TS AFC Minchinhampton 1918

D4168   Sold to Japanese Government; To Imperial Japanese Navy

D4169   Sold to Japanese Government; To Imperial Japanese Navy

D4170   5 TS AFC Minchinhampton; 6 TS AFC Minchinhampton; 8 TS AFC Leighterton, mid-air collision with Camel C6746 (2/Lt DA Ferguson killed) while practising aerial fighting 18.8.18 (Lt H Taylor MC MM killed)

D4171   5th (T) Sqdn AFC Minchinhampton 1918; 6th (T) Sqdn AFC Minchinhampton 1918

D4172   No information

D4173   8th (T) Sqdn AFC Leighterton, engine failure, crashed 26.10.18 (Lt JTP Stephens slightly injured)

D4174   Hooton Park to Hucknall, but forced landed Stafford 14.10.18; Arr 15 TDS Hucknall 16.10.18 (Lt A Glynne)

D4175   No information

D4176   29 TDS Beaulieu, forming up in formation, mid-air collision with 504 D7649 4.8.18 (Lt W Jones slightly injured)

D4177   27 TS London Colney from 7.5.18; WO 31.5.18

D4178   No information

D4179   8th (T) Sqdn AFC Leighterton, engine trouble, hit tree, crashed 14.8.18 (Lt DN Rees AFC slightly injured)

D4180   No information

D4181   70 TS Beaulieu by 6.18

D4182   Southern Training Brigade by 5.18 – 6.18 (flown by Mjr GI Carmichael DSO); Beaulieu by 25.5.18; To Boscombe to be reduced to produce 6.1.19; Last flown 12.2.19, then scrapped

D4183   27 TS London Colney from 7.5.18

D4184   Deld 18th Wing ARS Hounslow 29.4.18; 86 Sqdn Northolt 15.5.18; WO 2.6.18

D4185   Named 'PELUSIUM' [not known why, but this was the Roman name for an Egyptian town at the eastern mouth of the River Nile] Deld 18th Wing ARS Hounslow 29.4.18

D4186   91 Sqdn Tangmere from 4.5.18; 30 TDS Northolt by 4.10.18

D4187   2 TS Northolt from 7.5.18

D4188   No information

D4189   27 TS London Colney from 7.5.18

D4190   No information

D4191   8 TS AFC Leighterton, engine failure, forced landed, struck trees 10.1.19

D4192   Deld 18th Wing ARS Hounslow 29.4.18; 42 TDS Hounslow to AFI Schoool Manston 16.8.18; South Eastern Area Flying Instructors School Shoreham by 13.11.18

D4193-4 No information

D4195   62 TS Hounslow from 8.5.18; 92 Sqdn Tangmere by 5.18; Crashed 12.5.18 (2/Lt G Exley); 42 TDS Hounslow to Artillery & Infantry Co-operation School Worthy Down 10.8.18 to at least 12.18

D4196   27 TS London Colney from 7.5.18; Possibly 34 TDS Scampton 1918

D4197-9 No information

D4200-1 No information

D4202   67 TS North Shotwick 1918

D4203-6 No information

D4207   54 TS Eastbourne by 7.18; Tangmere to 94 Sqdn Upper Heyford 21.8.18

D4208-9 No information

D4210   No information

200 SOPWITH PUP ordered under unknown contract from unidentifed builder, to be numbered D8581 to D8780. Cancelled and serials reallotted.

1 SOPWITH PUP aircraft built up from spares and numbered in the range E9986 to E9996

E9996   (80hp Gnome) By 7th Wing ARS Thetford, serial allotted 30.4.18; 55 TDS Narborough by 11.18

Reservation for rebuilds by No.2 (Northern) Aircraft Repair Depot, Coal Aston, to be numbered F321 to F350, included at least one Sopwith Pup

F321   (Gnome Monosoupape) No information

GROUND INSTRUCTIONAL AIRFRAMES numbered F1 onwards, included this Pup
[These "serials" duplicated those issued to D.H.9s]

F12   Issued to [sic] W/E 14.1.18

50 SOPWITH PUP rebuilds by 3(W)ARD Yate from salvage numbered F4170 to F4220, included this Pup

F4220   By 17th Wing ARS Beaulieu, serial allotted 5.7.18

1 SOPWITH PUP numbered N503, to be built at Kingston-upon-Thames. (110hp Clerget 9Z) [Put forward W/E 21.7.16 for information of Beardmore]

N503   Not built

20 SOPWITH PUP (ADMIRALTY 9901 TYPE) put forward 7.16 and ordered under Contract number C.P.119901/16, numbered N5180 to N5199 & built Kingston-upon-Thames. Delivered from Brooklands. (Ordered with 80hp Le Rhône but some fitted 80hp Gnome)

N5180   (80hp Le Rhône) Deld Chingford 31.8.16 (transit); AD Dunkirk (via Dover) 6.9.16; 'C' Sqdn 1 (Naval) Wing 7.9.16; Crashed, completely wrecked 9.16; AD Dunkirk by 14.9.16 (repair) Surveyed 17.9.16; Deleted 13.10.16 wrecked
         [NOTE. The spurious serial number 'N5180' was later carried by converted Sopwith Dove G-EBKY, which was not this aircraft]

N5181   (80hp Gnome) Deld Chingford 31.8.16 (transit); Aircraft Park Dover 7.9.16; AD Dunkirk 11.9.16; 4 Flt 'B' Sqdn 1 (Naval) Wing 11.9.16; Detached Sqdn 'D' Flt by 2.11.16; AD Dunkirk to 8 (N) Sqdn (coded 'T') 16.11.16; Halberstadt shot down nr Remy 10.50 and 2-str nr Fontaine 11.30 20.12.16 (all FSL RR Soar); 2-str out of control Bapaume-Gommecourt 11.45 23.1.17; Left 14.00, escorting 15 Sqdn BE2s on photo recce, forced landed after combat with enemy aircraft, wrecked Picquigny, north-west of Amiens 26.1.17 (F/L RR Soar); 3 (N) Sqdn 3.2.17; Aircraft Park Dover 28.3.17 (overhaul); War School RNAS Manston 6.10.17; Crashed 10.10.17; Repaired; Still at Manston 3.18; Also reported at Freiston

N5182   Deld Chingford 5.9.16 (transit); AD Dunkirk (via Dover) 6.9.16; Allotted to RFC (Military Wing) as A8736 at Dunkirk but not taken up; 'C' Sqdn 1 (Naval) Wing 7.9.16; Seaplane broke up & into sea 6m off Ostende c.12.00 25.9.16 (FSL ER Grange) [Sablatnig SF2 Nr609, Seeflug 1 (Lt ZS Soltenborn & Lt ZS Rothig killed]; 'C' Flt 8 (N) Sqdn 26.10.16 (detached flight initially); Allotted FSL RA Little 14.11.16 and named 'LADY MAUD'; Roland or LVG 2-str shot down in flames, crashed nr wood north of Courcelette 09.50 23.11.16; 'B' Flt 8 (N) Sqdn 25.11.16; Halberstadt D shot down southeast of Bapaume 11.30 4.12.16; Albatros D.II out of control Fontaine 11.15 20.12.16 (all FSL RA Little (Aus)); 3 (N) Sqdn 3.2.17; AD Dunkirk 10.2.17 (repair); 9 (N) Sqdn 27.2.17; Overturned landing 16.3.17 (FSL AR Brown OK); AD Dunkirk by 22.3.17 (repair); Aircraft Park Dover 28.3.17 to at least 30.4.17; Walmer Defence Flt by 5.17; 2 Anti-Zeppelin patrols 23.5.17; Left 18.53 for Anti-Gotha patrol, landed 19.38 25.5.17 (all FSL WH Chisam); Dover Defence Flt 5.6.17 to at least 9.17; Left 18.20 for Anti-Gotha patrol, landed 9.45 5.6.17; Wings, propeller and undercarriage damaged 6.7.17; Walmer, badly damaged 11.8.17; War Flt/School Manston W/E 20.10.17; Deleted W/E 23.2.18

N5183   Deld Aircraft Park Dover (via Chingford) 13.9.16; AD Dunkirk 15.9.16; Allotted to RFC (Military Wing) as A8735 at Dunkirk but not taken up; 'C' Sqdn 1 (Naval) Wing by 17.9.16; Attacked by enemy aircraft and damaged by AA, engine failure, forced landed Malo 25.9.16 (F/L SV Trapp), flying again 26.9.16; Brown seaplane into sea 10m off Ostende 16.00 23.10.16 (F/L N Keeble); 8 (N) Sqdn 26.10.16 (detached flight initially); Travelling to join 2 (Naval) Wing, damaged Fienvillers 28.10.16 (F/L SJ Goble); ARS 2 AD 30.10.16; 3 (N) Sqdn 7.2.17; Crashed on landing Rue, north of mouth of Somme 14.2.17 (FSL AT Whealy), retd 15.2.17; ARS 2 AD 18.2.17; Aircraft Park Dover 23.2.17 (repair and overhaul); AD Dunkirk 17.3.17; 4 (N) Sqdn 21.3.17; Crashed on landing 26.4.17; AD Dunkirk by 28.4.17; Aircraft Park Dover 2.5.17 (repair); AD Dunkirk 31.5.17; 9 (N) Sqdn 19.6.17; ARS 2 AD 2.7.17; ARS 1 AD 11.7.17; AD Dunkirk 12.7.17; Deleted 16.7.17 Assessed as very old, not worth repairing

N5184   Deld Chingford (via Hendon) 9.9.16 (transit); Aircraft Park Dover 13.9.16; AD Dunkirk 15.9.16; 'C' Sqdn 1 (Naval) Wing by 17.9.16; Deld Vert Galant 23.10.16; AD Dunkirk by 9.11.16 (repair); 'C' Sqdn 1 (Naval) Wing 11.11.16; AD Dunkirk to 'C' Flt 8 (N) Sqdn 16.11.16; White biplane dived smoking north-east of Bapaume 20.12.16 (F/L GE Hervey); 3 (N) Sqdn 3.2.17; AD Dunkirk 10.2.17; 4 (N) Sqdn by 1.3.17; Wrecked on ground 10.4.17; For survey by 12.4.17; Deletion recommended AD Dunkirk 27.4.17; Approved 28.4.17; Implemented 4.5.17

Lt G.P.Taylor of No.66 Squadron, well padded against the cold, including a face mask, climbing into his Pup before departing on patrol. After WW1, Gordon Taylor, an Australian, became a famous record-breaking pilot and was eventually knighted. (Frank Cheesman)

N5185   Deld AD Dunkirk (via Manston) 15.9.16; 'C' Sqdn 1 (Naval) Wing 21.9.16; Hit flare lorry landing in strong wind 3.11.16; AD Dunkirk (defects reported 26.10.16); AD Dunkirk by 9.11.16; 3 (N) Sqdn (named 'BINKY II') 30.11.16 (in 'A' Flt 4.1.17); AD Dunkirk via ARS 2 AD to 8 (N) Sqdn 23.12.16; 3 (N) Sqdn 3.2.17; Forced landed Filescamp Farm 25.2.17 (FSL LH Rochford); Escort duty, forced landed Filescamp, hit bad ground taking off again, crashed and overturned in soft ground 4.3.17 (FSL E Pierce); Still 3 (N) Sqdn 8.3.17; 2 AD by 29.3.17 (overhaul); 3 (N) Sqdn by 5.4.17; Wrecked 11.4.17; AD Dunkirk by 12.4.17 (repair); Deletion recommended AD Dunkirk 27.4.17; Approved 28.4.17; Implemented 4.5.17

N5186   (80hp Le Rhône) Deld Chingford 16.9.16; Design Flt Eastchurch 12.10.16; Fitted with Le Prieur rocket and mg armament and wide centre section cut-out at Eastchurch; Flown 17.10.16 (S/Cdr HR Busteed); AD Dunkirk 23.10.16; 4 Flt 'B' Sqdn 1 (Naval) Wing 4.11.16; Became 3 (N) Sqdn 5.11.16; 8 (N) Sqdn (coded '4') 16.11.16 (faulty assembly workmanship reported 4.11.16 & 7.1.17); Albatros shot down Ypres 26.12.16 (F/Cdr BL Huskisson); 2-str shot down Arras 23.1.17 (F/Cdr BL Huskisson injured); 3 (N) Sqdn 3.2.17; Crashed on landing nr Talmus, south of Vert Galant 14.2.17 (FSL R Collishaw unhurt); ARS 2 AD 22.2.17; AD Dunkirk 1.3.17; 4 (N) Sqdn 21.3.17; Wrecked 10.4.17; AD Dunkirk by 12.4.17; Deletion recommended AD Dunkirk 27.4.17; Approved 28.4.17

N5187   Deld Aircraft Park Dover 22.9.16; AD Dunkirk 23.9.16; 4 Flt 'B' Sqdn 1 (Naval) Wing 24.9.16; Became 3 (N) Sqdn 5.11.16 to at least 9.11.16; Engine failure, forced landed on beach La Panne 24.9.16 (FSL HR Wambolt); AD Dunkirk (defects reported 26.10.16); 'C' Sqdn 1 (Naval) Wing by 16.11.16; AD Dunkirk to 8 (N) Sqdn (named 'TICKIE' or 'VICKIE', believed with 8 (N) Sqdn) 22.12.16; 3 (N) Sqdn 3.2.17; Withdrawn u/s 14.2.17; AD Dunkirk by 15.2.17; 4 (N) Sqdn 16.3.17; Wrecked 10.4.17; For survey by 12.4.17; Deletion recommended AD Dunkirk 27.4.17; Approved 28.4.17; Implemented 4.5.17

N5188   (80hp Gnome); Deld Chingford (via Northolt and Hendon) 24.9.16; Hendon to Dover for Dunkirk 14.10.16 but damaged Harty Ferry (Isle of Sheppey); Tested Hendon 20.10.16; AD Dunkirk (via Eastchurch and Dover) 2.11.16 (repair); 'C' Sqdn 1 (Naval) Wing 4.11.16; Became 3 (N) Sqdn 5.11.16; AD Dunkirk to 8 (N) Sqdn 20.12.16; 3 (N) Sqdn 3.2.17; Roland driven down Bapaume, shared with 9898 13.45 16.2.17 (FSL HF Beamish); Escort, shot up in combat, crashed on landing 4.3.17 (FSL HF Beamish unhurt); Aircraft Park Dover 8.3.17 (repair and overhaul); AD Dunkirk 7.4.17; 'C' Flt 9 (N) Sqdn 16.4.17; 2-str shot down off Middelkerke, shared with 9916 20.30 2.5.17 (FSL HE Mott); Forced landed on beach east of Calais 2.5.17; retd 3.5.17; 11 (N) Sqdn 3.6.17; 'A' Flt 12 (N) Sqdn 13.6.17 to at least 28.6.17; AD Dunkirk to Dover 4.7.17; War School RNAS Manston 23.9.17; Engine failure, forced landed on beach 4.12.17 (repaired); Became Pool of Pilots Manston 1.4.18

N5189   (80hp Le Rhône) Deld AD Dunkirk (via Dover) 9.11.16; 3 (N) Sqdn 10.11.16; Chased enemy seaplane from Ghistelles, then engine failure, forced landed in sea, picked up by French patrol boat Capricorn and towed into Calais 12.11.16 (FSL N Keeble); AD Dunkirk by 16.11.16 (repair); 3 (N) Sqdn 5.1.17; To 8 (N) Sqdn but crashed 5m from Vert Galant on delivery 7.1.17 (FSL HG Travers); Repaired; 3 (N) Sqdn 3.2.17; Crashed, to AD Dunkirk 14.2.17; Deletion recommended 22.2.17; Approved 24.3.17 Damaged beyond repair

N5190   (80hp Le Rhône) Deld Aircraft Park Dover 16.10.16; AD Dunkirk 17.10.16; In reserve 19.10.16; Allotted to RFC (Military Wing) as A8734 at Dunkirk but not taken up; 'C' Sqdn 1 (Naval) Wing (coded '2') 23.10.16; Defects reported 26.10.16; 'B' Flt 8 (N) Sqdn (coded '2') 26.10.16; Shot down by enemy aircraft east of lines nr Moeuvres 23.11.16 (F/L W Lush-Hope PoW, died of wounds 24.11.16) [Claimed Haplincourt 10.10 by Ltn F Ray, Jasta 1]

N5191   Deld Aircraft Park Dover 16.11.16; AD Dunkirk 21.11.16 (in reserve); 3 (N) Sqdn 28.11.16; 'A' Flt 8 (N) Sqdn 20.12.16; Photographic escort to Bapaume-Cambrai, shot down nr Hermies by Offrstlvtr F Kosmahl & Ltn d R Schultz, Fl.A(A).261 2.2.17 (FSL WE Traynor killed - he was 3 (N) Sqdn, attd 8 (N) Sqdn); For survey by 8.2.17; Deleted 11.5.17
Perhaps replaced by a resurrected replacement from salvage/spares as recorded again 5.10.17; Surveyed 17.10.17; AD Dunkirk to 8 (N) Sqdn 20.12.17; Deleted 23.10.17 Total loss

N5192   (80hp Le Rhône) Deld AD Dunkirk (via Dover) 20.10.16; Allotted to RFC (Military Wing) as A8737 at Dunkirk but not taken up; 'C' Sqdn 1 (Naval) Wing 23.10.16; 'C' Flt 8 (N) Sqdn 26.10.16 (detached flight initially); 2-str in flames 1m north-east of La Bassée 09.50 23.11.16 (FSL RA Little); Wings collapsed at 150ft over aerodrome pulling out of dive in test flight Vert Galant 10.12.16 (FSL SV Trapp killed); ARS 2 AD 12.12.16; SOC 13.12.16; Surveyed and deletion recommended 5.1.17; Approved 22.2.17

N5193   (80hp Le Rhône) Deld Aircraft Park Dover 21.10.16; AD Dunkirk 22.10.16; Allotted to RFC (Military Wing) as A8732 at Dunkirk but not taken up (defects reported 26.10.16); 'C' Sqdn 1 (Naval) Wing 23.10.16; 'C' Flt 8 (N) Sqdn 26.10.16 (detached flight initially); Roland DII out of control nr Bapaume 14.50 10.11.16; LVG C out of control Pys-Miraumont 15.30 16.11.16 (both FSL DMB Galbraith); With 'B' Flt 8 (N) Sqdn by 23.11.16; "Type K" (Albatros D.II?) shot down out of control in spinning nose dive 20.12.16 (FSL AS Todd); Left 14.30 on OP to Achiet-le-Grand, combat with 7 enemy aircraft, last seen attacking 3 enemy aircraft, shot down nr Bapaume 15.15 4.1.17 (F/L AS Todd killed) [claimed Metz-en-Couture 15.15 by Rittm Manfred von Richtofen (his 16th victory), Jasta Boelcke]; For survey 11.1.17; Deleted 24.3.17

N5194   Deld Aircraft Park Dover 19.10.16; AD Dunkirk 20.10.16; Allotted to RFC (Military Wing) as A8733 at Dunkirk but not taken up (defects reported 26.10.16); 'C' Sqdn 1 (Naval) Wing 23.10.16; 'C' Flt 8 (N) Sqdn 26.10.16 (detached flight initially); LVG 2-str out of control Gommecourt 10.55 16.11.16; 2-str destroyed Bapaume 15.35 17.11.16; With 'B' Flt 8 (N) Sqdn by 23.11.16; 2-str down on fire south-east of Bapaume 09.50 27.11.16; Halberstadt DII shot down south-east of Bapaume 11.00 4.12.16 (all F/L SJ Goble); Albatros D.II out of control south of Bapaume 15.00 4.1.17 (FSL ER Grange DSC); Albatros D.II out of control Grevillers 11.00 7.1.17 (FSL RA Little DSC); 'A' Flt 3 (N) Sqdn 3.2.17; Forced landed Cramont 26.2.17 (FSL ST Hosken); Enemy aircraft down smoking behind Bapaume on 12.30 - 13.45 patrol, then lost, ran out of fuel, forced landed, crashed Le Crotoy 4.3.17 (FSL HEP Wigglesworth unhurt); 2 AD by 15.3.17 to at least 29.3.17 (rebuilt); 3 (N) Sqdn by 5.4.17; Albatros D.III out of control Croiselles 06.30 23.4.17 (FSL GB Anderson); 2 AD by 26.4.17; 3 (N) Sqdn to AD Dunkirk 28.4.17; Aircraft Park Dover 12.5.17; Left 18.20 for Anti-Gotha patrol but returned 18.43 with engine trouble 25.5.17; Wings and undercarriage slightly damaged 15.6.17; Completely wrecked 20.8.17 (FSL CB Cook); Deleted in field 20.8.17

N5195   (80hp Gnome) Deld AD Dunkirk by 11.16 (not by 2.11.16); 3 (N) Sqdn 5.11.16; Forced landed Oost Dunkirk 7.1.17; retd Sqdn on/by 18.1.17; AD Dunkirk to 8 (N) Sqdn 26.1.17; 3 (N) Sqdn 3.2.17; Crashed 14.2.17; AD Dunkirk 14.2.17 (repair); Aircraft Park Dover 16.3.17 (overhaul); Undercarriage damaged 25.4.17; Wrecked 24.5.17; Repaired; Damaged 24.7.17; War School RNAS Manston 29.9.17; Became Pool of Pilots Manston 1.4.18

N5196   Deld AD Dunkirk by 9.11.16 (in reserve); 'D' Flt 3 (N) Sqdn 10.11.16; AD Dunkirk to 'C' Flt 8 (N) Sqdn (coded 'T') 16.11.16; In solo combat with 6 enemy aircraft, LVG C crashed east of Cambrai 14.40 23.11.16 (FSL DMB Galbraith); 2-str out of control east of Bucquoy 10.10 11.12.16 (F/L SJ Goble); 3 (N) Sqdn 3.2.17; Wheel gave way after landing, went on nose 6.2.17 (FSL E Pierce); Attacked by 3 Halberstadts 4.3.17 (FSL E Pierce); 2 AD 21.3.17 to at least 29.3.17; AD Dunkirk by 5.4.17; 'A' Flt 4 (N) Sqdn 24.4.17; Orange 2-str (Aviatik?) with green and brown wings & 260hp Maybach engine broke up at 9,000ft Rosendael, shared with N6462 12.20 2.5.17 (FSL FV Hall); With 'C' Flt 4 (N) Sqdn 3.5.17; 2-str out of control 7.5.17 (FSL EW Busby); Seaplane out of control Blankenberghe 07.45 12.5.17; Gotha crashed in sea 15m north of Westende, shared with N6168, N6176 & N6198 18.30 25.5.17; 2-str out of control Ostende, shared with N6462 17.35 28.5.17 (all FSL EW Busby); 11 (N) Sqdn 7.6.17; 12 (N) Sqdn 13.6.17; Wrecked 7.7.17; AD Dunkirk by 12.7.17; Deletion recommended 14.7.17; Approved 18.7.17

N5197   (80hp Gnome) Deld Brooklands direct to 'D' Flt 3 (N) Sqdn 10.11.16; AD Dunkirk to 8 (N) Sqdn 16.11.16; Halberstadt shot down north of Bapaume, shared with 3691 26.12.16 (F/L GE Hervey); Albatros C out of control smoking north-east of Bapaume 11.35 23.1.17 (F/L CD Booker); 3 (N) Sqdn 3.2.17; Crashed on landing Campigneulles, south-west of Montreuil 14.2.17 (FSL LH Rochford unhurt); ARS 2 AD 18.2.17; To AD Dunkirk 2.17; Aircraft Park Dover 23.2.17 (repair and overhaul); AD Dunkirk 11.3.17 (damaged in transit) [Casualty Report dated 13.3.17 says badly damaged in transit by road from AD Dunkirk to 3 (N) Sqdn, returned to AD Dunkirk]; Dover 28.3.17; Left 18.15 for Anti-Gotha patrol, landed 19.26 25.5.17; Crashed and damaged 25.7.17; War Flt Manston 23.9.17 to at least 3.18; Later at Freiston Gunnery School

N5198   (80hp Le Rhône) Deld AD Dunkirk (via Dover) 22.11.16; 3 (N) Sqdn 30.11.16; 'A' Flt 8 (N) Sqdn 20.12.16; D shot down Achiet le Petit 27.12.16 (F/L CR Mackenzie DSO); Shot up in combat with enemy aircraft 7.1.17 (FSL AHS Lawson wounded); Left 11.25 for OP to Bapaume, seen 12.00 going east after enemy aircraft over Bapaume, shot down in combat nr Favreuil 12.10 24.1.17 (F/Cdr CR Mackenzie DSO killed) [claimed Bihucourt by Ltn H von Keudall, Jasta 1]; Deleted AD Dunkirk 24.3.17

N5199   Deld Aircraft Park Dover 26.11.16; AD Dunkirk 28.11.16; 3 (N) Sqdn 30.11.16; AD Dunkirk to 8 (N) Sqdn 5.1.17; In combat 7.1.17 (FSL ER Grange wounded); 'B' Flt 3 (N) Sqdn 3.2.17; Albatros D.I spun out of control and crashed nr Manoncourt 11.15 4.3.17 (FSL LH Rochford); Halberstadt DII crashed nr Bourlon Wood 10.20 6.4.17 (F/Cdr LS Breadner); Shot up 11.4.17 (FSL S Bennett OK); AD Dunkirk 12.4.17; Deletion recommended 27.4.17; Approved 28.4.17; Implemented 4.5.17

30 SOPWITH PUP ordered 7.6.16 under Contract number C.P.18681 from Sir William Beardmore & Co Ltd, to be numbered N6100 to N6129 & built Dalmuir

N6100 to N6129 cancelled and order changed to W.B.III

50 SOPWITH PUP (ADMIRALTY 9901 TYPE) put forward 1.17, ordered under Contract number C.P.100785/16, numbered N6160 to N6209 & built Kingston-upon-Thames. (80hp Le Rhône)

N6160   Deld Aircraft Park Dover for erection 22.1.17; AD Dunkirk 29.1.17 (in Repair Section 8.2.17); 'A' Flt 3 (N) Sqdn by road 11.2.17; Halberstadt DII down in spin Bapaume at 9,000ft, then engine failure as following it down, forced landed 12.10 15.2.17; Forced landed at RFC aerodrome 25.2.17; Halberstadt DII out of control in spin nr Hermies 11.05 4.3.17 (all FSL R Collishaw); Albatros C out of control Cambrai 19.00 22.4.17; 2 Albatros D.III collided taking evasive action Le Pave 17.30 23.4.17 (all FSL HS Kerby); AD Dunkirk 18.5.17; Aircraft Park Dover 21.8.17 (overhaul); Re-allotted from Dunkirk to Dover 11.10.17; RNASTE Cranwell 27.10.17; Became 201/202 TDS Cranwell 1.4.18; School of Aerial Fighting & Bomb Dropping Freiston 24.4.18 (now 80hp Gnome); Became 4 School of Aerial Fighting & Gunnery Freiston 6.5.18; Mid-air collision 18.5.18 (Capt JC Tanner died of injuries 1.8.18)

N6161   Deld Aircraft Park Dover 22.1.17; AD Dunkirk 25.1.17; 'B' Flt 3 (N) Sqdn 25.1.17; Shot down nr Blankenberghe 1.2.17 (FSL GL Elliott PoW) [believed by Obfm K Meyer, SFS1]; Aircraft captured essentially intact and given German markings

N6162   Deld Aircraft Park Dover for erection 4.4.17; AD Dunkirk 8.4.17 (in Reserve 12.4.17); 'A' Flt 3 (N) Sqdn by 26.4.17; Damaged by explosive bullet 29.4.17 (FSL ET Hayne); In combat 11.5.17 (FSL HS Broad); Large 2-str seaplane in sea smoking 6-12m north of Ostende, shared with N6183, N6465, N6477 & N6479 c.11.10 7.7.17 (F/L LH Rochford); Forced landed on delivery to 11 (N) Sqdn 24.7.17 (FSL WH Chisam); Arrived 11 (N) Sqdn by 26.7.17; AD Dunkirk by 2.8.17 to at least 27.9.17; Aircraft Park Dover by 4.10.17; Surveyed 16.10.17; Deleted 19.10.17 Wear & tear

N6163   Deld Aircraft Park Dover for erection 24.1.17; AD Dunkirk 29.1.17; 9 (N) Sqdn 1.2.17; Wrecked Malo 13.2.17 (FSL S Bennett); AD Dunkirk by 15.2.17 (repair); 'A' Flt 3 (N) Sqdn by 8.3.17; Left 09.45, Halberstadt DII at 14,000ft out of control north-east of Bapaume 10.40, then forced landed nr Contalmaison Chateau, wrecked 17.3.17 (FSL FD Casey unhurt); Deleted from Sqdn 20.3.17; Recommended for deletion 27.4.17; Approved 28.4.17; Implemented 4.5.17

N6164   Deld Aircraft Park Dover for erection 24.1.17; AD Dunkirk 29.1.17; 9 (N) Sqdn 6.2.17; Damaged by shell splinters after fight with two enemy seaplanes, one of which he shot down, then forced landed in sea, overturned, nr Cadzand, Zeeland 1.3.17 (FSL FV Branford interned); Deleted 11.5.17; Interned by Dutch, repaired and eventually purchased by *Luchtvaart Afdeling*, renumbered as *LA41* (later *S212*)

N6165   Deld Hendon for erection 26.1.17; Accepted 6.2.17; Dover en route AD Dunkirk 8.2.17; Slightly damaged at RFC aerodrome, Dover 9.2.17; Listed on strength of 3 (N) Sqdn 15.2.17, but actually from AD Dunkirk to 3 (N) Sqdn by road 21.2.17; Left 11.15, line patrol Gommecourt-Le Transloy, in combat with enemy aircraft, shot down nr Vis-en-Artois by Obltn Hans Kummetz, Jasta 1 13.05 4.3.17 (FSL JP White killed); Deleted 11.5.17

N6166   Deld Hendon for erection 26.1.17; AD Dunkirk (via Dover) 6.2.17 (in repair 8.2.17); 3 (N) Sqdn by road 11.2.17 (with 'B' Flt 8.3.17, then 'A' Flt by 26.4.17); Line patrol, shot up in combat with enemy aircraft, landed Bertangles 4.3.17 (FSL LA Powell died of wounds 7.3.17); Albatros D out of control Cambrai 09.00 11.4.17 (FSL PG McNeil); Forced landed Allonville 11.5.17 (FSL OC Le Boutillier); AD Dunkirk 22.5.17; ARS 2AD by 1.6.17; 9 (N) Sqdn 19.6.17; 'B' Flt 11 (N) Sqdn 13.7.17 to at least 25.8.17; AD Dunkirk by 30.8.17; Aircraft Park Dover 11.10.17; Surveyed 16.10.17; Deleted 26.10.17 Wear & tear

N6167   Deld Hendon for erection 26.1.17; Accepted 6.2.17; AD Dunkirk 9.2.17; 9 (N) Sqdn 14.2.17; Forced landed 15.2.17 (FSL JC Tanner); AD Dunkirk by 22.2.17; 9 (N) Sqdn 26.2.17 (coded 'B' Flt by 29.3.17); Halberstadt DII out of control 12.30 9.5.17 (FSL AT Whealy); 11 (N) Sqdn 19.5.17; 4 (N) Sqdn 6.6.17 (temporarily attached); 11 (N) Sqdn 8.6.17 to at least 10.6.17; 'A' Flt 12 (N) Sqdn by 21.6.17 ('B' Flt by 21.6.17); Aircraft Park Dover 4.12.17; Allotted for experiments 10.12.17; Experimental Constructive Dept, Grain 15.12.17; Tested with sprung skid undercarriage 6.2.18; Still at Grain 6.18

N6168   Deld Hendon for erection 26.1.17; Accepted 6.2.17; Dover (transit) 8.2.17; AD Dunkirk 9.2.17; 9 (N) Sqdn 10.2.17; 4 (N) Sqdn 22.4.17; Orange Albatros D.III out of control east of Nieuport 12.45 30.4.17; Kite balloon driven down Ghistelles 08.00 9.5.17; Aviatik C crashed 1m south-east of Ghistelles aerodrome shared with N6200 17.15 9.5.17; Albatros D.III destroyed off Zeebrugge 07.30 12.5.17; Gotha broke up & spun into sea 15m north of Westende shared with N5196, N6176 & N6198 18.30 25.5.17; Kite balloon fell to ground Ostende 04.40 5.6.17; Albatros D.V crashed and another out of control north of Handzaeme 15.20 6.6.17 (all FSL LFW Smith); AD Dunkirk 24.6.17; 'A' Flt 11 (N) Sqdn 11.7.17 to at least 26.7.17; Forced landed, damaged 23.7.17 (FSL EGA Eyre); AD Dunkirk 2.8.17; Aircraft Park Dover W/E 27.9.17; RNASTE Cranwell 27.10.17 (later 80hp Gnome by 30.3.18); Became 201/202 TDS Cranwell 1.4.18

N6169   (80hp Gnome) Deld Hendon for erection 26.1.17; Accepted 3.2.17; AD Dunkirk (via Dover) 6.2.17; 'A' Flt 3 (N) Sqdn 10.2.17; Albatros D.III out of control Vaux 11.30 11.3.17; Albatros in flames north-east of Bapaume 10.35 & Halberstadt DII out of control Ecoust-St.Mein 10.50 17.3.17; Blue Halberstadt DII out of control east of Arras 11.30 24.3.17 (all F/Cdr BC Bell); Albatros D.III out of control north-east of Pronville 15.10 8.4.17; DFW CV forced down Morchies-Louverval 16.50 21.4.17 (numbered *G22*, Uffz Max Haase PoW & Ltn Karl Kelm killed, both of FA26); Albatros D.III out of control Cagnicourt 17.30 21.4.17; Albatros out of control Cagnicourt to south of Havrincourt Wood, shared with N6182 & N6208 (q.v.) 06.30 23.4.17; DFW CV forced to land, captured Morchies-Louverval 16.50 24.4.17 (all F/L HG Travers); Albatros Scout out of control map ref 11.30-11.45 13.5.17 (FSL LS Breadner); Crashed 20.6.17 (FSL MG Woodhouse); AD Dunkirk 21.6.17; Aircraft Park Dover 4.7.17; Damaged 31.8.17; Instructional Flight, War School RNAS Manston W/E 20.10.17; Became Pool of Pilots Manston 1.4.18; 204 TDS Eastchurch by 9.18; Stalled in on turn after take-off 18.9.18 (F/Cdt MH Bottomley slightly injured)

N6170   Deld Hendon for erection 26.1.17; Accepted 6.2.17; AD Dunkirk (via Dover) 10.2.17 to at least 22.2.17 (in Reserve); 3 (N) Sqdn by 27.2.17; Left 11.15, line patrol

Gommecourt-Le Transloy, in combat with enemy aircraft, shot down nr Vis-en-Artois, claimed by Ltn H Schröder, Jasta 1 at Inchy - Sains-les-Marquion 12.50 4.3.17 (F/L HR Wambolt killed); [For survey, "missing" 8.3.17]; Machine recovered by Germans (sic)

N6170   Serial number evidently re-allotted to another Pup, possibly one returned from French evaluation, or a rebuilt aircraft. 2 AD RFC by 22.3.17; 3 (N) Sqdn 19.3.17; Tested 22.3.17 (Rochford); In 'A' Flt by 26.4.17; Crashed and wrecked Hesdigneul 30.4.17 (FSL J Bampfylde-Daniell); AD Dunkirk 1.5.17; Deleted 14.5.17
[NB A Pup numbered N6170 was reported (perhaps in error) on strength of RNAS Dover on 1.6.17]

N6171   Deld AD Dunkirk by @6.2.17 (in Repair 8.2.17; In Reserve 15.2.17); 3 (N) Sqdn Marieux by 1.3.17 (coded 'P', named 'BLACK ARROW') (in 'C' Flt 8.3.17; In 'B' Flt 12.4.17); Damaged in storm; Albatros D.II out of control Pronville, shared with N6178 10.30 12.4.17; Caught by wind in front of sheds and crashed 14.4.17; Flying again 19.4.17; Albatros D.III out of control nr Cambrai 19.15 22.4.17; Albatros D.III out of control Croiselles 06.30 23.4.17; Albatros in flames Bourlon Wood, shared with N6178 & N6194 07.00 2.5.17 (All FSL E Pierce); Crashed on landing Ficheaux 6.5.17 (FSL OC Le Boutillier); AD Dunkirk by 10.5.17; Aircraft Park Dover W/E 31.5.17; AD Dunkirk 27.6.17; Seaplane Defence Flt St.Pol 3.7.17; AD Dunkirk 17.8.17; Aircraft Park Dover W/E 6.9.17; RNASTE Cranwell 27.10.17 (erecting with 80hp Gnome 30.3.18); Became 201/202 TDS Cranwell 1.4.18

N6172   Deld AD Dunkirk 1.17; 3 (N) Sqdn 10.2.17 (coded 'M', named 'BLACK TULIP') (in 'C' Flt 8.3.17; In 'B' Flt 12.4.17); 2-str driven down in dive nr Warlencourt 13.35 14.2.17 (F/L RG Mack); Photo escort, Albatros D.II shot down, then himself shot down, forced landed east of lines at Queant-Pronville 12.4.17 (A/F/Cdr RG Mack, PoW wounded) [claimed Marquion-Bourlon by Hptm Paul von Osterroht, Jasta 12]; Deleted 11.5.17

N6173   Deld Hendon for erection 31.1.17; Forced landed on aerodrome on acceptance test 7.2.17 (F/Cdr TD Hallam DSC); Sent for repair 24.3.17; Surveyed, deletion

N6161 of No.3 (Naval) Squadron was captured on 1st February 1917 when Flt Sub-Lt G.L.Elliott was shot down nr Blankenberghe 1.2.17, probably by Obfm K Meyer of SFS1. As can be seen here, it was captured essentially intact and given German markings with non-standard rudder cross.

(via Frank Cheesman)

Overturned N6171, coded "P" and named BLACK ARROW, is possibly seen here on 14th April 1917 when it was caught by the wind in from of the sheds. Damage was slight and it was soon flying again with 'C' Flight of No.3 (Naval) Squadron, Flt Sub-Lt E.Pierce claiming two victories and another shared before it was crashed by another pilot on 6th May. After repair it went to the Seaplane Defence Flight at St.Pol for a time, before returning to England to join the RNASTE at Cranwell. *(via Philip Jarrett)*

recommended 20.4.17, but apparently not implemented; Instead restored; 2 AAP Comm Flt Hendon by 25.1.18 [ex works?] (for use by Air Dept officers who made visits to stations in UK and GHQ France); Fitted 100hp Monosoupape when erecting 30.3.18; At Hendon to at least 4.7.18; Expeditionary Force to Lympne 31.7.18; Retd Rec Pk but Crashed on landing Marquise 1.8.18; SOC Rep Pk 1 ASD 11.8.18 Not worth repair

N6174 Deld AD Dunkirk 2.17 (in Repair 8.2.17); 3 (N) Sqdn by road 11.2.17; 2-str out of control east of Arras (probably indecisive) 11.30 24.3.17 (FSL FD Casey); Crashed on landing, overturned 06.05 2.4.17 (FSL FD Casey); Albatros D.III crashed Pronville 15.00 8.4.17 (FSL FD Casey); AD Dunkirk 22.5.17; ARS 2AD by 1.6.17; 9 (N) Sqdn 19.6.17; Albatros D.V out of control south-west of Haynecourt 16.00-18.37 patrol 7.7.17 (FSL JW Pinder); 'B' Flt 11 (N) Sqdn 13.7.17; Albatros out of control south of Nieuport 18.45 17.7.17 (FSL AR Brown); Engine cut out while diving on enemy aircraft at 7,000ft, forced landed in sea 17m north of Ostende 27.7.17 (FSL EJK Buckley unhurt; aircraft and pilot salved and to Dunkirk on board TBD *Francis Garnier*) ["Nieuport" claimed in combat Ostunkerkirk by FlM B Heinrich, MFJa1]; Aircraft Park Dover 11.10.17; Surveyed 16.10.17; Deleted 19.10.17 Wear & tear

N6175 Deld Aircraft Park Dover (via Hastings) 7.2.17; AD Dunkirk 8.2.17 (in Reserve); 3 (N) Sqdn 11.2.17 (in 'A' Flt 8.3.17; 'B' Flt 26.4.17); Photo escort, Albatros C out of control Vaux at 10,000ft 11.50, drove off another enemy aircraft steeply 11.55 11.3.17; Albatros D.III out of control nr Pronville 10.50 17.3.17 (both F/L HG Travers); Crashed landing at ARS 2 AD 2.4.17 (FSL GB Anderson); ARS 2 AD repair; 3 (N) Sqdn 26.4.17; Left 16.15, shot down Roumaucourt, west of Cambrai 17.30 30.4.17 (FSL JJ Malone DSO killed) [claimed by Ltn P Billik, Jasta 12]; Deleted 2.6.17

N6176 Deld AD Dunkirk 2.17; 3 (N) Sqdn c.3.17; AD Dunkirk by 26.4.17; 'A' Flt 4 (N) Sqdn 12.5.17; Albatros C broke up, in sea 10m north of Bray Dunes 05.35 25.5.17; Gotha in sea 15m north of Westende, shared with N5196, N6168, & N6198 18.30 25.5.17; 2-str crashed south-west of Furnes, shared with N6187 08.45 26.5.17; White

Albatros D.V crashed nr Courtemarck 16.40 3.6.17 (all FSL AJ Chadwick); Forced landed in mist nr Calais, dismantled and retd by road 29.6.17; AD Dunkirk 26.8.17; 12 (N) Sqdn 25.9.17 (in 'B' Flt 1.11.17); Aircraft Park Dover 23.11.17; Allotted to Grain for experiments 7.12.17; Experimental Constructive Dept, Grain 10.12.17 to at least 6.18 (held at Eastbourne for CTD Grain 30.3.18)

N6177 (later 80hp Gnome) Deld AD Dunkirk (via Dover) 26.2.17; 9 (N) Sqdn 28.2.17 (in 'A' Flt 29.3.17); Seaplane destroyed Wenduyne 24.3.17 (FSL HS Kerby); 'A' Flt 4 (N) Sqdn 22.4.17; White 1-str (Siemens-Schuckert DI?) into sea 5m north-east of Zeebrugge 07.20 12.5.17 (FSL GW Hemming); Last mention with Sqdn 26.5.17; AD Dunkirk 5.17; Dover 13.6.17; Left 10.30 for Anti-Gotha patrol, retd with engine trouble 7.7.17; Crashed 11.7.17; Transferred to Dover 9.8.17; War School RNAS Manston W/E 20.10.17; Crashed there 14.10.17; Deleted W/E 2.3.18

N6178 Deld AD Dunkirk 2.17; 3 (N) Sqdn 15.2.17 (in 'C' Flt 8.3.17); Crashed on landing 4.3.17 (FSL FC Armstrong); Halberstadt DII out of control (possibly indecisive) Bourlon Wood 10.20 6.4.17; Enemy aircraft out of control, then Albatros D.II out of control Pronville, shared with N6171 10.30 12.4.17; Albatros C in flames Bourlon Wood, shared with N6171 & N6194 07.00 2.5.17; Albatros D.III out of control Bourlon Wood, shared with N6465 19.05 6.5.17 (all FSL FC Armstrong); AD Dunkirk 22.5.17; ARS 2AD by 1.6.17; 9 (N) Sqdn 9.7.17; 'A' Flt 11 (N) Sqdn 13.7.17; Crashed on landing 16.7.17 (FSL LA Sands); Crashed on take-off 10.8.17 (FSL LA Sands); Aircraft Park Dover 11.10.17; Surveyed 16.10.17; Deleted 19.10.17 Wear & tear

N6179 (80hp Gnome) Deld AD Dunkirk 2.17; 3 (N) Sqdn 15.2.17 (named 'BABY MINE') (in 'B' Flt 12.4.17); Albatros D.II fell vertically Achiet-le-Grand 4.3.17 (F/Cdr TC Vernon); Albatros D.III out of control Epinoy 17.30 & another out of control Epinoy 18.00 23.4.17; Albatros D.III down smoking south of Cambrai 10.30 29.4.17 (all FSL AW Carter); AD Dunkirk to Dover 9.5.17 (repair); AD Dunkirk 24.6.17; Seaplane Defence Flt St.Pol 3.7.17; AD Dunkirk 4.8.17; Aircraft Park

Dover 21.8.17; Seaplane Defence Flt 31.8.17; AD Dunkirk 1.9.17; Seaplane Defence Flt 4.9.17; Gotha damaged and forced to land 29.9.17 (FSL LH Slatter); Aircraft Park Dover 12.10.17; Instructional Flight, War School RNAS Manston W/E 27.10.17 to at least 30.3.18 (for another station by 3.18)

N6180   Deld AD Dunkirk (via Dover) 2.6.17; 11 (N) Sqdn 20.7.17; Crashed on landing 25.7.17 (FSL WC Wilson injured); Last mention on Sqdn 22.8.17, but Sqdn disbanded 27.8.17 [still shown with 11 (N) Sqdn in AD Report 6.9.17]; AD Dunkirk by 13.9.17; 12 (N) Sqdn 2.10.17 (in 'A' Flt 1.11.17]; To Aircraft Park Dover, but on arrival crashed in cemetery west of Dover, completely wrecked 4.12.17 (FSL OP Adam injured); Deleted W/E 15.12.17

N6181   Deld AD Dunkirk (via Dover) 9.3.17; 'B' Flt 3 (N) Sqdn by 15.3.17 (named 'HMA HAPPY'); Albatros D.III broke up & Albatros C in flames Cambrai 08.45 - 08.55 11.4.17; Gotha G.IV Nr G610/16 driven down and landed intact south-east of Vron 10.30 23.4.17 (numbered *G23* Ltn K Schweren, Ltn O Wirsch & Offstlvtr A Hecher of KG III/15 PoWs); Albatros D.III down smoking Bourlon Wood 17.30 23.4.17; Albatros D.III out of control Bois du Gaard, south-east of Cambrai 11.15 29.4.17 (all F/L LS Breadner); Last mention 2.5.17; AD Dunkirk to Dover 8.5.17 (repair); AD Dunkirk 31.5.17; 3 (N) Sqdn 4.6.17; Dived in from 1,000ft into wheat field nr Furnes, between Oost Dunkirk and Coxyde 6.7.17 (FSL H Allan killed); AD Dunkirk 10.7.17 (completely wrecked); For survey 12.7.17; Deletion recommended 3.9.17; Implemented 15.9.17

N6182   Deld Aircraft Park Dover 24.3.17; AD Dunkirk 25.3.17; 3 (N) Sqdn by 29.3.17 (in 'C' Flt 12.4.17; 'B' Flt 26.4.17); Albatros D.III out of control north-east of Pronville 15.00 8.4.17; Albatros D.III out of control Villers-lez-Cagnicourt 18.40 21.4.17; Albatros D.III out of control Saudemont 17.15-18.30 & Albatros C out of control Pronville 18.40 23.4.17; Forced DFW CV to land Morchies-Louverval, shared with N6169 & N6208 (q.v) 16.50 24.4.17; Albatros D.III out of control north of Cambrai 19.15 26.4.17; Albatros D.III in flames Bantouzelle-Cambrai 11.00 29.4.17; Albatros D.III out of control Moeuvres 11.10 2.5.17 (all FSL FD Casey); AD Dunkirk 12.5.17; 12 (N) Sqdn 11.7.17; To Dover but shot down in sea nr Kentish Knock LV 4.12.17 (FSL JA Morell rescued by MTB); Deleted 14.12.17 Total loss

N6183   Deld Aircraft Park Dover 24.3.17; AD Dunkirk 16.4.17; ARS 2 AD and on to 3 (N) Sqdn (named 'MILDRED H') 30.4.17 (in 'B' Flt by 12.7.17); Albatros D.III out of control, pilot believed shot Bourlon-Fontaine-Notre-Dame 13.40 23.5.17; Albatros D.III crashed & burnt Ecourt-St.Quentin 07.30 27.5.17; 2 seaplanes in sea 6-12m off Ostende, 1 shared with N6162, N6465, N6477 & N6479 c.11.10 7.7.17 (all FSL JA Glen); AD Dunkirk 16.7.17; 11 (N) Sqdn by 30.7.17; Forced landed in sea 14.8.17 (FSL FR Johnson rescued); AD Dunkirk by 16.8.17; Deletion recommended and approved 20.8.17; Implemented 25.8.17

N6184   Deld Aircraft Park Dover 24.3.17; AD Dunkirk 4.4.17; 'B' Flt 9 (N) Sqdn 5.4.17 ('C' Flt by 12.4.17); 'B' Flt 11 (N) Sqdn 19.5.17; 'C' Flt 4 (N) Sqdn 6.6.17 to at least 21.6.17 (temp attd); Retd 11 (N) Sqdn by 28.6.17; Forced landed, damaged 17.7.17 (FSL ECR Stoneman); Aircraft Park Dover by 26.7.17 (officially transferred from Dunkirk to Dover 9.8.17); Surveyed 13.10.17; Deleted 18.10.17 wrecked

N6185   Tested Brooklands 2.3.17; Deld Aircraft Park Dover 16.3.17; AD Dunkirk 17.3.17; 4 (N) Sqdn 22.3.17

(coded 'A', named 'ANZAC'); Albatros D.V out of control south-east of Dixmude 19.15 26.4.17; Enemy aircraft out of control over floods south of Nieuport 19.00 30.4.17 (both FSL CJ Moir); Bomber escort, left pm, shot down nr Zeebrugge 10.5.17 (T/F/L CJ Moir killed); Deleted 21.5.17

N6186   Listed on strength of 'C' Flt 3 (N) Sqdn 15.2.17, but not deld Dover for erection until 7.3.17; AD Dunkirk 17.3.17; 3 (N) Sqdn from/by 21.3.17 (test of new machine); Test flight, crashed on landing Marieux 28.3.17 (FSL S Bennett); ARS 2 AD by 5.4.17; 3 (N) Sqdn by 26.4.17; Left 09.20, escort reconnaissance F.E.s, to Caudry, shot down, forced landed, crashed nr Ecourt-St.Quentin 1.5.17 (FSL AS Mather PoW) [Sopwith claimed 10.40 nr Cantaing by Obltn A Ritter von Tutschek, Jasta 12]; Deleted 11.5.17

N6187   Deld Aircraft Park Dover for erection 7.3.17; AD Dunkirk 23.3.17; 4 (N) Sqdn 28.3.17 (in 'B' Flt 12.4.17); Aviatik C out of control Westende 07.30 9.5.17; 2-str crashed Furnes, shared with N6176 08.45 26.5.17; At Dover 1.6.17; 1-str broke up off Ostende, crashed 2m north-east of Nieuport 19.15 5.6.17 (all FSL AJ Enstone); AD Dunkirk 17.6.17; 'B' Flt 11 (N) Sqdn 11.7.17; Enemy aircraft down in spin 18.7.17 (FSL ND Hall); Last mention with Sqdn 30.8.17; 12 (N) Sqdn, wrecked 12.9.17; AD Dunkirk 12.9.17; Deletion recommended 17.9.17; Deleted 22.9.17

N6188   Deld Aircraft Park Dover for erection 7.3.17; AD Dunkirk 23.3.17; 'C' Flt 9 (N) Sqdn 25.3.17; 2-str out of control Furnes-Nieuport, shared with 9916 & N6193 09.15 31.5.17; LVG out of control Westende-Ghistelles 09.15 1.6.17 (both FSL FE Banbury); 11 (N) Sqdn 11.6.17; 'B' Flt 4 (N) Sqdn 13.6.17 (temporarily attached); At Dover 16.6.17; 11 (N) Sqdn 4.7.17 (in 'A' Flt 12.7.17); AD Dunkirk 24.7.17; Aircraft Park Dover 26.8.17 (overhaul) (officially transferred from Dunkirk to Dover 11.10.17); War School RNAS Manston W/E 20.10.17; Serviceable with 80hp Gnome by 30.3.18; Became Pool of Pilots Manston 1.4.18

N6189   Recorded as "In Repair" at AD Dunkirk 8.3.17, but not deld Dover for erection until 10.3.17; AD Dunkirk 15.3.17; 'B' Flt 9 (N) Sqdn 18.3.17 to at least 1.4.17; AD Dunkirk by 5.4.17; Aircraft Park Dover 10.5.17 (repair); AD Dunkirk by 31.5.17; Dover War Flt 25.6.17 [sic]; Left 12.14 for Anti-Gotha patrol, landed 13.45 13.6.17; Officially transferred from Dunkirk to Dover 9.8.17; Left 10.20 for Anti-Gotha patrol, returned with engine trouble 10.45 22.8.17; Still Dover War Flt 13.10.17; War School RNAS Manston by 20.10.17; Engineless and awaiting deletion by 30.3.18

N6190   Deld Aircraft Park Dover for erection 9.3.17; AD Dunkirk 17.3.17 (in Reserve 12.4.17); 'B' Flt 4 (N) Sqdn 24.4.17 ('C' Flt by 3.5.17); AD Dunkirk 24.6.17; 'B' Flt 11 (N) Sqdn 9.7.17 to at least 30.8.17; Damaged 12.7.17; Crashed on landing 17.8.17 (FSL LA Sands); Aircraft Park Dover by 6.9.17 (officially transferred from Dunkirk to Dover 11.10.17); War School RNAS Manston W/E 20.10.17; Experimental Constructive & Armament Dept, Grain W/E 2.3.18 (deck arrester gear experiments); Deck landing experiments with skids & wheel undercarriage; Deck landing experiments with staggered 15-in wing struts 16.3.18; Allotted to Grain Acceptance Depot for Manston 30.3.18, but instead retained Grain for deck landing experiments until the end of the war; Deck landing experiment with skids 13.9.18

N6191   Recorded as "In Repair" at AD Dunkirk 8.3.17, but not deld Dover for erection until 10.3.17; AD Dunkirk 15.3.17; 9 (N) Sqdn 18.3.17 (in 'C' Flt 29.3.17);

The scene at the edge of the beach at St.Pol on 15th August 1917 after N6192 'A-C' of 'A' Flight, No.11 (Naval) Squadron overturned, presumably during a forced landing. After repair at the Aircraft Depot Dunkirk it was returned to England to serve as a training aircraft at Cranwell.

(J.M.Bruce/G.S.Leslie collection)

Unsuccessfully attacked U-boat 15m off Ostende 7.5.17 (F/Cdr GE Hervey); Crashed on landing 9.6.17 (FSL FJW Mellersh); AD Dunkirk by 14.6.17; Dover War Flt W/E 5.7.17; Left 08.30 for Anti-Gotha patrol, retd 10.20 22.7.17; Left 17.25 for Anti-Gotha patrol, gun jammed, retd, left again 17.40, landed 19.00 12.8.17; Left 10.20 for Anti-Gotha patrol, with N6440 attacked Gotha which went down in slow spin and believed it crashed in sea half mile off Margate 22.8.17 (all F/Cdr GE Hervey); War School RNAS Manston 27.10.17; Deleted W/E 23.3.18

N6192 Recorded as "In Repair" at AD Dunkirk 8.3.17, but not deld Dover for erection until 10.3.17; AD Dunkirk 15.3.17; 9 (N) Sqdn 25.3.17 (in 'C' Flt 25.3.17); 11 (N) Sqdn 3.6.17; 4 (N) Sqdn 6.6.17 (temporarily attached); 2-str out of control 4m north-east of Dixmude shared with N6476 16.00 6.6.17 (FSL EJK Buckley); 'A' Flt 11 (N) Sqdn (coded 'A-C') 4.7.17; Overturned on beach St.Pol 15.8.17; AD Dunkirk 16.8.17; Aircraft Park Dover by 6.9.17 (officially transferred from Dunkirk to Dover 11.10.17); RNASTE Cranwell 27.10.17 (erecting with 80hp Gnome 30.8.17); Became 201/202 TDS Cranwell 1.4.18

N6193 Deld Aircraft Park Dover for erection 14.3.17; AD Dunkirk 15.3.17; 9 (N) Sqdn 16.3.17 (in 'A' Flt 29.3.17; 'C' Flt 31.5.17); Halberstadt out of control Zeebrugge 07.15 12.5.17; 2-str down in near vertical dive 5m off Nieuport 09.20 28.5.17; 2-str out of control Furnes-Nieuport, shared with 9916 & N6188 16.15 31.5.17 (both FSL TR Shearer); 2-str on fire off Ostende 17.00 5.6.17 (FSL HE Mott); Badly shot up in combat 6.6.17 (FSL HF Stackard unhurt); AD Dunkirk 7.6.17; Aircraft Park Dover 4.7.17 (officially transferred from Dunkirk to Dover 9.8.17); Badly damaged 22.8.17; War Flt Manston 29.9.17; At Surveyed 3.1.18; At Chingford 5.1.18; War Flight Manston 11.1.18; Deleted 15.1.18 Wear & tear

N6194 Recorded as "In Repair" at AD Dunkirk 8.3.17, but does deld Dover for erection until 14.3.17; AD Dunkirk 15.3.17; 3 (N) Sqdn by 18.3.17 (in 'C' Flt 26.4.17); Halberstadt DII out of control Queant-Bourlon 10.30 12.4.17; Albatros D.III out of control north of Cambrai-Arras road 18.00 23.4.17; Albatros C in flames Bourlon Wood, shared with N6178 & N6171 07.00 2.5.17 (all FSL AT Whealy); Albatros D.III, shared with 18 Sqdn

RFC 23.5.17 (FSL WE Orchard); Left 08.25, travelling flight, shot up, wounded then lost control, overshot landing Fremicourt ALG, crashed, completely wrecked 2.6.17 (FSL WE Orchard died of wounds), believed credited Fl-Maat Kunstler, Marine Jasta 1; Surveyed 17.10.17; Deletion recommended 18.10.17; Implemented 24.10.17 Wrecked

N6195 Deld Aircraft Park Dover for erection 15.3.17; AD Dunkirk 17.3.17; 9 (N) Sqdn 17.3.17; Blown over on landing 23.3.17 (FSL J Bampfylde-Daniell unhurt); AD Dunkirk by 29.3.17 (repair); 3 (N) Sqdn Marieux (coded 'G', named GAB...' [name not clear in photo]) 12.5.17; Crashed on nose St.Pol 5.17; Still 3 (N) Sqdn 7.7.17; AD Dunkirk by 12.7.17; Aircraft Park Dover W/E 26.7.17 (officially transferred from Dunkirk to Dover 9.8.17); War School RNAS Manston 23.9.17; Deleted W/E 23.3.18

N6196 Deld Aircraft Park Dover for erection 16.3.17; AD Dunkirk 18.3.17; 9 (N) Sqdn 21.3.17 (with 'A' Flt 29.3.17); 4 (N) Sqdn 22.4.17 (in 'B' Flt 19.4.17; 'C' Flt 3.5.17); 11 (N) Sqdn 7.6.17; 12 (N) Sqdn 15.6.17 to at least 14.7.17; AD Dunkirk by 19.7.17; Aircraft Park Dover W/E 27.9.17 (officially transferred from Dunkirk to Dover 11.10.17); RNASTE Cranwell 27.10.17 (fitted 80hp Gnome); Became 201/202 TDS Cranwell 1.4.18

N6197 Deld Aircraft Park Dover for erection 13.4.17; AD Dunkirk 20.4.17; 3 (N) Sqdn 1.5.17; Forced landed nr Doullens 11.5.17; Albatros D.II out of control Awoingt-Bourlon 13.30-14.00 23.5.17; Crashed on landing 2.6.17 (all FSL LS Breadner) [flown again 4.6.17]; AD Dunkirk by 18.6.17; Aircraft Park Dover W/E 26.7.17 (officially transferred from Dunkirk to Dover 9.8.17); Instructional Flight, War School RNAS Manston 6.10.17 (80hp Le Rhône by 11.1.18, 80hp Gnome by 30.3.18); Became Pool of Pilots Manston 1.4.18; 41 TDS London Colney 6.8.18

N6198 (80hp Gnome) Deld Aircraft Park Dover for test 21.3.17; AD Dunkirk 30.3.17; 'A' Flt 4 (N) Sqdn from 9.4.17; Gotha spun into sea 15m north of Westende, shared with N5196, N6168, N6176 & N6198 18.30 25.5.17; Caught by wind after landing, overturned 3.6.17 (both FSL GMT Rouse); AD Dunkirk by 7.6.17; Aircraft Park Dover 4.7.17 (officially transferred from Dunkirk to Dover

9.8.17); Instructional Flight, War School RNAS Manston 13.10.17; With 80hp Gnome by 30.3.18; Became Pool of Pilots Manston 1.4.18; 41 TDS London Colney to Pilots & Observers AG&FS Lerysdown 3.9.18

N6199 (80hp Gnome) Deld Aircraft Park Dover for erection 20.3.17; AD Dunkirk 23.3.17; 9 (N) Sqdn 25.3.17 (in 'B' Flt 29.3.17); 'B' Flt 11 (N) Sqdn 25.5.17; Siemens-Schuckert DI destroyed & another out of control north-east of Dixmude 16.00 6.6.17 (by FSL GW Hemming of 4 (N) Sqdn (sic)); 4 (N) Sqdn 15.6.17 (temp attd); 11 (N) Sqdn 4.7.17; Aircraft Park Dover 9.8.17 (officially transferred from Dunkirk to Dover 9.8.17); War School RNAS 13.10.17; Became Pool of Pilots Manston 1.4.18; 206 TDS Eastbourne 8.5.18 to at least 29.5.18; South-Eastern Area Flying Instructors School Shoreham by 12.10.18 to at least 9.11.18

N6200 (80hp Gnome) Deld Aircraft Park Dover for erection 21.3.17; AD Dunkirk 30.3.17; 'B' Flt 4 (N) Sqdn Bray Dunes (name 'BOBS') 8.4.17; Fokker DII out of control Ghistelles 10.10 24.4.17; Aviatik C crashed 1m south-east of Ghistelles, shared with N6168, and 1-str out of control down in spin Westende 17.15 9.5.17; Seaplane into sea off Zeebrugge 07.30 12.5.17 (all F/L later A/F/Cdr AM Shook); Engine failure, forced landed in sea 4m north of Bray Dunes 08.40, picked up by French destroyer *Oriflamme* and towed into Dunkirk, brought ashore 19.5.17 (A/F/Cdr AM Shook unhurt); AD Dunkirk 19.5.17 (repair); Aircraft Park Dover 4.6.17 (officially transferred from Dunkirk to Dover 9.8.17); Crashed 11.7.17; Left 09.05 for Anti-Gotha patrol, landed 10.00 22.7.17; Spun twice, crashed on landing 12.8.17 (FSL AM Alexander); War Flt Manston 29.9.17; For deletion engineless by 30.3.18

N6201 (80hp Gnome) Deld Aircraft Park Dover for erection 23.3.17; AD Dunkirk 30.3.17; 9 (N) Sqdn 5.4.17 to at least 8.4.17; Believed the aircraft which crashed on take-off 9.4.17; AD Dunkirk by 12.4.17 (repair); Aircraft Park Dover 2.5.17 (repair); AD Dunkirk 31.5.17; 12 (N) Sqdn 18.6.17; AD Dunkirk by 21.6.17; Aircraft Park Dover 4.7.17; Badly damaged 7.8.17; Officially transferred from Dunkirk to Dover 9.8.17; War School RNAS Manston 6.10.17; For deletion engineless by 30.3.18

N6202 Deld Aircraft Park Dover for erection 25.3.17; AD Dunkirk by 5.4.17; 'C' Flt 3 (N) Sqdn W/E 12.4.17; Albatros D.III out of control Croiselles 06.30 23.4.17 (FSL HF Beamish); Albatros D.III crashed north of Cambrai (probably Vzfw Emil Eisenhuth, Jasta 3, killed) 19.15 26.4.17 (FSL JJ Malone DSO); AD Dunkirk by 3.5.17; Aircraft Park Dover 8.5.17 (repair); Left 12.14 for Anti-Gotha patrol, landed 13.35 13.6.17; Badly damaged 19.6.17; Left 07.40 for Anti-Gotha patrol, landed 08.45 4.7.17; Officially transferred from Dunkirk

N6203 was flown by the Seaplane Defence Flt at St.Pol in July 1917. It was flown by Flt Sub-Lt L.H.Slatter, who named it "MINA". [see also page 199] (via Frank Cheesman)

to Dover 9.8.17; 12 (N) Sqdn by 25.8.17; Aircraft Park Dover by 9.17; War School RNAS Manston W/E 20.10.17 [with Testing Sqdn Martlesham Heath 29.12.17]; With 80hp Gnome by 30.3.18; Became Pool of Pilots Manston 1.4.18; Also reported at Freiston; 6th Wing from 27.7.18

N6203 Deld Aircraft Park Dover for erection 24.3.17; AD Dunkirk 4.4.17; 3 (N) Sqdn 13.4.17 ('C' Flt by 21.4.17); Albatros D.III out of control Hendicourt 17.50 21.4.17; Albatros D.III down smoking south of Cambrai 10.30 29.4.17 (both FSL HS Broad); Last mention with Sqdn 5.5.17; AD Dunkirk by 10.5.17; Aircraft Park Dover by 31.5.17; AD Dunkirk 25.6.17; Seaplane Defence Flt St.Pol (coded 'S', named 'MINA') 3.7.17; AD Dunkirk 4.8.17; 12 (N) Sqdn by 25.8.17 (in 'A' Flt by 13.9.17; Aeroplane Park Dover 23.11.17; Allotted Grain for experiments 7.12.17; Arrived Experimental Constructive Dept, Grain 10.12.17 to at least 6.18; [Deck landing set fitted to first of new batch of Pups 15.12.17]; Crashed on nose at one time

N6204 Allotted for transfer to Russian Government 21.3.17; Official Air Department lists clearly account for this Pup having gone there, yet it has also been reported as being allotted to store on 3.12.17

N6205 Deld Aircraft Park Dover for erection 31.3.17; AD Dunkirk 13.4.17; 'C' Flt 3 (N) Sqdn (named 'BETTY') by 19.4.17; Albatros D.III out of control Bourlon Wood, south-east of Cambrai 17.30 23.4.17; Albatros D.III crashed Bois du Gaard 11.00 29.4.17; Albatros D.III out of control north-east of Cambrai 10.45 1.5.17; Damaged Marieux 11.5.17 (all FSL JST Fall); AD Dunkirk 12.5.17 to at least 24.5.17; Aircraft Park Dover by 1.6.17; Badly damaged 6.8.17; Repaired; Walmer 6.10.17; Eastbourne (via Dover) W/E 9.11.17; Grain, fitting deck landing gear from 22.12.17 [therefore became 9901a Ships Pup];
BUT East Fortune Naval Flying School from/by 24.11.17; Became 208 TDS East Fortune 1.4.18; 1 FS Ayr by 11.7.18

N6206 Deld Aircraft Park Dover for erection 31.3.17; AD Dunkirk 4.6.17; Seaplane Defence Flt 21.7.17; Crashed on landing 8.8.17 (F/L GW Price); AD Dunkirk 17.8.17; Aircraft Park Dover W/E 13.10.17; Surveyed 16.10.17; Deleted 19.10.17 Wear & tear

N6207 Deld Aircraft Park Dover for erection 31.3.17; AD Dunkirk 7.4.17; 3 (N) Sqdn 13.4.17 (named 'BLACK BESS') (in 'C' Flt 26.4.17); Offensive patrol, last seen Ecourt-St.Quentin 19.40 4.5.17 (FSL HS Murton PoW) [claimed Fresnes-Vitry by Obltn Adolf, Ritter von Tutschek, Jasta 12]; Deleted 21.5.17

N6208 Deld Aircraft Park Dover for erection 31.3.17; AD Dunkirk 8.4.17 (in Reserve); 3 (N) Sqdn 13.4.17; 2-str out of control 5m north of Queant 17.40 21.4.17; 3 Albatros D.III, 1 destroyed Croiselles 06.30, 1 out of control Croiselles 07.15 & 1 out of control Croiselles-Havrincourt 07.45 23.4.17; With N6169 & N6182 forced DFW C5297/16 of *FA26* to land Morchies-Louverval 16.50, then own aircraft suffered engine failure, landed alongside enemy aircraft then both destroyed by German shell fire 24.4.17 (all FSL JJ Malone DSO) [numbered *G25*, Uffz Max Haase slightly wounded, observer Ltn Karl Keim died after 10 min]; Deletion recommended by AD Dunkirk 26.4.17; Approved 28.4.17; Implemented 4.5.17

N6209 Deld Oxted to Hendon for erection 10.2.17; Ready 19.2.17; Aircraft Park Dover 26.2.17; AD Dunkirk 27.2.17; 'A' Flt 3 (N) Sqdn 13.3.17; Offensive patrol, engine failure, forced landed Beauvais 5.4.17 (FSL HF Beamish unhurt); 2 AD 12.4.17; 3 (N) Sqdn 9.5.17; 'B' Flt 11 (N) Sqdn 11.7.17; AD Dunkirk 20.7.17; Aircraft Park Dover 26.8.17 (officially transferred from Dunkirk to Dover 11.10.17); RNASTE Cranwell 27.10.17 (fitted 80hp Gnome by 5.1.18); In course of re-erection 30.3.18; Became 201/202 TDS Cranwell 1.4.18

30 SOPWITH SHIPS PUP (ADMIRALTY 9901a TYPE) ordered 16.2.17 (later 14.3.17) under Cont Nos A.S.19598/17 & A.S.775 from Sir William Beardmore & Co Ltd, numbered N6430 to N6459 & built Dalmuir. Fitted airbags and alternative Lewis gun and/or rocket armament. First flights usually at Inchinnan airfield by A.Dukinfield Jones. (Apparently intended to have 80hp Clerget but delivered with 80hp Le Rhône) [wheel undercarriage, but some later converted to skid undercarriage]

N6430 (Engine No.100257, propeller No.917); FF 24.4.17; Deld East Fortune for HMS *Manxman* 4.5.17; HMS *Manxman* 11.5.17 but damaged in transit and retd Turnhouse for repair; HMS *Manxman* 8.6.17; Fleet Aeroplane Depot Turnhouse by 8-14.6.17; HMS *Yarmouth* 23.7.17?; Shot down airship L23 in sea in flames off Lodbjerg, Denmark, then ditched 21.8.17 (FSL BA Smart picked up by TBD *Prince*, retd next day); Only the engine and gun salvaged, to Rosyth 7.9.17

N6431 (Engine No.100274, propeller No.891); FF 24.4.17; Deld East Fortune for HMS *Manxman* 4.5.17; HMS *Manxman* 11.5.17; HMS *Yarmouth* 23.8.17; Rosyth 7.9.17; Scapa 29.9.17 for recovery and truing up for HMS *Yarmouth*; HMS *Yarmouth* 29.9.17; Scapa 29.10.17; HMS *Dublin* 10.12.17; Houton Bay on/by 13.12.17; Rosyth W/E 15.12.17; HMAS *Sydney* to HMS *Campania* W/E 22.12.17; Houton Bay W/E 29.12.17; HMS *Dublin* 26.1.18; Rosyth 4.2.18; Fleet Aeroplane Depot Turnhouse W/E 16.3.18; Deleted W/E 19.12.18

N6432 (Engine No.100278, propeller No.888); FF 7.5.17; Allotted Aegean 12.4.17; Shipped to Aegean; Tested Stavros 9.10.17; Marsh Aerodrome 26.11.17 to at least 9.12.17; Mudros Base by 1.1.18; 'G' Sqdn 2 (Naval) Wing Mudros by 3.18; Became 'G' Sqdn 62 (Naval)

Wing Mudros 1.4.18; 'F' Sqdn Hadzi Junas; Marsh Aerodrome by 1.10.18; Sold to Greek Government; Transferred RHNAS for training by 1.19

N6433 (Engine No.100277, propeller No.893); FF & accepted 7.5.17; Allotted Aegean 12.4.17; Shipped to Aegean; Stavros by 1.12.17; Mudros Base by 1.1.18; 'C' Sqdn 2 (Naval) Wing Mudros; Sold to Greek Government; Transferred to RHNAS for training by 10.18 to at least 30.1.19

N6434 (Engine No.100279, propeller No.920); FF 15.5.17; Deld Killingholme store 22.5.17; East Fortune by rail 15.9.17 (for carriers); Damaged but repairable by 6.1.18; Deleted W/E 30.3.18; ALSO reported HMS *Renown* (unconfirmed)

N6435 (Engine No.100252, propeller No.1212); FF 15.5.17; Deld Killingholme store 22.5.17; AD Dunkirk (via Eastchurch) 17.7.17; Seaplane Defence Flt St.Pol 31.7.17 to at least 2.9.17; AD Dunkirk by 6.9.17; Aircraft Park Dover by 13.9.17 (officially transferred from Dunkirk to Dover 11.10.17); RNASTE Cranwell W/E 1.11.17; Crashed, badly damaged, Cranwell South 11.3.18 (pilot unhurt); U/s at Cranwell 30.3.18

N6436 (Engine No.5161, propeller No.LP11797); FF 15.5.17; Deld Killingholme store 27.5.17; AD Dunkirk 3.7.17 to at least 19.7.17; Seaplane Defence Flt St.Pol by 24.7.17; AD Dunkirk 17.8.17 to at least 30.8.17; Aircraft Park Dover by 6.9.17 (officially transferred from Dunkirk to Dover 11.10.17); RNASTE Cranwell W/E 1.11.17; Still there being erected with 80hp Gnome 30.3.18; Became 201/202 TDS Cranwell 1.4.18

N6437 (Engine No.100285, propeller No.1213); FF 15.5.17; Deld Killingholme store 27.5.17; Wyton 16.7.17 (transit); AD Dunkirk (via Chingford) 18.7.17; Seaplane Defence Flt St.Pol 31.7.17; Seaplane destroyed off Ostende, shared with N6459 & N6478 17.45 12.8.17 (F/L PS Fisher) [FF33L No.1246 (Flgm Walter Paatz & Vzfw Putz, Seeflug 1 both killed)]; Badly damaged landing 5.9.17 (FSL FG Horstmann); AD Dunkirk 5.9.17; Deleted 13.9.17 Damaged beyond repair

Possibly N6431, thus Pup is being hoisted to or from a pontoon. N6431 was initially flown from HMS Manxman from May 1917, later serving in HMS Yarmouth, HMS Dublin and HMS Campania at various times, *(via Frank Cheesman)*

N6438   (Engine No.8316, propeller No.LP11796); FF 16.5.17; accepted 23.5.17; Deld Aircraft Park Dover for Walmer 1.6.17; Walmer Defence Flt 5.6.17; Left 18.15 for Anti-Gotha patrol, landed 19.25 5.6.17; Enemy aircraft patrol 8.6.17 & 16.6.17x2; Left 08.10 for Anti-Gotha patrol, landed 09.15 4.7.17; (all FSL WH Chisham); Left 08.40 for Anti-Gotha patrol, landed 10.35 22.7.17 (F/L HS Kerby); Badly damaged landing Dover 11.8.17 (F/L RA Little); Remained Dover for repair; Anti-Gotha patrol from Dover, left 10.15, landed Walmer 12.00 21.8.17 (F/Cdr CT MacLaren); Enemy aircraft patrol at Walmer 8.9.17 (F/L RA Little); Aircraft Park Dover 29.9.17; Donibristle (named 'EXCUSE ME!') by 5.10.17; Rosyth W/E 13.12.17; HMS *Pegasus* W/E 20.12.17 (by 17.12.17); HMS *Repulse* W/E 20.12.17; HMS *Pegasus* to HMS *Tiger* 27.12.17; HMS *Pegasus* 6.1.18; Donibristle by 1.18 (for HMS *Tiger*); Rosyth W/E 18.1.18; Donibristle 7.2.18; HMS *Nairana* W/E 8.2.18; Fleet Aeroplane Depot Turnhouse W/E 9.3.18 (for HMS *Nairana*) (with Depot Flt to W/E 30.3.18); HMS *Furious* (still marked 'EXCUSE ME!') mid 4.18 (for deck landing experiments with skid undercarriage – see photos on pages 119-120); Damaged in deck landing 16.4.18; Surveyed 3.5.18; Deleted 15.5.18 wrecked
ALSO Grain 1918 (arrester gear experiments)

N6439   (Engine No.100297, propeller No.1216); FF & accepted 23.5.17; Deld Aircraft Park Dover for Walmer 1.6.17; Walmer Defence Flt 4.6.17; 2 Enemy aircraft patrols 7.6.17 (FSL WM Lusby); Anti-Gotha patrol, left 11.10, landed 13.10 13.6.17 (FSL WH Chisham); Hostile aircraft patrol 14.6.17 (FSL JA Shaw); Anti-Gotha patrol, left 07.50, landed 08.25 4.7.17 (FSL WM Lusby); Anti-Gotha patrol, left 09.30, landed 10.25 7.7.17 (FSL WM Lusby); Anti-Gotha patrol, left 10.50, landed 12.10 7.7.17 (FSL WH Chisham); Anti-Gotha patrol, left 08.35, landed 10.25 22.7.17 (F/L S Kemball); Anti-Gotha patrol, left 17.30 12.8.17; Anti-Gotha patrol 21.8.17; Anti-Gotha patrol, left 10.20, landed 19.33 22.8.17; Anti-Gotha patrol 9.9.17 (all FSL MR Kingsford); Aircraft Park Dover 29.9.17; Donibristle by 5.10.17; Aircraft Park Dover by 23.10.17; Donibristle by 27.10.17 to at least 3.11.17; Rosyth to HMS *Pegasus* W/E 10.11.17; Donibristle to HMS *Pegasus* W/E 15.11.17; Rosyth W/E 27.12.17; Fleet Aeroplane Depot Turnhouse W/E 21.3.18; Engineless by 30.3.18; Fitted 80hp Le Rhône by 7.11.18; Remained at Turnhouse to at least 30.1.19

N6440 mounted on the turret platform of HMS New Zealand with the pilot seated in the cockpit, probably some time in 1918. During earlier service with the Walmer Defence Flight, this aircraft shot down a Gotha bomber on 12th August 1917 and shared in a victory over another Gotha ten days later, in both cases piloted by Flt Sub-Lt H.S.Kerby.   (RAF Museum P.21728)

N6440   (Engine No.100284, propeller No.1217); FF & accepted 23.5.17; Deld Aircraft Park Dover for Walmer 1.6.17; Walmer Defence Flt 27.7.17; Anti-Gotha patrol 12.8.17 (F/L HS Kerby); Anti-Gotha patrol, left 17.30, attacked lagging Gotha GIV 656/16 which crashed into sea off Southend c.20.00 12.8.17 (F/L HS Kerby) [Ltn Kurl Rolin, Uffz Rudi Stolle & Uffz Otto Rosinsky, 16 Staffel, Kampfgeschwader all killed]; Anti-Gotha patrol, with 9901 shot down Gotha GIV 663/16 of Kagohl 3 off Margate c.10.45 22.8.17 [Ltn d R Werner Joschkowitz & Ltn Walter Latowsky killed; Uffz Bruno Schneider PoW]; Enemy aircraft patrols 3.9.17x2, 5.9.17 & 9.9.17 (all F/L HS Kerby); Aircraft Park Dover 30.9.17; Rosyth by 22.10.17 to at least 3.11.17; Donibristle W/E 9.11.17; HMS *Nairana* W/E 7.12.17; HMS *Princess Royal* by 12.17; Rosyth W/E 14.12.17; HMS *Pegasus* 13.1.18; Rosyth W/E 8.2.18; Fleet Aeroplane Depot Turnhouse by 6.4.18; Deleted W/E 12.9.18
ALSO reported HMS *New Zealand* [dates unknown]

N6441   (Engine No.100295, propeller No.LP11796); FF & accepted 23.5.17; Deld Aircraft Park Dover for Walmer 1.6.17; Walmer Defence Flt 6.6.17; Anti-Gotha patrol, left 11.50, landed 12.45 13.6.17 (FSL WM Lusby); Anti-Gotha patrol, left 09.30, landed Furnes 7.7.17 (F/Cdr TC Vernon); Anti-Gotha patrol, left 08.30, landed 09.45 22.7.17 (F/Cdr TC Vernon); Anti-Gotha patrol, left 17.30, landed 18.50 12.8.17 (F/Cdr TC Vernon); Then Anti-Gotha patrol 12.8.17 (FSL S Kemball); Enemy aircraft patrols 3.9.17x2 & 9.9.17 (F/Cdr CT MacLaren); Aircraft Park Dover 6.10.17; Donibristle by 27.10.17 (@5.10.17?); Turnhouse W/E 21.2.18 (to Depot Flt W/E 22.3.18); HMS *Furious* to Rosyth to W/E 28.3.18; Fleet Aeroplane Depot Turnhouse W/E 4.4.18 to at least 3.5.18; Deleted W/E 27.4.18

N6442   (Engine No.100296, propeller No.1220); FF & accepted 23.5.17; Deld Aircraft Park Dover for Walmer (named 'JULIA') 1.6.17; Walmer Defence Flt 3.6.17; Anti-Gotha patrol, left 18.25, landed 19.35 5.6.17; Anti-Gotha patrol, left 12.35, landed 13.41 13.6.17 (FSL JA Shaw); Enemy aircraft patrol 16.6.17 (FSL JA Shaw); Anti-Gotha patrol, left 09.30, landed 11.35 7.7.17 (FSL JA Shaw); Anti-Gotha patrol, left 08.35, landed 10.50 22.7.17 (FSL JA Shaw); Taxied into by RFC B.E.2 (2/Lt Rice) and badly damaged 26.7.17; Aircraft Park Dover 28.7.17 (repair); [Walmer Defence Flt by 3.11.17?]; East Fortune Naval Flying School by 29.12.17 to at least 30.3.18

N6443   (Engine No.6683, propeller No.1225); FF & accepted 30.5.17; Acceptance test 30.5.17; Deld Fleet Aeroplane Depot Turnhouse 9.7.17 (for HMS *Manxman*); transported to HMS *Pegasus* 1.9.17; HMS *Repulse* 7.11.17; Flew off turret at anchor 14.11.17; HMS *Pegasus* 14.11.17; Donibristle 14.11.17; *Pegasus* W/E 22.11.17; HMS *Tiger* 11.17; HMS *Renown*, ditched after take-off from forecastle ramp 1.12.17; Flew off HMS *Repulse* turret ramp at anchor 8.12.17; HMS *Pegasus* by 8.12.17; HMS *Yarmouth* 11.12.17; Rosyth to HMS *Yarmouth* 15.12.17; Rosyth by 28.12.17 to at least 29.12.17; *Pegasus* 1.18; Rosyth W/E 11.1.18; Donibristle 1.18; Rosyth W/E 17.1.18; HMS *Nairana* by 17.1.18; Donibristle 22.1.18; HMS *Nairana* by ? 18; HMS *Princess Royal* W/E 7.2.18; HMS *Nairana* 2.18; Rosyth W/E 8.2.18; Fleet Aeroplane Depot Turnhouse W/E 28.2.18; Donibristle W/E 20.4.18; Rosyth W/E 20.6.18; Fleet Aeroplane Depot Turnhouse W/E 11.7.18; Deleted W/E 15.8.18

N6444 (Engine No.6617, propeller No.1221); FF & accepted 30.5.17; Deld Fleet Aeroplane Depot Turnhouse 9.7.17 (for HMS *Manxman*); Rosyth 7.9.17; Donibristle by 5.10.17; HMS *Renown* by 11.17; Rosyth W/E 9.11.17; Donibristle W/E 7.12.17; HMS *Pegasus* W/E 13.1.18; Engine trouble, retd aerodrome 31.1.18; HMS *Pegasus* to HMS *Campania* W/E 7.2.18; Houton Bay (overhaul ex HMS *Pegasus*) W/E 16.2.18; Damaged beyond repair when Bessonneau tent blew down in gale 2.3.18; Deleted W/E 9.3.18, though still listed in Houton Bay Reserve "for deletion" 30.3.18

[NOTE - N6444 to N6456 were all tested by A.Dukinfeild Jones with propeller No.1221]

N6445 (Engine No.6746, propeller No.1221); FF & accepted 30.5.17; Deld Grain for Special Service 14.6.17 (deck landing trials); Undercarriage collapsed 24.6.17; Packed for East Fortune 8.9.17; arr East Fortune 14.9.17 (not listed 22.9.or 29.9) Donibristle by 5.10.17 to at least 3.11.17; HMS *Manxman*; Rosyth to HMS *Nairana* W/E 30.11.17; HMS *Princess Royal* 11.12.17; Lost overboard in heavy squall 15.12.17; Surveyed 19.12.17; Deleted 28.12.17 Total loss

N6446 (Engine No.2586, propeller No.1221); FF & accepted 5.6.17; Deld Grain W/E 1.7.17 (deck landing trials); Hendon 20.8.17; Grain 22.8.17; East Fortune by rail 1.9.17 (arr 8.9.17); Donibristle 15.9.17; Rosyth 16.9.17; Donibristle W/E 15.11.17; Rosyth W/E 13.12.17; HMS *Pegasus* W/E 14.12.17; Rosyth to Donibristle W/E 14.12.17; HMAS *Australia* W/E 20.12.17; HMS *Pegasus* 1.18; HMS *Repulse* W/E 3.1.18; Donibristle W/E 18.1.18; Rosyth W/E 18.1.18; HMS *Pegasus* 13.2.18; Donibristle by 2.18; Fleet Aeroplane Depot Turnhouse W/E 21.2.18 to at least 1.3.18; Rosyth to HMS *Furious* W/E 4.4.18; Rosyth W/E 2.5.18; HMS *Furious* W/E 11.5.18; Rosyth W/E 18.5.18; Deleted W/E 20.6.18

ALSO reported HMAS *Sydney* [date unknown]

N6447 (Engine No.2830, propeller No.1221); FF & accepted 30.5.17; Deld War Flt Grain for Special Service 14.6.17 (Fleet use); Allotted Grain to Rosyth 29.12.17 & again 30.3.18 (NTU?); Deleted W/E 25.5.18

N6448 (Engine No.7658, propeller No.1221); FF & accepted 5.6.17; Deld East Fortune 27.6.17; Donibristle 25.9.17; HMS *Nairana* by 29.9.17; HMS *Renown* W/E 30.11.17; Forced landed in sea on take-off from twin-trough launching track, capsized, sank 1.12.17 (F/Cdr RE Penny); Surveyed 4.12.17; Deleted 8.12.17 wrecked

N6449 (Engine No.2058, propeller No.1221); FF & accepted 5.6.17; Deld East Fortune 27.6.17; Donibristle 24.9.17; HMS *Dublin* 7.11.17; Houton Bay W/E 14.12.17 (overhaul); HMS *Campania* W/E 22.12.17; Scapa by 29.12.17 (overhaul); HMS *Dublin* 1.18; HMS *Campania* W/E 19.1.18; Houton Bay @2.2.18; HMS Chatham to Scapa W/E 23.2.18; For deletion by 9.3.18 ALSO reported HMAS *Sydney* [date unknown]

N6450 (Engine No.2610, propeller No.1221); FF & accepted 6.6.17; Deld Armstrongs for HMS *Furious* 9.7.17; Abortive Anti-Zeppelin patrol, ditched on return 11.9.17 (S/Cdr WG Moore rescued by *Mystic*); Deleted W/E 22.9.17

N6451 (Engine No.4797, propeller No.1221); FF & accepted 11.6.17; Deld Armstrongs for HMS *Furious* 9.7.17; East Fortune 10.11.17 (for carriers); 'F' Sqdn East Fortune Naval Flying School by 21.12.17; Rosyth W/E 18.1.18; Fleet Aeroplane Depot Turnhouse W/E 9.3.18; Deleted W/E 11.7.18

A Pup, possibly N6444, on the Y-turret of HMS Renown, possibly in November 1917. This aircraft flew from several ships until being damaged beyond repair on 2nd March 1918 when a Bessonneau tent blew down in a gale while it was in reserve at Houton Bay.
(FAA Museum)

N6452 (Engine No.5522, propeller No.1221); FF & accepted 11.6.17; Deld HMS *Furious* 11.7.17 (deck landing experiments); World's first deck landing on carrier under way 2.8.17 (S/Cdr EH Dunning DSC); Stalled on overshoot and crashed in sea 7.8.17 (S/Cdr EH Dunning DSC drowned); Deleted 20.8.17

N6453 (Engine No.6690, propeller No.1221); FF & accepted 11.6.17; Deld HMS *Furious* 11.7.17; Tail damaged 7.8.17 (S/Cdr EH Dunning DSC); Deck landing experiments 27.8.17 (F/Cdr HR Busteed); 'F' Sqdn East Fortune Naval Flying School 10.11.17; Donibristle W/E 12.1.18; Rosyth W/E 16.2.18; Fleet Aeroplane Depot Turnhouse W/E 16.3.18; HMS *Furious* to Rosyth W/E 21.3.18; Fleet Aeroplane Depot Turnhouse W/E 4.4.18; Deleted W/E 11.7.18 ALSO HMS *Repulse* 2.18

N6454 (Engine No.3225, propeller No.1221); FF & accepted 15.6.17; Deld HMS *Furious* 11.7.17; Surveyed 14.11.17; Deleted 21.11.17 wrecked

N6455 (Engine No.7563, propeller No.1221); FF & accepted 20.6.17; Deld Fleet Aeroplane Depot Turnhouse for HMS *Manxman* 9.7.17; HMS *Pegasus* 1.9.17; HMS *Lion* 8.11.17; HMS *Pegasus* 16.11.17 to at least 26.11.17 (at Rosyth for erection by 29.11.17); Donibristle to HMS *Nairana* W/E 30.11.17; HMS *Pegasus* to HMS *Tiger* 10.12.17; HMS *Pegasus* 17.12.17; Rosyth 19.12.17; HMS *Tiger* to Rosyth W/E 21.12.17; HMS *Pegasus* 13.1.18 [@19.1.18]; HMS *Repulse* to Donibristle W/E 18.1.18; HMS *Pegasus* W/E 8.2.18; Donibristle 24.2.18; Fleet Aeroplane Depot Turnhouse W/E 28.2.18 (storage during ship's refit); HMS *Pegasus* 13.3.18; Donibristle W/E 21.3.18; Fleet Aeroplane Depot Turnhouse by 6.4.18 to at least 10.5.18; HMS *Furious* W/E 15.8.18; Fleet Aeroplane Depot Turnhouse W/E 17.10.18 to at least 30.1.19

N6456 (Engine No.3752, propeller No.1221); FF & accepted 20.6.17; Deld Fleet Aeroplane Depot Turnhouse for HMS *Manxman* 9.7.17; HMS *Pegasus* 1.9.17; Donibristle W/E 30.11.17; HMS *Pegasus* W/E 7.12.17; HMS *Repulse* 11.12.17; Rosyth W/E 20.12.17; HMS *Pegasus* 22.12.17; To HMS *Tiger* then flew off ship at anchor 3.1.18; HMS *Tiger* to HMS *Pegasus* W/E 17.1.18 to at least 24.1.18; Rosyth by 2.18; HMS *Pegasus* W/E 2.2.18; Fleet Aeroplane Depot Turnhouse 24.2.18 (storage during ship's refit); HMS *Pegasus* 15.3.18; Fleet Aeroplane Depot Turnhouse 8.4.18; Donibristle W/E 9.5.18; HMS *Pegasus* W/E 9.5.18; Donibristle 16.5.18; HMS *Pegasus* 16.5.18; Donibristle 5.18; HMS *Pegasus* W/E 23.5.18 Rosyth W/E 23.5.18; HMS *Pegasus* 8.7.18; Rosyth W/E 22.9.18; Donibristle W/E 17.10.18; Fleet Aeroplane Depot Turnhouse W/E 30.1.19; HMS *Furious* by 7.19

Pup N6454 being brought up from the hold of HMS Furious, in which it was carried from July 1917 until being wrecked in unknown circumstances four months later.

(IWM Q20638)

N6457   (Engine No.3154, propeller No.1220); FF & accepted 20.6.17; Deld Felixstowe by rail 5.7.17 (to erect for Martlesham Heath for HMS *Vindex*); Yarmouth 20.7.17; HMS *Vindex* 21.7.17 to at least 9.9.17; Martlesham Heath by 22.9.17 (for HMS *Vindex*); HMS *Vindex* by 28.9.17; RNASTE Cranwell by 31.10.17 to at least 1.11.17; Martlesham Heath by 3.11.17 to at least 23.2.18 (for HMS *Vindex*); BUT RNASTE Cranwell by 29.12.17 & @19.1.18 & @23.2.18; Crashed and wrecked 25.2.18 (pilot unhurt); U/s at Cranwell 30.3.18; Cranwell from 4.19

N6458   (Engine No.7363, propeller No.1247); FF & accepted 26.6.17; Deld Felixstowe by rail for erection 5.7.17; Martlesham Heath 25.8.17; HMS *Vindex* by 29.12.17; Martlesham Heath by 5.1.18 to at least 23.2.18 (hangared for HMS *Vindex*); Allotted Manston; U/s and engineless at Manston 30.3.18; 204 TDS Eastchurch by 7.18; Propeller accident on start-up 20.7.18 (2/Lt WP Wemple seriously injured)

N6459   (Engine No.5838, propeller No.125); FF & accepted 29.6.17; Deld Aircraft Park Dover 11.7.17; AD Dunkirk 15.7.17; Seaplane Defence Flt St.Pol 31.7.17; FF33L No.1246 destroyed off Ostende, shared with N6437 (q.v.) & N6478 17.45 12.8.17 (FSL LH Slatter); Crashed on landing 8.9.17; AD Dunkirk 20.9.17 to at least 4.10.17; Aircraft Park Dover 10.17 (officially transferred from Dunkirk to Dover 18.10.17); Surveyed 16.10.17; Deleted 19.10.17 Wear & tear

70 SOPWITH PUP (ADMIRALTY 9901 TYPE) ordered 27.7.17 under Contract number C.P.102622, numbered N6460 to N6529 & built Kingston-upon-Thames. Delivered from Brooklands. (Apparently originally intended to have 80hp Clerget, but delivered with 80hp Le Rhône)

N6460   Deld Aircraft Park Dover 15.4.17; AD Dunkirk 29.4.17; 3 (N) Sqdn 5.5.17; (To Manston overnight 4.7.17; Walmer 6.7.17 then returned Furnes); Went up to intercept returning aircraft from raid on London by 22 Gothas, engine failure, forced landed in sea and sank 1m south-west of Nieuport 7.7.17 (FSL LL Lindsay rescued by French TBD) [believed by Ltn G Sachsenberg, Marinejasta 1]; Deleted 8.8.17

N6461   Deld Aircraft Park Dover for erection 17.4.17; AD Dunkirk 11.5.17; 3 (N) Sqdn 19.5.17; Albatros D.III out of control north-east of Bullecourt 09.30 20.5.17 (FSL LH Rochford); Hit another aircraft on take-off, crashed in ditch 3.7.17; To AD Dunkirk; Surveyed 17.10.17; Deleted 23.10.17 wrecked

N6462   Deld Aircraft Park Dover 18.4.17; AD Dunkirk 22.4.17; 'C' Flt 4 (N) Sqdn 30.4.17; Enemy aircraft broke up Rosendale, shared with N5196 (q.v) 12.20 2.5.17; 2-str out of control Ostende, shared with N5196 17.35 28.5.17 (both F/Cdr JD Newberry); AD Dunkirk 18.6.17; 9 (N) Sqdn 19.6.17; Albatros D.V out of control south-west of Haynecourt, shared with N6469 & N6475 c.17.30 7.7.17 (F/Cdr GE Hervey); 2-str crashed Bullecourt 17.30, then spun in from 1,500/2,000ft landing 7.7.17 (FSL JC Tanner died of injuries) [by Ltn F Anders, Jasta 4]; Deletion recommended by AD Dunkirk 16.7.17; Approved 18.7.17; Implemented 24.7.17

N6463   Shipped to Aegean; Deld Mudros 30.6.17

N6464   Deld Aircraft Park Dover 24.4.17; AD Dunkirk 25.4.17; 3 (N) Sqdn (coded 'D') 3.5.17; Escort, shot down, last seen nr Bourlon 11.5.17 (FSL J Bampfylde-Daniell, POW wounded) [possibly Sopwith shot down 14.40 by Obltn A Rt von Tutschek, Jasta 12]; Deleted 21.5.17

N6465   Deld Aircraft Park Dover 29.4.17; AD Dunkirk 1.5.17; 3 (N) Sqdn 5.5.17; Albatros D.III out of control Bourlon Wood shared with N6178 & Albatros D.III out of control Lagnicourt 19.05 6.5.17; Albatros D.III crashed and burnt Villers 07.50 27.5.17 (all FSL HS Kerby); Large 2-str seaplane in sea 6-12m off Ostende, shared with N6162, N6183, N6477 & N6479 c.11.10 7.7.17 (F/L FC Armstrong); AD Dunkirk 16.7.17; 'A' Flt 12 (N) Sqdn by

A crowd of German soldiers surrounding the wreckage of N6464 'D' of No.3 (Naval) Squadron on 11th May 1917. It had been shot down in the Bourlon area whilst on escort duty, Flt Sub-Lt J.Bampfylde-Daniell, who was wounded, being taken prisoner. (via Philip Jarrett)

19.7.17; AD Dunkirk 23.8.17; Aircraft Park Dover by 13.9.17 (officially transferred from Dunkirk to Dover 11.10.17); RNASTE Cranwell 27.10.17 (fitted 80hp Gnome by 5.1.18); Erecting at Cranwell 30.3.18; Became 201/202 TDS Cranwell 1.4.18

N6466 Deld Aircraft Park Dover for erection 29.4.17; AD Dunkirk 2.5.17; 3 (N) Sqdn 12.5.17; Crashed on landing Dunkirk Bains 19.6.17 (F/L FC Armstrong); still at AD Dunkirk 21.6.17; Aircraft Park Dover 4.7.17; Walmer, badly damaged 11.8.17; War School RNAS Manston 6.10.17; Possibly collided with Sopwith Triplane N5382 [F/L AF Brandon DSC killed] 26.10.17 (Lt DW Gray unhurt); Surveyed 10.11.17; Deleted 14.11.17 wrecked

N6467 Deld Aircraft Park Dover 30.4.17; AD Dunkirk 10.5.17; 3 (N) Sqdn 19.5.17 (in 'B' Flt 12.7.17); AD Dunkirk 16.7.17; 'B' Flt 12 (N) Sqdn by 19.7.17; Aircraft Park Dover W/E 13.9.17; RNASTE Cranwell 27.10.17 (fitted 80hp Gnome by 5.1.18); Erecting at Cranwell 30.3.18; Became 201/202 TDS Cranwell 1.4.18

N6468 Deld Aircraft Park Dover 2.5.17; AD Dunkirk 29.6.17 to at least 12.7.17; 11 (N) Sqdn by 17.7.17; AD Dunkirk W/E 6.9.17; 12 (N) Sqdn 25.9.17 ('C' Flt by 1.11.17); Aircraft Park Dover 23.11.17; Experimental Constructive Dept, Grain 10.12.17 (conversion to 9901a Ships Pup); Skid chassis completed 19.12.17; Deck landing gear fitted 21.12.17; Flown at East Fortune 21.1.18; Deleted Grain 13.3.18 Damaged beyond repair, but still on charge 6.18

N6469 Deld Aircraft Park Dover for erection 30.4.17; AD Dunkirk 2.6.17; 9 (N) Sqdn 19.6.17; Albatros D.V out of control south-west of Haynecourt, shared with N6462 &

N6475 '9' of 11 (Naval) Squadron after nosing up on landing Hondschoote on 13th July 1917, when piloted by Flt Sub-Lt E.C.R.Stoneman. *(via Frank Cheesman)*

N6475 c.17.30 7.7.17 (FSL HE Mott); 11 (N) Sqdn 13.7.17; Aircraft Park Dover W/E 6.9.17 (officially transferred from Dunkirk to Dover 11.10.17); War School RNAS Manston W/E 3.11.17; Surveyed Manston 4.1.18; Deleted 15.1.18 Wear & tear

N6470 Allotted Mudros 23.4.17; Shipped to Aegean; Mudros by 9.17; Marsh Aerodrome 29.9.17; On nose landing 4.10.17 (F/L JLA Sinclair); 'C' Sqdn 2 (Naval) Wing Mudros by 1.12.17 to at least 1.1.18; Sold to Greek Government for training by 3.18 to at least 30.1.19, but still with 2 (Naval) Wing for Greek training 1.10.18

N6471 Allotted Mudros 23.4.17; Shipped to Aegean; Mudros by 7.17; 'C' Sqdn 2 (Naval) Wing Imbros 13.7.17; Tipped on nose by ratings at Tenedos 4.8.17; Retd Imbros 13.8.17 (repair); Tested after re-erection 10.9.17; Sold to Greek Government for training 3.18 to at least 30.1.19, but still with 2 (Naval) Wing for Greek training 1.10.18

N6472 Deld RNASTE Cranwell 12.5.17; Redcar Naval Flying School 6.7.17; RNASTE Cranwell 8.7.17; Caught by gust, undercarriage collapsed 22.10.17 (A/F/L WW Wakefield); Parachute dropping experiments 12.12.17; Crashed and badly damaged Waddington 9.3.18 (pilot unhurt); Became 201/202 TDS Cranwell 1.4.18; School of Aerial Fighting & Bomb Dropping Freiston 20.4.18

N6473 Deld RNASTE Cranwell 12.5.17; Crashed in a wood c.10.17 - 11.17; Deleted W/E 23.11.17

N6474 Deld Aircraft Park Dover for erection 18.4.17; AD Dunkirk 23.4.17; 3 (N) Sqdn (named 'EXCUSE ME' by FSL AW Carter) 3.5.17; Albatros D.III out of control east of Bullecourt 07.40 27.5.17 (FSL AW Carter); Fouled kite balloon rope at 300ft on take-off, crashed on back 4.6.17 (FSL AW Carter unhurt); AD Dunkirk by 7.6.17; Aircraft Park Dover 4.7.17; Instructional Flight, War School RNAS Manston 6.10.17; Deleted W/E 2.3.18

N6475 Deld Aircraft Park Dover for erection 18.4.17; AD Dunkirk 25.4.17; 4 (N) Sqdn 29.4.17; Albatros D.III crashed in field 2m south-east of Ghistelles 16.00 25.5.17 (FSL SE Ellis); 2-str [or Albatros D.III?] destroyed 3-4m east of Dixmude 08.30 4.6.17 (FSL SE Ellis); AD Dunkirk to 9 (N) Sqdn 19.6.17; Albatros D.III out of control south-west of Haynecourt 17.30 7.7.17 (FSL JW Pinder); To 11 (N) Sqdn (coded '9') but nosed up on landing Hondschoote 13.7.17 (FSL ECR Stoneman); last mention on Sqdn 16.7.17; Aircraft Park Dover by 26.7.17 (officially transferred from Dunkirk to Dover 9.8.17); War School RNAS Manston 6.10.17 (by 11.1.18 fitted 80hp Gnome); For deletion by 30.3.18

N6476 Deld Aircraft Park Dover 30.4.17; AD Dunkirk 2.5.17; 4 (N) Sqdn 20.5.17 (in 'A' Flt by 7.6.17); 2-str out of control 4m north-east of Dixmude shared with N6192 16.00 6.6.17 (F/L GMT Rouse); AD Dunkirk 3.9.17; 12 (N) Sqdn 3.10.17 (in 'C' Flt by 1.11.17); Aircraft Park Dover 4.12.17; Eastbourne W/E 15.12.17; To Aircraft Park Dover but crashed on landing 3.2.18 (pilot unhurt); Deleted 9.2.18

N6477 Deld Aircraft Park Dover for erection 19.4.17; AD Dunkirk 25.4.17; 3 (N) Sqdn 1.5.17; Large 2-str seaplane in sea 6-12m north of Ostende, shared with N6162, N6183, N6465 & N6479 c.11.10 7.7.17 (FSL RFP Abbott); 'A' Flt 11 (N) Sqdn 11.7.17; Last mention by Sqdn 24.7.17; Dunkirk to Dover 26.7.17 (officially transferred from Dunkirk to Dover 9.8.17); RNASTE Cranwell 27.10.17; Erecting with 80hp Gnome 30.3.18; Became 201/202 TDS Cranwell 1.4.18

N6478   Deld Aircraft Park Dover for erection 19.4.17; AD Dunkirk 22.4.17; 'B' Flt 4 (N) Sqdn 29.4.17 to at least 10.5.17; Aircraft Park Dover by 31.5.17; AD Dunkirk 20.6.17; Seaplane Defence Flt St.Pol 4.7.17; FF33L No.1246 destroyed off Ostende, shared with N6437 (q.v.) & N6459 17.45 12.8.17 (FSL R Graham); Became Seaplane Defence Sqdn St.Pol 23.9.17; Aircraft Park Dover 15.10.17; East Fortune Naval Flying School 2.11.17 (used for practice landings); Ran into post turning, badly damaged 1.3.18 (FSL DH Lees); Surveyed 23.3.18; Deleted 27.3.18 wreck

N6479   Deld Aircraft Park Dover for erection 19.4.17; AD Dunkirk 20.4.17; 'A' Flt 3 (N) Sqdn 13.5.17; Albatros D.III out of control west of Bourlon 13.45 23.5.17 (FSL JST Fall); DFW C out of control north-east of Ypres, landed 06.30 17.6.17 (FSL JA Glen); Large 2-str seaplane in sea 6-12m north of Ostende, shared with N6162, N6183, N6465 & N6477 c.11.10 7.7.17; Landed from previous patrol, took off again, Albatros D.V in sea smoking 1m north-west of Ostende Piers 12.20 7.7.17 (both FSL JST Fall); AD Dunkirk 30.7.17; Aircraft Park Dover W/E 20.9.17 (officially transferred from Dunkirk to Dover 11.10.17); RNASTE Cranwell 27.10.17; To RN College Greenwich 15.12.18 without engine as ground instructional airframe

N6480 to N6529   Cancelled

Unidentified incidents

17.3.17   54 Sqdn, 2-str out of control 3m east of Roye, shared by 2/Lt NA Phillips/A669, Capt RGH Pixley/A649 & 2/Lt JW Sheridan 11.35 (Lt GA Hyde)

7.7.17   62 TS Dover, Anti-Gotha patrol (2/Lt JC Hopkins)

14.7.17   54 Sqdn, OP (2/Lt LW Osman wounded)

12.8.17   54 Sqdn, Albatros D.V out of control (2/Lt HH Maddocks)

14.9.17   54 Sqdn, OP (Lt JW Sheridan injured)

18.11.17   (80hp Gnome) 6 TS Catterick, pilot not strapped in, thrown forward onto control stick, a/c dived in (pilot killed)

Messrs Rochford, Nelson, Haynes, Broad and Beamish (in fur coat) [left to right] of No.3 (Naval) Squadron in front of Beamish's Pup at Marieux in April 1917. After WW1, Broad became Chief Test Pilot for de Havilland and later Hawker until the end of WW2.   (via Frank Cheesman)

A Pup taking off successfully from a turret platform of a warship in September 1918.   *(via Philip Jarrett)*

Two Japanese Army Pups in front of hangars at Spasskaya airfield.   *(via Toshio Fujita)*

Appendix 14

Military Exports

Australia

12 aircraft (C521-C532) ordered 2.10.18 for use by the Central Flying School, Australian Flying Corps at Point Cook (the corps was renamed Australian Air Corps 1.1.20, then Australian Air Force 31.3.21 and Royal Australian Air Force 8.21). C521-C528 & C530-C532 became *A4-1* to *A4-11* in that sequence, as follows, with known engine useage:

C521 (80hp Le Rhône No.10176/WD18076) Allotted to Australian Government 26.10.18, for CFS; 'C' Flt 1 HT Sqdn to ARS 22.9.19; 'C' Flt 1 HT Sqdn 23.9.19; ARS to 'A' Flt CFS 8.1.20; 1 FTS Laverton 31.3.21; Became *A4-1* by 3.10.21; to 'A' Flt 1 FTS 1.7.22; WFS 1925; To 3 Sqdn, Richmond, NSW c.1926 as GI; To East Sydney Technical Collage, Ultimo, NSW 30.6.30 *[these last entries may actually relate to A4-10]*

C522 (80hp Le Rhône No.10300/WD18200) Allotted to Australian Government 26.10.18, for CFS; ARS to 'C' Flt 1 HQ Sqdn 22.9.19; ARS to 'A' Flt CFS 8.1.20; 1 FTS Laverton 31.3.21; To 1 FTS Laverton 31.3.21; Became *A4-2* by 3.10.21; With 'C' Flt 1 FTS by 17.10.21; To 'B" Flt 1 FTS 1.7.22;

C523 (80hp Le Rhône No.10188/WD18088) Allotted to Australian Government 26.10.18; ARS to 'C' Flt 1 HT Sqdn 8.7.19; CFS Point Cook to Commandant 6th Military District 20.8.19; Reported crashed 19.9.19; To Laverton for repair; On display at the Exhibition Buildings, Melbourn 6.20; ARS to 'A' Flt CFS 14.12.20; 1 FTS Laverton 31.3.21; Became *A4-3* by 3.10.21; Accident 9.22 (F/O Bostock); Crashed Port Melbourne, Vic 5.2.25; WFS, airframe & engine log books retd HQ 24.4.25

C524 (80hp Le Rhône No.10353/WD18253) Allotted to Australian Government 26.10.18; ARS to 'A' Flt 1 HT Sqdn 15.10.19; ARS to 'A' Flt CFS 8.1.20; 1 FTS Laverton 31.3.21; Became *A4-4* by 13.9.21; Collided with Hangar on TO, Point Cook 4.12.24 (F/O Simpson injured); Board of Survey cnvened by 1 AD 27.1.25; Recommended to be reduced to spares 13.2.25

C525 (80hp Le Rhône No.56448/WD80730) Allotted to Australian Government 26.10.18; CFS to Commandant 2nd Military District in connection with 1st Peace Loan Flight ops in NSW 6.9.19; Prop damaged landing 18.9.19, retd to Laverton by rail; CFS 13.10.19; ARS to 'A' Flt CFS 8.1.20; 1 FTS Laverton 31.3.21; Became *A4-5* by 3.10.21; Damaged at Point Cook 29.11.21; Reduction to spares authorised 29.3.22

C526 Allotted to Australian Government 26.10.18; To CFS; Landing accident, Point Cook c.1919; To 1 FTS Laverton 31.3.21; Became *A4-6* by 3.10.21; WFS, airframe & engine log books retd HQ 24.4.25

C527 (80hp Le Rhône No.10334/WD18234) Allotted to Australian Government 26.10.18; To AAF at CFS, Point Cook 31.3.21; To 1 FTS Laverton 31.3.21; Became A4-7 3.10.21; Accident report 15.3.22; Reduction to spares authorised 29.3.22; Airframe & engine log books retd HQ 24.4.25

C528 (80hp Le Rhône No.10273/WD18173) Allotted to Australian Government 26.10.18; 'C' Flt 1 HT Sqdn to ARS 28.7.19; 'C' Flt 1 HT Sqdn 7.8.19; ARS 1.9.19; 'C' Flt 1 HT Sqdn 2.9.19; ARS 21.9.29; 'C' Flt 1 HT Sqdn 15.10.19; ARS to 'A' Flt CFS 8.1.20; To Stores 30.11.20; 1 FTS Laverton 31.3.21; Became *A4-8* by 3.10.21 (now engine No WD80730); Stalled on right hand vertical turn, spun into Bessoneau hangar 4.8.22 (F/L HF de la Rue) (fitted with engine No 10305/WD18205); Strike off approved 23.8.22; Airframe log books retd HQ 21.11.22

C529 Allotted to Australian Government 26.10.18; Damaged during shipment; At 1 ARS Point Cook by 26.4.19 (u/s); SOC 8.4.20

C530 (80hp Le Rhône No.10176/WD18076) Allotted to Australian Government 26.10.18; 'C' Flt 1 HT Sqdn to ARS 21.8.19; To 'C' Flt 1 HQ Sqdn W/E 5.9.19 (now engine No.10304/WD19204); To AAF 31.3.21; CFS, Point Cook to 1 FTS Laverton 31.3.21; Became *A4-9* by 3.10.21; With 'B' Flt 1 FTS by 17.10.21 (now engine No.10350/WD18250; Later to storage, but flying again by 6.3.24; WFS, airframe & engine log books retd HQ 24.4.25

C531 (80hp Le Rhône No.56439/WD80724) Allotted to Australian Government 26.10.18; From 'C' Flt CFS 28.7.19; ARS to 'B' Flt 1 HT Sqdn 15.10.19; ARS to 'A' Flt CFS 8.1.20; 1 FTS Laverton 31.3.21; Became *A4-10* by 3.10.21 'C' Flt 1 FTS by 17.10.21 (now engine No.10188/WD18088); Crashed at Point Cook 13.2.23 (F/O CC Matheson); WFS 1925; To 3 Sqdn, Richmond, NSW as GI c.1926; To East Sydney Technical College, Ultimo, NSW 30.6.30 *[these last entries may actually relate to A4-1]*

C532 (80hp Le Rhône No.10350/WD18250?) Allotted to Australian Government 26.10.18; Recd 1 ARS Point Cook 26.4.19; 'B' Flt 1 HT Sqdn CFS 21.10.19; ARS to 'A' Flt CFS 20.4.20; 1 FTS Laverton 31.3.21; Became *A4-11* by 3.10.21; Reduction to spares authorised 29.3.22

Belgium

6 aircraft in 1918 under contract No.A.S.24542
SB1 - SB4 plus two others [*SB5* and *SB6*?].

Greece

4 aircraft in 1918:
N6432, N6433, N6470, N6471.

Japan

Army use
50 Pups were imported by the Army as the Sopwith Type 3
in 1918:
Ex C481-C499, C503-C509, C533-C537, C1496,
D4144-D4152, D4155, D4156, D4160, D4161,
D4163, D4165, D4168, D4169.

They were used by Nos.1, 2 and 4 Daitai [Wings],
and by the Vladivostok Expeditionary Force air units.

Known individual service details:
C486 at Tokorozawa Field.
C488 at Vladivostok.

After the collapse of Imperial Russia, the Allied nations sent an Allied Siberia Expeditionary Force to the Vladivostok area in August 1918, this being known by the Japanese as the Vladivostok Expeditionary Force. The Japanese Army component included No.1 Aero Squadron, equipped with nine Maurice Farman and Sopwith aircraft (probably Type 1, single-seat French-built 1½ Strutters). In addition No.2 Aero Squadron was sent to support operations in the Zabaikale area, equipped with nine Maurice Farmans and three Sopwiths (also probably Type 1s). However, these two squadrons were the main strength of the Japanese Army Air Corps, and both were ordered to return home early in 1919 to receive tuition from a French aviation training mission. No.1 Squadron returned to Japan in February 1919, but about half of No.2 Squadron remained in Russia to form No.1 Aero Flight in May 1919.

In February 1920, Russian aircraft appeared on the east coast of Lake Baikal. As a consequence, No.1 Aero Flight, now equipped with six Maurice Farmans, one Sopwith Type 1 and one Sopwith Type 3 (Pup) was sent to Chita, where it arrived at the end of March. Three further Sopwith 3s were later added to the strength and these undertook reconnaissance and bombing sorties in support of Army operations, a maximum of two sorties being made by each pilot.

To fill the gap left by the transfer of No.1 Aero Flight, a new No.2 Aero Flight was formed in Japan equipped with six Sopwith Type 3s and having 33 personnel. This was sent to Russia, arriving at Spasskaya, near Lake Khank, to undertake sorties in support of Army operations towards Kabarovsk, to where the main strength of the flight moved in May 1920.

Both flights continued to fly reconnaissance, bombing, liaison and demonstration flights in support of the Army until November 1920, when they were both disbanded. In their place a new Vladivostok Expedition Aero Flight was formed with six aircraft, type unknown, but assumed to be Sopwith Type 3s since they came from No.2 Aero Flight. This flight was based at Spasskaya, small numbers of aircraft being detached to various places for support operations until returning to Japan in October 1922.

The Army Air Corps' role had proved rather limited, lacking at that time sufficient experience, equipment and training to be able to carry our successful military operations. No aerial encounters had occurred, but the aerial reconnaissance activities had been of great value to the Army. The bombing activities were less successful due to the inadequate number of aircraft and proper bombing equipment.

The Pup did not go into production for the Army in Japan as after accepting the French Training Mission of January to September 1919, the Japanese Army decided to standardise on French-built aircraft. Apart from its service in Russia, it was used mainly for training. Japanese Army pilots liked flying the Pup and one of them, Lt Kawaida, reportedly made 456 successive loops in 1921!

Naval use
The Japanese Navy also had some Pups for intended shipboard use from platforms on battleships and cruisers. Some appear to have been built by the Yokosuka Navy Arsenal Factory, others were ex-Army imports. Trials were successful but the plan was rejected by the Fleet and flying squadron.

The first use by the Navy was when one Pup one Yokosho reconnaissance seaplane were loaded on the battleship *Mikas* on 30th January 1920 and went to sea in conjunction with the Army Siberia Expedition. According to the recollection of Vice Admiral Takeo Kuwabawa this Pup had been built by the Yokosuka Navy Arsenal Factory. As the ship was not fitted with a launching platform, the Pup had to be unloaded onto ice for assembly and take-off. On 9th May it was transferred to the battleship *Shikishima*, then to the heavy cruiser *Kurama* on 30th June before being finally off-loaded on 9th July.

The next naval use of a Pup for a trial launch from the seaplane tender *Wakamiya*, to determine how long a platform would be needed for this purpose. An initial trial took place on 22nd June 1920 off an 18m-long platform, from which it was judged that a 12m platform would give sufficient safety margin. Accordingly a platform of this length was fitted on the second main gun turret of the battleship *Yamagi*, and several trial launches took place in October, piloted by Captain Kuwabara.

Between September 1920 and March 1921, a Pup and a Yokosho reconnaissance seaplane were loaded on to the special duty ship *Manto*, for similar usage to that on the *Mikasa*.

[Bibliography:
  Japanese Naval Aviation History,
      Volume 1 – Operations, Jiji Tsushinsha 1969.
  Naval Aviation Recollections, Takeo Kuwabara,
      Koku newspaper 1964.
  Recollections of an old Admiral, Kazuho Ueno, 1970.]

Russia

1 aircraft in 1917:
N6204.

U.S.A.

Two naval aircraft supplied by the Admiralty to the US Navy at Hampton Roads and numbered A5655 and A5656. Described as "with landing gear", and authorised for sale 22.11.2[0?].

Appendix 15

Civil and Museum Aircraft

Great Britain

G-EAVF Registered 20.8.20 to M.E.Tanner of South Harrow with two airframe numbers, 3210 and 764 quoted; No CofA issued. Regn lapsed 8.21

G-EAVV (ex C440) Registered 4.11.20 to Handley Page Ltd who were a major particpant in the syndicate which owned The Aircraft Disposal Co Ltd, Croydon. No CofA issued and regn lapsed 11.21

G-EAVW (ex C312) Registered 27.10.20 to Flt Lt Trygve Gran of the Air Pilotage School, RAF Andover. No CofA issued and regn lapsed 10.21

G-EAVX (ex B1807) Registered 2.11.20 to A.R.M. Rickards, Fairford, Glos. Damaged when nosed over at Hendon 16.7.21 while being piloted in the Aerial Derby by D.L.Forestier-Walker (believed only slightly damaged). No CofA issued and regn lapsed 11.21. It was known to be stored at Hendon 1922. Airframe reportedly found by Kelvyn A.M.Baker on a Dorset farm in 1977, minus engine and wings. Believed still on rebuild in Somerset. [The "official" identity is E1807 which was an Avro 504]

G-EAVY (ex C438) Registered 4.1 1.20 to Handley Page Ltd/ Aircraft Disposal Co Ltd. No CofA issued and regn lapsed 11.21

G-EAVZ (ex C540) Registered 22.11.20 to Handley Page Transport Ltd., Cricklewood/ Aircraft Disposal Co. Ltd. No CofA issued and regn lapsed 11.21. [An alternative serial of C546 has been quoted]

G-EBAZ (ex C1524) Registered 9.1.22 to Herbert Sykes of London NW6 [and based Kingsbury]. No CofA issued. Regd 7.6.23 to P.T.Capon of Upper Clapton, London E5 [and based Hendon and also Erith, Kent]. Flown by P.W.M.Swann. flown to Stag Lane by Sykes in 1924. Regn lapsed 6.24. [80 hp Le Rhône]

G-EBFJ (ex C242) Registered 22.2.23 to J.T.Norquay of Thurso. No CofA issued and regn lapsed 2.24.

G-EBKY (c/n W/O 3004/14), converted from Sopwith Dove, q.v., by R.O.Shuttleworth from 7.37; first flown as Pup 26.2.38; Authorisation to Fly issued 14.3.38; preserved in airworthy condition by the Shuttleworth Trust as "N5184", later "N5180", then "N6181" ('Happy'); registration and Permit current, extant at Old Warden

G-APUP (c/n "B.5292", PFA.1582) Construction of replica begun in 1958 at Luton, then Horley, with some parts of B5292. Registered as replica 13.2.59 to K.C.D.St.Cyrien, Dorking. Le Rhône engine and parts of N5182 aquired from France and according to owner the replica components were disposed of to Canada and USA. Designation changed to Sopwith Pup 7.5.73 and first flown 11.8.73 at Fairoaks, named 'Sheila'. CofA issued 27.3.74, based Blackbushe.

G-EAVX started life as B1807, flying with various Home Defence squadrons until being withdrawn from service in 1919. After being placed in storage it was sold for civilian flying, being registered as G-EAVX on 2nd November 1920 by the Aircraft Disposal Company. Owned by Mr A.R.M.Rickards, it went on its nose at Hendon on 21st July 1921, as seen here, and was never repaired.   (via Philip Jarrett)

Converted from a surviving Sopwith Dove, G-EBKY was first flown as a Pup in February 1938. Seen here at the Royal Aeronautical Society Garden Party at White Waltham in 1949, it has been preserved in airworthy condition by the Shuttleworth Trust as "N5184", later "N5180", then "N6181" (named "HAPPY"), it is still extant at Old Warden.   (via Philip Jarrett)

Dove conversion G-EBKY is seen he flying in one of its later guises as "N5180", probably at Old Warden.   *(via Philip Jarrett)*

Accident .78, CofA expired 28.6.78; registered to D.W.Arnold, Blackbushe 7.6.79; sold to RAF Museum, Hendon 6.82, displayed as "N5182"; registration cancelled 4.10.84. Allotted 9213M in 1994, not worn; extant as "N5182"

Others known:

James Palethorpe [probably Capt Palethorpe of Brokencote Hall, Kidderminster – a WWI pilot at Martlesham and Farnborough] announced in October 1925 that he was presenting the newly re-formed Midland Aero Club with three Sopwith Pups. Nothing more has been found but it was speculated that they "might" have been the three Handley Page Pups.

In 1923, Monique Agazarian's mother bought a Sopwith Pup at a Croydon auction for £5 for use by her and her brothers as a plaything.

In February 1919, Mr Russell of Alexandra Road, Farnborough, Hants had a brand new Pup for sale, minus engine and instruments for £150.

In November 1925, R.C.Shelley of High St, Billericay was advertising for a Pup tailplane. He had earlier that year bought Harry Hawker's personal experimental Sopwith SL.TBP from a garage in Chelmsford and he converted this to a 2-seater before selling it in 1926. He later bought back the Gnome engine which he sold on to Richard Shuttleworth for fitting to the Blackburn Monoplane. In February 1927, Shelley advertised for sale a "non-airworthy Sopwith biplane"; however this is believed to have been a Camel.

Australia

G-AUCK (ex C476) (Clerget No.61701/1299) ex RAAF stock, CofR No.24 28.6.21 by C.D.Pratt, Geelong Air Service, Belmont Common, Vic; CofA No53 issued 7.4.22; Last flown 24.6.23, to storage [TFH 10.05] Regn cancelled 14.7.31; Genet Major installed, test-flown 14.10.39 as *VH-UCK*; Regd to J.L.Roche, Carnegie, Vic 21.5.41; Sold to W.O.Stillard, Deniliquin, NSW 4.12.43; Final CofA expired 5.11.44 [TFH 50.15]; Damaged in gale 1945, ended up inverted on homestead roof, *Marboc*, Cobram, Vic; Owner requested cancellation 4.9.45; Engine fitted to an 'air-boat' on Lake Yarrawonga; Remains burned 9.45

Canada

"N5182"   Parts sold to G.Neale, Canada [see G-APUP]

France

"N5182"   Held in Musée de l'Air store, later sold in U.K. 1958 to form basis of G-APUP (q.v.)

Japan

Known as the Sopwith 3 in Japan (the single-seat 1½-Strutter bomber built by Lioré et Olivier was known as the Sopwith 1 and the two-seat reconnaisance version as the Sopwith 2). Some were new [?] builds by the Yokosuka Navy Arsenal Factory, others were ex-Army imports.

J-HUBD   (80hp Le Rhône) (c/n Yokosuka Navy Arsenal Factory 11) CofA 2.25 to S.Ogawa, expired 8.25

J-HUDF   (80hp Le Rhône) (c/n Yokosuka Navy Arsenal Factory 2) CofA 10.25 to Miyagi Flying Association; Owner changed to T.Ooba and new CofA 5.26, but expired 6.26

J-HUPQ   (c/n 534) CofA 3.24 to H.Noriike; Owner changed to K.Umemoto and new CofA 4.24, expired 2.25; Re-regd J-TALO

J-HUXY   (c/n Mizuta Special 2) Ex J-TETV. CofA 10.23 to K.Mizuta, expired 4.24; Owner change to Z.Ueda and new CofA issued 6.26, but cancelled 9.7.26 as aircraft damaged

J-TALO   (80hp Le Rhône) (c/n 534, ex J-HUPQ) CofA issued 2.25 to K.Uememoto, expired 12.25

J-TAWY   (ex Navy) (c/n Yokosuka Arsenal Factory 5). CofA 12.23, to Miyagi Flying Association; Owner changed to K.Aizawa and new CofA issued 5.27, expired 11.27

J-TAWZ   (c/n Whitehead 4169) CofA 11.25; Destroyed 25.11.25. Regd to NKYK

J-TEPT   (c/n Yokosuka Arsenal Factory 11) CofA 1.24 to S.Ogawa; CofA expired 1.25

J-TETV   (80hp Le Rhône) CofA 9.22 to K.Mizuta. Modified, possibly at Nakajima. Damaged, Wakamatsu City 14.10.22; CofA cancelled 20.10.22; new CofA 30.1.23 (accident date also reported as 3.12.22) Re-regd J-HUXY (q.v.)

J-TIMR   (Ex Navy, 80hp Le Rhône) (c/n 505). CofA 2.24 to A.Fukunaga; To S.Okura 11.24; CofA expired 2.25

J-TITY   (80hp Le Rhône) (c/n 536) CofA 4.24, to T.Aiba (Nippon Flying School); CofA expired 7.25

J-TIXC   (80hp Le Rhône) (c/n 509) CofA 5.24, to Nippon Central Flying School; CofA expired 4.25

J-TIYD   (80hp Le Rhône) (c/n 4) CofA 4.24; CofA returned 10.24 as no longer airworthy

J-TOPT   (80hp Le Rhône) (c/n Yokosuka Navy Arsenal Factory 12) CofA 12.23 to S.Ri; Fate unknown

J-TOSX   (80hp Le Rhône) (c/n 481) CofA 9.25 to K.Takahashi; CofA returned 4.26 as aircraft damaged

J-TOUZ   (80hp Le Rhône) (c/n Yokosuka Navy Arsenal Factory 2) CofA 11.23 to K.Takahashi; CofA expired 5.24

J-TUJQ   (80hp Le Rhône) (c/n Yokosuka Navy Arsenal Factory 15) CofA 9.24 to Osaka Mainichi newspaper. CofA returned 4.25 as aircraft destroyed

U.S.A.

"N5182"   Parts sold to USA [see G-APUP]

REPLICAS

Built in UK

G-AVPA   c/n CJW.1   Regd 13.6.67 to C.J.Warrilow, Harrow and under construction at High Wycombe in 1974. Project abandoned and some components to RAF Museum 1982.

G-ABOX   Regd 12.9.84 to K.C.D.St.Cyrien, Blackbushe [and stated to be original, although this is unconfirmed]; painted as "N5195". Permit to Fly issued 19.9.85; lapsed 22.4.93. On loan to Museum of Army Flying, Middle Wallop. Extant.

G-BIAT   c/n EMK.001 Regd 3.12.82 to Guy A.Black. Built by EMK Aeroplanes Ltd/Skysport Engineering 1978-83. Painted as "N6160". Regn cld 9.8.89 and sold Australia in damaged condition and never regd. Traded to RNZAF Museum, Christchurch for P-47D during 1995, under restoration for display. [Believed crashed on first flight]

J-TETV was registered to K.Mizuta who later modified it as a 'Mizuta Special' within the restricted flying category as J-HUXY. See also photograph on page 160. *("Aireview")*

This Pup replica was built by EMK Aeroplanes Ltd/Skysport Engineering from 1980 and registered G-BIAU, and made its first flight on 12th April 1983, painted as "N6452" as seen here when it was put up for auction at Duxford on 14th April 1983. It initially went to the Whitehall Theatre of War in London 8.83, then later to the Fleet Air Arm Museum, Yeovilton, now painted as "N5492". *(via Philip Jarrett)*

G-BIAU   c/n EMK.002 Regd 4.1.83 to C.D.Jarman. Built by EMK Aeroplanes Ltd/Skysport Engineering 1980-83. First flight 12.4.83; painted as "N6452". Permit to Fly issued 26.3.83. To Whitehall Theatre of War, London 8.83. Permit expired 13.9.89. To Fleet Air Arm Museum, Yeovilton by 3.96; now painted as "N5492". Regn cld as wfu 10.3.97. Extant.

G-BZND   Built by Brendan Goddard, Southampton with a 5-cylinder Salmson engine. Regd 27.9.00. Complete and rigged October 2000, but not yet flown.

BAPC.179 Non-flying replica for "Wings" film; painted as "A7317". To Waltham Abbey. To North Weald. To Midland Air Museum, Baginton. Extant.

PFA.1591 Under construction by D.Cooper-Maguire c.1972/3. Abandoned before completion.

Built in Australia

VH-PSP   c/n TSP-1. Built by Transavia. Genet engine. Regd 1.7.81 to Meil Cottee, Beverley Hills, NSW; to J.L.Petit, Geelong, Vic 23.4.82; to RAAF Museum, Point Cook, Vic 28.7.89. On loan to RAAF Historic Flight, Point Cook. Current.

VH-SOR   c/n TSP-1-02. Built by Transavia. Genet Major engine. Regd 16.10.92 to Ron H.Jackson, Riddell, Vic. No CofA issued, damaged in forced landing, current.

-         Replica marked "N5182" in the Australian Museum of Flight, Nowra by 11.00.

Built in Canada

CF-RFC(1) Built by Stan Green and Tom Sigrist of Calgary. Sold to US owner in Seattle, pre 1963.

CF-RFC(2) c/n C552. Built 1967 by George A.Neal [allegedly incorporating parts from N5182 from France, but see G-APUP]. Flown until purchased by National Aviation Museum, Ottawa, Ont., to whom registered 6.12.73. Displayed as "B2167" in RFC No.66 Sqdn colours. Extant, on loan to Canadian Warplane Heritage Museum, Hamilton.

-         Non-flying replica; marks unknown. Built by and displayed in Ontario Science Centre, North York, nr Toronto.

Built in South Africa

ZS-PUP   c/n NCH.1. Regd 1.73 to N.C.Harrison. Believed Genet engine. No longer current.

Built in USA

N2RF   c/n 10201. Built by Funkhouser. Amateur expermental. On display Ryders Replica Fighter Museum, Guntersville, Alabama. Collection closed on his death a few years ago. Regd to A.J.Parks, Aurora, Colorado 13.7.99; current.

N54T   c/n 101. Ex N542? Built 1961. "Pfeifer-Sopwith". Regd 3.6.80 to R.K.Pfeifer, Columbia, California; current, not active. On display California Antique Aircraft Museum, San Jose, California.

N158RC   c/n 5459. Built 1962. Le Rhône C engine. Regd to Kermit Weeks, Polk City, Florida 27.8.91;

Replica N54T was built in 1961 and described as a "Pfeifer-Sopwith". It went on display at the California Antique Aircraft Museum, San Jose, California.

current. On display Fantasy of Flight, Polk City, Florida; painted as "N5452". Stored in the restoration area to at least 12.00. Reported as "N6452", but this is Weeks' Camel replica.

N914W   c/n NCH.1. Built 1985. Warner SS165 engine. Current, "sale reported" to Dallas, Texas, 2002.

N1612U   c/n 1917. Built by Bevins. Kinner B6 engine. Regd 9.6.75 to C.R.Anger, Fairfax, Virginia; current.

N1915K   c/n 3. Built 1992 by Ken Pruitt. Warner Scarab engine. On display Ryders Replica Fighter Museum, Guntersville, Alabama. Collection closed on his death a few years ago. "Sale reported" to Netherlands. Arrived at Lelystad, The Netherlands, April 1998 and extant in the Early Birds collection there.

N4308   c/n OE1. Built by Tallmantz Aviation Co, Santa Ana, California,1972. Current, no other details.

N4781   c/n WRP-1. Built 1973. Warner Scarab engine. Current, "sale reported" to Oklahoma.

N5139   c/n 83213. Built 1967. Ex Old Rheinbeck? On display at Owls Head Transportation Museum, Owls Head, Maine, to whom regd 19.7.90.

N5192   c/n 01. Built 1968. Regd to A.I.Stix Sr, St.Louis, Missouri 19.7.99; current.

NX6018   c/n A-635. Built 1971. Le Rhone C engine. On display Champlin Fighter Museum, Mesa, Arizona; painted as "B1843". Currently owned by Windward Aviation Inc, Enid, Oklahoma.

N6086K   c/n 85444. Built by Ronald Bloomquist. Regd 25.5.00 to R.Bloomquist, Mooresburg, Tennessee; current.

N6179   c/n 008. Built 1993 by AJD Engineering (from a kit). Le Rhône C engine. Regd 27.1.93 to C C Air Corpn., Port Hueneme, California; current. On display Arango Collection, Los Angeles.

N6459   c/n AA.103. Built 1978 by Jim Appleby of Antique Aero Inc, California. Warner SS50A engine. Regd to E.Doyle, Hampton, Iowa 19.2.81; current. On display Ed Doyle Museum, Hampton, Iowa.

-         Non-flying replica [?] Originally marked as "4781". Repainted as "B5371". To Dover AFB, Delaware. On display Bolling Heritage Centre, Bolling AFB, DC. Still at Dover AFB marked "4781" until at least 9.00.

-         Non-flying replica [?]; marks unknown. Sometime displayed Castle Air Museum, Atwater, California; "taken back" by USAF, early 1990s.

Appendix 16

Individual Beardmore W.B.III histories

30 BEARDMORE W.B.III ordered 12.2.17 under Cont Nos A.S.775/17 & A.S.14757 from Sir William Beardmore & Co Ltd, numbered N6100 to N6129 & built Dalmuir. [N6101 and N6102 S.B.IIIF with folding undercarriage, remainder S.B.IIID with dropping undercarriage. These designations promulgated in AWO 2499/17 dated 6.7.17] [N6100 to N6112 believed originally to have been S.B.IIIF with folding wings]. First flights usually at Inchinnan airfield by A.Dukinfield Jones. (All 80hp Le Rhône 9c initially)

N6100   (Engine No.7320, propeller No.1220) FF 25.6.17; Accepted 26.6.17; Allotted Vickers 5.6.17; Flown again at Inchinnan, apparently after modification, 23.10.17 (conversion to have dropping undercarriage?); Deld Rosyth W/E 3.11.17; Donibristle W/E 9.11.17; HMS *Cassandra* 3.12.17; Donibristle 21.3.18; HMS *Nairana* W/E 27.4.18; Rosyth W/E 2.5.18; HMS *Nairana* W/E 2.5.18; Donibristle to HMS *Nairana* W/E 2.5.18; To Turnhouse 5.18; Rosyth to HMS *Nairana* W/E 9.5.18; Donibristle W/E 9.5.18; For deletion by 15.8.18

N6101   (Engine No.2615, propeller No.1252) FF & accepted 6.7.17; Deld East Fortune 15.7.17; HMS *Manxman* 24.7.17; East Fortune 27.7.17; Undercarriage broken on landing 10.10.17 (F/Cdr JCP Wood); Reported damaged but repairable at East Fortune 6.1.18; Deleted W/E 9.3.18

N6102   (Engine No.4686, propeller No.1256) FF & accepted 11.6.17; Deld ECD Grain for erection 24.7.17; Type test 6.8.17 (S/Cdr HR Busteed); Tested with jettisonable undercarriage 10.17; Acceptance Dept Grain W/E 1.12.17; Rosyth by rail 12.12.17; Donibristle W/E 28.12.17; Turnhouse W/E 21.2.18; Engineless by 30.3.18; Still there 30.1.19

N6103   (Engine No.684, propeller No.1243) Allotted Grain 20.6.17; FF & accepted 10.7.17 (Dukinfield Jones); Erecting Grain from/by 26.7.17; Tested 28.7.17; Fitting 100hp Gnome Monosoupape 27.8.17; Acceptance Dept Grain W/E 1.12.17; Rosyth by 18.1.18 (ex Port Victoria); East Fortune Naval Flying School W/E 31.1.18; Engineless and u/s at East Fortune

by 30.3.18; Became 208 TDS East Fortune 1.4.18; Deleted W/E 27.6.18

N6104   (Engine No.4536, propeller No.1248) Allotted HMS *Cassandra* 21.6.17 (NTU?); FF 10.8.17, then flown 11.8.17 & 13.8.17; Accepted 15.8.17; Deld HMS *Pegasus* W/E 27.8.17; Transported to Turnhouse 1.9.17; Donibristle by 5.10.17; Rosyth W/E 8.11.17; Deleted for spares 11.17

N6105   (Engine No.3626, propeller No.1258) FF & accepted 15.8.17; Allotted HMS *Nairana* (NTU?); Deld HMS *Pegasus* W/E 27.8.17; Transported to Turnhouse 1.9.17; Donibristle by 5.10.17; Rosyth W/E 8.11.17; Surveyed 2.11.17; Deleted for spares 6.11.17

N6106   (Engine No.1562, propeller No.1249) FF & accepted 11.6.17; Deld HMS *Pegasus* W/E 27.8.17; Transported to Turnhouse 1.9.17; Donibristle by 25.10.17; Rosyth W/E 8.11.17; Surveyed 2.11.17; Deleted for spares 6.11.17

N6107   (Engine No.6715, propeller No.1255) FF & accepted 17.8.17; Deld HMS *Pegasus* W/E 27.8.17; Transported to Turnhouse 1.9.17; Donibristle by 5.10.17; Rosyth W/E 27.10.17; Surveyed 2.11.17; Deleted 6.11.17 for spares

N6108   (Engine and propeller details not known) Allotted HMS *Nairana* (NTU?); FF 21.8.17; Accepted 23.8.17; Deld Donibristle W/E 5.10.17; Beardmore 18.10.17 (ex Donibristle?); Rosyth by 2.11.17; Surveyed 2.11.17; Deleted for spares 6.11.17

N6109   (Engine No.1523, propeller No.1299); FF 21.8.17; Flown again same day ranging Glasgow AA guns but engine failed, forced landing in Dalmuir Park 21.8.17; Repaired (now fitted engine No.1002, propeller No.1345); Tested again 2.10.17; Accepted 5.10.17; Deld by rail to East Fortune, held for *Manxman* 10.10.17; Donibristle W/E 3.11.17 (reported to have flown 7.11.17 & 14.11.17); HMS *Pegasus* (via Rosyth) W/E 10.11.17; Rosyth W/E 16.11.17; Donibristle to HMS *Nairana* W/E 7.12.17; HMS *Renown* W/E 14.12.17; Unsuccessful attempt to fly from trackway on ships forecastle 12.17; Rosyth W/E 21.12.17; Surveyed 16.12.17; Deleted 22.12.17 wrecked

N6110 (Engine No.2364, propeller No.1261) Allotted HMS *Nairana* (NTU?); FF & accepted 23.8.17; Deld Donibristle W/E 5.10.17; Rosyth W/E 27.10.17; Surveyed 2.11.17; Deleted for spares 6.11.17

N6111 (Engine No.1144, propeller No.1301); FF 19..9.17; Accepted 26.9.17; Deld Donibristle W/E 27.10.17; Rosyth W/E 13.12.17; Surveyed 12.12.17; Deleted 19.12.17 wrecked

N6112 (Engine No.764, propeller No.1237); FF & accepted 26.9.17; Deld Donibristle W/E 27.10.17; Turnhouse W/E 9.3.18; HMS *Nairana* W/E 20.4.18; Donibristle W/E 2.5.18; Turnhouse W/E 2.5.18; Donibristle W/E 23.5.18; For deletion by 29.8.18

N6113 (Engine No.8207, propeller No.1334); FF & accepted 26.9.17; Donibristle by 27.10.17; HMS *Nairana* W/E 25.1.18; Donibristle W/E 7.2.18; Rosyth W/E 16.2.18; HMS *Nairana* W/E 28.2.18; Donibristle W/E 16.3.18; Rosyth W/E 16.5.18; HMS *Pegasus* W/E 23.5.18; Donibristle W/E 23.5.18; For deletion W/E 15.9.18

N6114 (Engine No.5077, propeller No.1300); FF & accepted 5.10.17; Deld Rosyth W/E 10.10.17; Donibristle W/E 15.11.17; Rosyth W/E 23.11.17; Donibristle W/E 28.12.17; HMS *Pegasus* 15.3.18; Rosyth 18.3.18 Donibristle W/E 21.3.18; Rosyth 3.18; Donibristle W/E 4.4.18; Rosyth W/E 20.4.18; HMS *Nairana* W/E 2.5.18; Rosyth W/E 2.5.18; HMS *Nairana* W/E 9.5.18; Rosyth W/E 9.5.18; HMS *Nairana* to Donibristle W/E 9.5.18; HMS *Nairana* W/E 16.5.18; Rosyth W/E 16.5.18; HMS *Nairana* W/E 16.5.18; HMS *Pegasus* W/E 16.5.18; Rosyth W/E 16.5.18; Donibristle to Rosyth W/E 16.5.18 (twice); Rosyth to Donibristle W/E 23.5.18; Deleted W/E 1.8.18

N6115 (Engine No.10025, propeller No.1325); FF & accepted 5.10.17; Deld Donibristle W/E 10.10.17; HMS *Nairana* W/E 30.11.17; HMS *Renown* 11.17; Rosyth W/E 7.12.17; HMS *Nairana* 20.12.17; HMS *Princess Royal* by 1.18; HMS *Pegasus* 1.18; Donibristle W/E 4.1.18; Rosyth W/E 18.1.18; Donibristle to Rosyth again W/E 18.1.18; HMS *Nairana* W/E 17.1.18; Donibristle W/E 31.1.18; For deletion W/E 15.8.18

N6116 (Engine No.5148, propeller No.1260); FF & accepted 5.10.17; Donibristle by 27.10.17; HMS *Nairana* W/E 30.11.17; ALSO Rosyth to HMS *Nairana* W/E 30.11.17; HMS *Renown* 14.12.17; Rosyth W/E 21.12.17; HMS *Nairana* to Rosyth W/E 20.12.17; Donibristle W/E 11.1.18 - @23.2.18; HMS *Nairana* 2.18; Rosyth W/E 28.2.18; Turnhouse by 30.3.18; Deleted 1.8.18; Selected for preservation, delivered engineless to Agricultural Hall, Islington 16.8.18 (not preserved)

N6117 (Engine No.2602, propeller No.1298); FF & accepted 5.10.17; Deld Grain Test Depot 17.10.17; Deleted 3.1.18 wrecked, but still recorded as engineless at Test Depot 5.1.18

N6118 (Engine No.1394, propeller No.1304); FF & accepted 12.10.17; Deld Rosyth W/E 27.10.17; Engineless by 11.1.18; Turnhouse W/E 21.3.18; Erecting 30.3.18; Deleted W/E 11.7.18

N6119 (Engine No.2371, propeller No.1254); FF & accepted 12.10.17; Deld Donibristle W/E 27.10.17; Rosyth W/E 23.11.17; HMS *Pegasus* 12.17; Rosyth W/E 20.12.17; Surveyed 22.12.17; Deleted 31.12.17 wrecked

N6120 (Engine No.2540, propeller No.1306); FF & accepted 12.10.17; Deld Rosyth W/E 27.10.17; Donibristle W/E 22.11.17; Rosyth W/E 28.3.18; HMS *Nairana* W/E 28.3.18; Rosyth to HMS *Pegasus* W/E 28.3.18; Donibristle W/E 4.4.18; Turnhouse by 4.18; HMS *Nairana* by 4.18; Donibristle W/E 4.4.18; HMS *Nairana* by 5.4.18; Rosyth 5.18; Turnhouse W/E 9.5.18; Deleted W/E 4.7.18

N6121 (Engine No.3704, propeller No.1302); FF & accepted 12.10.17; Deld Donibristle W/E 27.10.17; HMS *Pegasus* W/E 13.12.17; Rosyth to HMS *Pegasus* W/E 14.12.17 - @17.12.17; Rosyth W/E 20.12.17; HMS *Nairana* W/E 21.12.17; Donibristle W/E 28.12.17; HMS *Pegasus* to Donibristle W/E 28.12.17; Rosyth W/E 4.4.18; Donibristle W/E 2.5.18; For deletion W/E 15.8.18

N6122 (Engine No.705, propeller No.1330); FF & accepted 12.10.17; Deld Rosyth W/E 27.10.17; Donibristle W/E 15.11.17; HMS *Nairana* W/E 30.11.17; Rosyth W/E 7.12.17; Donibristle 11.1.18; East Fortune Naval Flying School for carriers W/E 31.1.18; Became 208 TDS East Fortune 1.4.18; For deletion W/E 27.6.18

Two successive photographs of W.B.III N6115, taking off rather lopsidedly from an arrangement of troughs laid out on the fo'c'sle of HMS Renown in the Firth of Forth in November 1917, the famous railway bridge being visible in the background. The aircraft evidently avoided a ditching, as it survived until being deleted in August 1918. Not surprisingly, the arrangement was not a success, and by early 1918 Renown had been fitted with a turret-mounted platform.

(H.H.Dannreuther/FAA Museum)

N6123   No engine nor propeller fitted at works, no test flight; Deld Rosyth for erection W/E 27.10.17; Still erecting 29.12.17; Engine No.1076 by 11.1.18; Donibristle W/E 25.1.18; HMS *Pegasus* W/E 15.2.18 [@15.2.18]; Rosyth W/E 15.2.18; HMS *Dublin* to Rosyth W/E 15.2.18; HMS *Pegasus* W/E 15.2.18; Donibristle W/E 21.2.18; HMS *Pegasus* by 15.3.18; Donibristle 18.3.18; HMS *Nairana* W/E 28.3.18; Donibristle W/E 4.4.18; Rosyth W/E 4.4.18; HMS *Pegasus* W/E 4.4.18; W/E 4.4.18 = Donibristle ex *Nairana, Nairana, Pegasus, Nairana, Pegasus* ALSO Donibristle to Rosyth, *Nairana, Pegasus, Nairana* [i.e. a series of movements to and from Donibristle, exact details not clear in records]; Rosyth to HMS *Nairana* W/E 2.5.18; Rosyth W/E 2.5.18; HMS *Nairana* W/E 9.5.18; Donibristle W/E 9.5.18; HMS *Nairana* W/E 9.5.18; Donibristle to Rosyth W/E 16.5.18 (twice); to HMS *Nairana* W/E 16.5.18; Donibristle W/E 16.5.18; Rosyth to HMS *Pegasus* W/E 16.5.18; Rosyth W/E 16.5.18; HMS *Nairana* to Donibristle W/E 23.5.18; HMS *Pegasus* W/E 23.5.18; HMS *Pegasus* to Donibristle W/E 23.5.18 (twice); Donibristle to Rosyth W/E 23.5.18 (twice); Rosyth to HMS *Pegasus* W/E 23.5.18; Rosyth by 6.18; Donibristle 8.18 W/E 15.8.18; Deleted W/E 12.9.18

N6124   No engine nor propeller fitted at works, no test flight; Deld Rosyth for erection W/E 3.11.17; Still erecting 29.12.17; HMS *Nairana* W/E 25.1.18; Donibristle W/E 26.1.18; HMS *Nairana* W/E 31.1.18; Donibristle W/E 21.2.18 - @23.2.18; HMS *Nairana* to Donibristle W/E 28.2.18; For deletion W/E 15.8.18

N6125   (Engine No.1059, propeller No.1482); FF & accepted 23.10.17; Deld Rosyth W/E 3.11.17; Donibristle W/E 15.11.17; HMS *Pegasus* W/E 13.12.17 - @17.12.17; Rosyth W/E 20.12.17; Donibristle W/E 28.12.17; Fitted 80hp Clerget No.11061 by 11.1.18; HMS *Nairana* W/E 8.2.18; Turnhouse W/E 9.3.18 (for HMS *Nairana*); HMS *Nairana* from 3.18; Turnhouse by 30.3.18; Donibristle W/E 4.4.18; Rosyth W/E 20.4.18; Turnhouse W/E 9.5.18; Deleted W/E 27.6.18

N6126   (Engine No.1060, propeller No.1628); FF & accepted 23.10.17; Deld Rosyth W/E 3.11.17; Donibristle W/E 15.11.17; HMS *Pegasus* W/E 28.12.17; Donibristle to Rosyth W/E 28.12.17; Donibristle @29.12.17; HMS *Pegasus* by 31.12.17 - @7.1.18; Rosyth by @11.1.18; Fitted 80hp Clerget No.11061 by 11.1.18; Deleted 19.1.18

N6127   (Engine No.1058, propeller No.1614); FF & accepted 23.10.17; Deld Rosyth W/E 3.11.17; Donibristle W/E 15.11.17; HMS *Pegasus* W/E 13.12.17; HMS *Phaeton* 11.12.17; Rosyth W/E 20.12.17; Donibristle W/E 31.1.18 (now fitted 80hp Clerget); East Fortune Naval Flying School W/E 16.2.18; Deleted W/E 2.3.18

N6128   Deld Rosyth W/E 3.11.17; Erecting without engine 28.12.17; Still at Rosyth 19.1.18; Donibristle by 8.2.18; HMS *Pegasus* W/E 15.2.18 - @16.3.18; Donibristle @23.2.18; HMS *Pegasus* by 3.18; Donibristle 18.3.18; HMS *Cassandra* 21.3.18; Donibristle W/E 21.3.18; HMS *Cassandra* 29.3.18; Donibristle W/E 9.5.18; HMS *Cassandra* W/E 9.5.18; Rosyth to HMS *Cassandra* W/E 9.5.18; Donibristle by 25.5.18; HMS *Cassandra* W/E 13.6.18; Turnhouse W/E 11.7.18; Deleted W/E 25.7.18

N6129   Deld Rosyth W/E 9.11.17; Donibristle W/E 28.12.17; HMS *Nairana* W/E 4.1.18; HMS *Pegasus* to Donibristle W/E 3.1.18; HMS *Pegasus* 3.1.18; HMS *Yarmouth* W/E 31.1.18; HMS *Nairana* W/E 7.2.18; Scapa W/E 7.2.18; Houton Bay W/E 16.2.18 (for overhaul); Noted for deletion by 30.3.18, but to Scapa W/E 18.5.18; Smoogroo W/E 12.9.18; Scapa W/E 21.11.18; Still there 30.1.19

70 BEARDMORE W.B.III (SBIIID with jettisonable undercarriage) ordered under Cont Nos A.S.775 & A.S.12856, numbered N6680 to N6749 & built Dalmuir. First flights usually at Inchinnan airfield by A.Dukinfield Jones. 42 cancelled 5.2.18, presume reinstated but mostly to storage. (80hp Le Rhône)

N6680   Deld Donibristle W/E 9.11.17; Rosyth W/E 16.11.17; Donibristle W/E 22.11.17 (fitted 80hp Le Rhône No.3626 by 11.1.18); Rosyth W/E 21.3.18; Donibristle 3.18; HMS *Pegasus* W/E 21.3.18; Donibristle W/E 21.3.18; Rosyth W/E 28.3.18; HMS *Pegasus* W/E 28.3.18; Donibristle W/E 28.3.18; HMS *Pegasus* W/E 28.3.18 [@26-28.3.18]; Donibristle W/E 28.3.18; Rosyth W/E 13.6.18; Donibristle W/E 11.7.18; For deletion 15.8.18; Deleted W/E 12.9.18

N6681   Deld Donibristle W/E 9.11.17; Rosyth W/E 16.11.17 (fitted 80hp Le Rhône No.2058 by 11.1.18); HMS *Pegasus* 1.18; Donibristle W/E 11.1.18; HMS *Pegasus* W/E 21.3.18 [@18.3.18]; Donibristle W/E 21.3.18; Rosyth W/E 28.3.18; HMS *Pegasus* W/E 28.3.18; Donibristle W/E 28.3.18; For deletion by 15.8.18

N6682   Deld Donibristle W/E 9.11.17; Rosyth W/E 16.11.17; Erecting without engine 29.12.17; Donibristle W/E 8.2.18; Rosyth W/E 21.3.18; HMS *Nairana* W/E 28.3.18; Donibristle 30.3.18 (u/s with 80hp Le Rhône 30.3.18); HMS *Nairana* 30.3.18; Donibristle 4.4.18; Rosyth W/E 4.4.18; Donibristle to HMS *Nairana* W/E 4.4.18 (three times); Donibristle to HMS *Pegasus* W/E 4.4.18; a ship (*Pegasus*?) by 5.4.18; Rosyth by 2.5.18; Donibristle W/E 9.5.18; Rosyth W/E 16.5.18; HMS *Pegasus* to Donibristle W/E 23.5.18 (twice); Rosyth W/E 23.5.18 (twice); HMS *Pegasus* to Rosyth W/E 23.5.18;

Donibristle by 6.18; Rosyth W/E 11.7.18;
Donibristle W/E 15.8.18; Rosyth W/E 24.10.18;
Donibristle W/E 31.10.18; Still there 30.1.19

N6683 (Engine No.1066, propeller No.1303); FF 3.11.17; Accepted 6.11.17; Deld HMS *Campania* for erection 22.12.17; Houton Bay (for erection) W/E 29.12.17; Damaged when Bessonneau tent blown down in gale 27.2.18; Surveyed 2.3.18 (reported repairable); Erecting with 80hp Clerget at Houton Base Reserve, for Fleet use, 30.3.18; Deleted W/E 27.4.18

N6684 (Engine No.1065, propeller No.1253); FF & accepted 6.11.17; Deld HMS *Campania* for erection 22.12.17; Houton Bay (for erection) W/E 29.12.17; Erecting with 80hp Clerget at Houton Base Reserve, for Fleet use, 30.3.18; Deleted W/E 27.4.18

N6685 (Engine No.1699/5699, propeller No.1327); FF & accepted 12.10.17; Deld Houton Bay W/E 29.12.17 (at Scapa awaiting final truing up 29.12.17); Serviceable for Fleet in Houton Base Reserve 30.3.18; Scapa W/E 18.5.18; Smoogroo W/E 18.8.18; Scapa W/E 28.11.18; Still there 30.1.19

N6686 (Engine No.446, propeller No.1259); FF & accepted 6.11.17; Deld Houton Bay W/E 29.12.17 (repair wing by 23.2.18) (ex HMS *Royalist* by 9.3.18); Scapa W/E 18.5.18; Smoogroo W/E 1.8.18; Scapa W/E 19.12.18; Still there 30.1.19

N6687 Deld Rosyth for erection W/E 16.11.17; Donibristle W/E 5.1.18; At Donibristle with 80hp Le Rhône No.2371 for HMS *Nairana* by 11.1.18; HMS *Nairana* 11.1.18; Returned Donibristle but smashed undercarriage landing on snow 15.1.18; Rosyth W/E 18.1.18 (ex HMS *Pegasus*); Turnhouse W/E 21.3.18; Deleted W/E 11.7.18

N6688 Deld Rosyth for erection W/E 16.11.17; Erecting without engine 29.12.17; East Fortune Naval Flying School W/E 16.2.18 (for carriers); Engineless at 30.3.18; Became 208 TDS East Fortune 1.4.18; Deleted W/E 11.7.18

N6689 (Engine No.1068, propeller No.1394); FF 15.11.17; Accepted 21.11.17; Reported in transit to Houton Bay 29.12.17; Deld Houton Bay for erection W/E 2.2.18; Damaged when Bessonneau tent blown down in gale 27.2.18; Surveyed 2.3.18 (reported repairable); Erecting Houton Bay 30.3.18; Deleted W/E 27.4.18

N6690 Deld Rosyth for erection W/E 23.11.17; Erecting without engine 29.12.17; Donibristle 11.1.18; HMS *Pegasus* 13.2.18; Rosyth 15.2.18; For deletion by 21.2.18

N6691 Deld Rosyth W/E 23.11.17; Donibristle W/E 28.12.17; HMS *Pegasus* W/E 18.1.18; HMS *Nairana* W/E 17.1.18; Donibristle W/E 25.1.18; Rosyth W/E 25.1.18; Turnhouse W/E 21.3.18; Deleted W/E 11.7.18

N6692 Deld Rosyth W/E 23.11.17 - @29.12.17; HMS *Pegasus* with 80hp Le Rhône W/E 3.1.18 - @10.1.18; Donibristle to HMS *Pegasus*

W/E 11.1.18 [HMS *Pegasus* @7-11.1.18]; Donibristle W/E 17.1.18 - @19.1.18; HMS *Nairana* to Rosyth W/E 28.1.18; Donibristle to HMS *Pegasus* W/E 8.2.18 [by 8.2.18 at anchor]; Rosyth W/E 15.2.18; HMS *Pegasus* 13.2.18; Donibristle 15.2.18; HMS *Nairana* by 23.2.18; Donibristle W/E 28.2.18; HMS *Nairana* from 3.18; Donibristle by 30.3.18; HMS *Pegasus* to Donibristle W/E 4.4.18; HMS *Nairana* to Donibristle W/E 4.4.18; Still there 30.1.19

N6693 (Engine No.684/7964, propeller No.1424); FF 19.11.17; Accepted 10.12.17; Reported in transit to Houton Bay 29.12.17; Deld Houton Bay for erection W/E 23.2.18; Erecting for Fleet use 30.3.18; Scapa for erection W/E 4.5.18; Smoogroo W/E 8.8.18; HMS *Vindictive* 29.10.18; Scapa W/E 28.11.18; Smoogroo W/E 12.12.18; Scapa W/E 23.1.19; Still there 30.1.19

N6694 (Engine No.7581/5187, propeller No.1379); FF & accepted 21.11.17; Deld Houton Bay for erection W/E 29.12.17; Escaped damage when Bessonneau tent blown down in gale 27.2.18; Erecting for Fleet use 30.3.18; Deleted W/E 27.4.18

N6695 (Engine No.1316, propeller No.1403); FF & accepted 21.11.17; Deld Houton Bay (via Aberdeen) for erection W/E 12.12.17; Damaged when Bessoneau tent blown down in gale 27.2.18; Surveyed 2.3.18 (reported repairable); Erecting 30.3.18; Deleted W/E 27.4.18

N6696 Deld Rosyth for erection W/E 30.11.17; Erecting without engine 29.12.17; Donibristle W/E 16.2.18; Rosyth W/E 21.3.18; Donibristle 3.18; HMS *Pegasus* W/E 28.3.18 [by 26.3.18]; Donibristle W/E 4.4.18; Rosyth W/E 4.4.18; HMS *Nairana* W/E 4.4.18; Donibristle W/E 4.4.18; HMS *Pegasus* by 3-5.4.18; Donibristle by 2.5.18; HMS *Cassandra* 29.7.18; Donibristle 9.8.18; Deleted W/E 21.11.18

N6697 Deld Rosyth for erection W/E 30.11.17; Erecting without engine 29.12.17; Donibristle W/E 8.2.18 - @16.5.18; Rosyth 5.18; *Pegasus* W/E 23.5.18; Donibristle W/E 23.5.18; Rosyth W/E 23.5.18; Donibristle W/E 23.5.18; Rosyth W/E 23.5.18; Turnhouse W/E 11.7.18; Deleted W/E 15.8.18

N6698 (Engine No.35018, propeller No.1384); FF & accepted 10.12.17; Deld Houton Bay for erection W/E 29.12.17; Erecting for Fleet use 30.3.18; Scapa from W/E 4.5.18; Smoogroo W/E 8.8.18; Scapa W/E 28.11.18; Still there 30.1.19

N6699 Deld Rosyth for erection W/E 30.11.17; Erecting without engine 29.12.17; East Fortune Naval Flying School W/E 8.2.18 (for carriers); Became 208 TDS East Fortune 1.4.18; Deleted W/E 27.6.18

N6700 Deld Rosyth for erection W/E 30.11.17; Erecting without engine 29.12.17; Donibristle by 3.1.18; Rosyth by 18.1.18; Donibristle W/E 8.2.18; Turnhouse W/E 20.4.18; Donibristle W/E 23.5.18; HMS *Pegasus* W/E 1.8.18; Rosyth W/E 15.8.18; Donibristle W/E 21.11.18; Still there 30.1.19

N6701 (Engine No.5393, propeller No.1388); FF & accepted 10.12.17; Deld Houton Bay for erection W/E 29.12.17; Erecting 30.3.18; Scapa for erection from W/E 4.5.18; Smoogroo W/E 15.8.18; Scapa W/E 28.11.18; Smoogroo W/E 12.12.18; Scapa W/E 23.1.19; Still there 30.1.19

N6702   Deld Killingholme Reserve W/E 14.12.17; 6 AAP Renfrew W/E 27.4.18; Turnhouse W/E 13.6.18; Donibristle W/E 11.7.18; Rosyth W/E 29.8.18; Donibristle W/E 29.8.18; Still there 30.1.19

N6703   Deld Killingholme Reserve W/E 14.12.17; 6 AAP Renfrew W/E 27.4.18; Turnhouse W/E 13.6.18; HMS *Pegasus* W/E 1.8.18; Donibristle W/E 15.8.18; Rosyth W/E 22.8.18; Donibristle W/E 2.9.18; Rosyth W/E 24.10.18; Still there 30.1.19

N6704   Deld Killingholme Reserve W/E 14.12.17; 6 AAP Renfrew W/E 27.4.18; Turnhouse W/E 13.6.18; HMS *Pegasus* W/E 1.8.18; Rosyth W/E 15.8.18; Donibristle W/E 29.8.18; Rosyth W/E 26.9.18; Donibristle W/E 3.10.18; Rosyth W/E 17.10.18; Deleted W/E 31.10.18

N6705   Deld Killingholme Reserve W/E 14.12.17; 6 AAP Renfrew W/E 27.4.18; Turnhouse W/E 13.6.18; Donibristle W/E 11.7.18; Rosyth W/E 24.10.18; Donibristle W/E 31.10.18; Still there 30.1.19

N6706   Deld Killingholme Reserve W/E 12.12.17; 6 AAP Renfrew W/E 27.4.18; Turnhouse W/E 13.6.18; Donibristle W/E 15.8.18; Still there 30.1.19

N6707   Deld Killingholme Reserve W/E 12.12.17; 6 AAP Renfrew W/E 27.4.18; Turnhouse W/E 13.6.18; Donibristle W/E 17.10.18; Still there 30.1.19

N6708   Deld Grain Type Test Flt without engine 13.12.17; Weighed 20.12.17; By 5.1.18 had 80hp Le Rhône from N6117; Acceleration tests

c.18.1.18 [see page 134]; Rosyth W/E 15.2.18; Donibristle W/E 28.3.18; HMS *Nairana* W/E 13.4.18; Rosyth W/E 20.4.18; HMS *Nairana* W/E 22.4.18; Rosyth W/E 2.5.18; HMS *Nairana* W/E 11.5.18; Donibristle W/E 16.5.18; Rosyth W/E 23.5.18; For deletion W/E 15.8.18

N6709   Deld Killingholme Reserve W/E 12.12.17; 6 AAP Renfrew W/E 27.4.18; transit W/E 13.6.18; Turnhouse W/E 11.7.18; Donibristle W/E 22.8.18; Rosyth W/E 3.10.18; Donibristle W/E 17.10.18; Rosyth W/E 24.10.18; Donibristle W/E 14.11.18; Still there 30.1.19

N6710   Deld Killingholme Reserve W/E 12.12.17; 6 AAP Renfrew WE 27.4.18; transit W/E 13.6.18; Turnhouse W/E 11.7.18 (for HMS *Pegasus*); Donibristle W/E 15.8.18; Rosyth W/E 26.9.18; Donibristle W/E 3.10.18; Rosyth W/E 17.10.18; Donibristle W/E 31.10.18; Still there 30.1.19

N6711   Deld Killingholme Reserve W/E 12.12.17; 6 AAP Renfrew W/E 27.4.18; transit W/E 13.6.18; Turnhouse W/E 11.7.18; Donibristle W/E 15.8.18; Rosyth W/E 3.10.18; Donibristle W/E 17.10.18; Rosyth W/E 24.10.18; Donibristle W/E 14.11.18; Still there 30.1.19

N6712   Deld Killingholme Reserve W/E 12.12.17; 6 AAP Renfrew W/E 27.4.18; transit W/E 13.6.18; Turnhouse W/E 11.7.18; Donibristle W/E 15.8.18; Rosyth W/E 26.9.18; Donibristle W/E 3.10.18; Rosyth W/E 17.10.18; Deleted W/E 21.11.18

N6713   Deld Killingholme Reserve W/E 12.12.17; 6 AAP Renfrew W/E 27.4.18; transit W/E 13.6.18; Donibristle W/E 11.7.18; Rosyth W/E 22.8.18;

W.B.III N6717 probably spent its whole life in storage. It was initially delivered by Beardmore to the Killingholme Reserve in December 1917, being transferred to No.6 Aircraft Acceptance Park at Renfrew in April 1918 then finally to Donibristle in August 1918.   (via Frank Cheesman)

Donibristle W/E 29.8.18; Flew under Forth Bridge 28.8.18 (Capt WW Wakefield); Rosyth W/E 26.9.18; Donibristle W/E 3.10.18; Rosyth W/E 17.10.18; Donibristle W/E 31.10.18; Still there 30.1.19

N6714   Deld Killingholme Reserve W/E 19.12.17; 6 AAP Renfrew W/E 27.4.18; transit W/E 13.6.18; Turnhouse W/E 11.7.18 (for HMS *Pegasus*); Donibristle W/E 15.8.18; Rosyth W/E 22.8.18; Donibristle W/E 29.8.18; Deleted W/E 21.11.18

N6715   Deld Killingholme Reserve W/E 12.12.17; 6 AAP Renfrew W/E 27.4.18; transit W/E 11.7.18; Donibristle W/E 15.8.18; Still there 30.1.19

N6716   Deld Killingholme Reserve W/E 19.12.17; 6 AAP Renfrew W/E 27.4.18; transit W/E 11.7.18; Donibristle W/E 15.8.18; Still there 30.1.19

N6717   Deld Killingholme Reserve W/E 19.12.17; 6 AAP Renfrew W/E 27.4.18; transit W/E 11.7.18; Donibristle W/E 15.8.18; Still there 30.1.19

N6718   Deld Killingholme Reserve W/E 19.12.17; 6 AAP Renfrew W/E 27.4.18; transit W/E 11.7.18; Donibristle W/E 15.8.18; Engineless at 7.11.18; Still there 30.1.19

N6719   Deld Killingholme Reserve W/E 19.12.17; 6 AAP Renfrew W/E 27.4.18; transit W/E 11.7.18; Donibristle W/E 15.8.18; Engineless at 7.11.18; Still there 30.1.19

N6720   Deld Killingholme Reserve W/E 19.12.17; 6 AAP Renfrew W/E 27.4.18; transit W/E 11.7.18; Donibristle W/E 15.8.18; Engineless at 7.11.18; Still there 30.1.19

N6721   Deld Killingholme Reserve W/E 5.1.18; 6 AAP Renfrew W/E 27.4.18; transit W/E 11.7.18; Donibristle W/E 15.8.18; Engineless at 7.11.18; Engineless at 7.11.18; Still there 30.1.19

N6722   Deld Killingholme Reserve W/E 5.1.18; 6 AAP Renfrew W/E 27.4.18; transit W/E 11.7.18; Donibristle W/E 15.8.18; Engineless at 7.11.18; Still there 30.1.19

N6723   Deld Killingholme Reserve W/E 5.1.18; 6 AAP Renfrew W/E 27.4.18; transit W/E 11.7.18; Donibristle W/E 15.8.18; Engineless at 7.11.18; Still there 30.1.19

N6724   Deld Killingholme Reserve W/E 5.1.18; 6 AAP Renfrew W/E 27.4.18; transit W/E 11.7.18; Donibristle W/E 15.8.18; Engineless at 7.11.18; Still there 30.1.19
BUT 6 AAP Renfrew by 31.12.18

N6725   Deld Killingholme Reserve W/E 5.1.18; 6 AAP Renfrew W/E 27.4.18; transit W/E 11.7.18; Donibristle W/E 15.8.18; Turnhouse W/E 19.9.18; Engineless at 7.11.18; Still there 30.1.19

N6726   Deld Killingholme Reserve W/E 5.1.18; 6 AAP Renfrew W/E 27.4.18; transit W/E 11.7.18; Turnhouse W/E 15.8.18; Engineless at 7.11.18; Still there 30.1.19

N6727   Deld Killingholme Reserve W/E 5.1.18; 6 AAP Renfrew W/E 27.4.18; transit W/E 11.7.18; Turnhouse W/E 15.8.18; Engineless at 7.11.18; Still there 30.1.19

N6728   Deld Killingholme Reserve W/E 5.1.18; 6 AAP Renfrew W/E 27.4.18; transit W/E 11.7.18; Turnhouse W/E 15.8.18; Engineless at 7.11.18; Still there 30.1.19

N6729   Deld Killingholme Reserve W/E 5.1.18; 6 AAP Renfrew W/E 27.4.18; transit W/E 11.7.18; Turnhouse W/E 15.8.18; Engineless at 7.11.18; Still there 30.1.19

N6730   Deld Killingholme Reserve W/E 5.1.18; 6 AAP Renfrew W/E 27.4.18; transit W/E 11.7.18; Turnhouse W/E 15.8.18; Engineless at 7.11.18; Still there 30.1.19

N6731   Deld Killingholme Reserve W/E 26.1.18; 6 AAP Renfrew W/E 27.4.18; Allotted to Turnhouse engineless 7.11.18; Still at Renfrew 30.1.19 [HMS *Inconstant* 17.1.19 - 23.1.19? - listed as aeroplane 6371]

N6732   Deld Killingholme Reserve W/E 26.1.18; 6 AAP Renfrew W/E 27.4.18; Allotted to Turnhouse engineless 7.11.18; Still at Renfrew 30.1.19

N6733   Deld Killingholme Reserve W/E 26.1.18; 6 AAP Renfrew W/E 27.4.18; Allotted to Turnhouse engineless 7.11.18; Still at Renfrew 30.1.19

N6734   Deld Killingholme Reserve W/E 26.1.18; 6 AAP Renfrew W/E 27.4.18; Allotted to Turnhouse engineless 7.11.18; Still at Renfrew 30.1.19

N6735   (110-hp Le Rhône) Deld Killingholme Reserve W/E 26.1.18; 6 AAP Renfrew W/E 27.4.18; 6 SD Ascot 25.7.18; Transferred to Japanese Govt W/E 29.8.18

N6736   Deld Killingholme Reserve 26.1.18; 6 AAP Renfrew W/E 27.4.18; 6 SD Ascot W/E 18.7.18; Transferred to Japanese Govt W/E 29.8.18

N6737   Deld Killingholme Reserve W/E 26.1.18; 6 AAP Renfrew W/E 27.4.18; Still there 30.1.19

N6738   Deld Killingholme Reserve W/E 26.1.18; 6 AAP Renfrew W/E 27.4.18; Still there 30.1.19

N6739   Deld Killingholme Reserve W/E 26.1.18; 6 AAP Renfrew W/E 27.4.18; Still there 30.1.19

N6740   Deld Killingholme Reserve W/E 26.1.18; 6 AAP Renfrew W/E 27.4.18; Still there 30.1.19

N6741   Deld Killingholme Reserve W/E 26.1.18; 6 AAP Renfrew W/E 27.4.18; Still there 30.1.19

N6742   Deld Killingholme Reserve W/E 26.1.18; 6 AAP Renfrew W/E 27.4.18; Still there 30.1.19

N6743   Deld Killingholme Reserve W/E 23.2.18; 6 AAP Renfrew W/E 27.4.18; Still there 30.1.19

N6744   Deld Killingholme Reserve W/E 23.2.18; 6 AAP Renfrew W/E 27.4.18; Still there 30.1.19

N6745   Deld Killingholme Reserve W/E 23.2.18; 6 AAP Renfrew W/E 27.4.18; Still there 30.1.19

N6746   Deld Killingholme Reserve W/E 23.2.18; 6 AAP Renfrew W/E 27.4.18; Still there 30.1.19

N6747   Deld Killingholme Reserve W/E 23.2.18; 6 AAP Renfrew W/E 27.4.18; Still there 30.1.19

N6748   Deld Killingholme Reserve W/E 23.2.18; 6 AAP Renfrew W/E 27.4.18; Still there 30.1.19

N6749   Deld Grain Type Test Flt W/E 23.2.18 (engine test); Engineless at Grain 30.3.18; 6 AAP Renfrew W/E 8.8.18; Still there 30.1.19

Appendix 17

RFC, RNAS &
RAF Pup Units

Operational Squadrons partially or wholly equipped with Pups

No.28 Squadron
'B' Flight was equipped with Pups c.7.17 at Yatesbury in the 28th Wing whilst working up for departure to France with Sopwith Camels on 8 October 1917 ('A' Flight had D.H.5s and 'C' Flight had 504Ks). At least one Pup was later on strength in Italy shortly before the end of the war.

Commanding Officer (Pup period):
Mjr HF Glanville from 12.7.17

Known serial numbers – A6193, A7334, A7345, B803, B1753, B2196, D4143 (Italy).

No.34 Squadron
At least one Pup was on strength in Italy around the end of the war, the main equipment being R.E.8s. They were then based at Santa Luca as part of the 51st Wing in the 7th Brigade.

Commanding Officer (Pup period):
Mjr RJ Mounsey

Known serial number – D4143 (Italy).

No.36 Squadron
Based as a Home Defence squadron with headquarters at Cramlington as part of the 46th (Home Defence) Wing in the 6th Brigade with a number of Pups on strength from 4.18 until at least 1.19. The squadron moved to Usworth/Hylton on 1.7.18 and eventually Ashington leaving a detachment at Hylton before disbanding on 13.6.19. Throughout this period 'A' Flight was based at Usworth/Hylton, 'B' Flight at Ashington and 'C' Flight at Seaton Carew, all three flights having Pups on strength at various times.

Commanding Officers (Pup period):
Mjr SW Price MC to 25.7.18
Mjr WJ Tempest DSO MC 26.7.18 – 1.19

Known serial numbers – B849, B1763, B1805, B1807, B5905, B5906, C235, C291, C303, C326.

No.37 Squadron
A Home Defence squadron with headquarters at The Range, Woodham Mortimer as part of the 50th (Home Defence) Wing in the 6th Brigade with a number of Pups on strength from 4.17 until at least 5.18, and probably until being renumbered to become No.39 Squadron on 1.7.19. During this period 'A' Flight was based at Rochford until moving in 2.18 to Stow Maries, 'B' Flight was at Stow Maries throughout and 'C' Flight at Goldhanger throughout. The Pups appear to have been mainly flown at Stow Maries, though at least one was at Goldhanger.

Commanding Officers (Pup period):
Mjr WB Hargrave to 31.10.17
Mjr FW Honnett 1.11.17 to 2.19
Mjr J Sowrey 2.19 to 6.19
Mjr P Babington 6.19 to 1.7.19

Known serial numbers – A651, A653, A6244, A6246, B735, B1723, B1764, B1765, B1771, B2194, B5304, B5907.

No.39 Squadron
Based as a Home Defence squadron with headquarters at Salway Lodge, Woodford Green as part of the 50th (Home Defence)

Wing in the 6th Brigade with a variety of aircraft, including at least one Pup with 'A' Flight at North Weald from 7.17. The squadron reformed 1.7.19 from No.37 Squadron at Biggin Hill, with at least one Pup for a short period, the main equipment being D.H.9As.

Commanding Officers (Pup period):
Mjr JC Halahan in 7.17
Sqdn Ldr CA Ridley by 11.19

Known serial numbers – A6226 (7.17), B1807 (8.19).

No.46 Squadron
Formed 19.4.16 at Brooklands from a nucleus of 2 Reserve Squadron, moving next day to Wyton with various training aircraft. Re-equipped with Nieuport 2-seaters 9.16 - 10.16, then received its first Pups 20.4.17. To St.Omer 20.10.16, then to Droglandt 26.10.16 to join 2nd Corps Wing 2nd Brigade. 'A' Flight to Boisdinghem 16.4.17 to re-equip with Pups from 20.4.17, being joined there 25.4.17 by the remainder of the squadron to complete re-equipment, now under 11th Wing 2nd Brigade. To La Gorgue 12.5.17, transferring to 10th Wing 1st Brigade at midnight 12-13.6.17. To Bruay 6.7.17. To England for Home Defence duties 10.7.17, based at Sutton's Farm, Hornchurch. Returned to France 30.8.17, to be based at St.Marie Capelle with 11th Wing 2nd Brigade. To Le Hameau (Filescamp) 7.9.17, transferring to 13th Army Wing 3rd Brigade. Exchanged Pups for Camels between 8.11.17 and 13.12.17.

Commanding Officer (Pup period):
Mjr P Babington MC throughout.

Known serial numbers – A635, A648, A665, A673 ('5'), A6155, A6157 ('6'), A6159, A6164, A6188 ('4'), A6195, A6197, A6200, A6202, A6204, A6206, A6216, A6241, A7321, A7324, A7325 ('1'), A727 ('1'), A7330, A7331, A7332, A7333, A7334, A7335, A7337, A7344, A7346, A7347, A7348 ('3'), B1701, B1704, B1709, B1716, B1719, B1727 ('N' & '2'), B1728, B1747, B1754, B1758, B1759, B1766, B1776, B1777 ('X' & '4'), B1795 ('X'), B1799, B1802 ('W'), B1814, B1827, B1828, B1829, B1837, B1841, B1842, B1843, B2180, B2182, B2186, B2187, B2191, B2198, B5922.

Code markings:
'A' Flight, letters at the beginning of the alphabet.
'B' Flight, numbers '1' to '6'
'C' Flight, letters at the end of the alphabet.

Squadron identification markings:
Two vertical white bands around the rear fuselage, just in front of the tailplane.

No.50 Squadron
Based as a Home Defence squadron with headquarters at Harrietsham as part of the 49th (Home Defence) Wing in the 6th Brigade with a number of Pups on strength from some time in 6.17. At this time 'A' Flight was based at Dover, 'B' Flight at Bekesbourne and 'C' Flight at Throwley. Only 'C' Flight appears to have had Pups, but these were soon handed over to the newly formed No.112 (Home Defence) Squadron at Throwley on 30.7.17.

Commanding Officer (Pup period):
Mjr AT Watson

Known serial numbers – A638, A6153, B1711, B1763, B1769.

No.54 Squadron
Formed 15.5.16 out of 5 Reserve Squadron at Castle Bromwich with various training aircraft, including B.E.2c, B.E.12, Avro 504, D.H.6, 1½ Strutter and Bristol Scout D. Became the first RFC Pup squadron 11.16, the training aircraft being withdrawn 12.16. Moved to London Colney 22.12.16. Went to France 24.12.16, initially St.Omer (1 AD), then to Bertangles 26.12.16 to join 14th Wing 4th Brigade. To Chipilly 1.11.17. Two flights to Flez 22.4.17, followed next day by the third flight. To Bray Dunes 18.6.17, transferring to 3rd Wing 4th Brigade, returning to 14th Wing 4th Brigade 3.7.17. To Leffrinckhoucke 16.7.17. To Teteghem 8.9.17. To Bruay 6.12.17 and transferred to 10th Wing 1st Brigade (part of GHQ Reserve). Re-equipped with Camels 12.17, moving to La Houssoye 18.12.17 to join 22nd Wing 5th Brigade.

Commanding Officer (Pup period):
Mjr KK Horn throughout.

Known serial numbers – A627, A629 to A654, A661, A668, A669, A671, A672, A673, A6165 to A6168, A6171, A6172, A6174, A6182, A6183, A6184, A6189, A6192, A6196, A6199, A6202, A6203, A6205, A6209, A6210, A6211, A6215, A6217, A6238, A6240, A7306, A7307, A7308, A7312, A7315, A7330, A7331, A7334, A7339, A7344 ('F'), A7346, B1701, B1702, B1704, B1712, B1713, B1721 ('3'), B1726, B1729, B1730, B1732, B1742, B1744, B1757, B1759, B1761, B1770, B1776, B1779, B1780, B1782, B1783, B1784, B1791, B1792, B1793, B1796, B1799, B1800, B1814, B1834, B2151, B2155, B2156, B2160, B2161, B2174, B2223, B5911, B5912, B5913, B5916 to B5921, B5923 to B5926.

Squadron identification markings:
Horizontal white bar along the top edge of the fuselage sides.

No.61 Squadron
Reformed on 24.7.17 at Rochford from a nucleus of 37 Sqdn as a Home Defence squadron, being part of the 50th (Home Defence) Wing in the 6th Brigade with a variety of aircraft, the initial complement comprising 16 Pups. A few Pups were still on strength when it disbanded on 13.6.19.

Commanding Officers:
Mjr ER Pretyman 24.7.17 – 12.3.18
Mjr EM Murray MC 13.3.18 – 17.4.18
Mjr E Henty 18.4.18 – 24.9.18
Mjr EB Mason from 25.9.18

Known serial numbers – A653, A6243, A6245, A6246, A6248, A6249, B735, B1723, B1764, B1765, B1771, B1774, B1805, B1806, B1808 to B1812, B2157, B2159, B2194, B2216, B2222, B5307, B5904, B5905, B5907, B5927.

No.62 Squadron

Mainly equipped with F.E.2Bs, it had at least two Pups at Rendcomb in 10.17. Part of the 21st Wing, it eventually left for France on 21.1.18.

Commanding Officer (Pup period):
Mjr FW Smith

Known serial numbers – B1844, B2192.

No.64 Squadron
Stationed at Sedgeford in the 7th (Training) Wing and destined for the Western Front, it re-equipped from F.E.2Bs to D.H.5s in 6.17. A number of Pups and Avro 504As were also allotted at this time for training purposes, these being withdrawn shortly before the squadron left for France on 14.10.17.

Commanding Officer (Pup period):
Mjr BE Smythies throughout

Known serial numbers – A7311, B1786, B1787, B1788, B1789, B1839, B9440.

No.65 Squadron
Based at Wye in the 26th (Training) Wing from 6.17 and destined for the Western Front, it was equipped there until 10.17 with a miscellany of aircraft including some Pups. It re-equipped with Camels shortly before departing to France on 27.10.17.

Commanding Officer (Pup period):
Mjr Lord G Wellesley throughout.

Known serial numbers – A632, A6219, A6225, A6227, A6229, A6231, B2165, B2179?, B2199.

No.66 Squadron
Formed 30.6.16 at Filton under the 21st (Training) Wing with various training aircraft including B.E.2b, B.E.2c, B.E.2d, B.E.2e, B.E.12 and Avro 504A. It received its first Pups 1.2.17, and the training aircraft were withdrawn 5.2.17. The squadron started to move to France 3.3.17, its aircraft went 17.3.17, initially at St.Omer (1 AD). To Vert Galant 8.3.17 and joined 9th Wing GHQ Brigade. To Liettres (Estrée Blanche) 31.5.17. Temporarily left the front line for Home Defence duties 20.6.17, based at Calais and under the control of C-in-C Home Forces. Returned Liettres (Estrée Blanche) under 9th Wing 5th Brigade 6.7.17Exchanged Pups for Camels from 15.10.17 to 20.10.17.

Commanding Officers (Pup period):
Mjr OT Boyd MC 19.1.17 to 22.6.17
Mjr GLP Henderson MC 23.6.17 to 15.10.17
Mjr R Gregory MC 16.10.17 to 23.1.18

Squadron identification markings:
Full length horizontal white bar along the centre of the fuselage sides.

No.70 Squadron
Equipped with Sopwith 1½ Strutters, it briefly had one Pup on strength at Fienvillers in 11.16, the squadron being part of the 10th Wing at that time.

Commanding Officer (Pup period):
Mjr GAK Lawrence DSO

Known serial number – A626.

No.71 (Australian) Squadron
Formed 27.3.17 in the 21st (Training) Wing at Castle Bromwich, it was initially equipped with an assortment of training

aircraft, including at least one Pup. It re-equipped with Camels in 11.17, then left for France on 18.12.17, becoming No.4 Squadron, Australian Flying Corps on 14.1.18.

Commanding Officer (Pup period):
Mjr Sheldon throughout

Known serial number – B5943.

No.72 Squadron
Based in the 4th Wing at Netheravon from 7.17, it had a variety of aircraft, including several Pups. The squadron moved to Sedgeford on 1.11.17, then left for the Persian Gulf on 25.12.17.

Commanding Officer (Pup period):
Mjr HW von Poelnitz throughout
Known serial numbers – B5901, B5903, B5961?

No.73 Squadron
Based at Lilbourne in the 25th (Training) Wing from 7.17 and destined for the Western Front, it was equipped there with Camels. At this time it also received a number of Pups and Avro 504As which were discarded shortly before departing to France on 9.1.18.

Commanding Officer (Pup period):
Mjr HFA Gordon from 5.7.17 to 9.11.17
Mjr T O'Hubbard from 10.11.17.

Known serial numbers – A6222, A6231, A7317, A7343, B1705, B5932, B5956, B5957, B5965, B5966, B6040.

No.74 Squadron
Based in the 18th Wing at London Colney from 10.7.17 with a variety of aircraft including quite a number of Pups, it re-equipped with S.E.5As and moved to Goldhanger on 25. 3.18, then left for France on 30.3.18.

Commanding Officers:
Unknown to 28.2.18
Mjr AWS Dore DSO 1.3.18 to 7.3.18
Mjr KL Caldwell MC DFC & Bar from 8.3.18.

Known serial numbers – A662, A6222, A62632, A6235, B877, B1737, B2163, B5285, B5290, B5313, B5347, B5354, B5380, B7482, B7487, B7490, B7492, B7493, B7494.

No.76 Squadron
Based as a Home Defence squadron with headquarters at Racecourse Building, Ripon as part of the 46th (Home Defence) Wing in the 6th Brigade it had a motley collection of aircraft, these including a number of Pups by about 9.18 – 10.18. At this time 'A' Flight was based at Copmanthorpe, 'B' Flight at Helperby and 'C' Flight at Catterick. It is conjectured that the Pups were with 'A' Flight, since one aircraft was coded 'A7'.

Commanding Officers:
Mjr AC Wilson 1.2.18 to 3.19

Known serial numbers – B1807 ('A7'), B2209, C306.

No.80 Squadron
Based from 6.19 at Aboukir in Egypt with Snipes. The squadron was renumbered on 1.2.20 to become No.56 Squadron. A few Pups were on strength in this period.

Commanding Officers:
Mjr DV Bell to 1.19
Mjr G Allen 1.19 to 2.19.
Mjr CM Leman 2.19 to 1.2.20

Known serial numbers – C478, C480, D4082, D4115, D4116.

No.81 Squadron
Based at Scampton in the 23rd (Training) Wing by 7.17 with Camels and Pups, it was disbanded on 4.7.18 on being merged into No.34 TDS at the same base.

Commanding Officers:
Unknown

Known serial numbers – A627, A6224, A6226, B1801, B2164, B2166, B2231, B5352, B6124, B6126, B7499, B7502, B7504, B7539, C239, C257.

No.85 Squadron
Based at Hounslow in the 18th (Training) Wing from 27.11.17 and destined for the Western Front, it was equipped there with Avro 504s and Pups. It received S.E.5As shortly before departing to France on 22.5.18.

Commanding Officer (Pup period):
Mjr RA Archer to 3.18
Mjr WA Bishop VC DSO MC from 3.18.

Known serial numbers – A6239, B735, B1804, B2154, B2187, B5285, B5306, B5353, B5354, B5376, B5383, B5389, B7481, B7483, C273.

No.86 Squadron
Moved on 16.12.17 to Northolt in the 18th Wing with a mixture of Avro 504s, Camels and Pups, disbanding into No.30 TDS there on 4.7.18.

Commanding Officers:
Mjr DO Mulholland by 4.18 – 8.18

Known serial numbers – B850, B1774, B2159, B5285, B5325, B5333, B5348, B5356, B5380, B5920, B6133, B7492, D4184.

No.87 Squadron
Based at Sedgeford in the 7th (Training) Wing from 15.9.17 until moving on 19.12.17 to Hounslow and joining the 18th (Training) Wing. Destined for the Western Front, it was equipped during this period with a miscellany of aircraft including some Pups. Its main equipment of Dolphins arrived in 1.18, but some Pups were retained until shortly before departing to France on 24.4.18.

Commanding Officer (Pup period):
Capt CJW Darwin to 11.2.18
Mjr JC Callaghan from 12.2.18.

Known serial numbers – B1758, B1789, B1804, B1812, B2187, B2230, B2248, B2250, B5251, B5252, B5256, B5313, B5324, B5353, B5360, B5376, B5384, B5389, B5903, B7481, B9440, B9931, C273, C8653.

No.88 Squadron
Based at Harling Road in the 26th (Training) Wing with Bristol F.2Bs, at least two Pups were on strength around 12.17 – 1.18.

Commanding Officer (Pup period):
Unknown.

Known serial numbers – B5953, B6018.

No.89 Squadron
Based from 7.8.17 at Harling Road in the 26th (Training) Wing A' and 'B' Flights were equipped with Pups from 10.17, whilst 'C' Flight had Camels. The squadron later transferred to the 39th (Training) Wing when it formed on 27.10.17, then moved to Upper Heyford on 15.7.18 before disbanding there on 29.7.18

Commanding Officers:
Unknown to 25.12.17
Mjr AC Clarke 26.12.17 to 29.7.18

Known serial numbers – B5287, B5306, B5925, B5952, B5955, B6008, B6101.

No.90 Squadron
Some Pups on strength in 1.18 at North Shotwick (later renamed Sealand) in 37th (Training) Wing. It re-equipped with Dolphins on moving to Brockworth on 15.7.18, but disbanded there on 29.7.18.

Commanding Officers:
Mjr J Blackwood to 24.5.18   Capt Burdett 25.5.18 to 29.7.18

Known serial numbers – A6166, A6203, C224, C230, C231, C275, C276, C278, C279, C1522.

No.91 Squadron
Based from 14.9.17 at Chattis Hill in 34th (Training) Wing with some Pups on strength. Moved on 15.3.18 to Tangmere in 18th Wing, the Pups being discarded around the time it moved to Coventry on 27.7.18.

Commanding Officer:
Unknown

Known serial numbers – B2219, B5265, B5360, B5376, B6131, B6133, C267, C269, C272, D4186.

No.92 Squadron
Based from 3.10.17 at Chattis Hill in 34th (Training) Wing with some Pups on strength. Moved on 19.3.18 to Tangmere in 18th Wing, the Pups being discarded shortly before it went to France with S.E.5As on 2.7.18.

Commanding Officers:
Capt PAO Leask 1.9.17 to 4.18
Mjr A Coningham DSO MC from 4.18

Known serial numbers – B1804, B5255, B5269, B5270, B5303, B5311, B5324, B6019, B6067, B6131, C209, C233, D4145.

No.93 Squadron
Based from 14.9.17 at Chattis Hill in 34th (Training) Wing with some Pups on strength. Moved on 17.3.18 to Tangmere in 18th Wing, but disbanded there on 17.8.18.

Commanding Officers:
Mjr DJ Joy in 2.18

Known serial numbers – B1804, B5255, B5285, B5291, B5292, B5297, B5964, B7481, C266.

No.94 Squadron
Based from 2.8.17 at Harling Road in 26th (Training) Wing mainly with S.E.5As and Pups. Transferred to the newly-formed 39th (Training) Wing on 27.10.17, then moved on 27.7.18 to Shoreham and to Upper Heyford on 19.8.18 where it was fully equipped with S.E.5As before going overseas on 31.10.18

Commanding Officers:
Mjr AJ Capel to 28.2.18

Known serial numbers – A6229, A7318, B2165, B2199, B2223, B2248, B2250, B5289, B5363, B5368, B5369, B5383, B6010, B6095, B6139, B6140, B8829, C297, C300, C8654, C9993, D4207.

No.95 Squadron
North Shotwick 2.18 - 7.18

Commanding Officer:
Unknown

Known serial numbers – A6203, B5331, B6144, B7153, C202, C225, C231, C275, C278, C1531, D4166.

No.96 Squadron
North Shotwick 3.18 - 7.18
Equipped with Pups, Avro 504s and Dolphins by 3.18 at North Shotwick in 37th (Training) Wing, disbanding there on 4.7.18

Commanding Officer:
Unknown

Known serial numbers – A6203, C276, C279, C330, C331, C1531, D4013, D4154.

No.98 Squadron
Had a variety of aircraft including a small number of Pups by late 1917 at Old Sarum (formerly known as Ford Farm). It began re-equipping with D.H.9s in 2.18, then went overseas on 1.3.18.

Commanding Officers:
Mjr ELML Gower 21.9.17 to 18.12.17
Capt EAB Rice 19.12.17 to 18.2.18
Mjr HmacD O'Malley from 19.2.18

Known serial number – B2196.

No.100 Squadron
Briefly had one Pup on strength at Treizennes 9.17 – 10.17.

Commanding Officer:
Mjr MG Christie DSO MC

Known serial number – B1833.

No.102 Squadron
Briefly had one Pup on strength at Treizennes to 10.17.

Commanding Officer:
Mjr H Wyllie

Known serial number – A657.

No.103 Squadron
Briefly had one Pup on strength at Old Sarum 1.18.

Commanding Officer:
Mjr T Maxwell-Scott

Known serial number – B2196.

No.112 Squadron
Formed 25.7.17 from 'B' Flt No.50 Sqdn at Detling, then moved on 30.7.17 to Throwley in the 49th (Home Defence) Wing equipped mainly with Pups initially. Transferred to the newly-formed 53rd (Home Defence) Wing on 8.2.18, and began re-equipping with Camels, but still had some Pups in 5.18.

Commanding Officers:
Mjr G Allen 30.7.17 to 20.11.17
Mjr BF Moore from 21.11.17 but appointment not filled.
Mjr CA Ridley DSO MC 3.12.17 – 12.2.18
Mjr CJQ Brand DSO MC DFC from 13.2.18

Known serial numbers – A638, A6153, B1711, B1722, B1763, B1769, B1772, B1773, B1803, B1806 ('C6'), B1807, B1810, B2158, B2178, B2194, B2195, B2210, B5296, B5910.

No.141 Squadron
Formed 1.1.18 at Rochford in 49th (Home Defence) Wing. Briefly had one Pup on strength 1.18

Commanding Officer:
Mjr P Babington NC

Known serial numbers – none.

No.143 Squadron
Formed 1.2.18 from a flight of No.112 Squadron at Throwley in 53rd (Home Defence) Wing, moving on 14.2.18 to Detling where it disbanded on 31.10.19. Had a small number of Pups until 7.19.

Commanding Officers:
Mjr F Sowrey DSO MC 14.3.18 to 11.18.

Known serial numbers – A6245, B1724.

No.158 Squadron
Nucleus formed at Upper Heyford with a few Pups by 7.18 – 8.18. Officially formed there 4.9.18 intended for Sopwith Salamanders but disbanded on 20.11.18.

Known serial numbers – B2213, B5297, C266.

No.251 Squadron
One Pup known to have been with 506 Flt 251 Sqdn at Owthorne by 10.18 to at least 6.11.18.

Known serial number – B2218 (white fin with spitting cat).

No.1 Squadron Canadian Air Force
Formed 20.11.18 (also known as No.81 Sqdn RAF) equipped mainly with Dolphins plus various types including a few Pups. Moved 1.5.19 to Shoreham with S.E.5As, being reduced to a Number Plate basis 6.19 then disbanded 28.1.20.

Known serial numbers – B4158, B4338(?), B5333.

Other RFC/RAF units partially or wholly equipped with Pups

No.1 Reserve Squadron, became No.1 Training Squadron
In 17th Wing at Gosport, No.1 RS had an official establishment by 12.16 of 6 Bleriot XI, 6 Avro 504 and 6 Pup, but the earliest Pup know to have actually been flown by the unit was not until shortly after it became No.1 TS on 31.5.17. The unit was disbanded into the School of Special Flying at Gosport on 2.8.17.
No.1 TS reformed on 1.10.17 at Narborough in 7th Wing, moving to Port Meadow (21st Wing) on 10.10.17, then Beaulieu (17th Wing) on 6.12.17. Here it was equipped mainly with Pups and Camels, eventually disbanding into the newly-formed No.29 TDS on 27.7.18

Known serial numbers – A7345, B803, B2239, B5330, B5913, B5964, B5974, B7517, C201, D4075.

No.2 Training Squadron
Had a few Pups on strength in 1918 at Northolt.

Known serial numbers – B1758, C403, C404, D4187.

No.3 Training Squadron
Had a number of Pups on strength by 12.17 at Shoreham (7th Wing), until disbanding into No.21 TDS 15.7.18

Known serial numbers – A662, A6235, B1802, B1803, B2152, B5336, B5338, B5344, B5385 ('6'), N6096.

No.4 Training Squadron
Had a few Pups on strength in 1918 at Northolt.

Known serial numbers – C3500, D4016.

No.6 Training Squadron
Equipped by 10.17 with Avro 504, Camel and Pup at Catterick (19th Wing), moving 24.11.17 to Montrose where it disbanded into No.32 TDS 15.7.18

Known serial numbers – B1751, B2207, B4124, B4137, B4141, B5260, B5275, B5329, B6081, B7485, B7486, B7487, B7495, B7496, B7528, B7573, C381, C4295, D4030, D4032, D4141.

No.7 Training Squadron
It has been suggested that C242 was on the strength of 7 TS at Netheravon, but as this was mainly equipped with Bristol F.2b and Shorthorn it may be incorrect.

No.10 Training Squadron

Mainly equipped with Avro 504, Camel and Pup by 12.17 at Shawbury (29th Wing), moving 7.4.18 to Lilbourne (25th Wing), then 25.6.18 to Gosport where it may then have discarded its Pups.

Known serial numbers – B804, B1844, B1849 ('B'), B1850, B2191, B2192, B2245, B5295, B5335, B5341, B5381 ('A'), B6038, B6039, B6092, B6141.

No.11 Training Squadron
Had a mixture of type by 7.17 at Spittlegate (24th Wing) including a few Pups, moved to Scampton (23rd Wing) 15.9.17 and disbanded there into No.34 TDS 15.7.18.

Known serial numbers – A6218, B1743, B5322, B6128, B7542, D4127.

No.17 Training Squadron
Based at Yatesbury (28th Wing) in 1918 with D.H.6, R.E.8 and B.E.2e, at least one Pup (A7317) has been identified with this unit. Though confirmation is lacking.

No.18 Training Squadron
Equipped by 10.17 with Avro 504, Camel and Pup at Montrose (30th Wing), where it disbanded into No.32 TDS 15.7.18.

Known serial numbers – B5260, B5275, B5277, B5278, B5279, B5329, B5349, B5350, B5379, B6020, B6077, B6081, B6105, B7489, B7491, B7545, B7575, C287, C4295, D4024.

No.22 Training Squadron
Equipped by 5.18 with various types including Pups at Aboukir, Egypt (20th Wing). The unit became part of No.60 TDS on 1.12.18 but retained its identity until being reduced to cadre 14.6.19.

Known serial numbers – B6041, B6042, B6046, B6053, B6059, B6102, B6108, B6113, B6114, C414, C474, C475, C478, C479, C480, C1493, D4056, D4098, D4100, D4113, D4114.

No.23 Training Squadron
A few Pups on strength at Aboukir, Egypt (20th Wing). The unit became part of No.60 TDS on 1.12.18 but retained its identity until being reduced to cadre 14.6.19.

Known serial numbers – C1493, C1540, D4117.

No.25 Training Squadron
At least two Pups on strength in 1918 at Thetford (26th Wing). The unit disbanded into No.35 TDS.

Known serial numbers – B5351, C299.

No.27 Training Squadron
Reformed 22.3.18 with various types including Pups at London Colney (18th Wing), moving 7.18 to Driffield (19th Wing)

where it disbanded into No.21 TDS on 15.7.18.

Known serial numbers – A7324, B4189, B4196, B5353, B6087, C401, C402, D4177, D4183, D4189, D4196.

No.28 Training Squadron
Equipped with S.E.5A, Avro 504 and Pup by 12.17 at Castle Bromwich (25th Wing), possibly until moving 1.7.18 to Hounslow (18th Wing) where it disbanded into No.42 TDS on 15.7.18.
Known serial numbers – A6215, B2179, B5331, B5351, B5943, B5956,B5957, B5966, B7533.

No.29 Training Squadron (Australian Flying Corps)
(1) A few Pups on strength late 1917 at Shawbury, where it became 5th (Training) Sqdn AFC on 14.1.18.
(2) Reformed No.29 Training Squadron RAF on 1.8.18 at Hendon with at least one Pup.

Known serial numbers – (1) A6249, B1748, B2157, B2192, B4196; (2) B6074.

No.30 Training Squadron (Australian Flying Corps)
A few Pups on strength late 1917 at Ternhill, where it became 6th (Training) Sqdn AFC on 14.1.18.

Known serial numbers – A6249, B6089, B6090, B6191.

No.34 Training Squadron
Equipped with various types including a few Pups by 7.17 at Ternhill (29th Wing), moving 18.3.18 to Chattis Hill (34th Wing) where it disbanded into No.43 TDS on 15.7.18.

Known serial numbers – A651, A7310, B5283, B5293, B5314.

No.36 Training Squadron
Equipped from 1.18 with Avro 504, Camel and Pup at Montrose (30th Wing) where it disbanded into No.26 TDS at Edzell on 15.7.18.

Known serial numbers – B2207, B5260, B5278, B5351, B6077, B6079, B6080, B6081, B6104, B6105, B7485, B7489, B7495, B7496, B7529, B7572, C285, C288, C4295, D4035, D4135.

No.39 Training Squadron
A few Pups on strength by 4.18 at South Carlton (23rd Wing) where it disbanded into No.46 TDS on 27.7.18.

Known serial numbers – B2228, B6127, C261.

No.40 Reserve Squadron, became No.40 Training Squadron
Numerous Pups on strength from 4.17 at Port Meadow (Oxford) (21st Wing), being renamed from No.40 RS to No.40 TS on 31.5.17. Moved the following day to Croydon, then on 14.12.18 to Tangmere where it disbanded into No.61 TDS 15.12.18.

Known serial numbers – A649, A650, A6180, A6185, A6187, A6228, A6232, A7318, A7319, A7322, A7341, A7349, A7350, B1738, B5252, B5314, B5370, B6093, B6094, C210, C405, D4078.

No.41 Training Squadron
Possibly the only Pup on strength, A7311 was taken to Doncaster (8th Wing) by Lt J.T.B.McCudden on 7 May 1917.

No.42 Reserve Squadron, became No.42 Training Squadron
Equipped with various types including Pups from late 1917 at Hounslow (18th Wing), moving on 16.12.17 to Wye (6th Wing), where the type was flown until at least 5.18.

Known serial numbers – A7311, B2236, B5271, B5285, B5288, B5321, B5323, B7752, C3503, D4079.

No.43 Reserve Squadron, became No.43 Training Squadron
At Ternhill (25th Wing) by 12.16 with an establishment of 6 Avro 504, 6 Bristol Scout D and 6 Pup. Renamed from 43 RS to 43 TS on 31.5.17 and moved on 20.3.18 to Chattis Hill (34th Wing) where it disbanded into No.43 TDS on 15.7.18

Known serial numbers – A651, A653, A655, A656, A657, A7326, A7338, B1708, Bb1813, B2192, B5272, B5387, B6039, B6040, B6142, B7510, B7517.

No.45 Training Squadron
At least one Pup on strength in 1917 at South Carlton.

Known serial numbers – B1749.

No.48 Reserve Squadron, became No.48 Training Squadron
At least two Pups on strength of No.48 RS at Waddington in 5.17, this becoming No.48 TS on 31.5.17.

Known serial numbers – B1735, B1736.

No.54 Training Squadron
Some Pups on strength by 10.17 at Harlaxton (24th Wing). Moved on 12.12.17 to Castle Bromwich (25th Wing), then on 6.7.18 to Eastbourne (60th Wing) where it became No.50 TDS on 15.7.18.

Known serial numbers – A7317, A7343, B2243 to B2246, B5275, B5332, B5334, B5932, B7501, B7512, B7518, C213, C215, D4207.

No.55 Reserve Squadron, became No.55 Training Squadron
Had a few Pups at Yatesbury by 2.17, moving on 23.7.17 to Gosport where it was absorbed into the School of Special Flying on 2.8.17. Later reformed and had a few Pups at Lilbourne by 5.18.

Known serial numbers – A6193, A7334, B1753, B2196, B5990?, B7518?, B7535.

No.56 Reserve Squadron, became No.56 Training Squadron
No.56 RS London Colney had Pups on strength at the time it became No.56 TS on 31.5.17, until at least 6.18. It became No.41 TDS on 15.7.18 but no evidence has to come to light as to whether this new unit had Pups.

Known serial numbers – A6185, A6187, A6214, B1738, B1739, B1758, B2152 to B2154, B2185, B2214, B2233, B2234, B5259, B5281, B5284, B5288, B5386, B5942, B6006, B6007, B6085, B6086, B7482, B9931, C239, C269, C279.

No.58 Training Squadron
Had several Pups at Suez. Egypt (32nd Wing later 69th Wing) by 7.18 to at least 12.18.

Known serial numbers – B4121?, B6041, B6044, B6106, B6107, B6111, C254, C1546, D4103.

No.60 Training Squadron
Had Pups on strength by 3.18 at Scampton (23rd Wing) until becoming No.34 TDS on 15.7.18.

Known serial numbers – B5345, B5907, B725.

No.61 Training Squadron
Had several Pups on strength by 5.18 at South Carlton (23rd Wing), possibly until disbanding into No.28 TDS at Weston-on-the-Green on 27.7.18

Known serial numbers – B2218, B5282, B7500, B7505, B7520, C261.

No.62 Training Squadron
Formed 31.5.17 (28th Wing) and moved next day to Dover (6th Wing) with some Pups on strength. Moved again to Hounslow on 1.5.18, disbanding there on 15.7.18 into No.42 TDS Dover.

Known serial numbers – B1714, B1740, B6067, B6088, C273, C350, C367, C369, D4195.

No.63 Training Squadron
Formed 31.5.17 at Ternhill (25th Wing), moving next day to Joyce Green (6th Wing) where it had Pups on strength until at least 8.18.

Known serial numbers – A662, A674, A6221, A6223, A6230, A6231, A6233 to A6235, A7311, B2198, B9440.

No.65 Training Squadron
Based from 25.11.17 at Dover (6th Wing) where it had a few Pups on strength by 1.18 to at least 4.18.

Known serial numbers – B5312, B5297, B6069, C3502.

No.67 Training Squadron
Had Pups on strength by 12.17 at Shawbury (29th Wing), moving on 1.4.18 to North Shotwick where it disbanded into No.51 TDS on 15.7.18.

Known serial numbers – B804, B1844, B1850, B5399, B6090 to B6092, B6141, B6142, B6144, B6145, B7519, C216, C218, C219, D4014, D4202.

No.70 Training Squadron
Moved on 1.1.18 to Beaulieu (17th Wing) where it had several Pups on strength throughout, eventually disbanding into No.28 TDS at Weston-on-the-Green on 27.7.18.

Known serial numbers – B5310, B5901, B5974, B6015, B6074, C201, C294, D4076, D4077, D4181.

No.73 Training Squadron
Had Pups on strength by 12.17 at Turnhouse (30th Wing), moving on 20.2.18 to Beaulieu where it was disbanded into No.28 TDS at Weston-on-the-Green on 27.7.18.

Known serial numbers – B2247, B5274 to B5276, B5379, B5975, B6016, B6077, B6078, B6105, C275.

No.74 Training Squadron
Had Pups on strength by 2.18 at Castle Bromwich (25th Wing), moving on 27.6.18 to Tadcaster (8th Wing) until disbanding into No.26 TDS at Edzell on 15.7.18.

Known serial numbers – A7343, B2182, B2203, B2245, B5965, B7515, B7553.

No.187 (Night) Training Squadron
Believed to have had at least one Pup on strength when formed 1.4.18 at East Retford.

Commanding Officer (Pup period):
Mjr TR Irons.

Known serial numbers – none.

No.188 (Night) Training Squadron
Strength included 12 Pups in 4.18 at East Retford. Moved to Throwley 5.5.18 and still had Pups in 10.18.

Commanding Officers:
Mjr CB Cooke from 20.3.18 to at least 10.18

Known serial numbers – B1769, B2202, B2209, C303.

No.189 (Night) Training Squadron
Strength included Pups by 6.18 – 9.18 at Sutton's Farm.

Commanding Officers (Pup period):
Mjr HS Powell from 18.2.18 to at least 10.18

Known serial numbers – B5907, C303, C305, C306, C308, C309, C312.

No.190 (Night) Training Squadron
Strength included at least one Pups by 9.18 at Newmarket.

Commanding Officers (Pup period):
Mjr AdeB Brandon DSP MC

Known serial number –C309.

No.195 Training Squadron
Strength included Pups when absorbed into 19 TDS 21.7.18.

Known serial numbers – B6058, B6112.

No.198 (Night) Training Squadron
Formed 21.12.17 at Rochford with Pups on strength until disbanded 5.19

Commanding Officers:
Capt CO Usborne AFC (became Mjr 2.2.18) to 6.10.18
Capt LF Beynon from 7.10.18.

Known serial numbers – A6247, B849, B1803, B1807, B1848, B2194, B2216, B5304, B5905, B5907, C303, C306, C309.

5th (Training) Squadron, Australian Flying Corps
Formed 14.1.18 ex No.29 TS (AFC) at Shawbury with some Pups on strength, moving on 2.4.18 to Minchinhampton. (all pilots for 3rd Squadron AFC graduated from this unit from Septemebr 1918. Disbanded March 1919.

Known serial numbers – A6159, B1833, B2157, B4195, B7508, B7509, D4152, D4153, D4157, D4159, D4164, D4167, D4170, D4171.

6th (Training) Squadron, Australian Flying Corps
Formed 14.1.18 ex No.30 TS (AFC) at Ternhill with some Pups on strength, moving on 25.4.18 to Minchinhampton.

Known serial numbers – A6159, B1764, B1833, B2157, B7506, B7507, B5912, D4153, D4157, D4164, D4167, D4170, D4171.

8th (Training) Squadron, Australian Flying Corps
Formed 14.1.18 ex No.33 TS (AFC) at Minchinhampton with some Pups on strength, moving on 25.2.18 to Leighterton.

Known serial numbers – D4170, D4173, D4179, D4191.

No.1 Training Depot Station
Had at least one Pup at Stamford (Wittering) (35th Wing) by 8.18

Known serial number - C299.

No.2 Training Depot Station
Formed 14.4.18 at West Fenton (Gullane) (30th Wing) with some Pups on strength to at least 7.18.

Known serial numbers – B4135, B5260, B5349, B5350, B5379, B7486, B7496, D4027, D4028, D4031, D4032, D4135.

No.3 Training Depot Station
Formed 5.9.17 at Lopcombe Corner (34th Wing) with some Pups on strength until at least 10.18.

Known serial numbers – A7324, B1802, B2265, B5253, B5254, B5257, B5310, B5326, B5385, B5967, B5995, B6017, B6136, B9931, C264, C280, D4031.

No.4 Training Depot Station
Based at Hooton Park (37th Wing) from 19.9.17 with Dolphins, Avro 504s, Camels, and also Pups until at least 1.19.

Known serial numbers – A6166, A6203, A6238, B1742, B1743, B1850, B4159, B5921, B5972, B6035, B6036, B6039, B6085, B6089 to B6092, B6146 to B6148, B6150, B7513, C202 to C204, C206, C207, C216, C218, C219, C222, C224, C225, C227, C228, C230, C231, C234, C272, C275, D4011, D4012, D4106, D4109, D4111, D4158, D4159.

No.5 Training Depot Station
Based at Easton-on-the-Hill (Stamford) (35th Wing) with at least one Pup on strength by 5.18.

Known serial number – B5902.

No.7 Training Depot Station
Based at Feltwell (39th Wing) with Pups on strength by 6.18 to at least 7.18.

Known serial numbers – B1784, B5383, B6026, B6140, C299, C9990, C9991.

No.10 Training Depot Station
Based at Harling Road (39th Wing) with a small number of Pups on strength by 10.18

Known serial numbers – B2184, B5374?

No.11 Training Depot Station
Formed 1.4.18 at Old Sarum (33rd Wing) with Pups on strength, moving in 11.18 to Boscombe Down (33rd Wing) still with some Pups.

Known serial numbers – B5327, B5362, C263.

No.15 Training Depot Station
Based at Hucknall (27th Wing) with at least one Pup on strength in 10.18.

Known serial number – D4174.

No.16 Training Depot Station
Formed 21.7.18 ex No.194 TS at Amriya, Egypt (20th Wing) with a few Pups on strength until at least 10.18.

Known serial numbers – B6009, C324, C476.

No.18 Training Depot Station
Based at Ismailia, Egypt (32nd Wing) with at least one Pup on strength by 3.19.

Known serial number – B6047.

No.19 Training Depot Station
Formed 21.7.18 ex No.195 TS at El Rimal, Egypt (32nd Wing later 69th Wing) mainly with Avro 504 and Pups until 3.19.

Known serial numbers – B6046 to B6048, B6054, B6058, B6101, B6102, B6109, B6110, B6112, C246 to C251, C348, C349, C473, C1492, C1547, C1549, C1550, D4082, D4084.

No.20 Training Depot Station
Formed 21.7.18 with D.H.6s at Amriya (20th Wing), moving 21.8.18 to Shallufa (32nd Wing) and re-equipping with Avro 504s, S.E.5As and Pups. Returned to Amriya 11.18 and flew Pups until at least 2.19.

Known serial numbers – B6056, B6060, C473, C476, D4084, D4099, C4103, C4142.

No.26 Training Depot Station
Formed 15.7.18 frpom Nos.36 and 74 TSs at Edzell (20th Group) with a few Pups on strength.

Known serial numbers – B7523, B7573, B7575, C235.

No.27 Training Depot Station
Had a few Pups on strength at Crail by 10.18.

Known serial numbers – B6088, D4026.

No.28 Training Depot Station
Formed 27.7.18 from Nos.61, 70 and 73 TSs at Weston-on-the-Green (21st Wing) with a few Pups on strength until at least 8.18.

Known serial numbers – B5291, B5310.

No.29 Training Depot Station
Formed 27.7.18 from Nos.1 & 73 TSs at Beaulieu (17th Wing) with some Pups until at least 9.18.

Known serial numbers – B5291, B5306, D4176.

No.30 Training Depot Station
Formed 15.7.18 from Nos.2 & 4 TSs at Northolt (18th Wing) with some Pups on strength until at least 10.18.

Known serial numbers – B1796, B5354, B7752, C212, C403, C404, C3500, D4018, D4120, D4186.

No.31 Training Depot Station
Formed 19.8.18 from 58 TS at Wyton moving next day to Fowlmere (26th Wing) with at least one Pup on strength in 12.18.

Known serial number – B5902.

No.32 Training Depot Station
Formed 15.7.18 from Nos.6 & 18 TSs at Montrose (30th Group) with Avro 504s, S.E.5As, Camels and Pups, the Pups being in use until at least 11.18.

Known serial numbers - B2207, B5349, B5350, B5965, B6081, B6105, B7496, B7503, B7523, B7543, B7572, B7573, B7575, C235, C285, C288, C388, C4295, D4023 to D4025, D4027, D4028, D4030, D4032, D4037, D4133.

No.34 Training Depot Station
Formed 15.7.18 from No.11 TS, No.60 TS & No.81 Sqdn at Scampton (23rd Wing) with mainly with Avro 504s and Camels, with some Pups on strength until at least 12.18.

Known serial numbers – B2227, B2235, B2243, B5352, B62126, C234, D4127, D4128, D4129.

No.35 Training Depot Station
Formed 15.7.18 from Nos.12 & 25 TSs at Thetford (26th Wing), moving to Duxford 21.8.18. Some Pups on strength.

Known serial number – B6010.

No.37 Training Depot Station
Formed 15.7.18 from Nos.13 & 66 TSs at Yatesbury (28th Wing) with some Pups on strength until at least 9.18.

Known serial number – B2164.

No.38 Training Depot Station
Formed 15.7.18 from Nos.16 & 17 TSs at Tadcaster (28th Wing), with some Pups on strength until at least 11.18.

Known serial number – B4181, B6083.

No.41 Training Depot Station
Formed 15.7.18 from No.51 TS at London Colney (18th Wing until 18.9.18 then 56th Wing) with some Pups on strength until disbanded in 10.19.

Known serial numbers – A6239, A7324, B4158, B5234, B5932, B6138, C210, C256, C269, C1526, D4017, D4019, D4078, D4081, N6197, N6198.

No.42 Training Depot Station
Formed 15.7.18 from Nos.28 & 62 TSs at Hounslow (18th Wing) with Pups, 504s, Camels and Snipes on strength until disbanded in 7.19.

Known serial numbers – B1777, B1796, B4158, B5332, B5932, B7752, C212, C256, C280, C391 to C393, C1526, C3500, D4-81, D4192, D4195.

No.43 Training Depot Station
Formed 15.7.18 from Nos.34 & 43 TSs at Chattis Hill with Avro 504s, Camels and Pups on strength until disbanded 15.5.19.

Known serial numbers – B4123, B5271, B5276, B5314 ('C'), B5365, B5944, B6025, C431.

No.44 Training Depot Station
Formed 15.7.18 from Nos.35 & 71 TSs at Port Meadow (Oxford) (21st Wing), moving to Bicester 1.10.18. At least one Pup on strength 1.19

Known serial number – B6128.

No.46 Training Depot Station
Formed 27.7.18 from Nos.39 & 45 TSs at South Carlton (23rd Wing). At least one Pup on strength 10.18.

Known serial number – C258.

No.47 Training Depot Station
Formed 15.7.18 from Nos.41 & 49 TSs at Doncaster (8th wing later 23rd Wing) with some Pups on strength 9.18.

Known serial numbers – B4136, C420.

No.50 Training Depot Station
Formed 15.7.18 from No.54 TS & No.206 TDS at Eastbourne (60th Wing later 6th Wing) with some Pups until at least 1.19.

Known serial numbers – B2213, B5376, B6100, C215, C253, D4016.

No.51 Training Depot Station
Formed 15.7.18 from Nos.55 & 67 TSs at North Shotwick with Pups on strength until at least 8.18.

Known serial numbers – B4139, B7516, B7519, C218, D4013 to D4015, D4139.

No.53 Training Depot Station
Formed 15.7.18 from No.65 TS at Dover (60th Wing) with some Pups on strength.

Known serial numbers – D4018, D4019, D4081.

No.54 Training Depot Station
Formed 20.7.18 ex No.207 TDS at Chingford and Fairlop with a number of Pups on strength until at least 11.18.

Known serial numbers – B6085, B6097, B6098, C323, C1510, C1513 to C1515, C1519.

No.55 Training Depot Station
Formed 15.7.18 from Nos.55 & 67 TSs at Manston, moving to 12.9.18 to Narborough. At least one Pup on strength by 11.18.

Known serial number – E9996.

No.56 Training Depot Station
Formed 27.7.18 ex No.201 TDS at Cranwell (50th Wing) with Avro 504, Camels and Pups, disbanding 13.3.19.

Known serial numbers – B2181, B5391, B6061 to B6063, B6146, B8821, C265, C298, C324 to C326, C406, C408, C423, C424, D4018, D4091, D4092, D4095.

No.60 Training Depot Station
Formed 1.12.18 from Nos.22 & 23 TSs at Aboukir, Egypt (26th Group) with Pups until at least 1.19.

Known serial numbers – B4100, D474, C475, D4048, D4083, D4100, D4114.

Nos.201 & 202 Training Depot Stations
Formed 1.4.18 from RNASTE Cranwell with Pups on strength. Under a reorganisation on 17.6.18, No.201 TDS took over scout training with Avro 504s, Camels and Pups. Redesignated No.56 TDS 27.7.18.

Known serial numbers – 9903, 9925, 9935, 9936, B1825, B2173, B2181, B2183, B2202 to B2204, B2211, B2226, B5928, B5929, B5948 to B5950, B5978, B5979, B5989, B5990, B6013, B6014, B6021, B6023, B6032 to B6034, B6049, B6051 to B6054, B6075, B6076, B6143, B6146, B6149, N6160, N6168, N6171, N6192, N6196, N6209, N6436, N6465, N6467, N7227.

No.204 Training Depot Station
Formed 1.4.18 from RNAS Eastchurch Naval Flying School with a small number of Pups on strength until at least 9.18.

Known serial numbers – N6169, N6458.

No.205 Training Depot Station
Formed 1.4.18 from the RNAS Training Establishment at Vendôme with a number of Pups on strength until 10.18.

Known serial numbers – B5332, C307, C310, C313, C316, C319, C322, C325.

No.206 Training Depot Station
Formed 1.4.18 from the Eastbourne Naval Flying School, with Pups on strength, becoming No.50 TDS on 15.7.18.

Known serial numbers – B2213, B5958, B5991, B5994, B6001, B6099, B6100, C223, C229, C253, C257, C314, C320, N6199.

No.207 Training Depot Station
Formed 1.4.18 from the former naval school at Chingford and Fairlop with a number of Pups on strength. Became No.54 TDS on 20.7.18

Known serial numbers – B6018, B6086 to B6088, B6097, B6098, C304, C350, C363, C365, C367 to C370, C1513, C1515, C1519.

No.208 Training Depot Station
Formed by 6.18 (probably on 1.4.18) from the Naval Flying School at East Fortune, equipped with Pups. Redesignated the Grand Fleet School of Aerial Fighting & Gunnery on 19.7.18.

Known serial numbers – Pup 9946, B1822, B1825, B2211, C211, C220, C223, C226, C239, C283, C286, C289, C292, D4034, N6205, N6443.
Also SB.3D N6103, N6122, N6688, N6699.

No.211 Training Depot Station
Formed 1.4.18 at Portholme Meadow (26th Wing) with at least one Pup on strength; Became No.59 TDS 7.18.

Known serial number – B2202.

****

Armament Experimental Station Orfordness
Some Pups by 11.16 to at least 7.18.

Known serial numbers – A628, A6166, B1717, B1755, C1472.

Armament Experimental Station Martlesham Heath
Some Pups by 4.17 to at least 5.17.

Known serial numbers – A653, N6202.
(excluding aircraft held for carriers)

Artillery Co-operation Squadron
At least two Pups on strength at Tilshead in 1918.

Artillery and Infantry Co-operation School
Had Pups on strength at Worthy Down in 1918.

Known serial numbers – B1777, C431, D4195.

Artillery Observation School
Had Pups on strength at Almaza by 4.19 to at least 6.19.

Known serial numbers – B6044, B6107, C249, C473, C477, D4121, D4126.

No.3 (Auxiliary) School of Aerial Gunnery
A few Pups on strength by 12.17 at New Romney, disbanding into No.1 (Observers) School of Aerial Gunnery on 9.3.18.

Known serial number – B9440.

No.4 (Auxiliary) School of Aerial Gunnery
Formed 1.11.17 at Marske with Pups on strength in 1918, becoming No.2 Fighting School on 25.5.18

Known serial number – C414 ('103').

Central Flying School
Based at Upavon, had 3691 on strength for trials in 3.16 and A626 for trials in 10.16. Numerous Pups for training purposes from 12.16 until at least 7.18.

Known serial numbers – 3691, A626, A653, A658 to A660, A666, A6150, A7310, A7317, A7343, B1706, B1707, B1736, B1845, B2164, B2169, B2170, B2171, B2175, B220, B2229, B2232, B2237, B2238, B2240, B5267, B5271, B5301, B5314, B5317, B5320, B5321, B5326, B5364, B5365, B5367, B5387, B5933, B5936, B5937, B5967, B5998, B6116, B6117, C374, C376.

Experimental Depot Grain
Numerous Pups from 10.16 to at least 11.20.

Known serial numbers – 9497, 9498, 9901, 9912, 9921, 9922, 9939, 9940 (War Flight), 9949, B2212, B2217, B2217, B5939, B5940, B5968 to B5970, B6002 to B6004, N6167, N6176, N6190, N6203, N6205, N6438, N6445, N6446, N6447 (War Flight), N6468.
ALSO S.B.3D – N6102, N6103, N6117, N6708, N6749.

No.1 Fighting School
Formed 29.5.18 at Turnberry (and Ayr) with Pups on strength until at least 9.18.

Known serial numbers – B5287, B6034, C289, D4154, N6205.

No.2 Fighting School
Formed 29.5.18 ex No.4 (Auxiliary) School of Gunnery at Marske with Pups on strength until at least 11.18

Known serial numbers – B6008, C244, C247, C271, C411, C414 ('103'), C422, C428 to C430.

No.3 Fighting School
Formed 29.5.18 at Bircham Newton with at least one Pup on strength by 8.18 – 9.18.

Known serial numbers – C417.

No.4 Fighting School
Formed 1.4.18 from the RNAS Gunnery School (then a sub-unit of Cranwell based at Freiston) as the School of Aerial Fighting & Bomb Dropping Freiston with a number of Pups on strength. Became No.4 School of Aerial Fighting & Gunnery Freiston on 6.5.18 and then No.4 Fighting School on 29.5.18.

Known serial numbers – B5988, B6001, B6021, C268, N5181, N5197, N6160, N6202, N6472.

No.5 Fighting School
Formed 5.3.18 ex School of Aerial Fighting at Heliopolis with Pups until at least 3.19

Known serial numbers – B6041 to B6044, B6046, B6101, B6108, C248, C254, C255, C477, D4099, C4101, D4115, D4121, D4142.

Grand Fleet School of Aerial Fighting & Gunnery
Formed 19.7.18 ex No.208 TDS at East Fortune, moving to Leuchars 10.11.18 and using Pups until at least 7.19.

Known serial numbers – 9946, B2211, C223, C238, C283, C286, D4027, D4028, D4034.

Marine Observers School
At least one Pup on strength at Leysdown between 8.18 and 2.19.

Known serial number – C269.

North Eastern Area Flying Instructors School
Formed 1.7.18 ex No.2 School of Special Flying at Redcar with Pups until at least 8.18.

Known serial number – B6049.

No.1 (Observers) School of Aerial Gunnery
Formed 9.3.18 ex Nos.1 & 3 (Auxiliary) Schools of Aerial Gunnery at New Romney with a few Pups on strength until at least 11.18

Known serial numbers – A6220, B1815, B9440.

Pilots and Observers Air Gunnery amd Fighting School
Some Pups on strength at Leysdown in 1918.

Known serial numbers – C269, N6197.

Pool of Pilots
Formed 14.18 ex the RNAS War School at Manstone with Pups to at least 7.18.

Known serial numbers – B5938, B5958, B5960, B5991 to B5994, B6001, C212, C223, C229, C240, C244, C247, C250, C253, C256, C271, C274, C277, C280 ('18'), C514, D4192, N5188, N5195, N6169, N6188, N6197 to N6199, N6202.

School of Aerial Fighting, Heliopolis
At Heliopolis (38th Wing) with Pups on strength by 3.18 until disbanding into No.5 Fighting School on 5.9.18.

Known serial numbers – B6044 to B6046, B6057, D4124 to D4126.

No.4 School of Aerial Fighting & Gunnery
Formed 6.5.18 at Freiston with at least one Pup strength, becoming No.4 Fighting School on 29.5.18.

Known serial number – B5988, N6160.

School of Aerial Gunnery
A few Pups on strength at Aboukir (or Abu Qir), Egypt (38th Wing) when it disbanded into No.5 Fighting School on 5.9.18

Known serial numbers – B6042, B6043, B6101.

No.1 School of Military Aeronautics
One Pup on strength at Reading in 2.18 for ground instructional use.

Known serial number – B6121.

No.5 School of Military Aeronautics
One Pup on strength at Denham in 2.18 for ground instructional use.

Known serial number – B6121 ('G').

No.1 School of Navigation & Bomb Dropping
A few Pups on strength at Stonehenge between 3.18 and 3.19.

Known serial numbers – B7490, C284, D4021, D4022.

School of Special Flying
Formed 2.8.17 at Gosport with a few Pups on strength, becoming No.1 School of Special Flying on 18.5.18

Known serial numbers – B805, B1844, B2192, B2193, B4128?

Scout School, No.2 Aeroplane Depot (later Aeroplane Supply Depot from 1.11.17)
Formed 6.17 at Candas with Pups until 2.18.

Known serial numbers – A6165, A6167, A6241, A7309, A7324, B1710, B1724, B1742, B1827, B1832, B2182, B5922, B5983.

South Eastern Area Flying Instructors School
Formed 7.18 at Shoreham with Pups until at least 11.18.

Known serial numbers – B5390, C1510, D4192, N6210.

18th Wing Fighting School
At London Colney with some Pups in 9.17

Known serial numbers – A7311, B1847.

Wireless Experimental Establishment
Some Pups on strength at Biggin Hill during 1918.

Known serial numbers – A6228 ('C'), D4097 ('1'), D4118, D4119.

<u>Wireless and Observers School</u>
One Pup reported to be on strength at Brooklands in August 1917.

Known serial number – B1720.

Naval units partially or wholly equipped with Pups

<u>No.1 (Naval) Wing</u>
Had a number of Pups on strength from 6.16, these being formed into numbered naval squadrons in 10.16 & 11.16.

Known serial numbers – 3691, 9496, 9899, N5180 to N5188, N5190, N5192 to N5194.

<u>No.2 (Naval) Wing RNAS (later No.62 (Naval) Wing RAF)</u>
Headquarters at Mudros, had a few Pups on strength between 9.17 and 10.18.

Known serial numbers – 9941, 9942, N6432, N6433, N6470, N6471.

<u>No.5 (Naval) Wing</u>
Pup 3691 on strength at Coudekerque for a few days in 6.16.

<u>No.3 (Naval) Squadron</u>
Formed 5.11.16 in No.1 (Naval) Wing by redesignating 'C' Sqdn No.1 (Naval) Wing at St.Pol with 1½ Strutters and Pups, the Pups having all been replaced by Camels by 10.17.

Known serial numbers – 3691, 9898 to 9900, A6158, A6160, N5182 to N5189, N5191, N5194 to N5199, N6160 to N6163, N6165, N6166, N6169 to N6172, N6174 to N6176, N6178, N6179, N6181 to N6183, N6185, N6186, N6194, N6195, N6197, N6202, N6203, N6205, N6207 to N6209, N6460, N6461, N6464 to N6467, N6474, N6477, N6479.

<u>No.4 (Naval) Squadron</u>
Formed 31.12.16 in No.4 (Naval) Wing at Coudekerque, moving to Bray Dunes (Frontier aerodrome) on 1.4.18. Pups were flown between 3.17 and 8.17.

Known serial numbers – 9899, 9929, N5183, N5184, N5186, N5187, N5196, N6167, N6168, N6176, N6177, N6184, N6185, N6187, N6188, N6190, N6192, N6196, N6198 to N6200, N6462, N6475, N6476, N6478.

<u>No.8 (Naval) Squadron</u>
Formed 25.10.16 at St.Pol, with Pups equipping 'B' Flight. Moved to Vert Galant 26.10.16 and joined the 22nd Army Wing in the 5 Brigade, RFC. The Pups were handed over to No.3 (Naval) Squadron on 3.2.17, when the squadron was withdrawn to St.Pol for a rest and re-equipment with Camels.

Known serial numbers – 3691, 9898, 9899, A626, N5181 to N5199.

<u>No.9 (Naval) Squadron</u>
Formed 1.2.17 in No.1 (Naval) Wing at St.Pol with Pups on strength, these being handed over to No.11 (Naval) Sqdn on 13.7.17.

Known serial numbers – 9900, 9915, 9916, 9928, N5182, N5183, N5188, N6163, N6164, N6166, N6167, N6168, N6174, N6177, N6178, N6184, N6188, N6189, N6191 to N6193, N6195, N6196, N6199, N6201, N6462, N6469, N6475.

<u>No.11 (Naval) Squadron</u>
Had Pups on strength from 5.17 in No.4 (Naval) Wing at Hondschoote. Moved to Bray Dunes (Frontier aerodrome) 6.7.17 but disbanded 27.8.17 owing to a shortage of pilots.

Known serial numbers – 9898, 9899, 9915, B1816 to B1818, N5196, N6162, N6166 to N6168, N6174, N6178, N6180, N6183, N6184, N6187, N6188, N6190, N6192, N6196, N6199, N6209, N6468, N6469, N6475, N6477.

<u>No.12 (Naval) Squadron</u>
Formed 8.6.17 in No.5 (Naval) Wing as a training squadron at Hondschoote with some Pups on strength, moving on 1.7.17 to Petite Synthe where they were replaced by Camels in 12.17.

Known serial numbers – 9898, 9900, 9916, 9929, B1816 to B1818, B1820, N5188, N5196, N6167, N6176, N6180, N6182, N6187, N6196, N6201 to N6203, N6465, N6467, N6468, N6476.

<u>Seaplane Defence Flight</u>
Formed 30.6.17 at St.Pol with some Pups on strength, these having been replaced by Camels by 11.17.

Known serial numbers – 9899, 9916, 9929, B1819 to B1821, N6171, N6179, N6203 ('S'), N6206, N6435 to N6437, N6459, N6478.

<u>Shipboard use</u>
The following table lists Pups and S.B.3Ds known to have been aboard, or allotted to, the ships concerned. Such associations of aircraft and ships could be very brief and subject to frequent changes, therefore the table is probably incomplete.

Warships:
HMS *Cassandra*:   S.B.3D N6100, N6104, N6128, N6696.
HMS *Dublin*:   Pup 9931, N6431, N6449; S.B.3D N6123.
HMS *Inconstant*:   S.B.3D N6371?
HMS *Phaeton*:   S.B.3D N6127.
HMS *Princess Royal*: Pup N6440, N6443, N6445; S.B.3D N6115
HMS *Renown*:   Pup 9947, 9949, N6434, N6443, N6444, N6448; S.B.3D N6109, N6115, N6116
HMS *Repulse*:   Pup 9944, 9945, N6438, N6443, N6446, N6453, N6455, N6456.
HMAS *Sydney*:   Pup 9931, 9932, N6431, N6446, N6449
HMS *Tiger*:   Pup 9934, 9944, N6438, N6443, N6455, N6456.
HMS *Yarmouth*:   Pup 9901, 9904, 9905, 9910, 9911, 9932, 9944, N6430, N6431, N6443; S.B.3D N6129.

Carriers:
HMS *Argus*:   Pup 9949
HMS *Campania*: Pup 9931 to 9934, N6431, N6444, N6449; S.B.3D N6683, N6684.
HMS *Furious*:   Pup 9940, 9943, 9949, C214, N6438, N6441, N6446, N6450 to N6456.
HMS *Manxman*:   Pup 9901, 9913, 9914, 9917 to 9920, 9943 to 9945, N6430, N6431, N6443 to N6445, N6455, N6456;
                 S.B.3D N6100, N6109.
HMS *Nairana*:   Pup 9917, 9945, 9947, 9949, N6438, N6440, N6443, N6445, N6448, N6455; S.B.3D N6100, N6105, N6108
                 to N6110, N6112 to N6116, N6620 to N6625, N6629, N6682, N6687, N6691, N6692, N6696, N6708.
HMS *Pegasus*:   Pup 9944, N6438 to N6440, N6443, N6444, N6446, N6455, N6456; S.B.3D N6104 to N6107, N6109,
                 N6113 to N6115, N6119 to N6121, N6123, N6125 to N6129, N6680 to N6682, N6687, N6690 to N6692,
                 N6696, N6697, N6700, N6703, N6704, N6710, N6714.
HMS *Vindex*:   Pup 9910, 9911, 9921, 9926, 9927, 9930, N6457, N6458.
HMS *Vindictive*: Pup 9944.

RNAS Training Stations (to 1.4.18):

Chingford/Fairlop,
Several Pups for training from 12.17 (also others in transit) until became No.207 TDS 1.4.18.

Known serial numbers – B6085 to B6088, B6097, B6098, C304.

Cranwell/Freiston
The RNAS Training Establishment at Cranwell had a large number of Pups on strength from 11.16 until becoming Nos.201 and 202 TDSs on 1.4.18. A sub-station at Freiston was used for bomb dropping and gunnery training.

Known serial numbers – 9902, 9903, 9908, 9909, 9923 to 9925, 9935 to 9938, 9946, B1819, B1824, B1825, B2173, B2181, B2183, B2202 to B2205, B2208, B2211, B2226, B5928, B5929, B5948 to B5950, B5978 to B5980, B5988 to B5990, B6013, B6014, B6021 to B6024, B6031 to B6034, B6075, B6076, B6143, B6146, B6149, C201, C202, C205, C208, C232, C235, C235, C238, C241, C259, C262, C265, C295, C298, C301, N6160, N6168, N6171, N6192, N6196, N6209, N6435, N6436, N6457, N6465, N6467, N6472, N6473, N6477, N6479.

Eastbourne
The Naval Flying School had a few Pups from 12.17, becoming No.206 TDS on 1.4.18.

Known serial numbers – B1821, B6099, B6100, N6476.

East Fortune
The Naval Flying School flew Pups from 9.17 for practice landings by carrier pilots, 'F' Squadron being earmarked for aircraft ashore from HMS *Furious*. It had become No.206 TDS by 6.18, and probably from 1.4.18.

Known serial numbers – 9915, 9940, 9943, 9946, 9948, B1822, B1823, C211, C214, C217, C220, C223, C226, C283, C286, C289, C292, N6025, N6451, N6453, N6478; Also SB.3D N6103, N6122, N6127, N6688, N6699.

Manstone
Pups used by the War School (and also the War Flight) from 1.17. Became Pool of Pilots 1.4.18.

Known serial numbers – 9907, 9911, 9921, 9928, 9931, B2212 ('6'), B2213, B5930, B5938, B5958 to B5960, B5991 to B5994, B6001, C229, C244, C247, C250, C253, C256, C271, C274, C277, C280, N5181, N5182, N5188, N5195, N5197, N6169, N6177, N6179, N6188 to N6191, N6193, N6195, N6197 to N6202, N6458, N6466, N6469, N6474, N6475.

Redcar
The Naval Flying School had a number of Pups on strength between 7.17 and 5.18 when it closed down as such, the station being taken over by a School of Special Flying and other units.

Known serial numbers – B6049 to B6052, N6472, N6473.

Vendôme
The RNAS Training Establishment at Vendôme in France had several Pups on strength from 11.17 until this element became No.205 TDS on 1.4.18.

Known serial numbers – B1817 to B1820, C307, C310, C313, C316, C319, C322, C325.

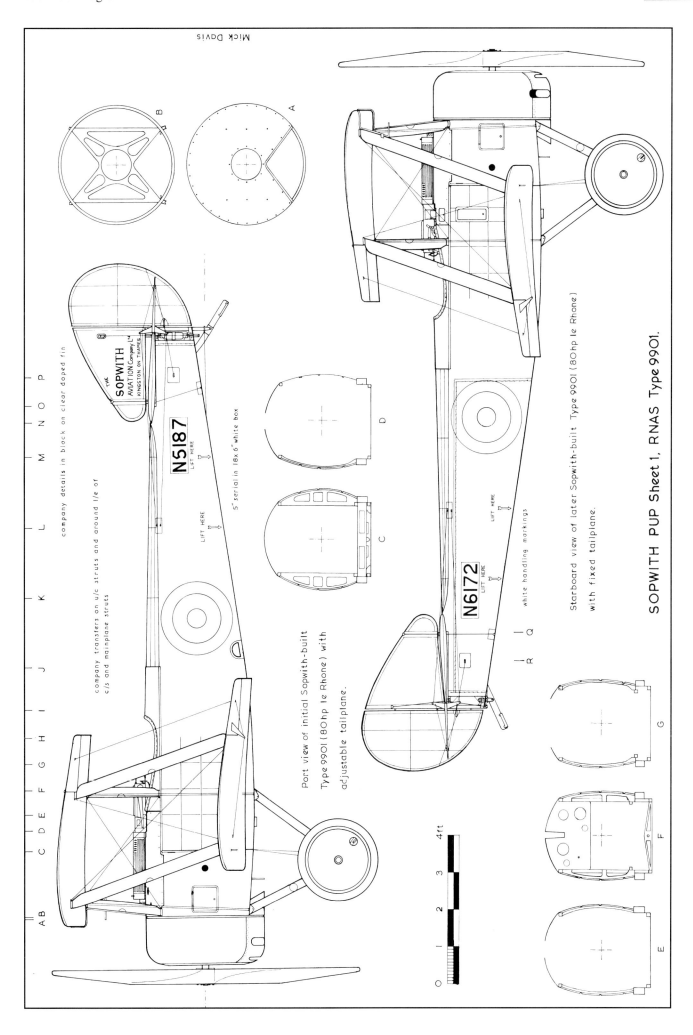

Mick Davis

company details in black on clear doped fin

company transfers on u/c struts and around l/e of c/s and mainplane struts

SOPWITH
AVIATION Company Ltd
KINGSTON ON THAMES

N5187
LIFT HERE

LIFT HERE

5" serial in 18x6" white box

Port view of initial Sopwith-built
Type 9901 (80hp le Rhone) with
adjustable tailplane.

N6172
LIFT HERE

LIFT HERE

white handling markings

Starboard view of later Sopwith-built Type 9901 (80hp le Rhone)
with fixed tailplane.

SOPWITH PUP Sheet 1, RNAS Type 9901.

4ft
3
2
1
0

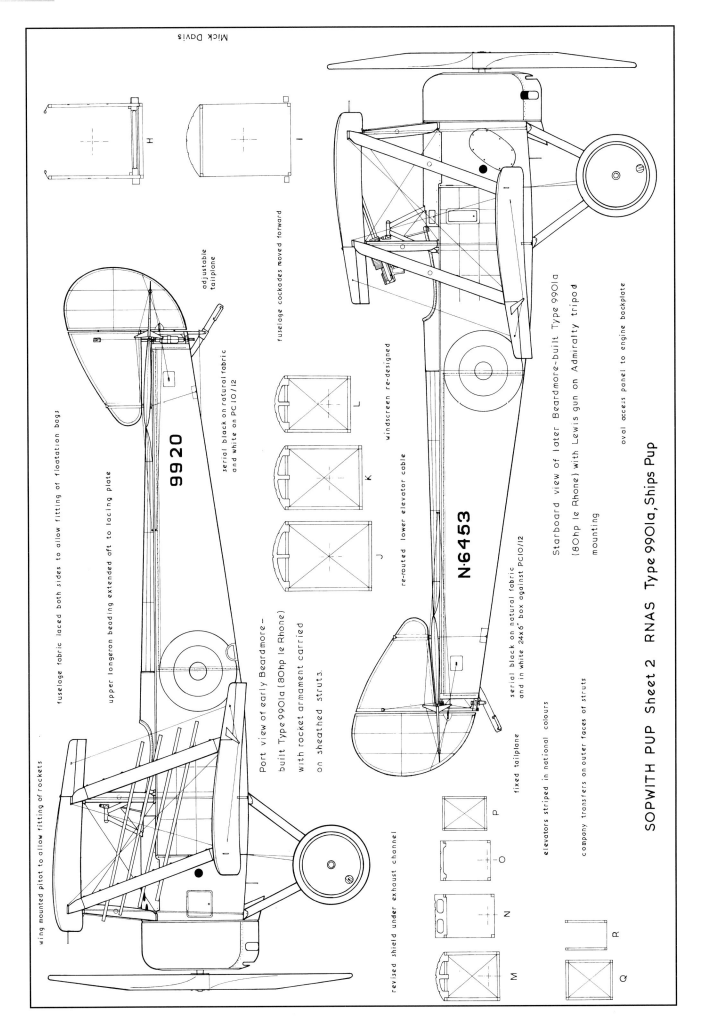

Mick Davis

adjustable tailplane

serial black on natural fabric and white on PC10/12

fuselage cockades moved forward

windscreen re-designed

re-routed lower elevator cable

Starboard view of later Beardmore-built Type 9901a (80hp le Rhone) with Lewis gun on Admiralty tripod mounting

oval access panel to engine backplate

fuselage fabric laced both sides to allow fitting of floatation bags

upper longeron beading extended aft to lacing plate

Port view of early Beardmore-built Type 9901a (80hp le Rhone) with rocket armament carried on sheathed struts.

wing mounted pitot to allow fitting of rockets

9920

N-6453

revised shield under exhaust channel

fixed tailplane

serial black on natural fabric and in white 24x6" box against PC10/12

elevators striped in national colours

company transfers on outer faces of struts

SOPWITH PUP Sheet 2 RNAS Type 9901a, Ships Pup

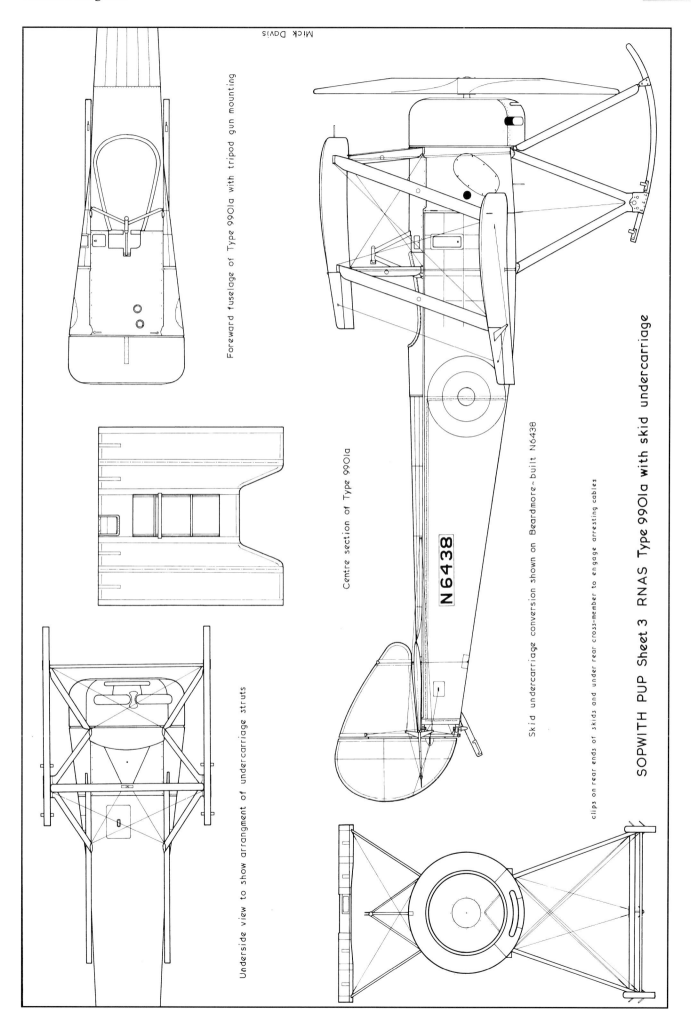

Mick Davis

Forward fuselage of Type 9901a with tripod gun mounting

Centre section of Type 9901a

Underside view to show arrangment of undercarriage struts

Skid undercarriage conversion shown on Beardmore-built N6438

clips on rear ends of skids and under rear cross-member to engage arresting cables

N6438

SOPWITH PUP Sheet 3 RNAS Type 9901a with skid undercarriage

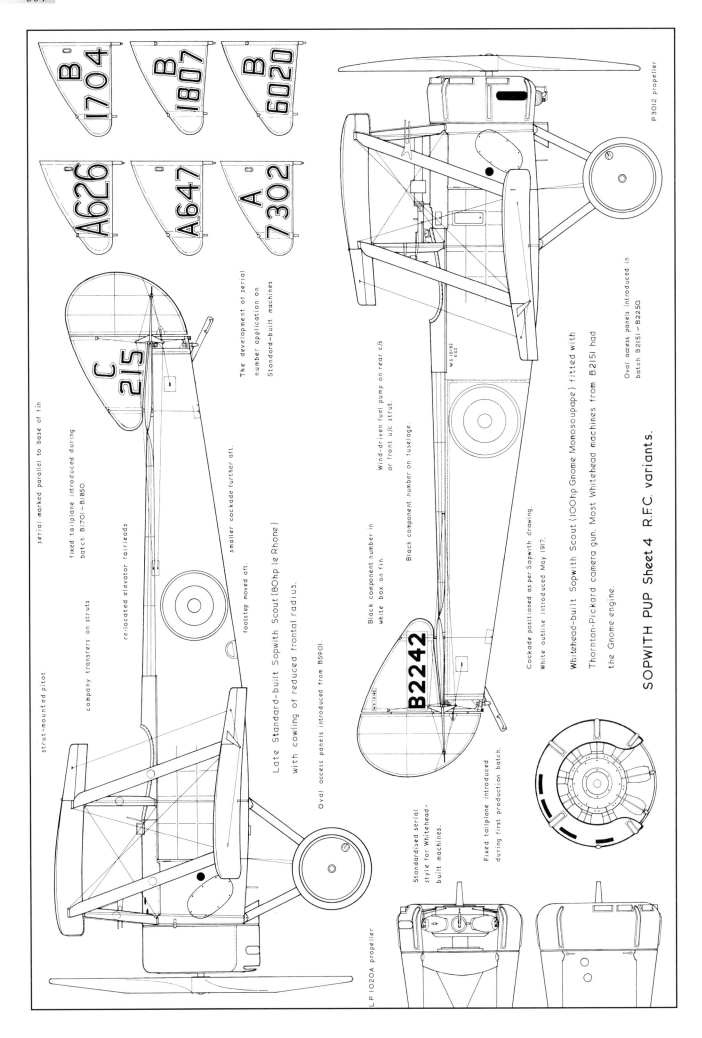

B 1704 B 1807 B 6020
A 626 A 647 A 7302

strut-mounted pitot

serial marked parallel to base of fin

fixed tailplane introduced during
batch B1701–B1850

company transfers on struts

re-located elevator fairleads

smaller cockade further aft.

footstep moved aft.

The development of serial
number application on
Standard-built machines

Late Standard-built Sopwith Scout (80hp le Rhone)
with cowling of reduced frontal radius.

Oval access panels introduced from B5901.

C 215

W.S.10192

Wind-driven fuel pump on rear c/s
or front u/c strut.

Black component number in
white box on fin.

Black component number on fuselage.

B2242

W.S.10192
EGZ

Cockade positioned as per Sopwith drawing.
White outline introduced May 1917.

Whitehead-built Sopwith Scout (100hp Gnome Monosoupape) fitted with
Thornton-Pickard camera gun. Most Whitehead machines from B2151 had
the Gnome engine.

Oval access panels introduced in
batch B2151–B2250.

Standardised serial
style for Whitehead-
built machines.

Fixed tailplane introduced
during first production batch.

SOPWITH PUP Sheet 4 R.F.C. variants.

P3012 propeller

LP 1020A propeller

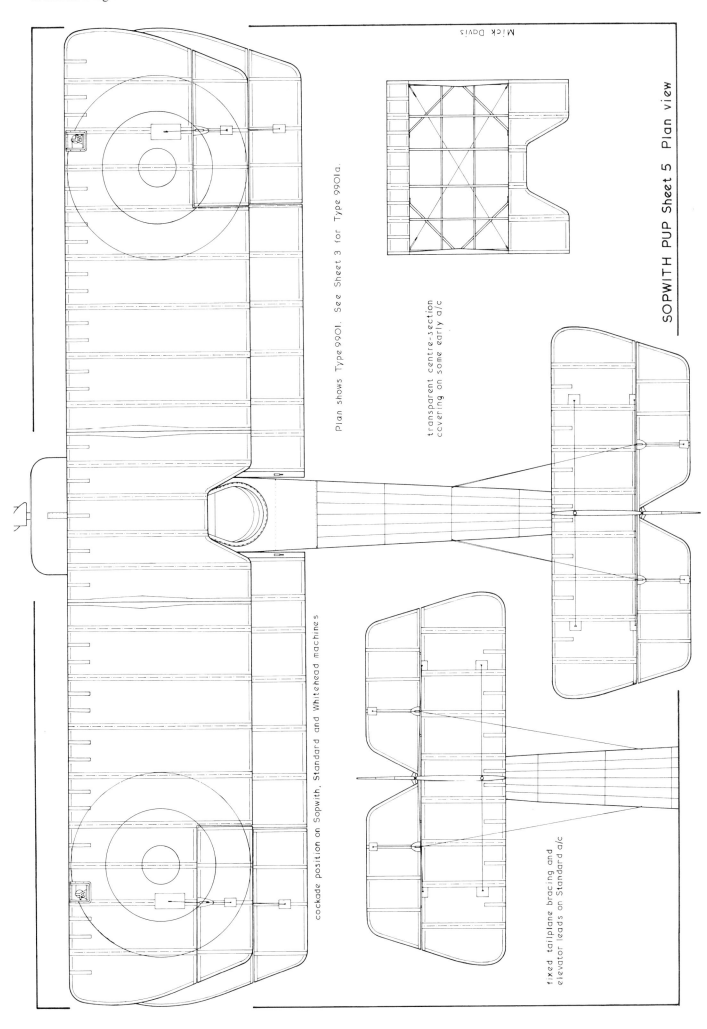

Mick Davis

SOPWITH PUP Sheet 5   Plan view

Plan shows Type 9901. See Sheet 3 for Type 9901a.

transparent centre-section
covering on some early a/c

cockade position on Sopwith, Standard and Whitehead machines

fixed tailplane bracing and
elevator leads on Standard a/c

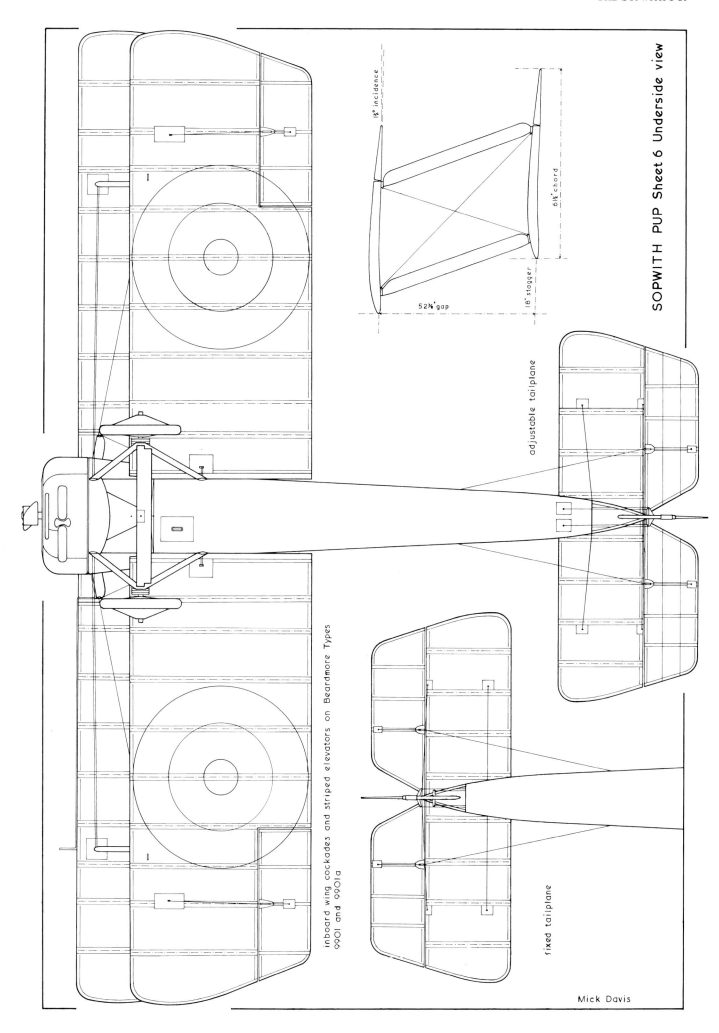

SOPWITH PUP Sheet 6 Underside view

1¼° incidence

6¼° chord

18° stagger

52¾° gap

adjustable tailplane

fixed tailplane

inboard wing cockades and striped elevators on Beardmore Types
9901 and 9901a

Mick Davis

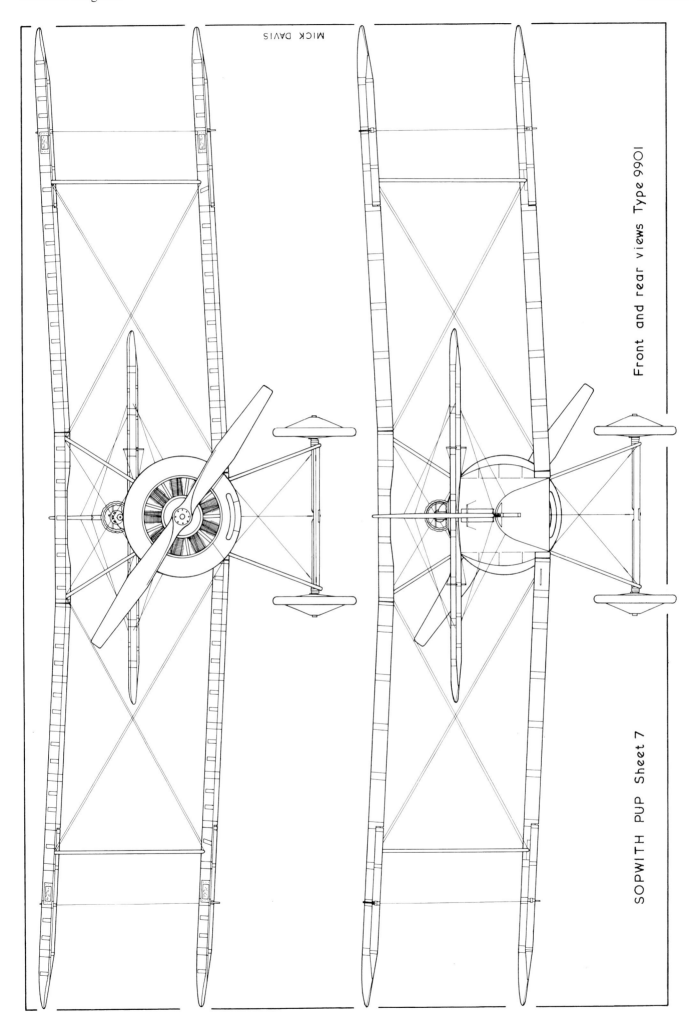

MICK DAVIS

Front and rear views Type 9901

SOPWITH PUP Sheet 7

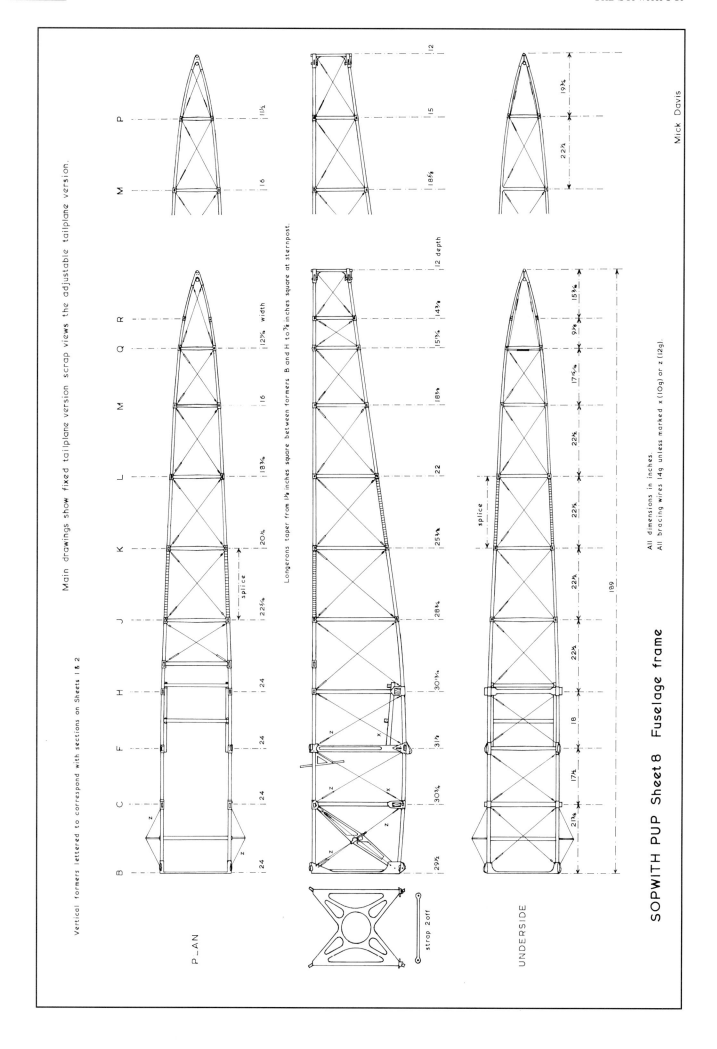

Vertical formers lettered to correspond with sections on Sheets 1 & 2

Main drawings show fixed tailplane version scrap views the adjustable tailplane version.

Longerons taper from 1⅛ inches square between formers B and H to ⅞ inches square at sternpost.

All dimensions in inches.
All bracing wires 14g unless marked x (10g) or z (12g).

SOPWITH PUP Sheet 8 Fuselage frame

Mick Davis

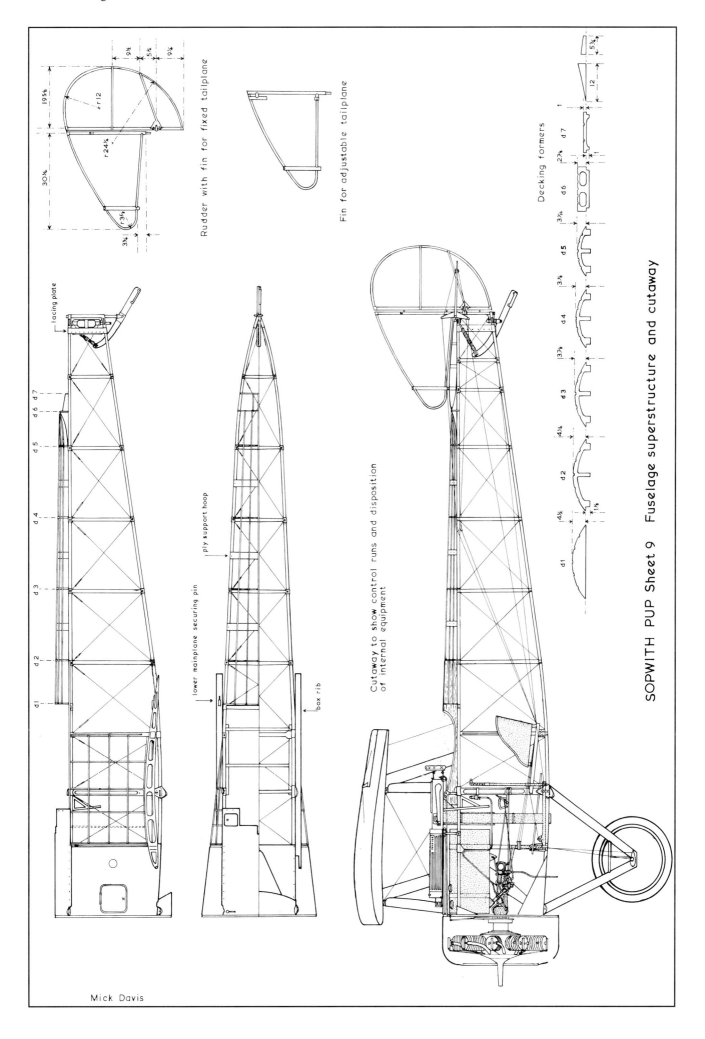

Rudder with fin for fixed tailplane

Fin for adjustable tailplane

Decking formers

lacing plate

ply support hoop

lower mainplane securing pin

box rib

Cutaway to show control runs and disposition of internal equipment

SOPWITH PUP Sheet 9   Fuselage superstructure and cutaway

Mick Davis

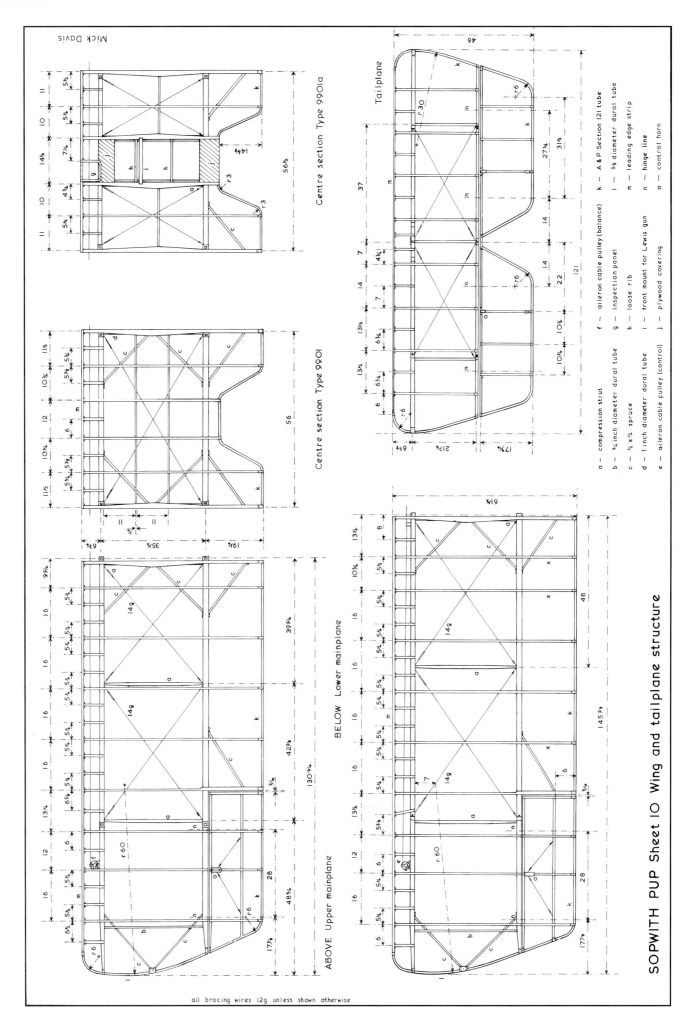

SOPWITH PUP Sheet 10 Wing and tailplane structure

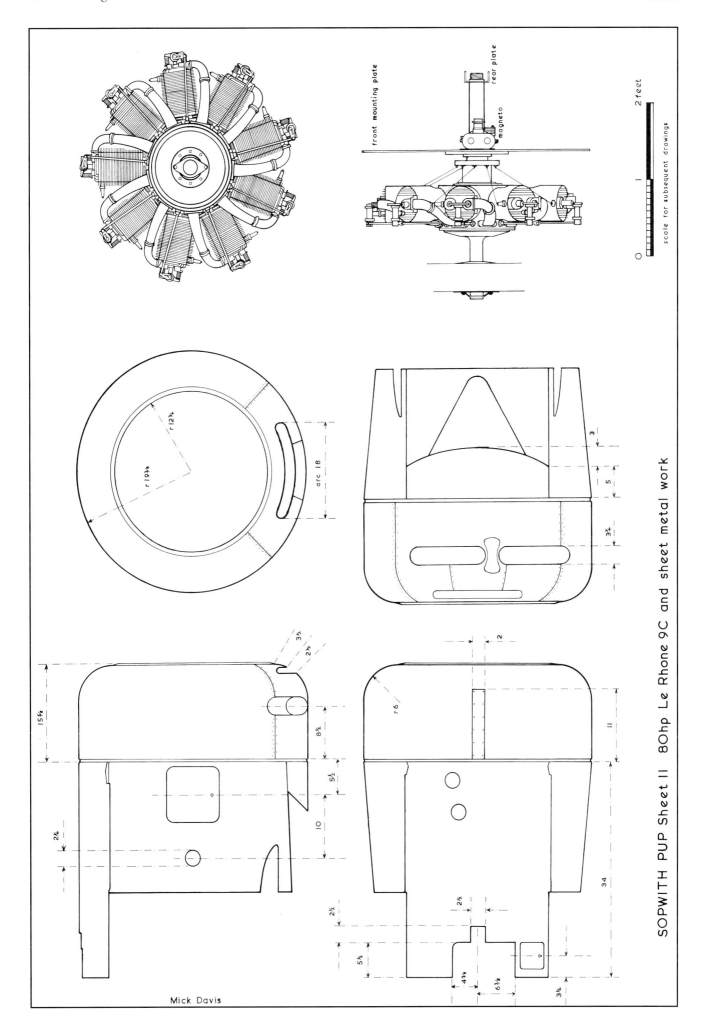

front mounting plate

rear plate

magneto

2 feet

scale for subsequent drawings

r 12¾

r 19¾

arc 18

3

5

3¾

3½

2½

15⅝

8½

5½

10

2¼

2½

5½

2

r 6

11

34

2½

4¾

6¾

3½

SOPWITH PUP Sheet II   80hp Le Rhone 9C and sheet metal work

Mick Davis

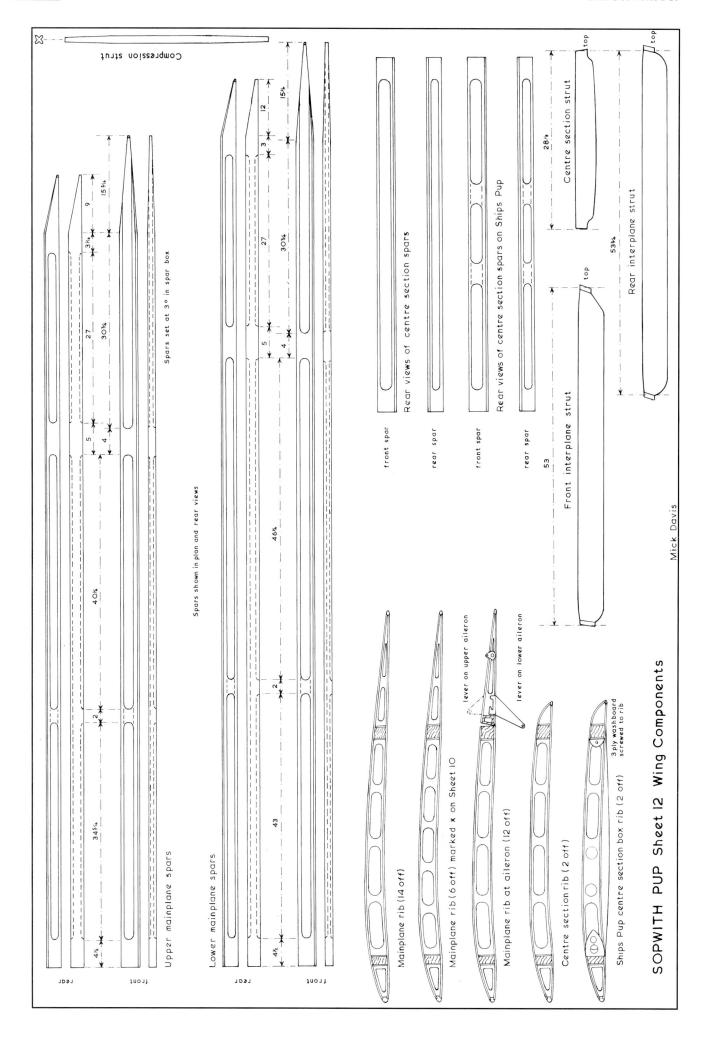

SOPWITH PUP Sheet 12 Wing Components

Mick Davis

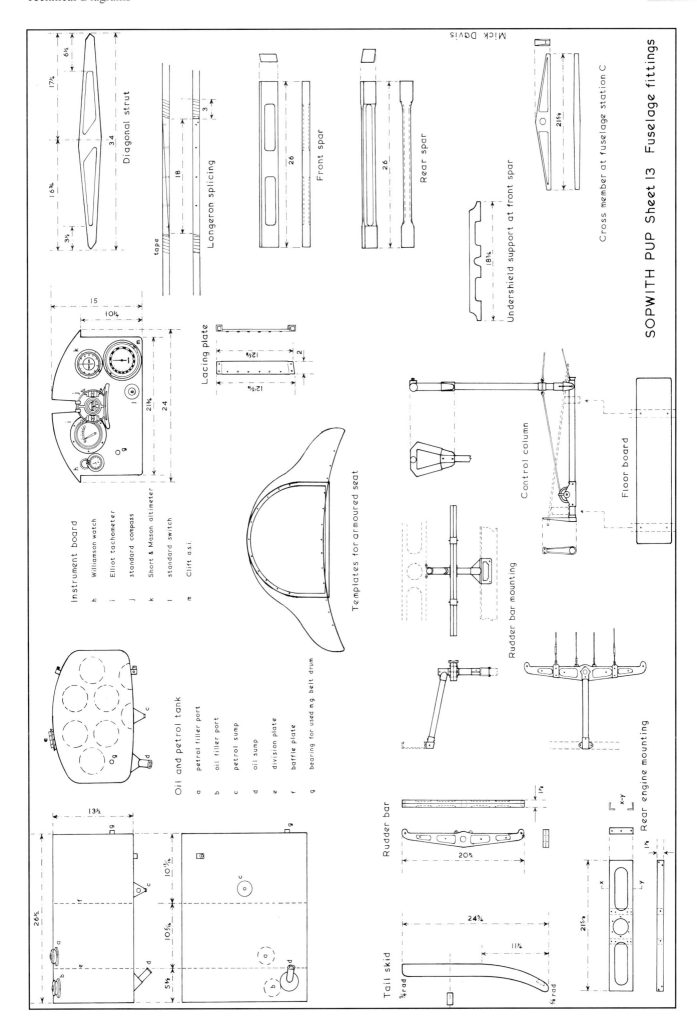

SOPWITH PUP Sheet 13 Fuselage fittings

Mick Davis

Diagonal strut

Longeron splicing

Front spar

Rear spar

Cross member at fuselage station C

Undershield support at front spar

Instrument board

h   Williamson watch
i   Elliot tachometer
j   standard compass
k   Short & Mason altimeter
l   standard switch
m   Clift a.s.i.

Lacing plate

Templates for armoured seat

Control column

Floor board

Rudder bar mounting

Rear engine mounting

Oil and petrol tank

a   petrol filler port
b   oil filler port
c   petrol sump
d   oil sump
e   division plate
f   baffle plate
g   bearing for used m.g. belt drum

Rudder bar

Tail skid

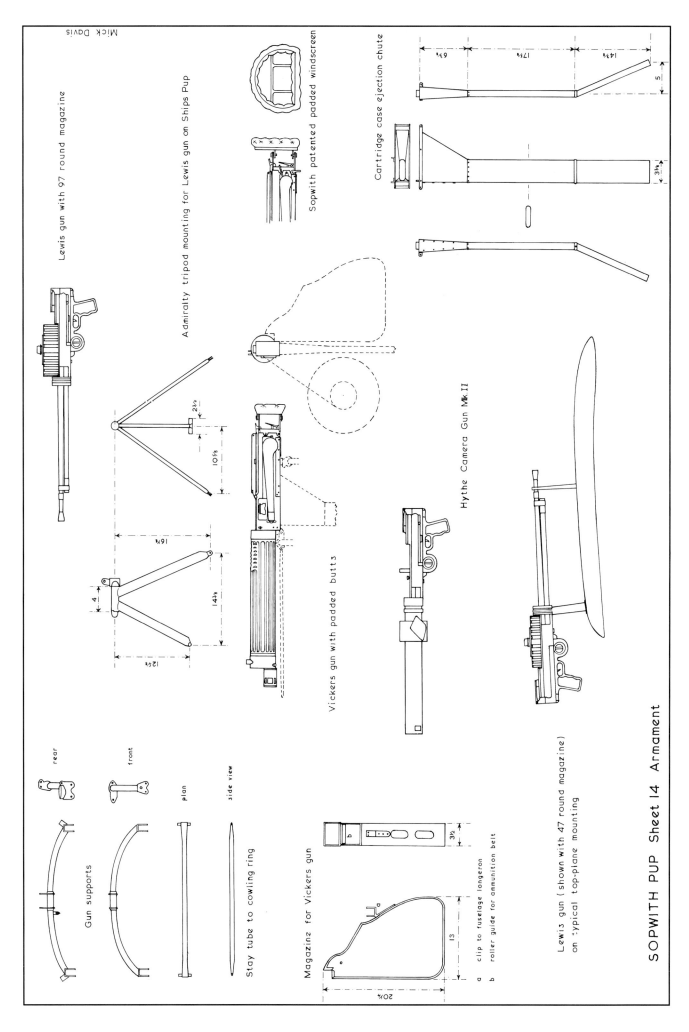

Mick Davis

Lewis gun with 97 round magazine

Admiralty tripod mounting for Lewis gun on Ships Pup

Sopwith patented padded windscreen

Cartridge case ejection chute

Vickers gun with padded butts

Hythe Camera Gun Mk.II

Gun supports

rear

front

plan

side view

Stay tube to cowling ring

Magazine for Vickers gun

a   clip to fuselage longeron
b   roller guide for ammunition belt

Lewis gun (shown with 47 round magazine)
on typical top-plane mounting

SOPWITH PUP Sheet 14 Armament

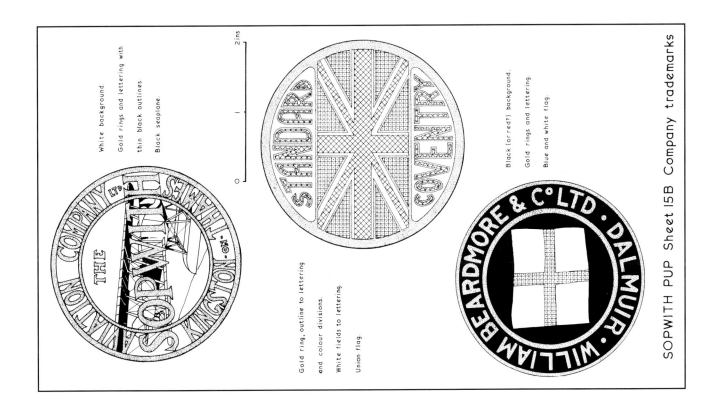

White background

Gold rings and lettering with

thin black outlines.

Black seaplane.

Gold ring, outline to lettering

and colour divisions.

White fields to lettering.

Union flag.

Black (or red?) background.

Gold rings and lettering.

Blue and white flag.

SOPWITH PUP Sheet 15B Company trademarks

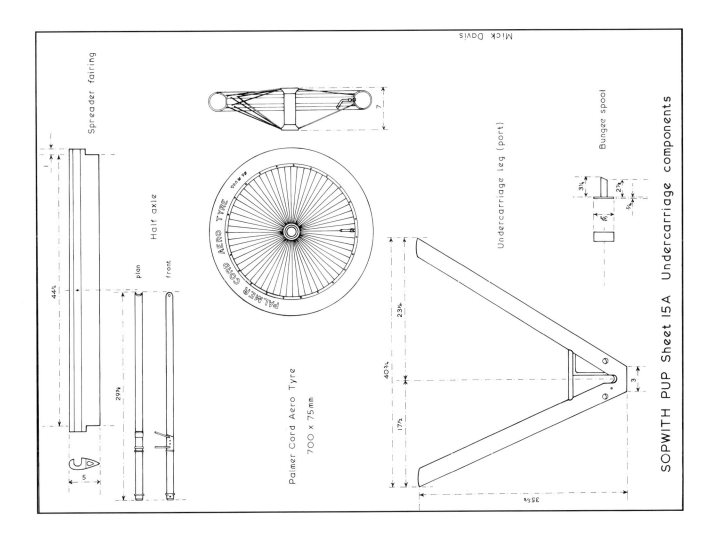

Spreader fairing

Half axle

plan

front

5

44¾

29¾

Palmer Cord Aero Tyre

700 x 75 mm

Undercarriage leg (port)

Bungee spools

7

23¾

40¾

17½

3

35⅝

3¼

2⅞

⁵⁄₈

³⁄₈

Mick Davis

SOPWITH PUP Sheet 15A Undercarriage components

Bibliography

The greater part of this book's factual content derives from many of the official files (mainly those in the Air 1 series) in the Public Record Office, Kew, from early volumes of the weekly magazines *Flight* and *The Aeroplane*, articles in the Journal of Cross & Cockade International, and from log books and other documents in the Royal Air Force Museum, Hendon, and the Fleet Air Arm Museum, Yeovilton. Relevant matter, much of it substantial, has also come from the books listed hereunder.

Balfour of Inchrye, Lord (Harold Balfour)   *An Airman Marches;* Greenhill Books, 1985

Bartlett, C.P.O.   *Bomber Pilot 1916-1918;* Ian Allan, 1974

Bridgman, L., and Stewart, Major O.   *The Clouds Remember;* Gale & Polden

Cole, C., & Cheesman, E.F.   *The Air Defence of Britain 1914-18;* Putnam, 1984

Coppens de Houthulst, Baron Willy   *Days on the Wing;* Aviation Book Club/John Hamilton

Cronin, Dick   *Royal Navy Shipboard Aircraft Developments 1912-1931;* Air-Britain,1990

Crundall, Wing Commander D.   *Fighter Pilot on the Western Front;* William Kimber, 1975

Fujita, Toshio   *The Japanese Civil Register 1919-45;* Air-Britain Archive (various issues)

Grey, C.G.   *Jane's All the World's Aircraft,* Sampson Low, Marston, 1920 & 1922 editions

Hawker, Muriel   *HG Hawker, Airman, his life and work;* Hutchinson, 1922

Isaacs, Wing Commander K.   *Military Aircraft of Australia 1909-1918;* Australian War Memorial, 1971

Jackson, A.J.   *British Civil Aircraft since 1919;* Putnam, 1974

Johnson, Brian   *Fly Navy;* David & Charles, 1981

Johnstone, E.G. (Ed)   *Naval Eight;* Arms & Armour Press edition, 1972

King, H.F.   *Sopwith Aircraft, 1912-20;* Putnam, 1980

Lee, Air Vice-Marshall A.S.G.   *Open Cockpit;* Jarrolds, 1969

Lewis, Cecil   *Farewell to Wings;* Temple Press Books, 1964

Macmillan, Wing Commander N.   *Into the Blue* (revised edition); Jarrolds, 1969

McCudden, Major J.T.B.   *Five Years in the RFC;* The Aeroplane & General Publishing Co, Ltd 1918

Moore, Major W.G.   *Early Bird;* Putnam, 1963

Navy Records Society (ed Capt SW Roskill)   *The Naval Air Service, 1908-1919;* 1969

Parnell, Neville and Boughton, Trevor   *Flypast - A Record of Aviation in Australia;* Australian Government Publishing Service, 1988

Penrose, Harald   *British Aviation: The Great War and Armistice:* Putnam 1969

Raleigh, Sir Walter, and Jones, H.A.   *The War in the Air;* Oxford University Press, 1922-1937

Rimell, R.L.   *Zeppelin!;* Conway Maritime Press, 1984

Rochford, Leonard H.   *I chose the Sky;* William Kimber, 1977

Robertson, Bruce   *Sopwith – the man and his aircraft;* Harleyford, 1976

Samson, Air Commodore C.R.   *Fights and Flights;* Benn, 1930

Strange, Colonel L.A.   *Recollections of an Airman;* Hamilton, 1933

Sturtivant, Ray and Page, Gordon   *RNAS Serials & Units 1911-1919;* Air-Britain, 1992

Taylor, Sir Gordon   *Sopwith Scout 7309;* Cassell, 1968

Young, Brigadier D.   *Rutland of Jutland;* Cassell, 1963

Index of names

AIR-BRITAIN – THE INTERNATIONAL ASSOCIATION OF AVIATION HISTORIANS – FOUNDED 1948

Since 1948, Air-Britain has recorded aviation events as they have happened, because today's events are tomorrow's history. In addition, considerable research into the past has been undertaken to provide historians with the background to aviation history. Over 18,000 members have contributed to our aims and efforts in that time and many have become accepted authorities in their own fields.

Every month, *AIR-BRITAIN NEWS* covers the current civil and military scene. Quarterly, each member receives *AIR-BRITAIN DIGEST* which is a fully-illustrated journal containing articles on various subjects, both past and present.

For those interested in military aviation history, there is the quarterly *AEROMILITARIA* which is designed to delve more deeply into the background of, mainly, British and Commonwealth military aviation than is possible in commercial publications and whose format permits it to be used as components of a filing system which suits the readers' requirements. This publication is responsible for the production of the present volume and other monographs on military subjects. Also published quarterly is *ARCHIVE*, produced in a similar format but covering civil aviation history in depth on a world-wide basis. Both magazines are well-illustrated by photographs and drawings.

In addition to these regular publications, there are monographs covering type histories, both military and civil, airline fleets, Royal Air Force registers, squadron histories and the civil registers of a large number of countries. Although our publications are available to non-members, prices are considerably lower for Air-Britain members, who have priority over non-members when availability is limited. The accumulated price discounts for which members qualify when buying Air-Britain books can far exceed the annual subscription rates.

A large team of aviation experts is available to answer members' queries on most aspects of aviation. If you have made a study of any particular subject, you may be able to expand your knowledge by joining those with similar interests. Also available to members are libraries of colour slides and photographs which supply slides and prints at prices considerably lower than those charged by commercial firms.

There are local branches of the Association in Blackpool, Bournemouth, Chiltern, Heston, London, Luton, Manchester, Merseyside, North-East England, Rugby, Scotland, Severnside, Solent, South-West Essex, Stansted, West Cornwall and West Midlands. Overseas in France and the Netherlands.

If you would like to receive samples of Air-Britain magazines, please write to the following address enclosing 50p and stating your particular interests. If you would like only a brochure, please send a stamped self-addressed envelope to the same address (preferably 230mm by 160mm or over) - **Air-Britain Membership Enquiries (Mil), 1 Rose Cottages, 179 Penn Road, Hazlemere, High Wycombe, Bucks., HP15 7NE.**

Our website may be found at **www.air-britain.com**

MILITARY AVIATION PUBLICATIONS IN PRINT
(prices are for members/non-members and are post-free)

Royal Air Force Aircraft series

J1-J9999	(£8.00/£10.00)	K1000-K9999	(see The K-File)	L1000-N9999	(£12.00/£15.00)
P1000-R9999	(£11.00/£14.00)	T1000-V9999	(£12.00/£15.00)	W1000-Z9999	(£13.00/£16.50)
AA100-AZ999	(£13.00/£16.50)	BA100-BZ999	(New edition in preparation)	DA100-DZ999	(£5.00/£6.00)
EA100-EZ999	(£5.00/£6.00)	FA100-FZ999	(£5.00/£6.00)	HA100-HZ999	(£6.00/£7.50)
JA100-JZ999	(£6.00/£7.50)	KA100-KZ999	(£6.00/£7.50)	LA100-LZ999	(£7.00/£8.50)
MA100-MZ999	(£8.00/£10.00)	NA100-NZ999	(£8.00/£10.00)	PA100-RZ999	(£10.00/£12.50)
WA100-WZ999	(New edition in preparation)	XA100-XZ999	(£9.00/£11.00)		

Type Histories

The Battle File	(£20.00/£25.00)	The Beaufort File	(£11.00/£13.50)	The Camel File	(£13.00/£16.00)
The Defiant File	(£12.50/£16.00)	The DH4/DH9 File	(£24.00/£30.00)	The S.E.5 File	(£16.00/£20.00)
The Harvard File	(£8.00/£9.50)	The Hoverfly File	(£16.50/£19.50)	The Martinsyde File	(£24.00/£30.00)
The Norman Thompson File	(£13.50/£17.00)	The Oxford, Consul & Envoy File	(£25.00/£32.00)	The Scimitar File	(£26.00/£32.00)

Individual R.A.F. Squadron Histories

Hawks Rising – The History of No.25 Squadron (£25.00/£32.00)
United in Effort – The Story of No.53 Squadron (£15.00/£19.00)
Always Prepared – The History of No.207 Squadron (£22.00/£27.50)
Rise from the East – The History of No.247 Squadron (£13.00/£16.50)

Flat Out – The History of No.30 Squadron (£27.00/£34.00)
Scorpions Sting – The Story of No.84 Squadron (£12.00/£16.50)
The Hornet Strikes – The Story of No.213 Squadron (£20.00/£25.00)
Strong By Night – The History of No.149 Squadron (£15.00/£19.00)

Naval Aviation titles

The Squadrons of the Fleet Air Arm (£24.00/£30.00)
Royal Navy Aircraft Serials and Units 1911 - 1919 (£12.00)
Fleet Air Arm Aircraft 1939 - 1945 (New edition in preparation)

Royal Navy Shipboard Aircraft Developments 1912 - 1931 (£12.00)
Fleet Air Arm Aircraft, Units and Ships 1920 - 1939 (£26.00/£32.50)
Fleet Air Arm Fixed Wing Aircraft since 1946 (In preparation)

Royal Navy Instructional Airframes (£14.00/£17.50)

Other titles

The K-File (the RAF of the 1930s) (£23.00/£30.00)
Aviation in Cornwall (£14.00/£17.50)
Aerial Refuelling at Farnborough 1924 - 1937 (£11.00/£14.00)
World Military Transport Fleets 2002 (£15.00/£19.00)

The British Aircraft Specifications File (£20.00/£25.00)
British Air Commission and Lend-Lease (£23.00/£29.00)
Broken Wings – Post-War RAF accidents (£21.00/£26.00)
U.K. Flight Testing Accidents 1940 - 1971 (£16.50/£20.50)

Spitfire International (£32.50/£39.50)

The above are available from Air-Britain (Historians) Ltd, 41 Penshurst Rd, Leigh, Tonbridge, Kent TN11 8HL
or by e-mail to mike@sales.demon.co.uk. Payment in Sterling only. Overseas carriage 15% of book price, minimum £1.50.
Visa, Mastercard, Delta/Visa accepted with card number and expiry date, also Switch (with Issue number).